Blackstone's

EU Treaties & Legislation

34th edition

edited by

Professor Nigel Foster, FRSA

Professor of EU Law, South East European Law School Network (SEELS) online EU Modules

LLM Degrees Dissertation Supervisor, Robert Kennedy College, Zürich, Switzerland

OXFORD
UNIVERSITY PRESS

OXFORD
UNIVERSITY PRESS

Great Clarendon Street, Oxford, OX2 6DP,
United Kingdom

Oxford University Press is a department of the University of Oxford.
It furthers the University's objective of excellence in research, scholarship,
and education by publishing worldwide. Oxford is a registered trade mark of
Oxford University Press in the UK and in certain other countries

First published by Blackstone Press 1990

Thirtieth edition 2019
Thirty-first edition 2020
Thirty-second edition 2021
Thirty-third edition 2022
Thirty-fourth edition 2023

Published in the United States of America by Oxford University Press
198 Madison Avenue, New York, NY 10016, United States of America

British Library Cataloguing in Publication Data
Data available

ISBN 978–0–19–889042–3

Printed in the UK by
Bell & Bain Ltd., Glasgow

Blackstone's Statutes
Unsurpassed in authority, reliability, and accuracy

The titles in the Blackstone's Statutes series are collections of carefully reviewed and selected unannotated legislative material and official documents.

We make every effort to ensure titles in the series meet the needs of their target market. They are reviewed by lecturers to match university courses closely and are expertly edited to be manageable in size, whilst retaining their comprehensive coverage.

The editors only include material that will be valuable to students and lecturers and it is therefore abridged where necessary.

Contents

Thematic Contents xi
Editor's preface to the 34th edition xv
Extracts from the editor's preface to the 1st edition xvi
New to this edition xviii

Part I EU Treaties 1

Treaty on European Union (Consolidated version) 1
Preamble 1
Title I Common provisions 2
Title II Provisions on democratic principles 4
Title III Provisions on the institutions 5
Title IV Provisions on enhanced cooperation 9
Title V General provisions on the Union's external action and specific provisions on the common foreign and security policy 10
Chapter 1 General provisions on the Union's external action 10
Chapter 2 Specific provisions on the common foreign and security policy 11
Section 1 Common provisions 11
Section 2 Provisions on the common security and defence policy 16
Title VI Final provisions 18

Treaty on the Functioning of the European Union (Consolidated version) 21
Preamble 21
Part One Principles 22
Title I Categories and areas of Union competence 22
Title II Provisions having general application 23
Part Two Non-discrimination and citizenship of the Union 25
Part Three Union policies and internal actions 27
Title I The internal market 27
Title II Free movement of goods 27
Chapter 1 The customs union 28
Chapter 2 Customs cooperation 28
Chapter 3 Prohibition of quantitative restrictions between Member States 28
Title III Agriculture and fisheries 29
Title IV Free movement of persons, services and capital 31
Chapter 1 Workers 31
Chapter 2 Right of establishment 32
Chapter 3 Services 33
Chapter 4 Capital and payments 34
Title V Area of freedom, security and justice 35
Chapter 1 General provisions 35
Chapter 2 Policies on border checks, asylum and immigration 37
Chapter 3 Judicial cooperation in civil matters 38

Chapter 4 Judicial cooperation in criminal matters 39
Chapter 5 Police cooperation 41
Title VI Transport 42
Title VII Common rules on competition, taxation and approximation of laws 44
Chapter 1 Rules on competition 44
Section 1 Rules applying to undertakings 44
Section 2 Aids granted by States 46
Chapter 2 Tax provisions 47
Chapter 3 Approximation of laws 48
Title VIII Economic and monetary policy 49
Chapter 1 Economic policy 50
Chapter 2 Monetary policy 53
Chapter 3 Institutional provisions 54
Chapter 4 Provisions specific to Member States whose currency is the euro 55
Chapter 5 Transitional provisions 56
Title IX Employment 58
Title X Social policy 60
Title XI The European Social Fund 63
Title XII Education, vocational training, youth and sport 63
Title XIII Culture 64
Title XIV Public health 65
Title XV Consumer protection 66
Title XVI Trans-European networks 66
Title XVII Industry 67
Title XVIII Economic, social and territorial cohesion 68
Title XIX Research and technological development and space 69
Title XX Environment 71
Title XXI Energy 72
Title XXII Tourism 73
Title XXIII Civil protection 73
Title XXIV Administrative cooperation 73
Part Four Association of the overseas countries and territories 74
Part Five External action by the Union 75
Title I General provisions on the Union's external action 75
Title II Common commercial policy 75
Title III Cooperation with third countries and humanitarian aid 76
Chapter 1 Development cooperation 76
Chapter 2 Economic, financial and technical cooperation with third countries 77
Chapter 3 Humanitarian aid 77
Title IV Restrictive measures 78
Title V International agreements 78
Title VI The Union's relations with international organisations and third countries and Union delegations 80
Title VII Solidarity clause 80
Part Six Institutional and financial provisions 81
Title I Institutional provisions 81
Chapter 1 The institutions 81
Section 1 The European Parliament 81
Section 2 The European Council 83

Section 3 The Council 84
Section 4 The Commission 85
Section 5 The Court of Justice of the European Union 86
Section 6 The European Central Bank 92
Section 7 The Court of Auditors 93
Chapter 2 Legal acts of the Union, adoption procedures and other provisions 95
Section 1 The legal acts of the Union 95
Section 2 Procedures for the adoption of acts and other provisions 96
Chapter 3 The Union's advisory bodies 98
Section 1 The Economic and Social Committee 99
Section 2 The Committee of the Regions 99
Chapter 4 The European Investment Bank 100
Title II Financial provisions 101
Chapter 1 The Union's own resources 101
Chapter 2 The multiannual financial framework 101
Chapter 3 The Union's annual budget 102
Chapter 4 Implementation of the budget and discharge 104
Chapter 5 Common provisions 105
Chapter 6 Combating fraud 105
Title III Enhanced cooperation 106
Part Seven General and final provisions 108

Charter of Fundamental Rights of the European Union **112**

European Convention on Human Rights (Article 1 and Section 1) **119**

Selected Protocols attached to the Treaties by the Lisbon Treaty **123**

Protocol (No 1) on the Role of National Parliaments in the European Union 123
Protocol (No 2) on the Application of the Principles of Subsidiarity and Proportionality 124
Protocol (No 3) on the Statute of the Court of Justice of the European Union (extracts) as amended 127
Protocol (No 8) Relating to Article 6(2) of the Treaty on European Union on the Accession of the Union to the European Convention on the Protection of Human Rights and Fundamental Freedoms 131
Protocol (No 25) on the Exercise of Shared Competence 131
Protocol (No 33) Concerning Article 157 of the Treaty on the Functioning of the European Union 132

Selected Declarations concerning provisions of the Treaties **132**

Declaration 1. concerning the Charter of Fundamental Rights of the European Union 132
Declaration 2. on Article 6(2) of the Treaty on European Union 132
Declaration 17. concerning primacy 132
Declaration 18. in relation to the delimitation of competences 133
Declaration 41. on Article 352 of the Treaty on the Functioning of the European Union 133
Declaration 42. on Article 352 of the Treaty on the Functioning of the European Union 133

Additional legislation and agreements affecting the institutions **134**

Majority voting procedure extract from the Luxembourg Accords 134
Regulation (EC) No 1049/2001 of the European Parliament and of the Council of 30 May 2001 regarding public access to European Parliament, Council and Commission documents (extracts) 134
Joint declaration relating to Regulation 1049/2001 of the European Parliament and of the Council regarding public access to European Parliament, Council and Commission documents 136
Joint declaration on practical arrangements for the codecision procedure (Article 251 of the EC Treaty) 137
Regulation (EU) No 182/2011 of the European Parliament and of the Council of 16 February 2011 laying down the rules and general principles concerning mechanisms for control by Member States of the Commission's exercise of implementing powers (extracts) 141

Court of Justice of the European Union **145**

Recommendations to national courts and tribunals, in relation to the initiation of preliminary ruling proceedings (2019) 145
Rules of Procedure of the Court of Justice (extracts to 2019) 152

Part II Secondary Legislation **169**

Free movement of goods **169**

Commission Directive 70/50 (Quantitative restrictions on imports) 169
Commission Practice Note on Import Prohibitions ('Cassis de Dijon') 171
Council Regulation 2679/98 (Free movement of goods) 172
European Parliament and Council Directive 2015/1535 (Technical regulations) (extracts) 174
European Parliament and Council Regulation 2019/515 (Mutual recognition of goods) (extracts) 180

Free movement of persons **185**

Council Directive 77/249 (Exercise by lawyers of freedom to provide services) as amended 185
European Parliament and Council Directive 96/71 (Posting of workers) 188
European Parliament and Council Directive 98/5 (Practice of profession of lawyer in another Member State) as amended (extracts) 193
Council Directive 2003/86 (On the right to family reunification) 196
Council Directive 2003/109 (Concerning the status of third-country nationals who are long-term residents) as amended 203
European Parliament and Council Directive 2004/38 (Citizens' free movement rights) as corrected and amended 213
European Parliament and Council Directive 2005/36 (Recognition of professional qualifications) as amended and corrected (extracts) 225
European Parliament and Council Directive 2006/123 (Services) (extracts) 240

European Parliament and Council Regulation (EU) No 492/2011 (Freedom of movement for workers within the Union) as amended (extracts) 257

Social policy: equal pay and treatment **259**

Council Directive 79/7 (Social security, equal treatment) 259
Council Directive 2000/43 (Equal treatment between persons irrespective of racial or ethnic origin) 261
Council Directive 2000/78 (Equal treatment in employment and occupation) (extracts) 265
Council Directive 2004/113 (Equal treatment between men and women in the access to and supply of goods and services) 268
European Parliament and Council Directive 2006/54 (Equal opportunities and equal treatment of men and women in matters of employment and occupation) recast (extracts) 272
European Parliament and Council Directive 2010/41 (Equal treatment in an activity in a self-employed capacity) (extracts) 278

Social policy: worker protection **281**

Council Directive 2001/23 (Transfers of undertakings) replacing the amended Directive 77/187 (extracts) 281
Council Directive 92/85 (Pregnant workers and working mothers) as amended (extracts) 283
Council Directive 98/59 (Collective redundancies) as amended and corrected 285
European Parliament and Council Directive 2003/88 (Working time) replacing Directives 93/104 and 2000/34 (extracts) 288

Competition **291**

Council Regulation No 17, Article 8 only 291
Commission (De Minimis) Notice (Minor agreements) 2014 291
Commission Notice 97/C 372/03 (Definition of relevant market) 294
Council Regulation (EC) No 1/2003 (Implementation of rules on competition) as amended (extracts) 303
Council Regulation (EC) No 139/2004 (Merger control) replacing Regulations 4064/89 and 1310/97 (extracts) 312
Commission Regulation (EC) No 773/2004 (Competition proceedings) as amended (extracts) 325
Commission Regulation (EU) No 2022/720 (Vertical agreements and concerted practices) 330
Summary of the 2004 Commission notice 'Guidelines on the effect on trade concept' 336
Commission 2006 Notice on Immunity from fines and reduction of fines in cartel cases as amended 337

Part III UK Brexit-Related Legislation **345**

European Communities Act 1972 (Extracts as amended) 345
European Union (Withdrawal) Act 2018 (Extracts) 346
EU–UK Withdrawal Agreement 2020 (Extracts) 365

The Irish Protocol/Windsor Framework 384
European Union (Withdrawal Agreement) Act 2020 392
The EU–UK Trade and Cooperation Agreement 2020 (Selected Extracts) 402
Part One: Common and Institutional Provisions 402
Title I: General provisions 402
Title II: Principles of interpretation and definitions 403
Title III: Institutional framework 404
Part Two: Trade, Transport, Fisheries and Other Arrangements 407
Heading One: Trade 407
Title I: Trade in goods 407
Title II: Services and investment 419
Title III: Digital trade 444
Title V: Intellectual property 449
Title IX: Transparency 460
Title X: Good regulatory practices and regulatory cooperation 461
Title XI: Level playing field for open and fair competition and sustainable development 465
Heading Four: Social Security Coordination and Visas for Short-Term Visits 472
Title I: Social security coordination 472
Title II: Visas for short-term visits 472
Part Six: Dispute Settlement and Horizontal Provisions 473
Title I: Dispute settlement 473
Title II: Basis for cooperation 482
Title III: Fulfillment of obligations and safeguard measures 483
Part Seven: Final Provisions 484

Index *487*

Thematic Contents

Competition Law

TFEU
Title VII Common rules on competition, taxation and approximation of laws 44
Chapter 1 Rules on competition 44
Section 1 Rules applying to undertakings 44
Section 2 Aids granted by States 46
Chapter 2 Tax provisions 47
Chapter 3 Approximation of laws 48

Council Regulation No 17, Article 8 only 291
Commission (De Minimis) Notice (Minor agreements) 2014 291
Commission Notice 97/C 372/03 (Definition of relevant market) 294
Council Regulation (EC) No 1/2003 (Implementation of rules on competition) 303
Council Regulation (EC) No 139/2004 (Merger control) 312
Commission Regulation (EC) No 773/2004 (Competition proceedings) 325
Summary of the 2004 Commission Notice 'Guidelines on the effect on trade concept' 336
Commission 2006 Notice on Immunity from fines and reduction of fines in cartel cases 337
Commission Regulation (EU) No 2022/720 (Vertical agreements and concerted practices) 330

Court of Justice of the European Union 145

Recommendations to national courts and tribunals, in relation to the initiation of preliminary ruling proceedings (2019) 145
Rules of Procedure of the Court of Justice (extracts to 2019) 152

Free movement of goods 169

TFEU
Title I The internal market 27
Title II Free movement of goods 27
Chapter 1 The customs union 28
Chapter 2 Customs cooperation 28
Chapter 3 Prohibition of quantitative restrictions between Member States 28

Commission Directive 70/50 (Quantitative restrictions on imports) 169
Commission Practice Note on Import Prohibitions ('Cassis de Dijon') 171
Council Regulation 2679/98 (Internal Market) 172
European Parliament and Council Directive 2015/1535 (Technical regulations) 174
European Parliament and Council Regulation 2019/515 (Mutual recognition of goods) 180

Free movement of persons 185

TFEU
Title IV Free movement of persons, services and capital 31
Chapter 1 Workers 31
Chapter 2 Right of establishment 32
Chapter 3 Services 33

Council Directive 77/249 (Exercise by lawyers of freedom to provide services) 185
European Parliament and Council Directive 96/71 (Posting of workers) 188
European Parliament and Council Directive 98/5 (Practice of profession of lawyer in another Member State) 193
Council Directive 2003/86 (On the right to family reunification) 196
Council Directive 2003/109 (Concerning the status of third-country nationals who are long-term residents) 203
European Parliament and Council Directive 2004/38 (Citizens' free movement rights) 213
European Parliament and Council Directive 2005/36 (Recognition of professional qualifications) 225
European Parliament and Council Directive 2006/123 (Services) 240

European Parliament and Council Regulation (EU) No 492/2011 (Freedom of movement for workers within the Union) 257

Institutional Law

TEU
Title III Provisions on the institutions 5
Title IV Provisions on enhanced cooperation 9

TFEU
Part Six Institutional and financial provisions 81
Title I Institutional provisions 81
Chapter 1 The institutions 81
Section 1 The European Parliament 81
Section 2 The European Council 83
Section 3 The Council 84
Section 4 The Commission 85
Section 5 The Court of Justice of the European Union 86
Section 6 The European Central Bank 92
Section 7 The Court of Auditors 93
Chapter 2 Legal acts of the Union, adoption procedures and other provisions 95
Section 1 The legal acts of the Union 95
Section 2 Procedures for the adoption of acts and other provisions 96
Chapter 3 The Union's advisory bodies 98
Section 1 The Economic and Social Committee 99
Section 2 The Committee of the Regions 99
Chapter 4 The European Investment Bank 100

Majority voting procedure extract from the Luxembourg Accords 134
Regulation (EC) No 1049/2001 of the European Parliament and of the Council of 30 May 2001 regarding public access to European Parliament, Council and Commission documents 134
Joint declaration relating to Regulation 1049/2001 of the European Parliament and of the Council regarding public access to European Parliament, Council and Commission documents 136
Joint declaration on practical arrangements for the codecision procedure 137
Regulation (EU) No 182/2011 of the European Parliament and of the Council of 16 February 2011 laying down the rules and general principles concerning mechanisms for control by Member States of the Commission's exercise of implementing powers 141

Selected Declarations concerning provisions of the Treaties 132

Declaration 1. concerning the Charter of Fundamental Rights of the European Union 132
Declaration 2. on Article 6(2) of the Treaty on European Union 132
Declaration 17. concerning primacy 132
Declaration 18. in relation to the delimitation of competences 133
Declaration 41. on Article 352 of the Treaty on the Functioning of the European Union 133
Declaration 42. on Article 352 of the Treaty on the Functioning of the European Union 133

Selected Protocols attached to the Treaties by the Lisbon Treaty 123

Protocol (No 1) on the Role of National Parliaments in the European Union 123
Protocol (No 2) on the Application of the Principles of Subsidiarity and Proportionality 124
Protocol (No 3) on the Statute of the Court of Justice of the European Union 127
Protocol (No 8) Relating to Article 6(2) of the Treaty on European Union on the Accession of the Union to the European Convention on the Protection of Human Rights and Fundamental Freedoms 131
Protocol (No 25) on the Exercise of Shared Competence 131
Protocol (No 33) Concerning Article 157 of the Treaty on the Functioning of the European Union 132

Social policy: Equal pay and treatment 259

TFEU
Title X Social policy 60

Council Directive 79/7 (Social security, equal treatment) 259
Council Directive 2000/43 (Equal treatment between persons irrespective of racial or ethnic origin) 261
Council Directive 2000/78 (Equal treatment in employment and occupation) 265
Council Directive 2004/113 (Equal treatment between men and women in the access to and supply of goods and services) 268
European Parliament and Council Directive 2006/54 (Equal opportunities and equal treatment of men and women in matters of employment and occupation) recast 272
European Parliament and Council Directive 2010/41 (Equal treatment in an activity in a self-employed capacity) 278

Social policy: Worker protection 281

TFEU
Title X Social policy 60

Council Directive 92/85 (Pregnant workers and working mothers) 283
Council Directive 98/59 (Collective redundancies) 285
Council Directive 2001/23 (Transfers of undertakings) 281
European Parliament and Council Directive 2003/88 (Working time) 288

Treaties 1

European Convention on Human Rights (Article 1 and Section 1) 119
Treaty on European Union (Consolidated version) 1
Treaty on the Functioning of the European Union (Consolidated version) 21
Charter of Fundamental Rights of the European Union 112

UK & Brexit-Related Legislation 345

European Communities Act 1972 (Extracts) 345
European Union (Withdrawal) Act 2018 346
EU–UK Withdrawal Agreement 2020 (Extracts: Arts 1–29; 40–50; and 86–91) 365
The Irish Protocol/Windsor Framework 384
European Union (Withdrawal Agreement) Act 2020 392
The EU–UK Trade and Cooperation Agreement 2020 (Selected Extracts) 402

Editor's preface to the 34th edition

Dear lecturer, student buying this book, reviewer, or reader,

This 34th edition is based on the foundations of the editions before and has been reviewed and updated subject, as ever, to space constraints, helpful advice from the editorial support team at OUP and the annual review amongst lecturers on the volume overall and its contents.

It is the third edition following the UK exit from the EU. With regard to Brexit-related material, I have included both the European Union (Withdrawal) Act 2018 and the European Union (Withdrawal Agreement) Act 2020, now in edited versions. There are also selected extracts from the EU–UK Trade and Cooperation Agreement 2020, the now to be amended Brexit Protocol on Ireland/Northern Ireland and select extracts from the December 2020 Trade and Cooperation Agreement. Strictly, the last three as EU instruments should appear in Part I of this collection but because they are so obviously UK Brexit-associated they are included in Part III. Those materials introduced into the last editions have now been edited further as the extent to which Brexit and reliance on the copious materials relating to it is included in EU law courses is becoming clearer. Hence, the decisions to omit or retain Articles are based on the Editor's view on their relevance to subjects covered in EU law modules. Another year may reveal whether courses, in fact, do pay great, if any, attention to the remaining materials. However, there have been significant developments in the Brexit story in the last year. The Protocol on Ireland/Northern Ireland has been the subject of fundamental discussion and amendment now by the Windsor Framework Agreement between the EU and the UK. The parties revisited the Protocol and considered closely the everyday application of the previous rules relating to customs, goods and agriculture. As a consequence, many of these rules, which are contained predominantly in annexes, will be removed or replaced once implementing legislation comes into force. Only the Protocol itself, now re-titled The Windsor Framework, is included (latest version: https://assets.publishing.service.gov.uk/government/uploads/system/uploads/attachment_data/file/1138989/The_Windsor_Framework_a_new_way_forward.pdf). A Statutory Instrument has now been drafted to put the Framework into law: https://www.legislation.gov.uk/ukdsi/2023/9780348246322.

The Retained EU Law (Revocation and Reform) Bill (REUL) (latest version: https://bills.parliament.uk/bills/3340) when enacted will also make changes to EUWA 2018. At the time of writing, the bill is a few weeks away from becoming law, hence the amendments have not been made but I have included Editor's Notes to indicate content which will be subject to amendment or repeal. As of 22 May 2023, the Commons were reviewing the Lords amendments to the bill at 2rd Reading stage.

The contents of this edition of *Blackstone's EU Treaties & Legislation* were chosen based on material frequently used in university EU law courses and modules. Originally the updating was undertaken by consulting the printed version of the Official Journal to check for new material in the subject areas selected and amendments to the existing stock. Unsurprisingly, this is now undertaken entirely electronically, especially as the electronic version of the OJ is now the official version.

In order to keep this collection to a manageable length, there has been a thorough review of the entire contents and legislation considered not to be mainstream for EU law courses has been removed. Other legislation has been presented as extracts by the removal of those articles and occasionally paragraphs equally considered as not required in EU law courses. The omissions to full articles are, hopefully, obvious. Article paragraph removals have been indicated by ellipses. The contents also show those items of legislation presented as extracts. The preambles and recitals in secondary EU legislation have been removed universally.

The core material taught in EU law modules has remained extremely stable for decades now. However, Brexit may well change that in the future. In the competition law section, because

I receive advice that it has been repealed, I wish to repeat my advice from a number of previous years that Article 8(3) of the largely repealed Regulation 17 has not been repealed and remains in force because it continues the Commission's powers in respect of being able to review past Decisions. If you don't believe me, look it up in 'EU Legislation in force'.

As usual, I have made various corrections and amendments to the existing stock as required and as are noted throughout the volume. I acknowledge with thanks the permission of the European Union to reproduce material taken historically from the OJ printed volumes. More recent provisions and additions have been taken from the online EUR-Lex website and, likewise, permission to reproduce these is gratefully acknowledged but with the clear proviso that from 1 July 2013 'only the Official Journal published in electronic form shall be authentic and shall produce legal effects' (Art 1 Regulation 216/2013). UK legislation is reproduced with the permission of HMSO (legislation.gov.uk) under the following terms: 'You may use and re-use the information featured on this website (not including logos) free of charge in any format or medium, under the terms of the Open Government Licence'. I am grateful to both for those permissions.

I am really thankful for the extensive support work and close attention to detail undertaken by the staff of OUP, Katherine Jones and Helen Swann, for another year of important and necessary behind-the-scenes editor work and support, and for conducting a thorough review of the volume and its contents. Thanks also to the copy-edit and proof stage staff and other persons for their input in the production of this edition.

As ever, I would be most grateful to receive any comments, suggestions, hints, criticisms, or advice on the content, style, or indeed any other aspect of this publication or just to point out plain errors where they are noticed. Suggestions for additional material to be included are also most welcome. Whilst for each edition I am able to spot a few errors from the OJ and eradicate them, it is also perfectly possible that I introduce, inadvertently, some of my own. Thanks to those of you who have made such comments or provided much appreciated advice. I do reflect on each piece of advice provided.

Nigel Foster
Buckingham, UK
April 2023

Extracts from the editor's preface to the 1st edition

This collection of European Community legislation has been compiled with two main considerations in mind.

First, to compile an up-to-date selection of the Community primary and secondary legislation which is the subject of frequent reference and is therefore appropriate to include in an accessible reference work which will be useful to both students of Community law and the many others who now come into contact with it.

Secondly, to furnish a basic set of unannotated legislative provisions for those students of Community law who are permitted to take materials into examinations.

In attempting to fulfil these twin tasks, I have been acutely aware of the growing mass of Community law and the danger of trying to incorporate everything which may be considered relevant. Therefore, as demanded by a compilation attempting to achieve specific aims, I have been very selective in the material chosen, particularly with regard to the primary source material of the European Communities.

The first part of the compilation contains Community Treaty and other primary materials. The second part of the book includes secondary Community legislation taken from a number of areas of substantive law. Once again I have been necessarily selective and confined the scope to areas most commonly covered in Community law courses, although I am certain that I shall be unable to entirely satisfy all courses or perhaps even any course.

Finally I have included as a matter of necessity extracts from the European Communities Act 1972. For the latter item, I gratefully acknowledge HMSO.

The Community source material was taken predominantly from the Official Journal of the European Communities unless where otherwise stated and likewise I gratefully acknowledge the permission of the European Commission to reproduce those materials. Wherever they were noticed, errors in this material have been corrected; all other errors and omissions are my responsibility.

Nigel Foster
Cardiff
February 1990

New to this edition

The 34th edition of *Blackstone's EU Treaties & Legislation* has been fully revised and updated with all relevant developments through to April 2023 including:

- The change of the Vertical Agreement block exemption Regulation in the competition law section.
- The considerable changes to Part 3, the UK & Brexit as a result of both the Windsor Framework Agreement and Retained EU Law (Revocation and Reform) Bill (RUEL).

Conventions used in *Blackstone's EU Treaties & Legislation*

The material in this book is reproduced in its most up-to-date form. Supplementary notes and details of amending provisions are generally not included.

Useful websites

Tables of equivalences for the Treaties on European Union and the Functioning of the European Union replacing the previous Treaty on European Union and the European Community Treaty as referred to in Article 5 of the Lisbon Treaty:

- Treaty on European Union and Treaty on the Functioning of the European Union: https://eur-lex.europa.eu/resource.html?uri=cellar:8d1c14fc-6be7-4d4e-8416-f28cfc7b3b60.0006.01/DOC_17&format=PDF

Tables of equivalences for the Treaty on European Union and for the European Community Treaty as referred to in Article 12 of the Treaty of Amsterdam:

- Treaty on European Union (pre-Lisbon) and Treaty establishing the European Community: https://eur-lex.europa.eu/LexUriServ/LexUriServ.do?uri=CELEX:11997DNA:EN:HTML

EU Treaties

Consolidated Version of the Treaty on European Union*

Preamble

RESOLVED to mark a new stage in the process of European integration undertaken with the establishment of the European Communities,

DRAWING INSPIRATION from the cultural, religious and humanist inheritance of Europe, from which have developed the universal values of the inviolable and inalienable rights of the human person, freedom, democracy, equality and the rule of law,

RECALLING the historic importance of the ending of the division of the European continent and the need to create firm bases for the construction of the future Europe,

CONFIRMING their attachment to the principles of liberty, democracy and respect for human rights and fundamental freedoms and of the rule of law,

CONFIRMING their attachment to fundamental social rights as defined in the European Social Charter signed at Turin on 18 October 1961 and in the 1989 Community Charter of the Fundamental Social Rights of Workers,

DESIRING to deepen the solidarity between their peoples while respecting their history, their culture and their traditions,

DESIRING to enhance further the democratic and efficient functioning of the institutions so as to enable them better to carry out, within a single institutional framework, the tasks entrusted to them,

RESOLVED to achieve the strengthening and the convergence of their economies and to establish an economic and monetary union including, in accordance with the provisions of this Treaty and of the Treaty on the Functioning of the European Union, a single and stable currency,

DETERMINED to promote economic and social progress for their peoples, taking into account the principle of sustainable development and within the context of the accomplishment of the internal market and of reinforced cohesion and environmental protection, and to implement policies ensuring that advances in economic integration are accompanied by parallel progress in other fields,

RESOLVED to establish a citizenship common to nationals of their countries,

RESOLVED to implement a common foreign and security policy including the progressive framing of a common defence policy, which might lead to a common defence in accordance with the provisions of Article 42, thereby reinforcing the European identity and its independence in order to promote peace, security and progress in Europe and in the world,

RESOLVED to facilitate the free movement of persons, while ensuring the safety and security of their peoples, by establishing an area of freedom, security and justice, in accordance with the provisions of this Treaty and of the Treaty on the Functioning of the European Union,

* **Editor's Note:** Incorporating Lisbon Treaty changes. Signatures and contents omitted. This version incorporates the minor changes as reproduced in OJ 2016 C202/1 of 7 June 2016 and as amended by the Croatian Accession Treaty (OJ 2012 L112/1). See https://eur-lex.europa.eu/collection/eu-law/treaties/treaties-force.html#new-2-51. List of member states omitted.

RESOLVED to continue the process of creating an ever closer union among the peoples of Europe, in which decisions are taken as closely as possible to the citizen in accordance with the principle of subsidiarity,

IN VIEW of further steps to be taken in order to advance European integration,

HAVE DECIDED to establish a European Union and to this end have designated as their Plenipotentiaries:

(List of plenipotentiaries not reproduced.)

WHO, having exchanged their full powers, found in good and due form, have agreed as follows:

Title I Common provisions

Article 1 (ex Article 1 TEU)[1]

By this Treaty, the HIGH CONTRACTING PARTIES establish among themselves a EUROPEAN UNION, hereinafter called 'the Union' on which the Member States confer competences to attain objectives they have in common.

This Treaty marks a new stage in the process of creating an ever closer union among the peoples of Europe, in which decisions are taken as openly as possible and as closely as possible to the citizen.

The Union shall be founded on the present Treaty and on the Treaty on the Functioning of the European Union (hereinafter referred to as 'the Treaties'). Those two Treaties shall have the same legal value. The Union shall replace and succeed the European Community.

Article 2

The Union is founded on the values of respect for human dignity, freedom, democracy, equality, the rule of law and respect for human rights, including the rights of persons belonging to minorities. These values are common to the Member States in a society in which pluralism, non-discrimination, tolerance, justice, solidarity and equality between women and men prevail.

Article 3 (ex Article 2 TEU)

1. The Union's aim is to promote peace, its values and the well-being of its peoples.

2. The Union shall offer its citizens an area of freedom, security and justice without internal frontiers, in which the free movement of persons is ensured in conjunction with appropriate measures with respect to external border controls, asylum, immigration and the prevention and combating of crime.

3. The Union shall establish an internal market. It shall work for the sustainable development of Europe based on balanced economic growth and price stability, a highly competitive social market economy, aiming at full employment and social progress, and a high level of protection and improvement of the quality of the environment. It shall promote scientific and technological advance.

It shall combat social exclusion and discrimination, and shall promote social justice and protection, equality between women and men, solidarity between generations and protection of the rights of the child.

It shall promote economic, social and territorial cohesion, and solidarity among Member States.

It shall respect its rich cultural and linguistic diversity, and shall ensure that Europe's cultural heritage is safeguarded and enhanced.

4. The Union shall establish an economic and monetary union whose currency is the euro.

5. In its relations with the wider world, the Union shall uphold and promote its values and interests and contribute to the protection of its citizens. It shall contribute to peace, security, the sustainable development of the Earth, solidarity and mutual respect among peoples, free and fair trade, eradication of poverty and the protection of human rights, in particular the rights of the child, as

[1] These references are merely indicative. For more ample information, please refer to the tables of equivalences between the old and the new numbering of the Treaties.

well as to the strict observance and the development of international law, including respect for the principles of the United Nations Charter.

6. The Union shall pursue its objectives by appropriate means commensurate with the competences which are conferred upon it in the Treaties.

Article 4

1. In accordance with Article 5, competences not conferred upon the Union in the Treaties remain with the Member States.

2. The Union shall respect the equality of Member States before the Treaties as well as their national identities, inherent in their fundamental structures, political and constitutional, inclusive of regional and local self-government. It shall respect their essential State functions, including ensuring the territorial integrity of the State, maintaining law and order and safeguarding national security. In particular, national security remains the sole responsibility of each Member State.

3. Pursuant to the principle of sincere cooperation, the Union and the Member States shall, in full mutual respect, assist each other in carrying out tasks which flow from the Treaties.

The Member States shall take any appropriate measure, general or particular, to ensure fulfilment of the obligations arising out of the Treaties or resulting from the acts of the institutions of the Union.

The Member States shall facilitate the achievement of the Union's tasks and refrain from any measure which could jeopardise the attainment of the Union's objectives.

Article 5 (ex Article 5 TEC)

1. The limits of Union competences are governed by the principle of conferral. The use of Union competences is governed by the principles of subsidiarity and proportionality.

2. Under the principle of conferral, the Union shall act only within the limits of the competences conferred upon it by the Member States in the Treaties to attain the objectives set out therein. Competences not conferred upon the Union in the Treaties remain with the Member States.

3. Under the principle of subsidiarity, in areas which do not fall within its exclusive competence, the Union shall act only if and in so far as the objectives of the proposed action cannot be sufficiently achieved by the Member States, either at central level or at regional and local level, but can rather, by reason of the scale or effects of the proposed action, be better achieved at Union level.

The institutions of the Union shall apply the principle of subsidiarity as laid down in the Protocol on the application of the principles of subsidiarity and proportionality. National Parliaments ensure compliance with the principle of subsidiarity in accordance with the procedure set out in that Protocol.

4. Under the principle of proportionality, the content and form of Union action shall not exceed what is necessary to achieve the objectives of the Treaties.

The institutions of the Union shall apply the principle of proportionality as laid down in the Protocol on the application of the principles of subsidiarity and proportionality.

Article 6 (ex Article 6 TEU)

1. The Union recognises the rights, freedoms and principles set out in the Charter of Fundamental Rights of the European Union of 7 December 2000, as adapted at Strasbourg, on 12 December 2007, which shall have the same legal value as the Treaties.

The provisions of the Charter shall not extend in any way the competences of the Union as defined in the Treaties.

The rights, freedoms and principles in the Charter shall be interpreted in accordance with the general provisions in Title VII of the Charter governing its interpretation and application and with due regard to the explanations referred to in the Charter, that set out the sources of those provisions.

2. The Union shall accede to the European Convention for the Protection of Human Rights and Fundamental Freedoms. Such accession shall not affect the Union's competences as defined in the Treaties.

3. Fundamental rights, as guaranteed by the European Convention for the Protection of Human Rights and Fundamental Freedoms and as they result from the constitutional traditions common to the Member States, shall constitute general principles of the Union's law.

Article 7 (ex Article 7 TEU)

1. On a reasoned proposal by one-third of the Member States, by the European Parliament or by the European Commission, the Council, acting by a majority of four-fifths of its members after obtaining the consent of the European Parliament, may determine that there is a clear risk of a serious breach by a Member State of the values referred to in Article 2. Before making such a determination, the Council shall hear the Member State in question and may address recommendations to it, acting in accordance with the same procedure.

The Council shall regularly verify that the grounds on which such a determination was made continue to apply.

2. The European Council, acting by unanimity on a proposal by one-third of the Member States or by the Commission and after obtaining the consent of the European Parliament, may determine the existence of a serious and persistent breach by a Member State of the values referred to in Article 2, after inviting the Member State in question to submit its observations.

3. Where a determination under paragraph 2 has been made, the Council, acting by a qualified majority, may decide to suspend certain of the rights deriving from the application of the Treaties to the Member State in question, including the voting rights of the representative of the government of that Member State in the Council. In doing so, the Council shall take into account the possible consequences of such a suspension on the rights and obligations of natural and legal persons.

The obligations of the Member State in question under this Treaty shall in any case continue to be binding on that State.

4. The Council, acting by a qualified majority, may decide subsequently to vary or revoke measures taken under paragraph 3 in response to changes in the situation which led to their being imposed.

5. The voting arrangements applying to the European Parliament, the European Council and the Council for the purposes of this Article are laid down in Article 354 of the Treaty on the Functioning of the European Union.

Article 8

1. The Union shall develop a special relationship with neighbouring countries, aiming to establish an area of prosperity and good neighbourliness, founded on the values of the Union and characterised by close and peaceful relations based on cooperation.

2. For the purposes of paragraph 1, the Union may conclude specific agreements with the countries concerned. These agreements may contain reciprocal rights and obligations as well as the possibility of undertaking activities jointly. Their implementation shall be the subject of periodic consultation.

Title II Provisions on democratic principles

Article 9

In all its activities, the Union shall observe the principle of the equality of its citizens, who shall receive equal attention from its institutions, bodies, offices and agencies. Every national of a Member State shall be a citizen of the Union. Citizenship of the Union shall be additional to national citizenship and shall not replace it.

Article 10

1. The functioning of the Union shall be founded on representative democracy.
2. Citizens are directly represented at Union level in the European Parliament.

Member States are represented in the European Council by their Heads of State or Government and in the Council by their governments, themselves democratically accountable either to their national Parliaments, or to their citizens.

3. Every citizen shall have the right to participate in the democratic life of the Union. Decisions shall be taken as openly and as closely as possible to the citizen.

4. Political parties at European level contribute to forming European political awareness and to expressing the will of citizens of the Union.

Article 11

1. The institutions shall, by appropriate means, give citizens and representative associations the opportunity to make known and publicly exchange their views in all areas of Union action.

2. The institutions shall maintain an open, transparent and regular dialogue with representative associations and civil society.

3. The European Commission shall carry out broad consultations with parties concerned in order to ensure that the Union's actions are coherent and transparent.

4. Not less than one million citizens who are nationals of a significant number of Member States may take the initiative of inviting the European Commission, within the framework of its powers, to submit any appropriate proposal on matters where citizens consider that a legal act of the Union is required for the purpose of implementing the Treaties.

The procedures and conditions required for such a citizens' initiative shall be determined in accordance with the first paragraph of Article 24 of the Treaty on the Functioning of the European Union.

Article 12

National Parliaments contribute actively to the good functioning of the Union:

(a) through being informed by the institutions of the Union and having draft legislative acts of the Union forwarded to them in accordance with the Protocol on the role of national Parliaments in the European Union;

(b) by seeing to it that the principle of subsidiarity is respected in accordance with the procedures provided for in the Protocol on the application of the principles of subsidiarity and proportionality;

(c) by taking part, within the framework of the area of freedom, security and justice, in the evaluation mechanisms for the implementation of the Union policies in that area, in accordance with Article 70 of the Treaty on the Functioning of the European Union, and through being involved in the political monitoring of Europol and the evaluation of Eurojust's activities in accordance with Articles 88 and 85 of that Treaty;

(d) by taking part in the revision procedures of the Treaties, in accordance with Article 48 of this Treaty;

(e) by being notified of applications for accession to the Union, in accordance with Article 49 of this Treaty;

(f) by taking part in the inter-parliamentary cooperation between national Parliaments and with the European Parliament, in accordance with the Protocol on the role of national Parliaments in the European Union.

Title III Provisions on the institutions

Article 13

1. The Union shall have an institutional framework which shall aim to promote its values, advance its objectives, serve its interests, those of its citizens and those of the Member States, and ensure the consistency, effectiveness and continuity of its policies and actions.

The Union's institutions shall be:

- the European Parliament,
- the European Council,

- the Council,
- the European Commission (hereinafter referred to as 'the Commission'),
- the Court of Justice of the European Union,
- the European Central Bank,
- the Court of Auditors.

2. Each institution shall act within the limits of the powers conferred on it in the Treaties, and in conformity with the procedures, conditions and objectives set out in them. The institutions shall practice mutual sincere cooperation.

3. The provisions relating to the European Central Bank and the Court of Auditors and detailed provisions on the other institutions are set out in the Treaty on the Functioning of the European Union.

4. The European Parliament, the Council and the Commission shall be assisted by an Economic and Social Committee and a Committee of the Regions acting in an advisory capacity.

Article 14

1. The European Parliament shall, jointly with the Council, exercise legislative and budgetary functions. It shall exercise functions of political control and consultation as laid down in the Treaties. It shall elect the President of the Commission.

2. The European Parliament shall be composed of representatives of the Union's citizens. They shall not exceed seven hundred and fifty in number, plus the President. Representation of citizens shall be degressively proportional, with a minimum threshold of six members per Member State. No Member State shall be allocated more than ninety-six seats.

The European Council shall adopt by unanimity, on the initiative of the European Parliament and with its consent, a decision establishing the composition of the European Parliament, respecting the principles referred to in the first subparagraph.

3. The members of the European Parliament shall be elected for a term of five years by direct universal suffrage in a free and secret ballot.

4. The European Parliament shall elect its President and its officers from among its members.

Article 15

1. The European Council shall provide the Union with the necessary impetus for its development and shall define the general political directions and priorities thereof. It shall not exercise legislative functions.

2. The European Council shall consist of the Heads of State or Government of the Member States, together with its President and the President of the Commission. The High Representative of the Union for Foreign Affairs and Security Policy shall take part in its work.

3. The European Council shall meet twice every six months, convened by its President. When the agenda so requires, the members of the European Council may decide each to be assisted by a minister and, in the case of the President of the Commission, by a member of the Commission. When the situation so requires, the President shall convene a special meeting of the European Council.

4. Except where the Treaties provide otherwise, decisions of the European Council shall be taken by consensus.

5. The European Council shall elect its President, by a qualified majority, for a term of two and a half years, renewable once. In the event of an impediment or serious misconduct, the European Council can end the President's term of office in accordance with the same procedure.

6. The President of the European Council:

(a) shall chair it and drive forward its work;
(b) shall ensure the preparation and continuity of the work of the European Council in cooperation with the President of the Commission, and on the basis of the work of the General Affairs Council;
(c) shall endeavour to facilitate cohesion and consensus within the European Council;
(d) shall present a report to the European Parliament after each of the meetings of the European Council.

The President of the European Council shall, at his level and in that capacity, ensure the external representation of the Union on issues concerning its common foreign and security policy, without prejudice to the powers of the High Representative of the Union for Foreign Affairs and Security Policy.

The President of the European Council shall not hold a national office.

Article 16

1. The Council shall, jointly with the European Parliament, exercise legislative and budgetary functions. It shall carry out policy-making and coordinating functions as laid down in the Treaties.

2. The Council shall consist of a representative of each Member State at ministerial level, who may commit the government of the Member State in question and cast its vote.

3. The Council shall act by a qualified majority except where the Treaties provide otherwise.

4. As from 1 November 2014, a qualified majority shall be defined as at least 55 % of the members of the Council, comprising at least fifteen of them and representing Member States comprising at least 65 % of the population of the Union.

A blocking minority must include at least four Council members, failing which the qualified majority shall be deemed attained.

The other arrangements governing the qualified majority are laid down in Article 238(2) of the Treaty on the Functioning of the European Union.

5. The transitional provisions relating to the definition of the qualified majority which shall be applicable until 31 October 2014 and those which shall be applicable from 1 November 2014 to 31 March 2017 are laid down in the Protocol on transitional provisions.

6. The Council shall meet in different configurations, the list of which shall be adopted in accordance with Article 236 of the Treaty on the Functioning of the European Union.

The General Affairs Council shall ensure consistency in the work of the different Council configurations. It shall prepare and ensure the follow-up to meetings of the European Council, in liaison with the President of the European Council and the Commission.

The Foreign Affairs Council shall elaborate the Union's external action on the basis of strategic guidelines laid down by the European Council and ensure that the Union's action is consistent.

7. A Committee of Permanent Representatives of the Governments of the Member States shall be responsible for preparing the work of the Council.

8. The Council shall meet in public when it deliberates and votes on a draft legislative act. To this end, each Council meeting shall be divided into two parts, dealing respectively with deliberations on Union legislative acts and non-legislative activities.

9. The Presidency of Council configurations, other than that of Foreign Affairs, shall be held by Member State representatives in the Council on the basis of equal rotation, in accordance with the conditions established in accordance with Article 236 of the Treaty on the Functioning of the European Union.

Article 17

1. The Commission shall promote the general interest of the Union and take appropriate initiatives to that end. It shall ensure the application of the Treaties, and of measures adopted by the institutions pursuant to them. It shall oversee the application of Union law under the control of the Court of Justice of the European Union. It shall execute the budget and manage programmes. It shall exercise coordinating, executive and management functions, as laid down in the Treaties. With the exception of the common foreign and security policy, and other cases provided for in the Treaties, it shall ensure the Union's external representation. It shall initiate the Union's annual and multiannual programming with a view to achieving interinstitutional agreements.

2. Union legislative acts may only be adopted on the basis of a Commission proposal, except where the Treaties provide otherwise. Other acts shall be adopted on the basis of a Commission proposal where the Treaties so provide.

3. The Commission's term of office shall be five years.

The members of the Commission shall be chosen on the ground of their general competence and European commitment from persons whose independence is beyond doubt.

In carrying out its responsibilities, the Commission shall be completely independent. Without prejudice to Article 18(2), the members of the Commission shall neither seek nor take instructions from any Government or other institution, body, office or entity. They shall refrain from any action incompatible with their duties or the performance of their tasks.

4. The Commission appointed between the date of entry into force of the Treaty of Lisbon and 31 October 2014, shall consist of one national of each Member State, including its President and the High Representative of the Union for Foreign Affairs and Security Policy who shall be one of its Vice-Presidents.

5. As from 1 November 2014, the Commission shall consist of a number of members, including its President and the High Representative of the Union for Foreign Affairs and Security Policy, corresponding to two-thirds of the number of Member States, unless the European Council, acting unanimously, decides to alter this number.

The members of the Commission shall be chosen from among the nationals of the Member States on the basis of a system of strictly equal rotation between the Member States, reflecting the demographic and geographical range of all the Member States. This system shall be established unanimously by the European Council in accordance with Article 244 of the Treaty on the Functioning of the European Union.

6. The President of the Commission shall:

(a) lay down guidelines within which the Commission is to work;

(b) decide on the internal organisation of the Commission, ensuring that it acts consistently, efficiently and as a collegiate body;

(c) appoint Vice-Presidents, other than the High Representative of the Union for Foreign Affairs and Security Policy, from among the members of the Commission.

A member of the Commission shall resign if the President so requests. The High Representative of the Union for Foreign Affairs and Security Policy shall resign, in accordance with the procedure set out in Article 18(1), if the President so requests.

7. Taking into account the elections to the European Parliament and after having held the appropriate consultations, the European Council, acting by a qualified majority, shall propose to the European Parliament a candidate for President of the Commission. This candidate shall be elected by the European Parliament by a majority of its component members. If he does not obtain the required majority, the European Council, acting by a qualified majority, shall within one month propose a new candidate who shall be elected by the European Parliament following the same procedure.

The Council, by common accord with the President-elect, shall adopt the list of the other persons whom it proposes for appointment as members of the Commission. They shall be selected, on the basis of the suggestions made by Member States, in accordance with the criteria set out in paragraph 3, second subparagraph, and paragraph 5, second subparagraph.

The President, the High Representative of the Union for Foreign Affairs and Security Policy and the other members of the Commission shall be subject as a body to a vote of consent by the European Parliament. On the basis of this consent the Commission shall be appointed by the European Council, acting by a qualified majority.

8. The Commission, as a body, shall be responsible to the European Parliament. In accordance with Article 234 of the Treaty on the Functioning of the European Union, the European Parliament may vote on a motion of censure of the Commission. If such a motion is carried, the members of the Commission shall resign as a body and the High Representative of the Union for Foreign Affairs and Security Policy shall resign from the duties that he carries out in the Commission.

Article 18

1. The European Council, acting by a qualified majority, with the agreement of the President of the Commission, shall appoint the High Representative of the Union for Foreign Affairs and Security Policy. The European Council may end his term of office by the same procedure.

2. The High Representative shall conduct the Union's common foreign and security policy. He shall contribute by his proposals to the development of that policy, which he shall carry out as mandated by the Council. The same shall apply to the common security and defence policy.

3. The High Representative shall preside over the Foreign Affairs Council.

4. The High Representative shall be one of the Vice-Presidents of the Commission. He shall ensure the consistency of the Union's external action. He shall be responsible within the Commission for responsibilities incumbent on it in external relations and for coordinating other aspects of the Union's external action. In exercising these responsibilities within the Commission, and only for these responsibilities, the High Representative shall be bound by Commission procedures to the extent that this is consistent with paragraphs 2 and 3.

Article 19

1. The Court of Justice of the European Union shall include the Court of Justice, the General Court and specialised courts. It shall ensure that in the interpretation and application of the Treaties the law is observed.

Member States shall provide remedies sufficient to ensure effective legal protection in the fields covered by Union law.

2. The Court of Justice shall consist of one judge from each Member State. It shall be assisted by Advocates-General.

The General Court shall include at least one judge per Member State.

The Judges and the Advocates-General of the Court of Justice and the Judges of the General Court shall be chosen from persons whose independence is beyond doubt and who satisfy the conditions set out in Articles 253 and 254 of the Treaty on the Functioning of the European Union. They shall be appointed by common accord of the governments of the Member States for six years. Retiring Judges and Advocates-General may be reappointed.

3. The Court of Justice of the European Union shall, in accordance with the Treaties:

(a) rule on actions brought by a Member State, an institution or a natural or legal person;

(b) give preliminary rulings, at the request of courts or tribunals of the Member States, on the interpretation of Union law or the validity of acts adopted by the institutions;

(c) rule in other cases provided for in the Treaties.

Title IV Provisions on enhanced cooperation

Article 20 (ex Articles 27a to 27e, 40 to 40b and 43 to 45 TEU and ex Articles 11 and 11a TEC)

1. Member States which wish to establish enhanced cooperation between themselves within the framework of the Union's non-exclusive competences may make use of its institutions and exercise those competences by applying the relevant provisions of the Treaties, subject to the limits and in accordance with the detailed arrangements laid down in this Article and in Articles 326 to 334 of the Treaty on the Functioning of the European Union.

Enhanced cooperation shall aim to further the objectives of the Union, protect its interests and reinforce its integration process. Such cooperation shall be open at any time to all Member States, in accordance with Article 328 of the Treaty on the Functioning of the European Union.

2. The decision authorising enhanced cooperation shall be adopted by the Council as a last resort, when it has established that the objectives of such cooperation cannot be attained within a reasonable period by the Union as a whole, and provided that at least nine Member States participate in it. The Council shall act in accordance with the procedure laid down in Article 329 of the Treaty on the Functioning of the European Union.

3. All members of the Council may participate in its deliberations, but only members of the Council representing the Member States participating in enhanced cooperation shall take part in the vote. The voting rules are set out in Article 330 of the Treaty on the Functioning of the European Union.

4. Acts adopted in the framework of enhanced cooperation shall bind only participating Member States. They shall not be regarded as part of the *acquis* which has to be accepted by candidate States for accession to the Union.

Title V General provisions on the Union's external action and specific provisions on the common foreign and security policy

Chapter 1 General provisions on the Union's external action

Article 21

1. The Union's action on the international scene shall be guided by the principles which have inspired its own creation, development and enlargement, and which it seeks to advance in the wider world: democracy, the rule of law, the universality and indivisibility of human rights and fundamental freedoms, respect for human dignity, the principles of equality and solidarity, and respect for the principles of the United Nations Charter and international law.

The Union shall seek to develop relations and build partnerships with third countries, and international, regional or global organisations which share the principles referred to in the first subparagraph. It shall promote multilateral solutions to common problems, in particular in the framework of the United Nations.

2. The Union shall define and pursue common policies and actions, and shall work for a high degree of cooperation in all fields of international relations, in order to:

(a) safeguard its values, fundamental interests, security, independence and integrity;
(b) consolidate and support democracy, the rule of law, human rights and the principles of international law;
(c) preserve peace, prevent conflicts and strengthen international security, in accordance with the purposes and principles of the United Nations Charter, with the principles of the Helsinki Final Act and with the aims of the Charter of Paris, including those relating to external borders;
(d) foster the sustainable economic, social and environmental development of developing countries, with the primary aim of eradicating poverty;
(e) encourage the integration of all countries into the world economy, including through the progressive abolition of restrictions on international trade;
(f) help develop international measures to preserve and improve the quality of the environment and the sustainable management of global natural resources, in order to ensure sustainable development;
(g) assist populations, countries and regions confronting natural or man-made disasters; and
(h) promote an international system based on stronger multilateral cooperation and good global governance.

3. The Union shall respect the principles and pursue the objectives set out in paragraphs 1 and 2 in the development and implementation of the different areas of the Union's external action covered by this Title and by Part Five of the Treaty on the Functioning of the European Union, and of the external aspects of its other policies.

The Union shall ensure consistency between the different areas of its external action and between these and its other policies. The Council and the Commission, assisted by the High Representative of the Union for Foreign Affairs and Security Policy, shall ensure that consistency and shall cooperate to that effect.

Article 22

1. On the basis of the principles and objectives set out in Article 21, the European Council shall identify the strategic interests and objectives of the Union.

Decisions of the European Council on the strategic interests and objectives of the Union shall relate to the common foreign and security policy and to other areas of the external action of the Union. Such decisions may concern the relations of the Union with a specific country or region or may be thematic in approach. They shall define their duration, and the means to be made available by the Union and the Member States.

The European Council shall act unanimously on a recommendation from the Council, adopted by the latter under the arrangements laid down for each area. Decisions of the European Council shall be implemented in accordance with the procedures provided for in the Treaties.

2. The High Representative of the Union for Foreign Affairs and Security Policy, for the area of common foreign and security policy, and the Commission, for other areas of external action, may submit joint proposals to the Council.

Chapter 2 Specific provisions on the common foreign and security policy

Section 1 Common provisions

Article 23

The Union's action on the international scene, pursuant to this Chapter, shall be guided by the principles, shall pursue the objectives of, and be conducted in accordance with, the general provisions laid down in Chapter 1.

Article 24 (ex Article 11 TEU)

1. The Union's competence in matters of common foreign and security policy shall cover all areas of foreign policy and all questions relating to the Union's security, including the progressive framing of a common defence policy that might lead to a common defence.

The common foreign and security policy is subject to specific rules and procedures. It shall be defined and implemented by the European Council and the Council acting unanimously, except where the Treaties provide otherwise. The adoption of legislative acts shall be excluded. The common foreign and security policy shall be put into effect by the High Representative of the Union for Foreign Affairs and Security Policy and by Member States, in accordance with the Treaties. The specific role of the European Parliament and of the Commission in this area is defined by the Treaties. The Court of Justice of the European Union shall not have jurisdiction with respect to these provisions, with the exception of its jurisdiction to monitor compliance with Article 40 of this Treaty and to review the legality of certain decisions as provided for by the second paragraph of Article 275 of the Treaty on the Functioning of the European Union.

2. Within the framework of the principles and objectives of its external action, the Union shall conduct, define and implement a common foreign and security policy, based on the development of mutual political solidarity among Member States, the identification of questions of general interest and the achievement of an ever-increasing degree of convergence of Member States' actions.

3. The Member States shall support the Union's external and security policy actively and unreservedly in a spirit of loyalty and mutual solidarity and shall comply with the Union's action in this area.

The Member States shall work together to enhance and develop their mutual political solidarity. They shall refrain from any action which is contrary to the interests of the Union or likely to impair its effectiveness as a cohesive force in international relations.

The Council and the High Representative shall ensure compliance with these principles.

Article 25 (ex Article 12 TEU)

The Union shall conduct the common foreign and security policy by:

- (a) defining the general guidelines;
- (b) adopting decisions defining:
  - (i) actions to be undertaken by the Union;
  - (ii) positions to be taken by the Union;
  - (iii) arrangements for the implementation of the decisions referred to in points (i) and (ii); and by
- (c) strengthening systematic cooperation between Member States in the conduct of policy.

Article 26 (ex Article 13 TEU)

1. The European Council shall identify the Union's strategic interests, determine the objectives of and define general guidelines for the common foreign and security policy, including for matters with defence implications. It shall adopt the necessary decisions.

If international developments so require, the President of the European Council shall convene an extraordinary meeting of the European Council in order to define the strategic lines of the Union's policy in the face of such developments.

2. The Council shall frame the common foreign and security policy and take the decisions necessary for defining and implementing it on the basis of the general guidelines and strategic lines defined by the European Council.

The Council and the High Representative of the Union for Foreign Affairs and Security Policy shall ensure the unity, consistency and effectiveness of action by the Union.

3. The common foreign and security policy shall be put into effect by the High Representative and by the Member States, using national and Union resources.

Article 27

1. The High Representative of the Union for Foreign Affairs and Security Policy, who shall chair the Foreign Affairs Council, shall contribute through his proposals towards the preparation of the common foreign and security policy and shall ensure implementation of the decisions adopted by the European Council and the Council.

2. The High Representative shall represent the Union for matters relating to the common foreign and security policy. He shall conduct political dialogue with third parties on the Union's behalf and shall express the Union's position in international organisations and at international conferences.

3. In fulfilling his mandate, the High Representative shall be assisted by a European External Action Service. This service shall work in cooperation with the diplomatic services of the Member States and shall comprise officials from relevant departments of the General Secretariat of the Council and of the Commission as well as staff seconded from national diplomatic services of the Member States. The organisation and functioning of the European External Action Service shall be established by a decision of the Council. The Council shall act on a proposal from the High Representative after consulting the European Parliament and after obtaining the consent of the Commission.

Article 28 (ex Article 14 TEU)

1. Where the international situation requires operational action by the Union, the Council shall adopt the necessary decisions. They shall lay down their objectives, scope, the means to be made available to the Union, if necessary their duration, and the conditions for their implementation.

If there is a change in circumstances having a substantial effect on a question subject to such a decision, the Council shall review the principles and objectives of that decision and take the necessary decisions.

2. Decisions referred to in paragraph 1 shall commit the Member States in the positions they adopt and in the conduct of their activity.

3. Whenever there is any plan to adopt a national position or take national action pursuant to a decision as referred to in paragraph 1, information shall be provided by the Member State concerned in time to allow, if necessary, for prior consultations within the Council. The obligation to provide prior information shall not apply to measures which are merely a national transposition of Council decisions.

4. In cases of imperative need arising from changes in the situation and failing a review of the Council decision as referred to in paragraph 1, Member States may take the necessary measures as a matter of urgency having regard to the general objectives of that decision. The Member State concerned shall inform the Council immediately of any such measures.

5. Should there be any major difficulties in implementing a decision as referred to in this Article, a Member State shall refer them to the Council which shall discuss them and seek appropriate solutions. Such solutions shall not run counter to the objectives of the decision referred to in paragraph 1 or impair its effectiveness.

Article 29 (ex Article 15 TEU)
The Council shall adopt decisions which shall define the approach of the Union to a particular matter of a geographical or thematic nature. Member States shall ensure that their national policies conform to the Union positions.

Article 30 (ex Article 22 TEU)
1. Any Member State, the High Representative of the Union for Foreign Affairs and Security Policy, or the High Representative with the Commission's support, may refer any question relating to the common foreign and security policy to the Council and may submit to it initiatives or proposals as appropriate.

2. In cases requiring a rapid decision, the High Representative, of his own motion, or at the request of a Member State, shall convene an extraordinary Council meeting within 48 hours or, in an emergency, within a shorter period.

Article 31 (ex Article 23 TEU)
1. Decisions under this Chapter shall be taken by the European Council and the Council acting unanimously, except where this Chapter provides otherwise. The adoption of legislative acts shall be excluded.

When abstaining in a vote, any member of the Council may qualify its abstention by making a formal declaration under the present subparagraph. In that case, it shall not be obliged to apply the decision, but shall accept that the decision commits the Union. In a spirit of mutual solidarity, the Member State concerned shall refrain from any action likely to conflict with or impede Union action based on that decision and the other Member States shall respect its position. If the members of the Council qualifying their abstention in this way represent at least one third of the Member States comprising at least one-third of the population of the Union, the decision shall not be adopted.

2. By derogation from the provisions of paragraph 1, the Council shall act by qualified majority:

- when adopting a decision defining a Union action or position on the basis of a decision of the European Council relating to the Union's strategic interests and objectives, as referred to in Article 22(1),
- when adopting a decision defining a Union action or position, on a proposal which the High Representative of the Union for Foreign Affairs and Security Policy has presented following a specific request from the European Council, made on its own initiative or that of the High Representative,
- when adopting any decision implementing a decision defining a Union action or position,
- when appointing a special representative in accordance with Article 33.

If a member of the Council declares that, for vital and stated reasons of national policy, it intends to oppose the adoption of a decision to be taken by qualified majority, a vote shall not be taken. The High Representative will, in close consultation with the Member State involved, search for a solution acceptable to it. If he does not succeed, the Council may, acting by a qualified majority, request that the matter be referred to the European Council for a decision by unanimity.

3. The European Council may unanimously adopt a decision stipulating that the Council shall act by a qualified majority in cases other than those referred to in paragraph 2.

4. Paragraphs 2 and 3 shall not apply to decisions having military or defence implications.

5. For procedural questions, the Council shall act by a majority of its members.

Article 32 (ex Article 16 TEU)
Member States shall consult one another within the European Council and the Council on any matter of foreign and security policy of general interest in order to determine a common approach. Before undertaking any action on the international scene or entering into any commitment which could affect the Union's interests, each Member State shall consult the others within the European Council or the Council. Member States shall ensure, through the convergence of their actions, that the Union is able to assert its interests and values on the international scene. Member States shall show mutual solidarity.

When the European Council or the Council has defined a common approach of the Union within the meaning of the first paragraph, the High Representative of the Union for Foreign Affairs and Security Policy and the Ministers for Foreign Affairs of the Member States shall coordinate their activities within the Council.

The diplomatic missions of the Member States and the Union delegations in third countries and at international organisations shall cooperate and shall contribute to formulating and implementing the common approach.

Article 33 (ex Article 18 TEU)

The Council may, on a proposal from the High Representative of the Union for Foreign Affairs and Security Policy, appoint a special representative with a mandate in relation to particular policy issues. The special representative shall carry out his mandate under the authority of the High Representative.

Article 34 (ex Article 19 TEU)

1. Member States shall coordinate their action in international organisations and at international conferences. They shall uphold the Union's positions in such forums. The High Representative of the Union for Foreign Affairs and Security Policy shall organise this coordination.

In international organisations and at international conferences where not all the Member States participate, those which do take part shall uphold the Union's positions.

2. In accordance with Article 24(3), Member States represented in international organisations or international conferences where not all the Member States participate shall keep the other Member States and the High Representative informed of any matter of common interest.

Member States which are also members of the United Nations Security Council will concert and keep the other Member States and the High Representative fully informed. Member States which are members of the Security Council will, in the execution of their functions, defend the positions and the interests of the Union, without prejudice to their responsibilities under the provisions of the United Nations Charter.

When the Union has defined a position on a subject which is on the United Nations Security Council agenda, those Member States which sit on the Security Council shall request that the High Representative be invited to present the Union's position.

Article 35 (ex Article 20 TEU)

The diplomatic and consular missions of the Member States and the Union delegations in third countries and international conferences, and their representations to international organisations, shall cooperate in ensuring that decisions defining Union positions and actions adopted pursuant to this Chapter are complied with and implemented.

They shall step up cooperation by exchanging information and carrying out joint assessments.

They shall contribute to the implementation of the right of citizens of the Union to protection in the territory of third countries as referred to in Article 20(2)(c) of the Treaty on the Functioning of the European Union and of the measures adopted pursuant to Article 23 of that Treaty.

Article 36 (ex Article 21 TEU)

The High Representative of the Union for Foreign Affairs and Security Policy shall regularly consult the European Parliament on the main aspects and the basic choices of the common foreign and security policy and the common security and defence policy and inform it of how those policies evolve. He shall ensure that the views of the European Parliament are duly taken into consideration. Special representatives may be involved in briefing the European Parliament.

The European Parliament may ask questions of the Council or make recommendations to it and to the High Representative. Twice a year it shall hold a debate on progress in implementing the common foreign and security policy, including the common security and defence policy.

Article 37 (ex Article 24 TEU)

The Union may conclude agreements with one or more States or international organisations in areas covered by this Chapter.

Article 38 (ex Article 25 TEU)

Without prejudice to Article 240 of the Treaty on the Functioning of the European Union, a Political and Security Committee shall monitor the international situation in the areas covered by the common foreign and security policy and contribute to the definition of policies by delivering opinions to the Council at the request of the Council or of the High Representative of the Union for Foreign Affairs and Security Policy or on its own initiative. It shall also monitor the implementation of agreed policies, without prejudice to the powers of the High Representative.

Within the scope of this Chapter, the Political and Security Committee shall exercise, under the responsibility of the Council and of the High Representative, the political control and strategic direction of the crisis management operations referred to in Article 43.

The Council may authorise the Committee, for the purpose and for the duration of a crisis management operation, as determined by the Council, to take the relevant decisions concerning the political control and strategic direction of the operation.

Article 39

In accordance with Article 16 of the Treaty on the Functioning of the European Union and by way of derogation from paragraph 2 thereof, the Council shall adopt a decision laying down the rules relating to the protection of individuals with regard to the processing of personal data by the Member States when carrying out activities which fall within the scope of this Chapter, and the rules relating to the free movement of such data. Compliance with these rules shall be subject to the control of independent authorities.

Article 40 (ex Article 47 TEU)

The implementation of the common foreign and security policy shall not affect the application of the procedures and the extent of the powers of the institutions laid down by the Treaties for the exercise of the Union competences referred to in Articles 3 to 6 of the Treaty on the Functioning of the European Union.

Similarly, the implementation of the policies listed in those Articles shall not affect the application of the procedures and the extent of the powers of the institutions laid down by the Treaties for the exercise of the Union competences under this Chapter.

Article 41 (ex Article 28 TEU)

1. Administrative expenditure to which the implementation of this Chapter gives rise for the institutions shall be charged to the Union budget.

2. Operating expenditure to which the implementation of this Chapter gives rise shall also be charged to the Union budget, except for such expenditure arising from operations having military or defence implications and cases where the Council acting unanimously decides otherwise.

In cases where expenditure is not charged to the Union budget, it shall be charged to the Member States in accordance with the gross national product scale, unless the Council acting unanimously decides otherwise. As for expenditure arising from operations having military or defence implications, Member States whose representatives in the Council have made a formal declaration under Article 31(1), second subparagraph, shall not be obliged to contribute to the financing thereof.

3. The Council shall adopt a decision establishing the specific procedures for guaranteeing rapid access to appropriations in the Union budget for urgent financing of initiatives in the framework of the common foreign and security policy, and in particular for preparatory activities for the tasks referred to in Article 42(1) and Article 43. It shall act after consulting the European Parliament.

Preparatory activities for the tasks referred to in Article 42(1) and Article 43 which are not charged to the Union budget shall be financed by a start-up fund made up of Member States' contributions.

The Council shall adopt by a qualified majority, on a proposal from the High Representative of the Union for Foreign Affairs and Security Policy, decisions establishing:

(a) the procedures for setting up and financing the start-up fund, in particular the amounts allocated to the fund;
(b) the procedures for administering the start-up fund;
(c) the financial control procedures.

When the task planned in accordance with Article 42(1) and Article 43 cannot be charged to the Union budget, the Council shall authorise the High Representative to use the fund. The High Representative shall report to the Council on the implementation of this remit.

Section 2 Provisions on the common security and defence policy

Article 42 (ex Article 17 TEU)

1. The common security and defence policy shall be an integral part of the common foreign and security policy. It shall provide the Union with an operational capacity drawing on civilian and military assets. The Union may use them on missions outside the Union for peace-keeping, conflict prevention and strengthening international security in accordance with the principles of the United Nations Charter. The performance of these tasks shall be undertaken using capabilities provided by the Member States.

2. The common security and defence policy shall include the progressive framing of a common Union defence policy. This will lead to a common defence, when the European Council, acting unanimously, so decides. It shall in that case recommend to the Member States the adoption of such a decision in accordance with their respective constitutional requirements.

The policy of the Union in accordance with this Section shall not prejudice the specific character of the security and defence policy of certain Member States and shall respect the obligations of certain Member States, which see their common defence realised in the North Atlantic Treaty Organisation (NATO), under the North Atlantic Treaty and be compatible with the common security and defence policy established within that framework.

3. Member States shall make civilian and military capabilities available to the Union for the implementation of the common security and defence policy, to contribute to the objectives defined by the Council. Those Member States which together establish multinational forces may also make them available to the common security and defence policy.

Member States shall undertake progressively to improve their military capabilities. The Agency in the field of defence capabilities development, research, acquisition and armaments (hereinafter referred to as 'the European Defence Agency') shall identify operational requirements, shall promote measures to satisfy those requirements, shall contribute to identifying and, where appropriate, implementing any measure needed to strengthen the industrial and technological base of the defence sector, shall participate in defining a European capabilities and armaments policy, and shall assist the Council in evaluating the improvement of military capabilities.

4. Decisions relating to the common security and defence policy, including those initiating a mission as referred to in this Article, shall be adopted by the Council acting unanimously on a proposal from the High Representative of the Union for Foreign Affairs and Security Policy or an initiative from a Member State. The High Representative may propose the use of both national resources and Union instruments, together with the Commission where appropriate.

5. The Council may entrust the execution of a task, within the Union framework, to a group of Member States in order to protect the Union's values and serve its interests. The execution of such a task shall be governed by Article 44.

6. Those Member States whose military capabilities fulfil higher criteria and which have made more binding commitments to one another in this area with a view to the most demanding missions shall establish permanent structured cooperation within the Union framework. Such cooperation shall be governed by Article 46. It shall not affect the provisions of Article 43.

7. If a Member State is the victim of armed aggression on its territory, the other Member States shall have towards it an obligation of aid and assistance by all the means in their power, in

accordance with Article 51 of the United Nations Charter. This shall not prejudice the specific character of the security and defence policy of certain Member States.

Commitments and cooperation in this area shall be consistent with commitments under the North Atlantic Treaty Organisation, which, for those States which are members of it, remains the foundation of their collective defence and the forum for its implementation.

Article 43

1. The tasks referred to in Article 42(1), in the course of which the Union may use civilian and military means, shall include joint disarmament operations, humanitarian and rescue tasks, military advice and assistance tasks, conflict prevention and peace-keeping tasks, tasks of combat forces in crisis management, including peace-making and post-conflict stabilisation. All these tasks may contribute to the fight against terrorism, including by supporting third countries in combating terrorism in their territories.

2. The Council shall adopt decisions relating to the tasks referred to in paragraph 1, defining their objectives and scope and the general conditions for their implementation. The High Representative of the Union for Foreign Affairs and Security Policy, acting under the authority of the Council and in close and constant contact with the Political and Security Committee, shall ensure coordination of the civilian and military aspects of such tasks.

Article 44

1. Within the framework of the decisions adopted in accordance with Article 43, the Council may entrust the implementation of a task to a group of Member States which are willing and have the necessary capability for such a task. Those Member States, in association with the High Representative of the Union for Foreign Affairs and Security Policy, shall agree among themselves on the management of the task.

2. Member States participating in the task shall keep the Council regularly informed of its progress on their own initiative or at the request of another Member State. Those States shall inform the Council immediately should the completion of the task entail major consequences or require amendment of the objective, scope and conditions determined for the task in the decisions referred to in paragraph 1. In such cases, the Council shall adopt the necessary decisions.

Article 45

1. The European Defence Agency referred to in Article 42(3), subject to the authority of the Council, shall have as its task to:

(a) contribute to identifying the Member States' military capability objectives and evaluating observance of the capability commitments given by the Member States;

(b) promote harmonisation of operational needs and adoption of effective, compatible procurement methods;

(c) propose multilateral projects to fulfil the objectives in terms of military capabilities, ensure coordination of the programmes implemented by the Member States and management of specific cooperation programmes;

(d) support defence technology research, and coordinate and plan joint research activities and the study of technical solutions meeting future operational needs;

(e) contribute to identifying and, if necessary, implementing any useful measure for strengthening the industrial and technological base of the defence sector and for improving the effectiveness of military expenditure.

2. The European Defence Agency shall be open to all Member States wishing to be part of it. The Council, acting by a qualified majority, shall adopt a decision defining the Agency's statute, seat and operational rules. That decision should take account of the level of effective participation in the Agency's activities. Specific groups shall be set up within the Agency bringing together Member States engaged in joint projects. The Agency shall carry out its tasks in liaison with the Commission where necessary.

Article 46

1. Those Member States which wish to participate in the permanent structured cooperation referred to in Article 42(6), which fulfil the criteria and have made the commitments on military

capabilities set out in the Protocol on permanent structured cooperation, shall notify their intention to the Council and to the High Representative of the Union for Foreign Affairs and Security Policy.

2. Within three months following the notification referred to in paragraph 1 the Council shall adopt a decision establishing permanent structured cooperation and determining the list of participating Member States. The Council shall act by a qualified majority after consulting the High Representative.

3. Any Member State which, at a later stage, wishes to participate in the permanent structured cooperation shall notify its intention to the Council and to the High Representative.

The Council shall adopt a decision confirming the participation of the Member State concerned which fulfils the criteria and makes the commitments referred to in Articles 1 and 2 of the Protocol on permanent structured cooperation. The Council shall act by a qualified majority after consulting the High Representative. Only members of the Council representing the participating Member States shall take part in the vote.

A qualified majority shall be defined in accordance with Article 238(3)(a) of the Treaty on the Functioning of the European Union.

4. If a participating Member State no longer fulfils the criteria or is no longer able to meet the commitments referred to in Articles 1 and 2 of the Protocol on permanent structured cooperation, the Council may adopt a decision suspending the participation of the Member State concerned.

The Council shall act by a qualified majority. Only members of the Council representing the participating Member States, with the exception of the Member State in question, shall take part in the vote.

A qualified majority shall be defined in accordance with Article 238(3)(a) of the Treaty on the Functioning of the European Union.

5. Any participating Member State which wishes to withdraw from permanent structured cooperation shall notify its intention to the Council, which shall take note that the Member State in question has ceased to participate.

6. The decisions and recommendations of the Council within the framework of permanent structured cooperation, other than those provided for in paragraphs 2 to 5, shall be adopted by unanimity. For the purposes of this paragraph, unanimity shall be constituted by the votes of the representatives of the participating Member States only.

Title VI Final provisions

Article 47

The Union shall have legal personality.

Article 48 (ex Article 48 TEU)

1. The Treaties may be amended in accordance with an ordinary revision procedure. They may also be amended in accordance with simplified revision procedures.

Ordinary revision procedure

2. The Government of any Member State, the European Parliament or the Commission may submit to the Council proposals for the amendment of the Treaties. These proposals may, *inter alia*, serve either to increase or to reduce the competences conferred on the Union in the Treaties. These proposals shall be submitted to the European Council by the Council and the national Parliaments shall be notified.

3. If the European Council, after consulting the European Parliament and the Commission, adopts by a simple majority a decision in favour of examining the proposed amendments, the President of the European Council shall convene a Convention composed of representatives of the national Parliaments, of the Heads of State or Government of the Member States, of the European Parliament and of the Commission. The European Central Bank shall also be consulted in the case of institutional changes in the monetary area. The Convention shall examine the proposals for

amendments and shall adopt by consensus a recommendation to a conference of representatives of the governments of the Member States as provided for in paragraph 4.

The European Council may decide by a simple majority, after obtaining the consent of the European Parliament, not to convene a Convention should this not be justified by the extent of the proposed amendments. In the latter case, the European Council shall define the terms of reference for a conference of representatives of the governments of the Member States.

4. A conference of representatives of the governments of the Member States shall be convened by the President of the Council for the purpose of determining by common accord the amendments to be made to the Treaties.

The amendments shall enter into force after being ratified by all the Member States in accordance with their respective constitutional requirements.

5. If, two years after the signature of a treaty amending the Treaties, four fifths of the Member States have ratified it and one or more Member States have encountered difficulties in proceeding with ratification, the matter shall be referred to the European Council.

Simplified revision procedures

6. The Government of any Member State, the European Parliament or the Commission may submit to the European Council proposals for revising all or part of the provisions of Part Three of the Treaty on the Functioning of the European Union relating to the internal policies and action of the Union.

The European Council may adopt a decision amending all or part of the provisions of Part Three of the Treaty on the Functioning of the European Union. The European Council shall act by unanimity after consulting the European Parliament and the Commission, and the European Central Bank in the case of institutional changes in the monetary area. That decision shall not enter into force until it is approved by the Member States in accordance with their respective constitutional requirements.

The decision referred to in the second subparagraph shall not increase the competences conferred on the Union in the Treaties.

7. Where the Treaty on the Functioning of the European Union or Title V of this Treaty provides for the Council to act by unanimity in a given area or case, the European Council may adopt a decision authorising the Council to act by a qualified majority in that area or in that case. This subparagraph shall not apply to decisions with military implications or those in the area of defence.

Where the Treaty on the Functioning of the European Union provides for legislative acts to be adopted by the Council in accordance with a special legislative procedure, the European Council may adopt a decision allowing for the adoption of such acts in accordance with the ordinary legislative procedure.

Any initiative taken by the European Council on the basis of the first or the second subparagraph shall be notified to the national Parliaments. If a national Parliament makes known its opposition within six months of the date of such notification, the decision referred to in the first or the second subparagraph shall not be adopted. In the absence of opposition, the European Council may adopt the decision.

For the adoption of the decisions referred to in the first and second subparagraphs, the European Council shall act by unanimity after obtaining the consent of the European Parliament, which shall be given by a majority of its component members.

Article 49 (ex Article 49 TEU)

Any European State which respects the values referred to in Article 2 and is committed to promoting them may apply to become a member of the Union. The European Parliament and national Parliaments shall be notified of this application. The applicant State shall address its application to the Council, which shall act unanimously after consulting the Commission and after receiving the consent of the European Parliament, which shall act by a majority of its component members. The conditions of eligibility agreed upon by the European Council shall be taken into account.

The conditions of admission and the adjustments to the Treaties on which the Union is founded, which such admission entails, shall be the subject of an agreement between the Member States and the applicant State. This agreement shall be submitted for ratification by all the contracting States in accordance with their respective constitutional requirements.

Article 50

1. Any Member State may decide to withdraw from the Union in accordance with its own constitutional requirements.

2. A Member State which decides to withdraw shall notify the European Council of its intention. In the light of the guidelines provided by the European Council, the Union shall negotiate and conclude an agreement with that State, setting out the arrangements for its withdrawal, taking account of the framework for its future relationship with the Union. That agreement shall be negotiated in accordance with Article 218(3) of the Treaty on the Functioning of the European Union. It shall be concluded on behalf of the Union by the Council, acting by a qualified majority, after obtaining the consent of the European Parliament.

3. The Treaties shall cease to apply to the State in question from the date of entry into force of the withdrawal agreement or, failing that, two years after the notification referred to in paragraph 2, unless the European Council, in agreement with the Member State concerned, unanimously decides to extend this period.

4. For the purposes of paragraphs 2 and 3, the member of the European Council or of the Council representing the withdrawing Member State shall not participate in the discussions of the European Council or Council or in decisions concerning it.

A qualified majority shall be defined in accordance with Article 238(3)(b) of the Treaty on the Functioning of the European Union.

5. If a State which has withdrawn from the Union asks to rejoin, its request shall be subject to the procedure referred to in Article 49.

Article 51

The Protocols and Annexes to the Treaties shall form an integral part thereof.

Article 52

1. The Treaties shall apply to the Kingdom of Belgium, the Republic of Bulgaria, the Czech Republic, the Kingdom of Denmark, the Federal Republic of Germany, the Republic of Estonia, Ireland, the Hellenic Republic, the Kingdom of Spain, the French Republic, the Republic of Croatia, the Italian Republic, the Republic of Cyprus, the Republic of Latvia, the Republic of Lithuania, the Grand Duchy of Luxembourg, the Republic of Hungary, the Republic of Malta, the Kingdom of the Netherlands, the Republic of Austria, the Republic of Poland, the Portuguese Republic, Romania, the Republic of Slovenia, the Slovak Republic, the Republic of Finland, the Kingdom of Sweden and the United Kingdom of Great Britain and Northern Ireland.

2. The territorial scope of the Treaties is specified in Article 355 of the Treaty on the Functioning of the European Union.

Article 53 (ex Article 51 TEU)

This Treaty is concluded for an unlimited period.

Article 54 (ex Article 52 TEU)

1. This Treaty shall be ratified by the High Contracting Parties in accordance with their respective constitutional requirements. The instruments of ratification shall be deposited with the Government of the Italian Republic.

2. This Treaty shall enter into force on 1 January 1993, provided that all the Instruments of ratification have been deposited, or, failing that, on the first day of the month following the deposit of the Instrument of ratification by the last signatory State to take this step.

Article 55 (ex Article 53 TEU)

1. This Treaty, drawn up in a single original in the Bulgarian, Croatian, Czech, Danish, Dutch, English, Estonian, Finnish, French, German, Greek, Hungarian, Irish, Italian, Latvian, Lithuanian, Maltese, Polish, Portuguese, Romanian, Slovak, Slovenian, Spanish and Swedish languages, the texts in each of these languages being equally authentic, shall be deposited in the archives of the Government of the Italian Republic, which will transmit a certified copy to each of the governments of the other signatory States.

2. This Treaty may also be translated into any other languages as determined by Member States among those which, in accordance with their constitutional order, enjoy official status in all or part of their territory. A certified copy of such translations shall be provided by the Member States concerned to be deposited in the archives of the Council.

IN WITNESS WHEREOF the undersigned Plenipotentiaries have signed this Treaty.

Done at Maastricht on the seventh day of February in the year one thousand nine hundred and ninety-two.

(List of signatories not reproduced.)

Consolidated Version of the Treaty on the Functioning of the European Union*

Preamble

DETERMINED to lay the foundations of an ever closer union among the peoples of Europe,

RESOLVED to ensure the economic and social progress of their States by common action to eliminate the barriers which divide Europe,

AFFIRMING as the essential objective of their efforts the constant improvements of the living and working conditions of their peoples,

RECOGNISING that the removal of existing obstacles calls for concerted action in order to guarantee steady expansion, balanced trade and fair competition,

ANXIOUS to strengthen the unity of their economies and to ensure their harmonious development by reducing the differences existing between the various regions and the backwardness of the less favoured regions,

DESIRING to contribute, by means of a common commercial policy, to the progressive abolition of restrictions on international trade,

INTENDING to confirm the solidarity which binds Europe and the overseas countries and desiring to ensure the development of their prosperity, in accordance with the principles of the Charter of the United Nations,

RESOLVED by thus pooling their resources to preserve and strengthen peace and liberty, and calling upon the other peoples of Europe who share their ideal to join in their efforts,

DETERMINED to promote the development of the highest possible level of knowledge for their peoples through a wide access to education and through its continuous updating,

and to this end have designated as their Plenipotentiaries:

(List of plenipotentiaries not reproduced.)

WHO, having exchanged their full powers, found in good and due form, have agreed as follows.

* **Editor's Note**: Incorporating Lisbon Treaty changes. Signatures, list of States and contents omitted. This version incorporates the changes as reproduced in OJ 2016 C202/1 of 7 June 2016 and as amended by the Croatian Accession Treaty (OJ 2012 L112/1). See https://eur-lex.europa.eu/legal-content/EN/TXT/?uri=OJ:C:2016:202:TOC.

PART ONE PRINCIPLES

Article 1

1. This Treaty organises the functioning of the Union and determines the areas of, delimitation of, and arrangements for exercising its competences.

2. This Treaty and the Treaty on European Union constitute the Treaties on which the Union is founded. These two Treaties, which have the same legal value, shall be referred to as 'the Treaties'.

Title I Categories and areas of Union competence

Article 2

1. When the Treaties confer on the Union exclusive competence in a specific area, only the Union may legislate and adopt legally binding acts, the Member States being able to do so themselves only if so empowered by the Union or for the implementation of Union acts.

2. When the Treaties confer on the Union a competence shared with the Member States in a specific area, the Union and the Member States may legislate and adopt legally binding acts in that area. The Member States shall exercise their competence to the extent that the Union has not exercised its competence. The Member States shall again exercise their competence to the extent that the Union has decided to cease exercising its competence.

3. The Member States shall coordinate their economic and employment policies within arrangements as determined by this Treaty, which the Union shall have competence to provide.

4. The Union shall have competence, in accordance with the provisions of the Treaty on European Union, to define and implement a common foreign and security policy, including the progressive framing of a common defence policy.

5. In certain areas and under the conditions laid down in the Treaties, the Union shall have competence to carry out actions to support, coordinate or supplement the actions of the Member States, without thereby superseding their competence in these areas.

Legally binding acts of the Union adopted on the basis of the provisions of the Treaties relating to these areas shall not entail harmonisation of Member States' laws or regulations.

6. The scope of and arrangements for exercising the Union's competences shall be determined by the provisions of the Treaties relating to each area.

Article 3

1. The Union shall have exclusive competence in the following areas:

(a) customs union;
(b) the establishing of the competition rules necessary for the functioning of the internal market;
(c) monetary policy for the Member States whose currency is the euro;
(d) the conservation of marine biological resources under the common fisheries policy;
(e) common commercial policy.

2. The Union shall also have exclusive competence for the conclusion of an international agreement when its conclusion is provided for in a legislative act of the Union or is necessary to enable the Union to exercise its internal competence, or in so far as its conclusion may affect common rules or alter their scope.

Article 4

1. The Union shall share competence with the Member States where the Treaties confer on it a competence which does not relate to the areas referred to in Articles 3 and 6.

2. Shared competence between the Union and the Member States applies in the following principal areas:

(a) internal market;
(b) social policy, for the aspects defined in this Treaty;

(c) economic, social and territorial cohesion;
(d) agriculture and fisheries, excluding the conservation of marine biological resources;
(e) environment;
(f) consumer protection;
(g) transport;
(h) trans-European networks;
(i) energy;
(j) area of freedom, security and justice;
(k) common safety concerns in public health matters, for the aspects defined in this Treaty.

3. In the areas of research, technological development and space, the Union shall have competence to carry out activities, in particular to define and implement programmes; however, the exercise of that competence shall not result in Member States being prevented from exercising theirs.

4. In the areas of development cooperation and humanitarian aid, the Union shall have competence to carry out activities and conduct a common policy; however, the exercise of that competence shall not result in Member States being prevented from exercising theirs.

Article 5

1. The Member States shall coordinate their economic policies within the Union. To this end, the Council shall adopt measures, in particular broad guidelines for these policies.

Specific provisions shall apply to those Member States whose currency is the euro.

2. The Union shall take measures to ensure coordination of the employment policies of the Member States, in particular by defining guidelines for these policies.

3. The Union may take initiatives to ensure coordination of Member States' social policies.

Article 6

The Union shall have competence to carry out actions to support, coordinate or supplement the actions of the Member States. The areas of such action shall, at European level, be:

(a) protection and improvement of human health;
(b) industry;
(c) culture;
(d) tourism;
(e) education, vocational training, youth and sport;
(f) civil protection;
(g) administrative cooperation.

Title II Provisions having general application

Article 7

The Union shall ensure consistency between its policies and activities, taking all of its objectives into account and in accordance with the principle of conferral of powers.

Article 8 (ex Article 3(2) TEC)[1]

In all its activities, the Union shall aim to eliminate inequalities, and to promote equality, between men and women.

Article 9

In defining and implementing its policies and activities, the Union shall take into account requirements linked to the promotion of a high level of employment, the guarantee of adequate social protection, the fight against social exclusion, and a high level of education, training and protection of human health.

[1] These references are merely indicative. For more ample information, please refer to the tables of equivalences between the old and the new numbering of the Treaties.

Article 10
In defining and implementing its policies and activities, the Union shall aim to combat discrimination based on sex, racial or ethnic origin, religion or belief, disability, age or sexual orientation.

Article 11 (ex Article 6 TEC)
Environmental protection requirements must be integrated into the definition and implementation of the Union policies and activities, in particular with a view to promoting sustainable development.

Article 12 (ex Article 153(2) TEC)
Consumer protection requirements shall be taken into account in defining and implementing other Union policies and activities.

Article 13
In formulating and implementing the Union's agriculture, fisheries, transport, internal market, research and technological development and space policies, the Union and the Member States shall, since animals are sentient beings, pay full regard to the welfare requirements of animals, while respecting the legislative or administrative provisions and customs of the Member States relating in particular to religious rites, cultural traditions and regional heritage.

Article 14 (ex Article 16 TEC)
Without prejudice to Article 4 of the Treaty on European Union or to Articles 93, 106 and 107 of this Treaty, and given the place occupied by services of general economic interest in the shared values of the Union as well as their role in promoting social and territorial cohesion, the Union and the Member States, each within their respective powers and within the scope of application of the Treaties, shall take care that such services operate on the basis of principles and conditions, particularly economic and financial conditions, which enable them to fulfil their missions. The European Parliament and the Council, acting by means of regulations in accordance with the ordinary legislative procedure, shall establish these principles and set these conditions without prejudice to the competence of Member States, in compliance with the Treaties, to provide, to commission and to fund such services.

Article 15 (ex Article 255 TEC)

1. In order to promote good governance and ensure the participation of civil society, the Union institutions, bodies, offices and agencies shall conduct their work as openly as possible.

2. The European Parliament shall meet in public, as shall the Council when considering and voting on a draft legislative act.

3. Any citizen of the Union, and any natural or legal person residing or having its registered office in a Member State, shall have a right of access to documents of the Union institutions, bodies, offices and agencies, whatever their medium, subject to the principles and the conditions to be defined in accordance with this paragraph.

General principles and limits on grounds of public or private interest governing this right of access to documents shall be determined by the European Parliament and the Council, by means of regulations, acting in accordance with the ordinary legislative procedure.

Each institution, body, office or agency shall ensure that its proceedings are transparent and shall elaborate in its own Rules of Procedure specific provisions regarding access to its documents, in accordance with the regulations referred to in the second subparagraph.

The Court of Justice of the European Union, the European Central Bank and the European Investment Bank shall be subject to this paragraph only when exercising their administrative tasks.

The European Parliament and the Council shall ensure publication of the documents relating to the legislative procedures under the terms laid down by the regulations referred to in the second subparagraph.

Article 16 (ex Article 286 TEC)

1. Everyone has the right to the protection of personal data concerning them.

2. The European Parliament and the Council, acting in accordance with the ordinary legislative procedure, shall lay down the rules relating to the protection of individuals with regard to the

processing of personal data by Union institutions, bodies, offices and agencies, and by the Member States when carrying out activities which fall within the scope of Union law, and the rules relating to the free movement of such data.

Compliance with these rules shall be subject to the control of independent authorities.

The rules adopted on the basis of this Article shall be without prejudice to the specific rules laid down in Article 39 of the Treaty on European Union.

Article 17

1. The Union respects and does not prejudice the status under national law of churches and religious associations or communities in the Member States.

2. The Union equally respects the status under national law of philosophical and non-confessional organisations.

3. Recognising their identity and their specific contribution, the Union shall maintain an open, transparent and regular dialogue with these churches and organisations.

PART TWO NON-DISCRIMINATION AND CITIZENSHIP OF THE UNION

Article 18 (ex Article 12 TEC)

Within the scope of application of the Treaties, and without prejudice to any special provisions contained therein, any discrimination on grounds of nationality shall be prohibited.

The European Parliament and the Council, acting in accordance with the ordinary legislative procedure, may adopt rules designed to prohibit such discrimination.

Article 19 (ex Article 13 TEC)

1. Without prejudice to the other provisions of the Treaties and within the limits of the powers conferred by them upon the Union, the Council, acting unanimously in accordance with a special legislative procedure and after obtaining the consent of the European Parliament, may take appropriate action to combat discrimination based on sex, racial or ethnic origin, religion or belief, disability, age or sexual orientation.

2. By way of derogation from paragraph 1, the European Parliament and the Council, acting in accordance with the ordinary legislative procedure, may adopt the basic principles of Union incentive measures, excluding any harmonisation of the laws and regulations of the Member States, to support action taken by the Member States in order to contribute to the achievement of the objectives referred to in paragraph 1.

Article 20 (ex Article 17 TEC)

1. Citizenship of the Union is hereby established. Every person holding the nationality of a Member State shall be a citizen of the Union. Citizenship of the Union shall be additional to and not replace national citizenship.

2. Citizens of the Union shall enjoy the rights and be subject to the duties provided for in the Treaties. They shall have, *inter alia*:

(a) the right to move and reside freely within the territory of the Member States;

(b) the right to vote and to stand as candidates in elections to the European Parliament and in municipal elections in their Member State of residence, under the same conditions as nationals of that State;

(c) the right to enjoy, in the territory of a third country in which the Member State of which they are nationals is not represented, the protection of the diplomatic and consular authorities of any Member State on the same conditions as the nationals of that State;

(d) the right to petition the European Parliament, to apply to the European Ombudsman, and to address the institutions and advisory bodies of the Union in any of the Treaty languages and to obtain a reply in the same language.

These rights shall be exercised in accordance with the conditions and limits defined by the Treaties and by the measures adopted thereunder.

Article 21 (ex Article 18 TEC)

1. Every citizen of the Union shall have the right to move and reside freely within the territory of the Member States, subject to the limitations and conditions laid down in the Treaties and by the measures adopted to give them effect.

2. If action by the Union should prove necessary to attain this objective and the Treaties have not provided the necessary powers, the European Parliament and the Council, acting in accordance with the ordinary legislative procedure, may adopt provisions with a view to facilitating the exercise of the rights referred to in paragraph 1.

3. For the same purposes as those referred to in paragraph 1 and if the Treaties have not provided the necessary powers, the Council, acting in accordance with a special legislative procedure, may adopt measures concerning social security or social protection. The Council shall act unanimously after consulting the European Parliament.

Article 22 (ex Article 19 TEC)

1. Every citizen of the Union residing in a Member State of which he is not a national shall have the right to vote and to stand as a candidate at municipal elections in the Member State in which he resides, under the same conditions as nationals of that State. This right shall be exercised subject to detailed arrangements adopted by the Council, acting unanimously in accordance with a special legislative procedure and after consulting the European Parliament; these arrangements may provide for derogations where warranted by problems specific to a Member State.

2. Without prejudice to Article 223(1) and to the provisions adopted for its implementation, every citizen of the Union residing in a Member State of which he is not a national shall have the right to vote and to stand as a candidate in elections to the European Parliament in the Member State in which he resides, under the same conditions as nationals of that State. This right shall be exercised subject to detailed arrangements adopted by the Council, acting unanimously in accordance with a special legislative procedure and after consulting the European Parliament; these arrangements may provide for derogations where warranted by problems specific to a Member State.

Article 23 (ex Article 20 TEC)

Every citizen of the Union shall, in the territory of a third country in which the Member State of which he is a national is not represented, be entitled to protection by the diplomatic or consular authorities of any Member State, on the same conditions as the nationals of that State. Member States shall adopt the necessary provisions and start the international negotiations required to secure this protection.

The Council, acting in accordance with a special legislative procedure and after consulting the European Parliament, may adopt directives establishing the coordination and cooperation measures necessary to facilitate such protection.

Article 24 (ex Article 21 TEC)

The European Parliament and the Council, acting by means of regulations in accordance with the ordinary legislative procedure, shall adopt the provisions for the procedures and conditions required for a citizens' initiative within the meaning of Article 11 of the Treaty on European Union, including the minimum number of Member States from which such citizens must come.

Every citizen of the Union shall have the right to petition the European Parliament in accordance with Article 227.

Every citizen of the Union may apply to the Ombudsman established in accordance with Article 228.

Every citizen of the Union may write to any of the institutions, bodies, offices or agencies referred to in this Article or in Article 13 of the Treaty on European Union in one of the languages mentioned in Article 55(1) of the Treaty on European Union and have an answer in the same language.

Article 25 (ex Article 22 TEC)
The Commission shall report to the European Parliament, to the Council and to the Economic and Social Committee every three years on the application of the provisions of this Part. This report shall take account of the development of the Union.

On this basis, and without prejudice to the other provisions of the Treaties, the Council, acting unanimously in accordance with a special legislative procedure and after obtaining the consent of the European Parliament, may adopt provisions to strengthen or to add to the rights listed in Article 20(2). These provisions shall enter into force after their approval by the Member States in accordance with their respective constitutional requirements.

PART THREE UNION POLICIES AND INTERNAL ACTIONS

Title I The internal market

Article 26 (ex Article 14 TEC)
1. The Union shall adopt measures with the aim of establishing or ensuring the functioning of the internal market, in accordance with the relevant provisions of the Treaties.

2. The internal market shall comprise an area without internal frontiers in which the free movement of goods, persons, services and capital is ensured in accordance with the provisions of the Treaties.

3. The Council, on a proposal from the Commission, shall determine the guidelines and conditions necessary to ensure balanced progress in all the sectors concerned.

Article 27 (ex Article 15 TEC)
When drawing up its proposals with a view to achieving the objectives set out in Article 26, the Commission shall take into account the extent of the effort that certain economies showing differences in development will have to sustain for the establishment of the internal market and it may propose appropriate provisions.

If these provisions take the form of derogations, they must be of a temporary nature and must cause the least possible disturbance to the functioning of the internal market.

Title II Free movement of goods

Article 28 (ex Article 23 TEC)
1. The Union shall comprise a customs union which shall cover all trade in goods and which shall involve the prohibition between Member States of customs duties on imports and exports and of all charges having equivalent effect, and the adoption of a common customs tariff in their relations with third countries.

2. The provisions of Article 30 and of Chapter 3 of this Title shall apply to products originating in Member States and to products coming from third countries which are in free circulation in Member States.*

Article 29 (ex Article 24 TEC)
Products coming from a third country shall be considered to be in free circulation in a Member State if the import formalities have been complied with and any customs duties or charges having equivalent effect which are payable have been levied in that Member State, and if they have not benefited from a total or partial drawback of such duties or charges.

* **Editor's Note**: Second paragraph as corrected in the Consolidated Treaties' version published in OJ 2012 C326/60.

Chapter 1 The customs union

Article 30 (ex Article 25 TEC)
Customs duties on imports and exports and charges having equivalent effect shall be prohibited between Member States. This prohibition shall also apply to customs duties of a fiscal nature.

Article 31 (ex Article 26 TEC)
Common Customs Tariff duties shall be fixed by the Council on a proposal from the Commission.

Article 32 (ex Article 27 TEC)
In carrying out the tasks entrusted to it under this Chapter the Commission shall be guided by:

(a) the need to promote trade between Member States and third countries;
(b) developments in conditions of competition within the Union in so far as they lead to an improvement in the competitive capacity of undertakings;
(c) the requirements of the Union as regards the supply of raw materials and semi-finished goods; in this connection the Commission shall take care to avoid distorting conditions of competition between Member States in respect of finished goods;
(d) the need to avoid serious disturbances in the economies of Member States and to ensure rational development of production and an expansion of consumption within the Union.

Chapter 2 Customs cooperation

Article 33 (ex Article 135 TEC)
Within the scope of application of the Treaties, the European Parliament and the Council, acting in accordance with the ordinary legislative procedure, shall take measures in order to strengthen customs cooperation between Member States and between the latter and the Commission.

Chapter 3 Prohibition of quantitative restrictions between Member States

Article 34 (ex Article 28 TEC)
Quantitative restrictions on imports and all measures having equivalent effect shall be prohibited between Member States.

Article 35 (ex Article 29 TEC)
Quantitative restrictions on exports, and all measures having equivalent effect, shall be prohibited between Member States.

Article 36 (ex Article 30 TEC)
The provisions of Articles 34 and 35 shall not preclude prohibitions or restrictions on imports, exports or goods in transit justified on grounds of public morality, public policy or public security; the protection of health and life of humans, animals or plants; the protection of national treasures possessing artistic, historic or archaeological value; or the protection of industrial and commercial property. Such prohibitions or restrictions shall not, however, constitute a means of arbitrary discrimination or a disguised restriction on trade between Member States.

Article 37 (ex Article 31 TEC)
1. Member States shall adjust any State monopolies of a commercial character so as to ensure that no discrimination regarding the conditions under which goods are procured and marketed exists between nationals of Member States.

The provisions of this Article shall apply to any body through which a Member State, in law or in fact, either directly or indirectly supervises, determines or appreciably influences imports or exports between Member States. These provisions shall likewise apply to monopolies delegated by the State to others.

2. Member States shall refrain from introducing any new measure which is contrary to the principles laid down in paragraph 1 or which restricts the scope of the articles dealing with the prohibition of customs duties and quantitative restrictions between Member States.

3. If a State monopoly of a commercial character has rules which are designed to make it easier to dispose of agricultural products or obtain for them the best return, steps should be taken in applying the rules contained in this Article to ensure equivalent safeguards for the employment and standard of living of the producers concerned.

Title III Agriculture and fisheries

Article 38 (ex Article 32 TEC)

1. The Union shall define and implement a common agriculture and fisheries policy.

'The internal market' shall extend to agriculture, fisheries and trade in agricultural products. 'Agricultural products' means the products of the soil, of stockfarming and of fisheries and products of first-stage processing directly related to these products. References to the common agricultural policy or to agriculture, and the use of the term 'agricultural', shall be understood as also referring to fisheries, having regard to the specific characteristics of this sector.

2. Save as otherwise provided in Articles 39 to 44, the rules laid down for the establishment and functioning of the internal market shall apply to agricultural products.

3. The products subject to the provisions of Articles 39 to 44 are listed in Annex I.

4. The operation and development of the internal market for agricultural products must be accompanied by the establishment of a common agricultural policy.

Article 39 (ex Article 33 TEC)

1. The objectives of the common agricultural policy shall be:

(a) to increase agricultural productivity by promoting technical progress and by ensuring the rational development of agricultural production and the optimum utilisation of the factors of production, in particular labour;

(b) thus to ensure a fair standard of living for the agricultural community, in particular by increasing the individual earnings of persons engaged in agriculture;

(c) to stabilise markets;

(d) to assure the availability of supplies;

(e) to ensure that supplies reach consumers at reasonable prices.

2. In working out the common agricultural policy and the special methods for its application, account shall be taken of:

(a) the particular nature of agricultural activity, which results from the social structure of agriculture and from structural and natural disparities between the various agricultural regions;

(b) the need to effect the appropriate adjustments by degrees;

(c) the fact that in the Member States agriculture constitutes a sector closely linked with the economy as a whole.

Article 40 (ex Article 34 TEC)

1. In order to attain the objectives set out in Article 39, a common organisation of agricultural markets shall be established.

This organisation shall take one of the following forms, depending on the product concerned:

(a) common rules on competition;

(b) compulsory coordination of the various national market organisations;

(c) a European market organisation.

2. The common organisation established in accordance with paragraph 1 may include all measures required to attain the objectives set out in Article 39, in particular regulation of prices, aids for the production and marketing of the various products, storage and carryover arrangements and common machinery for stabilising imports or exports.

The common organisation shall be limited to pursuit of the objectives set out in Article 39 and shall exclude any discrimination between producers or consumers within the Union.

Any common price policy shall be based on common criteria and uniform methods of calculation.

3. In order to enable the common organisation referred to in paragraph 1 to attain its objectives, one or more agricultural guidance and guarantee funds may be set up.

Article 41 (ex Article 35 TEC)

To enable the objectives set out in Article 39 to be attained, provision may be made within the framework of the common agricultural policy for measures such as:

(a) an effective coordination of efforts in the spheres of vocational training, of research and of the dissemination of agricultural knowledge; this may include joint financing of projects or institutions;

(b) joint measures to promote consumption of certain products.

Article 42 (ex Article 36 TEC)

The provisions of the Chapter relating to rules on competition shall apply to production of and trade in agricultural products only to the extent determined by the European Parliament and the Council within the framework of Article 43(2) and in accordance with the procedure laid down therein, account being taken of the objectives set out in Article 39.

The Council, on a proposal from the Commission, may authorise the granting of aid:

(a) for the protection of enterprises handicapped by structural or natural conditions;

(b) within the framework of economic development programmes.

Article 43 (ex Article 37 TEC)

1. The Commission shall submit proposals for working out and implementing the common agricultural policy, including the replacement of the national organisations by one of the forms of common organisation provided for in Article 40(1), and for implementing the measures specified in this Title.

These proposals shall take account of the interdependence of the agricultural matters mentioned in this Title.

2. The European Parliament and the Council, acting in accordance with the ordinary legislative procedure and after consulting the Economic and Social Committee, shall establish the common organisation of agricultural markets provided for in Article 40(1) and the other provisions necessary for the pursuit of the objectives of the common agricultural policy and the common fisheries policy.

3. The Council, on a proposal from the Commission, shall adopt measures on fixing prices, levies, aid and quantitative limitations and on the fixing and allocation of fishing opportunities.

4. In accordance with paragraph 1, the national market organisations may be replaced by the common organisation provided for in Article 40(1) if:

(a) the common organisation offers Member States which are opposed to this measure and which have an organisation of their own for the production in question equivalent safeguards for the employment and standard of living of the producers concerned, account being taken of the adjustments that will be possible and the specialisation that will be needed with the passage of time;

(b) such an organisation ensures conditions for trade within the Union similar to those existing in a national market.

5. If a common organisation for certain raw materials is established before a common organisation exists for the corresponding processed products, such raw materials as are used for processed products intended for export to third countries may be imported from outside the Union.

Article 44 (ex Article 38 TEC)

Where in a Member State a product is subject to a national market organisation or to internal rules having equivalent effect which affect the competitive position of similar production in another Member State, a countervailing charge shall be applied by Member States to imports of this product coming from the Member State where such organisation or rules exist, unless that State applies a countervailing charge on export.

The Commission shall fix the amount of these charges at the level required to redress the balance; it may also authorise other measures, the conditions and details of which it shall determine.

Title IV Free movement of persons, services and capital

Chapter 1 Workers

Article 45 (ex Article 39 TEC)

1. Freedom of movement for workers shall be secured within the Union.

2. Such freedom of movement shall entail the abolition of any discrimination based on nationality between workers of the Member States as regards employment, remuneration and other conditions of work and employment.

3. It shall entail the right, subject to limitations justified on grounds of public policy, public security or public health:

(a) to accept offers of employment actually made;
(b) to move freely within the territory of Member States for this purpose;
(c) to stay in a Member State for the purpose of employment in accordance with the provisions governing the employment of nationals of that State laid down by law, regulation or administrative action;
(d) to remain in the territory of a Member State after having been employed in that State, subject to conditions which shall be embodied in regulations to be drawn up by the Commission.

4. The provisions of this Article shall not apply to employment in the public service.

Article 46 (ex Article 40 TEC)

The European Parliament and the Council shall, acting in accordance with the ordinary legislative procedure and after consulting the Economic and Social Committee, issue directives or make regulations setting out the measures required to bring about freedom of movement for workers, as defined in Article 45, in particular:

(a) by ensuring close cooperation between national employment services;
(b) by abolishing those administrative procedures and practices and those qualifying periods in respect of eligibility for available employment, whether resulting from national legislation or from agreements previously concluded between Member States, the maintenance of which would form an obstacle to liberalisation of the movement of workers;
(c) by abolishing all such qualifying periods and other restrictions provided for either under national legislation or under agreements previously concluded between Member States as imposed on workers of other Member States conditions regarding the free choice of employment other than those imposed on workers of the State concerned;
(d) by setting up appropriate machinery to bring offers of employment into touch with applications for employment and to facilitate the achievement of a balance between supply and demand in the employment market in such a way as to avoid serious threats to the standard of living and level of employment in the various regions and industries.

Article 47 (ex Article 41 TEC)

Member States shall, within the framework of a joint programme, encourage the exchange of young workers.

Article 48 (ex Article 42 TEC)

The European Parliament and the Council shall, acting in accordance with the ordinary legislative procedure, adopt such measures in the field of social security as are necessary to provide freedom of movement for workers; to this end, they shall make arrangements to secure for employed and self-employed migrant workers and their dependants:

(a) aggregation, for the purpose of acquiring and retaining the right to benefit and of calculating the amount of benefit, of all periods taken into account under the laws of the several countries;

(b) payment of benefits to persons resident in the territories of Member States.

Where a member of the Council declares that a draft legislative act referred to in the first subparagraph would affect important aspects of its social security system, including its scope, cost or financial structure, or would affect the financial balance of that system, it may request that the matter be referred to the European Council. In that case, the ordinary legislative procedure shall be suspended. After discussion, the European Council shall, within four months of this suspension, either:

(a) refer the draft back to the Council, which shall terminate the suspension of the ordinary legislative procedure; or

(b) take no action or request the Commission to submit a new proposal; in that case, the act originally proposed shall be deemed not to have been adopted.

Chapter 2 Right of establishment

Article 49 (ex Article 43 TEC)

Within the framework of the provisions set out below, restrictions on the freedom of establishment of nationals of a Member State in the territory of another Member State shall be prohibited. Such prohibition shall also apply to restrictions on the setting-up of agencies, branches or subsidiaries by nationals of any Member State established in the territory of any Member State.

Freedom of establishment shall include the right to take up and pursue activities as self-employed persons and to set up and manage undertakings, in particular companies or firms within the meaning of the second paragraph of Article 54, under the conditions laid down for its own nationals by the law of the country where such establishment is effected, subject to the provisions of the Chapter relating to capital.

Article 50 (ex Article 44 TEC)

1. In order to attain freedom of establishment as regards a particular activity, the European Parliament and the Council, acting in accordance with the ordinary legislative procedure and after consulting the Economic and Social Committee, shall act by means of directives.

2. The European Parliament, the Council and the Commission shall carry out the duties devolving upon them under the preceding provisions, in particular:

(a) by according, as a general rule, priority treatment to activities where freedom of establishment makes a particularly valuable contribution to the development of production and trade;

(b) by ensuring close cooperation between the competent authorities in the Member States in order to ascertain the particular situation within the Union of the various activities concerned;

(c) by abolishing those administrative procedures and practices, whether resulting from national legislation or from agreements previously concluded between Member States, the maintenance of which would form an obstacle to freedom of establishment;

(d) by ensuring that workers of one Member State employed in the territory of another Member State may remain in that territory for the purpose of taking up activities therein as self-employed persons, where they satisfy the conditions which they would be required to satisfy if they were entering that State at the time when they intended to take up such activities;

(e) by enabling a national of one Member State to acquire and use land and buildings situated in the territory of another Member State, in so far as this does not conflict with the principles laid down in Article 39(2);

(f) by effecting the progressive abolition of restrictions on freedom of establishment in every branch of activity under consideration, both as regards the conditions for setting up agencies, branches or subsidiaries in the territory of a Member State and as regards the subsidiaries in the territory of a Member State and as regards the conditions governing the entry of personnel belonging to the main establishment into managerial or supervisory posts in such agencies, branches or subsidiaries;

(g) by coordinating to the necessary extent the safeguards which, for the protection of the interests of members and others, are required by Member States of companies or firms within the meaning of the second paragraph of Article 54 with a view to making such safeguards equivalent throughout the Union;

(h) by satisfying themselves that the conditions of establishment are not distorted by aids granted by Member States.

Article 51 (ex Article 45 TEC)

The provisions of this Chapter shall not apply, so far as any given Member State is concerned, to activities which in that State are connected, even occasionally, with the exercise of official authority.

The European Parliament and the Council, acting in accordance with the ordinary legislative procedure, may rule that the provisions of this Chapter shall not apply to certain activities.

Article 52 (ex Article 46 TEC)

1. The provisions of this Chapter and measures taken in pursuance thereof shall not prejudice the applicability of provisions laid down by law, regulation or administrative action providing for special treatment for foreign nationals on grounds of public policy, public security or public health.

2. The European Parliament and the Council shall, acting in accordance with the ordinary legislative procedure, issue directives for the coordination of the abovementioned provisions.

Article 53 (ex Article 47 TEC)

1. In order to make it easier for persons to take up and pursue activities as self-employed persons, the European Parliament and the Council shall, acting in accordance with the ordinary legislative procedure, issue directives for the mutual recognition of diplomas, certificates and other evidence of formal qualifications and for the coordination of the provisions laid down by law, regulation or administrative action in Member States concerning the taking-up and pursuit of activities as self-employed persons.

2. In the case of the medical and allied and pharmaceutical professions, the progressive abolition of restrictions shall be dependent upon coordination of the conditions for their exercise in the various Member States.

Article 54 (ex Article 48 TEC)

Companies or firms formed in accordance with the law of a Member State and having their registered office, central administration or principal place of business within the Union shall, for the purposes of this Chapter, be treated in the same way as natural persons who are nationals of Member States.,

'Companies or firms' means companies or firms constituted under civil or commercial law, including cooperative societies, and other legal persons governed by public or private law, save for those which are non-profit-making.

Article 55 (ex Article 294 TEC)

Member States shall accord nationals of the other Member States the same treatment as their own nationals as regards participation in the capital of companies or firms within the meaning of Article 54, without prejudice to the application of the other provisions of the Treaties.

Chapter 3 Services

Article 56 (ex Article 49 TEC)

Within the framework of the provisions set out below, restrictions on freedom to provide services within the Union shall be prohibited in respect of nationals of Member States who are established in a Member State other than that of the person for whom the services are intended.

The European Parliament and the Council, acting in accordance with the ordinary legislative procedure, may extend the provisions of the Chapter to nationals of a third country who provide services and who are established within the Union.

Article 57 (ex Article 50 TEC)

Services shall be considered to be 'services' within the meaning of the Treaties where they are normally provided for remuneration, in so far as they are not governed by the provisions relating to freedom of movement for goods, capital and persons.

'Services' shall in particular include:

(a) activities of an industrial character;
(b) activities of a commercial character;
(c) activities of craftsmen;
(d) activities of the professions.

Without prejudice to the provisions of the Chapter relating to the right of establishment, the person providing a service may, in order to do so, temporarily pursue his activity in the Member State where the service is provided, under the same conditions as are imposed by that State on its own nationals.

Article 58 (ex Article 51 TEC)

1. Freedom to provide services in the field of transport shall be governed by the provisions of the Title relating to transport.

2. The liberalisation of banking and insurance services connected with movements of capital shall be effected in step with the liberalisation of movement of capital.

Article 59 (ex Article 52 TEC)

1. In order to achieve the liberalisation of a specific service, the European Parliament and the Council, acting in accordance with the ordinary legislative procedure and after consulting the Economic and Social Committee, shall issue directives.

2. As regards the directives referred to in paragraph 1, priority shall as a general rule be given to those services which directly affect production costs or the liberalisation of which helps to promote trade in goods.

Article 60 (ex Article 53 TEC)

The Member States shall endeavour to undertake the liberalisation of services beyond the extent required by the directives issued pursuant to Article 59(1), if their general economic situation and the situation of the economic sector concerned so permit.

To this end, the Commission shall make recommendations to the Member States concerned.

Article 61 (ex Article 54 TEC)

As long as restrictions on freedom to provide services have not been abolished, each Member State shall apply such restrictions without distinction on grounds of nationality or residence to all persons providing services within the meaning of the first paragraph of Article 56.

Article 62 (ex Article 55 TEC)

The provisions of Articles 51 to 54 shall apply to the matters covered by this Chapter.

Chapter 4 Capital and payments

Article 63 (ex Article 56 TEC)

1. Within the framework of the provisions set out in this Chapter, all restrictions on the movement of capital between Member States and between Member States and third countries shall be prohibited.

2. Within the framework of the provisions set out in this Chapter, all restrictions on payments between Member States and between Member States and third countries shall be prohibited.

Article 64 (ex Article 57 TEC)

1. The provisions of Article 63 shall be without prejudice to the application to third countries of any restrictions which exist on 31 December 1993 under national or Union law adopted in respect of the movement of capital to or from third countries involving direct investment—including in

real estate—establishment, the provision of financial services or the admission of securities to capital markets. In respect of restrictions existing under national law in Bulgaria, Estonia and Hungary, the relevant date shall be 31 December 1999. In respect of restrictions existing under national law in Croatia, the relevant date shall be 31 December 2002.

2. Whilst endeavouring to achieve the objective of free movement of capital between Member States and third countries to the greatest extent possible and without prejudice to the other Chapters of the Treaties, the European Parliament and the Council, acting in accordance with the ordinary legislative procedure, shall adopt the measures on the movement of capital to or from third countries involving direct investment—including investment in real estate—establishment, the provision of financial services or the admission of securities to capital markets.

3. Notwithstanding paragraph 2, only the Council, acting in accordance with a special legislative procedure, may unanimously, and after consulting the European Parliament, adopt measures which constitute a step backwards in Union law as regards the liberalisation of the movement of capital to or from third countries.

Article 65 (ex Article 58 TEC)

1. The provisions of Article 63 shall be without prejudice to the right of Member States:
   (a) to apply the relevant provisions of their tax law which distinguish between taxpayers who are not in the same situation with regard to their place of residence or with regard to the place where their capital is invested;
   (b) to take all requisite measures to prevent infringements of national law and regulations, in particular in the field of taxation and the prudential supervision of financial institutions, or to lay down procedures for the declaration of capital movements for purposes of administrative or statistical information, or to take measures which are justified on grounds of public policy or public security.

2. The provisions of this Chapter shall be without prejudice to the applicability of restrictions on the right of establishment which are compatible with the Treaties.

3. The measures and procedures referred to in paragraphs 1 and 2 shall not constitute a means of arbitrary discrimination or a disguised restriction on the free movement of capital and payments as defined in Article 63.

4. In the absence of measures pursuant to Article 64(3), the Commission or, in the absence of a Commission decision within three months from the request of the Member State concerned, the Council, may adopt a decision stating that restrictive tax measures adopted by a Member State concerning one or more third countries are to be considered compatible with the Treaties in so far as they are justified by one of the objectives of the Union and compatible with the proper functioning of the internal market. The Council shall act unanimously on application by a Member State.

Article 66 (ex Article 59 TEC)

Where, in exceptional circumstances, movements of capital to or from third countries cause, or threaten to cause, serious difficulties for the operation of economic and monetary union, the Council, on a proposal from the Commission and after consulting the European Central Bank, may take safeguard measures with regard to third countries for a period not exceeding six months if such measures are strictly necessary.

Title V Area of freedom, security and justice

Chapter 1 General provisions

Article 67 (ex Article 61 TEC and ex Article 29 TEU)

1. The Union shall constitute an area of freedom, security and justice with respect for fundamental rights and the different legal systems and traditions of the Member States.

2. It shall ensure the absence of internal border controls for persons and shall frame a common policy on asylum, immigration and external border control, based on solidarity between Member

States, which is fair towards third-country nationals. For the purpose of this Title, stateless persons shall be treated as third-country nationals.

3. The Union shall endeavour to ensure a high level of security through measures to prevent and combat crime, racism and xenophobia, and through measures for coordination and cooperation between police and judicial authorities and other competent authorities, as well as through the mutual recognition of judgments in criminal matters and, if necessary, through the approximation of criminal laws.

4. The Union shall facilitate access to justice, in particular through the principle of mutual recognition of judicial and extrajudicial decisions in civil matters.

Article 68

The European Council shall define the strategic guidelines for legislative and operational planning within the area of freedom, security and justice.

Article 69

National Parliaments ensure that the proposals and legislative initiatives submitted under Chapters 4 and 5 comply with the principle of subsidiarity, in accordance with the arrangements laid down by the Protocol on the application of the principles of subsidiarity and proportionality.

Article 70

Without prejudice to Articles 258, 259 and 260, the Council may, on a proposal from the Commission, adopt measures laying down the arrangements whereby Member States, in collaboration with the Commission, conduct objective and impartial evaluation of the implementation of the Union policies referred to in this Title by Member States' authorities, in particular in order to facilitate full application of the principle of mutual recognition. The European Parliament and national Parliaments shall be informed of the content and results of the evaluation.

Article 71 (ex Article 36 TEU)

A standing committee shall be set up within the Council in order to ensure that operational cooperation on internal security is promoted and strengthened within the Union. Without prejudice to Article 240, it shall facilitate coordination of the action of Member States' competent authorities. Representatives of the Union bodies, offices and agencies concerned may be involved in the proceedings of this committee. The European Parliament and national Parliaments shall be kept informed of the proceedings.

Article 72 (ex Article 64(1) TEC and ex Article 33 TEU)

This Title shall not affect the exercise of the responsibilities incumbent upon Member States with regard to the maintenance of law and order and the safeguarding of internal security.

Article 73

It shall be open to Member States to organise between themselves and under their responsibility such forms of cooperation and coordination as they deem appropriate between the competent departments of their administrations responsible for safeguarding national security.

Article 74 (ex Article 66 TEC)

The Council shall adopt measures to ensure administrative cooperation between the relevant departments of the Member States in the areas covered by this Title, as well as between those departments and the Commission. It shall act on a Commission proposal, subject to Article 76, and after consulting the European Parliament.

Article 75 (ex Article 60 TEC)

Where necessary to achieve the objectives set out in Article 67, as regards preventing and combating terrorism and related activities, the European Parliament and the Council, acting by means of regulations in accordance with the ordinary legislative procedure, shall define a framework for administrative measures with regard to capital movements and payments, such as the freezing of funds, financial assets or economic gains belonging to, or owned or held by, natural or legal persons, groups or non-State entities.

The Council, on a proposal from the Commission, shall adopt measures to implement the framework referred to in the first paragraph.

The acts referred to in this Article shall include necessary provisions on legal safeguards.

Article 76

The acts referred to in Chapters 4 and 5, together with the measures referred to in Article 74 which ensure administrative cooperation in the areas covered by these Chapters, shall be adopted:

(a) on a proposal from the Commission, or
(b) on the initiative of a quarter of the Member States.

Chapter 2 Policies on border checks, asylum and immigration

Article 77 (ex Article 62 TEC)

1. The Union shall develop a policy with a view to:
   (a) ensuring the absence of any controls on persons, whatever their nationality, when crossing internal borders;
   (b) carrying out checks on persons and efficient monitoring of the crossing of external borders;
   (c) the gradual introduction of an integrated management system for external borders.

2. For the purposes of paragraph 1, the European Parliament and the Council, acting in accordance with the ordinary legislative procedure, shall adopt measures concerning:
   (a) the common policy on visas and other short-stay residence permits;
   (b) the checks to which persons crossing external borders are subject;
   (c) the conditions under which nationals of third countries shall have the freedom to travel within the Union for a short period;
   (d) any measure necessary for the gradual establishment of an integrated management system for external borders;
   (e) the absence of any controls on persons, whatever their nationality, when crossing internal borders.

3. If action by the Union should prove necessary to facilitate the exercise of the right referred to in Article 20(2)(a), and if the Treaties have not provided the necessary powers, the Council, acting in accordance with a special legislative procedure, may adopt provisions concerning passports, identity cards, residence permits or any other such document. The Council shall act unanimously after consulting the European Parliament.

4. This Article shall not affect the competence of the Member States concerning the geographical demarcation of their borders, in accordance with international law.

Article 78 (ex Articles 63, points 1 and 2, and 64(2) TEC)

1. The Union shall develop a common policy on asylum, subsidiary protection and temporary protection with a view to offering appropriate status to any third-country national requiring international protection and ensuring compliance with the principle of *non-refoulement*. This policy must be in accordance with the Geneva Convention of 28 July 1951 and the Protocol of 31 January 1967 relating to the status of refugees, and other relevant treaties.

2. For the purposes of paragraph 1, the European Parliament and the Council, acting in accordance with the ordinary legislative procedure, shall adopt measures for a common European asylum system comprising:
   (a) a uniform status of asylum for nationals of third countries, valid throughout the Union;
   (b) a uniform status of subsidiary protection for nationals of third countries who, without obtaining European asylum, are in need of international protection;
   (c) a common system of temporary protection for displaced persons in the event of a massive inflow;

(d) common procedures for the granting and withdrawing of uniform asylum or subsidiary protection status;
(e) criteria and mechanisms for determining which Member State is responsible for considering an application for asylum or subsidiary protection;
(f) standards concerning the conditions for the reception of applicants for asylum or subsidiary protection;
(g) partnership and cooperation with third countries for the purpose of managing inflows of people applying for asylum or subsidiary or temporary protection.

3. In the event of one or more Member States being confronted by an emergency situation characterised by a sudden inflow of nationals of third countries, the Council, on a proposal from the Commission, may adopt provisional measures for the benefit of the Member State(s) concerned. It shall act after consulting the European Parliament.

Article 79 (ex Article 63, points 3 and 4, TEC)

1. The Union shall develop a common immigration policy aimed at ensuring, at all stages, the efficient management of migration flows, fair treatment of third-country nationals residing legally in Member States, and the prevention of, and enhanced measures to combat, illegal immigration and trafficking in human beings.

2. For the purposes of paragraph 1, the European Parliament and the Council, acting in accordance with the ordinary legislative procedure, shall adopt measures in the following areas:

(a) the conditions of entry and residence, and standards on the issue by Member States of long-term visas and residence permits, including those for the purpose of family reunification;
(b) the definition of the rights of third-country nationals residing legally in a Member State, including the conditions governing freedom of movement and of residence in other Member States;
(c) illegal immigration and unauthorised residence, including removal and repatriation of persons residing without authorisation;
(d) combating trafficking in persons, in particular women and children.

3. The Union may conclude agreements with third countries for the readmission to their countries of origin or provenance of third-country nationals who do not or who no longer fulfil the conditions for entry, presence or residence in the territory of one of the Member States.

4. The European Parliament and the Council, acting in accordance with the ordinary legislative procedure, may establish measures to provide incentives and support for the action of Member States with a view to promoting the integration of third-country nationals residing legally in their territories, excluding any harmonisation of the laws and regulations of the Member States.

5. This Article shall not affect the right of Member States to determine volumes of admission of third-country nationals coming from third countries to their territory in order to seek work, whether employed or self-employed.

Article 80

The policies of the Union set out in this Chapter and their implementation shall be governed by the principle of solidarity and fair sharing of responsibility, including its financial implications, between the Member States. Whenever necessary, the Union acts adopted pursuant to this Chapter shall contain appropriate measures to give effect to this principle.

Chapter 3 Judicial cooperation in civil matters

Article 81 (ex Article 65 TEC)

1. The Union shall develop judicial cooperation in civil matters having cross-border implications, based on the principle of mutual recognition of judgments and of decisions in extrajudicial cases. Such cooperation may include the adoption of measures for the approximation of the laws and regulations of the Member States.

2. For the purposes of paragraph 1, the European Parliament and the Council, acting in accordance with the ordinary legislative procedure, shall adopt measures, particularly when necessary for the proper functioning of the internal market, aimed at ensuring:

- (a) the mutual recognition and enforcement between Member States of judgments and of decisions in extrajudicial cases;
- (b) the cross-border service of judicial and extrajudicial documents;
- (c) the compatibility of the rules applicable in the Member States concerning conflict of laws and of jurisdiction;
- (d) cooperation in the taking of evidence;
- (e) effective access to justice;
- (f) the elimination of obstacles to the proper functioning of civil proceedings, if necessary by promoting the compatibility of the rules on civil procedure applicable in the Member States;
- (g) the development of alternative methods of dispute settlement;
- (h) support for the training of the judiciary and judicial staff.

3. Notwithstanding paragraph 2, measures concerning family law with cross-border implications shall be established by the Council, acting in accordance with a special legislative procedure. The Council shall act unanimously after consulting the European Parliament.

The Council, on a proposal from the Commission, may adopt a decision determining those aspects of family law with cross-border implications which may be the subject of acts adopted by the ordinary legislative procedure. The Council shall act unanimously after consulting the European Parliament.

The proposal referred to in the second subparagraph shall be notified to the national Parliaments. If a national Parliament makes known its opposition within six months of the date of such notification, the decision shall not be adopted. In the absence of opposition, the Council may adopt the decision.

Chapter 4 Judicial cooperation in criminal matters

Article 82 (ex Article 31 TEU)

1. Judicial cooperation in criminal matters in the Union shall be based on the principle of mutual recognition of judgments and judicial decisions and shall include the approximation of the laws and regulations of the Member States in the areas referred to in paragraph 2 and in Article 83.

The European Parliament and the Council, acting in accordance with the ordinary legislative procedure, shall adopt measures to:

- (a) lay down rules and procedures for ensuring recognition throughout the Union of all forms of judgments and judicial decisions;
- (b) prevent and settle conflicts of jurisdiction between Member States;
- (c) support the training of the judiciary and judicial staff;
- (d) facilitate cooperation between judicial or equivalent authorities of the Member States in relation to proceedings in criminal matters and the enforcement of decisions.

2. To the extent necessary to facilitate mutual recognition of judgments and judicial decisions and police and judicial cooperation in criminal matters having a cross-border dimension, the European Parliament and the Council may, by means of directives adopted in accordance with the ordinary legislative procedure, establish minimum rules. Such rules shall take into account the differences between the legal traditions and systems of the Member States.

They shall concern:

- (a) mutual admissibility of evidence between Member States;
- (b) the rights of individuals in criminal procedure;
- (c) the rights of victims of crime;
- (d) any other specific aspects of criminal procedure which the Council has identified in advance by a decision; for the adoption of such a decision, the Council shall act unanimously after obtaining the consent of the European Parliament.

Adoption of the minimum rules referred to in this paragraph shall not prevent Member States from maintaining or introducing a higher level of protection for individuals.

3. Where a member of the Council considers that a draft directive as referred to in paragraph 2 would affect fundamental aspects of its criminal justice system, it may request that the draft directive be referred to the European Council. In that case, the ordinary legislative procedure shall be suspended. After discussion, and in case of a consensus, the European Council shall, within four months of this suspension, refer the draft back to the Council, which shall terminate the suspension of the ordinary legislative procedure.

Within the same timeframe, in case of disagreement, and if at least nine Member States wish to establish enhanced cooperation on the basis of the draft directive concerned, they shall notify the European Parliament, the Council and the Commission accordingly. In such a case, the authorisation to proceed with enhanced cooperation referred to in Article 20(2) of the Treaty on European Union and Article 329(1) of this Treaty shall be deemed to be granted and the provisions on enhanced cooperation shall apply.

Article 83 (ex Article 31 TEU)

1. The European Parliament and the Council may, by means of directives adopted in accordance with the ordinary legislative procedure, establish minimum rules concerning the definition of criminal offences and sanctions in the areas of particularly serious crime with a cross-border dimension resulting from the nature or impact of such offences or from a special need to combat them on a common basis.

These areas of crime are the following: terrorism, trafficking in human beings and sexual exploitation of women and children, illicit drug trafficking, illicit arms trafficking, money laundering, corruption, counterfeiting of means of payment, computer crime and organised crime.

On the basis of developments in crime, the Council may adopt a decision identifying other areas of crime that meet the criteria specified in this paragraph. It shall act unanimously after obtaining the consent of the European Parliament.

2. If the approximation of criminal laws and regulations of the Member States proves essential to ensure the effective implementation of a Union policy in an area which has been subject to harmonisation measures, directives may establish minimum rules with regard to the definition of criminal offences and sanctions in the area concerned.

Such directives shall be adopted by the same ordinary or special legislative procedure as was followed for the adoption of the harmonisation measures in question, without prejudice to Article 76.

3. Where a member of the Council considers that a draft directive as referred to in paragraph 1 or 2 would affect fundamental aspects of its criminal justice system, it may request that the draft directive be referred to the European Council. In that case, the ordinary legislative procedure shall be suspended. After discussion, and in case of a consensus, the European Council shall, within four months of this suspension, refer the draft back to the Council, which shall terminate the suspension of the ordinary legislative procedure.

Within the same timeframe, in case of disagreement, and if at least nine Member States wish to establish enhanced cooperation on the basis of the draft directive concerned, they shall notify the European Parliament, the Council and the Commission accordingly. In such a case, the authorisation to proceed with enhanced cooperation referred to in Article 20(2) of the Treaty on European Union and Article 329(1) of this Treaty shall be deemed to be granted and the provisions on enhanced cooperation shall apply.

Article 84

The European Parliament and the Council, acting in accordance with the ordinary legislative procedure, may establish measures to promote and support the action of Member States in the field of crime prevention, excluding any harmonisation of the laws and regulations of the Member States.

Article 85 (ex Article 31 TEU)

1. Eurojust's mission shall be to support and strengthen coordination and cooperation between national investigating and prosecuting authorities in relation to serious crime affecting two or more Member States or requiring a prosecution on common bases, on the basis of operations conducted and information supplied by the Member States' authorities and by Europol.

In this context, the European Parliament and the Council, by means of regulations adopted in accordance with the ordinary legislative procedure, shall determine Eurojust's structure, operation, field of action and tasks. These tasks may include:

(a) the initiation of criminal investigations, as well as proposing the initiation of prosecutions conducted by competent national authorities, particularly those relating to offences against the financial interests of the Union;
(b) the coordination of investigations and prosecutions referred to in point (a);
(c) the strengthening of judicial cooperation, including by resolution of conflicts of jurisdiction and by close cooperation with the European Judicial Network.

These regulations shall also determine arrangements for involving the European Parliament and national Parliaments in the evaluation of Eurojust's activities.

2. In the prosecutions referred to in paragraph 1, and without prejudice to Article 86, formal acts of judicial procedure shall be carried out by the competent national officials.

Article 86

1. In order to combat crimes affecting the financial interests of the Union, the Council, by means of regulations adopted in accordance with a special legislative procedure, may establish a European Public Prosecutor's Office from Eurojust. The Council shall act unanimously after obtaining the consent of the European Parliament.

In the absence of unanimity in the Council, a group of at least nine Member States may request that the draft regulation be referred to the European Council. In that case, the procedure in the Council shall be suspended. After discussion, and in case of a consensus, the European Council shall, within four months of this suspension, refer the draft back to the Council for adoption.

Within the same timeframe, in case of disagreement, and if at least nine Member States wish to establish enhanced cooperation on the basis of the draft regulation concerned, they shall notify the European Parliament, the Council and the Commission accordingly. In such a case, the authorisation to proceed with enhanced cooperation referred to in Article 20(2) of the Treaty on European Union and Article 329(1) of this Treaty shall be deemed to be granted and the provisions on enhanced cooperation shall apply.

2. The European Public Prosecutor's Office shall be responsible for investigating, prosecuting and bringing to judgment, where appropriate in liaison with Europol, the perpetrators of, and accomplices in, offences against the Union's financial interests, as determined by the regulation provided for in paragraph 1. It shall exercise the functions of prosecutor in the competent courts of the Member States in relation to such offences.

3. The regulations referred to in paragraph 1 shall determine the general rules applicable to the European Public Prosecutor's Office, the conditions governing the performance of its functions, the rules of procedure applicable to its activities, as well as those governing the admissibility of evidence, and the rules applicable to the judicial review of procedural measures taken by it in the performance of its functions.

4. The European Council may, at the same time or subsequently, adopt a decision amending paragraph 1 in order to extend the powers of the European Public Prosecutor's Office to include serious crime having a cross-border dimension and amending accordingly paragraph 2 as regards the perpetrators of, and accomplices in, serious crimes affecting more than one Member State. The European Council shall act unanimously after obtaining the consent of the European Parliament and after consulting the Commission.

Chapter 5 Police cooperation

Article 87 (ex Article 30 TEU)

1. The Union shall establish police cooperation involving all the Member States' competent authorities, including police, customs and other specialised law enforcement services in relation to the prevention, detection and investigation of criminal offences.

2. For the purposes of paragraph 1, the European Parliament and the Council, acting in accordance with the ordinary legislative procedure, may establish measures concerning:

(a) the collection, storage, processing, analysis and exchange of relevant information;

(b) support for the training of staff, and cooperation on the exchange of staff, on equipment and on research into crime-detection;

(c) common investigative techniques in relation to the detection of serious forms of organised crime.

3. The Council, acting in accordance with a special legislative procedure, may establish measures concerning operational cooperation between the authorities referred to in this Article. The Council shall act unanimously after consulting the European Parliament.

In case of the absence of unanimity in the Council, a group of at least nine Member States may request that the draft measures be referred to the European Council. In that case, the procedure in the Council shall be suspended. After discussion, and in case of a consensus, the European Council shall, within four months of this suspension, refer the draft back to the Council for adoption.

Within the same timeframe, in case of disagreement, and if at least nine Member States wish to establish enhanced cooperation on the basis of the draft measures concerned, they shall notify the European Parliament, the Council and the Commission accordingly. In such a case, the authorisation to proceed with enhanced cooperation referred to in Article 20(2) of the Treaty on European Union and Article 329(1) of this Treaty shall be deemed to be granted and the provisions on enhanced cooperation shall apply.

The specific procedure provided for in the second and third subparagraphs shall not apply to acts which constitute a development of the Schengen *acquis*.

Article 88 (ex Article 30 TEU)

1. Europol's mission shall be to support and strengthen action by the Member States' police authorities and other law enforcement services and their mutual cooperation in preventing and combating serious crime affecting two or more Member States, terrorism and forms of crime which affect a common interest covered by a Union policy.

2. The European Parliament and the Council, by means of regulations adopted in accordance with the ordinary legislative procedure, shall determine Europol's structure, operation, field of action and tasks. These tasks may include:

(a) the collection, storage, processing, analysis and exchange of information, in particular that forwarded by the authorities of the Member States or third countries or bodies;

(b) the coordination, organisation and implementation of investigative and operational action carried out jointly with the Member States' competent authorities or in the context of joint investigative teams, where appropriate in liaison with Eurojust.

These regulations shall also lay down the procedures for scrutiny of Europol's activities by the European Parliament, together with national Parliaments.

3. Any operational action by Europol must be carried out in liaison and in agreement with the authorities of the Member State or States whose territory is concerned. The application of coercive measures shall be the exclusive responsibility of the competent national authorities.

Article 89 (ex Article 32 TEU)

The Council, acting in accordance with a special legislative procedure, shall lay down the conditions and limitations under which the competent authorities of the Member States referred to in Articles 82 and 87 may operate in the territory of another Member State in liaison and in agreement with the authorities of that State. The Council shall act unanimously after consulting the European Parliament.

Title VI Transport

Article 90 (ex Article 70 TEC)

The objectives of the Treaties shall, in matters governed by this Title, be pursued within the framework of a common transport policy.

Article 91 (ex Article 71 TEC)

1. For the purpose of implementing Article 90, and taking into account the distinctive features of transport, the European Parliament and the Council shall, acting in accordance with the ordinary legislative procedure and after consulting the Economic and Social Committee and the Committee of the Regions, lay down:

(a) common rules applicable to international transport to or from the territory of a Member State or passing across the territory of one or more Member States;

(b) the conditions under which non-resident carriers may operate transport services within a Member State;

(c) measures to improve transport safety;

(d) any other appropriate provisions.

2. When the measures referred to in paragraph 1 are adopted, account shall be taken of cases where their application might seriously affect the standard of living and level of employment in certain regions, and the operation of transport facilities.

Article 92 (ex Article 72 TEC)

Until the provisions referred to in Article 91(1) have been laid down, no Member State may, unless the Council has unanimously adopted a measure granting a derogation, make the various provisions governing the subject on 1 January 1958 or, for acceding States, the date of their accession less favourable in their direct or indirect effect on carriers of other Member States as compared with carriers who are nationals of that State.

Article 93 (ex Article 73 TEC)

Aids shall be compatible with the Treaties if they meet the needs of coordination of transport or if they represent reimbursement for the discharge of certain obligations inherent in the concept of a public service.

Article 94 (ex Article 74 TEC)

Any measures taken within the framework of the Treaties in respect of transport rates and conditions shall take account of the economic circumstances of carriers.

Article 95 (ex Article 75 TEC)

1. In the case of transport within the Union, discrimination which takes the form of carriers charging different rates and imposing different conditions for the carriage of the same goods over the same transport links on grounds of the country of origin or of destination of the goods in question shall be prohibited.

2. Paragraph 1 shall not prevent the European Parliament and the Council from adopting other measures pursuant to Article 91(1).

3. The Council shall, on a proposal from the Commission and after consulting the European Parliament and the Economic and Social Committee, lay down rules for implementing the provisions of paragraph 1.

The Council may in particular lay down the provisions needed to enable the institutions of the Union to secure compliance with the rule laid down in paragraph 1 and to ensure that users benefit from it to the full.

4. The Commission shall, acting on its own initiative or on application by a Member State, investigate any cases of discrimination falling within paragraph 1 and, after consulting any Member State concerned, shall take the necessary decisions within the framework of the rules laid down in accordance with the provisions of paragraph 3.

Article 96 (ex Article 76 TEC)

1. The imposition by a Member State, in respect of transport operations carried out within the Union, of rates and conditions involving any element of support or protection in the interest of one or more particular undertakings or industries shall be prohibited, unless authorised by the Commission.

2. The Commission shall, acting on its own initiative or on application by a Member State, examine the rates and conditions referred to in paragraph 1, taking account in particular of the requirements of an appropriate regional economic policy, the needs of underdeveloped areas and the problems of areas seriously affected by political circumstances on the one hand, and of the effects of such rates and conditions on competition between the different modes of transport on the other.

After consulting each Member State concerned, the Commission shall take the necessary decisions.

3. The prohibition provided for in paragraph 1 shall not apply to tariffs fixed to meet competition.

Article 97 (ex Article 77 TEC)

Charges or dues in respect of the crossing of frontiers which are charged by a carrier in addition to the transport rates shall not exceed a reasonable level after taking the costs actually incurred thereby into account.

Member States shall endeavour to reduce these costs progressively.

The Commission may make recommendations to Member States for the application of this Article.

Article 98 (ex Article 78 TEC)

The provisions of this Title shall not form an obstacle to the application of measures taken in the Federal Republic of Germany to the extent that such measures are required in order to compensate for the economic disadvantages caused by the division of Germany to the economy of certain areas of the Federal Republic affected by that division. Five years after the entry into force of the Treaty of Lisbon, the Council, acting on a proposal from the Commission, may adopt a decision repealing this Article.

Article 99 (ex Article 79 TEC)

An Advisory Committee consisting of experts designated by the governments of Member States shall be attached to the Commission. The Commission, whenever it considers it desirable, shall consult the Committee on transport matters.

Article 100 (ex Article 80 TEC)

1. The provisions of this Title shall apply to transport by rail, road and inland waterway.

2. The European Parliament and the Council, acting in accordance with the ordinary legislative procedure, may lay down appropriate provisions for sea and air transport. They shall act after consulting the Economic and Social Committee and the Committee of the Regions.

Title VII Common rules on competition, taxation and approximation of laws

Chapter 1 Rules on competition

Section 1 Rules applying to undertakings

Article 101 (ex Article 81 TEC)

1. The following shall be prohibited as incompatible with the internal market: all agreements between undertakings, decisions by associations of undertakings and concerted practices which may affect trade between Member States and which have as their object or effect the prevention, restriction or distortion of competition within the internal market, and in particular those which:

(a) directly or indirectly fix purchase or selling prices or any other trading conditions;
(b) limit or control production, markets, technical development, or investment;
(c) share markets or sources of supply;
(d) apply dissimilar conditions to equivalent transactions with other trading parties, thereby placing them at a competitive disadvantage;
(e) make the conclusion of contracts subject to acceptance by the other parties of supplementary obligations which, by their nature or according to commercial usage, have no connection with the subject of such contracts.

2. Any agreements or decisions prohibited pursuant to this Article shall be automatically void.

3. The provisions of paragraph 1 may, however, be declared inapplicable in the case of:

- any agreement or category of agreements between undertakings,
- any decision or category of decisions by associations of undertakings,
- any concerted practice or category of concerted practices,

which contributes to improving the production or distribution of goods or to promoting technical or economic progress, while allowing consumers a fair share of the resulting benefit, and which does not:

(a) impose on the undertakings concerned restrictions which are not indispensable to the attainment of these objectives;

(b) afford such undertakings the possibility of eliminating competition in respect of a substantial part of the products in question.

Article 102 (ex Article 82 TEC)

Any abuse by one or more undertakings of a dominant position within the internal market or in a substantial part of it shall be prohibited as incompatible with the internal market in so far as it may affect trade between Member States.

Such abuse may, in particular, consist in:

(a) directly or indirectly imposing unfair purchase or selling prices or other unfair trading conditions;

(b) limiting production, markets or technical development to the prejudice of consumers;

(c) applying dissimilar conditions to equivalent transactions with other trading parties, thereby placing them at a competitive disadvantage;

(d) making the conclusion of contracts subject to acceptance by the other parties of supplementary obligations which, by their nature or according to commercial usage, have no connection with the subject of such contracts.

Article 103 (ex Article 83 TEC)

1. The appropriate regulations or directives to give effect to the principles set out in Articles 101 and 102 shall be laid down by the Council, on a proposal from the Commission and after consulting the European Parliament.

2. The regulations or directives referred to in paragraph 1 shall be designed in particular:

(a) to ensure compliance with the prohibitions laid down in Article 101(1) and in Article 102 by making provision for fines and periodic penalty payments;

(b) to lay down detailed rules for the application of Article 101(3), taking into account the need to ensure effective supervision on the one hand, and to simplify administration to the greatest possible extent on the other;

(c) to define, if need be, in the various branches of the economy, the scope of the provisions of Articles 101 and 102;

(d) to define the respective functions of the Commission and of the Court of Justice of the European Union in applying the provisions laid down in this paragraph;

(e) to determine the relationship between national laws and the provisions contained in this Section or adopted pursuant to this Article.

Article 104 (ex Article 84 TEC)

Until the entry into force of the provisions adopted in pursuance of Article 103, the authorities in Member States shall rule on the admissibility of agreements, decisions and concerted practices and on abuse of a dominant position in the internal market in accordance with the law of their country and with the provisions of Article 101, in particular paragraph 3, and of Article 102.

Article 105 (ex Article 85 TEC)

1. Without prejudice to Article 104, the Commission shall ensure the application of the principles laid down in Articles 101 and 102. On application by a Member State or on its own initiative, and in cooperation with the competent authorities in the Member States, which shall give it their

assistance, the Commission shall investigate cases of suspected infringement of these principles. If it finds that there has been an infringement, it shall propose appropriate measures to bring it to an end.

2. If the infringement is not brought to an end, the Commission shall record such infringement of the principles in a reasoned decision. The Commission may publish its decision and authorise Member States to take the measures, the conditions and details of which it shall determine, needed to remedy the situation.

3. The Commission may adopt regulations relating to the categories of agreement in respect of which the Council has adopted a regulation or a directive pursuant to Article 103(2)(b).

Article 106 (ex Article 86 TEC)

1. In the case of public undertakings and undertakings to which Member States grant special or exclusive rights, Member States shall neither enact nor maintain in force any measure contrary to the rules contained in the Treaties, in particular to those rules provided for in Article 18 and Articles 101 to 109.

2. Undertakings entrusted with the operation of services of general economic interest or having the character of a revenue-producing monopoly shall be subject to the rules contained in the Treaties, in particular to the rules on competition, in so far as the application of such rules does not obstruct the performance, in law or in fact, of the particular tasks assigned to them. The development of trade must not be affected to such an extent as would be contrary to the interests of the Union.

3. The Commission shall ensure the application of the provisions of this Article and shall, where necessary, address appropriate directives or decisions to Member States.

Section 2 Aids granted by States

Article 107 (ex Article 87 TEC)

1. Save as otherwise provided in the Treaties, any aid granted by a Member State or through State resources in any form whatsoever which distorts or threatens to distort competition by favouring certain undertakings or the production of certain goods shall, in so far as it affects trade between Member States, be incompatible with the internal market.

2. The following shall be compatible with the internal market:
   - (a) aid having a social character, granted to individual consumers, provided that such aid is granted without discrimination related to the origin of the products concerned;
   - (b) aid to make good the damage caused by natural disasters or exceptional occurrences;
   - (c) aid granted to the economy of certain areas of the Federal Republic of Germany affected by the division of Germany, in so far as such aid is required in order to compensate for the economic disadvantages caused by that division. Five years after the entry into force of the Treaty of Lisbon, the Council, acting on a proposal from the Commission, may adopt a decision repealing this point.

3. The following may be considered to be compatible with the internal market:
   - (a) aid to promote the economic development of areas where the standard of living is abnormally low or where there is serious underemployment, and of the regions referred to in Article 349, in view of their structural, economic and social situation;
   - (b) aid to promote the execution of an important project of common European interest or to remedy a serious disturbance in the economy of a Member State;
   - (c) aid to facilitate the development of certain economic activities or of certain economic areas, where such aid does not adversely affect trading conditions to an extent contrary to the common interest;
   - (d) aid to promote culture and heritage conservation where such aid does not affect trading conditions and competition in the Union to an extent that is contrary to the common interest;
   - (e) such other categories of aid as may be specified by decision of the Council on a proposal from the Commission.

Article 108 (ex Article 88 TEC)

1. The Commission shall, in cooperation with Member States, keep under constant review all systems of aid existing in those States. It shall propose to the latter any appropriate measures required by the progressive development or by the functioning of the internal market.

2. If, after giving notice to the parties concerned to submit their comments, the Commission finds that aid granted by a State or through State resources is not compatible with the internal market having regard to Article 107, or that such aid is being misused, it shall decide that the State concerned shall abolish or alter such aid within a period of time to be determined by the Commission.

If the State concerned does not comply with this decision within the prescribed time, the Commission or any other interested State may, in derogation from the provisions of Articles 258 and 259, refer the matter to the Court of Justice of the European Union direct.

On application by a Member State, the Council may, acting unanimously, decide that aid which that State is granting or intends to grant shall be considered to be compatible with the internal market, in derogation from the provisions of Article 107 or from the regulations provided for in Article 109, if such a decision is justified by exceptional circumstances. If, as regards the aid in question, the Commission has already initiated the procedure provided for in the first subparagraph of this paragraph, the fact that the State concerned has made its application to the Council shall have the effect of suspending that procedure until the Council has made its attitude known.

If, however, the Council has not made its attitude known within three months of the said application being made, the Commission shall give its decision on the case.

3. The Commission shall be informed, in sufficient time to enable it to submit its comments, of any plans to grant or alter aid. If it considers that any such plan is not compatible with the internal market having regard to Article 107, it shall without delay initiate the procedure provided for in paragraph 2. The Member State concerned shall not put its proposed measures into effect until this procedure has resulted in a final decision.

4. The Commission may adopt regulations relating to the categories of State aid that the Council has, pursuant to Article 109, determined may be exempted from the procedure provided for by paragraph 3 of this Article.

Article 109 (ex Article 89 TEC)

The Council, on a proposal from the Commission and after consulting the European Parliament, may make any appropriate regulations for the application of Articles 107 and 108 and may in particular determine the conditions in which Article 108(3) shall apply and the categories of aid exempted from this procedure.

Chapter 2 Tax provisions

Article 110 (ex Article 90 TEC)

No Member State shall impose, directly or indirectly, on the products of other Member States any internal taxation of any kind in excess of that imposed directly or indirectly on similar domestic products.

Furthermore, no Member State shall impose on the products of other Member States any internal taxation of such a nature as to afford indirect protection to other products.

Article 111 (ex Article 91 TEC)

Where products are exported to the territory of any Member State, any repayment of internal taxation shall not exceed the internal taxation imposed on them whether directly or indirectly.

Article 112 (ex Article 92 TEC)

In the case of charges other than turnover taxes, excise duties and other forms of indirect taxation, remissions and repayments in respect of exports to other Member States may not be granted and countervailing charges in respect of imports from Member States may not be imposed unless the measures contemplated have been previously approved for a limited period by the Council on a proposal from the Commission.

Article 113 (ex Article 93 TEC)
The Council shall, acting unanimously in accordance with a special legislative procedure and after consulting the European Parliament and the Economic and Social Committee, adopt provisions for the harmonisation of legislation concerning turnover taxes, excise duties and other forms of indirect taxation to the extent that such harmonisation is necessary to ensure the establishment and the functioning of the internal market and to avoid distortion of competition.

Chapter 3 Approximation of laws

Article 114 (ex Article 95 TEC)

1. Save where otherwise provided in the Treaties, the following provisions shall apply for the achievement of the objectives set out in Article 26. The European Parliament and the Council shall, acting in accordance with the ordinary legislative procedure and after consulting the Economic and Social Committee, adopt the measures for the approximation of the provisions laid down by law, regulation or administrative action in Member States which have as their object the establishment and functioning of the internal market.

2. Paragraph 1 shall not apply to fiscal provisions, to those relating to the free movement of persons nor to those relating to the rights and interests of employed persons.

3. The Commission, in its proposals envisaged in paragraph 1 concerning health, safety, environmental protection and consumer protection, will take as a base a high level of protection, taking account in particular of any new development based on scientific facts. Within their respective powers, the European Parliament and the Council will also seek to achieve this objective.

4. If, after the adoption of a harmonisation measure by the European Parliament and the Council, by the Council or by the Commission, a Member State deems it necessary to maintain national provisions on grounds of major needs referred to in Article 36, or relating to the protection of the environment or the working environment, it shall notify the Commission of these provisions as well as the grounds for maintaining them.

5. Moreover, without prejudice to paragraph 4, if, after the adoption of a harmonisation measure by the European Parliament and the Council, by the Council or by the Commission, a Member State deems it necessary to introduce national provisions based on new scientific evidence relating to the protection of the environment or the working environment on grounds of a problem specific to that Member State arising after the adoption of the harmonisation measure, it shall notify the Commission of the envisaged provisions as well as the grounds for introducing them.

6. The Commission shall, within six months of the notifications as referred to in paragraphs 4 and 5, approve or reject the national provisions involved after having verified whether or not they are a means of arbitrary discrimination or a disguised restriction on trade between Member States and whether or not they shall constitute an obstacle to the functioning of the internal market.

In the absence of a decision by the Commission within this period the national provisions referred to in paragraphs 4 and 5 shall be deemed to have been approved.

When justified by the complexity of the matter and in the absence of danger for human health, the Commission may notify the Member State concerned that the period referred to in this paragraph may be extended for a further period of up to six months.

7. When, pursuant to paragraph 6, a Member State is authorised to maintain or introduce national provisions derogating from a harmonisation measure, the Commission shall immediately examine whether to propose an adaptation to that measure.

8. When a Member State raises a specific problem on public health in a field which has been the subject of prior harmonisation measures, it shall bring it to the attention of the Commission which shall immediately examine whether to propose appropriate measures to the Council.

9. By way of derogation from the procedure laid down in Articles 258 and 259, the Commission and any Member State may bring the matter directly before the Court of Justice of the European Union if it considers that another Member State is making improper use of the powers provided for in this Article.

10. The harmonisation measures referred to above shall, in appropriate cases, include a safeguard clause authorising the Member States to take, for one or more of the non-economic reasons referred to in Article 36, provisional measures subject to a Union control procedure.

Article 115 (ex Article 94 TEC)

Without prejudice to Article 114, the Council shall, acting unanimously in accordance with a special legislative procedure and after consulting the European Parliament and the Economic and Social Committee, issue directives for the approximation of such laws, regulations or administrative provisions of the Member States as directly affect the establishment or functioning of the internal market.

Article 116 (ex Article 96 TEC)

Where the Commission finds that a difference between the provisions laid down by law, regulation or administrative action in Member States is distorting the conditions of competition in the internal market and that the resultant distortion needs to be eliminated, it shall consult the Member States concerned.

If such consultation does not result in an agreement eliminating the distortion in question, the European, Parliament and the Council, acting in accordance with the ordinary legislative procedure, shall issue the necessary directives. Any other appropriate measures provided for in the Treaties may be adopted.

Article 117 (ex Article 97 TEC)

1. Where there is a reason to fear that the adoption or amendment of a provision laid down by law, regulation or administrative action may cause distortion within the meaning of Article 116, a Member State desiring to proceed therewith shall consult the Commission. After consulting the Member States, the Commission shall recommend to the States concerned such measures as may be appropriate to avoid the distortion in question.

2. If a State desiring to introduce or amend its own provisions does not comply with the recommendation addressed to it by the Commission, other Member States shall not be required, pursuant to Article 116, to amend their own provisions in order to eliminate such distortion. If the Member State which has ignored the recommendation of the Commission causes distortion detrimental only to itself, the provisions of Article 116 shall not apply.

Article 118

In the context of the establishment and functioning of the internal market, the European Parliament and the Council, acting in accordance with the ordinary legislative procedure, shall establish measures for the creation of European intellectual property rights to provide uniform protection of intellectual property rights throughout the Union and for the setting up of centralised Union-wide authorisation, coordination and supervision arrangements.

The Council, acting in accordance with a special legislative procedure, shall by means of regulations establish language arrangements for the European intellectual property rights. The Council shall act unanimously after consulting the European Parliament.

Title VIII Economic and monetary policy

Article 119 (ex Article 4 TEC)

1. For the purposes set out in Article 3 of the Treaty on European Union, the activities of the Member States and the Union shall include, as provided in the Treaties, the adoption of an economic policy which is based on the close coordination of Member States' economic policies, on the internal market and on the definition of common objectives, and conducted in accordance with the principle of an open market economy with free competition.

2. Concurrently with the foregoing, and as provided in the Treaties and in accordance with the procedures set out therein, these activities shall include a single currency, the euro, and the definition and conduct of a single monetary policy and exchange-rate policy the primary objective of both of which shall be to maintain price stability and, without prejudice to this objective, to support the

general economic policies in the Union, in accordance with the principle of an open market economy with free competition.

3. These activities of the Member States and the Union shall entail compliance with the following guiding principles: stable prices, sound public finances and monetary conditions and a sustainable balance of payments.

Chapter 1 Economic policy

Article 120 (ex Article 98 TEC)

Member States shall conduct their economic policies with a view to contributing to the achievement of the objectives of the Union, as defined in Article 3 of the Treaty on European Union, and in the context of the broad guidelines referred to in Article 121(2). The Member States and the Union shall act in accordance with the principle of an open market economy with free competition, favouring an efficient allocation of resources, and in compliance with the principles set out in Article 119.

Article 121 (ex Article 99 TEC)

1. Member States shall regard their economic policies as a matter of common concern and shall coordinate them within the Council, in accordance with the provisions of Article 120.

2. The Council shall, on a recommendation from the Commission, formulate a draft for the broad guidelines of the economic policies of the Member States and of the Union, and shall report its findings to the European Council.

The European Council shall, acting on the basis of the report from the Council, discuss a conclusion on the broad guidelines of the economic policies of the Member States and of the Union.

On the basis of this conclusion, the Council shall adopt a recommendation setting out these broad guidelines. The Council shall inform the European Parliament of its recommendation.

3. In order to ensure closer coordination of economic policies and sustained convergence of the economic performances of the Member States, the Council shall, on the basis of reports submitted by the Commission, monitor economic developments in each of the Member States and in the Union as well as the consistency of economic policies with the broad guidelines referred to in paragraph 2, and regularly carry out an overall assessment.

For the purpose of this multilateral surveillance, Member States shall forward information to the Commission about important measures taken by them in the field of their economic policy and such other information as they deem necessary.

4. Where it is established, under the procedure referred to in paragraph 3, that the economic policies of a Member State are not consistent with the broad guidelines referred to in paragraph 2 or that they risk jeopardising the proper functioning of economic and monetary union, the Commission may address a warning to the Member State concerned. The Council, on a recommendation from the Commission, may address the necessary recommendations to the Member State concerned. The Council may, on a proposal from the Commission, decide to make its recommendations public.

Within the scope of this paragraph, the Council shall act without taking into account the vote of the member of the Council representing the Member State concerned.

A qualified majority of the other members of the Council shall be defined in accordance with Article 238(3)(a).

5. The President of the Council and the Commission shall report to the European Parliament on the results of multilateral surveillance. The President of the Council may be invited to appear before the competent committee of the European Parliament if the Council has made its recommendations public.

6. The European Parliament and the Council, acting by means of regulations in accordance with the ordinary legislative procedure, may adopt detailed rules for the multilateral surveillance procedure referred to in paragraphs 3 and 4.

Article 122 (ex Article 100 TEC)

1. Without prejudice to any other procedures provided for in the Treaties, the Council, on a proposal from the Commission, may decide, in a spirit of solidarity between Member States, upon the

measures appropriate to the economic situation, in particular if severe difficulties arise in the supply of certain products, notably in the area of energy.

2. Where a Member State is in difficulties or is seriously threatened with severe difficulties caused by natural disasters or exceptional occurrences beyond its control, the Council, on a proposal from the Commission, may grant, under certain conditions, Union financial assistance to the Member State concerned. The President of the Council shall inform the European Parliament of the decision taken.

Article 123 (ex Article 101 TEC)

1. Overdraft facilities or any other type of credit facility with the European Central Bank or with the central banks of the Member States (hereinafter referred to as 'national central banks') in favour of Union institutions, bodies, offices or agencies, central governments, regional, local or other public authorities, other bodies governed by public law, or public undertakings of Member States shall be prohibited, as shall the purchase directly from them by the European Central Bank or national central banks of debt instruments.

2. Paragraph 1 shall not apply to publicly owned credit institutions which, in the context of the supply of reserves by central banks, shall be given the same treatment by national central banks and the European Central Bank as private credit institutions.

Article 124 (ex Article 102 TEC)

Any measure, not based on prudential considerations, establishing privileged access by Union institutions, bodies, offices or agencies, central governments, regional, local or other public authorities, other bodies governed by public law, or public undertakings of Member States to financial institutions, shall be prohibited.

Article 125 (ex Article 103 TEC)

1. The Union shall not be liable for or assume the commitments of central governments, regional, local or other public authorities, other bodies governed by public law, or public undertakings of any Member State, without prejudice to mutual financial guarantees for the joint execution of a specific project. A Member State shall not be liable for or assume the commitments of central governments, regional, local or other public authorities, other bodies governed by public law, or public undertakings of another Member State, without prejudice to mutual financial guarantees for the joint execution of a specific project.

2. The Council, on a proposal from the Commission and after consulting the European Parliament, may, as required, specify definitions for the application of the prohibitions referred to in Articles 123 and 124 and in this Article.

Article 126 (ex Article 104 TEC)

1. Member States shall avoid excessive government deficits.

2. The Commission shall monitor the development of the budgetary situation and of the stock of government debt in the Member States with a view to identifying gross errors. In particular it shall examine compliance with budgetary discipline on the basis of the following two criteria:

(a) whether the ratio of the planned or actual government deficit to gross domestic product exceeds a reference value, unless:
- either the ratio has declined substantially and continuously and reached a level that comes close to the reference value,
- or, alternatively, the excess over the reference value is only exceptional and temporary and the ratio remains close to the reference value;

(b) whether the ratio of government debt to gross domestic product exceeds a reference value, unless the ratio is sufficiently diminishing and approaching the reference value at a satisfactory pace.

The reference values are specified in the Protocol on the excessive deficit procedure annexed to the Treaties.

3. If a Member State does not fulfil the requirements under one or both of these criteria, the Commission shall prepare a report. The report of the Commission shall also take into account

whether the government deficit exceeds government investment expenditure and take into account all other relevant factors, including the medium-term economic and budgetary position of the Member State.

The Commission may also prepare a report if, notwithstanding the fulfilment of the requirements under the criteria, it is of the opinion that there is a risk of an excessive deficit in a Member State.

4. The Economic and Financial Committee shall formulate an opinion on the report of the Commission.

5. If the Commission considers that an excessive deficit in a Member State exists or may occur, it shall address an opinion to the Member State concerned and shall inform the Council accordingly.

6. The Council shall, on a proposal from the Commission, and having considered any observations which the Member State concerned may wish to make, decide after an overall assessment whether an excessive deficit exists.

7. Where the Council decides, in accordance with paragraph 6, that an excessive deficit exists, it shall adopt, without undue delay, on a recommendation from the Commission, recommendations addressed to the Member State concerned with a view to bringing that situation to an end within a given period. Subject to the provisions of paragraph 8, these recommendations shall not be made public.

8. Where it establishes that there has been no effective action in response to its recommendations within the period laid down, the Council may make its recommendations public.

9. If a Member State persists in failing to put into practice the recommendations of the Council, the Council may decide to give notice to the Member State to take, within a specified time limit, measures for the deficit reduction which is judged necessary by the Council in order to remedy the situation.

In such a case, the Council may request the Member State concerned to submit reports in accordance with a specific timetable in order to examine the adjustment efforts of that Member State.

10. The rights to bring actions provided for in Articles 258 and 259 may not be exercised within the framework of paragraphs 1 to 9 of this Article.

11. As long as a Member State fails to comply with a decision taken in accordance with paragraph 9, the Council may decide to apply or, as the case may be, intensify one or more of the following measures:

- to require the Member State concerned to publish additional information, to be specified by the Council, before issuing bonds and securities,
- to invite the European Investment Bank to reconsider its lending policy towards the Member State concerned,
- to require the Member State concerned to make a non-interest-bearing deposit of an appropriate size with the Union until the excessive deficit has, in the view of the Council, been corrected,
- to impose fines of an appropriate size.

The President of the Council shall inform the European Parliament of the decisions taken.

12. The Council shall abrogate some or all of its decisions or recommendations referred to in paragraphs 6 to 9 and 11 to the extent that the excessive deficit in the Member State concerned has, in the view of the Council, been corrected. If the Council has previously made public recommendations, it shall, as soon as the decision under paragraph 8 has been abrogated, make a public statement that an excessive deficit in the Member State concerned no longer exists.

13. When taking the decisions or recommendations referred to in paragraphs 8, 9, 11 and 12, the Council shall act on a recommendation from the Commission.

When the Council adopts the measures referred to in paragraphs 6 to 9, 11 and 12, it shall act without taking into account the vote of the member of the Council representing the Member State concerned.

A qualified majority of the other members of the Council shall be defined in accordance with Article 238(3)(a).

14. Further provisions relating to the implementation of the procedure described in this Article are set out in the Protocol on the excessive deficit procedure annexed to the Treaties.

The Council shall, acting unanimously in accordance with a special legislative procedure and after consulting the European Parliament and the European Central Bank, adopt the appropriate provisions which shall then replace the said Protocol.

Subject to the other provisions of this paragraph, the Council shall, on a proposal from the Commission and after consulting the European Parliament, lay down detailed rules and definitions for the application of the provisions of the said Protocol.

Chapter 2 Monetary policy

Article 127 (ex Article 105 TEC)

1. The primary objective of the European System of Central Banks (hereinafter referred to as 'the ESCB') shall be to maintain price stability. Without prejudice to the objective of price stability, the ESCB shall support the general economic policies in the Union with a view to contributing to the achievement of the objectives of the Union as laid down in Article 3 of the Treaty on European Union. The ESCB shall act in accordance with the principle of an open market economy with free competition, favouring an efficient allocation of resources, and in compliance with the principles set out in Article 119.

2. The basic tasks to be carried out through the ESCB shall be:
   - to define and implement the monetary policy of the Union,
   - to conduct foreign-exchange operations consistent with the provisions of Article 219,
   - to hold and manage the official foreign reserves of the Member States,
   - to promote the smooth operation of payment systems.

3. The third indent of paragraph 2 shall be without prejudice to the holding and management by the governments of Member States of foreign-exchange working balances.

4. The European Central Bank shall be consulted:
   - on any proposed Union act in its fields of competence,
   - by national authorities regarding any draft legislative provision in its fields of competence, but within the limits and under the conditions set out by the Council in accordance with the procedure laid down in Article 129(4).

The European Central Bank may submit opinions to the appropriate Union institutions, bodies, offices or agencies or to national authorities on matters in its fields of competence.

5. The ESCB shall contribute to the smooth conduct of policies pursued by the competent authorities relating to the prudential supervision of credit institutions and the stability of the financial system.

6. The Council, acting by means of regulations in accordance with a special legislative procedure, may unanimously, and after consulting the European Parliament and the European Central Bank, confer specific tasks upon the European Central Bank concerning policies relating to the prudential supervision of credit institutions and other financial institutions with the exception of insurance undertakings.

Article 128 (ex Article 106 TEC)

1. The European Central Bank shall have the exclusive right to authorise the issue of euro banknotes within the Union. The European Central Bank and the national central banks may issue such notes. The banknotes issued by the European Central Bank and the national central banks shall be the only such notes to have the status of legal tender within the Union.

2. Member States may issue euro coins subject to approval by the European Central Bank of the volume of the issue. The Council, on a proposal from the Commission and after consulting the European Parliament and the European Central Bank, may adopt measures to harmonise the denominations and technical specifications of all coins intended for circulation to the extent necessary to permit their smooth circulation within the Union.

Article 129 (ex Article 107 TEC)

1. The ESCB shall be governed by the decision-making bodies of the European Central Bank which shall be the Governing Council and the Executive Board.

2. The Statute of the European System of Central Banks and of the European Central Bank (hereinafter referred to as 'the Statute of the ESCB and of the ECB') is laid down in a Protocol annexed to the Treaties.

3. Articles 5.1, 5.2, 5.3, 17, 18, 19.1, 22, 23, 24, 26, 32.2, 32.3, 32.4, 32.6, 33.1(a) and 36 of the Statute of the ESCB and of the ECB may be amended by the European Parliament and the Council, acting in accordance with the ordinary legislative procedure. They shall act either on a recommendation from the European Central Bank and after consulting the Commission or on a proposal from the Commission and after consulting the European Central Bank.

4. The Council, either on a proposal from the Commission and after consulting the European Parliament and the European Central Bank or on a recommendation from the European Central Bank and after consulting the European Parliament and the Commission, shall adopt the provisions referred to in Articles 4, 5.4, 19.2, 20, 28.1, 29.2, 30.4 and 34.3 of the Statute of the ESCB and of the ECB.

Article 130 (ex Article 108 TEC)

When exercising the powers and carrying out the tasks and duties conferred upon them by the Treaties and the Statute of the ESCB and of the ECB, neither the European Central Bank, nor a national central bank, nor any member of their decision-making bodies shall seek or take instructions from Union institutions, bodies, offices or agencies, from any government of a Member State or from any other body. The Union institutions, bodies, offices or agencies and the governments of the Member States undertake to respect this principle and not to seek to influence the members of the decision-making bodies of the European Central Bank or of the national central banks in the performance of their tasks.

Article 131 (ex Article 109 TEC)

Each Member State shall ensure that its national legislation including the statutes of its national central bank is compatible with the Treaties and the Statute of the ESCB and of the ECB.

Article 132 (ex Article 110 TEC)

1. In order to carry out the tasks entrusted to the ESCB, the European Central Bank shall, in accordance with the provisions of the Treaties and under the conditions laid down in the Statute of the ESCB and of the ECB:

- make regulations to the extent necessary to implement the tasks defined in Article 3.1, first indent, Articles 19.1, 22 and 25.2 of the Statute of the ESCB and of the ECB in cases which shall be laid down in the acts of the Council referred to in Article 129(4),
- take decisions necessary for carrying out the tasks entrusted to the ESCB under the Treaties and the Statute of the ESCB and of the ECB,
- make recommendations and deliver opinions.

2. The European Central Bank may decide to publish its decisions, recommendations and opinions.

3. Within the limits and under the conditions adopted by the Council under the procedure laid down in Article 129(4), the European Central Bank shall be entitled to impose fines or periodic penalty payments on undertakings for failure to comply with obligations under its regulations and decisions.

Article 133

Without prejudice to the powers of the European Central Bank, the European Parliament and the Council, acting in accordance with the ordinary legislative procedure, shall lay down the measures necessary for the use of the euro as the single currency. Such measures shall be adopted after consultation of the European Central Bank.

Chapter 3 Institutional provisions

Article 134 (ex Article 114 TEC)

1. In order to promote coordination of the policies of Member States to the full extent needed for the functioning of the internal market, an Economic and Financial Committee is hereby set up.

2. The Economic and Financial Committee shall have the following tasks:

- to deliver opinions at the request of the Council or of the Commission, or on its own initiative for submission to those institutions,

- to keep under review the economic and financial situation of the Member States and of the Union and to report regularly thereon to the Council and to the Commission, in particular on financial relations with third countries and international institutions,
- without prejudice to Article 240, to contribute to the preparation of the work of the Council referred to in Articles 66, 75, 121(2), (3), (4) and (6), 122, 124, 125, 126, 127(6), 128(2), 129(3) and (4), 138, 140(2) and (3), 143, 144(2) and (3), and in Article 219, and to carry out other advisory and preparatory tasks assigned to it by the Council,
- to examine, at least once a year, the situation regarding the movement of capital and the freedom of payments, as they result from the application of the Treaties and of measures adopted by the Council; the examination shall cover all measures relating to capital movements and payments; the Committee shall report to the Commission and to the Council on the outcome of this examination.

The Member States, the Commission and the European Central Bank shall each appoint no more than two members of the Committee.

3. The Council shall, on a proposal from the Commission and after consulting the European Central Bank and the Committee referred to in this Article, lay down detailed provisions concerning the composition of the Economic and Financial Committee. The President of the Council shall inform the European Parliament of such a decision.

4. In addition to the tasks set out in paragraph 2, if and as long as there are Member States with a derogation as referred to in Article 139, the Committee shall keep under review the monetary and financial situation and the general payments system of those Member States and report regularly thereon to the Council and to the Commission.

Article 135 (ex Article 115 TEC)

For matters within the scope of Articles 121(4), 126 with the exception of paragraph 14, 138, 140(1), 140(2), first subparagraph, 140(3) and 219, the Council or a Member State may request the Commission to make a recommendation or a proposal, as appropriate. The Commission shall examine this request and submit its conclusions to the Council without delay.

Chapter 4 Provisions specific to Member States whose currency is the euro

Article 136*

1. In order to ensure the proper functioning of economic and monetary union, and in accordance with the relevant provisions of the Treaties, the Council shall, in accordance with the relevant procedure from among those referred to in Articles 121 and 126, with the exception of the procedure set out in Article 126(14), adopt measures specific to those Member States whose currency is the euro:

(a) to strengthen the coordination and surveillance of their budgetary discipline;

(b) to set out economic policy guidelines for them, while ensuring that they are compatible with those adopted for the whole of the Union and are kept under surveillance.

2. For those measures set out in paragraph 1, only members of the Council representing Member States whose currency is the euro shall take part in the vote.

A qualified majority of the said members shall be defined in accordance with Article 238(3)(a).

3. The Member States whose currency is the euro may establish a stability mechanism to be activated if indispensable to safeguard the stability of the euro area as a whole. The granting of any required financial assistance under the mechanism will be made subject to strict conditionality.

Article 137

Arrangements for meetings between ministers of those Member States whose currency is the euro are laid down by the Protocol on the Euro Group.

* **Editor's Note:** As amended by Decision 2011/199 (OJ 2011 L91/1).

Article 138 (ex Article 111(4), TEC)

1. In order to secure the euro's place in the international monetary system, the Council, on a proposal from the Commission, shall adopt a decision establishing common positions on matters of particular interest for economic and monetary union within the competent international financial institutions and conferences. The Council shall act after consulting the European Central Bank.

2. The Council, on a proposal from the Commission, may adopt appropriate measures to ensure unified representation within the international financial institutions and conferences. The Council shall act after consulting the European Central Bank.

3. For the measures referred to in paragraphs 1 and 2, only members of the Council representing Member States whose currency is the euro shall take part in the vote.

A qualified majority of the said members shall be defined in accordance with Article 238(3)(a).

Chapter 5 Transitional provisions

Article 139

1. Member States in respect of which the Council has not decided that they fulfil the necessary conditions for the adoption of the euro shall hereinafter be referred to as 'Member States with a derogation'.

2. The following provisions of the Treaties shall not apply to Member States with a derogation:

(a) adoption of the parts of the broad economic policy guidelines which concern the euro area generally (Article 121(2));
(b) coercive means of remedying excessive deficits (Article 126(9) and (11));
(c) the objectives and tasks of the ESCB (Article 127(1) to (3) and (5));
(d) issue of the euro (Article 128);
(e) acts of the European Central Bank (Article 132);
(f) measures governing the use of the euro (Article 133);
(g) monetary agreements and other measures relating to exchange-rate policy (Article 219);
(h) appointment of members of the Executive Board of the European Central Bank (Article 283(2));
(i) decisions establishing common positions on issues of particular relevance for economic and monetary union within the competent international financial institutions and conferences (Article 138(1));
(j) measures to ensure unified representation within the international financial institutions and conferences (Article 138(2)).

In the Articles referred to in points (a) to (j), 'Member States' shall therefore mean Member States whose currency is the euro.

3. Under Chapter IX of the Statute of the ESCB and of the ECB, Member States with a derogation and their national central banks are excluded from rights and obligations within the ESCB.

4. The voting rights of members of the Council representing Member States with a derogation shall be suspended for the adoption by the Council of the measures referred to in the Articles listed in paragraph 2, and in the following instances:

(a) recommendations made to those Member States whose currency is the euro in the framework of multilateral surveillance, including on stability programmes and warnings (Article 121(4));
(b) measures relating to excessive deficits concerning those Member States whose currency is the euro (Article 126(6), (7), (8), (12) and (13)).

A qualified majority of the other members of the Council shall be defined in accordance with Article 238(3)(a).

Article 140 (ex Articles 121(1), 122(2), second sentence, and 123(5) TEC)

1. At least once every two years, or at the request of a Member State with a derogation, the Commission and the European Central Bank shall report to the Council on the progress made by the Member States with a derogation in fulfilling their obligations regarding the achievement of economic

and monetary union. These reports shall include an examination of the compatibility between the national legislation of each of these Member States, including the statutes of its national central bank, and Articles 130 and 131 and the Statute of the ESCB and of the ECB. The reports shall also examine the achievement of a high degree of sustainable convergence by reference to the fulfilment by each Member State of the following criteria:

- the achievement of a high degree of price stability; this will be apparent from a rate of inflation which is close to that of, at most, the three best performing Member States in terms of price stability,
- the sustainability of the government financial position; this will be apparent from having achieved a government budgetary position without a deficit that is excessive as determined in accordance with Article 126(6),
- the observance of the normal fluctuation margins provided for by the exchange-rate mechanism of the European Monetary System, for at least two years, without devaluing against the euro,
- the durability of convergence achieved by the Member State with a derogation and of its participation in the exchange-rate mechanism being reflected in the long-term interest-rate levels.

The four criteria mentioned in this paragraph and the relevant periods over which they are to be respected are developed further in a Protocol annexed to the Treaties. The reports of the Commission and the European Central Bank shall also take account of the results of the integration of markets, the situation and development of the balances of payments on current account and an examination of the development of unit labour costs and other price indices.

2. After consulting the European Parliament and after discussion in the European Council, the Council shall, on a proposal from the Commission, decide which Member States with a derogation fulfil the necessary conditions on the basis of the criteria set out in paragraph 1, and abrogate the derogations of the Member States concerned.

The Council shall act having received a recommendation of a qualified majority of those among its members representing Member States whose currency is the euro. These members shall act within six months of the Council receiving the Commission's proposal.

The qualified majority of the said members, as referred to in the second subparagraph, shall be defined in accordance with Article 238(3)(a).

3. If it is decided, in accordance with the procedure set out in paragraph 2, to abrogate a derogation, the Council shall, acting with the unanimity of the Member States whose currency is the euro and the Member State concerned, on a proposal from the Commission and after consulting the European Central Bank, irrevocably fix the rate at which the euro shall be substituted for the currency of the Member State concerned, and take the other measures necessary for the introduction of the euro as the single currency in the Member State concerned.

Article 141 (ex Articles 123(3) and 117(2) first five indents, TEC)

1. If and as long as there are Member States with a derogation, and without prejudice to Article 129(1), the General Council of the European Central Bank referred to in Article 44 of the Statute of the ESCB and of the ECB shall be constituted as a third decision-making body of the European Central Bank.

2. If and as long as there are Member States with a derogation, the European Central Bank shall, as regards those Member States:

- strengthen cooperation between the national central banks,
- strengthen the coordination of the monetary policies of the Member States, with the aim of ensuring price stability,
- monitor the functioning of the exchange-rate mechanism,
- hold consultations concerning issues falling within the competence of the national central banks and affecting the stability of financial institutions and markets,
- carry out the former tasks of the European Monetary Cooperation Fund which had subsequently been taken over by the European Monetary Institute.

Article 142 (ex Article 124(1) TEC)

Each Member State with a derogation shall treat its exchange-rate policy as a matter of common interest. In so doing, Member States shall take account of the experience acquired in cooperation within the framework of the exchange-rate mechanism.

Article 143 (ex Article 119 TEC)

1. Where a Member State with a derogation is in difficulties or is seriously threatened with difficulties as regards its balance of payments either as a result of an overall disequilibrium in its balance of payments, or as a result of the type of currency at its disposal, and where such difficulties are liable in particular to jeopardise the functioning of the internal market or the implementation of the common commercial policy, the Commission shall immediately investigate the position of the State in question and the action which, making use of all the means at its disposal, that State has taken or may take in accordance with the provisions of the Treaties. The Commission shall state what measures it recommends the State concerned to take.

If the action taken by a Member State with a derogation and the measures suggested by the Commission do not prove sufficient to overcome the difficulties which have arisen or which threaten, the Commission shall, after consulting the Economic and Financial Committee, recommend to the Council the granting of mutual assistance and appropriate methods therefore.

The Commission shall keep the Council regularly informed of the situation and of how it is developing.

2. The Council shall grant such mutual assistance; it shall adopt directives or decisions laying down the conditions and details of such assistance, which may take such forms as:

(a) a concerted approach to or within any other international organisations to which Member States with a derogation may have recourse;

(b) measures needed to avoid deflection of trade where the Member State with a derogation which is in difficulties maintains or reintroduces quantitative restrictions against third countries;

(c) the granting of limited credits by other Member States, subject to their agreement.

3. If the mutual assistance recommended by the Commission is not granted by the Council or if the mutual assistance granted and the measures taken are insufficient, the Commission shall authorise the Member State with a derogation which is in difficulties to take protective measures, the conditions and details of which the Commission shall determine.

Such authorisation may be revoked and such conditions and details may be changed by the Council.

Article 144 (ex Article 120 TEC)

1. Where a sudden crisis in the balance of payments occurs and a decision within the meaning of Article 143(2) is not immediately taken, a Member State with a derogation may, as a precaution, take the necessary protective measures. Such measures must cause the least possible disturbance in the functioning of the internal market and must not be wider in scope than is strictly necessary to remedy the sudden difficulties which have arisen.

2. The Commission and the other Member States shall be informed of such protective measures not later than when they enter into force. The Commission may recommend to the Council the granting of mutual assistance under Article 143.

3. After the Commission has delivered a recommendation and the Economic and Financial Committee has been consulted, the Council may decide that the Member State concerned shall amend, suspend or abolish the protective measures referred to above.

Title IX Employment

Article 145 (ex Article 125 TEC)

Member States and the Union shall, in accordance with this Title, work towards developing a coordinated strategy for employment and particularly for promoting a skilled, trained and adaptable workforce and labour markets responsive to economic change with a view to achieving the objectives defined in Article 3 of the Treaty on European Union.

Article 146 (ex Article 126 TEC)

1. Member States, through their employment policies, shall contribute to the achievement of the objectives referred to in Article 145 in a way consistent with the broad guidelines of the economic policies of the Member States and of the Union adopted pursuant to Article 121(2).

2. Member States, having regard to national practices related to the responsibilities of management and labour, shall regard promoting employment as a matter of common concern and shall coordinate their action in this respect within the Council, in accordance with the provisions of Article 148.

Article 147 (ex Article 127 TEC)

1. The Union shall contribute to a high level of employment by encouraging cooperation between Member States and by supporting and, if necessary, complementing their action. In doing so, the competences of the Member States shall be respected.

2. The objective of a high level of employment shall be taken into consideration in the formulation and implementation of Union policies and activities.

Article 148 (ex Article 128 TEC)

1. The European Council shall each year consider the employment situation in the Union and adopt conclusions thereon, on the basis of a joint annual report by the Council and the Commission.

2. On the basis of the conclusions of the European Council, the Council, on a proposal from the Commission and after consulting the European Parliament, the Economic and Social Committee, the Committee of the Regions and the Employment Committee referred to in Article 150, shall each year draw up guidelines which the Member States shall take into account in their employment policies. These guidelines shall be consistent with the broad guidelines adopted pursuant to Article 121(2).

3. Each Member State shall provide the Council and the Commission with an annual report on the principal measures taken to implement its employment policy in the light of the guidelines for employment as referred to in paragraph 2.

4. The Council, on the basis of the reports referred to in paragraph 3 and having received the views of the Employment Committee, shall each year carry out an examination of the implementation of the employment policies of the Member States in the light of the guidelines for employment. The Council, on a recommendation from the Commission, may, if it considers it appropriate in the light of that examination, make recommendations to Member States.

5. On the basis of the results of that examination, the Council and the Commission shall make a joint annual report to the European Council on the employment situation in the Union and on the implementation of the guidelines for employment.

Article 149 (ex Article 129 TEC)

The European Parliament and the Council, acting in accordance with the ordinary legislative procedure and after consulting the Economic and Social Committee and the Committee of the Regions, may adopt incentive measures designed to encourage cooperation between Member States and to support their action in the field of employment through initiatives aimed at developing exchanges of information and best practices, providing comparative analysis and advice as well as promoting innovative approaches and evaluating experiences, in particular by recourse to pilot projects.

Those measures shall not include harmonisation of the laws and regulations of the Member States.

Article 150 (ex Article 130 TEC)

The Council, acting by a simple majority after consulting the European Parliament, shall establish an Employment Committee with advisory status to promote coordination between Member States on employment and labour market policies. The tasks of the Committee shall be:

- to monitor the employment situation and employment policies in the Member States and the Union,

- without prejudice to Article 240, to formulate opinions at the request of either the Council or the Commission or on its own initiative, and to contribute to the preparation of the Council proceedings referred to in Article 148.

In fulfilling its mandate, the Committee shall consult management and labour.

Each Member State and the Commission shall appoint two members of the Committee.

Title X Social policy

Article 151 (ex Article 136 TEC)

The Union and the Member States, having in mind fundamental social rights such as those set out in the European Social Charter signed at Turin on 18 October 1961 and in the 1989 Community Charter of the Fundamental Social Rights of Workers, shall have as their objectives the promotion of employment, improved living and working conditions, so as to make possible their harmonisation while the improvement is being maintained, proper social protection, dialogue between management and labour, the development of human resources with a view to lasting high employment and the combating of exclusion.

To this end the Union and the Member States shall implement measures which take account of the diverse forms of national practices, in particular in the field of contractual relations, and the need to maintain the competitiveness of the Union economy.

They believe that such a development will ensue not only from the functioning of the internal market, which will favour the harmonisation of social systems, but also from the procedures provided for in the Treaties and from the approximation of provisions laid down by law, regulation or administrative action.

Article 152

The Union recognises and promotes the role of the social partners at its level, taking into account the diversity of national systems. It shall facilitate dialogue between the social partners, respecting their autonomy.

The Tripartite Social Summit for Growth and Employment shall contribute to social dialogue.

Article 153 (ex Article 137 TEC)

1. With a view to achieving the objectives of Article 151, the Union shall support and complement the activities of the Member States in the following fields:
   (a) improvement in particular of the working environment to protect workers' health and safety;
   (b) working conditions;
   (c) social security and social protection of workers;
   (d) protection of workers where their employment contract is terminated;
   (e) the information and consultation of workers;
   (f) representation and collective defence of the interests of workers and employers, including co-determination, subject to paragraph 5;
   (g) conditions of employment for third-country nationals legally residing in Union territory;
   (h) the integration of persons excluded from the labour market, without prejudice to Article 166;
   (i) equality between men and women with regard to labour market opportunities and treatment at work;
   (j) the combating of social exclusion;
   (k) the modernisation of social protection systems without prejudice to point (c).
2. To this end, the European Parliament and the Council:
   (a) may adopt measures designed to encourage cooperation between Member States through initiatives aimed at improving knowledge, developing exchanges of information and best practices, promoting innovative approaches and evaluating experiences, excluding any harmonisation of the laws and regulations of the Member States;

(b) may adopt, in the fields referred to in paragraph 1(a) to (i), by means of directives, minimum requirements for gradual implementation, having regard to the conditions and technical rules obtaining in each of the Member States. Such directives shall avoid imposing administrative, financial and legal constraints in a way which would hold back the creation and development of small and medium-sized undertakings.

The European Parliament and the Council shall act in accordance with the ordinary legislative procedure after consulting the Economic and Social Committee and the Committee of the Regions.

In the fields referred to in paragraph 1(c), (d), (f) and (g), the Council shall act unanimously, in accordance with a special legislative procedure, after consulting the European Parliament and the said Committees.

The Council, acting unanimously on a proposal from the Commission, after consulting the European Parliament, may decide to render the ordinary legislative procedure applicable to paragraph 1(d), (f) and (g).

3. A Member State may entrust management and labour, at their joint request, with the implementation of directives adopted pursuant to paragraph 2, or, where appropriate, with the implementation of a Council decision adopted in accordance with Article 155.

In this case, it shall ensure that, no later than the date on which a directive or a decision must be transposed or implemented, management and labour have introduced the necessary measures by agreement, the Member State concerned being required to take any necessary measure enabling it at any time to be in a position to guarantee the results imposed by that directive or that decision.

4. The provisions adopted pursuant to this Article:

- shall not affect the right of Member States to define the fundamental principles of their social security systems and must not significantly affect the financial equilibrium thereof,
- shall not prevent any Member State from maintaining or introducing more stringent protective measures compatible with the Treaties.

5. The provisions of this Article shall not apply to pay, the right of association, the right to strike or the right to impose lock-outs.

Article 154 (ex Article 138 TEC)

1. The Commission shall have the task of promoting the consultation of management and labour at Union level and shall take any relevant measure to facilitate their dialogue by ensuring balanced support for the parties.

2. To this end, before submitting proposals in the social policy field, the Commission shall consult management and labour on the possible direction of Union action.

3. If, after such consultation, the Commission considers Union action advisable, it shall consult management and labour on the content of the envisaged proposal.

Management and labour shall forward to the Commission an opinion or, where appropriate, a recommendation.

4. On the occasion of the consultation referred to in paragraphs 2 and 3, management and labour may inform the Commission of their wish to initiate the process provided for in Article 155. The duration of this process shall not exceed nine months, unless the management and labour concerned and the Commission decide jointly to extend it.

Article 155 (ex Article 139 TEC)

1. Should management and labour so desire, the dialogue between them at Union level may lead to contractual relations, including agreements.

2. Agreements concluded at Union level shall be implemented either in accordance with the procedures and practices specific to management and labour and the Member States or, in matters covered by Article 153, at the joint request of the signatory parties, by a Council decision on a proposal from the Commission. The European Parliament shall be informed.

The Council shall act unanimously where the agreement in question contains one or more provisions relating to one of the areas for which unanimity is required pursuant to Article 153(2).

Article 156 (ex Article 140 TEC)

With a view to achieving the objectives of Article 151 and without prejudice to the other provisions of the Treaties, the Commission shall encourage cooperation between the Member States and facilitate the coordination of their action in all social policy fields under this Chapter, particularly in matters relating to:

- employment,
- labour law and working conditions,
- basic and advanced vocational training,
- social security,
- prevention of occupational accidents and diseases,
- occupational hygiene,
- the right of association and collective bargaining between employers and workers.

To this end, the Commission shall act in close contact with Member States by making studies, delivering opinions and arranging consultations both on problems arising at national level and on those of concern to international organisations, in particular initiatives aiming at the establishment of guidelines and indicators, the organisation of exchange of best practice, and the preparation of the necessary elements for periodic monitoring and evaluation. The European Parliament shall be kept fully informed.

Before delivering the opinions provided for in this Article, the Commission shall consult the Economic and Social Committee.

Article 157 (ex Article 141 TEC)

1. Each Member State shall ensure that the principle of equal pay for male and female workers for equal work or work of equal value is applied.

2. For the purpose of this Article, 'pay' means the ordinary basic or minimum wage or salary and any other consideration, whether in cash or in kind, which the worker receives directly or indirectly, in respect of his employment, from his employer.

Equal pay without discrimination based on sex means:

(a) that pay for the same work at piece rates shall be calculated on the basis of the same unit of measurement;

(b) that pay for work at time rates shall be the same for the same job.

3. The European Parliament and the Council, acting in accordance with the ordinary legislative procedure, and after consulting the Economic and Social Committee, shall adopt measures to ensure the application of the principle of equal opportunities and equal treatment of men and women in matters of employment and occupation, including the principle of equal pay for equal work or work of equal value.

4. With a view to ensuring full equality in practice between men and women in working life, the principle of equal treatment shall not prevent any Member State from maintaining or adopting measures providing for specific advantages in order to make it easier for the underrepresented sex to pursue a vocational activity or to prevent or compensate for disadvantages in professional careers.

Article 158 (ex Article 142 TEC)

Member States shall endeavour to maintain the existing equivalence between paid holiday schemes.

Article 159 (ex Article 143 TEC)

The Commission shall draw up a report each year on progress in achieving the objectives of Article 151, including the demographic situation in the Union. It shall forward the report to the European Parliament, the Council and the Economic and Social Committee.

Article 160 (ex Article 144 TEC)

The Council, acting by a simple majority after consulting the European Parliament, shall establish a Social Protection Committee with advisory status to promote cooperation on social protection policies between Member States and with the Commission. The tasks of the Committee shall be:

- to monitor the social situation and the development of social protection policies in the Member States and the Union,

- to promote exchanges of information, experience and good practice between Member States and with the Commission,
- without prejudice to Article 240, to prepare reports, formulate opinions or undertake other work within its fields of competence, at the request of either the Council or the Commission or on its own initiative.

In fulfilling its mandate, the Committee shall establish appropriate contacts with management and labour.

Each Member State and the Commission shall appoint two members of the Committee.

Article 161 (ex Article 145 TEC)

The Commission shall include a separate chapter on social developments within the Union in its annual report to the European Parliament.

The European Parliament may invite the Commission to draw up reports on any particular problems concerning social conditions.

Title XI The European Social Fund

Article 162 (ex Article 146 TEC)

In order to improve employment opportunities for workers in the internal market and to contribute thereby to raising the standard of living, a European Social Fund is hereby established in accordance with the provisions set out below; it shall aim to render the employment of workers easier and to increase their geographical and occupational mobility within the Union, and to facilitate their adaptation to industrial changes and to changes in production systems, in particular through vocational training and retraining.

Article 163 (ex Article 147 TEC)

The Fund shall be administered by the Commission.

The Commission shall be assisted in this task by a Committee presided over by a Member of the Commission and composed of representatives of governments, trade unions and employers' organisations.

Article 164 (ex Article 148 TEC)

The European Parliament and the Council, acting in accordance with the ordinary legislative procedure and after consulting the Economic and Social Committee and the Committee of the Regions, shall adopt implementing regulations relating to the European Social Fund.

Title XII Education, vocational training, youth and sport

Article 165 (ex Article 149 TEC)

1. The Union shall contribute to the development of quality education by encouraging cooperation between Member States and, if necessary, by supporting and supplementing their action, while fully respecting the responsibility of the Member States for the content of teaching and the organisation of education systems and their cultural and linguistic diversity.

The Union shall contribute to the promotion of European sporting issues, while taking account of the specific nature of sport, its structures based on voluntary activity and its social and educational function.

2. Union action shall be aimed at:
   - developing the European dimension in education, particularly through the teaching and dissemination of the languages of the Member States,
   - encouraging mobility of students and teachers, by encouraging *inter alia*, the academic recognition of diplomas and periods of study,
   - promoting cooperation between educational establishments,

- developing exchanges of information and experience on issues common to the education systems of the Member States,
- encouraging the development of youth exchanges and of exchanges of socio-educational instructors, and encouraging the participation of young people in democratic life in Europe,
- encouraging the development of distance education,
- developing the European dimension in sport, by promoting fairness and openness in sporting competitions and cooperation between bodies responsible for sports, and by protecting the physical and moral integrity of sportsmen and sportswomen, especially the youngest sportsmen and sportswomen.

3. The Union and the Member States shall foster cooperation with third countries and the competent international organisations in the field of education and sport, in particular the Council of Europe.

4. In order to contribute to the achievement of the objectives referred to in this Article:
- the European Parliament and the Council, acting in accordance with the ordinary legislative procedure, after consulting the Economic and Social Committee and the Committee of the Regions, shall adopt incentive measures, excluding any harmonisation of the laws and regulations of the Member States,
- the Council, on a proposal from the Commission, shall adopt recommendations.

Article 166 (ex Article 150 TEC)

1. The Union shall implement a vocational training policy which shall support and supplement the action of the Member States, while fully respecting the responsibility of the Member States for the content and organisation of vocational training.

2. Union action shall aim to:
- facilitate adaptation to industrial changes, in particular through vocational training and retraining,
- improve initial and continuing vocational training in order to facilitate vocational integration and reintegration into the labour market,
- facilitate access to vocational training and encourage mobility of instructors and trainees and particularly young people,
- stimulate cooperation on training between educational or training establishments and firms,
- develop exchanges of information and experience on issues common to the training systems of the Member States.

3. The Union and the Member States shall foster cooperation with third countries and the competent international organisations in the sphere of vocational training.

4. The European Parliament and the Council, acting in accordance with the ordinary legislative procedure and after consulting the Economic and Social Committee and the Committee of the Regions, shall adopt measures to contribute to the achievement of the objectives referred to in this Article, excluding any harmonisation of the laws and regulations of the Member States, and the Council, on a proposal from the Commission, shall adopt recommendations.

Title XIII Culture

Article 167 (ex Article 151 TEC)

1. The Union shall contribute to the flowering of the cultures of the Member States, while respecting their national and regional diversity and at the same time bringing the common cultural heritage to the fore.

2. Action by the Union shall be aimed at encouraging cooperation between Member States and, if necessary, supporting and supplementing their action in the following areas:
- improvement of the knowledge and dissemination of the culture and history of the European peoples,

- conservation and safeguarding of cultural heritage of European significance,
- non-commercial cultural exchanges,
- artistic and literary creation, including in the audiovisual sector.

3. The Union and the Member States shall foster cooperation with third countries and the competent international organisations in the sphere of culture, in particular the Council of Europe.

4. The Union shall take cultural aspects into account in its action under other provisions of the Treaties, in particular in order to respect and to promote the diversity of its cultures.

5. In order to contribute to the achievement of the objectives referred to in this Article:

- the European Parliament and the Council acting in accordance with the ordinary legislative procedure and after consulting the Committee of the Regions, shall adopt incentive measures, excluding any harmonisation of the laws and regulations of the Member States.
- the Council, on a proposal from the Commission, shall adopt recommendations.

Title XIV Public health

Article 168 (ex Article 152 TEC)

1. A high level of human health protection shall be ensured in the definition and implementation of all Union policies and activities.

Union action, which shall complement national policies, shall be directed towards improving public health, preventing physical and mental illness and diseases, and obviating sources of danger to physical and mental health. Such action shall cover the fight against the major health scourges, by promoting research into their causes, their transmission and their prevention, as well as health information and education, and monitoring, early warning of and combating serious cross-border threats to health.

The Union shall complement the Member States' action in reducing drugs-related health damage, including information and prevention.

2. The Union shall encourage cooperation between the Member States in the areas referred to in this Article and, if necessary, lend support to their action. It shall in particular encourage cooperation between the Member States to improve the complementarity of their health services in cross-border areas.

Member States shall, in liaison with the Commission, coordinate among themselves their policies and programmes in the areas referred to in paragraph 1. The Commission may, in close contact with the Member States, take any useful initiative to promote such coordination, in particular initiatives aiming at the establishment of guidelines and indicators, the organisation of exchange of best practice, and the preparation of the necessary elements for periodic monitoring and evaluation. The European Parliament shall be kept fully informed.

3. The Union and the Member States shall foster cooperation with third countries and the competent international organisations in the sphere of public health.

4. By way of derogation from Article 2(5) and Article 6(a) and in accordance with Article 4(2)(k) the European Parliament and the Council, acting in accordance with the ordinary legislative procedure and after consulting the Economic and Social Committee and the Committee of the Regions, shall contribute to the achievement of the objectives referred to in this Article through adopting in order to meet common safety concerns:

(a) measures setting high standards of quality and safety of organs and substances of human origin, blood and blood derivatives; these measures shall not prevent any Member State from maintaining or introducing more stringent protective measures;

(b) measures in the veterinary and phytosanitary fields which have as their direct objective the protection of public health;

(c) measures setting high standards of quality and safety for medicinal products and devices for medical use.

5. The European Parliament and the Council, acting in accordance with the ordinary legislative procedure and after consulting the Economic and Social Committee and the Committee of the Regions, may also adopt incentive measures designed to protect and improve human health and in

particular to combat the major cross-border health scourges, measures concerning monitoring, early warning of and combating serious cross-border threats to health, and measures which have as their direct objective the protection of public health regarding tobacco and the abuse of alcohol, excluding any harmonisation of the laws and regulations of the Member States.

6. The Council, on a proposal from the Commission, may also adopt recommendations for the purposes set out in this Article.

7. Union action shall respect the responsibilities of the Member States for the definition of their health policy and for the organisation and delivery of health services and medical care. The responsibilities of the Member States shall include the management of health services and medical care and the allocation of the resources assigned to them. The measures referred to in paragraph 4(a) shall not affect national provisions on the donation or medical use of organs and blood.

Title XV Consumer protection

Article 169 (ex Article 153 TEC)

1. In order to promote the interests of consumers and to ensure a high level of consumer protection, the Union shall contribute to protecting the health, safety and economic interests of consumers, as well as to promoting their right to information, education and to organise themselves in order to safeguard their interests.

2. The Union shall contribute to the attainment of the objectives referred to in paragraph 1 through:

(a) measures adopted pursuant to Article 114 in the context of the completion of the internal market;

(b) measures which support, supplement and monitor the policy pursued by the Member States.

3. The European Parliament and the Council, acting in accordance with the ordinary legislative procedure and after consulting the Economic and Social Committee, shall adopt the measures referred to in paragraph 2(b).

4. Measures adopted pursuant to paragraph 3 shall not prevent any Member State from maintaining or introducing more stringent protective measures. Such measures must be compatible with the Treaties. The Commission shall be notified of them.

Title XVI Trans-European networks

Article 170 (ex Article 154 TEC)

1. To help achieve the objectives referred to in Articles 26 and 174 and to enable citizens of the Union, economic operators and regional and local communities to derive full benefit from the setting-up of an area without internal frontiers, the Union shall contribute to the establishment and development of trans-European networks in the areas of transport, telecommunications and energy infrastructures.

2. Within the framework of a system of open and competitive markets, action by the Union shall aim at promoting the interconnection and interoperability of national networks as well as access to such networks. It shall take account in particular of the need to link island, landlocked and peripheral regions with the central regions of the Union.

Article 171 (ex Article 155 TEC)

1. In order to achieve the objectives referred to in Article 170, the Union:

- shall establish a series of guidelines covering the objectives, priorities and broad lines of measures envisaged in the sphere of trans-European networks; these guidelines shall identify projects of common interest,

- shall implement any measures that may prove necessary to ensure the interoperability of the networks, in particular in the field of technical standardisation,
- may support projects of common interest supported by Member States, which are identified in the framework of the guidelines referred to in the first indent, particularly through feasibility studies, loan guarantees or interest-rate subsidies; the Union may also contribute, through the Cohesion Fund set up pursuant to Article 177, to the financing of specific projects in Member States in the area of transport infrastructure.

The Union's activities shall take into account the potential economic viability of the projects.

2. Member States shall, in liaison with the Commission, coordinate among themselves the policies pursued at national level which may have a significant impact on the achievement of the objectives referred to in Article 170. The Commission may, in close cooperation with the Member State, take any useful initiative to promote such coordination.

3. The Union may decide to cooperate with third countries to promote projects of mutual interest and to ensure the interoperability of networks.

Article 172 (ex Article 156 TEC)

The guidelines and other measures referred to in Article 171(1) shall be adopted by the European Parliament and the Council, acting in accordance with the ordinary legislative procedure and after consulting the Economic and Social Committee and the Committee of the Regions.

Guidelines and projects of common interest which relate to the territory of a Member State shall require the approval of the Member State concerned.

Title XVII Industry

Article 173 (ex Article 157 TEC)

1. The Union and the Member States shall ensure that the conditions necessary for the competitiveness of the Union's industry exist.

For that purpose, in accordance with a system of open and competitive markets, their action shall be aimed at:

- speeding up the adjustment of industry to structural changes,
- encouraging an environment favourable to initiative and to the development of undertakings throughout the Union, particularly small and medium-sized undertakings,
- encouraging an environment favourable to cooperation between undertakings,
- fostering better exploitation of the industrial potential of policies of innovation, research and technological development.

2. The Member States shall consult each other in liaison with the Commission and, where necessary, shall coordinate their action. The Commission may take any useful initiative to promote such coordination, in particular initiatives aiming at the establishment of guidelines and indicators, the organisation of exchange of best practice, and the preparation of the necessary elements for periodic monitoring and evaluation. The European Parliament shall be kept fully informed.

3. The Union shall contribute to the achievement of the objectives set out in paragraph 1 through the policies and activities it pursues under other provisions of the Treaties. The European Parliament and the Council, acting in accordance with the ordinary legislative procedure and after consulting the Economic and Social Committee, may decide on specific measures in support of action taken in the Member States to achieve the objectives set out in paragraph 1, excluding any harmonisation of the laws and regulations of the Member States.

This Title shall not provide a basis for the introduction by the Union of any measure which could lead to a distortion of competition or contains tax provisions or provisions relating to the rights and interests of employed persons.

Title XVIII Economic, social and territorial cohesion

Article 174 (ex Article 158 TEC)

In order to promote its overall harmonious development, the Union shall develop and pursue its actions leading to the strengthening of its economic, social and territorial cohesion.

In particular, the Union shall aim at reducing disparities between the levels of development of the various regions and the backwardness of the least favoured regions.

Among the regions concerned, particular attention shall be paid to rural areas, areas affected by industrial transition, and regions which suffer from severe and permanent natural or demographic handicaps such as the northernmost regions with very low population density and island, cross-border and mountain regions.

Article 175 (ex Article 159 TEC)

Member States shall conduct their economic policies and shall coordinate them in such a way as, in addition, to attain the objectives set out in Article 174. The formulation and implementation of the Union's policies and actions and the implementation of the internal market shall take into account the objectives set out in Article 174 and shall contribute to their achievement. The Union shall also support the achievement of these objectives by the action it takes through the Structural Funds (European Agricultural Guidance and Guarantee Fund, Guidance Section; European Social Fund; European Regional Development Fund), the European Investment Bank and the other existing Financial Instruments.

The Commission shall submit a report to the European Parliament, the Council, the Economic and Social Committee and the Committee of the Regions every three years on the progress made towards achieving economic, social and territorial cohesion and on the manner in which the various means provided for in this Article have contributed to it. This report shall, if necessary, be accompanied by appropriate proposals.

If specific actions prove necessary outside the Funds and without prejudice to the measures decided upon within the framework of the other Union policies, such actions may be adopted by the Council acting in accordance with the ordinary legislative procedure and after consulting the Economic and Social Committee and the Committee of the Regions.

Article 176 (ex Article 160 TEC)

The European Regional Development Fund is intended to help to redress the main regional imbalances in the Union through participation in the development and structural adjustment of regions whose development is lagging behind and in the conversion of declining industrial regions.

Article 177 (ex Article 161 TEC)

Without prejudice to Article 178, the European Parliament and the Council, acting by means of regulations in accordance with the ordinary legislative procedure and consulting the Economic and Social Committee and the Committee of the Regions, shall define the tasks, priority objectives and the organisation of the Structural Funds, which may involve grouping the Funds. The general rules applicable to them and the provisions necessary to ensure their effectiveness and the coordination of the Funds with one another and with the other existing Financial Instruments shall also be defined by the same procedure.

A Cohesion Fund set up in accordance with the same procedure shall provide a financial contribution to projects in the fields of environment and trans-European networks in the area of transport infrastructure.

Article 178 (ex Article 162 TEC)

Implementing regulations relating to the European Regional Development Fund shall be taken by the European Parliament and the Council, acting in accordance with the ordinary legislative procedure and after consulting the Economic and Social Committee and the Committee of the Regions.

With regard to the European Agricultural Guidance and Guarantee Fund, Guidance Section, and the European Social Fund, Articles 43 and 164 respectively shall continue to apply.

Title XIX Research and technological development and space

Article 179 (ex Article 163 TEC)

1. The Union shall have the objective of strengthening its scientific and technological bases by achieving a European research area in which researchers, scientific knowledge and technology circulate freely, and encouraging it to become more competitive, including in its industry, while promoting all the research activities deemed necessary by virtue of other Chapters of the Treaties.

2. For this purpose the Union shall, throughout the Union, encourage undertakings, including small and medium-sized undertakings, research centres and universities in their research and technological development activities of high quality; it shall support their efforts to cooperate with one another, aiming, notably, at permitting researchers to cooperate freely across borders and at enabling undertakings to exploit the internal market potential to the full, in particular through the opening-up of national public contracts, the definition of common standards and the removal of legal and fiscal obstacles to that cooperation.

3. All Union activities under the Treaties in the area of research and technological development, including demonstration projects, shall be decided on and implemented in accordance with the provisions of this Title.

Article 180 (ex Article 164 TEC)

In pursuing these objectives, the Union shall carry out the following activities, complementing the activities carried out in the Member States:

(a) implementation of research, technological development and demonstration programmes, by promoting cooperation with and between undertakings, research centres and universities;
(b) promotion of cooperation in the field of Union research, technological development and demonstration with third countries and international organisations;
(c) dissemination and optimisation of the results of activities in Union research, technological development and demonstration;
(d) stimulation of the training and mobility of researchers in the Union.

Article 181 (ex Article 165 TEC)

1. The Union and the Member States shall coordinate their research and technological development activities so as to ensure that national policies and Union policy are mutually consistent.

2. In close cooperation with the Member State, the Commission may take any useful initiative to promote the coordination referred to in paragraph 1, in particular initiatives aiming at the establishment of guidelines and indicators, the organisation of exchange of best practice, and the preparation of the necessary elements for periodic monitoring and evaluation. The European Parliament shall be kept fully informed.

Article 182 (ex Article 166 TEC)

1. A multiannual framework programme, setting out all the activities of the Union, shall be adopted by the European Parliament and the Council, acting in accordance with the ordinary legislative procedure after consulting the Economic and Social Committee.

The framework programme shall:

- establish the scientific and technological objectives to be achieved by the activities provided for in Article 180 and fix the relevant priorities,
- indicate the broad lines of such activities,
- fix the maximum overall amount and the detailed rules for Union financial participation in the framework programme and the respective shares in each of the activities provided for.

2. The framework programme shall be adapted or supplemented as the situation changes.

3. The framework programme shall be implemented through specific programmes developed within each activity. Each specific programme shall define the detailed rules for implementing it, fix its duration and provide for the means deemed necessary. The sum of the amounts deemed necessary, fixed in the specific programmes, may not exceed the overall maximum amount fixed for the framework programme and each activity.

4. The Council, acting in accordance with a special legislative procedure and after consulting the European Parliament and the Economic and Social Committee, shall adopt the specific programmes.

5. As a complement to the activities planned in the multiannual framework programme, the European Parliament and the Council, acting in accordance with the ordinary legislative procedure and after consulting the Economic and Social Committee, shall establish the measures necessary for the implementation of the European research area.

Article 183 (ex Article 167 TEC)

For the implementation of the multiannual framework programme the Union shall:

- determine the rules for the participation of undertakings, research centres and universities,
- lay down the rules governing the dissemination of research results.

Article 184 (ex Article 168 TEC)

In implementing the multiannual framework programme, supplementary programmes may be decided on involving the participation of certain Member States only, which shall finance them subject to possible Union participation.

The Union shall adopt the rules applicable to supplementary programmes, particularly as regards the dissemination of knowledge and access by other Member States.

Article 185 (ex Article 169 TEC)

In implementing the multiannual framework programme, the Union may make provision, in agreement with the Member States concerned, for participation in research and development programmes undertaken by several Member States, including participation in the structures created for the execution of those programmes.

Article 186 (ex Article 170 TEC)

In implementing the multiannual framework programme the Union may make provision for cooperation in Union research, technological development and demonstration with third countries or international organisations.

The detailed arrangements for such cooperation may be the subject of agreements between the Union and the third parties concerned.

Article 187 (ex Article 171 TEC)

The Union may set up joint undertakings or any other structure necessary for the efficient execution of Union research, technological development and demonstration programmes.

Article 188 (ex Article 172 TEC)

The Council, on a proposal from the Commission and after consulting the European Parliament and the Economic and Social Committee, shall adopt the provisions referred to in Article 187.

The European Parliament and the Council, acting in accordance with the ordinary legislative procedure and after consulting the Economic and Social Committee, shall adopt the provisions referred to in Articles 183, 184 and 185. Adoption of the supplementary programmes shall require the agreement of the Member States concerned.

Article 189

1. To promote scientific and technical progress, industrial competitiveness and the implementation of its policies, the Union shall draw up a European space policy. To this end, it may promote joint

initiatives, support research and technological development and coordinate the efforts needed for the exploration and exploitation of space.

2. To contribute to attaining the objectives referred to in paragraph 1, the European Parliament and the Council, acting in accordance with the ordinary legislative procedure, shall establish the necessary measures, which may take the form of a European space programme, excluding any harmonisation of the laws and regulations of the Member States.

3. The Union shall establish any appropriate relations with the European Space Agency.

4. This Article shall be without prejudice to the other provisions of this Title.

Article 190 (ex Article 173 TEC)

At the beginning of each year the Commission shall send a report to the European Parliament and to the Council. The report shall include information on research and technological development activities and the dissemination of results during the previous year, and the work programme for the current year.

Title XX Environment

Article 191 (ex Article 174 TEC)

1. Union policy on the environment shall contribute to pursuit of the following objectives:
   - preserving, protecting and improving the quality of the environment,
   - protecting human health,
   - prudent and rational utilisation of natural resources,
   - promoting measures at international level to deal with regional or worldwide environmental problems, and in particular combating climate change.

2. Union policy on the environment shall aim at a high level of protection taking into account the diversity of situations in the various regions of the Union. It shall be based on the precautionary principle and on the principles that preventive action should be taken, that environmental damage should as a priority be rectified at source and that the polluter should pay.

In this context, harmonisation measures answering environmental protection requirements shall include, where appropriate, a safeguard clause allowing Member States to take provisional measures, for non-economic environmental reasons, subject to a procedure of inspection by the Union.

3. In preparing its policy on the environment, the Union shall take account of:
   - available scientific and technical data,
   - environmental conditions in the various regions of the Union,
   - the potential benefits and costs of action or lack of action,
   - the economic and social development of the Union as a whole and the balanced development of its regions.

4. Within their respective spheres of competence, the Union and the Member States shall cooperate with third countries and with the competent international organisations. The arrangements for Union cooperation may be the subject of agreements between the Union and the third parties concerned.

The previous subparagraph shall be without prejudice to Member States' competence to negotiate in international bodies and to conclude international agreements.

Article 192 (ex Article 175 TEC)

1. The European Parliament and the Council, acting in accordance with the ordinary legislative procedure and after consulting the Economic and Social Committee and the Committee of the Regions, shall decide what action is to be taken by the Union in order to achieve the objectives referred to in Article 191.

2. By way of derogation from the decision-making procedure provided for in paragraph 1 and without prejudice to Article 114, the Council acting unanimously in accordance with a special legislative

procedure and after consulting the European Parliament, the Economic and Social Committee and the Committee of the Regions, shall adopt:

(a) provisions primarily of a fiscal nature;

(b) measures affecting:

- town and country planning,
- quantitative management of water resources or affecting, directly or indirectly, the availability of those resources,
- land use, with the exception of waste management;

(c) measures significantly affecting a Member State's choice between different energy sources and the general structure of its energy supply.

The Council, acting unanimously on a proposal from the Commission and after consulting the European Parliament, the Economic and Social Committee and the Committee of the Regions, may make the ordinary legislative procedure applicable to the matters referred to in the first subparagraph.

3. General action programmes setting out priority objectives to be attained shall be adopted by the European Parliament and the Council, acting in accordance with the ordinary legislative procedure and after consulting the Economic and Social Committee and the Committee of the Regions.

The measures necessary for the implementation of these programmes shall be adopted under the terms of paragraph 1 or 2, as the case may be.

4. Without prejudice to certain measures adopted by the Union, the Member States shall finance and implement the environment policy.

5. Without prejudice to the principle that the polluter should pay, if a measure based on the provisions of paragraph 1 involves costs deemed disproportionate for the public authorities of a Member State, such measure shall lay down appropriate provisions in the form of:

- temporary derogations, and/or
- financial support from the Cohesion Fund set up pursuant to Article 177.

Article 193 (ex Article 176 TEC)

The protective measures adopted pursuant to Article 192 shall not prevent any Member State from maintaining or introducing more stringent protective measures. Such measures must be compatible with the Treaties. They shall be notified to the Commission.

Title XXI Energy

Article 194

1. In the context of the establishment and functioning of the internal market and with regard for the need to preserve and improve the environment, Union policy on energy shall aim, in a spirit of solidarity between Member States, to:

(a) ensure the functioning of the energy market;

(b) ensure security of energy supply in the Union;

(c) promote energy efficiency and energy saving and the development of new and renewable forms of energy; and

(d) promote the interconnection of energy networks.

2. Without prejudice to the application of other provisions of the Treaties, the European Parliament and the Council, acting in accordance with the ordinary legislative procedure, shall establish the measures necessary to achieve the objectives in paragraph 1. Such measures shall be adopted after consultation of the Economic and Social Committee and the Committee of the Regions.

Such measures shall not affect a Member State's right to determine the conditions for exploiting its energy resources, its choice between different energy sources and the general structure of its energy supply, without prejudice to Article 192(2)(c).

3. By way of derogation from paragraph 2, the Council, acting in accordance with a special legislative procedure, shall unanimously and after consulting the European Parliament, establish the measures referred to therein when they are primarily of a fiscal nature.

Title XXII Tourism

Article 195

1. The Union shall complement the action of the Member States in the tourism sector, in particular by promoting the competitiveness of Union undertakings in that sector.

To that end, Union action shall be aimed at:

(a) encouraging the creation of a favourable environment for the development of undertakings in this sector;

(b) promoting cooperation between the Member States, particularly by the exchange of good practice.

2. The European Parliament and the Council, acting in accordance with the ordinary legislative procedure, shall establish specific measures to complement actions within the Member States to achieve the objectives referred to in this Article, excluding any harmonisation of the laws and regulations of the Member States.

Title XXIII Civil protection

Article 196

1. The Union shall encourage cooperation between Member States in order to improve the effectiveness of systems for preventing and protecting against natural or man-made disasters.

Union action shall aim to:

(a) support and complement Member States' action at national, regional and local level in risk prevention, in preparing their civil-protection personnel and in responding to natural or man-made disasters within the Union;

(b) promote swift, effective operational cooperation within the Union between national civil-protection services;

(c) promote consistency in international civil-protection work.

2. The European Parliament and the Council, acting in accordance with the ordinary legislative procedure shall establish the measures necessary to help achieve the objectives referred to in paragraph 1, excluding any harmonisation of the laws and regulations of the Member States.

Title XXIV Administrative cooperation

Article 197

1. Effective implementation of Union law by the Member States, which is essential for the proper functioning of the Union, shall be regarded as a matter of common interest.

2. The Union may support the efforts of Member States to improve their administrative capacity to implement Union law. Such action may include facilitating the exchange of information and of civil servants as well as supporting training schemes. No Member State shall be obliged to avail itself of such support. The European Parliament and the Council, acting by means of regulations in accordance with the ordinary legislative procedure, shall establish the necessary measures to this end, excluding any harmonisation of the laws and regulations of the Member States.

3. This Article shall be without prejudice to the obligations of the Member States to implement Union law or to the prerogatives and duties of the Commission. It shall also be without prejudice to other provisions of the Treaties providing for administrative cooperation among the Member States and between them and the Union.

PART FOUR ASSOCIATION OF THE OVERSEAS COUNTRIES AND TERRITORIES

Article 198 (ex Article 182 TEC)

The Member States agree to associate with the Union the non-European countries and territories which have special relations with Denmark, France, the Netherlands and the United Kingdom. These countries and territories (hereinafter called the 'countries and territories') are listed in Annex II.

The purpose of association shall be to promote the economic and social development of the countries and territories and to establish close economic relations between them and the Union as a whole.

In accordance with the principles set out in the preamble to this Treaty, association shall serve primarily to further the interests and prosperity of the inhabitants of these countries and territories in order to lead them to the economic, social and cultural development to which they aspire.

Article 199 (ex Article 183 TEC)

Association shall have the following objectives.

1. Member States shall apply to their trade with the countries and territories the same treatment as they accord each other pursuant to the Treaties.
2. Each country or territory shall apply to its trade with Member States and with the other countries and territories the same treatment as that which it applies to the European State with which it has special relations.
3. The Member States shall contribute to the investments required for the progressive development of these countries and territories.
4. For investments financed by the Union, participation in tenders and supplies shall be open on equal terms to all natural and legal persons who are nationals of a Member State or of one of the countries and territories.
5. In relations between Member States and the countries and territories the right of establishment of nationals and companies or firms shall be regulated in accordance with the provisions and procedures laid down in the Chapter relating to the right of establishment and on a non-discriminatory basis, subject to any special provisions laid down pursuant to Article 203.

Article 200 (ex Article 184 TEC)

1. Customs duties on imports into the Member States of goods originating in the countries and territories shall be prohibited in conformity with the prohibition of customs duties between Member States in accordance with the provisions of the Treaties.
2. Customs duties on imports into each country or territory from Member States or from the other countries or territories shall be prohibited in accordance with the provisions of Article 30.
3. The countries and territories may, however, levy customs duties which meet the needs of their development and industrialisation or produce revenue for their budgets.

The duties referred to in the preceding subparagraph may not exceed the level of those imposed on imports of products from the Member State with which each country or territory has special relations.

4. Paragraph 2 shall not apply to countries and territories which, by reason of the particular international obligations by which they are bound, already apply a non-discriminatory customs tariff.
5. The introduction of or any change in customs duties imposed on goods imported into the countries and territories shall not, either in law or in fact, give rise to any direct or indirect discrimination between imports from the various Member States.

Article 201 (ex Article 185 TEC)

If the level of the duties applicable to goods from a third country on entry into a country or territory is liable, when the provisions of Article 200(1) have been applied, to cause deflections of trade to the detriment of any Member State, the latter may request the Commission to propose to the other Member States the measures needed to remedy the situation.

Article 202 (ex Article 186 TEC)
Subject to the provisions relating to public health, public security or public policy, freedom of movement within Member States for workers from the countries and territories, and within the countries and territories for workers from Member States, shall be regulated by acts adopted in accordance with Article 203.

Article 203 (ex Article 187 TEC)
The Council, acting unanimously on a proposal from the Commission, shall, on the basis of the experience acquired under the association of the countries and territories with the Union and of the principles set out in the Treaties, lay down provisions as regards the detailed rules and the procedure for the association of the countries and territories with the Union. Where the provisions in question are adopted by the Council in accordance with a special legislative procedure, it shall act unanimously on a proposal from the Commission and after consulting the European Parliament.

Article 204 (ex Article 188 TEC)
The provisions of Articles 198 to 203 shall apply to Greenland, subject to the specific provisions for Greenland set out in the Protocol on special arrangements for Greenland, annexed to the Treaties.

PART FIVE EXTERNAL ACTION BY THE UNION

Title I General provisions on the Union's external action

Article 205
The Union's action on the international scene, pursuant to this Part, shall be guided by the principles, pursue the objectives and be conducted in accordance with the general provisions laid down in Chapter 1 of Title V of the Treaty on European Union.

Title II Common commercial policy

Article 206 (ex Article 131 TEC)
By establishing a customs union in accordance with Articles 28 to 32, the Union shall contribute, in the common interest, to the harmonious development of world trade, the progressive abolition of restrictions on international trade and on foreign direct investment, and the lowering of customs and other barriers.

Article 207 (ex Article 133 TEC)
1. The common commercial policy shall be based on uniform principles, particularly with regard to changes in tariff rates, the conclusion of tariff and trade agreements relating to trade in goods and services, and the commercial aspects of intellectual property, foreign direct investment, the achievement of uniformity in measures of liberalisation, export policy and measures to protect trade such as those to be taken in the event of dumping or subsidies. The common commercial policy shall be conducted in the context of the principles and objectives of the Union's external action.

2. The European Parliament and the Council, acting by means of regulations in accordance with the ordinary legislative procedure, shall adopt the measures defining the framework for implementing the common commercial policy.

3. Where agreements with one or more third countries or international organisations need to be negotiated and concluded, Article 218 shall apply, subject to the special provisions of this Article.

The Commission shall make recommendations to the Council, which shall authorise it to open the necessary negotiations. The Council and the Commission shall be responsible for ensuring that the agreements negotiated are compatible with internal Union policies and rules.

The Commission shall conduct these negotiations in consultation with a special committee appointed by the Council to assist the Commission in this task and within the framework of such directives as the Council may issue to it. The Commission shall report regularly to the special committee and to the European Parliament on the progress of negotiations.

4. For the negotiation and conclusion of the agreements referred to in paragraph 3, the Council shall act by a qualified majority.

For the negotiation and conclusion of agreements in the fields of trade in services and the commercial aspects of intellectual property, as well as foreign direct investment, the Council shall act unanimously where such agreements include provisions for which unanimity is required for the adoption of internal rules.

The Council shall also act unanimously for the negotiation and conclusion of agreements:

(a) in the field of trade in cultural and audiovisual services, where these agreements risk prejudicing the Union's cultural and linguistic diversity;

(b) in the field of trade in social, education and health services, where these agreements risk seriously disturbing the national organisation of such services and prejudicing the responsibility of Member States to deliver them.

5. The negotiation and conclusion of international agreements in the field of transport shall be subject to Title VI of Part Three and to Article 218.

6. The exercise of the competences conferred by this Article in the field of the common commercial policy shall not affect the delimitation of competences between the Union and the Member States, and shall not lead to harmonisation of legislative or regulatory provisions of the Member States in so far as the Treaties exclude such harmonisation.

Title III Cooperation with third countries and humanitarian aid

Chapter 1 Development cooperation

Article 208 (ex Article 177 TEC)

1. Union policy in the field of development cooperation shall be conducted within the framework of the principles and objectives of the Union's external action. The Union's development cooperation policy and that of the Member States complement and reinforce each other.

Union development cooperation policy shall have as its primary objective the reduction and, in the long term, the eradication of poverty. The Union shall take account of the objectives of development cooperation in the policies that it implements which are likely to affect developing countries.

2. The Union and the Member States shall comply with the commitments and take account of the objectives they have approved in the context of the United Nations and other competent international organisations.

Article 209 (ex Article 179 TEC)

1. The European Parliament and the Council, acting in accordance with the ordinary legislative procedure, shall adopt the measures necessary for the implementation of development cooperation policy, which may relate to multiannual cooperation programmes with developing countries or programmes with a thematic approach.

2. The Union may conclude with third countries and competent international organisations any agreement helping to achieve the objectives referred to in Article 21 of the Treaty on European Union and in Article 208 of this Treaty.

The first subparagraph shall be without prejudice to Member States' competence to negotiate in international bodies and to conclude agreements.

3. The European Investment Bank shall contribute, under the terms laid down in its Statute, to the implementation of the measures referred to in paragraph 1.

Article 210 (ex Article 180 TEC)

1. In order to promote the complementarity and efficiency of their action, the Union and the Member States shall coordinate their policies on development cooperation and shall consult each other on their aid programmes, including in international organisations and during international conferences. They may undertake joint action. Member States shall contribute if necessary to the implementation of Union aid programmes.

2. The Commission may take any useful initiative to promote the coordination referred to in paragraph 1.

Article 211 (ex Article 181 TEC)

Within their respective spheres of competence, the Union and the Member States shall cooperate with third countries and with the competent international organisations.

Chapter 2 Economic, financial and technical cooperation with third countries

Article 212 (ex Article 181a TEC)

1. Without prejudice to the other provisions of the Treaties, and in particular Articles 208 to 211, the Union shall carry out economic, financial and technical cooperation measures, including assistance, in particular financial assistance, with third countries other than developing countries. Such measures shall be consistent with the development policy of the Union and shall be carried out within the framework of the principles and objectives of its external action. The Union's operations and those of the Member States shall complement and reinforce each other.

2. The European Parliament and the Council, acting in accordance with the ordinary legislative procedure, shall adopt the measures necessary for the implementation of paragraph 1.

3. Within their respective spheres of competence, the Union and the Member States shall cooperate with third countries and the competent international organisations. The arrangements for Union cooperation may be the subject of agreements between the Union and the third parties concerned.

The first subparagraph shall be without prejudice to the Member States' competence to negotiate in international bodies and to conclude international agreements.

Article 213

When the situation in a third country requires urgent financial assistance from the Union, the Council shall adopt the necessary decisions on a proposal from the Commission.

Chapter 3 Humanitarian aid

Article 214

1. The Union's operations in the field of humanitarian aid shall be conducted within the framework of the principles and objectives of the external action of the Union. Such operations shall be intended to provide *ad hoc* assistance and relief and protection for people in third countries who are victims of natural or man-made disasters, in order to meet the humanitarian needs resulting from these different situations. The Union's measures and those of the Member States shall complement and reinforce each other.

2. Humanitarian aid operations shall be conducted in compliance with the principles of international law and with the principles of impartiality, neutrality and non-discrimination.

3. The European Parliament and the Council, acting in accordance with the ordinary legislative procedure, shall establish the measures defining the framework within which the Union's humanitarian aid operations shall be implemented.

4. The Union may conclude with third countries and competent international organisations any agreement helping to achieve the objectives referred to in paragraph 1 and in Article 21 of the Treaty on European Union.

The first subparagraph shall be without prejudice to Member States' competence to negotiate in international bodies and to conclude agreements.

5. In order to establish a framework for joint contributions from young Europeans to the humanitarian aid operations of the Union, a European Voluntary Humanitarian Aid Corps shall be set up. The European Parliament and the Council, acting by means of regulations in accordance with the ordinary legislative procedure, shall determine the rules and procedures for the operation of the Corps.

6. The Commission may take any useful initiative to promote coordination between actions of the Union and those of the Member States, in order to enhance the efficiency and complementarity of Union and national humanitarian aid measures.

7. The Union shall ensure that its humanitarian aid operations are coordinated and consistent with those of international organisations and bodies, in particular those forming part of the United Nations system.

Title IV Restrictive measures

Article 215 (ex Article 301 TEC)

1. Where a decision, adopted in accordance with Chapter 2 of Title V of the Treaty on European Union, provides for the interruption or reduction, in part or completely, of economic and financial relations with one or more third countries, the Council, acting by a qualified majority on a joint proposal from the High Representative of the Union for Foreign Affairs and Security Policy and the Commission, shall adopt the necessary measures. It shall inform the European Parliament thereof.

2. Where a decision adopted in accordance with Chapter 2 of Title V of the Treaty on European Union so provides, the Council may adopt restrictive measures under the procedure referred to in paragraph 1 against natural or legal persons and groups or non-State entities.

3. The acts referred to in this Article shall include necessary provisions on legal safeguards.

Title V International agreements

Article 216

1. The Union may conclude an agreement with one or more third countries or international organisations where the Treaties so provide or where the conclusion of an agreement is necessary in order to achieve, within the framework of the Union's policies, one of the objectives referred to in the Treaties, or is provided for in a legally binding Union act or is likely to affect common rules or alter their scope.

2. Agreements concluded by the Union are binding upon the institutions of the Union and on its Member States.

Article 217 (ex Article 310 TEC)

The Union may conclude with one or more third countries or international organisations agreements establishing an association involving reciprocal rights and obligations, common action and special procedure.

Article 218 (ex Article 300 TEC)

1. Without prejudice to the specific provisions laid down in Article 207, agreements between the Union and third countries or international organisations shall be negotiated and concluded in accordance with the following procedure.

2. The Council shall authorise the opening of negotiations, adopt negotiating directives, authorise the signing of agreements and conclude them.

3. The Commission, or the High Representative of the Union for Foreign Affairs and Security Policy where the agreement envisaged relates exclusively or principally to the common foreign and security policy, shall submit recommendations to the Council, which shall adopt a decision authorising

the opening of negotiations and, depending on the subject of the agreement envisaged, nominating the Union negotiator or the head of the Union's negotiating team.

4. The Council may address directives to the negotiator and designate a special committee in consultation with which the negotiations must be conducted.

5. The Council, on a proposal by the negotiator, shall adopt a decision authorising the signing of the agreement and, if necessary, its provisional application before entry into force.

6. The Council, on a proposal by the negotiator, shall adopt a decision concluding the agreement.

Except where agreements relate exclusively to the common foreign and security policy, the Council shall adopt the decision concluding the agreement:

(a) after obtaining the consent of the European Parliament in the following cases:
 (i) association agreements;
 (ii) agreement on Union accession to the European Convention for the Protection of Human Rights and Fundamental Freedoms;
 (iii) agreements establishing a specific institutional framework by organising cooperation procedures;
 (iv) agreements with important budgetary implications for the Union;
 (v) agreements covering fields to which either the ordinary legislative procedure applies, or the special legislative procedure where consent by the European Parliament is required.

 The European Parliament and the Council may, in an urgent situation, agree upon a time-limit for consent.

(b) after consulting the European Parliament in other cases. The European Parliament shall deliver its opinion within a time-limit which the Council may set depending on the urgency of the matter. In the absence of an opinion within that time-limit, the Council may act.

7. When concluding an agreement, the Council may, by way of derogation from paragraphs 5, 6 and 9, authorise the negotiator to approve on the Union's behalf modifications to the agreement where it provides for them to be adopted by a simplified procedure or by a body set up by the agreement. The Council may attach specific conditions to such authorisation.

8. The Council shall act by a qualified majority throughout the procedure.

However, it shall act unanimously when the agreement covers a field for which unanimity is required for the adoption of a Union act as well as for association agreements and the agreements referred to in Article 212 with the States which are candidates for accession. The Council shall also act unanimously for the agreement on accession of the Union to the European Convention for the Protection of Human Rights and Fundamental Freedoms; the decision concluding this agreement shall enter into force after it has been approved by the Member States in accordance with their respective constitutional requirements.

9. The Council, on a proposal from the Commission or the High Representative of the Union for Foreign Affairs and Security Policy, shall adopt a decision suspending application of an agreement and establishing the positions to be adopted on the Union's behalf in a body set up by an agreement, when that body is called upon to adopt acts having legal effects, with the exception of acts supplementing or amending the institutional framework of the agreement.

10. The European Parliament shall be immediately and fully informed at all stages of the procedure.

11. A Member State, the European Parliament, the Council or the Commission may obtain the opinion of the Court of Justice as to whether an agreement envisaged is compatible with the Treaties. Where the opinion of the Court is adverse, the agreement envisaged may not enter into force unless it is amended or the Treaties are revised.

Article 219 (ex Article 111(1) to (3) and (5) TEC)

1. By way of derogation from Article 218, the Council, either on a recommendation from the European Central Bank or on a recommendation from the Commission and after consulting the European Central Bank, in an endeavour to reach a consensus consistent with the objective of price

stability, may conclude formal agreements on an exchange-rate system for the euro in relation to the currencies of third States. The Council shall act unanimously after consulting the European Parliament and in accordance with the procedure provided for in paragraph 3.

The Council may, either on a recommendation from the European Central Bank or on a recommendation from the Commission, and after consulting the European Central Bank, in an endeavour to reach a consensus consistent with the objective of price stability, adopt, adjust or abandon the central rates of the euro within the exchange-rate system. The President of the Council shall inform the European Parliament of the adoption, adjustment or abandonment of the euro central rates.

2. In the absence of an exchange-rate system in relation to one or more currencies of third States as referred to in paragraph 1, the Council, either on a recommendation from the Commission and after consulting the European Central Bank or on a recommendation from the European Central Bank, may formulate general orientations for exchange-rate policy in relation to these currencies. These general orientations shall be without prejudice to the primary objective of the ESCB to maintain price stability.

3. By way of derogation from Article 218, where agreements concerning monetary or foreign exchange regime matters need to be negotiated by the Union with one or more third States or international organisations, the Council, on a recommendation from the Commission and after consulting the European Central Bank, shall decide the arrangements for the negotiation and for the conclusion of such agreements. These arrangements shall ensure that the Union expresses a single position. The Commission shall be fully associated with the negotiations.

4. Without prejudice to Union competence and Union agreements as regards economic and monetary union, Member States may negotiate in international bodies and conclude international agreements.

Title VI The Union's relations with international organisations and third countries and Union delegations

Article 220 (ex Articles 302 to 304 TEC)

1. The Union shall establish all appropriate forms of cooperation with the organs of the United Nations and its specialised agencies, the Council of Europe, the Organisation for Security and Cooperation in Europe and the Organisation for Economic Cooperation and Development.

The Union shall also maintain such relations as are appropriate with other international organisations.

2. The High Representative of the Union for Foreign Affairs and Security Policy and the Commission shall be instructed to implement this Article.

Article 221

1. Union delegations in third countries and at international organisations shall represent the Union.

2. Union delegations shall be placed under the authority of the High Representative of the Union for Foreign Affairs and Security Policy. They shall act in close cooperation with Member States' diplomatic and consular missions.

Title VII Solidarity clause

Article 222

1. The Union and its Member States shall act jointly in a spirit of solidarity if a Member State is the object of a terrorist attack or the victim of a natural or man-made disaster. The Union shall mobilise all the instruments at its disposal, including the military resources made available by the Member States, to:

(a) – prevent the terrorist threat in the territory of the Member States;
– protect democratic institutions and the civilian population from any terrorist attack;

- assist a Member State in its territory, at the request of its political authorities, in the event of a terrorist attack;

(b) assist a Member State in its territory, at the request of its political authorities, in the event of a natural or man-made disaster.

2. Should a Member State be the object of a terrorist attack or the victim of a natural or man-made disaster, the other Member States shall assist it at the request of its political authorities. To that end, the Member States shall coordinate between themselves in the Council.

3. The arrangements for the implementation by the Union of the solidarity clause shall be defined by a decision adopted by the Council acting on a joint proposal by the Commission and the High Representative of the Union for Foreign Affairs and Security Policy. The Council shall act in accordance with Article 31(1) of the Treaty on European Union where this decision has defence implications. The European Parliament shall be informed.

For the purposes of this paragraph and without prejudice to Article 240, the Council shall be assisted by the Political and Security Committee with the support of the structures developed in the context of the common security and defence policy and by the Committee referred to in Article 71; the two committees shall, if necessary, submit joint opinions.

4. The European Council shall regularly assess the threats facing the Union in order to enable the Union and its Member States to take effective action.

PART SIX INSTITUTIONAL AND FINANCIAL PROVISIONS

Title I Institutional provisions

Chapter 1 The institutions

Section 1 The European Parliament

Article 223 (ex Article 190(4) and (5) TEC)

1. The European Parliament shall draw up a proposal to lay down the provisions necessary for the election of its Members by direct universal suffrage in accordance with a uniform procedure in all Member States or in accordance with principles common to all Member States.

The Council, acting unanimously in accordance with a special legislative procedure and after obtaining the consent of the European Parliament, which shall act by a majority of its component Members, shall lay down the necessary provisions. These provisions shall enter into force following their approval by the Member States in accordance with their respective constitutional requirements.

2. The European Parliament, acting by means of regulations on its own initiative in accordance with a special legislative procedure after seeking an opinion from the Commission and with the approval of the Council, shall lay down the regulations and general conditions governing the performance of the duties of its Members. All rules or conditions relating to the taxation of Members or former Members shall require unanimity within the Council.

Article 224 (ex Article 191, second subparagraph, TEC)

The European Parliament and the Council, acting in accordance with the ordinary legislative procedure, by means of regulations, shall lay down the regulations governing political parties at European level referred to in Article 10(4) of the Treaty on European Union and in particular the rules regarding their funding.

Article 225 (ex Article 192, second subparagraph, TEC)

The European Parliament may, acting by a majority of its component Members, request the Commission to submit any appropriate proposal on matters on which it considers that a Union act is required for the purpose of implementing the Treaties. If the Commission does not submit a proposal, it shall inform the European Parliament of the reasons.

Article 226 (ex Article 193 TEC)

In the course of its duties, the European Parliament may, at the request of a quarter of its component Members, set up a temporary Committee of Inquiry to investigate, without prejudice to the powers conferred by the Treaties on other institutions or bodies, alleged contraventions or maladministration in the implementation of Union law, except where the alleged facts are being examined before a court and while the case is still subject to legal proceedings.

The temporary Committee of Inquiry shall cease to exist on the submission of its report.

The detailed provisions governing the exercise of the right of inquiry shall be determined by the European Parliament, acting by means of regulations on its own initiative in accordance with a special legislative procedure, after obtaining the consent of the Council and the Commission.

Article 227 (ex Article 194 TEC)

Any citizen of the Union, and any natural or legal person residing or having its registered office in a Member State, shall have the right to address, individually or in association with other citizens or persons, a petition to the European Parliament on a matter which comes within the Union's fields of activity and which affects him, her or it directly.

Article 228 (ex Article 195 TEC)

1. A European Ombudsman, elected by the European Parliament, shall be empowered to receive complaints from any citizen of the Union or any natural or legal person residing or having its registered office in a Member State concerning instances of maladministration in the activities of the Union institutions, bodies, offices or agencies, with the exception of the Court of Justice of the European Union acting in its judicial role. He or she shall examine such complaints and report on them.

In accordance with his duties, the Ombudsman shall conduct inquiries for which he finds grounds, either on his own initiative or on the basis of complaints submitted to him direct or through a Member of the European Parliament, except where the alleged facts are or have been the subject of legal proceedings. Where the Ombudsman establishes an instance of maladministration, he shall refer the matter to the institution, body, office or agency concerned, which shall have a period of three months in which to inform him of its views. The Ombudsman shall then forward a report to the European Parliament and the institution, body, office or agency concerned. The person lodging the complaint shall be informed of the outcome of such inquiries.

The Ombudsman shall submit an annual report to the European Parliament on the outcome of his inquiries.

2. The Ombudsman shall be elected after each election of the European Parliament for the duration of its term of office. The Ombudsman shall be eligible for reappointment.

The Ombudsman may be dismissed by the Court of Justice at the request of the European Parliament if he no longer fulfils the conditions required for the performance of his duties or if he is guilty of serious misconduct.

3. The Ombudsman shall be completely independent in the performance of his duties. In the performance of those duties he shall neither seek nor take instructions from any Government, institution, body, office or entity. The Ombudsman may not, during his term of office, engage in any other occupation, whether gainful or not.

4. The European Parliament acting by means of regulations on its own initiative in accordance with a special legislative procedure shall, after seeking an opinion from the Commission and with the approval of the Council, lay down the regulations and general conditions governing the performance of the Ombudsman's duties.

Article 229 (ex Article 196 TEC)

The European Parliament shall hold an annual session. It shall meet, without requiring to be convened, on the second Tuesday in March.

The European Parliament may meet in extraordinary part-session at the request of a majority of its component Members or at the request of the Council or of the Commission.

Article 230 (ex Article 197, second, third and fourth paragraph, TEC)
The Commission may attend all the meetings and shall, at its request, be heard.

The Commission shall reply orally or in writing to questions put to it by the European Parliament or by its Members.

The European Council and the Council shall be heard by the European Parliament in accordance with the conditions laid down in the Rules of Procedure of the European Council and those of the Council.

Article 231 (ex Article 198 TEC)
Save as otherwise provided in the Treaties, the European Parliament shall act by a majority of the votes cast.

The Rules of Procedure shall determine the quorum.

Article 232 (ex Article 199 TEC)
The European Parliament shall adopt its Rules of Procedure, acting by a majority of its Members.

The proceedings of the European Parliament shall be published in the manner laid down in the Treaties and in its Rules of Procedure.

Article 233 (ex Article 200 TEC)
The European Parliament shall discuss in open session the annual general report submitted to it by the Commission.

Article 234 (ex Article 201 TEC)
If a motion of censure on the activities of the Commission is tabled before it, the European Parliament shall not vote thereon until at least three days after the motion has been tabled and only by open vote.

If the motion of censure is carried by a two-thirds majority of the votes cast, representing a majority of the component Members of the European Parliament, the members of the Commission shall resign as a body and the High Representative of the Union for Foreign Affairs and Security Policy shall resign from duties that he or she carries out in the Commission. They shall remain in office and continue to deal with current business until they are replaced in accordance with Article 17 of the Treaty on European Union. In this case, the term of office of the members of the Commission appointed to replace them shall expire on the date on which the term of office of the members of the Commission obliged to resign as a body would have expired.

Section 2 The European Council

Article 235

1. Where a vote is taken, any member of the European Council may also act on behalf of not more than one other member.

Article 16(4) of the Treaty on European Union and Article 238(2) of this Treaty shall apply to the European Council when it is acting by a qualified majority. Where the European Council decides by vote, its President and the President of the Commission shall not take part in the vote.

Abstentions by members present in person or represented shall not prevent the adoption by the European Council of acts which require unanimity.

2. The President of the European Parliament may be invited to be heard by the European Council.

3. The European Council shall act by a simple majority for procedural questions and for the adoption of its Rules of Procedure.

4. The European Council shall be assisted by the General Secretariat of the Council.

Article 236
The European Council shall adopt by a qualified majority:

(a) a decision establishing the list of Council configurations, other than those of the General Affairs Council and of the Foreign Affairs Council, in accordance with Article 16(6) of the Treaty on European Union;

(b) a decision on the Presidency of Council configurations, other than that of Foreign Affairs, in accordance with Article 16(9) of the Treaty on European Union.

Section 3 The Council

Article 237 (ex Article 204 TEC)

The Council shall meet when convened by its President on his own initiative or at the request of one of its Members or of the Commission.

Article 238 (ex Article 205(1) and (2), TEC)

1. Where it is required to act by a simple majority, the Council shall act by a majority of its component members.

2. By way of derogation from Article 16(4) of the Treaty on European Union, as from 1 November 2014 and subject to the provisions laid down in the Protocol on transitional provisions, where the Council does not act on a proposal from the Commission or from the High Representative of the Union for Foreign Affairs and Security Policy, the qualified majority shall be defined as at least 72 % of the members of the Council, representing Member States comprising at least 65 % of the population of the Union.

3. As from 1 November 2014 and subject to the provisions laid down in the Protocol on transitional provisions, in cases where, under the Treaties, not all the members of the Council participate in voting, a qualified majority shall be defined as follows:

(a) A qualified majority shall be defined as at least 55 % of the members of the Council representing the participating Member States, comprising at least 65 % of the population of these States.

A blocking minority must include at least the minimum number of Council members representing more than 35 % of the population of the participating Member States, plus one member, failing which the qualified majority shall be deemed attained;

(b) By way of derogation from point (a), where the Council does not act on a proposal from the Commission or from the High Representative of the Union for Foreign Affairs and Security Policy, the qualified majority shall be defined as at least 72 % of the members of the Council representing the participating Member States, comprising at least 65 % of the population of these States.

4. Abstentions by Members present in person or represented shall not prevent the adoption by the Council of acts which require unanimity.

Article 239 (ex Article 206 TEC)

Where a vote is taken, any Member of the Council may also act on behalf of not more than one other member.

Article 240 (ex Article 207 TEC)

1. A committee consisting of the Permanent Representatives of the Governments of the Member States shall be responsible for preparing the work of the Council and for carrying out the tasks assigned to it by the latter. The Committee may adopt procedural decisions in cases provided for in the Council's Rules of Procedure.

2. The Council shall be assisted by a General Secretariat, under the responsibility of a Secretary-General appointed by the Council.

The Council shall decide on the organisation of the General Secretariat by a simple majority.

3. The Council shall act by a simple majority regarding procedural matters and for the adoption of its Rules of Procedure.

Article 241 (ex Article 208 TEC)

The Council acting by a simple majority may request the Commission to undertake any studies the Council considers desirable for the attainment of the common objectives, and to submit to it any appropriate proposals. If the Commission does not submit a proposal, it shall inform the Council of the reasons.

Article 242 (ex Article 209 TEC)

The Council, acting by a simple majority shall, after consulting the Commission, determine the rules governing the committees provided for in the Treaties.

Article 243 (ex Article 210 TEC)

The Council shall determine the salaries, allowances and pensions of the President of the European Council, the President of the Commission, the High Representative of the Union for Foreign Affairs and Security Policy, the Members of the Commission, the Presidents, Members and Registrars of the Court of Justice of the European Union, and the Secretary-General of the Council. It shall also determine any payment to be made instead of remuneration.

Section 4 The Commission

Article 244

In accordance with Article 17(5) of the Treaty on European Union, the Members of the Commission shall be chosen on the basis of a system of rotation established unanimously by the European Council and on the basis of the following principles:

(a) Member States shall be treated on a strictly equal footing as regards determination of the sequence of, and the time spent by, their nationals as members of the Commission; consequently, the difference between the total number of terms of office held by nationals of any given pair of Member States may never be more than one;

(b) subject to point (a), each successive Commission shall be so composed as to reflect satisfactorily the demographic and geographical range of all the Member States.

Article 245 (ex Article 213 TEC)

The Members of the Commission shall refrain from any action incompatible with their duties. Member States shall respect their independence and shall not seek to influence them in the performance of their tasks.

The Members of the Commission may not, during their term of office, engage in any other occupation, whether gainful or not. When entering upon their duties they shall give a solemn undertaking that, both during and after their term of office, they will respect the obligations arising therefrom and in particular their duty to behave with integrity and discretion as regards the acceptance, after they have ceased to hold office, of certain appointments or benefits. In the event of any breach of these obligations, the Court of Justice may, on application by the Council acting by a simple majority or the Commission, rule that the Member concerned be, according to the circumstances, either compulsorily retired in accordance with Article 247 or deprived of his right to a pension or other benefits in its stead.

Article 246 (ex Article 215 TEC)

Apart from normal replacement, or death, the duties of a Member of the Commission shall end when he resigns or is compulsorily retired.

A vacancy caused by resignation, compulsory retirement or death shall be filled for the remainder of the Member's term of office by a new Member of the same nationality appointed by the Council, by common accord with the President of the Commission, after consulting the European Parliament and in accordance with the criteria set out in the second subparagraph of Article 17(3) of the Treaty on European Union.

The Council may, acting unanimously on a proposal from the President of the Commission, decide that such a vacancy need not be filled, in particular when the remainder of the Member's term of office is short.

In the event of resignation, compulsory retirement or death, the President shall be replaced for the remainder of his term of office. The procedure laid down in the first subparagraph of Article 17(7) of the Treaty on European Union shall be applicable for the replacement of the President.

In the event of resignation, compulsory retirement or death, the High Representative of the Union for Foreign Affairs and Security Policy shall be replaced, for the remainder of his or her term of office, in accordance with Article 18(1) of the Treaty on European Union.

In the case of the resignation of all the Members of the Commission, they shall remain in office and continue to deal with current business until they have been replaced, for the remainder of their term of office, in accordance with Article 17 of the Treaty on European Union.

Article 247 (ex Article 216 TEC)

If any Member of the Commission no longer fulfils the conditions required for the performance of his duties or if he has been guilty of serious misconduct, the Court of Justice may, on application by the Council acting by a simple majority or the Commission, compulsorily retire him.

Article 248 (ex Article 217(2), TEC)

Without prejudice to Article 18(4) of the Treaty on European Union, the responsibilities incumbent upon the Commission shall be structured and allocated among its members by its President, in accordance with Article 17(6) of that Treaty. The President may reshuffle the allocation of those responsibilities during the Commission's term of office. The Members of the Commission shall carry out the duties devolved upon them by the President under his authority.

Article 249 (ex Articles 218(2) and 212 TEC)

1. The Commission shall adopt its Rules of Procedure so as to ensure that both it and its departments operate. It shall ensure that these Rules are published.

2. The Commission shall publish annually, not later than one month before the opening of the session of the European Parliament, a general report on the activities of the Union.

Article 250 (ex Article 219 TEC)

The Commission shall act by a majority of its Members.

Its Rules of Procedure shall determine the quorum.

Section 5 The Court of Justice of the European Union

Article 251 (ex Article 221 TEC)

The Court of Justice shall sit in chambers or in a Grand Chamber, in accordance with the rules laid down for that purpose in the Statute of the Court of Justice of the European Union.

When provided for in the Statute, the Court of Justice may also sit as a full Court.

Article 252 (ex Article 222 TEC)

The Court of Justice shall be assisted by eight Advocates-General. Should the Court of Justice so request, the Council, acting unanimously, may increase the number of Advocates-General.*

It shall be the duty of the Advocate-General, acting with complete impartiality and independence, to make, in open court, reasoned submissions on cases which, in accordance with the Statute of the Court of Justice of the European Union, require his involvement.

Article 253 (ex Article 223 TEC)

The Judges and Advocates-General of the Court of Justice shall be chosen from persons whose independence is beyond doubt and who possess the qualifications required for appointment to the highest judicial offices in their respective countries or who are jurisconsults of recognised competence; they shall be appointed by common accord of the governments of the Member States for a term of six years, after consultation of the panel provided for in Article 255.

Every three years there shall be a partial replacement of the Judges and Advocates-General, in accordance with the conditions laid down in the Statute of the Court of Justice of the European Union.

* **Editor's Note**: Declaration 38 attached to the Treaties allows for the Court to request an increase in the number of Advocates-General, which has now taken place and has been unanimously approved by the Council in Decision 2013/336 (OJ 2013 L179/92), so the number of Advocates-General now stands at nine. Note though that the Decision also agreed an increase in the number of Advocates-General to 11 with effect from 7 October 2015.

The Judges shall elect the President of the Court of Justice from among their number for a term of three years. He may be re-elected.

Retiring Judges and Advocates-General may be reappointed.

The Court of Justice shall appoint its Registrar and lay down the rules governing his service.

The Court of Justice shall establish its Rules of Procedure. Those Rules shall require the approval of the Council.

Article 254 (ex Article 224 TEC)

The number of Judges of the General Court shall be determined by the Statute of the Court of Justice of the European Union. The Statute may provide for the General Court to be assisted by Advocates-General.

The members of the General Court shall be chosen from persons whose independence is beyond doubt and who possess the ability required for appointment to high judicial office. They shall be appointed by common accord of the governments of the Member States for a term of six years, after consultation of the panel provided for in Article 255. The membership shall be partially renewed every three years. Retiring members shall be eligible for reappointment.

The Judges shall elect the President of the General Court from among their number for a term of three years. He may be re-elected.

The General Court shall appoint its Registrar and lay down the rules governing his service.

The General Court shall establish its Rules of Procedure in agreement with the Court of Justice. Those Rules shall require the approval of the Council.

Unless the Statute of the Court of Justice of the European Union provides otherwise, the provisions of the Treaties relating to the Court of Justice shall apply to the General Court.

Article 255

A panel shall be set up in order to give an opinion on candidates' suitability to perform the duties of Judge and Advocate-General of the Court of Justice and the General Court before the governments of the Member States make the appointments referred to in Articles 253 and 254.

The panel shall comprise seven persons chosen from among former members of the Court of Justice and the General Court, members of national supreme courts and lawyers of recognised competence, one of whom shall be proposed by the European Parliament. The Council shall adopt a decision establishing the panel's operating rules and a decision appointing its members. It shall act on the initiative of the President of the Court of Justice.

Article 256 (ex Article 225 TEC)

1. The General Court shall have jurisdiction to hear and determine at first instance actions or proceedings referred to in Articles 263, 265, 268, 270 and 272, with the exception of those assigned to a specialised court set up under Article 257 and those reserved in the Statute for the Court of Justice. The Statute may provide for the General Court to have jurisdiction for other classes of action or proceeding.

Decisions given by the General Court under this paragraph may be subject to a right of appeal to the Court of Justice on points of law only, under the conditions and within the limits laid down by the Statute.

2. The General Court shall have jurisdiction to hear and determine actions or proceedings brought against decisions of the specialised courts.

Decisions given by the General Court under this paragraph may exceptionally be subject to review by the Court of Justice, under the conditions and within the limits laid down by the Statute, where there is a serious risk of the unity or consistency of Union law being affected.

3. The General Court shall have jurisdiction to hear and determine questions referred for a preliminary ruling under Article 267, in specific areas laid down by the Statute.

Where the General Court considers that the case requires a decision of principle likely to affect the unity or consistency of Union law, it may refer the case to the Court of Justice for a ruling.

Decisions given by the General Court on questions referred for a preliminary ruling may exceptionally be subject to review by the Court of Justice, under the conditions and within the limits laid down by the Statute, where there is a serious risk of the unity or consistency of Union law being affected.

Article 257 (ex Article 225a TEC)

The European Parliament and the Council, acting in accordance with the ordinary legislative procedure, may establish specialised courts attached to the General Court to hear and determine at first instance certain classes of action or proceeding brought in specific areas. The European Parliament and the Council shall act by means of regulations either on a proposal from the Commission after consultation of the Court of Justice or at the request of the Court of Justice after consultation of the Commission.

The regulation establishing a specialised court shall lay down the rules on the organisation of the court and the extent of the jurisdiction conferred upon it.

Decisions given by specialised courts may be subject to a right of appeal on points of law only or, when provided for in the regulation establishing the specialised court, a right of appeal also on matters of fact, before the General Court.

The members of the specialised courts shall be chosen from persons whose independence is beyond doubt and who possess the ability required for appointment to judicial office. They shall be appointed by the Council, acting unanimously.

The specialised courts shall establish their Rules of Procedure in agreement with the Court of Justice. Those Rules shall require the approval of the Council.

Unless the regulation establishing the specialised court provides otherwise, the provisions of the Treaties relating to the Court of Justice of the European Union and the provisions of the Statute of the Court of Justice of the European Union shall apply to the specialised courts. Title I of the Statute and Article 64 thereof shall in any case apply to the specialised courts.

Article 258 (ex Article 226 TEC)

If the Commission considers that a Member State has failed to fulfil an obligation under the Treaties, it shall deliver a reasoned opinion on the matter after giving the State concerned the opportunity to submit its observations.

If the State concerned does not comply with the opinion within the period laid down by the Commission, the latter may bring the matter before the Court of Justice of the European Union.

Article 259 (ex Article 227 TEC)

A Member State which considers that another Member State has failed to fulfil an obligation under the Treaties may bring the matter before the Court of Justice of the European Union.

Before a Member State brings an action against another Member State for an alleged infringement of an obligation under the Treaties, it shall bring the matter before the Commission.

The Commission shall deliver a reasoned opinion after each of the States concerned has been given the opportunity to submit its own case and its observations on the other party's case both orally and in writing.

If the Commission has not delivered an opinion within three months of the date on which the matter was brought before it, the absence of such opinion shall not prevent the matter from being brought before the Court.

Article 260 (ex Article 228 TEC)

1. If the Court of Justice of the European Union finds that a Member State has failed to fulfil an obligation under the Treaties, the State shall be required to take the necessary measures to comply with the judgment of the Court.

2. If the Commission considers that the Member State concerned has not taken the necessary measures to comply with the judgment of the Court, it may bring the case before the Court after giving that State the opportunity to submit its observations. It shall specify the amount of the lump sum or penalty payment to be paid by the Member State concerned which it considers appropriate in the circumstances.

If the Court finds that the Member State concerned has not complied with its judgment it may impose a lump sum or penalty payment on it.

This procedure shall be without prejudice to Article 259.

3. When the Commission brings a case before the Court pursuant to Article 258 on the grounds that the Member State concerned has failed to fulfil its obligation to notify measures transposing

a directive adopted under a legislative procedure, it may, when it deems appropriate, specify the amount of the lump sum or penalty payment to be paid by the Member State concerned which it considers appropriate in the circumstances.

If the Court finds that there is an infringement it may impose a lump sum or penalty payment on the Member State concerned not exceeding the amount specified by the Commission. The payment obligation shall take effect on the date set by the Court in its judgment.

Article 261 (ex Article 229 TEC)

Regulations adopted jointly by the European Parliament and the Council, and by the Council, pursuant to the provisions of the Treaties, may give the Court of Justice of the European Union unlimited jurisdiction with regard to the penalties provided for in such regulations.

Article 262 (ex Article 229a TEC)

Without prejudice to the other provisions of the Treaties, the Council, acting unanimously in accordance with a special legislative procedure and after consulting the European Parliament, may adopt provisions to confer jurisdiction, to the extent that it shall determine, on the Court of Justice of the European Union in disputes relating to the application of acts adopted on the basis of the Treaties which create European intellectual property rights. These provisions shall enter into force after their approval by the Member States in accordance with their respective constitutional requirements.

Article 263 (ex Article 230 TEC)

The Court of Justice of the European Union shall review the legality of legislative acts, of acts of the Council, of the Commission and of the European Central Bank, other than recommendations and opinions, and of acts of the European Parliament and of the European Council intended to produce legal effects *vis-à-vis* third parties. It shall also review the legality of acts of bodies, offices or agencies of the Union intended to produce legal effects *vis-à-vis* third parties.

It shall for this purpose have jurisdiction in actions brought by a Member State, the European Parliament, the Council or the Commission on grounds of lack of competence, infringement of an essential procedural requirement, infringement of the Treaties or of any rule of law relating to their application, or misuse of powers.

The Court shall have jurisdiction under the same conditions in actions brought by the Court of Auditors, by the European Central Bank and by the Committee of the Regions for the purpose of protecting their prerogatives.

Any natural or legal person may, under the conditions laid down in the first and second paragraphs, institute proceedings against an act addressed to that person or which is of direct and individual concern to them, and against a regulatory act which is of direct concern to them and does not entail implementing measures.

Acts setting up bodies, offices and agencies of the Union may lay down specific conditions and arrangements concerning actions brought by natural or legal persons against acts of these bodies, offices or agencies intended to produce legal effects in relation to them.

The proceedings provided for in this Article shall be instituted within two months of the publication of the measure, or of its notification to the plaintiff, or, in the absence thereof, of the day on which it came to the knowledge of the latter, as the case may be.

Article 264 (ex Article 231 TEC)

If the action is well founded, the Court of Justice of the European Union shall declare the act concerned to be void.

However, the Court shall, if it considers this necessary, state which of the effects of the act which it has declared void shall be considered as definitive.

Article 265 (ex Article 232 TEC)

Should the European Parliament, the European Council, the Council, the Commission or the European Central Bank, in infringement of the Treaties, fail to act, the Member States and the other institutions of the Union may bring an action before the Court of Justice of the European Union to have the infringement established. This Article shall apply, under the same conditions, to bodies, offices and agencies of the Union which fail to act.

The action shall be admissible only if the institution, body, office or agency concerned has first been called upon to act. If, within two months of being so called upon, the institution, body, office or agency concerned has not defined its position, the action may be brought within a further period of two months.

Any natural or legal person may, under the conditions laid down in the preceding paragraphs, complain to the Court that an institution, body, office or agency of the Union has failed to address to that person any act other than a recommendation or an opinion.

Article 266 (ex Article 233 TEC)

The institution whose act has been declared void or whose failure to act has been declared contrary to the Treaties shall be required to take the necessary measures to comply with the judgment of the Court of Justice of the European Union.

This obligation shall not affect any obligation which may result from the application of the second paragraph of Article 340.

Article 267 (ex Article 234 TEC)

The Court of Justice of the European Union shall have jurisdiction to give preliminary rulings concerning:

(a) the interpretation of the Treaties;

(b) the validity and interpretation of acts of the institutions, bodies, offices or agencies of the Union;

Where such a question is raised before any court or tribunal of a Member State, that court or tribunal may, if it considers that a decision on the question is necessary to enable it to give judgment, request the Court to give a ruling thereon.

Where any such question is raised in a case pending before a court or tribunal of a Member State against whose decisions there is no judicial remedy under national law, that court or tribunal shall bring the matter before the Court.

If such a question is raised in a case pending before a court or tribunal of a Member State with regard to a person in custody, the Court of Justice of the European Union shall act with the minimum of delay.

Article 268 (ex Article 235 TEC)

The Court of Justice of the European Union shall have jurisdiction in disputes relating to compensation for damage provided for in the second and third paragraphs of Article 340.

Article 269

The Court of Justice shall have jurisdiction to decide on the legality of an act adopted by the European Council or by the Council pursuant to Article 7 of the Treaty on European Union solely at the request of the Member State concerned by a determination of the European Council or of the Council and in respect solely of the procedural stipulations contained in that Article.

Such a request must be made within one month from the date of such determination.

The Court shall rule within one month from the date of the request.

Article 270 (ex Article 236 TEC)

The Court of Justice of the European Union shall have jurisdiction in any dispute between the Union and its servants within the limits and under the conditions laid down in the Staff Regulations of Officials and the Conditions of Employment of other servants of the Union.

Article 271 (ex Article 237 TEC)

The Court of Justice of the European Union shall, within the limits hereinafter laid down, have jurisdiction in disputes concerning:

(a) the fulfilment by Member States of obligations under the Statute of the European Investment Bank. In this connection, the Board of Directors of the Bank shall enjoy the powers conferred upon the Commission by Article 258;

(b) measures adopted by the Board of Governors of the European Investment Bank. In this connection, any Member State, the Commission or the Board of Directors of the Bank may institute proceedings under the conditions laid down in Article 263;

(c) measures adopted by the Board of Directors of the European Investment Bank. Proceedings against such measures may be instituted only by Member States or by the Commission, under the conditions laid down in Article 263, and solely on the grounds of non-compliance with the procedure provided for in Article 19(2), (5), (6) and (7) of the Statute of the Bank;

(d) the fulfilment by national central banks of obligations under the Treaties and the Statute of the ESCB and of the ECB. In this connection the powers of the Governing Council of the European Central Bank in respect of national central banks shall be the same as those conferred upon the Commission in respect of Member States by Article 258. If the Court finds that a national central bank has failed to fulfil an obligation under the Treaties, that bank shall be required to take the necessary measures to comply with the judgment of the Court.

Article 272 (ex Article 238 TEC)

The Court of Justice of the European Union shall have jurisdiction to give judgment pursuant to any arbitration clause contained in a contract concluded by or on behalf of the Union, whether that contract be governed by public or private law.

Article 273 (ex Article 239 TEC)

The Court of Justice shall have jurisdiction in any dispute between Member States which relates to the subject matter of the Treaties if the dispute is submitted to it under a special agreement between the parties.

Article 274 (ex Article 240 TEC)

Save where jurisdiction is conferred on the Court of Justice of the European Union by the Treaties, disputes to which the Union is a party shall not on that ground be excluded from the jurisdiction of the courts or tribunals of the Member States.

Article 275

The Court of Justice of the European Union shall not have jurisdiction with respect to the provisions relating to the common foreign and security policy nor with respect to acts adopted on the basis of those provisions.

However, the Court shall have jurisdiction to monitor compliance with Article 40 of the Treaty on European Union and to rule on proceedings, brought in accordance with the conditions laid down in the fourth paragraph of Article 263 of this Treaty, reviewing the legality of decisions providing for restrictive measures against natural or legal persons adopted by the Council on the basis of Chapter 2 of Title V of the Treaty on European Union.

Article 276

In exercising its powers regarding the provisions of Chapters 4 and 5 of Title V of Part Three relating to the area of freedom, security and justice, the Court of Justice of the European Union shall have no jurisdiction to review the validity or proportionality of operations carried out by the police or other law-enforcement services of a Member State or the exercise of the responsibilities incumbent upon Member States with regard to the maintenance of law and order and the safeguarding of internal security.

Article 277 (ex Article 241 TEC)

Notwithstanding the expiry of the period laid down in Article 263, sixth paragraph, any party may, in proceedings in which an act of general application adopted by an institution, body, office or agency of the Union is at issue, plead the grounds specified in Article 263, second paragraph, in order to invoke before the Court of Justice of the European Union the inapplicability of that act.

Article 278 (ex Article 242 TEC)

Actions brought before the Court of Justice of the European Union shall not have suspensory effect. The Court may, however, if it considers that circumstances so require, order that application of the contested act be suspended.

Article 279 (ex Article 243 TEC)

The Court of Justice of the European Union may in any cases before it prescribe any necessary interim measures.

Article 280 (ex Article 244 TEC)

The judgments of the Court of Justice of the European Union shall be enforceable under the conditions laid down in Article 299.

Article 281 (ex Article 245 TEC)

The Statute of the Court of Justice of the European Union shall be laid down in a separate Protocol.

The European Parliament and the Council, acting in accordance with the ordinary legislative procedure, may amend the provisions of the Statute, with the exception of Title I and Article 64. The European Parliament and the Council shall act either at the request of the Court of Justice and after consultation of the Commission, or on a proposal from the Commission and after consultation of the Court of Justice.

Section 6 The European Central Bank

Article 282

1. The European Central Bank, together with the national central banks, shall constitute the European System of Central Banks (ESCB). The European Central Bank, together with the national central banks of the Member States whose currency is the euro, which constitute the Eurosystem, shall conduct the monetary policy of the Union.

2. The ESCB shall be governed by the decision-making bodies of the European Central Bank. The primary objective of the ESCB shall be to maintain price stability. Without prejudice to that objective, it shall support the general economic policies in the Union in order to contribute to the achievement of the latter's objectives.

3. The European Central Bank shall have legal personality. It alone may authorise the issue of the euro. It shall be independent in the exercise of its powers and in the management of its finances. Union institutions, bodies, offices and agencies and the governments of the Member States shall respect that independence.

4. The European Central Bank shall adopt such measures as are necessary to carry out its tasks in accordance with Articles 127 to 133, with Article 138, and with the conditions laid down in the Statute of the ESCB and of the ECB. In accordance with these same Articles, those Member States whose currency is not the euro, and their central banks, shall retain their powers in monetary matters.

5. Within the areas falling within its responsibilities, the European Central Bank shall be consulted on all proposed Union acts, and all proposals for regulation at national level, and may give an opinion.

Article 283 (ex Article 112 TEC)

1. The Governing Council of the European Central Bank shall comprise the members of the Executive Board of the European Central Bank and the Governors of the national central banks of the Member States whose currency is the euro.

2. The Executive Board shall comprise the President, the Vice-President and four other members.

The President, the Vice-President and the other members of the Executive Board shall be appointed by the European Council, acting by a qualified majority, from among persons of recognised standing and professional experience in monetary or banking matters, on a recommendation from the Council, after it has consulted the European Parliament and the Governing Council of the European Central Bank.

Their term of office shall be eight years and shall not be renewable.

Only nationals of Member States may be members of the Executive Board.

Article 284 (ex Article 113 TEC)

1. The President of the Council and a Member of the Commission may participate, without having the right to vote, in meetings of the Governing Council of the European Central Bank.

The President of the Council may submit a motion for deliberation to the Governing Council of the European Central Bank.

2. The President of the European Central Bank shall be invited to participate in Council meetings when the Council is discussing matters relating to the objectives and tasks of the ESCB.

3. The European Central Bank shall address an annual report on the activities of the ESCB and on the monetary policy of both the previous and current year to the European Parliament, the Council and the Commission, and also to the European Council. The President of the European Central Bank shall present this report to the Council and to the European Parliament, which may hold a general debate on that basis.

The President of the European Central Bank and the other members of the Executive Board may, at the request of the European Parliament or on their own initiative, be heard by the competent committees of the European Parliament.

Section 7 The Court of Auditors

Article 285 (ex Article 246 TEC)

The Court of Auditors shall carry out the Union's audit.

It shall consist of one national of each Member State. Its Members shall be completely independent in the performance of their duties, in the Union's general interest.

Article 286 (ex Article 247 TEC)

1. The Members of the Court of Auditors shall be chosen from among persons who belong or have belonged in their respective States to external audit bodies or who are especially qualified for this office. Their independence must be beyond doubt.

2. The Members of the Court of Auditors shall be appointed for a term of six years. The Council, after consulting the European Parliament, shall adopt the list of Members drawn up in accordance with the proposals made by each Member State. The term of office of the Members of the Court of Auditors shall be renewable.

They shall elect the President of the Court of Auditors from among their number for a term of three years. The President may be re-elected.

3. In the performance of these duties, the Members of the Court of Auditors shall neither seek nor take instructions from any government or from any other body. The Members of the Court of Auditors shall refrain from any action incompatible with their duties.

4. The Members of the Court of Auditors may not, during their term of office, engage in any other occupation, whether gainful or not. When entering upon their duties they shall give a solemn undertaking that, both during and after their term of office, they will respect the obligations arising therefrom and in particular their duty to behave with integrity and discretion as regards the acceptance, after they have ceased to hold office, of certain appointments or benefits.

5. Apart from normal replacement, or death, the duties of a Member of the Court of Auditors shall end when he resigns, or is compulsorily retired by a ruling of the Court of Justice pursuant to paragraph 6.

The vacancy thus caused shall be filled for the remainder of the Member's term of office.

Save in the case of compulsory retirement, Members of the Court of Auditors shall remain in office until they have been replaced.

6. A Member of the Court of Auditors may be deprived of his office or of his right to a pension or other benefits in its stead only if the Court of Justice, at the request of the Court of Auditors, finds that he no longer fulfils the requisite conditions or meets the obligations arising from his office.

7. The Council shall determine the conditions of employment of the President and the Members of the Court of Auditors and in particular their salaries, allowances and pensions. It shall also determine any payment to be made instead of remuneration.

8. The provisions of the Protocol on the privileges and immunities of the European Union applicable to the Judges of the Court of Justice of the European Union shall also apply to the Members of the Court of Auditors.

Article 287 (ex Article 248 TEC)

1. The Court of Auditors shall examine the accounts of all revenue and expenditure of the Union. It shall also examine the accounts of all revenue and expenditure of all bodies, offices or agencies set up by the Union in so far as the relevant constituent instrument does not preclude such examination.

The Court of Auditors shall provide the European Parliament and the Council with a statement of assurance as to the reliability of the accounts and the legality and regularity of the underlying transactions which shall be published in the *Official Journal of the European Union*. This statement may be supplemented by specific assessments for each major area of Union activity.

2. The Court of Auditors shall examine whether all revenue has been received and all expenditure incurred in a lawful and regular manner and whether the financial management has been sound. In doing so, it shall report in particular on any cases of irregularity.

The audit of revenue shall be carried out on the basis both of the amounts established as due and the amounts actually paid to the Union.

The audit of expenditure shall be carried out on the basis both of commitments undertaken and payments made.

These audits may be carried out before the closure of accounts for the financial year in question.

3. The audit shall be based on records and, if necessary, performed on the spot in the other institutions of the Union, on the premises of any body, office or agency which manages revenue or expenditure on behalf of the Union and in the Member States, including on the premises of any natural or legal person in receipt of payments from the budget. In the Member States the audit shall be carried out in liaison with national audit bodies or, if these do not have the necessary powers, with the competent national departments. The Court of Auditors and the national audit bodies of the Member States shall cooperate in a spirit of trust while maintaining their independence. These bodies or departments shall inform the Court of Auditors whether they intend to take part in the audit.

The other institutions of the Union, any bodies, offices or agencies managing revenue or expenditure on behalf of the Union, any natural or legal person in receipt of payments from the budget, and the national audit bodies or, if these do not have the necessary powers, the competent national departments, shall forward to the Court of Auditors, at its request, any document or information necessary to carry out its task.

In respect of the European Investment Bank's activity in managing Union expenditure and revenue, the Court's rights of access to information held by the Bank shall be governed by an agreement between the Court, the Bank and the Commission. In the absence of an agreement, the Court shall nevertheless have access to information necessary for the audit of Union expenditure and revenue managed by the Bank.

4. The Court of Auditors shall draw up an annual report after the close of each financial year. It shall be forwarded to the other institutions of the Union and shall be published, together with the replies of these institutions to the observations of the Court of Auditors, in the *Official Journal of the European Union*.

The Court of Auditors may also, at any time, submit observations, particularly in the form of special reports, on specific questions and deliver opinions at the request of one of the other institutions of the Union.

It shall adopt its annual reports, special reports or opinions by a majority of its Members. However, it may establish internal chambers in order to adopt certain categories of reports or opinions under the conditions laid down by its Rules of Procedure.

It shall assist the European Parliament and the Council in exercising their powers of control over the implementation of the budget.

The Court of Auditors shall draw up its Rules of Procedure. Those rules shall require the approval of the Council.

Chapter 2 Legal acts of the Union, adoption procedures and other provisions

Section 1 The legal acts of the Union

Article 288 (ex Article 249 TEC)

To exercise the Union's competences, the institutions shall adopt regulations, directives, decisions, recommendations and opinions.

A regulation shall have general application. It shall be binding in its entirety and directly applicable in all Member States.

A directive shall be binding, as to the result to be achieved, upon each Member State to which it is addressed, but shall leave to the national authorities the choice of form and methods.

A decision shall be binding in its entirety. A decision which specifies those to whom it is addressed shall be binding only on them.

Recommendations and opinions shall have no binding force.

Article 289

1. The ordinary legislative procedure shall consist in the joint adoption by the European Parliament and the Council of a regulation, directive or decision on a proposal from the Commission. This procedure is defined in Article 294.
2. In the specific cases provided for by the Treaties, the adoption of a regulation, directive or decision by the European Parliament with the participation of the Council, or by the latter with the participation of the European Parliament, shall constitute a special legislative procedure.
3. Legal acts adopted by legislative procedure shall constitute legislative acts.
4. In the specific cases provided for by the Treaties, legislative acts may be adopted on the initiative of a group of Member States or of the European Parliament, on a recommendation from the European Central Bank or at the request of the Court of Justice or the European Investment Bank.

Article 290

1. A legislative act may delegate to the Commission the power to adopt non-legislative acts of general application to supplement or amend certain non-essential elements of the legislative act.

The objectives, content, scope and duration of the delegation of power shall be explicitly defined in the legislative acts. The essential elements of an area shall be reserved for the legislative act and accordingly shall not be the subject of a delegation of power.

2. Legislative acts shall explicitly lay down the conditions to which the delegation is subject; these conditions may be as follows:
   (a) the European Parliament or the Council may decide to revoke the delegation;
   (b) the delegated act may enter into force only if no objection has been expressed by the European Parliament or the Council within a period set by the legislative act.

For the purposes of (a) and (b), the European Parliament shall act by a majority of its component members, and the Council by a qualified majority.

3. The adjective 'delegated' shall be inserted in the title of delegated acts.

Article 291

1. Member States shall adopt all measures of national law necessary to implement legally binding Union acts.

2. Where uniform conditions for implementing legally binding Union acts are needed, those acts shall confer implementing powers on the Commission, or, in duly justified specific cases and in the cases provided for in Articles 24 and 26 of the Treaty on European Union, on the Council.

3. For the purposes of paragraph 2, the European Parliament and the Council, acting by means of regulations in accordance with the ordinary legislative procedure, shall lay down in advance the rules and general principles concerning mechanisms for control by Member States of the Commission's exercise of implementing powers.

4. The word 'implementing' shall be inserted in the title of implementing acts.

Article 292

The Council shall adopt recommendations. It shall act on a proposal from the Commission in all cases where the Treaties provide that it shall adopt acts on a proposal from the Commission. It shall act unanimously in those areas in which unanimity is required for the adoption of a Union act. The Commission, and the European Central Bank in the specific cases provided for in the Treaties, shall adopt recommendations.

Section 2 Procedures for the adoption of acts and other provisions

Article 293 (ex Article 250 TEC)

1. Where, pursuant to the Treaties, the Council acts on a proposal from the Commission, it may amend that proposal only by acting unanimously, except in the cases referred to in paragraphs 10 and 13 of Article 294, in Articles 310, 312 and 314 and in the second paragraph of Article 315.

2. As long as the Council has not acted, the Commission may alter its proposal at any time during the procedures leading to the adoption of a Union act.

Article 294 (ex Article 251 TEC)

1. Where reference is made in the Treaties to the ordinary legislative procedure for the adoption of an act, the following procedure shall apply.

2. The Commission shall submit a proposal to the European Parliament and the Council.

First reading

3. The European Parliament shall adopt its position at first reading and communicate it to the Council.

4. If the Council approves the European Parliament's position, the act concerned shall be adopted in the wording which corresponds to the position of the European Parliament.

5. If the Council does not approve the European Parliament's position, it shall adopt its position at first reading and communicate it to the European Parliament.

6. The Council shall inform the European Parliament fully of the reasons which led it to adopt its position at first reading. The Commission shall inform the European Parliament fully of its position.

Second reading

7. If, within three months of such communication, the European Parliament:

(a) approves the Council's position at first reading or has not taken a decision, the act concerned shall be deemed to have been adopted in the wording which corresponds to the position of the Council;

(b) rejects, by a majority of its component members, the Council's position at first reading, the proposed act shall be deemed not to have been adopted;

(c) proposes, by a majority of its component members, amendments to the Council's position at first reading, the text thus amended shall be forwarded to the Council and to the Commission, which shall deliver an opinion on those amendments.

8. If, within three months of receiving the European Parliament's amendments, the Council, acting by a qualified majority:

(a) approves all those amendments, the act in question shall be deemed to have been adopted;

(b) does not approve all the amendments, the President of the Council, in agreement with the President of the European Parliament, shall within six weeks convene a meeting of the Conciliation Committee.

9. The Council shall act unanimously on the amendments on which the Commission has delivered a negative opinion.

Conciliation

10. The Conciliation Committee, which shall be composed of the members of the Council or their representatives and an equal number of members representing the European Parliament, shall have the task of reaching agreement on a joint text, by a qualified majority of the members of the Council or their representatives and by a majority of the members representing the European Parliament within six weeks of its being convened, on the basis of the positions of the European Parliament and the Council at second reading.

11. The Commission shall take part in the Conciliation Committee's proceedings and shall take all necessary initiatives with a view to reconciling the positions of the European Parliament and the Council.

12. If, within six weeks of its being convened, the Conciliation Committee does not approve the joint text, the proposed act shall be deemed not to have been adopted.

Third reading

13. If, within that period, the Conciliation Committee approves a joint text, the European Parliament, acting by a majority of the votes cast, and the Council, acting by a qualified majority, shall each have a period of six weeks from that approval in which to adopt the act in question in accordance with the joint text. If they fail to do so, the proposed act shall be deemed not to have been adopted.

14. The periods of three months and six weeks referred to in this Article shall be extended by a maximum of one month and two weeks respectively at the initiative of the European Parliament or the Council.

Special provisions

15. Where, in the cases provided for in the Treaties, a legislative act is submitted to the ordinary legislative procedure on the initiative of a group of Member States, on a recommendation by the European Central Bank, or at the request of the Court of Justice, paragraph 2, the second sentence of paragraph 6, and paragraph 9 shall not apply.

In such cases, the European Parliament and the Council shall communicate the proposed act to the Commission with their positions at first and second readings. The European Parliament or the Council may request the opinion of the Commission throughout the procedure, which the Commission may also deliver on its own initiative. It may also, if it deems it necessary, take part in the Conciliation Committee in accordance with paragraph 11.

Article 295

The European Parliament, the Council and the Commission shall consult each other and by common agreement make arrangements for their cooperation. To that end, they may, in compliance with the Treaties, conclude interinstitutional agreements which may be of a binding nature.

Article 296 (ex Article 253 TEC)

Where the Treaties do not specify the type of act to be adopted, the institutions shall select it on a case-by-case basis, in compliance with the applicable procedures and with the principle of proportionality.

Legal acts shall state the reasons on which they are based and shall refer to any proposals, initiatives, recommendations, requests or opinions required by the Treaties.

When considering draft legislative acts, the European Parliament and the Council shall refrain from adopting acts not provided for by the relevant legislative procedure in the area in question.

Article 297 (ex Article 254 TEC)

1. Legislative acts adopted under the ordinary legislative procedure shall be signed by the President of the European Parliament and by the President of the Council.

Legislative acts adopted under a special legislative procedure shall be signed by the President of the institution which adopted them.

Legislative acts shall be published in the *Official Journal of the European Union*. They shall enter into force on the date specified in them or, in the absence thereof, on the twentieth day following that of their publication.

2. Non-legislative acts adopted in the form of regulations, directives or decisions, when the latter do not specify to whom they are addressed, shall be signed by the President of the institution which adopted them.

Regulations and directives which are addressed to all Member States, as well as decisions which do not specify to whom they are addressed, shall be published in the *Official Journal of the European Union*. They shall enter into force on the date specified in them or, in the absence thereof, on the twentieth day following that of their publication.

Other directives, and decisions which specify to whom they are addressed, shall be notified to those to whom they are addressed and shall take effect upon such notification.

Article 298

1. In carrying out their missions, the institutions, bodies, offices and agencies of the Union shall have the support of an open, efficient and independent European administration.

2. In compliance with the Staff Regulations and the Conditions of Employment adopted on the basis of Article 336, the European Parliament and the Council, acting by means of regulations in accordance with the ordinary legislative procedure, shall establish provisions to that end.

Article 299 (ex Article 256 TEC)

Acts of the Council, the Commission or the European Central Bank which impose a pecuniary obligation on persons other than States, shall be enforceable.

Enforcement shall be governed by the rules of civil procedure in force in the State in the territory of which it is carried out. The order for its enforcement shall be appended to the decision, without other formality than verification of the authenticity of the decision, by the national authority which the government of each Member State shall designate for this purpose and shall make known to the Commission and to the Court of Justice of the European Union.

When these formalities have been completed on application by the party concerned, the latter may proceed to enforcement in accordance with the national law, by bringing the matter directly before the competent authority.

Enforcement may be suspended only by a decision of the Court. However, the courts of the country concerned shall have jurisdiction over complaints that enforcement is being carried out in an irregular manner.

Chapter 3 The Union's advisory bodies

Article 300

1. The European Parliament, the Council and the Commission shall be assisted by an Economic and Social Committee and a Committee of the Regions, exercising advisory functions.

2. The Economic and Social Committee shall consist of representatives of organisations of employers, of the employed, and of other parties representative of civil society, notably in socio-economic, civic, professional and cultural areas.

3. The Committee of the Regions shall consist of representatives of regional and local bodies who either hold a regional or local authority electoral mandate or are politically accountable to an elected assembly.

4. The members of the Economic and Social Committee and of the Committee of the Regions shall not be bound by any mandatory instructions. They shall be completely independent in the performance of their duties, in the Union's general interest.

5. The rules referred to in paragraphs 2 and 3 governing the nature of the composition of the Committees shall be reviewed at regular intervals by the Council to take account of economic, social and demographic developments within the Union. The Council, on a proposal from the Commission, shall adopt decisions to that end.

Section 1 The Economic and Social Committee

Article 301 (ex Article 258 TEC)

The number of members of the Economic and Social Committee shall not exceed 350.

The Council, acting unanimously on a proposal from the Commission, shall adopt a decision determining the Committee's composition.

The Council shall determine the allowances of members of the Committee.

Article 302 (ex Article 259 TEC)

1. The members of the Committee shall be appointed for five years The Council shall adopt the list of members drawn up in accordance with the proposals made by each Member State. The term of office of the members of the Committee shall be renewable.

2. The Council shall act after consulting the Commission. It may obtain the opinion of European bodies which are representative of the various economic and social sectors and of civil society to which the Union's activities are of concern.

Article 303 (ex Article 260 TEC)

The Committee shall elect its chairman and officers from among its members for a term of two and a half years.

It shall adopt its Rules of Procedure.

The Committee shall be convened by its chairman at the request of the European Parliament, the Council or of the Commission. It may also meet on its own initiative.

Article 304 (ex Article 262 TEC)

The Committee shall be consulted by the European Parliament, by the Council or by the Commission where the Treaties so provide. The Committee may be consulted by these institutions in all cases in which they consider it appropriate. It may issue an opinion on its own initiative in cases in which it considers such action appropriate.

The European Parliament, the Council or the Commission shall, if it considers it necessary, set the Committee, for the submission of its opinion, a time limit which may not be less than one month from the date on which the chairman receives notification to this effect. Upon expiry of the time limit, the absence of an opinion shall not prevent further action.

The opinion of the Committee, together with a record of the proceedings, shall be forwarded to the European Parliament, to the Council and to the Commission.

Section 2 The Committee of the Regions

Article 305 (ex Article 263, second, third and fourth paragraphs, TEC)

The number of members of the Committee of the Regions shall not exceed 350.

The Council, acting unanimously on a proposal from the Commission, shall adopt a decision determining the Committee's composition.

The members of the Committee and an equal number of alternate members shall be appointed for five years. Their term of office shall be renewable. The Council shall adopt the list of members and alternate members drawn up in accordance with the proposals made by each Member State. When the mandate referred to in Article 300(3) on the basis of which they were proposed comes to an end, the term of office of members of the Committee shall terminate automatically and they shall then be replaced for the remainder of the said term of office in accordance with the same procedure. No member of the Committee shall at the same time be a Member of the European Parliament.

Article 306 (ex Article 264 TEC)

The Committee of the Regions shall elect its chairman and officers from among its members for a term of two and a half years.

It shall adopt its Rules of Procedure.

The Committee shall be convened by its chairman at the request of the European Parliament, the Council or of the Commission. It may also meet on its own initiative.

Article 307 (ex Article 265 TEC)

The Committee of the Regions shall be consulted by the European Parliament, by the Council or by the Commission where the Treaties so provide and in all other cases, in particular those which concern cross-border cooperation, in which one of these institutions considers it appropriate.

The European Parliament, the Council or the Commission shall, if it considers it necessary, set the Committee, for the submission of its opinion, a time limit which may not be less than one month from the date on which the chairman receives notification to this effect. Upon expiry of the time limit, the absence of an opinion shall not prevent further action.

Where the Economic and Social Committee is consulted pursuant to Article 304, the Committee of the Regions shall be informed by the European Parliament, the Council or the Commission of the request for an opinion. Where it considers that specific regional interests are involved, the Committee of the Regions may issue an opinion on the matter.

It may issue an opinion on its own initiative in cases in which it considers such action appropriate.

The opinion of the Committee, together with a record of the proceedings, shall be forwarded to the European Parliament, to the Council and to the Commission.

Chapter 4 The European Investment Bank

Article 308 (ex Article 266 TEC)

The European Investment Bank shall have legal personality.

The members of the European Investment Bank shall be the Member States.

The Statute of the European Investment Bank is laid down in a Protocol annexed to the Treaties. The Council acting unanimously in accordance with a special legislative procedure, at the request of the European Investment Bank and after consulting the European Parliament and the Commission, or on a proposal from the Commission and after consulting the European Parliament and the European Investment Bank, may amend the Statute of the Bank.

Article 309 (ex Article 267 TEC)

The task of the European Investment Bank shall be to contribute, by having recourse to the capital market and utilising its own resources, to the balanced and steady development of the internal market in the interest of the Union. For this purpose the Bank shall, operating on a non-profit-making basis, grant loans and give guarantees which facilitate the financing of the following projects in all sectors of the economy:

(a) projects for developing less-developed regions;

(b) projects for modernising or converting undertakings or for developing fresh activities called for by the establishment or functioning of the internal market, where these projects are of such a size or nature that they cannot be entirely financed by the various means available in the individual Member States;

(c) projects of common interest to several Member States which are of such a size or nature that they cannot be entirely financed by the various means available in the individual Member States.

In carrying out its task, the Bank shall facilitate the financing of investment programmes in conjunction with assistance from the Structural Funds and other Union Financial Instruments.

Title II Financial provisions

Article 310 (ex Article 268 TEC)

1. All items of revenue and expenditure of the Union shall be included in estimates to be drawn up for each financial year and shall be shown in the budget.

The Union's annual budget shall be established by the European Parliament and the Council in accordance with Article 314.

The revenue and expenditure shown in the budget shall be in balance.

2. The expenditure shown in the budget shall be authorised for the annual budgetary period in accordance with the regulation referred to in Article 322.

3. The implementation of expenditure shown in the budget shall require the prior adoption of a legally binding Union act providing a legal basis for its action and for the implementation of the corresponding expenditure in accordance with the regulation referred to in Article 322, except in cases for which that law provides.

4. With a view to maintaining budgetary discipline, the Union shall not adopt any act which is likely to have appreciable implications for the budget without providing an assurance that the expenditure arising from such an act is capable of being financed within the limit of the Union's own resources and in compliance with the multiannual financial framework referred to in Article 312.

5. The budget shall be implemented in accordance with the principle of sound financial management. Member States shall cooperate with the Union to ensure that the appropriations entered in the budget are used in accordance with this principle.

6. The Union and the Member States, in accordance with Article 325, shall counter fraud and any other illegal activities affecting the financial interests of the Union.

Chapter 1 The Union's own resources

Article 311 (ex Article 269 TEC)

The Union shall provide itself with the means necessary to attain its objectives and carry through its policies.

Without prejudice to other revenue, the budget shall be financed wholly from own resources.

The Council, acting in accordance with a special legislative procedure, shall unanimously and after consulting the European Parliament adopt a decision laying down the provisions relating to the system of own resources of the Union. In this context it may establish new categories of own resources or abolish an existing category. That decision shall not enter into force until it is approved by the Member States in accordance with their respective constitutional requirements.

The Council, acting by means of regulations in accordance with a special legislative procedure, shall lay down implementing measures for the Union's own resources system in so far as this is provided for in the decision adopted on the basis of the third paragraph. The Council shall act after obtaining the consent of the European Parliament.

Chapter 2 The multiannual financial framework

Article 312

1. The multiannual financial framework shall ensure that Union expenditure develops in an orderly manner and within the limits of its own resources.

It shall be established for a period of at least five years.

The annual budget of the Union shall comply with the multiannual financial framework.

2. The Council, acting in accordance with a special legislative procedure, shall adopt a regulation laying down the multiannual financial framework. The Council shall act unanimously after obtaining the consent of the European Parliament, which shall be given by a majority of its component members.

The European Council may, unanimously, adopt a decision authorising the Council to act by a qualified majority when adopting the regulation referred to in the first subparagraph.

3. The financial framework shall determine the amounts of the annual ceilings on commitment appropriations by category of expenditure and of the annual ceiling on payment appropriations. The categories of expenditure, limited in number, shall correspond to the Union's major sectors of activity.

The financial framework shall lay down any other provisions required for the annual budgetary procedure to run smoothly.

4. Where no Council regulation determining a new financial framework has been adopted by the end of the previous financial framework, the ceilings and other provisions corresponding to the last year of that framework shall be extended until such time as that act is adopted.

5. Throughout the procedure leading to the adoption of the financial framework, the European Parliament, the Council and the Commission shall take any measure necessary to facilitate its adoption.

Chapter 3 The Union's annual budget

Article 313 (ex Article 272(1), TEC)

The financial year shall run from 1 January to 31 December.

Article 314 (ex Article 272(2) to (10), TEC)

The European Parliament and the Council, acting in accordance with a special legislative procedure, shall establish the Union's annual budget in accordance with the following provisions.

1. With the exception of the European Central Bank, each institution shall, before 1 July, draw up estimates of its expenditure for the following financial year. The Commission shall consolidate these estimates in a draft budget which may contain different estimates.

The draft budget shall contain an estimate of revenue and an estimate of expenditure.

2. The Commission shall submit a proposal containing the draft budget to the European Parliament and to the Council not later than 1 September of the year preceding that in which the budget is to be implemented.

The Commission may amend the draft budget during the procedure until such time as the Conciliation Committee, referred to in paragraph 5, is convened.

3. The Council shall adopt its position on the draft budget and forward it to the European Parliament not later than 1 October of the year preceding that in which the budget is to be implemented. The Council shall inform the European Parliament in full of the reasons which led it to adopt its position.

4. If, within forty-two days of such communication, the European Parliament:
   - (a) approves the position of the Council, the budget shall be adopted;
   - (b) has not taken a decision, the budget shall be deemed to have been adopted;
   - (c) adopts amendments by a majority of its component members, the amended draft shall be forwarded to the Council and to the Commission. The President of the European Parliament, in agreement with the President of the Council, shall immediately convene a meeting of the Conciliation Committee. However, if within ten days of the draft being forwarded the Council informs the European Parliament that it has approved all its amendments, the Conciliation Committee shall not meet.

5. The Conciliation Committee, which shall be composed of the members of the Council or their representatives and an equal number of members representing the European Parliament, shall have the task of reaching agreement on a joint text, by a qualified majority of the members of the Council or their representatives and by a majority of the representatives of the European Parliament within twenty-one days of its being convened, on the basis of the positions of the European Parliament and the Council.

The Commission shall take part in the Conciliation Committee's proceedings and shall take all the necessary initiatives with a view to reconciling the positions of the European Parliament and the Council.

6. If, within the twenty-one days referred to in paragraph 5, the Conciliation Committee agrees on a joint text, the European Parliament and the Council shall each have a period of fourteen days from the date of that agreement in which to approve the joint text.

7. If, within the period of fourteen days referred to in paragraph 6:

(a) the European Parliament and the Council both approve the joint text or fail to take a decision, or if one of these institutions approves the joint text while the other one fails to take a decision, the budget shall be deemed to be definitively adopted in accordance with the joint text; or

(b) the European Parliament, acting by a majority of its component members, and the Council both reject the joint text, or if one of these institutions rejects the joint text while the other one fails to take a decision, a new draft budget shall be submitted by the Commission; or

(c) the European Parliament, acting by a majority of its component members, rejects the joint text while the Council approves it, a new draft budget shall be submitted by the Commission; or

(d) the European Parliament approves the joint text whilst the Council rejects it, the European Parliament may, within fourteen days from the date of the rejection by the Council and acting by a majority of its component members and three-fifths of the votes cast, decide to confirm all or some of the amendments referred to in paragraph 4(c). Where a European Parliament amendment is not confirmed, the position agreed in the Conciliation Committee on the budget heading which is the subject of the amendment shall be retained. The budget shall be deemed to be definitively adopted on this basis.

8. If, within the twenty-one days referred to in paragraph 5, the Conciliation Committee does not agree on a joint text, a new draft budget shall be submitted by the Commission.

9. When the procedure provided for in this Article has been completed, the President of the European Parliament shall declare that the budget has been definitively adopted.

10. Each institution shall exercise the powers conferred upon it under this Article in compliance with the Treaties and the acts adopted thereunder, with particular regard to the Union's own resources and the balance between revenue and expenditure.

Article 315 (ex Article 273 TEC)

If, at the beginning of a financial year, the budget has not yet been definitively adopted, a sum equivalent to not more than one-twelfth of the budget appropriations for the preceding financial year may be spent each month in respect of any chapter of the budget in accordance with the provisions of the Regulations made pursuant to Article 322; that sum shall not, however, exceed one-twelfth of the appropriations provided for in the same chapter of the draft budget.

The Council on a proposal by the Commission, may, provided that the other conditions laid down in the first paragraph are observed, authorise expenditure in excess of one-twelfth in accordance with the regulations made pursuant to Article 322. The Council shall forward the decision immediately to the European Parliament.

The decision referred to in the second paragraph shall lay down the necessary measures relating to resources to ensure application of this Article, in accordance with the acts referred to in Article 311.

It shall enter into force thirty days following its adoption if the European Parliament, acting by a majority of its component Members, has not decided to reduce this expenditure within that time limit.

Article 316 (ex Article 271 TEC)

In accordance with conditions to be laid down pursuant to Article 322, any appropriations, other than those relating to staff expenditure, that are unexpended at the end of the financial year may be carried forward to the next financial year only.

Appropriations shall be classified under different chapters grouping items of expenditure according to their nature or purpose and subdivided in accordance with the regulations made pursuant to Article 322.

The expenditure of the European Parliament, the European Council and the Council, the Commission and the Court of Justice of the European Union shall be set out in separate parts of the budget, without prejudice to special arrangements for certain common items of expenditure.

Chapter 4 Implementation of the budget and discharge

Article 317 (ex Article 274 TEC)

The Commission shall implement the budget in cooperation with the Member States, in accordance with the provisions of the regulations made pursuant to Article 322, on its own responsibility and within the limits of the appropriations, having regard to the principles of sound financial management. Member States shall cooperate with the Commission to ensure that the appropriations are used in accordance with the principles of sound financial management.

The regulations shall lay down the control and audit obligations of the Member States in the implementation of the budget and the resulting responsibilities. They shall also lay down the responsibilities and detailed rules for each institution concerning its part in effecting its own expenditure.

Within the budget, the Commission may, subject to the limits and conditions laid down in the regulations made pursuant to Article 322, transfer appropriations from one chapter to another or from one subdivision to another.

Article 318 (ex Article 275 TEC)

The Commission shall submit annually to the European Parliament and to the Council the accounts of the preceding financial year relating to the implementation of the budget. The Commission shall also forward to them a financial statement of the assets and liabilities of the Union.

The Commission shall also submit to the European Parliament and to the Council an evaluation report on the Union's finances based on the results achieved, in particular in relation to the indications given by the European Parliament and the Council pursuant to Article 319.

Article 319 (ex Article 276 TEC)

1. The European Parliament, acting on a recommendation from the Council, shall give a discharge to the Commission in respect of the implementation of the budget. To this end, the Council and the European Parliament in turn shall examine the accounts, the financial statement and the evaluation report referred to in Article 318, the annual report by the Court of Auditors together with the replies of the institutions under audit to the observations of the Court of Auditors, the statement of assurance referred to in Article 287(1), second subparagraph and any relevant special reports by the Court of Auditors.

2. Before giving a discharge to the Commission, or for any other purpose in connection with the exercise of its powers over the implementation of the budget, the European Parliament may ask to hear the Commission give evidence with regard to the execution of expenditure or the operation of financial control systems. The Commission shall submit any necessary information to the European Parliament at the latter's request.

3. The Commission shall take all appropriate steps to act on the observations in the decisions giving discharge and on other observations by the European Parliament relating to the execution of expenditure, as well as on comments accompanying the recommendations on discharge adopted by the Council.

At the request of the European Parliament or the Council, the Commission shall report on the measures taken in the light of these observations and comments and in particular on the instructions given to the departments which are responsible for the implementation of the budget. These reports shall also be forwarded to the Court of Auditors.

Chapter 5 Common provisions

Article 320 (ex Article 277 TEC)

The multiannual financial framework and the annual budget shall be drawn up in euro.

Article 321 (ex Article 278 TEC)

The Commission may, provided it notifies the competent authorities of the Member States concerned, transfer into the currency of one of the Member States its holdings in the currency of another Member State, to the extent necessary to enable them to be used for purposes which come within the scope of the Treaties. The Commission shall as far as possible avoid making such transfers if it possesses cash or liquid assets in the currencies which it needs.

The Commission shall deal with each Member State through the authority designated by the State concerned. In carrying out financial operations the Commission shall employ the services of the bank of issue of the Member State concerned or of any other financial institution approved by that State.

Article 322 (ex Article 279 TEC)

1. The European Parliament and the Council, acting in accordance with the ordinary legislative procedure, and after consulting the Court of Auditors, shall adopt by means of regulations:

   (a) the financial rules which determine in particular the procedure to be adopted for establishing and implementing the budget and for presenting and auditing accounts;

   (b) rules providing for checks on the responsibility of financial actors, in particular authorising officers and accounting officers.

2. The Council, acting on a proposal from the Commission and after consulting the European Parliament and the Court of Auditors, shall determine the methods and procedure whereby the budget revenue provided under the arrangements relating to the Union's own resources shall be made available to the Commission, and determine the measures to be applied, if need be, to meet cash requirements.

Article 323

The European Parliament, the Council and the Commission shall ensure that the financial means are made available to allow the Union to fulfil its legal obligations in respect of third parties.

Article 324

Regular meetings between the Presidents of the European Parliament, the Council and the Commission shall be convened, on the initiative of the Commission, under the budgetary procedures referred to in this Title. The Presidents shall take all the necessary steps to promote consultation and the reconciliation of the positions of the institutions over which they preside in order to facilitate the implementation of this Title.

Chapter 6 Combating fraud

Article 325 (ex Article 280 TEC)

1. The Union and the Member States shall counter fraud and any other illegal activities affecting the financial interests of the Union through measures to be taken in accordance with this Article, which shall act as a deterrent and be such as to afford effective protection in the Member States, and in all the Union's institutions, bodies, offices and agencies.

2. Member States shall take the same measures to counter fraud affecting the financial interests of the Union as they take to counter fraud affecting their own financial interests.

3. Without prejudice to other provisions of the Treaties, the Member States shall coordinate their action aimed at protecting the financial interests of the Union against fraud. To this end they shall organise, together with the Commission, close and regular cooperation between the competent authorities.

4. The European Parliament and the Council, acting in accordance with the ordinary legislative procedure, after consulting the Court of Auditors, shall adopt the necessary measures in the fields of

the prevention of and fight against fraud affecting the financial interests of the Union with a view to affording effective and equivalent protection in the Member States and in all the Union's institutions, bodies, offices and agencies.

5. The Commission, in cooperation with Member States, shall each year submit to the European Parliament and to the Council a report on the measures taken for the implementation of this Article.

Title III Enhanced cooperation

Article 326 (ex Articles 27a to 27e, 40 to 40b and 43 to 45 TEU and ex Articles 11 and 11a TEC)

Any enhanced cooperation shall comply with the Treaties and Union law.

Such cooperation shall not undermine the internal market or economic, social and territorial cohesion. It shall not constitute a barrier to or discrimination in trade between Member States, nor shall it distort competition between them.

Article 327 (ex Articles 27a to 27e, 40 to 40b and 43 to 45 TEU and ex Articles 11 and 11a TEC)

Any enhanced cooperation shall respect the competences, rights and obligations of those Member States which do not participate in it. Those Member States shall not impede its implementation by the participating Member States.

Article 328 (ex Articles 27a to 27e, 40 to 40b and 43 to 45 TEU and ex Articles 11 and 11a TEC)

1. When enhanced cooperation is being established, it shall be open to all Member States, subject to compliance with any conditions of participation laid down by the authorising decision. It shall also be open to them at any other time, subject to compliance with the acts already adopted within that framework, in addition to those conditions.

The Commission and the Member States participating in enhanced cooperation shall ensure that they promote participation by as many Member States as possible.

2. The Commission and, where appropriate, the High Representative of the Union for Foreign Affairs and Security Policy shall keep the European Parliament and the Council regularly informed regarding developments in enhanced cooperation.

Article 329 (ex Articles 27a to 27e, 40 to 40b and 43 to 45 TEU and ex Articles 11 and 11a TEC)

1. Member States which wish to establish enhanced cooperation between themselves in one of the areas covered by the Treaties, with the exception of fields of exclusive competence and the common foreign and security policy, shall address a request to the Commission, specifying the scope and objectives of the enhanced cooperation proposed. The Commission may submit a proposal to the Council to that effect. In the event of the Commission not submitting a proposal, it shall inform the Member States concerned of the reasons for not doing so.

Authorisation to proceed with the enhanced cooperation referred to in the first subparagraph shall be granted by the Council, on a proposal from the Commission and after obtaining the consent of the European Parliament.

2. The request of the Member States which wish to establish enhanced cooperation between themselves within the framework of the common foreign and security policy shall be addressed to the Council. It shall be forwarded to the High Representative of the Union for Foreign Affairs and Security Policy, who shall give an opinion on whether the enhanced cooperation proposed is consistent with the Union's common foreign and security policy, and to the Commission, which shall give its opinion in particular on whether the enhanced cooperation proposed is consistent with other Union policies. It shall also be forwarded to the European Parliament for information.

Authorisation to proceed with enhanced cooperation shall be granted by a decision of the Council acting unanimously.

Article 330 (ex Articles 27a to 27e, 40 to 40b and 43 to 45 TEU and ex Articles 11 and 11a TEC)

All members of the Council may participate in its deliberations, but only members of the Council representing the Member States participating in enhanced cooperation shall take part in the vote.

Unanimity shall be constituted by the votes of the representatives of the participating Member States only.

A qualified majority shall be defined in accordance with Article 238(3).

Article 331 (ex Articles 27a to 27e, 40 to 40b and 43 to 45 TEU and ex Articles 11 and 11a TEC)

1. Any Member State which wishes to participate in enhanced cooperation in progress in one of the areas referred to in Article 329(1) shall notify its intention to the Council and the Commission.

The Commission shall, within four months of the date of receipt of the notification, confirm the participation of the Member State concerned. It shall note where necessary that the conditions of participation have been fulfilled and shall adopt any transitional measures necessary with regard to the application of the acts already adopted within the framework of enhanced cooperation.

However, if the Commission considers that the conditions of participation have not been fulfilled, it shall indicate the arrangements to be adopted to fulfil those conditions and shall set a deadline for re-examining the request. On the expiry of that deadline, it shall re-examine the request, in accordance with the procedure set out in the second subparagraph. If the Commission considers that the conditions of participation have still not been met, the Member State concerned may refer the matter to the Council, which shall decide on the request. The Council shall act in accordance with Article 330. It may also adopt the transitional measures referred to in the second subparagraph on a proposal from the Commission.

2. Any Member State which wishes to participate in enhanced cooperation in progress in the framework of the common foreign and security policy shall notify its intention to the Council, the High Representative of the Union for Foreign Affairs and Security Policy and the Commission.

The Council shall confirm the participation of the Member State concerned, after consulting the High Representative of the Union for Foreign Affairs and Security Policy and after noting, where necessary, that the conditions of participation have been fulfilled. The Council, on a proposal from the High Representative, may also adopt any transitional measures necessary with regard to the application of the acts already adopted within the framework of enhanced cooperation. However, if the Council considers that the conditions of participation have not been fulfilled, it shall indicate the arrangements to be adopted to fulfil those conditions and shall set a deadline for re-examining the request for participation.

For the purposes of this paragraph, the Council shall act unanimously and in accordance with Article 330.

Article 332 (ex Articles 27a to 27e, 40 to 40b and 43 to 45 TEU and ex Articles 11 and 11a TEC)

Expenditure resulting from implementation of enhanced cooperation, other than administrative costs entailed for the institutions, shall be borne by the participating Member States, unless all members of the Council, acting unanimously after consulting the European Parliament, decide otherwise.

Article 333 (ex Articles 27a to 27e, 40 to 40b and 43 to 45 TEU and ex Articles 11 and 11a TEC)

1. Where a provision of the Treaties which may be applied in the context of enhanced cooperation stipulates that the Council shall act unanimously, the Council, acting unanimously in accordance with the arrangements laid down in Article 330, may adopt a decision stipulating that it will act by a qualified majority.

2. Where a provision of the Treaties which may be applied in the context of enhanced cooperation stipulates that the Council shall adopt acts under a special legislative procedure, the Council, acting unanimously in accordance with the arrangements laid down in Article 330, may adopt a decision stipulating that it will act under the ordinary legislative procedure. The Council shall act after consulting the European Parliament.

3. Paragraphs 1 and 2 shall not apply to decisions having military or defence implications.

Article 334 (ex Articles 27a to 27e, 40 to 40b and 43 to 45 TEU and ex Articles 11 and 11a TEC)
The Council and the Commission shall ensure the consistency of activities undertaken in the context of enhanced cooperation and the consistency of such activities with the policies of the Union, and shall cooperate to that end.

PART SEVEN GENERAL AND FINAL PROVISIONS

Article 335 (ex Article 282 TEC)
In each of the Member States, the Union shall enjoy the most extensive legal capacity accorded to legal persons under their laws; it may, in particular, acquire or dispose of movable and immovable property and may be a party to legal proceedings. To this end, the Union shall be represented by the Commission. However, the Union shall be represented by each of the institutions, by virtue of their administrative autonomy, in matters relating to their respective operation.

Article 336 (ex Article 283 TEC)
The European Parliament and the Council shall, acting by means of regulations in accordance with the ordinary legislative procedure on a proposal from the Commission and after consulting the other institutions concerned, lay down the Staff Regulations of Officials of the European Union and the Conditions of Employment of other servants of the Union.

Article 337 (ex Article 284 TEC)
The Commission may, within the limits and under conditions laid down by the Council acting by a simple majority in accordance with the provisions of the Treaties, collect any information and carry out any checks required for the performance of the tasks entrusted to it.

Article 338 (ex Article 285 TEC)
1. Without prejudice to Article 5 of the Protocol on the Statute of the European System of Central Banks and of the European Central Bank, the European Parliament and the Council, acting in accordance with the ordinary legislative procedure, shall adopt measures for the production of statistics where necessary for the performance of the activities of the Union.

2. The production of Union statistics shall conform to impartiality, reliability, objectivity, scientific independence, cost-effectiveness and statistical confidentiality; it shall not entail excessive burdens on economic operators.

Article 339 (ex Article 287 TEC)
The members of the institutions of the Union, the members of committees, and the officials and other servants of the Union shall be required, even after their duties have ceased, not to disclose information of the kind covered by the obligation of professional secrecy, in particular information about undertakings, their business relations or their cost components.

Article 340 (ex Article 288 TEC)
The contractual liability of the Union shall be governed by the law applicable to the contract in question.

In the case of non-contractual liability, the Union shall, in accordance with the general principles common to the laws of the Member States, make good any damage caused by its institutions or by its servants in the performance of their duties.

Notwithstanding the second paragraph, the European Central Bank shall, in accordance with the general principles common to the laws of the Member States, make good any damage caused by it or by its servants in the performance of their duties.

The personal liability of its servants towards the Union shall be governed by the provisions laid down in their Staff Regulations or in the Conditions of Employment applicable to them.

Article 341 (ex Article 289 TEC)

The seat of the institutions of the Union shall be determined by common accord of the governments of the Member States.

Article 342 (ex Article 290 TEC)

The rules governing the languages of the institutions of the Union shall, without prejudice to the provisions contained in the Statute of the Court of Justice of the European Union, be determined by the Council, acting unanimously by means of regulations.

Article 343 (ex Article 291 TEC)

The Union shall enjoy in the territories of the Member States such privileges and immunities as are necessary for the performance of its tasks, under the conditions laid down in the Protocol of 8 April 1965 on the privileges and immunities of the European Union. The same shall apply to the European Central Bank and the European Investment Bank.

Article 344 (ex Article 292 TEC)

Member States undertake not to submit a dispute concerning the interpretation or application of the Treaties to any method of settlement other than those provided for therein.

Article 345 (ex Article 295 TEC)

The Treaties shall in no way prejudice the rules in Member States governing the system of property ownership.

Article 346 (ex Article 296 TEC)

1. The provisions of the Treaties shall not preclude the application of the following rules:
   (a) no Member State shall be obliged to supply information the disclosure of which it considers contrary to the essential interests of its security;
   (b) any Member State may take such measures as it considers necessary for the protection of the essential interests of its security which are connected with the production of or trade in arms, munitions and war material; such measures shall not adversely affect the conditions of competition in the internal market regarding products which are not intended for specifically military purposes.

2. The Council may, acting unanimously on a proposal from the Commission, make changes to the list, which it drew up on 15 April 1958, of the products to which the provisions of paragraph 1(b) apply.

Article 347 (ex Article 297 TEC)

Member States shall consult each other with a view to taking together the steps needed to prevent the functioning of the internal market being affected by measures which a Member State may be called upon to take in the event of serious internal disturbances affecting the maintenance of law and order, in the event of war, serious international tension constituting a threat of war, or in order to carry out obligations it has accepted for the purpose of maintaining peace and international security.

Article 348 (ex Article 298 TEC)

If measures taken in the circumstances referred to in Articles 346 and 347 have the effect of distorting the conditions of competition in the internal market, the Commission shall, together with the State concerned, examine how these measures can be adjusted to the rules laid down in the Treaties.

By way of derogation from the procedure laid down in Articles 258 and 259, the Commission or any Member State may bring the matter directly before the Court of Justice if it considers that another Member State is making improper use of the powers provided for in Articles 346 and 347. The Court of Justice shall give its ruling in camera.

Article 349 (ex Article 299(2), second, third and fourth subparagraphs, TEC)

Taking account of the structural social and economic situation of Guadeloupe, French Guiana, Martinique, Réunion, Saint-Barthélemy, Saint-Martin, the Azores, Madeira and the Canary Islands, which is compounded by their remoteness, insularity, small size, difficult topography and climate, economic dependence on a few products, the permanence and combination of which severely restrain their development, the Council, on a proposal from the Commission and after consulting the European Parliament, shall adopt specific measures aimed, in particular, at laying down the conditions of application of the Treaties to those regions, including common policies. Where the specific measures in question are adopted by the Council in accordance with a special legislative procedure, it shall also act on a proposal from the Commission and after consulting the European Parliament.

The measures referred to in the first paragraph concern in particular areas such as customs and trade policies, fiscal policy, free zones, agriculture and fisheries policies, conditions for supply of raw materials and essential consumer goods, State aids and conditions of access to structural funds and to horizontal Union programmes.

The Council shall adopt the measures referred to in the first paragraph taking into account the special characteristics and constraints of the outermost regions without undermining the integrity and the coherence of the Union legal order, including the internal market and common policies.

Article 350 (ex Article 306 TEC)

The provisions of the Treaties shall not preclude the existence or completion of regional unions between Belgium and Luxembourg, or between Belgium, Luxembourg and the Netherlands, to the extent that the objectives of these regional unions are not attained by application of the Treaties.

Article 351 (ex Article 307 TEC)

The rights and obligations arising from agreements concluded before 1 January 1958 or, for acceding States, before the date of their accession, between one or more Member States on the one hand, and one or more third countries on the other, shall not be affected by the provisions of the Treaties.

To the extent that such agreements are not compatible with the Treaties, the Member State or States concerned shall take all appropriate steps to eliminate the incompatibilities established. Member States shall, where necessary, assist each other to this end and shall, where appropriate, adopt a common attitude.

In applying the agreements referred to in the first paragraph, Member States shall take into account the fact that the advantages accorded under the Treaties by each Member State form an integral part of the establishment of the Union and are thereby inseparably linked with the creation of common institutions, the conferring of powers upon them and the granting of the same advantages by all the other Member States.

Article 352 (ex Article 308 TEC)

1. If action by the Union should prove necessary, within the framework of the policies defined in the Treaties, to attain one of the objectives set out in the Treaties, and the Treaties have not provided the necessary powers, the Council, acting unanimously on a proposal from the Commission and after obtaining the consent of the European Parliament, shall adopt the appropriate measures. Where the measures in question are adopted by the Council in accordance with a special legislative procedure, it shall also act unanimously on a proposal from the Commission and after obtaining the consent of the European Parliament.

2. Using the procedure for monitoring the subsidiarity principle referred to in Article 5(3) of the Treaty on European Union, the Commission shall draw national Parliaments' attention to proposals based on this Article.

3. Measures based on this Article shall not entail harmonisation of Member States' laws or regulations in cases where the Treaties exclude such harmonisation.

4. This Article cannot serve as a basis for attaining objectives pertaining to the common foreign and security policy and any acts adopted pursuant to this Article shall respect the limits set out in Article 40, second paragraph, of the Treaty on European Union.

Article 353

Article 48(7) of the Treaty on European Union shall not apply to the following Articles:

- Article 311, third and fourth paragraphs,
- Article 312(2), first subparagraph,
- Article 352, and
- Article 354.

Article 354 (ex Article 309 TEC)

For the purposes of Article 7 of the Treaty on European Union on the suspension of certain rights resulting from Union membership, the member of the European Council or of the Council representing the Member State in question shall not take part in the vote and the Member State in question shall not be counted in the calculation of the one-third or four-fifths of Member States referred to in paragraphs 1 and 2 of that Article. Abstentions by members present in person or represented shall not prevent the adoption of decisions referred to in paragraph 2 of that Article.

For the adoption of the decisions referred to in paragraphs 3 and 4 of Article 7 of the Treaty on European Union, a qualified majority shall be defined in accordance with Article 238(3)(b) of this Treaty.

Where, following a decision to suspend voting rights adopted pursuant to paragraph 3 of Article 7 of the Treaty on European Union, the Council acts by a qualified majority on the basis of a provision of the Treaties, that qualified majority shall be defined in accordance with Article 238(3)(b) of this Treaty, or, where the Council acts on a proposal from the Commission or from the High Representative of the Union for Foreign Affairs and Security Policy, in accordance with Article 238(3)(a).

For the purposes of Article 7 of the Treaty on European Union, the European Parliament shall act by a two-thirds majority of the votes cast, representing the majority of its component Members.

Article 355 (ex Article 299(2), first subparagraph, and Article 299(3) to (6) TEC)

In addition to the provisions of Article 52 of the Treaty on European Union relating to the territorial scope of the Treaties, the following provisions shall apply:

1. The provisions of the Treaties shall apply to Guadeloupe, French Guiana, Martinique, Réunion, Saint-Barthélemy, Saint-Martin, the Azores, Madeira and the Canary Islands in accordance with Article 349.

2. The special arrangements for association set out in Part Four shall apply to the overseas countries and territories listed in Annex II.

The Treaties shall not apply to those overseas countries and territories having special relations with the United Kingdom of Great Britain and Northern Ireland which are not included in the aforementioned list.

3. The provisions of the Treaties shall apply to the European territories for whose external relations a Member State is responsible.

4. The provisions of the Treaties shall apply to the Åland Islands in accordance with the provisions set out in Protocol 2 to the Act concerning the conditions of accession of the Republic of Austria, the Republic of Finland and the Kingdom of Sweden.

5. Notwithstanding Article 52 of the Treaty on European Union and paragraphs 1 to 4 of this Article:

(a) the Treaties shall not apply to the Faeroe Islands;

(b) the Treaties shall not apply to the United Kingdom Sovereign Base Areas of Akrotiri and Dhekelia in Cyprus except to the extent necessary to ensure the implementation of the arrangements set out in the Protocol on the Sovereign Base Areas of the United Kingdom of Great Britain and Northern Ireland in Cyprus annexed to the Act concerning the conditions of accession of the Czech Republic, the Republic of Estonia, the Republic of Cyprus, the Republic of Latvia, the Republic of Lithuania, the Republic of Hungary, the Republic of Malta, the Republic of Poland, the Republic of Slovenia and the Slovak Republic to the European Union and in accordance with the terms of that Protocol;

(c) the Treaties shall apply to the Channel Islands and the Isle of Man only to the extent necessary to ensure the implementation of the arrangements for those islands set out in the Treaty concerning the accession of new Member States to the European Economic Community and to the European Atomic Energy Community signed on 22 January 1972.

6. The European Council may, on the initiative of the Member State concerned, adopt a decision amending the status, with regard to the Union, of a Danish, French or Netherlands country or territory referred to in paragraphs 1 and 2. The European Council shall act unanimously after consulting the Commission.

Article 356 (ex Article 312 TEC)
This Treaty is concluded for an unlimited period.

Article 357 (ex Article 313 TEC)
This Treaty shall be ratified by the High Contracting Parties in accordance with their respective constitutional requirements. The Instruments of ratification shall be deposited with the Government of the Italian Republic.

This Treaty shall enter into force on the first day of the month following the deposit of the Instrument of ratification by the last signatory State to take this step. If, however, such deposit is made less than 15 days before the beginning of the following month, this Treaty shall not enter into force until the first day of the second month after the date of such deposit.

Article 358
The provisions of Article 55 of the Treaty on European Union shall apply to this Treaty.

IN WITNESS WHEREOF, the undersigned Plenipotentiaries have signed this Treaty.

Done at Rome this twenty-fifth day of March in the year one thousand nine hundred and fifty-seven.
(List of signatories not reproduced.)

Charter of Fundamental Rights of the European Union

[OJ 2016 C202/389]*

Preamble

The peoples of Europe, in creating an ever closer union among them, are resolved to share a peaceful future based on common values.

Conscious of its spiritual and moral heritage, the Union is founded on the indivisible, universal values of human dignity, freedom, equality and solidarity; it is based on the principles of democracy and the rule of law. It places the individual at the heart of its activities, by establishing the citizenship of the Union and by creating an area of freedom, security and justice.

The Union contributes to the preservation and to the development of these common values while respecting the diversity of the cultures and traditions of the peoples of Europe as well as the national identities of the Member States and the organisation of their public authorities at national, regional and local levels; it seeks to promote balanced and sustainable development and ensures free movement of persons, goods, services and capital, and the freedom of establishment.

To this end, it is necessary to strengthen the protection of fundamental rights in the light of changes in society, social progress and scientific and technological developments by making those rights more visible in a Charter.

This Charter reaffirms, with due regard for the powers and tasks of the Community and the Union and the principle of subsidiarity, the rights as they result, in particular, from the constitutional traditions and international obligations common to the Member States, the Treaty on European Union, the Community Treaties, the European Convention for the Protection of Human Rights and Fundamental Freedoms, the Social Charters adopted by the Community and by the Council of Europe and the case-law of the Court of Justice of the European Communities and of the European Court of Human Rights. In this context the Charter will be interpreted by the courts of the Union and the Member States with due regard to the explanations prepared under the authority of the Praesidium of the Convention which drafted the Charter and updated under the responsibility of the Praesidium of the European Convention.

* **Editor's Note:** Proclamations and signatures omitted. This is the version re-proclaimed in 2007 and subsequently published in the OJ in 2016. It remains, however, largely the text of 2000.

Enjoyment of these rights entails responsibilities and duties with regard to other persons, to the human community and to future generations.

The Union therefore recognises the rights, freedoms and principles set out hereafter.

Chapter I Dignity

Article 1 Human dignity

Human dignity is inviolable. It must be respected and protected.

Article 2 Right to life

1. Everyone has the right to life.
2. No one shall be condemned to the death penalty, or executed.

Article 3 Right to the integrity of the person

1. Everyone has the right to respect for his or her physical and mental integrity.
2. In the fields of medicine and biology, the following must be respected in particular:
   - the free and informed consent of the person concerned, according to the procedures laid down by law,
   - the prohibition of eugenic practices, in particular those aiming at the selection of persons,
   - the prohibition on making the human body and its parts as such a source of financial gain,
   - the prohibition of the reproductive cloning of human beings.

Article 4 Prohibition of torture and inhuman or degrading treatment or punishment

No one shall be subjected to torture or to inhuman or degrading treatment or punishment.

Article 5 Prohibition of slavery and forced labour

1. No one shall be held in slavery or servitude.
2. No one shall be required to perform forced or compulsory labour.
3. Trafficking in human beings is prohibited.

Chapter II Freedoms

Article 6 Right to liberty and security

Everyone has the right to liberty and security of person.

Article 7 Respect for private and family life

Everyone has the right to respect for his or her private and family life, home and communications.

Article 8 Protection of personal data

1. Everyone has the right to the protection of personal data concerning him or her.

2. Such data must be processed fairly for specified purposes and on the basis of the consent of the person concerned or some other legitimate basis laid down by law. Everyone has the right of access to data which has been collected concerning him or her, and the right to have it rectified.

3. Compliance with these rules shall be subject to control by an independent authority.

Article 9 Right to marry and right to found a family

The right to marry and the right to found a family shall be guaranteed in accordance with the national laws governing the exercise of these rights.

Article 10 Freedom of thought, conscience and religion

1. Everyone has the right to freedom of thought, conscience and religion. This right includes freedom to change religion or belief and freedom, either alone or in community with others and in public or in private, to manifest religion or belief, in worship, teaching, practice and observance.

2. The right to conscientious objection is recognised, in accordance with the national laws governing the exercise of this right.

Article 11 Freedom of expression and information

1. Everyone has the right to freedom of expression. This right shall include freedom to hold opinions and to receive and impart information and ideas without interference by public authority and regardless of frontiers.

2. The freedom and pluralism of the media shall be respected.

Article 12 Freedom of assembly and of association

1. Everyone has the right to freedom of peaceful assembly and to freedom of association at all levels, in particular in political, trade union and civic matters, which implies the right of everyone to form and to join trade unions for the protection of his or her interests.

2. Political parties at Union level contribute to expressing the political will of the citizens of the Union.

Article 13 Freedom of the arts and sciences

The arts and scientific research shall be free of constraint. Academic freedom shall be respected.

Article 14 Right to education

1. Everyone has the right to education and to have access to vocational and continuing training.

2. This right includes the possibility to receive free compulsory education.

3. The freedom to found educational establishments with due respect for democratic principles and the right of parents to ensure the education and teaching of their children in conformity with their religious, philosophical and pedagogical convictions shall be respected, in accordance with the national laws governing the exercise of such freedom and right.

Article 15 Freedom to choose an occupation and right to engage in work

1. Everyone has the right to engage in work and to pursue a freely chosen or accepted occupation.

2. Every citizen of the Union has the freedom to seek employment, to work, to exercise the right of establishment and to provide services in any Member State.

3. Nationals of third countries who are authorised to work in the territories of the Member States are entitled to working conditions equivalent to those of citizens of the Union.

Article 16 Freedom to conduct a business

The freedom to conduct a business in accordance with Union law and national laws and practices is recognised.

Article 17 Right to property

1. Everyone has the right to own, use, dispose of and bequeath his or her lawfully acquired possessions. No one may be deprived of his or her possessions, except in the public interest and in the cases and under the conditions provided for by law, subject to fair compensation being paid in good time for their loss. The use of property may be regulated by law in so far as is necessary for the general interest.

2. Intellectual property shall be protected.

Article 18 Right to asylum

The right to asylum shall be guaranteed with due respect for the rules of the Geneva Convention of 28 July 1951 and the Protocol of 31 January 1967 relating to the status of refugees and in accordance with the Treaty on European Union and the Treaty on the Functioning of the European Union (hereinafter referred to as 'the Treaties').

Article 19 Protection in the event of removal, expulsion or extradition

1. Collective expulsions are prohibited.

2. No one may be removed, expelled or extradited to a State where there is a serious risk that he or she would be subjected to the death penalty, torture or other inhuman or degrading treatment or punishment.

Chapter III Equality

Article 20 Equality before the law

Everyone is equal before the law.

Article 21 Non-discrimination

1. Any discrimination based on any ground such as sex, race, colour, ethnic or social origin, genetic features, language, religion or belief, political or any other opinion, membership of a national minority, property, birth, disability, age or sexual orientation shall be prohibited.

2. Within the scope of application of the Treaties and without prejudice to the special provisions of those Treaties, any discrimination on grounds of nationality shall be prohibited.

Article 22 Cultural, religious and linguistic diversity

The Union shall respect cultural, religious and linguistic diversity.

Article 23 Equality between men and women

Equality between men and women must be ensured in all areas, including employment, work and pay.

The principle of equality shall not prevent the maintenance or adoption of measures providing for specific advantages in favour of the under-represented sex.

Article 24 The rights of the child

1. Children shall have the right to such protection and care as is necessary for their well-being. They may express their views freely. Such views shall be taken into consideration on matters which concern them in accordance with their age and maturity.

2. In all actions relating to children, whether taken by public authorities or private institutions, the child's best interests must be a primary consideration.

3. Every child shall have the right to maintain on a regular basis a personal relationship and direct contact with both his or her parents, unless that is contrary to his or her interests.

Article 25 The rights of the elderly

The Union recognises and respects the rights of the elderly to lead a life of dignity and independence and to participate in social and cultural life.

Article 26 Integration of persons with disabilities

The Union recognises and respects the right of persons with disabilities to benefit from measures designed to ensure their independence, social and occupational integration and participation in the life of the community.

Chapter IV Solidarity

Article 27 Workers' right to information and consultation within the undertaking

Workers or their representatives must, at the appropriate levels, be guaranteed information and consultation in good time in the cases and under the conditions provided for by Community law and national laws and practices.

Article 28 Right of collective bargaining and action

Workers and employers, or their respective organisations, have, in accordance with Community law and national laws and practices, the right to negotiate and conclude collective agreements at the appropriate levels and, in cases of conflicts of interest, to take collective action to defend their interests, including strike action.

Article 29 Right of access to placement services

Everyone has the right of access to a free placement service.

Article 30 Protection in the event of unjustified dismissal

Every worker has the right to protection against unjustified dismissal, in accordance with Union law and national laws and practices.

Article 31 Fair and just working conditions

1. Every worker has the right to working conditions which respect his or her health, safety and dignity.

2. Every worker has the right to limitation of maximum working hours, to daily and weekly rest periods and to an annual period of paid leave.

Article 32 Prohibition of child labour and protection of young people at work

The employment of children is prohibited. The minimum age of admission to employment may not be lower than the minimum school-leaving age, without prejudice to such rules as may be more favourable to young people and except for limited derogations.

Young people admitted to work must have working conditions appropriate to their age and be protected against economic exploitation and any work likely to harm their safety, health or physical, mental, moral or social development or to interfere with their education.

Article 33 Family and professional life

1. The family shall enjoy legal, economic and social protection.

2. To reconcile family and professional life, everyone shall have the right to protection from dismissal for a reason connected with maternity and the right to paid maternity leave and to parental leave following the birth or adoption of a child.

Article 34 Social security and social assistance

1. The Union recognises and respects the entitlement to social security benefits and social services providing protection in cases such as maternity, illness, industrial accidents, dependency or old age, and in the case of loss of employment, in accordance with the rules laid down by Union law and national laws and practices.

2. Everyone residing and moving legally within the European Union is entitled to social security benefits and social advantages in accordance with Union law and national laws and practices.

3. In order to combat social exclusion and poverty, the Union recognises and respects the right to social and housing assistance so as to ensure a decent existence for all those who lack sufficient resources, in accordance with the rules laid down by Union law and national laws and practices.

Article 35 Health care

Everyone has the right of access to preventive health care and the right to benefit from medical treatment under the conditions established by national laws and practices. A high level of human health protection shall be ensured in the definition and implementation of all Union policies and activities.

Article 36 Access to services of general economic interest

The Union recognises and respects access to services of general economic interest as provided for in national laws and practices, in accordance with the Treaties, in order to promote the social and territorial cohesion of the Union.

Article 37 Environmental protection

A high level of environmental protection and the improvement of the quality of the environment must be integrated into the policies of the Union and ensured in accordance with the principle of sustainable development.

Article 38 Consumer protection

Union policies shall ensure a high level of consumer protection.

Chapter V Citizens' rights

Article 39 Right to vote and to stand as a candidate at elections to the European Parliament

1. Every citizen of the Union has the right to vote and to stand as a candidate at elections to the European Parliament in the Member State in which he or she resides, under the same conditions as nationals of that State.

2. Members of the European Parliament shall be elected by direct universal suffrage in a free and secret ballot.

Article 40 Right to vote and to stand as a candidate at municipal elections

Every citizen of the Union has the right to vote and to stand as a candidate at municipal elections in the Member State in which he or she resides under the same conditions as nationals of that State.

Article 41 Right to good administration

1. Every person has the right to have his or her affairs handled impartially, fairly and within a reasonable time by the institutions, bodies, offices and agencies of the Union.

2. This right includes:
   - the right of every person to be heard, before any individual measure which would affect him or her adversely is taken;
   - the right of every person to have access to his or her file, while respecting the legitimate interests of confidentiality and of professional and business secrecy;
   - the obligation of the administration to give reasons for its decisions.

3. Every person has the right to have the Community make good any damage caused by its institutions or by its servants in the performance of their duties, in accordance with the general principles common to the laws of the Member States.

4. Every person may write to the institutions of the Union in one of the languages of the Treaties and must have an answer in the same language.

Article 42 Right of access to documents

Any citizen of the Union, and any natural or legal person residing or having its registered office in a Member State, has a right of access to documents of the institutions, bodies, offices and agencies of the Union, whatever their medium.

Article 43 Ombudsman

Any citizen of the Union and any natural or legal person residing or having its registered office in a Member State has the right to refer to the European Ombudsman cases of maladministration in the activities of the institutions, bodies, offices or agencies of the Union, with the exception of the Court of Justice of the European Union acting in its judicial role.

Article 44 Right to petition

Any citizen of the Union and any natural or legal person residing or having its registered office in a Member State has the right to petition the European Parliament.

Article 45 Freedom of movement and of residence

1. Every citizen of the Union has the right to move and reside freely within the territory of the Member States.

2. Freedom of movement and residence may be granted, in accordance with the Treaties, to nationals of third countries legally resident in the territory of a Member State.

Article 46 Diplomatic and consular protection

Every citizen of the Union shall, in the territory of a third country in which the Member State of which he or she is a national is not represented, be entitled to protection by the diplomatic or consular authorities of any Member State, on the same conditions as the nationals of that Member State.

Chapter VI Justice

Article 47 Right to an effective remedy and to a fair trial

Everyone whose rights and freedoms guaranteed by the law of the Union are violated has the right to an effective remedy before a tribunal in compliance with the conditions laid down in this Article.

Everyone is entitled to a fair and public hearing within a reasonable time by an independent and impartial tribunal previously established by law. Everyone shall have the possibility of being advised, defended and represented.

Legal aid shall be made available to those who lack sufficient resources in so far as such aid is necessary to ensure effective access to justice.

Article 48 Presumption of innocence and right of defence

1. Everyone who has been charged shall be presumed innocent until proved guilty according to law.
2. Respect for the rights of the defence of anyone who has been charged shall be guaranteed.

Article 49 Principles of legality and proportionality of criminal offences and penalties

1. No one shall be held guilty of any criminal offence on account of any act or omission which did not constitute a criminal offence under national law or international law at the time when it was committed. Nor shall a heavier penalty be imposed than that which was applicable at the time the criminal offence was committed. If, subsequent to the commission of a criminal offence, the law provides for a lighter penalty, that penalty shall be applicable.
2. This Article shall not prejudice the trial and punishment of any person for any act or omission which, at the time when it was committed, was criminal according to the general principles recognised by the community of nations.
3. The severity of penalties must not be disproportionate to the criminal offence.

Article 50 Right not to be tried or punished twice in criminal proceedings for the same criminal offence

No one shall be liable to be tried or punished again in criminal proceedings for an offence for which he or she has already been finally acquitted or convicted within the Union in accordance with the law.

Chapter VII General provisions

Article 51 Scope

1. The provisions of this Charter are addressed to the institutions, bodies, offices and agencies of the Union with due regard for the principle of subsidiarity and to the Member States only when they are implementing Union law. They shall therefore respect the rights, observe the principles and promote the application thereof in accordance with their respective powers and respecting the limits of the powers of the Union as conferred on it in the Treaties.
2. The Charter does not extend the field of application of Union law beyond the powers of the Union or establish any new power or task for the Union, or modify powers and tasks as defined in the Treaties.

Article 52 Scope of guaranteed rights

1. Any limitation on the exercise of the rights and freedoms recognised by this Charter must be provided for by law and respect the essence of those rights and freedoms. Subject to the principle of proportionality, limitations may be made only if they are necessary and genuinely meet objectives of general interest recognised by the Union or the need to protect the rights and freedoms of others.
2. Rights recognised by this Charter for which provision is made in the Treaties shall be exercised under the conditions and within the limits defined by those Treaties.
3. In so far as this Charter contains rights which correspond to rights guaranteed by the Convention for the Protection of Human Rights and Fundamental Freedoms, the meaning and scope

of those rights shall be the same as those laid down by the said Convention. This provision shall not prevent Union law providing more extensive protection.

4. In so far as this Charter recognises fundamental rights as they result from the constitutional traditions common to the Member States, those rights shall be interpreted in harmony with those traditions.

5. The provisions of this Charter which contain principles may be implemented by legislative and executive acts taken by institutions, bodies, offices and agencies of the Union, and by acts of Member States when they are implementing Union law, in the exercise of their respective powers. They shall be judicially cognisable only in the interpretation of such acts and in the ruling on their legality.

6. Full account shall be taken of national laws and practices as specified in this Charter.

7. The explanations drawn up as a way of providing guidance in the interpretation of this Charter shall be given due regard by the courts of the Union and of the Member States.

Article 53 Level of protection

Nothing in this Charter shall be interpreted as restricting or adversely affecting human rights and fundamental freedoms as recognised, in their respective fields of application, by Union law and international law and by international agreements to which the Union, the Community or all the Member States are party, including the European Convention for the Protection of Human Rights and Fundamental Freedoms, and by the Member States' constitutions.

Article 54 Prohibition of abuse of rights

Nothing in this Charter shall be interpreted as implying any right to engage in any activity or to perform any act aimed at the destruction of any of the rights and freedoms recognised in this Charter or at their limitation to a greater extent than is provided for herein.

The above text adapts the wording of the Charter proclaimed on 7 December 2000, and will replace it as from the date of entry into force of the Treaty of Lisbon.

European Convention on Human Rights*

Article 1 Obligation to respect Human Rights

The High Contracting Parties shall secure to everyone within their jurisdiction the rights and freedoms defined in Section I of this Convention.

Section I Rights and Freedoms

Article 2 Right to life

1. Everyone's right to life shall be protected by law. No one shall be deprived of his life intentionally save in the execution of a sentence of a court following his conviction of a crime for which this penalty is provided by law.

2. Deprivation of life shall not be regarded as inflicted in contravention of this article when it results from the use of force which is no more than absolutely necessary:

(a) in defence of any person from unlawful violence;
(b) in order to effect a lawful arrest or to prevent escape of a person unlawfully detained;
(c) in action lawfully taken for the purpose of quelling a riot or insurrection.

Article 3 Prohibition of torture

No one shall be subjected to torture or to inhuman or degrading treatment or punishment.

* Rome, 4.XI.1950, as amended by Protocol Nos. 11, 14 and 15. https://www.echr.coe.int/Documents/Convention_ENG.pdf.

Article 4 Prohibition of slavery and forced labour

1. No one shall be held in slavery or servitude.
2. No one shall be required to perform forced or compulsory labour.
3. For the purpose of this article the term 'forced or compulsory labour' shall not include:
   (a) any work required to be done in the ordinary course of detention imposed according to the provisions of Article 5 of this Convention or during conditional release from such detention;
   (b) any service of a military character or, in case of conscientious objectors in countries where they are recognized, service exacted instead of compulsory military service;
   (c) any service exacted in case of an emergency or calamity threatening the life or well-being of the community;
   (d) any work or service which forms part of normal civic obligations.

Article 5 Right to liberty and security

1. Everyone has the right to liberty and security of person. No one shall be deprived of his liberty save in the following cases and in accordance with a procedure prescribed by law:
   (a) the lawful detention of a person after conviction by a competent court;
   (b) the lawful arrest or detention of a person for non-compliance with the lawful order of a court or in order to secure the fulfilment of any obligation prescribed by law;
   (c) the lawful arrest or detention of a person effected for the purpose of bringing him before the competent legal authority of reasonable suspicion of having committed and offence or when it is reasonably considered necessary to prevent his committing an offence or fleeing after having done so;
   (d) the detention of a minor by lawful order for the purpose of educational supervision or his lawful detention for the purpose of bringing him before the competent legal authority;
   (e) the lawful detention of persons for the prevention of the spreading of infectious diseases, of persons of unsound mind, alcoholics or drug addicts, or vagrants;
   (f) the lawful arrest or detention of a person to prevent his effecting an unauthorized entry into the country or of a person against whom action is being taken with a view to deportation or extradition.

2. Everyone who is arrested shall be informed promptly, in a language which he understands, of the reasons for his arrest and the charge against him.

3. Everyone arrested or detained in accordance with the provisions of paragraph 1(c) of this article shall be brought promptly before a judge or other officer authorized by law to exercise judicial power and shall be entitled to trial within a reasonable time or to release pending trial. Release may be conditioned by guarantees to appear for trial.

4. Everyone who is deprived of his liberty by arrest or detention shall be entitled to take proceedings by which the lawfulness of his detention shall be decided speedily by a court and his release ordered if the detention is not lawful.

5. Everyone who has been the victim of arrest or detention in contravention of the provisions of this article shall have an enforceable right to compensation.

Article 6 Right to a fair trial

1. In the determination of his civil rights and obligations or of any criminal charge against him, everyone is entitled to a fair and public hearing within a reasonable time by an independent and impartial tribunal established by law. Judgement shall be pronounced publicly by the press and public may be excluded from all or part of the trial in the interest of morals, public order or national security in a democratic society, where the interests of juveniles or the protection of the private life of the parties so require, or the extent strictly necessary in the opinion of the court in special circumstances where publicity would prejudice the interests of justice.

2. Everyone charged with a criminal offence shall be presumed innocent until proved guilty according to law.

3. Everyone charged with a criminal offence has the following minimum rights:

(a) to be informed promptly, in a language which he understands and in detail, of the nature and cause of the accusation against him;

(b) to have adequate time and the facilities for the preparation of his defence;

(c) to defend himself in person or through legal assistance of his own choosing or, if he has not sufficient means to pay for legal assistance, to be given it free when the interests of justice so require;

(d) to examine or have examined witnesses against him and to obtain the attendance and examination of witnesses on his behalf under the same conditions as witnesses against him;

(e) to have the free assistance of an interpreter if he cannot understand or speak the language used in court.

Article 7 No punishment without law

1. No one shall be held guilty of any criminal offence on account of any act or omission which did not constitute a criminal offence under national or international law at the time when it was committed. Nor shall a heavier penalty be imposed than the one that was applicable at the time the criminal offence was committed.

2. This article shall not prejudice the trial and punishment of any person for any act or omission which, at the time when it was committed, was criminal according the general principles of law recognized by civilized nations.

Article 8 Right to respect for private and family life

1. Everyone has the right to respect for his private and family life, his home and his correspondence.

2. There shall be no interference by a public authority with the exercise of this right except such as is in accordance with the law and is necessary in a democratic society in the interests of national security, public safety or the economic well-being of the country, for the prevention of disorder or crime, for the protection of health or morals, or for the protection of the rights and freedoms of others.

Article 9 Freedom of thought, conscience and religion

1. Everyone has the right to freedom of thought, conscience and religion; this right includes freedom to change his religion or belief, and freedom, either alone or in community with others and in public or private, to manifest his religion or belief, in worship, teaching, practice and observance.

2. Freedom to manifest one's religion or beliefs shall be subject only to such limitations as are prescribed by law and are necessary in a democratic society in the interests of public safety, for the protection of public order, health or morals, or the protection of the rights and freedoms of others.

Article 10 Freedom of expression

1. Everyone has the right to freedom of expression. this right shall include freedom to hold opinions and to receive and impart information an ideas without interference by public authority and regardless of frontiers. This article shall not prevent States from requiring the licensing of broadcasting, television or cinema enterprises.

2. The exercise of these freedoms, since it carries with it duties and responsibilities, may be subject to such formalities, conditions, restrictions or penalties as are prescribed by law and are necessary in a democratic society, in the interests of national security, territorial integrity or public safety, for the prevention of disorder or crime, for the protection of health or morals, for the protection of

the reputation or the rights of others, for preventing the disclosure of information received in confidence, or for maintaining the authority and impartiality of the judiciary.

Article 11 Freedom of assembly and association

1. Everyone has the right to freedom of peaceful assembly and to freedom of association with others, including the right to form and to join trade unions for the protection of his interests.

2. No restrictions shall be placed on the exercise of these rights other than such as are prescribed by law and are necessary in a democratic society in the interests of national security or public safety, for the prevention of disorder or crime, for the protection of health or morals or for the protection of the rights and freedoms of others. This article shall not prevent the imposition of lawful restrictions on the exercise of these rights by members of the armed forces, of the police or of the administration of the State.

Article 12 Right to marry

Men and women of marriageable age have the right to marry and to found a family, according to the national laws governing the exercise of this right.

Article 13 Right to an effective remedy

Everyone whose rights and freedoms as set forth in this Convention are violated shall have an effective remedy before a national authority notwithstanding that the violation has been committed by persons acting in an official capacity.

Article 14 Prohibition of discrimination

The enjoyment of the rights and freedoms set forth in this Convention shall be secured without discrimination on any ground such as sex, race, colour, language, religion, political or other opinion, national or social origin, association with a national minority, property, birth or other status.

Article 15 Derogation in time of emergency

1. In time of war or other public emergency threatening the life of the nation any High Contracting Party may take measures derogating from its obligations under this Convention to the extent strictly required by the exigencies of the situation, provided that such measures are not inconsistent with its other obligations under international law.

2. No derogation from Article 2, except in respect of deaths resulting from lawful acts of war, or from Articles 3, 4 (paragraph 1) and 7 shall be made under this provision.

3. Any High Contracting Party availing itself of this right of derogation shall keep the Secretary-General of the Council of Europe fully informed of the measures which it has taken and the reasons therefor. It shall also inform the Secretary-General of the Council of Europe when such measures have ceased to operate and the provisions of the Convention are again being fully executed.

Article 16 Restrictions on political activity of aliens

Nothing in Articles 10, 11, and 14 shall be regarded as preventing the High Contracting Parties from imposing restrictions on the political activity of aliens.

Article 17 Prohibition of abuse of rights

Nothing in this Convention may be interpreted as implying for any State, group or person any right to engage in any activity or perform any act aimed at the destruction on any of the rights and freedoms set forth herein or at their limitation to a greater extent than is provided for in the Convention.

Article 18 Limitation on use of restrictions on rights

The restrictions permitted under this Convention to the said rights and freedoms shall not be applied for any purpose other than those for which they have been prescribed.

Selected Protocols attached to the Treaties by the Lisbon Treaty*

Protocol (No 1) on the Role of National Parliaments in the European Union

THE HIGH CONTRACTING PARTIES

RECALLING that the way in which national Parliaments scrutinise their governments in relation to the activities of the Union is a matter for the particular constitutional organisation and practice of each Member State,

DESIRING to encourage greater involvement of national Parliaments in the activities of the European Union and to enhance their ability to express their views on draft legislative acts of the Union as well as on other matters which may be of particular interest to them,

HAVE AGREED UPON the following provisions, which shall be annexed to the Treaty on European Union, to the Treaty on the Functioning of the European Union and to the Treaty establishing the European Atomic Energy Community:

Title I Information for national Parliaments

Article 1

Commission consultation documents (green and white papers and communications) shall be forwarded directly by the Commission to national Parliaments upon publication. The Commission shall also forward the annual legislative programme as well as any other instrument of legislative planning or policy to national Parliaments, at the same time as to the European Parliament and the Council.

Article 2

Draft legislative acts sent to the European Parliament and to the Council shall be forwarded to national Parliaments.

For the purposes of this Protocol, 'draft legislative acts' shall mean proposals from the Commission, initiatives from a group of Member States, initiatives from the European Parliament, requests from the Court of Justice, recommendations from the European Central Bank and requests from the European Investment Bank for the adoption of a legislative act.

Draft legislative acts originating from the Commission shall be forwarded to national Parliaments directly by the Commission, at the same time as to the European Parliament and the Council.

Draft legislative acts originating from the European Parliament shall be forwarded to national Parliaments directly by the European Parliament.

Draft legislative acts originating from a group of Member States, the Court of Justice, the European Central Bank or the European Investment Bank shall be forwarded to national Parliaments by the Council.

Article 3

National Parliaments may send to the Presidents of the European Parliament, the Council and the Commission a reasoned opinion on whether a draft legislative act complies with the principle of subsidiarity, in accordance with the procedure laid down in the Protocol on the application of the principles of subsidiarity and proportionality.

If the draft legislative act originates from a group of Member States, the President of the Council shall forward the reasoned opinion or opinions to the governments of those Member States.

* **Editor's Note:** The protocols are those taken from the 2016 re-publication OJ 2016 C202/201.

If the draft legislative act originates from the Court of Justice, the European Central Bank or the European Investment Bank, the President of the Council shall forward the reasoned opinion or opinions to the institution or body concerned.

Article 4

An eight-week period shall elapse between a draft legislative act being made available to national Parliaments in the official languages of the Union and the date when it is placed on a provisional agenda for the Council for its adoption or for adoption of a position under a legislative procedure. Exceptions shall be possible in cases of urgency, the reasons for which shall be stated in the act or position of the Council. Save in urgent cases for which due reasons have been given, no agreement may be reached on a draft legislative act during those eight weeks. Save in urgent cases for which due reasons have been given, a ten-day period shall elapse between the placing of a draft legislative act on the provisional agenda for the Council and the adoption of a position.

Article 5

The agendas for and the outcome of meetings of the Council, including the minutes of meetings where the Council is deliberating on draft legislative acts, shall be forwarded directly to national Parliaments, at the same time as to Member States' governments.

Article 6

When the European Council intends to make use of the first or second subparagraphs of Article 48(7) of the Treaty on European Union, national Parliaments shall be informed of the initiative of the European Council at least six months before any decision is adopted.

Article 7

The Court of Auditors shall forward its annual report to national Parliaments, for information, at the same time as to the European Parliament and to the Council.

Article 8

Where the national Parliamentary system is not unicameral, Articles 1 to 7 shall apply to the component chambers.

Title II Interparliamentary cooperation

Article 9

The European Parliament and national Parliaments shall together determine the organisation and promotion of effective and regular interparliamentary cooperation within the Union.

Article 10

A conference of Parliamentary Committees for Union Affairs may submit any contribution it deems appropriate for the attention of the European Parliament, the Council and the Commission. That conference shall in addition promote the exchange of information and best practice between national Parliaments and the European Parliament, including their special committees. It may also organise interparliamentary conferences on specific topics, in particular to debate matters of common foreign and security policy, including common security and defence policy. Contributions from the conference shall not bind national Parliaments and shall not prejudge their positions.

Protocol (No 2) on the Application of the Principles of Subsidiarity and Proportionality

THE HIGH CONTRACTING PARTIES,

WISHING to ensure that decisions are taken as closely as possible to the citizens of the Union,

RESOLVED to establish the conditions for the application of the principles of subsidiarity and proportionality, as laid down in Article 5 of the Treaty on European Union, and to establish a system for monitoring the application of those principles,

HAVE AGREED UPON the following provisions, which shall be annexed to the Treaty on European Union and to the Treaty on the Functioning of the European Union:

Article 1

Each institution shall ensure constant respect for the principles of subsidiarity and proportionality, as laid down in Article 5 of the Treaty on European Union.

Article 2

Before proposing legislative acts, the Commission shall consult widely. Such consultations shall, where appropriate, take into account the regional and local dimension of the action envisaged. In cases of exceptional urgency, the Commission shall not conduct such consultations. It shall give reasons for its decision in its proposal.

Article 3

For the purposes of this Protocol, 'draft legislative acts' shall mean proposals from the Commission, initiatives from a group of Member States, initiatives from the European Parliament, requests from the Court of Justice, recommendations from the European Central Bank and requests from the European Investment Bank for the adoption of a legislative act.

Article 4

The Commission shall forward its draft legislative acts and its amended drafts to national Parliaments at the same time as to the Union legislator.

The European Parliament shall forward its draft legislative acts and its amended drafts to national Parliaments.

The Council shall forward draft legislative acts originating from a group of Member States, the Court of Justice, the European Central Bank or the European Investment Bank and amended drafts to national Parliaments.

Upon adoption, legislative resolutions of the European Parliament and positions of the Council shall be forwarded by them to national Parliaments.

Article 5

Draft legislative acts shall be justified with regard to the principles of subsidiarity and proportionality. Any draft legislative act should contain a detailed statement making it possible to appraise compliance with the principles of subsidiarity and proportionality. This statement should contain some assessment of the proposal's financial impact and, in the case of a directive, of its implications for the rules to be put in place by Member States, including, where necessary, the regional legislation. The reasons for concluding that a Union objective can be better achieved at Union level shall be substantiated by qualitative and, wherever possible, quantitative indicators. Draft legislative acts shall take account of the need for any burden, whether financial or administrative, falling upon the Union, national governments, regional or local authorities, economic operators and citizens, to be minimised and commensurate with the objective to be achieved.

Article 6

Any national Parliament or any chamber of a national Parliament may, within eight weeks from the date of transmission of a draft legislative act, in the official languages of the Union, send to the Presidents of the European Parliament, the Council and the Commission a reasoned opinion stating why it considers that the draft in question does not comply with the principle of subsidiarity. It will be for each national Parliament or each chamber of a national Parliament to consult, where appropriate, regional parliaments with legislative powers.

If the draft legislative act originates from a group of Member States, the President of the Council shall forward the opinion to the governments of those Member States.

If the draft legislative act originates from the Court of Justice, the European Central Bank or the European Investment Bank, the President of the Council shall forward the opinion to the institution or body concerned.

Article 7

1. The European Parliament, the Council and the Commission, and, where appropriate, the group of Member States, the Court of Justice, the European Central Bank or the European Investment Bank, if the draft legislative act originates from them, shall take account of the reasoned opinions issued by national Parliaments or by a chamber of a national Parliament.

Each national Parliament shall have two votes, shared out on the basis of the national Parliamentary system. In the case of a bicameral Parliamentary system, each of the two chambers shall have one vote.

2. Where reasoned opinions on a draft legislative act's non-compliance with the principle of subsidiarity represent at least one third of all the votes allocated to the national Parliaments in accordance with the second subparagraph of paragraph 1, the draft must be reviewed. This threshold shall be a quarter in the case of a draft legislative act submitted on the basis of Article 76 of the Treaty on the Functioning of the European Union on the area of freedom, security and justice.

After such review, the Commission or, where appropriate, the group of Member States, the European Parliament, the Court of Justice, the European Central Bank or the European Investment Bank, if the draft legislative act originates from them, may decide to maintain, amend or withdraw the draft. Reasons must be given for this decision.

3. Furthermore, under the ordinary legislative procedure, where reasoned opinions on the non-compliance of a proposal for a legislative act with the principle of subsidiarity represent at least a simple majority of the votes allocated to the national Parliaments in accordance with the second subparagraph of paragraph 1, the proposal must be reviewed. After such review, the Commission may decide to maintain, amend or withdraw the proposal.

If it chooses to maintain the proposal, the Commission will have, in a reasoned opinion, to justify why it considers that the proposal complies with the principle of subsidiarity. This reasoned opinion, as well as the reasoned opinions of the national Parliaments, will have to be submitted to the Union legislator, for consideration in the procedure:

(a) before concluding the first reading, the legislator (the European Parliament and the Council) shall consider whether the legislative proposal is compatible with the principle of subsidiarity, taking particular account of the reasons expressed and shared by the majority of national Parliaments as well as the reasoned opinion of the Commission;

(b) if, by a majority of 55 % of the members of the Council or a majority of the votes cast in the European Parliament, the legislator is of the opinion that the proposal is not compatible with the principle of subsidiarity, the legislative proposal shall not be given further consideration.

Article 8

The Court of Justice of the European Union shall have jurisdiction in actions on grounds of infringement of the principle of subsidiarity by a legislative act, brought in accordance with the rules laid down in Article 263 of the Treaty on the Functioning of the European Union by Member States, or notified by them in accordance with their legal order on behalf of their national Parliament or a chamber thereof.

In accordance with the rules laid down in the said Article, the Committee of the Regions may also bring such actions against legislative acts for the adoption of which the Treaty on the Functioning of the European Union provides that it be consulted.

Article 9

The Commission shall submit each year to the European Council, the European Parliament, the Council and national Parliaments a report on the application of Article 5 of the Treaty on European Union. This annual report shall also be forwarded to the Economic and Social Committee and the Committee of the Regions.

Protocol (No 3) on the Statute of the Court of Justice of the European Union*

Article 1
The Court of Justice of the European Union shall be constituted and shall function in accordance with the provisions of the Treaties, of the Treaty establishing the European Atomic Energy Community (EAEC Treaty) and of this Statute.

Title I Judges and Advocates-General

Article 2
Before taking up his duties each Judge shall, before the Court of Justice sitting in open court, take an oath to perform his duties impartially and conscientiously and to preserve the secrecy of the deliberations of the Court.

Article 3
The Judges shall be immune from legal proceedings. After they have ceased to hold office, they shall continue to enjoy immunity in respect of acts performed by them in their official capacity, including words spoken or written.

The Court of Justice, sitting as a full Court, may waive the immunity. If the decision concerns a member of the General Court or of a specialised court, the Court shall decide after consulting the court concerned.

Where immunity has been waived and criminal proceedings are instituted against a Judge, he shall be tried, in any of the Member States, only by the court competent to judge the members of the highest national judiciary.

Articles 11 to 14 and Article 17 of the Protocol on the privileges and immunities of the European Union shall apply to the Judges, Advocates-General, Registrar and Assistant Rapporteurs of the Court of Justice of the European Union, without prejudice to the provisions relating to immunity from legal proceedings of Judges which are set out in the preceding paragraphs.

Article 4
The Judges may not hold any political or administrative office.

They may not engage in any occupation, whether gainful or not, unless exemption is exceptionally granted by the Council, acting by a simple majority.

When taking up their duties, they shall give a solemn undertaking that, both during and after their term of office, they will respect the obligations arising therefrom, in particular the duty to behave with integrity and discretion as regards the acceptance, after they have ceased to hold office, of certain appointments or benefits.

Any doubt on this point shall be settled by decision of the Court of Justice. If the decision concerns a member of the General Court or of a specialised court, the Court shall decide after consulting the court concerned.

Article 5
Apart from normal replacement, or death, the duties of a Judge shall end when he resigns.

Where a Judge resigns, his letter of resignation shall be addressed to the President of the Court of Justice for transmission to the President of the Council. Upon this notification a vacancy shall arise on the bench.

Save where Article 6 applies, a Judge shall continue to hold office until his successor takes up his duties.

* **Editor's Note:** As published in OJ 2016 C202/210 and amended up to 17 April 2019 (OJ 2019 L111/1).

Article 6

A Judge may be deprived of his office or of his right to a pension or other benefits in its stead only if, in the unanimous opinion of the Judges and Advocates-General of the Court of Justice, he no longer fulfils the requisite conditions or meets the obligations arising from his office. The Judge concerned shall not take part in any such deliberations. If the person concerned is a member of the General Court or of a specialised court, the Court shall decide after consulting the court concerned.

The Registrar of the Court shall communicate the decision of the Court to the President of the European Parliament and to the President of the Commission and shall notify it to the President of the Council.

In the case of a decision depriving a Judge of his office, a vacancy shall arise on the bench upon this latter notification.

Article 7

A Judge who is to replace a member of the Court whose term of office has not expired shall be appointed for the remainder of his predecessor's term.

Article 8

The provisions of Articles 2 to 7 shall apply to the Advocates-General.

Title II Organisation of the Court of Justice

Article 9

When, every three years, the Judges are partially replaced, one half of the number of Judges shall be replaced. If the number of Judges is an uneven number, the number of Judges who shall be replaced shall alternately be the number which is the next above one half of the number of Judges and the number which is next below one half. The first paragraph shall also apply when the Advocates-General are partially replaced, every three years.

Article 9a

The Judges shall elect the President and the Vice-President of the Court of Justice from among their number for a term of three years. They may be re-elected.

The Vice-President shall assist the President in accordance with the conditions laid down in the Rules of Procedure. He shall take the President's place when the latter is prevented from attending or when the office of President is vacant.

Article 16

The Court of Justice shall form chambers consisting of three and five Judges. The Judges shall elect the Presidents of the chambers from among their number. The Presidents of the chambers of five Judges shall be elected for three years. They may be re-elected once.

The Grand Chamber shall consist of 15 Judges. It shall be presided over by the President of the Court. The Vice-President of the Court and, in accordance with the conditions laid down in the Rules of Procedure, three of the Presidents of the chambers of five Judges and other Judges shall also form part of the Grand Chamber.

The Court shall sit in a Grand Chamber when a Member State or an institution of the Union that is party to the proceedings so requests.

The Court shall sit as a full Court where cases are brought before it pursuant to Article 228(2), Article 245(2), Article 247 or Article 286(7) of the Treaty on the Functioning of the European Union.

Moreover, where it considers that a case before it is of exceptional importance, the Court may decide, after hearing the Advocate-General, to refer the case to the full Court.

Article 17

Decisions of the Court of Justice shall be valid only when an uneven number of its members is sitting in the deliberations.

Decisions of the chambers consisting of either three or five Judges shall be valid only if they are taken by three Judges.

Decisions of the Grand Chamber shall be valid only if 11 Judges are sitting.

Decisions of the full Court shall be valid only if 17 Judges are sitting.

In the event of one of the Judges of a chamber being prevented from attending, a Judge of another chamber may be called upon to sit in accordance with conditions laid down in the Rules of Procedure.

Title III Procedure before the Court of Justice

Article 19

The Member States and the institutions of the Union shall be represented before the Court of Justice by an agent appointed for each case; the agent may be assisted by an adviser or by a lawyer.

The States, other than the Member States, which are parties to the Agreement on the European Economic Area and also the EFTA Surveillance Authority referred to in that Agreement shall be represented in same manner.

Other parties must be represented by a lawyer.

Only a lawyer authorised to practise before a court of a Member State or of another State which is a party to the Agreement on the European Economic Area may represent or assist a party before the Court.

Such agents, advisers and lawyers shall, when they appear before the Court, enjoy the rights and immunities necessary to the independent exercise of their duties, under conditions laid down in the Rules of Procedure.

As regards such advisers and lawyers who appear before it, the Court shall have the powers normally accorded to courts of law, under conditions laid down in the Rules of Procedure.

University teachers being nationals of a Member State whose law accords them a right of audience shall have the same rights before the Court as are accorded by this Article to lawyers.

Article 20

The procedure before the Court of Justice shall consist of two parts: written and oral.

The written procedure shall consist of the communication to the parties and to the institutions of the Union whose decisions are in dispute, of applications, statements of case, defences and observations, and of replies, if any, as well as of all papers and documents in support or of certified copies of them.

Communications shall be made by the Registrar in the order and within the time laid down in the Rules of Procedure.

The oral procedure shall consist of the hearing by the Court of agents, advisers and lawyers and of the submissions of the Advocate-General, as well as the hearing, if any, of witnesses and experts.

Where it considers that the case raises no new point of law, the Court may decide, after hearing the Advocate-General, that the case shall be determined without a submission from the Advocate-General.

Title IV General Court

Article 47

The first paragraph of Article 9, Article 9a, Articles 14 and 15, the first, second, fourth and fifth paragraphs of Article 17 and Article 18 shall apply to the General Court and its members.

The fourth paragraph of Article 3 and Articles 10, 11 and 14 shall apply to the Registrar of the General Court *mutatis mutandis*.

Article 48*

The General Court shall consist of:

(a) 40 Judges as from 25 December 2015;

(b) 47 Judges as from 1 September 2016;

(c) two Judges per Member State as from 1 September 2019.

* **Editor's Note:** The details of the appointment process and terms of office are contained within Articles 2 and 3 of the amending Regulation.

Article 49

The Members of the General Court may be called upon to perform the task of an Advocate-General.

It shall be the duty of the Advocate-General, acting with complete impartiality and independence, to make, in open court, reasoned submissions on certain cases brought before the General Court in order to assist the General Court in the performance of its task.

The criteria for selecting such cases, as well as the procedures for designating the Advocates-General, shall be laid down in the Rules of Procedure of the General Court.

A Member called upon to perform the task of Advocate-General in a case may not take part in the judgment of the case.

Article 50

The General Court shall sit in chambers of three or five Judges. The Judges shall elect the Presidents of the chambers from among their number. The Presidents of the chambers of five Judges shall be elected for three years. They may be re-elected once.

The composition of the chambers and the assignment of cases to them shall be governed by the Rules of Procedure. In certain cases governed by the Rules of Procedure, the General Court may sit as a full court or be constituted by a single Judge.

The Rules of Procedure may also provide that the General Court may sit in a Grand Chamber in cases and under the conditions specified therein.

Article 50a

1. The General Court shall exercise at first instance jurisdiction in disputes between the Union and its servants as referred to in Article 270 of the Treaty on the Functioning of the European Union, including disputes between all institutions, bodies, offices or agencies, on the one hand, and their servants, on the other, in respect of which jurisdiction is conferred on the Court of Justice of the European Union.

2. At all stages of the procedure, including the time when the application is filed, the General Court may examine the possibilities of an amicable settlement of the dispute and may try to facilitate such settlement.

Article 51

By way of derogation from the rule laid down in Article 256(1) of the Treaty on the Functioning of the European Union, jurisdiction shall be reserved to the Court of Justice:

(a) in actions referred to in Articles 263 and 265 of the Treaty on the Functioning of the European Union which are brought by a Member State against:

(i) a legislative act, an act of the European Parliament, of the European Council or of the Council, or against a failure to act by one or more of those institutions, except for:

- decisions taken by the Council under the third subparagraph of Article 108(2) of the Treaty on the Functioning of the European Union,
- acts of the Council adopted pursuant to a Council regulation concerning measures to protect trade within the meaning of Article 207 of the Treaty on the Functioning of the European Union,
- acts of the Council by which the Council exercises implementing powers in accordance with Article 291(2) of the Treaty on the Functioning of the European Union;

(ii) an act of, or a failure to act by, the Commission under Article 331(1) of the Treaty on the Functioning of the European Union;

(b) in actions referred to in Articles 263 and 265 of the Treaty on the Functioning of the European Union which are brought by an institution of the Union against a legislative act, an act of the European Parliament, of the European Council, of the Council, of the Commission or of the European Central Bank, or against a failure to act by one or more of those institutions;

(c) in actions referred to in Article 263 of the Treaty on the Functioning of the European Union which are brought by a Member State against an act of the Commission relating to a failure to comply with a judgment delivered by the Court under the second subparagraph of Article 260(2), or the second subparagraph of Article 260(3), of the Treaty on the Functioning of the European Union.

Protocol (No 8) Relating to Article 6(2) of the Treaty on European Union on the Accession of the Union to the European Convention on the Protection of Human Rights and Fundamental Freedoms

THE HIGH CONTRACTING PARTIES,

HAVE AGREED UPON the following provisions, which shall be annexed to the Treaty on European Union and to the Treaty on the Functioning of the European Union:

Article 1

The agreement relating to the accession of the Union to the European Convention on the Protection of Human Rights and Fundamental Freedoms (hereinafter referred to as the 'European Convention') provided for in Article 6(2) of the Treaty on European Union shall make provision for preserving the specific characteristics of the Union and Union law, in particular with regard to:

(a) the specific arrangements for the Union's possible participation in the control bodies of the European Convention;

(b) the mechanisms necessary to ensure that proceedings by non-Member States and individual applications are correctly addressed to Member States and/or the Union as appropriate.

Article 2

The agreement referred to in Article 1 shall ensure that accession of the Union shall not affect the competences of the Union or the powers of its institutions. It shall ensure that nothing therein affects the situation of Member States in relation to the European Convention, in particular in relation to the Protocols thereto, measures taken by Member States derogating from the European Convention in accordance with Article 15 thereof and reservations to the European Convention made by Member States in accordance with Article 57 thereof.

Article 3

Nothing in the agreement referred to in Article 1 shall affect Article 344 of the Treaty on the Functioning of the European Union.

Protocol (No 25) on the Exercise of Shared Competence

THE HIGH CONTRACTING PARTIES,

HAVE AGREED UPON the following provisions, which shall be annexed to the Treaty on European Union and to the Treaty on the Functioning of the European Union:

Sole Article

With reference to Article 2 (2) of the Treaty on the Functioning of the European Union on shared competence, when the Union has taken action in a certain area, the scope of this exercise of competence only covers those elements governed by the Union act in question and therefore does not cover the whole area.

Protocol (No 33) Concerning Article 157 of the Treaty on the Functioning of the European Union

THE HIGH CONTRACTING PARTIES,

HAVE AGREED UPON the following provision, which shall be annexed to the Treaty on European Union and to the Treaty on the Functioning of the European Union:

For the purposes of Article 157 of the Treaty on the Functioning of the European Union, benefits under occupational social security schemes shall not be considered as remuneration if and in so far as they are attributable to periods of employment prior to 17 May 1990, except in the case of workers or those claiming under them who have before that date initiated legal proceedings or introduced an equivalent claim under the applicable national law.

Selected Declarations concerning provisions of the Treaties

1. Declaration concerning the Charter of Fundamental Rights of the European Union

The Charter of Fundamental Rights of the European Union, which has legally binding force, confirms the fundamental rights guaranteed by the European Convention for the Protection of Human Rights and Fundamental Freedoms and as they result from the constitutional traditions common to the Member States.

The Charter does not extend the field of application of Union law beyond the powers of the Union or establish any new power or task for the Union, or modify powers and tasks as defined by the Treaties.

2. Declaration on Article 6(2) of the Treaty on European Union

The Conference agrees that the Union's accession to the European Convention for the Protection of Human Rights and Fundamental Freedoms should be arranged in such a way as to preserve the specific features of Union law. In this connection, the Conference notes the existence of a regular dialogue between the Court of Justice of the European Union and the European Court of Human Rights; such dialogue could be reinforced when the Union accedes to that Convention.

17. Declaration concerning primacy

The Conference recalls that, in accordance with well settled case law of the Court of Justice of the European Union, the Treaties and the law adopted by the Union on the basis of the Treaties have primacy over the law of Member States, under the conditions laid down by the said case law.

The Conference has also decided to attach as an Annex to this Final Act the Opinion of the Council Legal Service on the primacy of EC law as set out in 11197/07 (JUR 260):

'Opinion of the Council Legal Service of 22 June 2007

It results from the case-law of the Court of Justice that primacy of EC law is a cornerstone principle of Community law. According to the Court, this principle is inherent to the specific nature of the European

Community. At the time of the first judgment of this established case law (Costa/ENEL,15 July 1964, Case 6/641[1]) there was no mention of primacy in the treaty. It is still the case today. The fact that the principle of primacy will not be included in the future treaty shall not in any way change the existence of the principle and the existing case-law of the Court of Justice.'

18. Declaration in relation to the delimitation of competences

The Conference underlines that, in accordance with the system of division of competences between the Union and the Member States as provided for in the Treaty on European Union and the Treaty on the Functioning of the European Union, competences not conferred upon the Union in the Treaties remain with the Member States.

When the Treaties confer on the Union a competence shared with the Member States in a specific area, the Member States shall exercise their competence to the extent that the Union has not exercised, or has decided to cease exercising, its competence. The latter situation arises when the relevant EU institutions decide to repeal a legislative act, in particular better to ensure constant respect for the principles of subsidiarity and proportionality. The Council may, at the initiative of one or several of its members (representatives of Member States) and in accordance with Article 241 of the Treaty on the Functioning of the European Union, request the Commission to submit proposals for repealing a legislative act. The Conference welcomes the Commission's declaration that it will devote particular attention to these requests.

Equally, the representatives of the governments of the Member States, meeting in an Intergovernmental Conference, in accordance with the ordinary revision procedure provided for in Article 48(2) to (5) of the Treaty on European Union, may decide to amend the Treaties upon which the Union is founded, including either to increase or to reduce the competences conferred on the Union in the said Treaties.

41. Declaration on Article 352 of the Treaty on the Functioning of the European Union

The Conference declares that the reference in Article 352(1) of the Treaty on the Functioning of the European Union to objectives of the Union refers to the objectives as set out in Article 3(2) and (3) of the Treaty on European Union and to the objectives of Article 3(5) of the said Treaty with respect to external action under Part Five of the Treaty on the Functioning of the European Union. It is therefore excluded that an action based on Article 352 of the Treaty on the Functioning of the European Union would only pursue objectives set out in Article 3(1) of the Treaty on European Union. In this connection, the Conference notes that in accordance with Article 31(1) of the Treaty on European Union, legislative acts may not be adopted in the area of the Common Foreign and Security Policy.

42. Declaration on Article 352 of the Treaty on the Functioning of the European Union

The Conference underlines that, in accordance with the settled case law of the Court of Justice of the European Union, Article 352 of the Treaty on the Functioning of the European Union, being an integral part of an institutional system based on the principle of conferred powers, cannot serve as

[1] *'It follows (. . .) that the law stemming from the treaty, an independent source of law, could not, because of its special and original nature, be overridden by domestic legal provisions, however framed, without being deprived of its character as Community law and without the legal basis of the Community itself being called into question.'*

a basis for widening the scope of Union powers beyond the general framework created by the provisions of the Treaties as a whole and, in particular, by those that define the tasks and the activities of the Union. In any event, this Article cannot be used as a basis for the adoption of provisions whose effect would, in substance, be to amend the Treaties without following the procedure which they provide for that purpose.

Additional legislation and agreements affecting the institutions

Majority voting procedure extract from the Luxembourg Accords

[EEC Bulletin 1966 No 3, p. 9]

I. Where, in the case of decisions which may be taken by majority vote on a proposal of the Commission, very important interests of one or more partners are at stake, the Members of the Council will endeavour, within a reasonable time, to reach solutions which can be adopted by all the Members of the Council while respecting their mutual interests and those of the Community, in accordance with Article 2 of the Treaty.

II. With regard to the preceding paragraph, the French delegation considers that where very important interests are at stake the discussion must be continued until unanimous agreement is reached.

III. The six delegations note that there is a divergence of views on what should be done in the event of a failure to reach complete agreement.

IV. The six delegations nevertheless consider that this divergence does not prevent the Community's work being resumed in accordance with the normal procedure.

Regulation (EC) No 1049/2001 of the European Parliament and of the Council of 30 May 2001 regarding public access to European Parliament, Council and Commission documents*

[OJ 2001 L145/43]

HAVE ADOPTED THIS REGULATION:

Article 1 Purpose

The purpose of this Regulation is:

(a) to define the principles, conditions and limits on grounds of public or private interest governing the right of access to European Parliament, Council and Commission (hereinafter referred to as 'the institutions') documents provided for in Article 255 of the EC Treaty in such a way as to ensure the widest possible access to documents,

(b) to establish rules ensuring the easiest possible exercise of this right, and

(c) to promote good administrative practice on access to documents.

Article 2 Beneficiaries and scope

1. Any citizen of the Union, and any natural or legal person residing or having its registered office in a Member State, has a right of access to documents of the institutions, subject to the principles, conditions and limits defined in this Regulation.

* **Editor's Note:** Preamble and recitals omitted.

2. The institutions may, subject to the same principles, conditions and limits, grant access to documents to any natural or legal person not residing or not having its registered office in a Member State.

3. This Regulation shall apply to all documents held by an institution, that is to say, documents drawn up or received by it and in its possession, in all areas of activity of the European Union.

4. Without prejudice to Articles 4 and 9, documents shall be made accessible to the public either following a written application or directly in electronic form or through a register. In particular, documents drawn up or received in the course of a legislative procedure shall be made directly accessible in accordance with Article 12.

5. Sensitive documents as defined in Article 9(1) shall be subject to special treatment in accordance with that Article.

6. This Regulation shall be without prejudice to rights of public access to documents held by the institutions which might follow from instruments of international law or acts of the institutions implementing them.

Article 3 Definitions

For the purpose of this Regulation:

(a) 'document' shall mean any content whatever its medium (written on paper or stored in electronic form or as a sound, visual or audiovisual recording) concerning a matter relating to the policies, activities and decisions falling within the institution's sphere of responsibility;

(b) 'third party' shall mean any natural or legal person, or any entity outside the institution concerned, including the Member States, other Community or non-Community institutions and bodies and third countries.

Article 4 Exceptions

1. The institutions shall refuse access to a document where disclosure would undermine the protection of:

(a) the public interest as regards:
- public security,
- defence and military matters,
- international relations,
- the financial, monetary or economic policy of the Community or a Member State;

(b) privacy and the integrity of the individual, in particular in accordance with Community legislation regarding the protection of personal data.

2. The institutions shall refuse access to a document where disclosure would undermine the protection of:
- commercial interests of a natural or legal person, including intellectual property,
- court proceedings and legal advice,
- the purpose of inspections, investigations and audits,

unless there is an overriding public interest in disclosure.

3. Access to a document, drawn up by an institution for internal use or received by an institution, which relates to a matter where the decision has not been taken by the institution, shall be refused if disclosure of the document would seriously undermine the institution's decision-making process, unless there is an overriding public interest in disclosure. Access to a document containing opinions for internal use as part of deliberations and preliminary consultations within the institution concerned shall be refused even after the decision has been taken if disclosure of the document would seriously undermine the institution's decision-making process, unless there is an overriding public interest in disclosure.

4. As regards third-party documents, the institution shall consult the third party with a view to assessing whether an exception in paragraph 1 or 2 is applicable, unless it is clear that the document shall or shall not be disclosed.

5. A Member State may request the institution not to disclose a document originating from that Member State without its prior agreement.

6. If only parts of the requested document are covered by any of the exceptions, the remaining parts of the document shall be released.

7. The exceptions as laid down in paragraphs 1 to 3 shall only apply for the period during which protection is justified on the basis of the content of the document. The exceptions may apply for a maximum period of 30 years. In the case of documents covered by the exceptions relating to privacy or commercial interests and in the case of sensitive documents, the exceptions may, if necessary, continue to apply after this period.

Article 13 Publication in the Official Journal

1. In addition to the acts referred to in Article 254(1) and (2) of the EC Treaty and the first paragraph of Article 163 of the Euratom Treaty, the following documents shall, subject to Articles 4 and 9 of this Regulation, be published in the Official Journal:

(a) Commission proposals;

(b) common positions adopted by the Council in accordance with the procedures referred to in Articles 251 and 252 of the EC Treaty and the reasons underlying those common positions, as well as the European Parliament's positions in these procedures;

(c) framework decisions and decisions referred to in Article 34(2) of the EU Treaty;

(d) conventions established by the Council in accordance with Article 34(2) of the EU Treaty;

(e) conventions signed between Member States on the basis of Article 293 of the EC Treaty;

(f) international agreements concluded by the Community or in accordance with Article 24 of the EU Treaty.

2. As far as possible, the following documents shall be published in the Official Journal:

(a) initiatives presented to the Council by a Member State pursuant to Article 67(1) of the EC Treaty or pursuant to Article 34(2) of the EU Treaty;

(b) common positions referred to in Article 34(2) of the EU Treaty;

(c) directives other than those referred to in Article 254(1) and (2) of the EC Treaty, decisions other than those referred to in Article 254(1) of the EC Treaty, recommendations and opinions.

3. Each institution may in its rules of procedure establish which further documents shall be published in the Official Journal.

Article 19 Entry into force

This Regulation shall enter into force on the third day following that of its publication in the Official Journal of the European Communities. It shall be applicable from 3 December 2001.

This Regulation shall be binding in its entirety and directly applicable in all Member States.

Done at Brussels, 30 May 2001.

Joint declaration relating to Regulation 1049/2001 of the European Parliament and of the Council regarding public access to European Parliament, Council and Commission documents

[OJ 2001 L173/5]

1. The European Parliament, the Council and the Commission agree that the agencies and similar bodies created by the legislator should have rules on access to their documents which conform to those of this Regulation. To this effect, the European Parliament and the Council welcome the Commission's intention to propose, as soon as possible, amendments to the acts

establishing the existing agencies and bodies and to include provisions in future proposals concerning the establishment of such agencies and bodies. They undertake to adopt the necessary acts rapidly.

2. The European Parliament, the Council and the Commission call on the institutions and bodies not covered by paragraph 1 to adopt internal rules on public access to documents which take account of the principles and limits in this Regulation.

Joint declaration on practical arrangements for the codecision procedure (Article 251 of the EC Treaty)*

[OJ 2007 C145/02]

General principles

1. The European Parliament, the Council and the Commission, hereinafter referred to collectively as 'the institutions', note that current practice involving talks between the Council Presidency, the Commission and the chairs of the relevant committees and/or rapporteurs of the European Parliament and between the co-chairs of the Conciliation Committee has proved its worth.

2. The institutions confirm that this practice, which has developed at all stages of the codecision procedure, must continue to be encouraged. The institutions undertake to examine their working methods with a view to making even more effective use of the full scope of the codecision procedure as established by the EC Treaty.

3. This Joint Declaration clarifies these working methods, and the practical arrangements for pursuing them. It complements the Interinstitutional Agreement on Better Lawmaking[1] and notably its provisions relating to the co-decision procedure. The institutions undertake fully to respect such commitments in line with the principles of transparency, accountability and efficiency. In this respect, the institutions should pay particular attention to making progress on simplification proposals while respecting the acquis communautaire.

4. The institutions shall cooperate in good faith throughout the procedure with a view to reconciling their positions as far as possible and thereby clearing the way, where appropriate, for the adoption of the act concerned at an early stage of the procedure.

5. With that aim in view, they shall cooperate through appropriate interinstitutional contacts to monitor the progress of the work and analyse the degree of convergence at all stages of the codecision procedure.

6. The institutions, in accordance with their internal rules of procedure, undertake to exchange information regularly on the progress of codecision files. They shall ensure that their respective calendars of work are coordinated as far as possible in order to enable proceedings to be conducted in a coherent and convergent fashion. They will therefore seek to establish an indicative timetable for the various stages leading to the final adoption of different legislative proposals, while fully respecting the political nature of the decision-making process.

7. Cooperation between the institutions in the context of codecision often takes the form of tripartite meetings ('trilogues'). This trilogue system has demonstrated its vitality and flexibility in increasing significantly the possibilities for agreement at first and second reading stages, as well as contributing to the preparation of the work of the Conciliation Committee.

8. Such trilogues are usually conducted in an informal framework. They may be held at all stages of the procedure and at different levels of representation, depending on the nature of the expected discussion. Each institution, in accordance with its own rules of procedure, will designate its participants for each meeting, define its mandate for the negotiations and inform the other institutions of arrangements for the meetings in good time.

* **Editor's Note:** Now Article 294 TFEU.

[1] OJ C 321, 31.12.2003, p. 1.

9. As far as possible, any draft compromise texts submitted for discussion at a forthcoming meeting shall be circulated in advance to all participants. In order to enhance transparency, trilogues taking place within the European Parliament and Council shall be announced, where practicable.

10. The Council Presidency will endeavour to attend the meetings of the parliamentary committees. It will carefully consider any request it receives to provide information related to the Council position, as appropriate.

FIRST READING

11. The institutions shall cooperate in good faith with a view to reconciling their positions as far as possible so that, wherever possible, acts can be adopted at first reading.

Agreement at the stage of first reading in the European Parliament

12. Appropriate contacts shall be established to facilitate the conduct of proceedings at first reading.

13. The Commission shall facilitate such contacts and shall exercise its right of initiative in a constructive manner with a view to reconciling the positions of the European Parliament and the Council, with due regard for the balance between the institutions and the role conferred on it by the Treaty.

14. Where an agreement is reached through informal negotiations in trilogues, the chair of Coreper shall forward, in a letter to the chair of the relevant parliamentary committee, details of the substance of the agreement, in the form of amendments to the Commission proposal. That letter shall indicate the Council's willingness to accept that outcome, subject to legal-linguistic verification, should it be confirmed by the vote in plenary. A copy of that letter shall be forwarded to the Commission.

15. In this context, where conclusion of a dossier at first reading is imminent, information on the intention to conclude an agreement should be made readily available as early as possible.

Agreement at the stage of Council common position

16. Where no agreement is reached at the European Parliament's first reading, contacts may be continued with a view to concluding an agreement at the common position stage.

17. The Commission shall facilitate such contacts and shall exercise its right of initiative in a constructive manner with a view to reconciling the positions of the European Parliament and the Council, with due regard for the balance between the institutions and the role conferred on it by the Treaty.

18. Where an agreement is reached at this stage, the chair of the relevant parliamentary committee shall indicate, in a letter to the chair of Coreper, his recommendation to the plenary to accept the Council common position without amendment, subject to confirmation of the common position by the Council and to legal-linguistic verification. A copy of the letter shall be forwarded to the Commission.

SECOND READING

19. In its statement of reasons, the Council shall explain as clearly as possible the reasons that led it to adopt its common position. During its second reading, the European Parliament shall take the greatest possible account of those reasons and of the Commission's position.

20. Before transmitting the common position, the Council shall endeavour to consider in consultation with the European Parliament and the Commission the date for its transmission in order to ensure the maximum efficiency of the legislative procedure at second reading.

Agreement at the stage of second reading in the European Parliament

21. Appropriate contacts will continue as soon as the Council common position is forwarded to the European Parliament, with a view to achieving a better understanding of the respective positions and thus to bringing the legislative procedure to a conclusion as quickly as possible.

22. The Commission shall facilitate such contacts and give its opinion with a view to reconciling the positions of the European Parliament and the Council, with due regard for the balance between the institutions and the role conferred on it by the Treaty.

23. Where an agreement is reached through informal negotiations in trilogues, the chair of Coreper shall forward, in a letter to the chair of the relevant parliamentary committee, details of the substance of the agreement, in the form of amendments to the Council common position. That letter shall indicate the Council's willingness to accept that outcome, subject to legal-linguistic verification, should it be confirmed by the vote in plenary. A copy of that letter shall be forwarded to the Commission.

CONCILIATION

24. If it becomes clear that the Council will not be in a position to accept all the amendments of the European Parliament at second reading and when the Council is ready to present its position, a first trilogue will be organised. Each institution, in accordance with its own rules of procedure, will designate its participants for each meeting and define its mandate for the negotiations. The Commission will indicate to both delegations at the earliest possible stage its intentions with regard to its opinion on the European Parliament's second reading amendments.

25. Trilogues shall take place throughout the conciliation procedure with the aim of resolving outstanding issues and preparing the ground for an agreement to be reached in the Conciliation Committee. The results of the trilogues shall be discussed and possibly approved at the meetings of the respective institutions.

26. The Conciliation Committee shall be convened by the President of the Council, with the agreement of the President of the European Parliament and with due regard to the provisions of the Treaty.

27. The Commission shall take part in the conciliation proceedings and shall take all the necessary initiatives with a view to reconciling the positions of the European Parliament and the Council. Such initiatives may include, draft compromise texts having regard to the positions of the European Parliament and of the Council and with due regard for the role conferred upon the Commission by the Treaty.

28. The Conciliation Committee shall be chaired jointly by the President of the European Parliament and the President of the Council. Committee meetings shall be chaired alternately by each co-chair.

29. The dates and the agendas for the Conciliation Committee's meetings shall be set jointly by the co-chairs with a view to the effective functioning of the Conciliation Committee throughout the conciliation procedure. The Commission shall be consulted on the dates envisaged. The European Parliament and the Council shall set aside, for guidance, appropriate dates for conciliation proceedings and shall notify the Commission thereof.

30. The co-chairs may put several dossiers on the agenda of any one meeting of the Conciliation Committee. As well as the principal topic ('B-item'), where agreement has not yet been reached, conciliation procedures on other topics may be opened and/or closed without discussion on these items ('A-item').

31. While respecting the Treaty provisions regarding time-limits, the European Parliament and the Council shall, as far as possible, take account of scheduling requirements, in particular those resulting from breaks in the institutions' activities and from the European Parliament's elections. At all events, the break in activities shall be as short as possible.

32. The Conciliation Committee shall meet alternately at the premises of the European Parliament and the Council, with a view to an equal sharing of facilities, including interpretation facilities.

33. The Conciliation Committee shall have available to it the Commission proposal, the Council common position and the Commission's opinion thereon, the amendments proposed by the European Parliament and the Commission's opinion thereon, and a joint working document by the European Parliament and Council delegations. This working document should enable users to identify the issues at stake easily and to refer to them efficiently. The Commission shall, as a general rule, submit

its opinion within three weeks of official receipt of the outcome of the European Parliament's vote and at the latest by the commencement of conciliation proceedings.

34. The co-chairs may submit texts for the Conciliation Committee's approval.

35. Agreement on a joint text shall be established at a meeting of the Conciliation Committee or, subsequently, by an exchange of letters between the co-chairs. Copies of such letters shall be forwarded to the Commission.

36. If the Conciliation Committee reaches agreement on a joint text, the text shall, after legal-linguistic finalisation, be submitted to the co-chairs for formal approval. However, in exceptional cases in order to respect the deadlines, a draft joint text may be submitted to the co-chairs for approval.

37. The co-chairs shall forward the approved joint text to the Presidents of the European Parliament and of the Council by means of a jointly signed letter. Where the Conciliation Committee is unable to agree on a joint text, the co-chairs shall notify the Presidents of the European Parliament and of the Council thereof in a jointly signed letter. Such letters shall serve as an official record. Copies of such letters shall be forwarded to the Commission for information. The working documents used during the conciliation procedure will be accessible in the Register of each institution once the procedure has been concluded.

38. The Secretariat of the European Parliament and the General-Secretariat of the Council shall act jointly as the Conciliation Committee's secretariat, in association with the Secretariat-General of the Commission.

GENERAL PROVISIONS

39. Should the European Parliament or the Council deem it essential to extend the time-limits referred to in Article 251 of the Treaty, they shall notify the President of the other institution and the Commission accordingly.

40. Where an agreement is reached at first or second reading, or during conciliation, the agreed text shall be finalised by the legal-linguistic services of the European Parliament and of the Council acting in close cooperation and by mutual agreement.

41. No changes shall be made to any agreed texts without the explicit agreement, at the appropriate level, of both the European Parliament and the Council.

42. Finalisation shall be carried out with due regard to the different procedures of the European Parliament and the Council, in particular with respect to deadlines for conclusion of internal procedures. The institutions undertake not to use the time-limits laid down for the legal-linguistic finalisation of acts to reopen discussions on substantive issues.

43. The European Parliament and the Council shall agree on a common presentation of the texts prepared jointly by those institutions.

44. As far as possible, the institutions undertake to use mutually acceptable standard clauses to be incorporated in the acts adopted under codecision in particular as regards provisions concerning the exercise of implementing powers (in accordance with the 'comitology' decision[2]), entry into force, transposition and the application of acts and respect for the Commission's right of initiative.

45. The institutions will endeavour to hold a joint press conference to announce the successful outcome of the legislative process at first or second reading or during conciliation. They will also endeavour to issue joint press releases.

46. Following adoption of a legislative act under the codecision procedure by the European Parliament and the Council, the text shall be submitted, for signature, to the President of the European Parliament and the President of the Council and to the Secretaries-General of those institutions.

47. The Presidents of the European Parliament and the Council shall receive the text for signature in their respective languages and shall, as far as possible, sign the text together at a joint

[2] Council Decision 1999/468/EC of 28 June 1999 laying down the procedures for the exercise of implementing powers conferred on the Commission (OJ L 184, 17.7.1999, p. 23). Decision as amended by Decision 2006/512/EC (OJ L 200, 27.7.2006, p. 11).

ceremony to be organised on a monthly basis with a view to signing important acts in the presence of the media.

48. The jointly signed text shall be forwarded for publication in the *Official Journal of the European Union*. Publication shall normally follow within two months of the adoption of the legislative act by the European Parliament and the Council.

49. If one of the institutions identifies a clerical or obvious error in a text (or in one of the language versions thereof), it shall immediately notify the other institutions. If the error concerns an act that has not yet been adopted by either the European Parliament or the Council, the legal-linguistic services of the European Parliament and the Council shall prepare the necessary corrigendum in close cooperation.

Where this error concerns an act that has already been adopted by one or both of those institutions, whether published or not, the European Parliament and the Council shall adopt, by common agreement, a corrigendum drawn up under their respective procedures.

Done at Brussels, on the thirteenth day of June in the year two thousand and seven.
(Signatures omitted.)

Regulation (EU) No 182/2011 of the European Parliament and of the Council of 16 February 2011 laying down the rules and general principles concerning mechanisms for control by Member States of the Commission's exercise of implementing powers*

[OJ 2011 L55/13]

HAVE ADOPTED THIS REGULATION:

Article 1 Subject-matter

This Regulation lays down the rules and general principles governing the mechanisms which apply where a legally binding Union act (hereinafter a 'basic act') identifies the need for uniform conditions of implementation and requires that the adoption of implementing acts by the Commission be subject to the control of Member States.

Article 2 Selection of procedures

1. A basic act may provide for the application of the advisory procedure or the examination procedure, taking into account the nature or the impact of the implementing act required.

2. The examination procedure applies, in particular, for the adoption of:
   (a) implementing acts of general scope;
   (b) other implementing acts relating to:
      (i) programmes with substantial implications;
      (ii) the common agricultural and common fisheries policies;
      (iii) the environment, security and safety, or protection of the health or safety, of humans, animals or plants;
      (iv) the common commercial policy;
      (v) taxation.

3. The advisory procedure applies, as a general rule, for the adoption of implementing acts not falling within the ambit of paragraph 2. However, the advisory procedure may apply for the adoption of the implementing acts referred to in paragraph 2 in duly justified cases.

* **Editor's Note:** Preamble and recitals omitted.

Article 3 Common provisions

1. The common provisions set out in this Article shall apply to all the procedures referred to in Articles 4 to 8.

2. The Commission shall be assisted by a committee composed of representatives of the Member States. The committee shall be chaired by a representative of the Commission. The chair shall not take part in the committee vote.

3. The chair shall submit to the committee the draft implementing act to be adopted by the Commission.

Except in duly justified cases, the chair shall convene a meeting not less than 14 days from submission of the draft implementing act and of the draft agenda to the committee. The committee shall deliver its opinion on the draft implementing act within a time limit which the chair may lay down according to the urgency of the matter. Time limits shall be proportionate and shall afford committee members early and effective opportunities to examine the draft implementing act and express their views.

4. Until the committee delivers an opinion, any committee member may suggest amendments and the chair may present amended versions of the draft implementing act.

The chair shall endeavour to find solutions which command the widest possible support within the committee. The chair shall inform the committee of the manner in which the discussions and suggestions for amendments have been taken into account, in particular as regards those suggestions which have been largely supported within the committee.

5. In duly justified cases, the chair may obtain the committee's opinion by written procedure. The chair shall send the committee members the draft implementing act and shall lay down a time limit for delivery of an opinion according to the urgency of the matter. Any committee member who does not oppose the draft implementing act or who does not explicitly abstain from voting thereon before the expiry of that time limit shall be regarded as having tacitly agreed to the draft implementing act.

Unless otherwise provided in the basic act, the written procedure shall be terminated without result where, within the time limit referred to in the first subparagraph, the chair so decides or a committee member so requests. In such a case, the chair shall convene a committee meeting within a reasonable time.

6. The committee's opinion shall be recorded in the minutes. Committee members shall have the right to ask for their position to be recorded in the minutes. The chair shall send the minutes to the committee members without delay.

7. Where applicable, the control mechanism shall include referral to an appeal committee.

The appeal committee shall adopt its own rules of procedure by a simple majority of its component members, on a proposal from the Commission.

Where the appeal committee is seised, it shall meet at the earliest 14 days, except in duly justified cases, and at the latest 6 weeks, after the date of referral. Without prejudice to paragraph 3, the appeal committee shall deliver its opinion within 2 months of the date of referral.

A representative of the Commission shall chair the appeal committee.

The chair shall set the date of the appeal committee meeting in close cooperation with the members of the committee, in order to enable Member States and the Commission to ensure an appropriate level of representation. By 1 April 2011, the Commission shall convene the first meeting of the appeal committee in order to adopt its rules of procedure.

Article 4 Advisory procedure

1. Where the advisory procedure applies, the committee shall deliver its opinion, if necessary by taking a vote. If the committee takes a vote, the opinion shall be delivered by a simple majority of its component members.

2. The Commission shall decide on the draft implementing act to be adopted, taking the utmost account of the conclusions drawn from the discussions within the committee and of the opinion delivered.

Article 5 Examination procedure

1. Where the examination procedure applies, the committee shall deliver its opinion by the majority laid down in Article 16(4) and (5) of the Treaty on European Union and, where applicable, Article 238(3) TFEU, for acts to be adopted on a proposal from the Commission. The votes of the representatives of the Member States within the committee shall be weighted in the manner set out in those Articles.

2. Where the committee delivers a positive opinion, the Commission shall adopt the draft implementing act.

3. Without prejudice to Article 7, if the committee delivers a negative opinion, the Commission shall not adopt the draft implementing act. Where an implementing act is deemed to be necessary, the chair may either submit an amended version of the draft implementing act to the same committee within 2 months of delivery of the negative opinion, or submit the draft implementing act within 1 month of such delivery to the appeal committee for further deliberation.

4. Where no opinion is delivered, the Commission may adopt the draft implementing act, except in the cases provided for in the second subparagraph. Where the Commission does not adopt the draft implementing act, the chair may submit to the committee an amended version thereof.

Without prejudice to Article 7, the Commission shall not adopt the draft implementing act where:

(a) that act concerns taxation, financial services, the protection of the health or safety of humans, animals or plants, or definitive multilateral safeguard measures;

(b) the basic act provides that the draft implementing act may not be adopted where no opinion is delivered; or

(c) a simple majority of the component members of the committee opposes it.

In any of the cases referred to in the second subparagraph, where an implementing act is deemed to be necessary, the chair may either submit an amended version of that act to the same committee within 2 months of the vote, or submit the draft implementing act within 1 month of the vote to the appeal committee for further deliberation.

5. By way of derogation from paragraph 4, the following procedure shall apply for the adoption of draft definitive anti-dumping or countervailing measures, where no opinion is delivered by the committee and a simple majority of its component members opposes the draft implementing act.

The Commission shall conduct consultations with the Member States. 14 days at the earliest and 1 month at the latest after the committee meeting, the Commission shall inform the committee members of the results of those consultations and submit a draft implementing act to the appeal committee. By way of derogation from Article 3(7), the appeal committee shall meet 14 days at the earliest and 1 month at the latest after the submission of the draft implementing act. The appeal committee shall deliver its opinion in accordance with Article 6. The time limits laid down in this paragraph shall be without prejudice to the need to respect the deadlines laid down in the relevant basic acts.

Article 6 Referral to the appeal committee

1. The appeal committee shall deliver its opinion by the majority provided for in Article 5(1).

2. Until an opinion is delivered, any member of the appeal committee may suggest amendments to the draft implementing act and the chair may decide whether or not to modify it.

The chair shall endeavour to find solutions which command the widest possible support within the appeal committee.

The chair shall inform the appeal committee of the manner in which the discussions and suggestions for amendments have been taken into account, in particular as regards suggestions for amendments which have been largely supported within the appeal committee.

3. Where the appeal committee delivers a positive opinion, the Commission shall adopt the draft implementing act.

Where no opinion is delivered, the Commission may adopt the draft implementing act.

Where the appeal committee delivers a negative opinion, the Commission shall not adopt the draft implementing act.

4. By way of derogation from paragraph 3, for the adoption of definitive multilateral safeguard measures, in the absence of a positive opinion voted by the majority provided for in Article 5(1), the Commission shall not adopt the draft measures.

5. By way of derogation from paragraph 1, until 1 September 2012, the appeal committee shall deliver its opinion on draft definitive anti-dumping or countervailing measures by a simple majority of its component members.

Article 7 Adoption of implementing acts in exceptional cases

By way of derogation from Article 5(3) and the second subparagraph of Article 5(4), the Commission may adopt a draft implementing act where it needs to be adopted without delay in order to avoid creating a significant disruption of the markets in the area of agriculture or a risk for the financial interests of the Union within the meaning of Article 325 TFEU.

In such a case, the Commission shall immediately submit the adopted implementing act to the appeal committee. Where the appeal committee delivers a negative opinion on the adopted implementing act, the Commission shall repeal that act immediately. Where the appeal committee delivers a positive opinion or no opinion is delivered, the implementing act shall remain in force.

Article 8 Immediately applicable implementing acts

1. By way of derogation from Articles 4 and 5, a basic act may provide that, on duly justified imperative grounds of urgency, this Article is to apply.

2. The Commission shall adopt an implementing act which shall apply immediately, without its prior submission to a committee, and shall remain in force for a period not exceeding 6 months unless the basic act provides otherwise.

3. At the latest 14 days after its adoption, the chair shall submit the act referred to in paragraph 2 to the relevant committee in order to obtain its opinion.

4. Where the examination procedure applies, in the event of the committee delivering a negative opinion, the Commission shall immediately repeal the implementing act adopted in accordance with paragraph 2.

5. Where the Commission adopts provisional anti-dumping or countervailing measures, the procedure provided for in this Article shall apply. The Commission shall adopt such measures after consulting or, in cases of extreme urgency, after informing the Member States. In the latter case, consultations shall take place 10 days at the latest after notification to the Member States of the measures adopted by the Commission.

Article 9 Rules of procedure

1. Each committee shall adopt by a simple majority of its component members its own rules of procedure on the proposal of its chair, on the basis of standard rules to be drawn up by the Commission following consultation with Member States. Such standard rules shall be published by the Commission in the *Official Journal of the European Union*.

In so far as may be necessary, existing committees shall adapt their rules of procedure to the standard rules.

2. The principles and conditions on public access to documents and the rules on data protection applicable to the Commission shall apply to the committees.

Article 10 Information on committee proceedings

1. The Commission shall keep a register of committee proceedings which shall contain:

(a) a list of committees;

(b) the agendas of committee meetings;

(c) the summary records, together with the lists of the authorities and organisations to which the persons designated by the Member States to represent them belong;

(d) the draft implementing acts on which the committees are asked to deliver an opinion;

(e) the voting results;

(f) the final draft implementing acts following delivery of the opinion of the committees;

(g) information concerning the adoption of the final draft implementing acts by the Commission; and

(h) statistical data on the work of the committees.

2. The Commission shall also publish an annual report on the work of the committees.

3. The European Parliament and the Council shall have access to the information referred to in paragraph 1 in accordance with the applicable rules.

4. At the same time as they are sent to the committee members, the Commission shall make available to the European Parliament and the Council the documents referred to in points (b), (d) and (f) of paragraph 1 whilst also informing them of the availability of such documents.

5. The references of all documents referred to in points (a) to (g) of paragraph 1 as well as the information referred to in paragraph 1(h) shall be made public in the register.

Article 11 Right of scrutiny for the European Parliament and the Council

Where a basic act is adopted under the ordinary legislative procedure, either the European Parliament or the Council may at any time indicate to the Commission that, in its view, a draft implementing act exceeds the implementing powers provided for in the basic act. In such a case, the Commission shall review the draft implementing act, taking account of the positions expressed, and shall inform the European Parliament and the Council whether it intends to maintain, amend or withdraw the draft implementing act.

Article 16 Entry into force

This Regulation shall enter into force on 1 March 2011.

This Regulation is binding in its entirety and directly applicable in all Member States.

Done at Strasbourg, 16 February 2011.
(Signatures omitted.)

Court of Justice of the European Union

RECOMMENDATIONS to national courts and tribunals, in relation to the initiation of preliminary ruling proceedings*

[OJ 2019 C830/01]

Introduction

1. The reference for a preliminary ruling, provided for in Article 19(3)(b) of the Treaty on European Union ('TEU') and Article 267 of the Treaty on the Functioning of the European Union ('TFEU'), is a fundamental mechanism of EU law. It is designed to ensure the uniform interpretation and application of EU law within the European Union, by offering the courts and tribunals of the Member States a means of bringing before the Court of Justice of the European Union ('the Court') for a preliminary ruling questions concerning the interpretation of EU law or the validity of acts adopted by the institutions, bodies, offices or agencies of the Union.

2. The preliminary ruling procedure is based on close cooperation between the Court and the courts and tribunals of the Member States. In order to ensure that that procedure is fully effective, it is necessary to recall its essential characteristics and to provide further information to clarify the provisions of the rules of procedure relating, in particular, to the originator, subject matter and

* **Editor's Note:** This version of the Recommendations is the version from 2019, OJ 2019/C380/01.

scope of a request for a preliminary ruling, as well as to the form and content of such a request. That information—which applies to all requests for a preliminary ruling (I)—is supplemented by provisions concerning requests for a preliminary ruling requiring particularly expeditious handling (II) and by an annex which summarises, by way of a reminder, all the elements that must be included in a request for a preliminary ruling.

I. Provisions which apply to all requests for a preliminary ruling

The originator of the request for a preliminary ruling

3. The jurisdiction of the Court to give a preliminary ruling on the interpretation or validity of EU law is exercised exclusively on the initiative of the national courts and tribunals, whether or not the parties to the main proceedings have expressed the wish that a question be referred to the Court. In so far as it is called upon to assume responsibility for the subsequent judicial decision, it is for the national court or tribunal before which a dispute has been brought—and for that court or tribunal alone—to determine, in the light of the particular circumstances of each case, both the need for a request for a preliminary ruling in order to enable it to deliver its decision and the relevance of the questions which it submits to the Court.

4. Status as a court or tribunal is interpreted by the Court as an autonomous concept of EU law. The Court takes account of a number of factors such as whether the body making the reference is established by law, whether it is permanent, whether its jurisdiction is compulsory, whether its procedure is *inter partes*, whether it applies rules of law and whether it is independent.

5. The courts and tribunals of the Member States may refer a question to the Court on the interpretation or validity of EU law where they consider that a decision of the Court on the question is necessary to enable them to give judgment (see second paragraph of Article 267 TFEU). A reference for a preliminary ruling may, inter alia, prove particularly useful when a question of interpretation is raised before the national court or tribunal that is new and of general interest for the uniform application of EU law, or where the existing case-law does not appear to provide the necessary guidance in a new legal context or set of facts.

6. Where a question is raised in the context of a case that is pending before a court or tribunal against whose decisions there is no judicial remedy under national law, that court or tribunal is nonetheless required to bring a request for a preliminary ruling before the Court (see third paragraph of Article 267 TFEU), unless there is already well-established case-law on the point or unless the correct interpretation of the rule of law in question admits of no reasonable doubt.

7. It follows, moreover, from settled case-law that although national courts and tribunals may reject pleas raised before them challenging the validity of acts of an institution, body, office or agency of the Union, the Court has exclusive jurisdiction to declare such acts invalid. When it has doubts about the validity of such an act, a court or tribunal of a Member State must therefore refer the matter to the Court, stating the reasons why it has such doubts.

The subject matter and scope of the request for a preliminary ruling

8. A request for a preliminary ruling must concern the interpretation or validity of EU law, not the interpretation of rules of national law or issues of fact raised in the main proceedings.

9. *The Court can give a preliminary ruling only if EU law applies to the case in the main proceedings.* It is essential, in that respect, that the referring court or tribunal set out all the relevant matters of fact and of law that have prompted it to consider that any provisions of EU law may be applicable in the case.

10. With regard to references for a preliminary ruling concerning the interpretation of the Charter of Fundamental Rights of the European Union, it must be noted that, under Article 51(1) of the Charter, the provisions of the Charter are addressed to the Member States only when they are implementing EU law. While the circumstances of such implementation can vary, it must nevertheless be clearly and unequivocally apparent from the request for a preliminary ruling that a rule of EU

law other than the Charter is applicable to the case in the main proceedings. Since the Court has no jurisdiction to give a preliminary ruling where a legal situation does not come within the scope of EU law, any *provisions of the Charter* that may be relied upon by the referring court or tribunal *cannot, of themselves, form the basis for such jurisdiction.*

11. Lastly, although, in order to deliver its decision, the Court necessarily takes into account the legal and factual context of the dispute in the main proceedings, as defined by the referring court or tribunal in its request for a preliminary ruling, it does not itself apply EU law to that dispute. When ruling on the interpretation or validity of EU law, the Court makes every effort to give a reply which will be of assistance in resolving the dispute in the main proceedings, but it is for the referring court or tribunal to draw case-specific conclusions, if necessary by disapplying the rule of national law that has been held to be incompatible with EU law.

The appropriate stage at which to make a reference for a preliminary ruling

12. A national court or tribunal may submit a request for a preliminary ruling to the Court as soon as it finds that a ruling on the interpretation or validity of EU law is necessary to enable it to give judgment. It is that court or tribunal which is in fact in the best position to decide at what stage of the national proceedings such a request should be made.

13. Since, however, that request will serve as the basis of the proceedings before the Court and the Court must therefore have available to it all the information that will enable it both to assess whether it has jurisdiction to give a reply to the questions raised and, if so, to give a useful reply to those questions, it is necessary that a decision to make a reference for a preliminary ruling be taken when the national proceedings have reached a stage at which the referring court or tribunal is able to *define, in sufficient detail, the legal and factual context of the case in the main proceedings, and the legal issues which it raises*. In the interests of the proper administration of justice, it may also be appropriate for the reference to be made only after both sides have been heard.

The form and content of the request for a preliminary ruling

14. The request for a preliminary ruling may be in any form allowed by national law, but it should be borne in mind that that request serves as the basis of the proceedings before the Court and is served on all the interested persons referred to in Article 23 of the Protocol on the Statute of the Court of Justice of the European Union ('the Statute') and, in particular, on all the Member States, with a view to obtaining any observations they may wish to make. Owing to the consequential need to translate it into all the official languages of the European Union, the request for a preliminary ruling should therefore be drafted simply, clearly and precisely by the referring court or tribunal, avoiding superfluous detail. As experience has shown, about 10 pages are often sufficient to set out adequately the legal and factual context of a request for a preliminary ruling and the grounds for making the reference to the Court.

15. The content of any request for a preliminary ruling is prescribed by Article 94 of the Rules of Procedure of the Court and is summarised, by way of a reminder, in the annex hereto. In addition to the text of the questions referred to the Court for a preliminary ruling, *the request for a preliminary ruling must contain*:

- a summary of the subject matter of the dispute in the main proceedings and the relevant findings of fact as determined by the referring court or tribunal, or, at the very least, an account of the facts on which the questions referred are based,
- the tenor of any national provisions applicable in the case and, where appropriate, the relevant national case-law, and
- a statement of the reasons which prompted the referring court or tribunal to inquire about the interpretation or validity of certain provisions of EU law, and the relationship between those provisions and the national legislation applicable to the main proceedings.

In the absence of one or more of the above, the Court may find it necessary, notably on the basis of Article 53(2) of the Rules of Procedure, to decline jurisdiction to give a preliminary ruling on the questions referred or dismiss the request for a preliminary ruling as inadmissible.

16. In its request for a preliminary ruling, the referring court or tribunal must provide the *precise references for the national provisions applicable to the facts of the dispute in the main proceedings and for the provisions of EU law* whose interpretation is sought or whose validity is challenged. Those references must, as far as possible, include both the exact title and date of adoption of the acts containing the provisions concerned and the publication references for those acts. When referring to case-law, the referring court or tribunal is also requested to mention the European Case Law Identifier (ECLI) of the decision concerned.

17. If it considers it necessary for the purpose of understanding the case, the referring court or tribunal may briefly set out the *main arguments of the parties to the main proceedings*. It should be borne in mind in that context that only the request for a preliminary ruling will be translated, not any annexes to that request.

18. The referring court or tribunal may also briefly state *its view on the answer to be given to the questions referred for a preliminary ruling*. That information may be useful to the Court, particularly where it is called upon to give a preliminary ruling in an expedited or urgent procedure.

19. Lastly, *the questions referred* to the Court for a preliminary ruling must appear *in a separate and clearly identified section of the order for reference*, preferably at the beginning or the end. It must be possible to understand them on their own terms, without it being necessary to refer to the statement of the grounds for the request.

20. In order to make the request for a preliminary ruling easier to read, it is essential that the Court receive it in typewritten form and that the pages and paragraphs of the order for reference be numbered. Handwritten requests for a preliminary ruling will not be processed by the Court.

Protection of personal data and anonymisation of the request for a preliminary ruling

21. In order to ensure optimal protection of personal data in the Court's handling of the case, service of the request for a preliminary ruling on the interested persons referred to in Article 23 of the Statute and the subsequent dissemination, in all official languages of the European Union, of the decision closing the proceedings, *the referring court or tribunal*—which alone has full knowledge of the file submitted to the Court—*is invited to anonymise the case by replacing, for example using initials or a combination of letters, the names of individuals* referred to in the request *and by redacting information that might enable them to be identified*. Given the increasing use of new information technologies and, in particular, the use of search engines, any anonymisation effected after the request for a preliminary ruling has been served on the interested persons referred to in Article 23 of the Statute and publication of the notice relating to the case in the *Official Journal of the European Union* is likely to be less effective.

22. If the referring court or tribunal has a nominative version of the request for a preliminary ruling, containing the full names and contact details of the parties to the main proceedings, and an anonymised version of that request, it is requested to send both versions to the Court to facilitate the Court's handling of the case.

Transmission to the Court of the request for a preliminary ruling and of the case file in the national proceedings

23. The request for a preliminary ruling must be dated and signed, then sent to the Court Registry electronically or by post (Registry of the Court of Justice, Rue du Fort Niedergrünewald, L-2925 Luxembourg). For reasons connected, in particular, with the need to ensure expeditious handling of the case and optimal communication with the referring court or tribunal, the Court recommends that national courts and tribunals use the e-Curia application. The rules on access to that application, which enables procedural documents to be lodged and served electronically, and the conditions of use of e-Curia may be viewed on the institution's website (https://curia.europa.eu/jcms/jcms/P_78957/en/). In order to facilitate the Court's processing of requests for a preliminary ruling and, in particular, their translation into all the official languages of the European Union, national courts and tribunals are requested, in addition to sending the original version of the request for a preliminary ruling via e-Curia, to send an editable version (word processing software such as 'Word', 'OpenOffice' or 'LibreOffice') of that request to the following address: DDP-GreffeCour@curia.europa.eu.

24. The request for a preliminary ruling must reach the Registry together with all the relevant documents and documents useful for the Court's handling of the case and, in particular, the precise contact details for the parties to the main proceedings and their representatives, if any, as well as the file of the case in the main proceedings or a copy of it. The file (or copy file)—which may be sent electronically or by post—will be retained at the Registry throughout the proceedings before the Court where, unless otherwise indicated by the referring court or tribunal, it may be consulted by the interested persons referred to in Article 23 of the Statute.

Interaction between the reference for a preliminary ruling and the national proceedings

25. Although the referring court or tribunal may still order protective measures, particularly in connection with a reference on determination of validity, the lodging of a request for a preliminary ruling nevertheless calls for the national proceedings to be stayed until the Court has given its ruling.

26. While the Court, in principle, remains seised of a request for a preliminary ruling for so long as that request is not withdrawn by the referring court or tribunal, it must nevertheless be borne in mind that the Court's role in the preliminary ruling procedure is to contribute to the effective administration of justice in the Member States, and not to give opinions on general or hypothetical questions. Since the preliminary ruling procedure is predicated on there being proceedings actually pending before the referring court or tribunal, it is incumbent on that court or tribunal to inform the Court of any procedural step that may affect the referral and, in particular, of any discontinuance or withdrawal or of any amicable settlement of the dispute in the main proceedings, and of any other event leading to the termination of the proceedings. The referring court or tribunal must also inform the Court of any decision delivered in the context of an appeal against the order for reference and of the consequences of that decision for the request for a preliminary ruling. In the interests of the proper conduct of the preliminary ruling proceedings before the Court and, in particular, to ensure that the Court does not devote time and resources to a case that is likely to be withdrawn or become devoid of purpose, it is important that such information is communicated to the Court with the minimum of delay.

27. National courts and tribunals should also note that the withdrawal of a request for a preliminary ruling may have an impact on the management of similar cases by the referring court or tribunal. Where the outcome of a number of cases pending before the referring court or tribunal depends on the reply to be given by the Court to the questions submitted by that court or tribunal, it is appropriate for that court or tribunal to join those cases before submitting to the Court its request for a preliminary ruling in order to enable the Court to reply to the questions referred notwithstanding any withdrawal of one or more cases.

Costs and legal aid

28. Preliminary ruling proceedings before the Court are free of charge and the Court does not rule on the costs of the parties to the proceedings pending before the referring court or tribunal. It is for the referring court or tribunal to rule on those costs.

29. If a party to the main proceedings has insufficient means, the Court may grant that party legal aid to cover the costs, particularly those in respect of its representation, which it incurs before the Court. That aid can, however, be granted only if the party in question is not already in receipt of aid under national rules or to the extent to which that aid does not cover, or covers only partly, costs incurred before the Court. That party is requested in any event to send to the Court all information and supporting documents that will enable his or her true financial situation to be assessed.

Conduct of the proceedings before the Court and the action taken by the referring court or tribunal upon the Court's decision

30. The Court Registry will remain in contact with the referring court or tribunal throughout the proceedings, and will send it copies of all procedural documents and any requests for information or clarification deemed necessary in order for a useful reply to be given to the questions referred by that court or tribunal.

31. At the end of the proceedings which, as a rule, comprise a written part and an oral part, the Court gives its ruling in the form of a judgment on the questions put by the referring court or tribunal. In some cases, however, the Court may find it necessary to rule on those questions without an oral part of the procedure, or even without seeking the written observations of the interested persons referred to in Article 23 of the Statute. That is the case, in particular, when the question referred for a preliminary ruling is identical to a question on which the Court has already ruled, or where the answer to such a question may be clearly deduced from existing case-law or admits of no reasonable doubt. In such cases, the Court will, on the basis of Article 99 of its Rules of Procedure, rule expeditiously on the question put, by a reasoned order which has the same scope and the same binding force as a judgment.

32. After the judgment has been delivered or the order closing the proceedings has been signed, the Registry will send the Court's decision to the referring court or tribunal, which is requested to inform the Court of the action taken upon that decision in the case in the main proceedings. The final decision of the referring court or tribunal must be sent, with an express reference to the case number of the case before the Court, to the following address: Follow-up-DDP@curia.europa.eu.

II. Provisions applicable to requests for a preliminary ruling requiring particularly expeditious handling

33. As provided in Article 23a of the Statute and Articles 105 to 114 of the Rules of Procedure, a reference for a preliminary ruling may, in certain circumstances, be determined pursuant to an expedited procedure or an urgent procedure. The Court will decide whether these procedures are to be applied, either on submission by the referring court or tribunal of a separate, duly reasoned, request setting out the matters of fact or of law which justify the application of such procedure(s), or, exceptionally, of its own motion, where that appears to be required by the nature or the particular circumstances of the case.

Conditions for the application of the expedited procedure and the urgent procedure

34. Article 105 of the Rules of Procedure provides that a reference for a preliminary ruling may thus be determined pursuant to *an expedited procedure*, derogating from the provisions of those rules, where the nature of the case requires that it be dealt with within a short time. Since that procedure imposes significant constraints on all those involved in it, and, in particular, on all the Member States called upon to lodge observations, whether written or oral, within much shorter time limits than would ordinarily apply, its application must be sought only when particular circumstances create an emergency that warrants the Court ruling quickly on the questions referred. That may be the case, inter alia, if there is a serious and immediate danger to public health or to the environment which a prompt decision by the Court might help to avert, or if particular circumstances require uncertainties concerning fundamental issues of national constitutional law and of EU law to be resolved within a very short time. According to settled case-law, the large number of persons or legal situations potentially affected by the decision that the referring court or tribunal has to deliver after bringing the matter before the Court for a preliminary ruling, the fact that there may be important economic issues at stake or that the referring court or tribunal is obliged to rule expeditiously do not, however, in themselves constitute exceptional circumstances that would justify the use of the expedited procedure.

35. The same applies *a fortiori* to *the urgent preliminary ruling procedure*, provided for in Article 107 of the Rules of Procedure. That procedure, which applies only in the areas covered by Title V of Part Three of the TFEU, relating to the area of freedom, security and justice, imposes even greater constraints on those concerned, since it limits the number of parties authorised to lodge written observations and, in cases of extreme urgency, allows the written part of the procedure before the Court to be omitted altogether. The application of the urgent procedure must therefore be requested only where it is absolutely necessary for the Court to give its ruling very quickly on the questions submitted by the referring court or tribunal.

36. Although it is not possible to provide an exhaustive list of such circumstances, particularly because of the varied and evolving nature of the rules of EU law governing the area of freedom, security

and justice, a national court or tribunal may, for example, consider submitting a request for the urgent preliminary ruling procedure to be applied in the case, referred to in the fourth paragraph of Article 267 TFEU, of a person in custody or deprived of his or her liberty, where the answer to the question raised is decisive as to the assessment of that person's legal situation, or in proceedings concerning parental authority or custody of young children, in so far, in particular, as the outcome of the dispute in the main proceedings depends on the answer to the question referred for a preliminary ruling and the use of the ordinary procedure could cause serious, and perhaps irreparable, harm to the relationship between a child and (one of) that child's parents or to the child's development and integration into his or her family and social environment. By contrast, mere economic interests, however substantial and legitimate they may be, the legal uncertainty affecting the parties to the main proceedings or other parties to similar disputes, the large number of persons or legal situations potentially affected by the decision that a referring court has to deliver after bringing a matter before the Court for a preliminary ruling, or the large number of cases that may be affected by the decision of the Court do not constitute, as such, circumstances that would justify the application of the urgent preliminary ruling procedure.

The request for application of the expedited procedure or the urgent procedure

37. To enable the Court to decide quickly whether the expedited procedure or the urgent preliminary ruling procedure should be applied, the request must *set out precisely the matters of fact and law which establish the urgency* and, in particular, the risks involved in following the ordinary procedure. In so far as it is possible to do so, the referring court or tribunal must also briefly state its view on the answer to be given to the questions referred. Such a statement makes it easier for the parties to the main proceedings and the other interested persons participating in the procedure to define their positions, and therefore contributes to the rapidity of the procedure.

38. The request for the application of the expedited procedure or the urgent procedure must in any event be submitted in an unambiguous form that enables the Registry to establish immediately that the file has to be dealt with in a particular way. Accordingly, the referring court or tribunal is requested to specify which of the two procedures is required in the particular case, and to mention in its request the relevant article of the Rules of Procedure (Article 105 for the expedited procedure or Article 107 for the urgent procedure). That mention must be included in a clearly identifiable place in its order for reference or in a separate letter from the referring court or tribunal.

39. As regards the order for reference itself, it is particularly important that it should be concise where the matter is urgent, as this will help to ensure the rapidity of the procedure.

Communication between the Court, the referring court or tribunal and the parties to the main proceedings

40. A court or tribunal submitting a request for the expedited procedure or the urgent procedure to be applied is requested to send that request and the order for reference itself—together with the text of the latter in an editable format (word processing software such as 'Word', 'Open Office' or 'LibreOffice')—by means of the e-Curia application or by email (DDP-GreffeCour@curia.europa.eu).

41. In order to facilitate subsequent communication by the Court with the referring court or tribunal and with the parties to the main proceedings, the referring court or tribunal is also requested to state its email address and any fax number which may be used by the Court, together with the email addresses and any fax numbers of the representatives of the parties to the main proceedings.

ANNEX

The essential elements of a request for a preliminary ruling

This annex summarises, by way of a reminder, the main elements that must be included in a request for a preliminary ruling. These are followed by an indication of the paragraphs in the present recommendations in which those elements are discussed in more detail.

Whether transmitted electronically or by post, all requests for a preliminary ruling must mention:

1. the identity of the court or tribunal making the reference and, where appropriate, the chamber or formation of the court or tribunal having jurisdiction (see, in that respect, paragraphs 3 to 7);

2. the precise identity of the parties to the main proceedings and of anyone representing them before the referring court or tribunal (with regard to the parties to the main proceedings, see, however, paragraphs 21 and 22 of the present recommendations, in relation to the protection of personal data);

3. the subject matter of the dispute in the main proceedings and the relevant facts (see paragraph 15);

4. the relevant provisions of national law and of EU law (see paragraphs 15 and 16);

5. the reasons that prompted the referring court or tribunal to inquire about the interpretation or validity of EU law (see paragraphs 8 to 11 and 15 to 18);

6. the questions referred for a preliminary ruling (see paragraph 19) and, if applicable,

7. the possible need for specific treatment of the request, related, for example, to the need to preserve the anonymity of individuals concerned by the dispute or to the particularly expeditious way in which the request should be dealt with by the Court (see paragraph 33 et seq.).

As regards form, requests for a preliminary ruling must be typewritten, dated and signed and must be received at the Court Registry, preferably electronically, together with all the documents that are relevant and useful for the handling of the case (see, in that respect, paragraphs 20 to 24 of the present recommendations and, with regard to requests requiring particularly expeditious treatment, paragraphs 40 and 41).

Transmission channels recommended by the Court

In order to ensure the best possible communication with courts and tribunals that have referred questions to the Court for a preliminary ruling, the Court recommends the use of the following transmission channels:

(1) Lodging of the request for a preliminary ruling (or of other relevant documents linked to that request):

- Signed original of the request for a preliminary ruling (or of the other documents linked to that request): to be sent via the e-Curia application. The rules on access to that application, which is free of charge and secure, and the conditions of use of e-Curia, are available here: https://curia.europa.eu/jcms/jcms/P_78957/en/
- Editable version of the request for a preliminary ruling (or of the other documents linked to it): DDP-GreffeCour@curia.europa.eu

(2) Transmission of the final decision of the referring court or tribunal (anonymised, if necessary, including for the purposes of being placed online), following the Court's decision on the request for a preliminary ruling: Follow-up-DDP@curia.europa.eu

Rules of Procedure of the Court of Justice*

Introductory provisions

Title I Organisation of the Court

Chapter 7 Formations of the Court

Section 1 Composition of the formations of the Court

Article 27 Composition of the Grand Chamber

1. The Grand Chamber shall, for each case, be composed of the President and the Vice-President of the Court, three Presidents of Chambers of five Judges, the Judge-Rapporteur and the number of Judges necessary to reach 15. The last-mentioned Judges and the three Presidents of Chambers of

* **Editor's Note:** Of 25 September 2012 (OJ 2012 L265/1) as amended to 18 June 2013 (OJ 2013 L173/65), 19 July 2016 (OJ 2016 L217/69), which replaced entirely the previously much amended rules of procedure from 1991, 9 April 2019 (OJ 2019 L111/73) and 26 November 2019 (OJ 2019 L316/103). Preamble and recitals omitted.

five Judges shall be designated from the lists referred to in paragraphs 3 and 4 of this Article, following the order laid down therein. The starting-point on each of those lists, in every case assigned to the Grand Chamber, shall be the name of the Judge immediately following the last Judge designated from the list concerned for the preceding case assigned to that formation of the Court.

2. After the election of the President and the Vice-President of the Court, and then of the Presidents of the Chambers of five Judges, a list of the Presidents of Chambers of five Judges and a list of the other Judges shall be drawn up for the purposes of determining the composition of the Grand Chamber.

3. The list of the Presidents of Chambers of five Judges shall be drawn up according to the order laid down in Article 7 of these Rules.

4. The list of the other Judges shall be drawn up according to the order laid down in Article 7 of these Rules, alternating with the reverse order: the first Judge on that list shall be the first according to the order laid down in that Article, the second Judge shall be the last according to that order, the third Judge shall be the second according to that order, the fourth Judge the penultimate according to that order, and so on.

5. The lists referred to in paragraphs 3 and 4 shall be published in the *Official Journal of the European Union*.

6. In cases which are assigned to the Grand Chamber between the beginning of a calendar year in which there is a partial replacement of Judges and the moment when that replacement has taken place, two substitute Judges may be designated to complete the formation of the Court for so long as the attainment of the quorum referred to in the third paragraph of Article 17 of the Statute is in doubt. Those substitute Judges shall be the two Judges appearing on the list referred to in paragraph 4 immediately after the last Judge designated for the composition of the Grand Chamber in the case.

7. The substitute Judges shall replace, in the order of the list referred to in paragraph 4, such Judges as are unable to take part in the determination of the case.

Article 28 Composition of the Chambers of five and of three Judges

1. The Chambers of five Judges and of three Judges shall, for each case, be composed of the President of the Chamber, the Judge-Rapporteur and the number of Judges required to attain the number of five and three Judges respectively. Those last-mentioned Judges shall be designated from the lists referred to in paragraphs 2 and 3, following the order laid down therein. The starting-point on those lists, in every case assigned to a Chamber, shall be the name of the Judge immediately following the last Judge designated from the list for the preceding case assigned to the Chamber concerned.

2. For the composition of the Chambers of five Judges, after the election of the Presidents of those Chambers lists shall be drawn up including all the Judges attached to the Chamber concerned, with the exception of its President. The lists shall be drawn up in the same way as the list referred to in Article 27(4).

3. For the composition of the Chambers of three Judges, after the election of the Presidents of those Chambers lists shall be drawn up including all the Judges attached to the Chamber concerned, with the exception of its President. The lists shall be drawn up according to the order laid down in Article 7.

4. The lists referred to in paragraphs 2 and 3 shall be published in the *Official Journal of the European Union*.

Section 2 Deliberations

Article 32 Procedures concerning deliberations

1. The deliberations of the Court shall be and shall remain secret.

2. When a hearing has taken place, only those Judges who participated in that hearing and, where relevant, the Assistant Rapporteur responsible for the consideration of the case shall take part in the deliberations.

3. Every Judge taking part in the deliberations shall state his opinion and the reasons for it.

4. The conclusions reached by the majority of the Judges after final discussion shall determine the decision of the Court.

Article 33 Number of Judges taking part in the deliberations
Where, by reason of a Judge being prevented from acting, there is an even number of Judges, the most junior Judge for the purposes of Article 7 of these Rules shall abstain from taking part in the deliberations unless he is the Judge-Rapporteur. In that case the Judge immediately senior to him shall abstain from taking part in the deliberations.

Article 34 Quorum of the Grand Chamber
1. If, for a case assigned to the Grand Chamber, it is not possible to attain the quorum referred to in the third paragraph of Article 17 of the Statute, the President of the Court shall designate one or more other Judges according to the order of the list referred to in Article 27(4) of these Rules.
2. If a hearing has taken place before that designation, the Court shall rehear oral argument from the parties and the Opinion of the Advocate General.

Article 35 Quorum of the Chambers of five and of three Judges
1. If, for a case assigned to a Chamber of five or of three Judges, it is not possible to attain the quorum referred to in the second paragraph of Article 17 of the Statute, the President of the Court shall designate one or more other Judges according to the order of the list referred to in Article 28(2) or (3), respectively, of these Rules. If it is not possible to replace the Judge prevented from acting by a Judge of the same Chamber, the President of that Chamber shall so inform the President of the Court forthwith who shall designate another Judge to complete the Chamber.
2. Article 34(2) shall apply, *mutatis mutandis*, to the Chambers of five and of three Judges.

Chapter 8 Languages

Article 36 Language of a case
The language of a case shall be Bulgarian, Croatian, Czech, Danish, Dutch, English, Estonian, Finnish, French, German, Greek, Hungarian, Irish, Italian, Latvian, Lithuanian, Maltese, Polish, Portuguese, Romanian, Slovak, Slovene, Spanish or Swedish.

Article 37 Determination of the language of a case
1. In direct actions, the language of a case shall be chosen by the applicant, except that:
   (a) where the defendant is a Member State, the language of the case shall be the official language of that State; where that State has more than one official language, the applicant may choose between them;
   (b) at the joint request of the parties, the use of another of the languages mentioned in Article 36 for all or part of the proceedings may be authorised;
   (c) at the request of one of the parties, and after the opposite party and the Advocate General have been heard, the use of another of the languages mentioned in Article 36 may be authorised as the language of the case for all or part of the proceedings by way of derogation from subparagraphs (a) and (b); such a request may not be submitted by one of the institutions of the European Union.

2. Without prejudice to the provisions of paragraph 1(b) and (c), and of Article 38(4) and (5) of these Rules,
   (a) in appeals against decisions of the General Court as referred to in Articles 56 and 57 of the Statute, the language of the case shall be the language of the decision of the General Court against which the appeal is brought;
   (b) where, in accordance with the second paragraph of Article 62 of the Statute, the Court decides to review a decision of the General Court, the language of the case shall be the language of the decision of the General Court which is the subject of review;
   (c) in the case of challenges concerning the costs to be recovered, applications to set aside judgments by default, third-party proceedings and applications for interpretation or revision of a judgment or for the Court to remedy a failure to adjudicate, the language of

the case shall be the language of the decision to which those applications or challenges relate.

3. In preliminary ruling proceedings, the language of the case shall be the language of the referring court or tribunal. At the duly substantiated request of one of the parties to the main proceedings, and after the other party to the main proceedings and the Advocate General have been heard, the use of another of the languages mentioned in Article 36 may be authorised for the oral part of the procedure. Where granted, the authorisation to use that other language shall apply in respect of all the interested persons referred to in Article 23 of the Statute.

4. Requests as above may be decided on by the President; the latter may, and where he wishes to accede to a request without the agreement of all the parties must, refer the request to the Court.

Article 38 Use of the language of the case

1. The language of the case shall in particular be used in the written and oral pleadings of the parties, including the items and documents produced or annexed to them, and also in the minutes and decisions of the Court.

2. Any item or document produced or annexed that is expressed in another language must be accompanied by a translation into the language of the case.

3. However, in the case of substantial items or lengthy documents, translations may be confined to extracts. At any time the Court may, of its own motion or at the request of one of the parties, call for a complete or fuller translation.

4. Notwithstanding the foregoing provisions, a Member State shall be entitled to use its official language when taking part in preliminary ruling proceedings, when intervening in a case before the Court or when bringing a matter before the Court pursuant to Article 259 TFEU. This provision shall apply both to written documents and to oral statements. The Registrar shall arrange in each instance for translation into the language of the case.

5. The States, other than the Member States, which are parties to the EEA Agreement, and also the EFTA Surveillance Authority, shall be entitled to use one of the languages mentioned in Article 36, other than the language of the case, when they take part in preliminary ruling proceedings or intervene in a case before the Court. This provision shall apply both to written documents and to oral statements. The Registrar shall arrange in each instance for translation into the language of the case.

6. Non-Member States taking part in preliminary ruling proceedings pursuant to the fourth paragraph of Article 23 of the Statute shall be entitled to use one of the languages mentioned in Article 36 other than the language of the case. This provision shall apply both to written documents and to oral statements. The Registrar shall arrange in each instance for translation into the language of the case.

7. Where a witness or expert states that he is unable adequately to express himself in one of the languages referred to in Article 36, the Court may authorise him to give his evidence in another language. The Registrar shall arrange for translation into the language of the case.

8. The President and the Vice-President of the Court and also the Presidents of Chambers in conducting oral proceedings, Judges and Advocates General in putting questions and Advocates General in delivering their Opinions may use one of the languages referred to in Article 36 other than the language of the case. The Registrar shall arrange for translation into the language of the case.

Title II Common procedural provisions

Chapter 3 Time-limits

Article 49 Calculation of time-limits

1. Any procedural time-limit prescribed by the Treaties, the Statute or these Rules shall be calculated as follows:

(a) where a time-limit expressed in days, weeks, months or years is to be calculated from the moment at which an event occurs or an action takes place, the day during which that event occurs or that action takes place shall not be counted as falling within the time-limit in question;

(b) a time-limit expressed in weeks, months or years shall end with the expiry of whichever day in the last week, month or year is the same day of the week, or falls on the same date, as the day during which the event or action from which the time-limit is to be calculated occurred or took place. If, in a time-limit expressed in months or years, the day on which it should expire does not occur in the last month, the time-limit shall end with the expiry of the last day of that month;

(c) where a time-limit is expressed in months and days, it shall first be calculated in whole months, then in days;

(d) time-limits shall include Saturdays, Sundays and the official holidays referred to in Article 24(6) of these Rules;

(e) time-limits shall not be suspended during the judicial vacations.

2. If the time-limit would otherwise end on a Saturday, Sunday or an official holiday, it shall be extended until the end of the first subsequent working day.

Article 50 Proceedings against a measure adopted by an institution

Where the time-limit allowed for initiating proceedings against a measure adopted by an institution runs from the publication of that measure, that time-limit shall be calculated, for the purposes of Article 49(1)(a), from the end of the 14th day after publication of the measure in the *Official Journal of the European Union*.

Article 51 Extension on account of distance

The procedural time-limits shall be extended on account of distance by a single period of 10 days.

Article 52 Setting and extension of time-limits

1. Any time-limit prescribed by the Court pursuant to these Rules may be extended.

2. The President and the Presidents of Chambers may delegate to the Registrar power of signature for the purposes of setting certain time-limits which, pursuant to these Rules, it falls to them to prescribe, or of extending such time-limits.

Title III References for a preliminary ruling

Chapter 1 General provisions

Article 93 Scope

The procedure shall be governed by the provisions of this Title:

(a) in the cases covered by Article 23 of the Statute,

(b) as regards references for interpretation which may be provided for by agreements to which the European Union or the Member States are parties.

Article 94 Content of the request for a preliminary ruling

In addition to the text of the questions referred to the Court for a preliminary ruling, the request for a preliminary ruling shall contain:

(a) a summary of the subject-matter of the dispute and the relevant findings of fact as determined by the referring court or tribunal, or, at least, an account of the facts on which the questions are based;

(b) the tenor of any national provisions applicable in the case and, where appropriate, the relevant national case-law;

(c) a statement of the reasons which prompted the referring court or tribunal to inquire about the interpretation or validity of certain provisions of European Union law, and the relationship between those provisions and the national legislation applicable to the main proceedings.

Article 95 Anonymity

1. Where anonymity has been granted by the referring court or tribunal, the Court shall respect that anonymity in the proceedings pending before it.

2. At the request of the referring court or tribunal, of a party to the main proceedings or of its own motion, the Court may also render anonymous one or more persons or entities concerned by the case.

Article 96 Participation in preliminary ruling proceedings

1. Pursuant to Article 23 of the Statute, the following shall be authorised to submit observations to the Court:

(a) the parties to the main proceedings,
(b) the Member States,
(c) the European Commission,
(d) the institution which adopted the act the validity or interpretation of which is in dispute,
(e) the States, other than the Member States, which are parties to the EEA Agreement, and also the EFTA Surveillance Authority, where a question concerning one of the fields of application of that Agreement is referred to the Court for a preliminary ruling,
(f) non-Member States which are parties to an agreement relating to a specific subject-matter, concluded with the Council, where the agreement so provides and where a court or tribunal of a Member State refers to the Court of Justice for a preliminary ruling a question falling within the scope of that agreement.

2. Non-participation in the written part of the procedure does not preclude participation in the oral part of the procedure.

Article 97 Parties to the main proceedings

1. The parties to the main proceedings are those who are determined as such by the referring court or tribunal in accordance with national rules of procedure.

2. Where the referring court or tribunal informs the Court that a new party has been admitted to the main proceedings, when the proceedings before the Court are already pending, that party must accept the case as he finds it at the time when the Court was so informed. That party shall receive a copy of every procedural document already served on the interested persons referred to in Article 23 of the Statute.

3. As regards the representation and attendance of the parties to the main proceedings, the Court shall take account of the rules of procedure in force before the court or tribunal which made the reference. In the event of any doubt as to whether a person may under national law represent a party to the main proceedings, the Court may obtain information from the referring court or tribunal on the rules of procedure applicable.

Article 98 Translation and service of the request for a preliminary ruling

1. The requests for a preliminary ruling referred to in this Title shall be served on the Member States in the original version, accompanied by a translation into the official language of the State to which they are being addressed. Where appropriate, on account of the length of the request, such translation shall be replaced by the translation into the official language of the State to which it is addressed of a summary of that request, which will serve as a basis for the position to be adopted by that State. The summary shall include the full text of the question or questions referred for a preliminary ruling. That summary shall contain, in particular, in so far as that information appears in the request for a preliminary ruling, the subject-matter of the main proceedings, the essential arguments of the parties to those proceedings, a succinct presentation of the reasons for the reference for a preliminary ruling and the case-law and the provisions of national law and European Union law relied on.

2. In the cases covered by the third paragraph of Article 23 of the Statute, the requests for a preliminary ruling shall be served on the States, other than the Member States, which are parties to the EEA Agreement and also on the EFTA Surveillance Authority in the original version,

accompanied by a translation of the request, or where appropriate of a summary, into one of the languages referred to in Article 36, to be chosen by the addressee.

3. Where a non-Member State has the right to take part in preliminary ruling proceedings pursuant to the fourth paragraph of Article 23 of the Statute, the original version of the request for a preliminary ruling shall be served on it accompanied by a translation of the request, or where appropriate of a summary, into one of the languages referred to in Article 36, to be chosen by the non-Member State concerned.

Article 99 Reply by reasoned order

Where a question referred to the Court for a preliminary ruling is identical to a question on which the Court has already ruled, where the reply to such a question may be clearly deduced from existing case-law or where the answer to the question referred for a preliminary ruling admits of no reasonable doubt, the Court may at any time, on a proposal from the Judge-Rapporteur and after hearing the Advocate General, decide to rule by reasoned order.

Article 100 Circumstances in which the Court remains seised

1. The Court shall remain seised of a request for a preliminary ruling for as long as it is not withdrawn by the court or tribunal which made that request to the Court. The withdrawal of a request may be taken into account until notice of the date of delivery of the judgment has been served on the interested persons referred to in Article 23 of the Statute.

2. However, the Court may at any time declare that the conditions of its jurisdiction are no longer fulfilled.

Article 101 Request for clarification

1. Without prejudice to the measures of organisation of procedure and measures of inquiry provided for in these Rules, the Court may, after hearing the Advocate General, request clarification from the referring court or tribunal within a time-limit prescribed by the Court.

2. The reply of the referring court or tribunal to that request shall be served on the interested persons referred to in Article 23 of the Statute.

Article 102 Costs of the preliminary ruling proceedings

It shall be for the referring court or tribunal to decide as to the costs of the preliminary ruling proceedings.

Article 103 Rectification of judgments and orders

1. Clerical mistakes, errors in calculation and obvious inaccuracies affecting judgments or orders may be rectified by the Court, of its own motion or at the request of an interested person referred to in Article 23 of the Statute made within two weeks after delivery of the judgment or service of the order.

2. The Court shall take its decision after hearing the Advocate General.

3. The original of the rectification order shall be annexed to the original of the rectified decision. A note of this order shall be made in the margin of the original of the rectified decision.

Article 104 Interpretation of preliminary rulings

1. Article 158 of these Rules relating to the interpretation of judgments and orders shall not apply to decisions given in reply to a request for a preliminary ruling.

2. It shall be for the national courts or tribunals to assess whether they consider that sufficient guidance is given by a preliminary ruling, or whether it appears to them that a further reference to the Court is required.

Chapter 2 Expedited preliminary ruling procedure

Article 105 Expedited procedure

1. At the request of the referring court or tribunal or, exceptionally, of his own motion, the President of the Court may, where the nature of the case requires that it be dealt with within a short

time, after hearing the Judge-Rapporteur and the Advocate General, decide that a reference for a preliminary ruling is to be determined pursuant to an expedited procedure derogating from the provisions of these Rules.

2. In that event, the President shall immediately fix the date for the hearing, which shall be communicated to the interested persons referred to in Article 23 of the Statute when the request for a preliminary ruling is served.

3. The interested persons referred to in the preceding paragraph may lodge statements of case or written observations within a time-limit prescribed by the President, which shall not be less than 15 days. The President may request those interested persons to restrict the matters addressed in their statement of case or written observations to the essential points of law raised by the request for a preliminary ruling.

4. The statements of case or written observations, if any, shall be communicated to all the interested persons referred to in Article 23 of the Statute prior to the hearing.

5. The Court shall rule after hearing the Advocate General.

Article 106 Transmission of procedural documents

1. The procedural documents referred to in the preceding Article shall be deemed to have been lodged on the transmission to the Registry, by telefax or any other technical means of communication available to the Court, of a copy of the signed original and the items and documents relied on in support of it, together with the schedule referred to in Article 57(4). The original of the document and the annexes referred to above shall be sent to the Registry immediately.

2. Where the preceding Article requires that a document be served on or communicated to a person, such service or communication may be effected by transmission of a copy of the document by telefax or any other technical means of communication available to the Court and the addressee.

Chapter 3 Urgent preliminary ruling procedure

Article 107 Scope of the urgent preliminary ruling procedure

1. A reference for a preliminary ruling which raises one or more questions in the areas covered by Title V of Part Three of the Treaty on the Functioning of the European Union may, at the request of the referring court or tribunal or, exceptionally, of the Court's own motion, be dealt with under an urgent procedure derogating from the provisions of these Rules.

2. The referring court or tribunal shall set out the matters of fact and law which establish the urgency and justify the application of that exceptional procedure and shall, in so far as possible, indicate the answer that it proposes to the questions referred.

3. If the referring court or tribunal has not submitted a request for the urgent procedure to be applied, the President of the Court may, if the application of that procedure appears, prima facie, to be required, ask the Chamber referred to in Article 108 to consider whether it is necessary to deal with the reference under that procedure.

Article 108 Decision as to urgency

1. The decision to deal with a reference for a preliminary ruling under the urgent procedure shall be taken by the designated Chamber, acting on a proposal from the Judge-Rapporteur and after hearing the Advocate General. The composition of that Chamber shall be determined in accordance with Article 28(2) on the day on which the case is assigned to the Judge-Rapporteur if the application of the urgent procedure is requested by the referring court or tribunal, or, if the application of that procedure is considered at the request of the President of the Court, on the day on which that request is made.

2. If the case is connected with a pending case assigned to a Judge-Rapporteur who is not a member of the designated Chamber, that Chamber may propose to the President of the Court that the case be assigned to that Judge-Rapporteur. Where the case is reassigned to that Judge-Rapporteur, the Chamber of five Judges which includes him shall carry out the duties of the designated Chamber in respect of that case. Article 29(1) shall apply.

Article 109 Written part of the urgent procedure

1. A request for a preliminary ruling shall, where the referring court or tribunal has requested the application of the urgent procedure or where the President has requested the designated Chamber to consider whether it is necessary to deal with the reference under that procedure, be served forthwith by the Registrar on the parties to the main proceedings, on the Member State from which the reference is made, on the European Commission and on the institution which adopted the act the validity or interpretation of which is in dispute.

2. The decision as to whether or not to deal with the reference for a preliminary ruling under the urgent procedure shall be served immediately on the referring court or tribunal and on the parties, Member State and institutions referred to in the preceding paragraph. The decision to deal with the reference under the urgent procedure shall prescribe the time-limit within which those parties or entities may lodge statements of case or written observations. The decision may specify the matters of law to which such statements of case or written observations must relate and may specify the maximum length of those documents.

3. Where a request for a preliminary ruling refers to an administrative procedure or judicial proceedings conducted in a Member State other than that from which the reference is made, the Court may invite that first Member State to provide all relevant information in writing or at the hearing.

4. As soon as the service referred to in paragraph 1 above has been effected, the request for a preliminary ruling shall also be communicated to the interested persons referred to in Article 23 of the Statute, other than the persons served, and the decision whether or not to deal with the reference for a preliminary ruling under the urgent procedure shall be communicated to those interested persons as soon as the service referred to in paragraph 2 has been effected.

5. The interested persons referred to in Article 23 of the Statute shall be informed as soon as possible of the likely date of the hearing.

6. Where the reference is not to be dealt with under the urgent procedure, the proceedings shall continue in accordance with the provisions of Article 23 of the Statute and the applicable provisions of these Rules.

Article 110 Service and information following the close of the written part of the procedure

1. Where a reference for a preliminary ruling is to be dealt with under the urgent procedure, the request for a preliminary ruling and the statements of case or written observations which have been lodged shall be served on the interested persons referred to in Article 23 of the Statute other than the parties and entities referred to in Article 109(1). The request for a preliminary ruling shall be accompanied by a translation, where appropriate of a summary, in accordance with Article 98.

2. The statements of case or written observations which have been lodged shall also be served on the parties and other interested persons referred to in Article 109(1).

3. The date of the hearing shall be communicated to the interested persons referred to in Article 23 of the Statute at the same time as the documents referred to in the preceding paragraphs are served.

Article 111 Omission of the written part of the procedure

The designated Chamber may, in cases of extreme urgency, decide to omit the written part of the procedure referred to in Article 109(2).

Article 112 Decision on the substance

The designated Chamber shall rule after hearing the Advocate General.

Article 113 Formation of the Court

1. The designated Chamber may decide to sit in a formation of three Judges. In that event, it shall be composed of the President of the designated Chamber, the Judge-Rapporteur and the first Judge or, as the case may be, the first two Judges designated from the list referred to in Article 28(2)

on the date on which the composition of the designated Chamber is determined in accordance with Article 108(1).

2. The designated Chamber may also request the Court to assign the case to a formation composed of a greater number of Judges. The urgent procedure shall continue before the new formation of the Court, where necessary after the reopening of the oral part of the procedure.

Article 114 Transmission of procedural documents

Procedural documents shall be transmitted in accordance with Article 106.

Title IV Direct actions

Chapter 1 Representation of the parties

Article 119 Obligation to be represented

1. A party may be represented only by his agent or lawyer.

2. Agents and lawyers must lodge at the Registry an official document or an authority to act issued by the party whom they represent.

3. The lawyer acting for a party must also lodge at the Registry a certificate that he is authorised to practise before a court of a Member State or of another State which is a party to the EEA Agreement.

4. If those documents are not lodged, the Registrar shall prescribe a reasonable time limit within which the party concerned is to produce them. If the party concerned fails to produce the required documents within the time limit prescribed, the President shall, after hearing the Judge-Rapporteur and the Advocate General, decide whether the non-compliance with that procedural requirement renders the application or written pleading formally inadmissible. If he considers it necessary, the President may refer that question to the Court of Justice.

Chapter 2 Written part of the procedure

Article 120 Content of the application

An application of the kind referred to in Article 21 of the Statute shall state:

(a) the name and address of the applicant;
(b) the name of the party against whom the application is made;
(c) the subject-matter of the proceedings, the pleas in law and arguments relied on and a summary of those pleas in law;
(d) the form of order sought by the applicant;
(e) where appropriate, any evidence produced or offered.

Article 121 Information relating to service

1. For the purpose of the proceedings, the application shall state an address for service. It shall indicate the name of the person who is authorised and has expressed willingness to accept service.

2. In addition to, or instead of, specifying an address for service as referred to in paragraph 1, the application may state that the lawyer or agent agrees that service is to be effected on him by telefax or any other technical means of communication.

3. If the application does not comply with the requirements referred to in paragraphs 1 or 2, all service on the party concerned for the purpose of the proceedings shall be effected, for so long as the defect has not been cured, by registered letter addressed to the agent or lawyer of that party. By way of derogation from Article 48, service shall then be deemed to be duly effected by the lodging of the registered letter at the post office of the place in which the Court has its seat.

Article 122 Annexes to the application

1. The application shall be accompanied, where appropriate, by the documents specified in the second paragraph of Article 21 of the Statute.

2. An application submitted under Article 273 TFEU shall be accompanied by a copy of the special agreement concluded between the Member States concerned.

3. If an application does not comply with the requirements set out in paragraphs 1 or 2 of this Article, the Registrar shall prescribe a reasonable time limit within which the applicant is to produce the abovementioned documents. If the applicant fails to put the application in order, the President shall, after hearing the Judge-Rapporteur and the Advocate General, decide whether the non-compliance with these conditions renders the application formally inadmissible. If he considers it necessary, the President may refer that question to the Court of Justice.

Article 123 Service of the application

The application shall be served on the defendant. In cases where Article 119(4) or Article 122(3) applies, service shall be effected as soon as the application has been put in order or the President or the Court has declared it admissible notwithstanding the failure to observe the requirements set out in those two Articles.

Article 124 Content of the defence

1. Within two months after service on him of the application, the defendant shall lodge a defence, stating:

    (a) the name and address of the defendant;
    (b) the pleas in law and arguments relied on;
    (c) the form of order sought by the defendant;
    (d) where appropriate, any evidence produced or offered.

2. Article 121 shall apply to the defence.

3. The time-limit laid down in paragraph 1 may exceptionally be extended by the President at the duly reasoned request of the defendant.

Article 125 Transmission of documents

Where the European Parliament, the Council or the European Commission is not a party to a case, the Court shall send to them copies of the application and of the defence, without the annexes thereto, to enable them to assess whether the inapplicability of one of their acts is being invoked under Article 277 TFEU.

Article 126 Reply and rejoinder

1. The application initiating proceedings and the defence may be supplemented by a reply from the applicant and by a rejoinder from the defendant.

2. The President shall prescribe the time-limits within which those procedural documents are to be produced. He may specify the matters to which the reply or the rejoinder should relate.

Chapter 5 Expedited procedure

Article 133 Decision relating to the expedited procedure

1. At the request of the applicant or the defendant, the President of the Court may, where the nature of the case requires that it be dealt with within a short time, after hearing the other party, the Judge-Rapporteur and the Advocate General, decide that a case is to be determined pursuant to an expedited procedure derogating from the provisions of these Rules.

2. The request for a case to be determined pursuant to an expedited procedure must be made by a separate document submitted at the same time as the application initiating proceedings or the defence, as the case may be, is lodged.

3. Exceptionally the President may also take such a decision of his own motion, after hearing the parties, the Judge-Rapporteur and the Advocate General.

Article 134 Written part of the procedure

1. Under the expedited procedure, the application initiating proceedings and the defence may be supplemented by a reply and a rejoinder only if the President, after hearing the Judge-Rapporteur and the Advocate General, considers this to be necessary.

2. An intervener may submit a statement in intervention only if the President, after hearing the Judge-Rapporteur and the Advocate General, considers this to be necessary.

Article 135 Oral part of the procedure

1. Once the defence has been submitted or, if the decision to determine the case pursuant to an expedited procedure is not made until after that pleading has been lodged, once that decision has been taken, the President shall fix a date for the hearing, which shall be communicated forthwith to the parties. He may postpone the date of the hearing where it is necessary to undertake measures of inquiry or where measures of organisation of procedure so require.

2. Without prejudice to Articles 127 and 128, a party may supplement his arguments and produce or offer evidence during the oral part of the procedure. The party must, however, give reasons for the delay in producing such further arguments or evidence.

Article 136 Decision on the substance

The Court shall give its ruling after hearing the Advocate General.

Article 159a Manifestly inadmissible or manifestly unfounded requests and applications

Where a request or an application referred to in this Chapter is, in whole or in part, manifestly inadmissible or manifestly unfounded, the Court may, having heard the Judge-Rapporteur and the Advocate General, at any time decide to dismiss it, in whole or in part, by reasoned order.

Chapter 10 Suspension of operation or enforcement and other interim measures

Article 160 Application for suspension or for interim measures

1. An application to suspend the operation of any measure adopted by an institution, made pursuant to Article 278 TFEU or Article 157 TEAEC, shall be admissible only if the applicant has challenged that measure in an action before the Court.

2. An application for the adoption of one of the other interim measures referred to in Article 279 TFEU shall be admissible only if it is made by a party to a case before the Court and relates to that case.

3. An application of a kind referred to in the preceding paragraphs shall state the subject-matter of the proceedings, the circumstances giving rise to urgency and the pleas of fact and law establishing a prima facie case for the interim measure applied for.

4. The application shall be made by a separate document and in accordance with the provisions of Articles 120 to 122 of these Rules.

5. The application shall be served on the opposite party, and the President shall prescribe a short time-limit within which that party may submit written or oral observations.

6. The President may order a preparatory inquiry.

7. The President may grant the application even before the observations of the opposite party have been submitted. This decision may be varied or cancelled even without any application being made by any party.

Article 161 Decision on the application

1. The President shall either decide on the application himself or refer it immediately to the Court.

2. If the President is prevented from acting, Articles 10 and 13 of these Rules shall apply.

3. Where the application is referred to it, the Court shall give a decision immediately, after hearing the Advocate General.

Article 162 Order for suspension of operation or for interim measures

1. The decision on the application shall take the form of a reasoned order, from which no appeal shall lie. The order shall be served on the parties forthwith.

2. The execution of the order may be made conditional on the lodging by the applicant of security, of an amount and nature to be fixed in the light of the circumstances.

3. Unless the order fixes the date on which the interim measure is to lapse, the measure shall lapse when the judgment which closes the proceedings is delivered.

4. The order shall have only an interim effect, and shall be without prejudice to the decision of the Court on the substance of the case.

Article 163 Change in circumstances

On application by a party, the order may at any time be varied or cancelled on account of a change in circumstances.

Article 164 New application

Rejection of an application for an interim measure shall not bar the party who made it from making a further application on the basis of new facts.

Title V Appeals against decisions of the General Court

Chapter 1 Form and content of the appeal, and form of order sought

Article 167 Lodging of the appeal

1. An appeal shall be brought by lodging an application at the Registry of the Court of Justice or of the General Court. When that application is lodged at the Registry of the General Court, it shall be transmitted forthwith to the Registry of the Court of Justice.

2. As soon as it is informed of the existence of an appeal, the Registry of the General Court shall forthwith transmit to the Registry of the Court of Justice the file in the case at first instance and any procedural file of the Board of Appeal transmitted to the General Court pursuant to the provisions of the Rules of Procedure of the General Court concerning proceedings relating to intellectual property rights.

Article 168 Content of the appeal

1. An appeal shall contain:
   (a) the name and address of the appellant;
   (b) a reference to the decision of the General Court appealed against;
   (c) the names of the other parties to the relevant case before the General Court;
   (d) the pleas in law and legal arguments relied on, and a summary of those pleas in law;
   (e) the form of order sought by the appellant.

2. Articles 119, 121 and 122(1) of these Rules shall apply to appeals.

3. The appeal shall state the date on which the decision appealed against was served on the appellant.

4. If an appeal does not comply with paragraphs 1 to 3 of this Article, the Registrar shall prescribe a reasonable time limit within which the appellant is to put the appeal in order. If the appellant fails to put the appeal in order within the time limit prescribed, the President shall, after hearing the Judge-Rapporteur and the Advocate General, decide whether the non-compliance with that formal requirement renders the appeal formally inadmissible. If he considers it necessary, the President may refer that question to the Court of Justice.

Article 169 Form of order sought, pleas in law and arguments of the appeal

1. An appeal shall seek to have set aside, in whole or in part, the decision of the General Court as set out in the operative part of that decision.

2. The pleas in law and legal arguments relied on shall identify precisely those points in the grounds of the decision of the General Court which are contested.

Article 170 Form of order sought in the event that the appeal is allowed

1. An appeal shall seek, in the event that it is declared well founded, the same form of order, in whole or in part, as that sought at first instance and shall not seek a different form of order. The subject-matter of the proceedings before the General Court may not be changed in the appeal.

2. Where the appellant requests that the case be referred back to the General Court if the decision appealed against is set aside, he shall set out the reasons why the state of the proceedings does not permit a decision by the Court of Justice.

Title VI Review of decisions of the General Court

Article 191 Reviewing Chamber

A Chamber of five Judges shall be designated for a period of one year for the purpose of deciding, in accordance with Articles 193 and 194 of these Rules, whether a decision of the General Court is to be reviewed in accordance with Article 62 of the Statute.

Article 192 Information and communication of decisions which may be reviewed

1. As soon as the date for the delivery or signature of a decision to be given under Article 256(2) or (3) TFEU is fixed, the Registry of the General Court shall inform the Registry of the Court of Justice.

2. The decision shall be communicated to the Registry of the Court of Justice immediately upon its delivery or signature, as shall the file in the case, which shall be made available forthwith to the First Advocate General.

Article 193 Review of decisions given on appeal

1. The proposal of the First Advocate General to review a decision of the General Court given under Article 256(2) TFEU shall be forwarded to the President of the Court of Justice and to the President of the reviewing Chamber. Notice of that transmission shall be given to the Registrar at the same time.

2. As soon as he is informed of the existence of a proposal, the Registrar shall communicate the file in the case before the General Court to the members of the reviewing Chamber.

3. As soon as the proposal to review has been received, the President of the Court shall designate the Judge-Rapporteur from among the Judges of the reviewing Chamber on a proposal from the President of that Chamber. The composition of the formation of the Court shall be determined in accordance with Article 28(2) of these Rules on the day on which the case is assigned to the Judge-Rapporteur.

4. That Chamber, acting on a proposal from the Judge-Rapporteur, shall decide whether the decision of the General Court is to be reviewed. The decision to review the decision of the General Court shall indicate only the questions which are to be reviewed.

5. The General Court, the parties to the proceedings before it and the other interested persons referred to in the second paragraph of Article 62a of the Statute shall forthwith be informed by the Registrar of the decision of the Court of Justice to review the decision of the General Court.

6. Notice of the date of the decision to review the decision of the General Court and of the questions which are to be reviewed shall be published in the *Official Journal of the European Union*.

Article 194 Review of preliminary rulings

1. The proposal of the First Advocate General to review a decision of the General Court given under Article 256(3) TFEU shall be forwarded to the President of the Court of Justice and to the President of the reviewing Chamber. Notice of that transmission shall be given to the Registrar at the same time.

2. As soon as he is informed of the existence of a proposal, the Registrar shall communicate the file in the case before the General Court to the members of the reviewing Chamber.

3. The Registrar shall also inform the General Court, the referring court or tribunal, the parties to the main proceedings and the other interested persons referred to in the second paragraph of Article 62a of the Statute of the existence of a proposal to review.

4. As soon as the proposal to review has been received, the President of the Court shall designate the Judge-Rapporteur from among the Judges of the reviewing Chamber on a proposal from the President of that Chamber. The composition of the formation of the Court shall be determined in accordance with Article 28(2) of these Rules on the day on which the case is assigned to the Judge-Rapporteur.

5. That Chamber, acting on a proposal from the Judge-Rapporteur, shall decide whether the decision of the General Court is to be reviewed. The decision to review the decision of the General Court shall indicate only the questions which are to be reviewed.

6. The General Court, the referring court or tribunal, the parties to the main proceedings and the other interested persons referred to in the second paragraph of Article 62a of the Statute shall forthwith be informed by the Registrar of the decision of the Court of Justice as to whether or not the decision of the General Court is to be reviewed.

7. Notice of the date of the decision to review the decision of the General Court and of the questions which are to be reviewed shall be published in the *Official Journal of the European Union*.

Article 195 Judgment on the substance of the case after a decision to review

1. The decision to review a decision of the General Court shall be served on the parties and other interested persons referred to in the second paragraph of Article 62a of the Statute. The decision served on the Member States, and the States, other than the Member States, which are parties to the EEA Agreement, as well as the EFTA Surveillance Authority, shall be accompanied by a translation of the decision of the Court of Justice in accordance with the provisions of Article 98 of these Rules. The decision of the Court of Justice shall also be communicated to the General Court and, if applicable, to the referring court or tribunal.

2. Within one month of the date of service referred to in paragraph 1, the parties and other interested persons on whom the decision of the Court of Justice has been served may lodge statements or written observations on the questions which are subject to review.

3. As soon as a decision to review a decision of the General Court has been taken, the First Advocate General shall assign the review to an Advocate General.

4. The reviewing Chamber shall rule on the substance of the case, after hearing the Advocate General.

5. It may, however, request the Court of Justice to assign the case to a formation of the Court composed of a greater number of Judges.

6. Where the decision of the General Court which is subject to review was given under Article 256(2) TFEU, the Court of Justice shall make a decision as to costs.

Title VII Requests for Opinions

Article 196 Written part of the procedure

1. In accordance with Article 218(11) TFEU, a request for an Opinion may be made by a Member State, by the European Parliament, by the Council or by the European Commission.

2. A request for an Opinion may relate both to whether the envisaged agreement is compatible with the provisions of the Treaties and to whether the European Union or any institution of the European Union has the power to enter into that agreement.

3. It shall be served on the Member States and on the institutions referred to in paragraph 1, and the President shall prescribe a time-limit within which they may submit written observations.

Article 197 Designation of the Judge-Rapporteur and of the Advocate General

As soon as the request for an Opinion has been submitted, the President shall designate a Judge-Rapporteur and the First Advocate General shall assign the case to an Advocate General.

Article 198 Hearing

The Court may decide that the procedure before it shall also include a hearing.

Article 199 Time-limit for delivering the Opinion

The Court shall deliver its Opinion as soon as possible, after hearing the Advocate General.

Article 200 Delivery of the Opinion

1. The Opinion, signed by the President, the Judges who took part in the deliberations and the Registrar, shall be delivered in open court.

2. It shall be served on all the Member States and on the institutions referred to in Article 196(1).

Done at Luxembourg, 25 September 2012.

Secondary Legislation

Free movement of goods

Commission Directive of 22 December 1969 based on the provisions of Article 33(7), on the abolition of measures which have an effect equivalent to quantitative restrictions on imports and are not covered by other provisions adopted in pursuance of the EEC Treaty (70/50/EEC)*

[OJ Sp. Ed. 1970, I No L13/29, p. 17]

Article 1

The purpose of this Directive is to abolish the measures referred to in Articles 2 and 3, which were operative at the date of entry into force of the EEC Treaty.

Article 2

1. This Directive covers measures, other than those applicable equally to domestic or imported products, which hinder imports which could otherwise take place, including measures which make importation more difficult or costly than the disposal of domestic production.

2. In particular, it covers measures which make imports or the disposal, at any marketing stage, of imported products subject to a condition—other than a formality—which is required in respect of imported products only, or a condition differing from that required for domestic products and more difficult to satisfy. Equally, it covers, in particular, measures which favour domestic products or grant them a preference, other than an aid, to which conditions may or may not be attached.

3. The measures referred to must be taken to include those measures which:

(a) lay down, for imported products only, minimum or maximum prices below or above which imports are prohibited, reduced or made subject to conditions liable to hinder importation;

(b) lay down less favourable prices for imported products than for domestic products;

(c) fix profit margins or any other price components for imported products only or fix these differently for domestic products and for imported products, to the detriment of the latter;

* **Editor's Note:** As clarified in the Preface, this is still in force. See http://data.europa.eu/eli/dir/1970/50/oj.

(d) preclude any increase in the price of the imported product corresponding to the supplementary costs and charges inherent in importation;
(e) fix the prices of products solely on the basis of the cost price or the quality of domestic products at such a level as to create a hindrance to importation;
(f) lower the value of an imported product, in particular by causing a reduction in its intrinsic value, or increase its costs;
(g) make access of imported products to the domestic market conditional upon having an agent or representative in the territory of the importing Member State;
(h) lay down conditions of payment in respect of imported products only, or subject imported products to conditions which are different from those laid down for domestic products and more difficult to satisfy;
(i) require, for imports only, the giving of guarantees or making of payments on account;
(j) subject imported products only to conditions, in respect, in particular of shape, size, weight, composition, presentation, identification or putting up, or subject imported products to conditions which are different from those for domestic products and more difficult to satisfy;
(k) hinder the purchase by private individuals of imported products only, or encourage, require or give preference to the purchase of domestic products only;
(l) totally or partially preclude the use of national facilities or equipment in respect of imported products only, or totally or partially confine the use of such facilities or equipment to domestic products only;
(m) prohibit or limit publicity in respect of imported products only, or totally or partially confine publicity to domestic products only;
(n) prohibit, limit or require stocking in respect of imported products only; totally or partially confine the use of stocking facilities to domestic products only, or make the stocking of imported products subject to conditions which are different from those required for domestic products and more difficult to satisfy;
(o) make importation subject to the granting of reciprocity by one or more Member States;
(p) prescribe that imported products are to conform, totally or partially, to rules other than those of the importing country;
(q) specify time limits for imported products which are insufficient or excessive in relation to the normal course of the various transactions to which these time limits apply;
(r) subject imported products to controls or, other than those inherent in the customs clearance procedure, to which domestic products are not subject or which are stricter in respect of imported products than they are in respect of domestic products, without this being necessary in order to ensure equivalent protection;
(s) confine names which are not indicative of origin or source to domestic products only.

Article 3

This Directive also covers measures governing the marketing of products which deal, in particular, with shape, size, weight, composition, presentation, identification or putting up and which are equally applicable to domestic and imported products, where the restrictive effect of such measures on the free movement of goods exceeds the effects intrinsic to trade rules.

This is the case, in particular, where:

- the restrictive effects on the free movement of goods are out of proportion to their purpose;
- the same objective can be attained by other means which are less of a hindrance to trade.

(All remaining provisions omitted.)

Commission Practice Note on Import Prohibitions

Communication from the Commission concerning the consequences of the judgment given by the Court of Justice on 20 February 1979 in Case 120/78 ('Cassis de Dijon')

[OJ 1980 C256/2]

The following is the text of a letter which has been sent to the Member States; the European Parliament and the Council have also been notified of it.

In the Commission's Communication of 6 November 1978 on 'Safeguarding free trade within the Community', it was emphasised that the free movement of goods is being affected by a growing number of restrictive measures.

The judgment delivered by the Court of Justice on 20 February 1979 in Case 120/78 (the 'Cassis de Dijon' case), and recently reaffirmed in the judgment of 26 June 1980 in Case 788/79, has given the Commission some interpretative guidance enabling it to monitor more strictly the application of the Treaty rules on the free movement of goods, particularly Articles 30 to 36 of the EEC Treaty.

The Court gives a very general definition of the barriers to free trade which are prohibited by the provisions of Article 30 et seq. of the EEC Treaty. These are taken to include 'any national measure capable of hindering, directly or indirectly, actually or potentially, intra-Community trade'.

In its judgment of 20 February 1979 the Court indicates the scope of this definition as it applies to technical and commercial rules.

Any product lawfully produced and marketed in one Member State must, in principle, be admitted to the market of any other Member State.

Technical and commercial rules, even those equally applicable to national and imported products, may create barriers to trade only where those rules are necessary to satisfy mandatory requirements and to serve a purpose which is in the general interest and for which they are an essential guarantee. This purpose must be such as to take precedence over the requirements of the free movement of goods, which constitutes one of the fundamental rules of the Community.

The conclusions in terms of policy which the Commission draws from this new guidance are set out below.

- Whereas Member States may, with respect to domestic products and in the absence of relevant Community provisions, regulate the terms on which such products are marketed, the case is different for products imported from other Member States.

Any product imported from another Member State must in principle be admitted to the territory of the importing Member State if it has been lawfully produced, that is, conforms to the rules and processes of manufacture that are customarily and traditionally accepted in the exporting country, and is marketed in the territory of the latter.

This principle implies that Member States, when drawing up commercial or technical rules liable to affect the free movement of goods, may not take an exclusively national viewpoint and take account only of requirements confined to domestic products. The proper functioning of the common market demands that each Member State also give consideration to the legitimate requirements of the other Member States.

- Only under very strict conditions does the Court accept exceptions to this principle; barriers to trade resulting from differences between commercial and technical rules are only admissible:

- if the rules are necessary, that is appropriate and not excessive, in order to satisfy mandatory requirements (public health, protection of consumers or the environment, the fairness of commercial transactions, etc.);
- if the rules serve a purpose in the general interest which is compelling enough to justify an exception to a fundamental rule of the Treaty such as the free movement of goods;
- if the rules are essential for such a purpose to be attained, i.e. are the means which are the most appropriate and at the same time least hinder trade.

The Court's interpretation has induced the Commission to set out a number of guidelines.

- The principles deduced by the Court imply that a Member State may not in principle prohibit the sale in its territory of a product lawfully produced and marketed in another Member State even if the product is produced according to technical or quality requirements which differ from those imposed on its domestic products. Where a product 'suitably and satisfactorily' fulfils the legitimate objective of a Member State's own rules (public safety, protection of the consumer or the environment, etc.), the importing country cannot justify prohibiting its sale in its territory by claiming that the way it fulfils the objective is different from that imposed on domestic products.

In such a case, an absolute prohibition of sale could not be considered 'necessary' to satisfy a 'mandatory requirement' because it would not be an 'essential guarantee' in the sense defined in the Court's judgment.

The Commission will therefore have to tackle a whole body of commercial rules which lay down that products manufactured and marketed in one Member State must fulfil technical or qualitative conditions in order to be admitted to the market of another and specifically in all cases where the trade barriers occasioned by such rules are inadmissible according to the very strict criteria set out by the Court.

The Commission is referring in particular to rules covering the composition, designation, presentation and packaging of products as well as rules requiring compliance with certain technical standards.

The Commission's work of harmonisation will henceforth have to be directed mainly at national laws having an impact on the functioning of the common market where barriers to trade to be removed arise from national provisions which are admissible under the criteria set by the Court.

The Commission will be concentrating on sectors deserving priority because of their economic relevance to the creation of a single internal market.

To forestall later difficulties, the Commission will be informing Member States of potential objections, under the terms of Community law, to provisions they may be considering introducing which come to the attention of the Commission.

It will be producing suggestions soon on the procedures to be followed in such cases.

The Commission is confident that this approach will secure greater freedom of trade for the Community's manufacturers, so strengthening the industrial base of the Community, while meeting the expectations of consumers.

Council Regulation 2679/98 of 7 December 1998 on the functioning of the internal market in relation to the free movement of goods among the Member States

[OJ 1998 L337/8]

Article 1

For the purpose of this Regulation:

1. the term 'obstacle' shall mean an obstacle to the free movement of goods among Member States which is attributable to a Member State, whether it involves action or inaction on its part, which may constitute a breach of Articles 30 to 36 of the Treaty and which:

(a) leads to serious disruption of the free movement of goods by physically or otherwise preventing, delaying or diverting their import into, export from or transport across a Member State,
(b) causes serious loss to the individuals affected, and
(c) requires immediate action in order to prevent any continuation, increase or intensification of the disruption or loss in question;

2. the term 'inaction' shall cover the case when the competent authorities of a Member State, in the presence of an obstacle caused by actions taken by private individuals, fail to take all necessary and proportionate measures within their powers with a view to removing the obstacle and ensuring the free movement of goods in their territory.

Article 2

This Regulation may not be interpreted as affecting in any way the exercise of fundamental rights as recognised in Member States, including the right or freedom to strike. These rights may also include the right or freedom to take other actions covered by the specific industrial relations systems in Member States.

Article 3

1. When an obstacle occurs or when there is a threat thereof
(a) any Member State (whether or not it is the Member State concerned) which has relevant information shall immediately transmit it to the Commission, and
(b) the Commission shall immediately transmit to the Member States that information and any information from any other source which it may consider relevant.

2. The Member State concerned shall respond as soon as possible to requests for information from the Commission and from other Member States concerning the nature of the obstacle or threat and the action which it has taken or proposes to take. Information exchange between Member States shall also be transmitted to the Commission.

Article 4

1. When an obstacle occurs, and subject to Article 2, the Member State concerned shall
(a) take all necessary and proportionate measures so that the free movement of goods is assured in the territory of the Member State in accordance with the Treaty, and
(b) inform the Commission of the actions which its authorities have taken or intend to take.

2. The Commission shall immediately transmit the information received under paragraph 1(b) to the other Member States.

Article 5

1. Where the Commission considers that an obstacle is occurring in a Member State, it shall notify the Member State concerned of the reasons that have led the Commission to such a conclusion and shall request the Member State to take all necessary and proportionate measures to remove the said obstacle within a period which it shall determine with reference to the urgency of the case.

2. In reaching its conclusion, the Commission shall have regard to Article 2.

3. The Commission may publish in the Official Journal of the European Communities the text of the notification which it has sent to the Member State concerned and shall immediately transmit the text to any party which requests it.

4. The Member State shall, within five working days of receipt of the text, either:
- inform the Commission of the steps which it has taken or intends to take to implement paragraph 1, or
- communicate a reasoned submission as to why there is no obstacle constituting a breach of Articles 30 to 36 of the Treaty.

5. In exceptional cases, the Commission may allow an extension of the deadline mentioned in paragraph 4 if the Member State submits a duly substantiated request and the grounds cited are deemed acceptable.

This Regulation shall be binding in its entirety and directly applicable in all Member States.

Done at Brussels, 7 December 1998.

Directive (EU) 2015/1535 of the European Parliament and of the Council of 9 September 2015 laying down a procedure for the provision of information in the field of technical regulations and of rules on Information Society services (codification)*

[OJ 2015 L241/1]

Article 1

1. For the purposes of this Directive, the following definitions apply:
   (a) 'product' means any industrially manufactured product and any agricultural product, including fish products;
   (b) 'service' means any Information Society service, that is to say, any service normally provided for remuneration, at a distance, by electronic means and at the individual request of a recipient of services.
      For the purposes of this definition:
      (i) 'at a distance' means that the service is provided without the parties being simultaneously present;
      (ii) 'by electronic means' means that the service is sent initially and received at its destination by means of electronic equipment for the processing (including digital compression) and storage of data, and entirely transmitted, conveyed and received by wire, by radio, by optical means or by other electromagnetic means;
      (iii) 'at the individual request of a recipient of services' means that the service is provided through the transmission of data on individual request.
      An indicative list of services not covered by this definition is set out in Annex I;
   (c) 'technical specification' means a specification contained in a document which lays down the characteristics required of a product such as levels of quality, performance, safety or dimensions, including the requirements applicable to the product as regards the name under which the product is sold, terminology, symbols, testing and test methods, packaging, marking or labelling and conformity assessment procedures.
      The term 'technical specification' also covers production methods and processes used in respect of agricultural products, as referred to in the second subparagraph of Article 38(1) of the Treaty on the Functioning of the European Union (TFEU), products intended for human and animal consumption, and medicinal products as defined in Article 1 of Directive 2001/83/EC of the European Parliament and of the Council[1], as well as production methods and processes relating to other products, where these have an effect on their characteristics;
   (d) 'other requirements' means a requirement, other than a technical specification, imposed on a product for the purpose of protecting, in particular, consumers or the environment, and which affects its life cycle after it has been placed on the market, such as conditions of use, recycling, reuse or disposal, where such conditions can significantly influence the composition or nature of the product or its marketing;
   (e) 'rule on services' means a requirement of a general nature relating to the taking-up and pursuit of service activities within the meaning of point (b), in particular provisions concerning the service provider, the services and the recipient of services, excluding any rules which are not specifically aimed at the services defined in that point.

* **Editor's Note:** Annex III omitted.

[1] Directive 2001/83/EC of the European Parliament and of the Council of 6 November 2001 on the Community code relating to medicinal products for human use (OJ L 311, 28.11.2001, p. 67).

For the purposes of this definition:

(i) a rule shall be considered to be specifically aimed at Information Society services where, having regard to its statement of reasons and its operative part, the specific aim and object of all or some of its individual provisions is to regulate such services in an explicit and targeted manner;

(ii) a rule shall not be considered to be specifically aimed at Information Society services if it affects such services only in an implicit or incidental manner;

(f) 'technical regulation' means technical specifications and other requirements or rules on services, including the relevant administrative provisions, the observance of which is compulsory, de jure or de facto, in the case of marketing, provision of a service, establishment of a service operator or use in a Member State or a major part thereof, as well as laws, regulations or administrative provisions of Member States, except those provided for in Article 7, prohibiting the manufacture, importation, marketing or use of a product or prohibiting the provision or use of a service, or establishment as a service provider.

De facto technical regulations shall include:

(i) laws, regulations or administrative provisions of a Member State which refer either to technical specifications or to other requirements or to rules on services, or to professional codes or codes of practice which in turn refer to technical specifications or to other requirements or to rules on services, compliance with which confers a presumption of conformity with the obligations imposed by the aforementioned laws, regulations or administrative provisions;

(ii) voluntary agreements to which a public authority is a contracting party and which provide, in the general interest, for compliance with technical specifications or other requirements or rules on services, excluding public procurement tender specifications;

(iii) technical specifications or other requirements or rules on services which are linked to fiscal or financial measures affecting the consumption of products or services by encouraging compliance with such technical specifications or other requirements or rules on services; technical specifications or other requirements or rules on services linked to national social security systems are not included.

This comprises technical regulations imposed by the authorities designated by the Member States and appearing on a list drawn up and updated, where appropriate, by the Commission, in the framework of the Committee referred to in Article 2.

The same procedure shall be used for amending this list;

(g) 'draft technical regulation' means the text of a technical specification or other requirement or of a rule on services, including administrative provisions, formulated with the aim of enacting it or of ultimately having it enacted as a technical regulation, the text being at a stage of preparation at which substantial amendments can still be made.

2. This Directive shall not apply to:

(a) radio broadcasting services;

(b) television broadcasting services covered by point (e) of Article 1(1) of Directive 2010/13/EU of the European Parliament and of the Council[2].

3. This Directive shall not apply to rules relating to matters which are covered by Union legislation in the field of telecommunications services, as covered by Directive 2002/21/EC of the European Parliament and of the Council[3].

4. This Directive shall not apply to rules relating to matters which are covered by Union legislation in the field of financial services, as listed non-exhaustively in Annex II to this Directive.

5. With the exception of Article 5(3), this Directive shall not apply to rules enacted by or for regulated markets within the meaning of Directive 2004/39/EC of the European Parliament and of

[2] Directive 2010/13/EU of the European Parliament and of the Council of 10 March 2010 on the coordination of certain provisions laid down by law, regulation or administrative action in Member States concerning the provision of audiovisual media services (Audiovisual Media Services Directive) (OJ L 95, 15.4.2010, p. 1).

[3] Directive 2002/21/EC of the European Parliament and of the Council of 7 March 2002 on a common regulatory framework for electronic communications networks and services (Framework Directive) (OJ L 108, 24.4.2002, p. 33).

the Council[4] or by or for other markets or bodies carrying out clearing or settlement functions for those markets.

6. This Directive shall not apply to those measures Member States consider necessary under the Treaties for the protection of persons, in particular workers, when products are used, provided that such measures do not affect the products.

Article 4

Member States shall communicate to the Commission, in accordance with Article 5(1), all requests made to standards institutions to draw up technical specifications or a standard for specific products for the purpose of enacting a technical regulation for such products in the form of draft technical regulations, and shall state the grounds for their enactment.

Article 5

1. Subject to Article 7, Member States shall immediately communicate to the Commission any draft technical regulation, except where it merely transposes the full text of an international or European standard, in which case information regarding the relevant standard shall suffice; they shall also let the Commission have a statement of the grounds which make the enactment of such a technical regulation necessary, where those grounds have not already been made clear in the draft.

Where appropriate, and unless it has already been sent with a prior communication, Member States shall simultaneously communicate the text of the basic legislative or regulatory provisions principally and directly concerned to the Commission, should knowledge of such text be necessary to assess the implications of the draft technical regulation.

Member States shall communicate the draft technical regulation again to the Commission under the conditions set out in the first and second subparagraphs of this paragraph if they make changes to the draft that have the effect of significantly altering its scope, shortening the timetable originally envisaged for implementation, adding specifications or requirements, or making the latter more restrictive.

Where, in particular, the draft technical regulation seeks to limit the marketing or use of a chemical substance, preparation or product on grounds of public health or of the protection of consumers or the environment, Member States shall also forward either a summary or the references of all relevant data relating to the substance, preparation or product concerned and to known and available substitutes, where such information may be available, and communicate the anticipated effects of the measure on public health and the protection of the consumer and the environment, together with an analysis of the risk carried out as appropriate in accordance with the principles provided for in the relevant part of Section II.3 of Annex XV to Regulation (EC) No 1907/2006 of the European Parliament and of the Council[5].

The Commission shall immediately notify the other Member States of the draft technical regulation and all documents which have been forwarded to it; it may also refer this draft, for an opinion, to the Committee referred to in Article 2 of this Directive and, where appropriate, to the committee responsible for the field in question.

With respect to the technical specifications or other requirements or rules on services referred to in point (iii) of the second subparagraph of point (f) of Article 1(1) of this Directive, the comments or detailed opinions of the Commission or Member States may concern only aspects which may hinder trade or, in respect of rules on services, the free movement of services or the freedom of establishment of service operators and not the fiscal or financial aspects of the measure.

[4] Directive 2004/39/EC of the European Parliament and of the Council of 21 April 2004 on markets in financial instruments amending Council Directives 85/611/EEC and 93/6/EEC and Directive 2000/12/EC of the European Parliament and of the Council and repealing Council Directive 93/22/EEC (OJ L 145, 30.4.2004, p. 1).

[5] Regulation (EC) No 1907/2006 of the European Parliament and of the Council of 18 December 2006 concerning the Registration, Evaluation, Authorisation and Restriction of Chemicals (REACH), establishing a European Chemicals Agency, amending Directive 1999/45/EC and repealing Council Regulation (EEC) No 793/93 and Commission Regulation (EC) No 1488/94 as well as Council Directive 76/769/EEC and Commission Directives 91/155/EEC, 93/67/EEC, 93/105/EC and 2000/21/EC (OJ L 396, 30.12.2006, p. 1).

2. The Commission and the Member States may make comments to the Member State which has forwarded a draft technical regulation; that Member State shall take such comments into account as far as possible in the subsequent preparation of the technical regulation.

3. Member States shall communicate the definitive text of a technical regulation to the Commission without delay.

4. Information supplied under this Article shall not be confidential except at the express request of the notifying Member State. Any such request shall be supported by reasons.

In cases of that kind, if the necessary precautions are taken, the Committee referred to in Article 2 and the national authorities may seek expert advice from physical or legal persons in the private sector.

5. When draft technical regulations form part of measures which are required to be communicated to the Commission at the draft stage under another Union act, Member States may make a communication within the meaning of paragraph 1 under that other act, provided that they formally indicate that the said communication also constitutes a communication for the purposes of this Directive.

The absence of a reaction from the Commission under this Directive to a draft technical regulation shall not prejudice any decision which might be taken under other Union acts.

Article 6

1. Member States shall postpone the adoption of a draft technical regulation for three months from the date of receipt by the Commission of the communication referred to in Article 5(1).

2. Member States shall postpone:

- for four months the adoption of a draft technical regulation in the form of a voluntary agreement within the meaning of point (ii) of the second subparagraph of point (f) of Article 1(1),
- without prejudice to paragraphs 3, 4 and 5 of this article, for six months the adoption of any other draft technical regulation except for draft rules on services,

from the date of receipt by the Commission of the communication referred to in Article 5(1), if the Commission or another Member State delivers a detailed opinion, within three months of that date, to the effect that the measure envisaged may create obstacles to the free movement of goods within the internal market,

- without prejudice to paragraphs 4 and 5, for four months the adoption of any draft rule on services, from the date of receipt by the Commission of the communication referred to in Article 5(1), if the Commission or another Member State delivers a detailed opinion, within three months of that date, to the effect that the measure envisaged may create obstacles to the free movement of services or to the freedom of establishment of service operators within the internal market.

With regard to draft rules on services, detailed opinions from the Commission or Member States may not affect any cultural policy measures, in particular in the audiovisual sphere, which Member States might adopt in accordance with the law of the Union, taking account of their linguistic diversity, their specific national and regional characteristics and their cultural heritage.

The Member State concerned shall report to the Commission on the action it proposes to take on such detailed opinions. The Commission shall comment on this reaction.

With respect to rules on services, the Member State concerned shall indicate, where appropriate, the reasons why the detailed opinions cannot be taken into account.

3. With the exclusion of draft rules relating to services, Member States shall postpone the adoption of a draft technical regulation for 12 months from the date of receipt by the Commission of the communication referred to in Article 5(1) of this Directive, if, within three months of that date, the Commission announces its intention to propose or adopt a directive, regulation or decision on the matter in accordance with Article 288 TFEU.

4. Member States shall postpone the adoption of a draft technical regulation for 12 months from the date of receipt by the Commission of the communication referred to in Article 5(1) of this Directive, if, within the three months following that date, the Commission announces its finding that the draft

technical regulation concerns a matter which is covered by a proposal for a directive, regulation or decision presented to the European Parliament and the Council in accordance with Article 288 TFEU.

5. If the Council adopts a position at first reading during the standstill period referred to in paragraphs 3 and 4, that period shall, subject to paragraph 6, be extended to 18 months.

6. The obligations referred to in paragraphs 3, 4 and 5 shall lapse:

(a) when the Commission informs the Member States that it no longer intends to propose or adopt a binding act;

(b) when the Commission informs the Member States of the withdrawal of its draft or proposal;

(c) when a binding act has been adopted by the European Parliament and the Council or by the Commission.

7. Paragraphs 1 to 5 shall not apply in cases where:

(a) for urgent reasons, occasioned by serious and unforeseeable circumstances relating to the protection of public health or safety, the protection of animals or the preservation of plants, and for rules on services, also for public policy, in particular the protection of minors, a Member State is obliged to prepare technical regulations in a very short space of time in order to enact and introduce them immediately without any consultations being possible; or

(b) for urgent reasons occasioned by serious circumstances relating to the protection of the security and the integrity of the financial system, in particular the protection of depositors, investors and insured persons, a Member State is obliged to enact and implement rules on financial services immediately.

In the communication referred to in Article 5, the Member State shall give reasons for the urgency of the measures taken. The Commission shall give its views on the communication as soon as possible. It shall take appropriate action in cases where improper use is made of this procedure. The European Parliament shall be kept informed by the Commission.

Article 7

1. Articles 5 and 6 shall not apply to those laws, regulations and administrative provisions of the Member States or voluntary agreements by means of which Member States:

(a) comply with binding Union acts which result in the adoption of technical specifications or rules on services;

(b) fulfil the obligations arising out of international agreements which result in the adoption of common technical specifications or rules on services in the Union;

(c) make use of safeguard clauses provided for in binding Union acts;

(d) apply Article 12(1) of Directive 2001/95/EC of the European Parliament and of the Council[6];

(e) restrict themselves to implementing a judgment of the Court of Justice of the European Union;

(f) restrict themselves to amending a technical regulation within the meaning of point (f) of Article 1(1), in accordance with a Commission request, with a view to removing a barrier to trade or, in the case of rules on services, to the free movement of services or the freedom of establishment of service operators.

2. Article 6 shall not apply to the laws, regulations and administrative provisions of the Member States prohibiting manufacture in so far as they do not impede the free movement of products.

3. Paragraphs 3 to 6 of Article 6 shall not apply to the voluntary agreements referred to in point (ii) of the second subparagraph of point (f) of Article 1(1).

4. Article 6 shall not apply to the technical specifications or other requirements or the rules on services referred to in point (iii) of the second subparagraph of point (f) of Article 1(1).

[6] Directive 2001/95/EC of the European Parliament and of the Council of 3 December 2001 on general product safety (OJ L 11, 15.1.2002, p. 4).

Article 11
This Directive shall enter into force on the twentieth day following that of its publication in the *Official Journal of the European Union*.

Article 12
This Directive is addressed to the Member States.

Done at Strasbourg, 9 September 2015.
(Signatures omitted.)

ANNEX I

Indicative list of services not covered by the second subparagraph of point (b) of Article 1(1)

1. Services not provided 'at a distance'

Services provided in the physical presence of the provider and the recipient, even if they involve the use of electronic devices:

(a) medical examinations or treatment at a doctor's surgery using electronic equipment where the patient is physically present;
(b) consultation of an electronic catalogue in a shop with the customer on site;
(c) plane ticket reservation at a travel agency in the physical presence of the customer by means of a network of computers;
(d) electronic games made available in a video arcade where the customer is physically present.

2. Services not provided 'by electronic means'

- services having material content even though provided via electronic devices:
  (a) automatic cash or ticket dispensing machines (banknotes, rail tickets);
  (b) access to road networks, car parks, etc., charging for use, even if there are electronic devices at the entrance/exit controlling access and/or ensuring correct payment is made,
- offline services: distribution of CD-ROMs or software on diskettes,
- services which are not provided via electronic processing/inventory systems:
  (a) voice telephony services;
  (b) telefax/telex services;
  (c) services provided via voice telephony or fax;
  (d) telephone/telefax consultation of a doctor;
  (e) telephone/telefax consultation of a lawyer;
  (f) telephone/telefax direct marketing.

3. Services not supplied 'at the individual request of a recipient of services'

Services provided by transmitting data without individual demand for simultaneous reception by an unlimited number of individual receivers (point to multipoint transmission):

(a) television broadcasting services (including near-video on-demand services), covered by point (e) of Article 1(1) of Directive 2010/13/EU;
(b) radio broadcasting services;
(c) (televised) teletext.

ANNEX II

Indicative list of the financial services covered by Article 1(4)

- Investment services,
- insurance and reinsurance operations,
- banking services,
- operations relating to pension funds,
- services relating to dealings in futures or options.

Such services include in particular:

(a) investment services referred to in the Annex to Directive 2004/39/EC; services of collective investment undertakings;

(b) services covered by the activities subject to mutual recognition referred to in Annex I to Directive 2013/36/EU of the European Parliament and of the Council[7];

(c) operations covered by the insurance and reinsurance activities referred to in Directive 2009/138/EC of the European Parliament and of the Council[8].

Regulation (EU) 2019/515 of the European Parliament and of the Council of 19 March 2019 on the mutual recognition of goods lawfully marketed in another Member State*

[OJ 2019 L91/1]

Chapter I General provisions

Article 1 Subject matter

1. The aim of this Regulation is to strengthen the functioning of the internal market by improving the application of the principle of mutual recognition and by removing unjustified barriers to trade.

2. This Regulation lays down rules and procedures concerning the application by Member States of the principle of mutual recognition in individual cases in relation to goods which are subject to Article 34 TFEU and which are lawfully marketed in another Member State, having regard to Article 36 TFEU and the case-law of the Court of Justice of the European Union.

3. This Regulation also provides for the establishment and maintenance of Product Contact Points in Member States and for cooperation and exchange of information in the context of the principle of mutual recognition.

Article 2 Scope

1. This Regulation applies to goods of any type, including agricultural products within the meaning of the second subparagraph of Article 38(1) TFEU, and to administrative decisions that have been taken or are to be taken by a competent authority of a Member State of destination in relation to any such goods that are lawfully marketed in another Member State, where the administrative decision meets the following criteria:

(a) the basis for the administrative decision is a national technical rule applicable in the Member State of destination; and

[7] Directive 2013/36/EU of the European Parliament and of the Council of 26 June 2013 on access to the activity of credit institutions and the prudential supervision of credit institutions and investment firms, amending Directive 2002/87/EC and repealing Directives 2006/48/EC and 2006/49/EC (OJ L 176, 27.6.2013, p. 338).

[8] Directive 2009/138/EC of the European Parliament and of the Council of 25 November 2009 on the taking-up and pursuit of the business of Insurance and Reinsurance (Solvency II) (OJ L 335, 17.12.2009, p. 1).

* **Editor's Note:** Repealing Regulation 764/2008.

(b) the direct or indirect effect of the administrative decision is to restrict or deny market access in the Member State of destination.

Administrative decision includes any administrative step that is based on a national technical rule and that has the same or substantially the same legal effect as the effect referred to in point (b).

2. For the purposes of this Regulation, a 'national technical rule' is any provision of a law, regulation or other administrative provision of a Member State which has the following characteristics:

(a) it covers goods or aspects of goods that are not the subject of harmonisation at Union level;

(b) it either prohibits the making available of goods, or goods of a given type, on the market in that Member State, or it makes compliance with the provision compulsory, de facto or de jure, whenever goods, or goods of a given type, are made available on that market; and

(c) it does at least one of the following:

(i) it lays down the characteristics required of goods or of goods of a given type, such as their levels of quality, performance or safety, or their dimensions, including the requirements applicable to those goods as regards the names under which they are sold, terminology, symbols, testing and test methods, packaging, marking or labelling and conformity assessment procedures;

(ii) for the purpose of protecting consumers or the environment, it imposes other requirements on goods or goods of a given type that affect the life-cycle of the goods after they have been made available on the market in that Member State, such as conditions of use, recycling, reuse or disposal, where such conditions can significantly influence either the composition or nature of those goods, or the making available of them on the market in that Member State.

3. Point (c)(i) of paragraph 2 of this Article also covers production methods and processes used in respect of agricultural products as referred to in the second subparagraph of Article 38(1) TFEU, and in respect of products intended for human or animal consumption, as well as production methods and processes relating to other products, where these have an effect on their characteristics.

4. A prior authorisation procedure does not itself constitute a national technical rule for the purposes of this Regulation, but a decision to refuse prior authorisation based on a national technical rule shall be considered to be an administrative decision to which this Regulation applies, if that decision fulfils the other requirements of the first subparagraph of paragraph 1.

5. This Regulation does not apply to:

(a) decisions of a judicial nature taken by national courts or tribunals;

(b) decisions of a judicial nature taken by law enforcement authorities in the course of the investigation or prosecution of a criminal offence as regards the terminology, symbols or any material reference to unconstitutional or criminal organisations or offences of a racist, discriminatory or xenophobic nature.

6. Articles 5 and 6 shall not affect the application of the following provisions:

(a) points (b) to (f) of Article 8(1) and Article 8(3) of Directive 2001/95/EC;

(b) point (a) of Article 50(3) and Article 54 of Regulation (EC) No 178/2002;

(c) Article 90 of Regulation (EU) No 1306/2013; and

(d) Article 138 of Regulation (EU) 2017/625.

7. This Regulation does not affect the obligation under Directive (EU) 2015/1535 to notify draft national technical regulations to the Commission and the Member States prior to their adoption.

Article 3 Definitions

For the purposes of this Regulation, the following definitions apply:

(1) 'lawfully marketed in another Member State' means that goods or goods of that type comply with the relevant rules applicable in that Member State or are not subject to any such rules in that Member State, and are made available to end users in that Member State;

(2) 'making available on the market' means any supply of goods for distribution, consumption or use on the market within the territory of a Member State in the course of a commercial activity, whether in return for payment or free of charge;

(3) 'restricting market access' means imposing conditions to be fulfilled before goods can be made available on the market in the Member State of destination, or conditions for keeping goods on that market, which in either case require the modification of one or more of the characteristics of those goods, as referred to in point (c)(i) of Article 2(2), or require the performance of additional testing;

(4) 'denying market access' means any of the following:

(a) prohibiting goods from being made available on the market in the Member State of destination or from being kept on that market; or

(b) requiring the withdrawal or recall of those goods from that market;

(5) 'withdrawal' means any measure aimed at preventing goods in the supply chain from being made available on the market;

(6) 'recall' means any measure aimed at achieving the return of goods that have already been made available to the end user;

(7) 'prior authorisation procedure' means an administrative procedure under the law of a Member State whereby the competent authority of that Member State is required, on the basis of an application by an economic operator, to give its formal approval before goods may be made available on the market in that Member State;

(8) 'producer' means:

(a) any natural or legal person who manufactures goods or has goods designed or manufactured, or who produces goods which were not the result of a manufacturing process, including agricultural products, and markets them under that person's name or trademark,

(b) any natural or legal person who modifies goods already lawfully marketed in a Member State in a way that might affect compliance with the relevant rules applicable in that Member State, or

(c) any other natural or legal person who, by putting its name, trademark or other distinguishing feature on goods or on the documents that accompany those goods, presents itself as the producer of those goods;

(9) 'authorised representative' means any natural or legal person established within the Union who has received a written mandate from a producer to act on that producer's behalf with regard to the making available of goods on the market in question;

(10) 'importer' means any natural or legal person established within the Union who makes goods from a third country available on the Union market for the first time;

(11) 'distributor' means any natural or legal person in the supply chain, other than the producer or the importer, who makes goods available on the market in a Member State;

(12) 'economic operator' means any of the following in relation to goods: the producer, the authorised representative, the importer or the distributor;

(13) 'end user' means any natural or legal person residing or established in the Union, to whom the goods have been made available or are being made available, either as a consumer outside of any trade, business, craft or profession or as a professional end user in the course of its industrial or professional activities;

(14) 'legitimate public interest grounds' means any of the grounds set out in Article 36 TFEU or any other overriding reasons of public interest;

(15) 'conformity assessment body' means a conformity assessment body as defined in point 13 of Article 2 of Regulation (EC) No 765/2008.

Chapter II Procedures concerning application of the principle of mutual recognition in individual cases

Article 4 Mutual recognition declaration

1. The producer of goods, or of goods of a given type, that are being made or are to be made available on the market in the Member State of destination may draw up a voluntary declaration of lawful marketing of goods for the purposes of mutual recognition ('mutual recognition declaration')

in order to demonstrate to the competent authorities of the Member State of destination that the goods, or the goods of that type, are lawfully marketed in another Member State.

The producer may mandate its authorised representative to draw up the mutual recognition declaration on its behalf.

The mutual recognition declaration shall follow the structure set out in Part I and Part II of the Annex and shall contain all the information specified therein.

The producer or its authorised representative, where mandated to do so, may fill in the mutual recognition declaration with only the information set out in Part I of the Annex. In such case the information set out in Part II of the Annex shall be filled in by the importer or by the distributor.

Alternatively, both parts of the mutual recognition declaration may be drawn up by the importer or by the distributor, provided that the signatory can supply the evidence referred to in point (a) of Article 5(4).

The mutual recognition declaration shall be drawn up in one of the official languages of the Union. Where that language is not the language required by the Member State of destination, the economic operator shall translate the mutual recognition declaration into a language required by the Member State of destination.

2. Economic operators who sign the mutual recognition declaration or a part of it shall be responsible for the content and accuracy of the information that they provide in the mutual recognition declaration, including the correctness of the information they translate. For the purposes of this paragraph, economic operators shall be liable in accordance with national laws.

3. Economic operators shall ensure that the mutual recognition declaration is kept up to date at all times, reflecting any changes in the information that they have provided in the mutual recognition declaration.

4. The mutual recognition declaration may be supplied to the competent authority of the Member State of destination for the purposes of an assessment to be carried out under Article 5. It may be supplied either in paper form or by electronic means or be made available online in accordance with the requirements of the Member State of destination.

5. Where economic operators make the mutual recognition declaration available online, the following conditions apply:

(a) the type of goods or the series to which the mutual recognition declaration applies shall be easily identifiable; and

(b) the technical means used shall ensure easy navigation and shall be monitored to ensure the availability of, and access to, the mutual recognition declaration.

6. Where the goods for which the mutual recognition declaration is being supplied are also subject to a Union act requiring an EU declaration of conformity, the mutual recognition declaration may be attached to the EU declaration of conformity.

Article 5 Assessment of goods

1. Where a competent authority of the Member State of destination intends to assess goods subject to this Regulation to establish whether the goods or goods of that type are lawfully marketed in another Member State, and, if so, whether the legitimate public interests covered by the applicable national technical rule of the Member State of destination are adequately protected, having regard to the characteristics of the goods in question, it shall contact the economic operator concerned without delay.

2. When entering into contact with the economic operator concerned, the competent authority of the Member State of destination shall inform the economic operator of the assessment, indicating the goods that are subject to that assessment and specifying the applicable national technical rule or prior authorisation procedure. The competent authority of the Member State of destination shall also inform the economic operator of the possibility of supplying a mutual recognition declaration in accordance with Article 4 for the purposes of that assessment.

3. The economic operator shall be allowed to make the goods available on the market in the Member State of destination while the competent authority carries out the assessment under

paragraph 1 of this Article, and may continue to do so unless the economic operator receives an administrative decision restricting or denying market access for those goods. This paragraph shall not apply where the assessment is carried out in the framework of a prior authorisation procedure, or where the competent authority temporary suspends the making available on the market of the goods that are subject to that assessment in accordance with Article 6.

4. If a mutual recognition declaration is supplied to a competent authority of the Member State of destination in accordance with Article 4, then for the purposes of the assessment under paragraph 1 of this Article:

(a) the mutual recognition declaration, together with supporting evidence necessary to verify the information contained in it that was provided in response to a request by the competent authority, shall be accepted by the competent authority as sufficient to demonstrate that the goods are lawfully marketed in another Member State; and

(b) the competent authority shall not require any other information or documentation from any economic operator for the purpose of demonstrating that the goods are lawfully marketed in another Member State.

5. If a mutual recognition declaration is not supplied to a competent authority of the Member State of destination in accordance with Article 4, then for the purposes of the assessment under paragraph 1 of this Article, the competent authority may request the economic operators concerned to provide documentation and information that is necessary for that assessment concerning the following:

(a) the characteristics of the goods or type of goods in question; and

(b) lawful marketing of the goods in another Member State.

6. The economic operator concerned shall be allowed at least 15 working days following the request of the competent authority of the Member State of destination in which to submit the documents and information referred to in point (a) of paragraph 4 or in paragraph 5, or to submit any arguments or comments that the economic operator might have.

7. For the purposes of the assessment under paragraph 1 of this Article, the competent authority of the Member State of destination, in accordance with Article 10(3), may contact the competent authorities or the Product Contact Points of the Member State in which an economic operator claims to be lawfully marketing its goods, if the competent authority needs to verify any information provided by the economic operator.

8. In carrying out the assessment under paragraph 1, the competent authorities of Member States of destination shall take due account of the content of test reports or certificates issued by a conformity assessment body that have been provided by any economic operator as part of the assessment. The competent authorities of Member States of destination shall not refuse test reports or certificates that were issued by a conformity assessment body accredited for the appropriate field of conformity assessment activity in accordance with Regulation (EC) No 765/2008 on grounds related to the competence of that body.

9. Where, on completion of an assessment under paragraph 1 of this Article, the competent authority of a Member State of destination takes an administrative decision with respect to the goods that it has assessed, it shall notify that administrative decision without delay to the economic operator referred to in paragraph 1 of this Article. The competent authority shall also notify that administrative decision to the Commission and to the other Member States no later than 20 working days after it took the decision. For that purpose, it shall use the system referred to in Article 11.

10. The administrative decision referred to in paragraph 9 shall set out the reasons for the decision in a manner that is sufficiently detailed and reasoned to facilitate an assessment of its compatibility with the principle of mutual recognition and with the requirements of this Regulation.

11. In particular, the following information shall be included in the administrative decision referred to in paragraph 9:

(a) the national technical rule on which the administrative decision is based;

(b) the legitimate public interest grounds justifying the application of the national technical rule on which the administrative decision is based;

(c) the technical or scientific evidence that the competent authority of the Member State of destination considered, including, where applicable, any relevant changes in the state of the art that have occurred since the national technical rule came into force;

(d) a summary of the arguments put forward by the economic operator concerned that are relevant for the assessment under paragraph 1, if any;

(e) the evidence demonstrating that the administrative decision is appropriate for the purpose of achieving the objective pursued and that the administrative decision does not go beyond what is necessary in order to attain that objective.

12. The administrative decision referred to in paragraph 9 of this Article shall specify the remedies available under the national law of the Member State of destination and the time limits applicable to those remedies. It shall also include a reference to the possibility for economic operators to use SOLVIT and the procedure under Article 8.

13. The administrative decision referred to in paragraph 9 shall not take effect before it has been notified to the economic operator concerned under that paragraph.

Article 6 Temporary suspension of market access

1. When the competent authority of a Member State is carrying out an assessment of goods pursuant to Article 5, it may temporarily suspend the making available of those goods on the market in that Member State only if:

(a) under normal or reasonably foreseeable conditions of use, the goods pose a serious risk to safety or health of persons or to the environment, including one where the effects are not immediate, which requires rapid intervention by the competent authority; or

(b) the making available of the goods, or of goods of that type, on the market in that Member State is generally prohibited in that Member State on grounds of public morality or public security.

2. The competent authority of the Member State shall immediately notify the economic operator concerned, the Commission and the other Member States of any temporary suspension pursuant to paragraph 1 of this Article. The notification to the Commission and the other Member States shall be made by means of the system referred to in Article 11. In cases falling within point (a) of paragraph 1 of this Article, the notification shall be accompanied by a detailed technical or scientific justification demonstrating why the case falls within the scope of that point.

Article 17 Entry into force and application

This Regulation shall enter into force on the twentieth day following that of its publication in the *Official Journal of the European Union*.

It shall apply from 19 April 2020.

This Regulation shall be binding in its entirety and directly applicable in all Member States.

Done at Brussels, 19 March 2019.

Free movement of persons

Council Directive of 22 March 1977 to facilitate the effective exercise by lawyers of freedom to provide services (77/249/EEC)*

[OJ 1977 L78/17]

Article 1

1. This Directive shall apply, within the limits and under the conditions laid down herein, to the activities of lawyers pursued by way of provision of services.

Notwithstanding anything contained in this Directive, Member States may reserve to prescribed categories of lawyers the preparation of formal documents for obtaining title to administer estates of deceased persons, and the drafting of formal documents creating or transferring interests in land.

* **Editor's Note:** As amended up to and including OJ 2013 L158/368.

2. 'Lawyers' means any person entitled to pursue his professional activities under one of the following designations:*

Belgium:	Avocat/Advocaat
Bulgaria:	адвокат
Croatia:	Odvjetnik/Odvjetnica
Czech Republic:	Advokát
Denmark:	Advokat
Germany:	Rechtsanwalt
Estonia:	Vandeadvokaat
Greece:	Δικηγόρος
France:	Avocat
Ireland:	Barrister
	Solicitor
Italy:	Avvocato
Cyprus:	Δικηγόρος
Latvia:	Zvērināts/advokāts
Lithuania:	Advokatas
Luxembourg:	Avocat-avoué
Hungary:	Ügyvéd
Malta:	Avukat/Prokuratur Legali
Netherlands:	Advocaat
Austria:	Rechtsanwalt
Poland:	Adwokat/Radca prawny
Portugal:	Advogado
Romania:	Avocat
Slovenia:	Odvetnik/Odvetnica
Slovakia	Advokát/Komerčný právnik
Finland:	Asianajaja—Advokat
Spain:	Abogado
Sweden:	Advokat
United Kingdom:	Advocate
	Barrister
	Solicitor

Article 2

Each Member State shall recognise as a lawyer for the purpose of pursuing the activities specified in Article 1(1) any person listed in paragraph 2 of that Article.

Article 3

A person referred to in Article 1 shall adopt the professional title used in the Member State from which he comes, expressed in the language or one of the languages, of that State, with an indication of the professional organisation by which he is authorised to practise or the court of law before which he is entitled to practise pursuant to the laws of that State.

Article 4

1. Activities relating to the representation of a client in legal proceedings or before public authorities shall be pursued in each host Member State under the conditions laid down for lawyers established in that State, with the exception of any conditions requiring residence, or registration with a professional organisation, in that State.

* **Editor's Note:** As amended by the Accession Acts.

2. A lawyer pursuing these activities shall observe the rules of professional conduct of the host Member State, without prejudice to his obligations in the Member State from which he comes.

3. When these activities are pursued in the United Kingdom, 'rules of professional conduct of the host Member State' means the rules of professional conduct applicable to solicitors, where such activities are not reserved for barristers and advocates. Otherwise the rules of professional conduct applicable to the latter shall apply. However, barristers from Ireland shall always be subject to the rules of professional conduct applicable in the United Kingdom to barristers and advocates.

When these activities are pursued in Ireland 'rules of professional conduct of the host Member State' means, in so far as they govern the oral presentation of a case in court, the rules of professional conduct applicable to barristers. In all other cases the rules of professional conduct applicable to solicitors shall apply. However, barristers and advocates from the United Kingdom shall always be subject to the rules of professional conduct applicable in Ireland to barristers.

4. A lawyer pursuing activities other than those referred to in paragraph 1 shall remain subject to the conditions and rules of professional conduct of the Member State from which he comes without prejudice to respect for the rules, whatever their source, which govern the profession in the host Member State, especially those concerning the incompatibility of the exercise of the activities of a lawyer with the exercise of other activities in that State, professional secrecy, relation with other lawyers, the prohibition on the same lawyer acting for parties with mutually conflicting interests, and publicity. The latter rules are applicable only if they are capable of being observed by a lawyer who is not established in the host Member State and to the extent to which their observance is objectively justified to ensure, in that State, the proper exercise of a lawyer's activities, the standing of the profession and respect for the rules concerning incompatibility.

Article 5

For the pursuit of activities relating to the representation of a client in legal proceedings, a Member State may require lawyers to whom Article 1 applies:

- to be introduced, in accordance with local rules or customs, to the presiding judge and, where appropriate, to the President of the relevant Bar in the host Member State;
- to work in conjunction with a lawyer who practises before the judicial authority in question and who would, where necessary, be answerable to that authority, or with an 'avoué' or 'procuratore' practising before it.

Article 6

Any Member State may exclude lawyers who are in the salaried employment of a public or private undertaking from pursuing activities relating to the representation of that undertaking in legal proceedings in so far as lawyers established in that State are not permitted to pursue those activities.

Article 7

1. The competent authority of the host Member State may request the person providing the services to establish his qualifications as a lawyer.

2. In the event of non-compliance with the obligations referred to in Article 4 and in force in the host Member State, the competent authority of the latter shall determine in accordance with its own rules and procedures the consequences of such non-compliance, and to this end may obtain an appropriate professional information concerning the person providing services. It shall notify the competent authority of the Member State from which the person comes of any decision taken. Such exchanges shall not affect the confidential nature of the information supplied.

(All remaining provisions omitted.)

Directive 96/71/EC of the European Parliament and of the Council of 16 December 1996 concerning the posting of workers in the framework of the provision of services*

[OJ 1997 L18/1]

Article 1 Subject-matter and scope

–1. This Directive shall ensure the protection of posted workers during their posting in relation to the freedom to provide services, by laying down mandatory provisions regarding working conditions and the protection of workers' health and safety that must be respected.

–1a. This Directive shall not in any way affect the exercise of fundamental rights as recognised in the Member States and at Union level, including the right or freedom to strike or to take other action covered by the specific industrial relations systems in Member States, in accordance with national law and/or practice. Nor does it affect the right to negotiate, to conclude and enforce collective agreements, or to take collective action in accordance with national law and/or practice.

1. This Directive shall apply to undertakings established in a Member State which, in the framework of the transnational provision of services, post workers, in accordance with paragraph 3, to the territory of a Member State.

2. This Directive shall not apply to merchant navy undertakings as regards seagoing personnel.

3. This Directive shall apply to the extent that the undertakings referred to in paragraph 1 take one of the following transnational measures:

(a) post workers to the territory of a Member State on their account and under their direction, under a contract concluded between the undertaking making the posting and the party for whom the services are intended, operating in that Member State, provided there is an employment relationship between the undertaking making the posting and the worker during the period of posting; or

(b) post workers to an establishment or to an undertaking owned by the group in the territory of a Member State, provided there is an employment relationship between the undertaking making the posting and the worker during the period of posting; or

(c) being a temporary employment undertaking or placement agency, hire out a worker to a user undertaking established or operating in the territory of a Member State, provided there is an employment relationship between the temporary employment undertaking or placement agency and the worker during the period of posting.

Where a worker who has been hired out by a temporary employment undertaking or placement agency to a user undertaking as referred to in point (c) is to carry out work in the framework of the transnational provision of services within the meaning of point (a), (b) or (c) by the user undertaking in the territory of a Member State other than where the worker normally works for the temporary employment undertaking or placement agency, or for the user undertaking, the worker shall be considered to be posted to the territory of that Member State by the temporary employment undertaking or placement agency with which the worker is in an employment relationship. The temporary employment undertaking or placement agency shall be considered to be an undertaking as referred to in paragraph 1 and shall fully comply with the relevant provisions of this Directive and Directive 2014/67/EU of the European Parliament and of the Council.

The user undertaking shall inform the temporary employment undertaking or placement agency which hired out the worker in due time before commencement of the work referred to in the second subparagraph.

4. Undertakings established in a non-member State must not be given more favourable treatment than undertakings established in a Member State.

* **Editor's Note:** As amended by Directive 2018/957 (OJ 2018 L173/16).

Article 2 Definition

1. For the purposes of this Directive, 'posted worker' means a worker who, for a limited period, carries out his work in the territory of a Member State other than the State in which he normally works.

2. For the purposes of this Directive, the definition of a worker is that which applies in the law of the Member State to whose territory the worker is posted.

Article 3 Terms and conditions of employment

1. Member States shall ensure, irrespective of which law applies to the employment relationship, that undertakings as referred to in Article 1(1) guarantee, on the basis of equality of treatment, workers who are posted to their territory the terms and conditions of employment covering the following matters which are laid down in the Member State where the work is carried out:

- by law, regulation or administrative provision, and/or
- by collective agreements or arbitration awards which have been declared universally applicable or otherwise apply in accordance with paragraph 8:

(a) maximum work periods and minimum rest periods;
(b) minimum paid annual leave;
(c) remuneration, including overtime rates; this point does not apply to supplementary occupational retirement pension schemes;
(d) the conditions of hiring-out of workers, in particular the supply of workers by temporary employment undertakings;
(e) health, safety and hygiene at work;
(f) protective measures with regard to the terms and conditions of employment of pregnant women or women who have recently given birth, of children and of young people;
(g) equality of treatment between men and women and other provisions on non-discrimination;
(h) the conditions of workers' accommodation where provided by the employer to workers away from their regular place of work;
(i) allowances or reimbursement of expenditure to cover travel, board and lodging expenses for workers away from home for professional reasons.

Point (i) shall apply exclusively to travel, board and lodging expenditure incurred by posted workers where they are required to travel to and from their regular place of work in the Member State to whose territory they are posted, or where they are temporarily sent by their employer from that regular place of work to another place of work.

For the purposes of this Directive, the concept of remuneration shall be determined by the national law and/or practice of the Member State to whose territory the worker is posted and means all the constituent elements of remuneration rendered mandatory by national law, regulation or administrative provision, or by collective agreements or arbitration awards which, in that Member State, have been declared universally applicable or otherwise apply in accordance with paragraph 8.

Without prejudice to Article 5 of Directive 2014/67/EU, Member States shall publish the information on the terms and conditions of employment, in accordance with national law and/or practice, without undue delay and in a transparent manner, on the single official national website referred to in that Article, including the constituent elements of remuneration as referred to in the third subparagraph of this paragraph and all the terms and conditions of employment in accordance with paragraph 1a of this Article.

Member States shall ensure that the information provided on the single official national website is accurate and up to date. The Commission shall publish on its website the addresses of the single official national websites.

Where, contrary to Article 5 of Directive 2014/67/EU, the information on the single official national website does not indicate which terms and conditions of employment are to be applied, that circumstance shall be taken into account, in accordance with national law and/or practice, in determining penalties in the event of infringements of the national provisions adopted pursuant to this Directive, to the extent necessary to ensure the proportionality thereof.

1a. Where the effective duration of a posting exceeds 12 months, Member States shall ensure, irrespective of which law applies to the employment relationship, that undertakings as referred to in Article 1(1) guarantee, on the basis of equality of treatment, workers who are posted to their territory, in addition to the terms and conditions of employment referred to in paragraph 1 of this Article, all the applicable terms and conditions of employment which are laid down in the Member State where the work is carried out:

- by law, regulation or administrative provision, and/or
- by collective agreements or arbitration awards which have been declared universally applicable or otherwise apply in accordance with paragraph 8.

The first subparagraph of this paragraph shall not apply to the following matters:

(a) procedures, formalities and conditions of the conclusion and termination of the employment contract, including non-competition clauses;

(b) supplementary occupational retirement pension schemes.

Where the service provider submits a motivated notification, the Member State where the service is provided shall extend the period referred to in the first subparagraph to 18 months.

Where an undertaking as referred to in Article 1(1) replaces a posted worker by another posted worker performing the same task at the same place, the duration of the posting shall, for the purposes of this paragraph, be the cumulative duration of the posting periods of the individual posted workers concerned.

The concept of 'the same task at the same place' referred to in the fourth subparagraph of this paragraph shall be determined taking into consideration, inter alia, the nature of the service to be provided, the work to be performed and the address(es) of the workplace.

1b. Member States shall provide that the undertakings referred to in point (c) of Article 1(3) guarantee posted workers the terms and conditions of employment which apply pursuant to Article 5 of Directive 2008/104/EC of the European Parliament and of the Council to temporary agency workers hired-out by temporary-work agencies established in the Member State where the work is carried out.

The user undertaking shall inform the undertakings referred to in point (c) of Article 1(3) of the terms and conditions of employment that it applies regarding the working conditions and remuneration to the extent covered by the first subparagraph of this paragraph.

2. In the case of initial assembly and/or first installation of goods where this is an integral part of a contract for the supply of goods and necessary for taking the goods supplied into use and carried out by the skilled and/or specialist workers of the supplying undertaking, the first subparagraph of paragraph 1(b) and (c) shall not apply, if the period of posting does not exceed eight days.

This provision shall not apply to activities in the field of building work listed in the Annex.

3. Member States may, after consulting employers and labour, in accordance with the traditions and practices of each Member State, decide not to apply the first subparagraph of paragraph 1(c) in the cases referred to in Article 1(3)(a) and (b) when the length of the posting does not exceed one month.

4. Member States may, in accordance with national laws and/or practices, provide that exemptions may be made from the first subparagraph of paragraph 1(c) in the cases referred to in Article 1(3)(a) and (b) and from a decision by a Member State within the meaning of paragraph 3 of this Article, by means of collective agreements within the meaning of paragraph 8 of this Article, concerning one or more sectors of activity, where the length of the posting does not exceed one month.

5. Member States may provide for exemptions to be granted from the first subparagraph of paragraph 1(b) and (c) in the cases referred to in Article 1(3)(a) and (b) on the grounds that the amount of work to be done is not significant.

Member States availing themselves of the option referred to in the first subparagraph shall lay down the criteria which the work to be performed must meet in order to be considered as 'non-significant'.

6. The length of the posting shall be calculated on the basis of a reference period of one year from the beginning of the posting.

For the purpose of such calculations, account shall be taken of any previous periods for which the post has been filled by a posted worker.

7. Paragraphs 1 to 6 shall not prevent the application of terms and conditions of employment which are more favourable to workers.

Allowances specific to the posting shall be considered to be part of remuneration, unless they are paid in reimbursement of expenditure actually incurred on account of the posting, such as expenditure on travel, board and lodging. The employer shall, without prejudice to point (h) of the first subparagraph of paragraph 1, reimburse the posted worker for such expenditure in accordance with the national law and/or practice applicable to the employment relationship.

Where the terms and conditions of employment applicable to the employment relationship do not determine whether and, if so, which elements of the allowance specific to the posting are paid in reimbursement of expenditure actually incurred on account of the posting or which are part of remuneration, then the entire allowance shall be considered to be paid in reimbursement of expenditure.

8. 'Collective agreements or arbitration awards which have been declared universally applicable' means collective agreements or arbitration awards which must be observed by all undertakings in the geographical area and in the profession or industry concerned.

In the absence of a system for declaring collective agreements or arbitration awards to be of universal application within the meaning of the first subparagraph, Member States may, if they so decide, base themselves on:

- collective agreements or arbitration awards which are generally applicable to all similar undertakings in the geographical area and in the profession or industry concerned, and/or
- collective agreements which have been concluded by the most representative employers and labour organizations at national level and which are applied throughout national territory,

provided that their application to undertakings as referred to in Article 1(1) ensures equality of treatment on matters listed in the first subparagraph of paragraph 1 of this Article and, where applicable, with regard to the terms and conditions of employment to be guaranteed posted workers in accordance with paragraph 1a of this Article, between those undertakings and the other undertakings referred to in this subparagraph which are in a similar position.

Equality of treatment, within the meaning of this Article, shall be deemed to exist where national undertakings in a similar position:

- are subject, in the place in question or in the sector concerned, to the same obligations as undertakings as referred to in Article 1(1) as regards the matters listed in the first subparagraph of paragraph 1 of this Article and, where applicable, as regards the terms and conditions of employment to be guaranteed posted workers in accordance with paragraph 1a of this Article, and
- are required to fulfil such obligations with the same effects.

9. Member States may require undertakings as referred to in Article 1(1) to guarantee workers referred to in point (c) of Article 1(3), in addition to the terms and conditions of employment referred to in paragraph 1b of this Article, other terms and conditions that apply to temporary agency workers in the Member State where the work is carried out.

10. This Directive shall not preclude the application by Member States, in compliance with the Treaties, to national undertakings and to the undertakings of other Member States, on the basis of equality of treatment, of terms and conditions of employment on matters other than those referred to in the first subparagraph of paragraph 1 in the case of public policy provisions.

Article 4 Cooperation on information

1. For the purposes of implementing this Directive, Member States shall, in accordance with national legislation and/or practice, designate one or more liaison offices or one or more competent national bodies.

2. Member States shall make provision for cooperation between the competent authorities or bodies, including public authorities, which, in accordance with national law, are responsible for monitoring the terms and conditions of employment referred to in Article 3, including at Union level. Such cooperation shall in particular consist in replying to reasoned requests from those authorities or bodies for information on the transnational hiring-out of workers, and in tackling manifest abuses or possible cases of unlawful activities, such as transnational cases of undeclared work and bogus self-employment linked to the posting of workers. Where the competent authority or body in the Member State from which the worker is posted does not possess the information requested by the competent authority or body of the Member State to whose territory the worker is posted, it shall seek to obtain that information from other authorities or bodies in that Member State. In the event of persistent delays in the provision of such information to the Member State to whose territory the worker is posted, the Commission shall be informed and shall take appropriate measures.

3. Each Member State shall take the appropriate measures to make the information on the terms and conditions of employment referred to in Article 3 generally available.

4. Each Member State shall notify the other Member States and the Commission of the liaison offices and/or competent bodies referred to in paragraph 1.

Article 5 Monitoring, control and enforcement

The Member State to whose territory the worker is posted and the Member State from which the worker is posted shall be responsible for the monitoring, control and enforcement of the obligations laid down in this Directive and in Directive 2014/67/EU and shall take appropriate measures in the event of failure to comply with this Directive.

Member States shall lay down the rules on penalties applicable to infringements of national provisions adopted pursuant to this Directive and shall take all measures necessary to ensure that they are implemented. The penalties provided for shall be effective, proportionate and dissuasive.

Member States shall in particular ensure that adequate procedures are available to workers and/or workers' representatives for the enforcement of obligations under this Directive.

Where, following an overall assessment made pursuant to Article 4 of Directive 2014/67/EU by a Member State, it is established that an undertaking is improperly or fraudulently creating the impression that the situation of a worker falls within the scope of this Directive, that Member State shall ensure that the worker benefits from relevant law and practice.

Member States shall ensure that this Article does not lead to the worker concerned being subject to less favourable conditions than those applicable to posted workers.

Article 6 Jurisdiction

In order to enforce the right to the terms and conditions of employment guaranteed in Article 3, judicial proceedings may be instituted in the Member State in whose territory the worker is or was posted, without prejudice, where applicable, to the right, under existing international conventions on jurisdiction, to institute proceedings in another State.

Article 7 Implementation

Member States shall adopt the laws, regulations and administrative provisions necessary to comply with this Directive by 16 December 1999 at the latest. They shall forthwith inform the Commission thereof.

When Member States adopt these provisions, they shall contain a reference to this Directive or shall be accompanied by such reference on the occasion of their official publication. The methods of making such reference shall be laid down by Member States.

Article 8 Commission review

By 16 December 2001 at the latest, the Commission shall review the operation of this Directive with a view to proposing the necessary amendments to the Council where appropriate.

Article 9

This Directive is addressed to the Member States.

Done at Brussels, 16 December 1996.

ANNEX

The activities referred to in Article 3(2) include all building work related to the construction, repair, upkeep, alteration or demolition of buildings, and in particular the following work:

1. excavation
2. earthmoving
3. actual building work
4. assembly and dismantling of prefabricated elements
5. fitting out or installation
6. alterations
7. renovation
8. repairs
9. dismantling
10. demolition
11. maintenance
12. upkeep, painting and cleaning work
13. improvements.

Directive 98/5/EC of the European Parliament and of the Council of 16 February 1998 to facilitate practice of the profession of lawyer on a permanent basis in a Member State other than that in which the qualification was obtained*

[OJ 1998 L77/36]

Article 2 Right to practise under the home-country professional title

Any lawyer shall be entitled to pursue on a permanent basis, in any other Member State under his home-country professional title, the activities specified in Article 5.

Integration into the profession of lawyer in the host Member State shall be subject to Article 10.

Article 3 Registration with the competent authority

1. A lawyer who wishes to practise in a Member State other than that in which he obtained his professional qualification shall register with the competent authority in that State.

2. The competent authority in the host Member State shall register the lawyer upon presentation of a certificate attesting to his registration with the competent authority in the home Member State. It may require that, when presented by the competent authority of the home Member State, the certificate be not more than three months old. It shall inform the competent authority in the home Member State of the registration.

* **Editor's Note:** As amended up to and including Directive 2013/25 (OJ 2013 L158/368).

3. For the purpose of applying paragraph 1:
- in the United Kingdom and Ireland, lawyers practising under a professional title other than those used in the United Kingdom or Ireland shall register either with the authority responsible for the profession of barrister or advocate or with the authority responsible for the profession of solicitor,
- in the United Kingdom, the authority responsible for a barrister from Ireland shall be that responsible for the profession of barrister or advocate, and the authority responsible for a solicitor from Ireland shall be that responsible for the profession of solicitor,
- in Ireland, the authority responsible for a barrister or an advocate from the United Kingdom shall be that responsible for the profession of barrister, and the authority responsible for a solicitor from the United Kingdom shall be that responsible for the profession of solicitor.

4. Where the relevant competent authority in a host Member State publishes the names of lawyers registered with it, it shall also publish the names of lawyers registered pursuant to this Directive.

Article 4 Practice under the home-country professional title

1. A lawyer practising in a host Member State under his home-country professional title shall do so under that title, which must be expressed in the official language or one of the official languages of his home Member State, in an intelligible manner and in such a way as to avoid confusion with the professional title of the host Member State.

2. For the purpose of applying paragraph 1, a host Member State may require a lawyer practising under his home-country professional title to indicate the professional body of which he is a member in his home Member State or the judicial authority before which he is entitled to practise pursuant to the laws of his home Member State. A host Member State may also require a lawyer practising under his home-country professional title to include a reference to his registration with the competent authority in that State.

Article 5 Area of activity

1. Subject to paragraphs 2 and 3, a lawyer practising under his home-country professional title carries on the same professional activities as a lawyer practising under the relevant processional title used in the host Member State and may, *inter alia*, give advice on the law of his home Member State, on Community law, on international law and on the law of the host Member State. He shall in any event comply with the rules of procedure applicable in the national courts.

2. Member States which authorise in their territory a prescribed category of lawyers to prepare deeds for obtaining title to administer estates of deceased persons and for creating or transferring interests in land which, in other Member States, are reserved for professions other than that of lawyer may exclude from such activities lawyers practising under a home-country professional title conferred in one of the latter Member States.

3. For the pursuit of activities relating to the representation or defence of a client in legal proceedings and insofar as the law of the host Member State reserves such activities to lawyers practising under the professional title of that State, the latter may require lawyers practising under their home-country professional titles to work in conjunction with a lawyer who practises before the judicial authority in question and who would, where necessary, be answerable to that authority or with an 'avoué' practising before it.

Nevertheless, in order to ensure the smooth operation of the justice system, Member States may lay down specific rules for access to supreme courts, such as the use of specialist lawyers.

Article 6 Rules of professional conduct applicable

1. Irrespective of the rules of professional conduct to which he is subject in his home Member State, a lawyer practising under his home-country professional title shall be subject to the same rules of professional conduct as lawyers practising under the relevant professional title of the host Member State in respect of all the activities he pursues in its territory.

2. Lawyers practising under their home-country professional titles shall be granted appropriate representation in the professional associations of the host Member State. Such representation shall involve at least the right to vote in elections to those associations' governing bodies.

3. The host Member State may require a lawyer practising under his home country professional title either to take out professional indemnity insurance or to become a member of a professional guarantee fund in accordance with the rules which that State lays down for professional activities pursued in its territory. Nevertheless, a lawyer practising under his home-country professional title shall be exempted from that requirement if he can prove that he is covered by insurance taken out or a guarantee provided in accordance with the rules of his home Member State, insofar as such insurance or guarantee is equivalent in terms of the conditions and extent of cover. Where the equivalence is only partial, the competent authority in the host Member State may require that additional insurance or an additional guarantee be contacted to cover the elements which are not already covered by the insurance or guarantee contracted in accordance with the rules of the home Member States.

Article 10 Like treatment as a lawyer of the host Member State

1. A lawyer practising under his home-country professional title who has effectively and regularly pursued for a period of at least three years an activity in the host Member State in the law of that State including Community law shall, with a view to gaining admission to the profession of lawyer in the host Member State, be exempted from the conditions set out in Article 4(1)(b) of Directive 89/48/EEC, 'Effective and regular pursuit' means actual exercise of the activity without any interruption other than that resulting from the events of everyday life.

It shall be for the lawyer concerned to furnish the competent authority in the host Member State with proof of such effective regular pursuit for a period of at least three years of an activity in the law of the host Member State. To that end:

(a) the lawyer shall provide the competent authority in the host Member State with any relevant information and documentation, notably on the number of matters he has dealt with and their nature;

(b) the competent authority of the host Member State may verify the effective and regular nature of the activity pursued and may, if need be, request the lawyer to provide, orally or in writing, clarification of or further details on the information and documentation mentioned in point (a).

Reasons shall be given for a decision by the competent authority in the host Member State not to grant an exemption where proof is not provided that the requirements laid down in the first subparagraph have been fulfilled, and the decision shall be subject to appeal under domestic law.

2. A lawyer practising under his home-country professional title in a host Member State may, at any time, apply to have his diploma recognised in accordance with Directive 89/48/ EEC with a view to gaining admission to the profession of lawyer in the host Member State and practising it under the professional title corresponding to the profession in that Member State.

3. A lawyer practising under his home-country professional title who has effectively and regularly pursued a professional activity in the host Member State for a period of at least three years but for a lesser period in the law of that Member State may obtain from the competent authority of that State admission to the profession of lawyer in the host Member State and the right to practise it under the professional title corresponding to the profession in that Member State, without having to meet the conditions referred to in Article 4(1)(b) of Directive 89/48/ EEC, under the conditions and in accordance with the procedures set out below:

(a) The competent authority of the host Member State shall take into account the effective and regular professional activity pursued during the abovementioned period and any knowledge and professional experience of the law of the host Member State, and any attendance at lectures or seminars on the law of the host Member State, including the rules regulating professional practice and conduct.

(b) The lawyer shall provide the competent authority of the host Member State with any relevant information and documentation, in particular on the matters he has dealt with. Assessment of the lawyer's effective and regular activity in the host Member State and assessment of his capacity to continue the activity he has pursued there shall be carried out by means of an interview with the competent authority of the host Member State in order to verify the regular and effective nature of the activity pursued.

Reasons shall be given for a decision by the competent authority in the host Member State not to grant authorisation where proof is not provided that the requirements laid down in the first subparagraph have been fulfilled, and the decision shall be subject to appeal under domestic law.

4. The competent authority of the host Member State may, by reasoned decision subject to appeal under domestic law, refuse to allow the lawyer the benefit of the provisions of this Article if it considers that this would be against public policy, in particular because of disciplinary proceedings, complaints or incidents of any kind.

5. The representatives of the competent authority entrusted with consideration of the application shall preserve the confidentiality of any information received.

6. A lawyer who gains admission to the profession of lawyer in the host Member State in accordance with paragraphs 1, 2 and 3 shall be entitled to use his home-country professional title, expressed in the official language or one of the official languages of his home Member State, alongside the professional title corresponding to the profession of lawyer in the host Member State.

Done at Brussels, 16 February 1998.

Council Directive 2003/86/EC of 22 September 2003 on the right to family reunification

[OJ 2003 L251/12]

Chapter I General provisions

Article 1

The purpose of this Directive is to determine the conditions for the exercise of the right to family reunification by third country nationals residing lawfully in the territory of the Member States.

Article 2

For the purposes of this Directive:

(a) 'third country national' means any person who is not a citizen of the Union within the meaning of Article 17(1) of the Treaty;

(b) 'refugee' means any third country national or stateless person enjoying refugee status within the meaning of the Geneva Convention relating to the status of refugees of 28 July 1951, as amended by the Protocol signed in New York on 31 January 1967;

(c) 'sponsor' means a third country national residing lawfully in a Member State and applying or whose family members apply for family reunification to be joined with him/her;

(d) 'family reunification' means the entry into and residence in a Member State by family members of a third country national residing lawfully in that Member State in order to preserve the family unit, whether the family relationship arose before or after the resident's entry;

(e) 'residence permit' means any authorisation issued by the authorities of a Member State allowing a third country national to stay legally in its territory, in accordance with the provisions of Article 1(2)(a) of Council Regulation (EC) No 1030/2002 of 13 June 2002 laying down a uniform format for residence permits for third country nationals;[1]

(f) 'unaccompanied minor' means third country nationals or stateless persons below the age of eighteen, who arrive on the territory of the Member States unaccompanied by an adult

[1] OJ L 157, 15.6.2002, p. 1.

responsible by law or custom, and for as long as they are not effectively taken into the care of such a person, or minors who are left unaccompanied after they entered the territory of the Member States.

Article 3

1. This Directive shall apply where the sponsor is holding a residence permit issued by a Member State for a period of validity of one year or more who has reasonable prospects of obtaining the right of permanent residence, if the members of his or her family are third country nationals of whatever status.

2. This Directive shall not apply where the sponsor is:
   (a) applying for recognition of refugee status whose application has not yet given rise to a final decision;
   (b) authorised to reside in a Member State on the basis of temporary protection or applying for authorisation to reside on that basis and awaiting a decision on his status;
   (c) authorised to reside in a Member State on the basis of a subsidiary form of protection in accordance with international obligations, national legislation or the practice of the Member States or applying for authorisation to reside on that basis and awaiting a decision on his status.

3. This Directive shall not apply to members of the family of a Union citizen.

4. This Directive is without prejudice to more favourable provisions of:
   (a) bilateral and multilateral agreements between the Community or the Community and its Member States, on the one hand, and third countries, on the other;
   (b) the European Social Charter of 18 October 1961, the amended European Social Charter of 3 May 1987 and the European Convention on the legal status of migrant workers of 24 November 1977.

5. This Directive shall not affect the possibility for the Member States to adopt or maintain more favourable provisions.

Chapter II Family members

Article 4

1. The Member States shall authorise the entry and residence, pursuant to this Directive and subject to compliance with the conditions laid down in Chapter IV, as well as in Article 16, of the following family members:
   (a) the sponsor's spouse;
   (b) the minor children of the sponsor and of his/her spouse, including children adopted in accordance with a decision taken by the competent authority in the Member State concerned or a decision which is automatically enforceable due to international obligations of that Member State or must be recognised in accordance with international obligations;
   (c) the minor children including adopted children of the sponsor where the sponsor has custody and the children are dependent on him or her. Member States may authorise the reunification of children of whom custody is shared, provided the other party sharing custody has given his or her agreement;
   (d) the minor children including adopted children of the spouse where the spouse has custody and the children are dependent on him or her. Member States may authorise the reunification of children of whom custody is shared, provided the other party sharing custody has given his or her agreement.

The minor children referred to in this Article must be below the age of majority set by the law of the Member State concerned and must not be married.

By way of derogation, where a child is aged over 12 years and arrives independently from the rest of his/her family, the Member State may, before authorising entry and residence under this

Directive, verify whether he or she meets a condition for integration provided for by its existing legislation on the date of implementation of this Directive.

2. The Member States may, by law or regulation, authorise the entry and residence, pursuant to this Directive and subject to compliance with the conditions laid down in Chapter IV, of the following family members:

(a) first-degree relatives in the direct ascending line of the sponsor or his or her spouse, where they are dependent on them and do not enjoy proper family support in the country of origin;

(b) the adult unmarried children of the sponsor or his or her spouse, where they are objectively unable to provide for their own needs on account of their state of health.

3. The Member States may, by law or regulation, authorise the entry and residence, pursuant to this Directive and subject to compliance with the conditions laid down in Chapter IV, of the unmarried partner, being a third country national, with whom the sponsor is in a duly attested stable long-term relationship, or of a third country national who is bound to the sponsor by a registered partnership in accordance with Article 5(2), and of the unmarried minor children, including adopted children, as well as the adult unmarried children who are objectively unable to provide for their own needs on account of their state of health, of such persons.

Member States may decide that registered partners are to be treated equally as spouses with respect to family reunification.

4. In the event of a polygamous marriage, where the sponsor already has a spouse living with him in the territory of a Member State, the Member State concerned shall not authorise the family reunification of a further spouse.

By way of derogation from paragraph 1(c), Member States may limit the family reunification of minor children of a further spouse and the sponsor.

5. In order to ensure better integration and to prevent forced marriages Member States may require the sponsor and his/her spouse to be of a minimum age, and at maximum 21 years, before the spouse is able to join him/her.

6. By way of derogation, Member States may request that the applications concerning family reunification of minor children have to be submitted before the age of 15, as provided for by its existing legislation on the date of the implementation of this Directive. If the application is submitted after the age of 15, the Member States which decide to apply this derogation shall authorise the entry and residence of such children on grounds other than family reunification.

Chapter III Submission and examination of the application

Article 5

1. Member States shall determine whether, in order to exercise the right to family reunification, an application for entry and residence shall be submitted to the competent authorities of the Member State concerned either by the sponsor or by the family member or members.

2. The application shall be accompanied by documentary evidence of the family relationship and of compliance with the conditions laid down in Articles 4 and 6 and, where applicable, Articles 7 and 8, as well as certified copies of family member(s)' travel documents.

If appropriate, in order to obtain evidence that a family relationship exists, Member States may carry out interviews with the sponsor and his/her family members and conduct other investigations that are found to be necessary.

When examining an application concerning the unmarried partner of the sponsor, Member States shall consider, as evidence of the family relationship, factors such as a common child, previous cohabitation, registration of the partnership and any other reliable means of proof.

3. The application shall be submitted and examined when the family members are residing outside the territory of the Member State in which the sponsor resides.

By way of derogation, a Member State may, in appropriate circumstances, accept an application submitted when the family members are already in its territory.

4. The competent authorities of the Member State shall give the person, who has submitted the application, written notification of the decision as soon as possible and in any event no later than nine months from the date on which the application was lodged.

In exceptional circumstances linked to the complexity of the examination of the application, the time limit referred to in the first subparagraph may be extended.

Reasons shall be given for the decision rejecting the application. Any consequences of no decision being taken by the end of the period provided for in the first subparagraph shall be determined by the national legislation of the relevant Member State.

5. When examining an application, the Member States shall have due regard to the best interests of minor children.

Chapter IV Requirements for the exercise of the right to family reunification

Article 6

1. The Member States may reject an application for entry and residence of family members on grounds of public policy, public security or public health.

2. Member States may withdraw or refuse to renew a family member's residence permit on grounds of public policy or public security or public health.

When taking the relevant decision, the Member State shall consider, besides Article 17, the severity or type of offence against public policy or public security committed by the family member, or the dangers that are emanating from such person.

3. Renewal of the residence permit may not be withheld and removal from the territory may not be ordered by the competent authority of the Member State concerned on the sole ground of illness or disability suffered after the issue of the residence permit.

Article 7

1. When the application for family reunification is submitted, the Member State concerned may require the person who has submitted the application to provide evidence that the sponsor has:

(a) accommodation regarded as normal for a comparable family in the same region and which meets the general health and safety standards in force in the Member State concerned;

(b) sickness insurance in respect of all risks normally covered for its own nationals in the Member State concerned for himself/herself and the members of his/her family;

(c) stable and regular resources which are sufficient to maintain himself/herself and the members of his/her family, without recourse to the social assistance system of the Member State concerned. Member States shall evaluate these resources by reference to their nature and regularity and may take into account the level of minimum national wages and pensions as well as the number of family members.

2. Member States may require third country nationals to comply with integration measures, in accordance with national law.

With regard to the refugees and/or family members of refugees referred to in Article 12 the integration measures referred to in the first subparagraph may only be applied once the persons concerned have been granted family reunification.

Article 8

Member States may require the sponsor to have stayed lawfully in their territory for a period not exceeding two years, before having his/her family members join him/her.

By way of derogation, where the legislation of a Member State relating to family reunification in force on the date of adoption of this Directive takes into account its reception capacity, the Member

State may provide for a waiting period of no more than three years between submission of the application for family reunification and the issue of a residence permit to the family members.

Chapter V Family reunification of refugees

Article 9

1. This Chapter shall apply to family reunification of refugees recognised by the Member States.
2. Member States may confine the application of this Chapter to refugees whose family relationships predate their entry.
3. This Chapter is without prejudice to any rules granting refugee status to family members.

Article 10

1. Article 4 shall apply to the definition of family members except that the third subparagraph of paragraph 1 thereof shall not apply to the children of refugees.
2. The Member States may authorise family reunification of other family members not referred to in Article 4, if they are dependent on the refugee.
3. If the refugee is an unaccompanied minor, the Member States:
   (a) shall authorise the entry and residence for the purposes of family reunification of his/her first-degree relatives in the direct ascending line without applying the conditions laid down in Article 4(2)(a);
   (b) may authorise the entry and residence for the purposes of family reunification of his/her legal guardian or any other member of the family, where the refugee has no relatives in the direct ascending line or such relatives cannot be traced.

Article 11

1. Article 5 shall apply to the submission and examination of the application, subject to paragraph 2 of this Article.
2. Where a refugee cannot provide official documentary evidence of the family relationship, the Member States shall take into account other evidence, to be assessed in accordance with national law, of the existence of such relationship. A decision rejecting an application may not be based solely on the fact that documentary evidence is lacking.

Article 12

1. By way of derogation from Article 7, the Member States shall not require the refugee and/or family member(s) to provide, in respect of applications concerning those family members referred to in Article 4(1), the evidence that the refugee fulfils the requirements set out in Article 7.

Without prejudice to international obligations, where family reunification is possible in a third country with which the sponsor and/or family member has special links, Member States may require provision of the evidence referred to in the first subparagraph.

Member States may require the refugee to meet the conditions referred to in Article 7(1) if the application for family reunification is not submitted within a period of three months after the granting of the refugee status.

2. By way of derogation from Article 8, the Member States shall not require the refugee to have resided in their territory for a certain period of time, before having his/her family members join him/her.

Chapter VI Entry and residence of family members

Article 13

1. As soon as the application for family reunification has been accepted, the Member State concerned shall authorise the entry of the family member or members. In that regard, the Member State concerned shall grant such persons every facility for obtaining the requisite visas.
2. The Member State concerned shall grant the family members a first residence permit of at least one year's duration. This residence permit shall be renewable.

3. The duration of the residence permits granted to the family member(s) shall in principle not go beyond the date of expiry of the residence permit held by the sponsor.

Article 14

1. The sponsor's family members shall be entitled, in the same way as the sponsor, to:

(a) access to education;

(b) access to employment and self-employed activity;

(c) access to vocational guidance, initial and further training and retraining.

2. Member States may decide according to national law the conditions under which family members shall exercise an employed or self-employed activity. These conditions shall set a time limit which shall in no case exceed 12 months, during which Member States may examine the situation of their labour market before authorising family members to exercise an employed or self-employed activity.

3. Member States may restrict access to employment or self-employed activity by first-degree relatives in the direct ascending line or adult unmarried children to whom Article 4(2) applies.

Article 15

1. Not later than after five years of residence, and provided that the family member has not been granted a residence permit for reasons other than family reunification, the spouse or unmarried partner and a child who has reached majority shall be entitled, upon application, if required, to an autonomous residence permit, independent of that of the sponsor.

Member States may limit the granting of the residence permit referred to in the first subparagraph to the spouse or unmarried partner in cases of breakdown of the family relationship.

2. The Member States may issue an autonomous residence permit to adult children and to relatives in the direct ascending line to whom Article 4(2) applies.

3. In the event of widowhood, divorce, separation, or death of first-degree relatives in the direct ascending or descending line, an autonomous residence permit may be issued, upon application, if required, to persons who have entered by virtue of family reunification. Member States shall lay down provisions ensuring the granting of an autonomous residence permit in the event of particularly difficult circumstances.

4. The conditions relating to the granting and duration of the autonomous residence permit are established by national law.

Chapter VII Penalties and redress

Article 16

1. Member States may reject an application for entry and residence for the purpose of family reunification, or, if appropriate, withdraw or refuse to renew a family member's residence permit, in the following circumstances:

(a) where the conditions laid down by this Directive are not or are no longer satisfied. When renewing the residence permit, where the sponsor has not sufficient resources without recourse to the social assistance system of the Member State, as referred to in Article 7(1)(c), the Member State shall take into account the contributions of the family members to the household income;

(b) where the sponsor and his/her family member(s) do not or no longer live in a real marital or family relationship;

(c) where it is found that the sponsor or the unmarried partner is married or is in a stable long-term relationship with another person.

2. Member States may also reject an application for entry and residence for the purpose of family reunification, or withdraw or refuse to renew the family member's residence permits, where it is shown that:

(a) false or misleading information, false or falsified documents were used, fraud was otherwise committed or other unlawful means were used;

(b) the marriage, partnership or adoption was contracted for the sole purpose of enabling the person concerned to enter or reside in a Member State.

When making an assessment with respect to this point, Member States may have regard in particular to the fact that the marriage, partnership or adoption was contracted after the sponsor had been issued his/her residence permit.

3. The Member States may withdraw or refuse to renew the residence permit of a family member where the sponsor's residence comes to an end and the family member does not yet enjoy an autonomous right of residence under Article 15.

4. Member States may conduct specific checks and inspections where there is reason to suspect that there is fraud or a marriage, partnership or adoption of convenience as defined by paragraph 2. Specific checks may also be undertaken on the occasion of the renewal of family members' residence permit.

Article 17

Member States shall take due account of the nature and solidity of the person's family relationships and the duration of his residence in the Member State and of the existence of family, cultural and social ties with his/her country of origin where they reject an application, withdraw or refuse to renew a residence permit or decide to order the removal of the sponsor or members of his family.

Article 18

The Member States shall ensure that the sponsor and/or the members of his/her family have the right to mount a legal challenge where an application for family reunification is rejected or a residence permit is either not renewed or is withdrawn or removal is ordered.

The procedure and the competence according to which the right referred to in the first subparagraph is exercised shall be established by the Member States concerned.

Chapter VIII Final provisions

Article 19

Periodically, and for the first time not later than 3 October 2007, the Commission shall report to the European Parliament and the Council on the application of this Directive in the Member States and shall propose such amendments as may appear necessary. These proposals for amendments shall be made by way of priority in relation to Articles 3, 4, 7, 8 and 13.

Article 20

Member States shall bring into force the laws, regulations and administrative provisions necessary to comply with this Directive by not later than 3 October 2005. They shall forthwith inform the Commission thereof.

When Member States adopt these measures, they shall contain a reference to this Directive or be accompanied by such a reference on the occasion of their official publication. The methods of making such reference shall be laid down by the Member States.

Article 21

This Directive shall enter into force on the day of its publication in the *Official Journal of the European Union*.

Article 22

This Directive is addressed to the Member States in accordance with the Treaty establishing the European Community.

Done at Brussels, 22 September 2003.

Council Directive 2003/109/EC of 25 November 2003 concerning the status of third-country nationals who are long-term residents*

[OJ 2004 L16/44]

Chapter I General provisions

Article 1 Subject matter

This Directive determines:

(a) the terms for conferring and withdrawing long-term resident status granted by a Member State in relation to third-country nationals legally residing in its territory, and the rights pertaining thereto; and

(b) the terms of residence in Member States other than the one which conferred long-term status on them for third-country nationals enjoying that status.

Article 2 Definitions

For the purposes of this Directive:

(a) 'third-country national' means any person who is not a citizen of the Union within the meaning of Article 17(1) of the Treaty;

(b) 'long-term resident' means any third-country national who has long-term resident status as provided for under Articles 4 to 7;

(c) 'first Member State' means the Member State which for the first time granted long-term resident status to a third-country national;

(d) 'second Member State' means any Member State other than the one which for the first time granted long-term resident status to a third-country national and in which that long-term resident exercises the right of residence;

(e) 'family members' means the third-country nationals who reside in the Member State concerned in accordance with Council Directive 2003/86/EC of 22 September 2003 on the right to family reunification;[1]

(f) 'international protection' means international protection as defined in Article 2(a) of Council Directive 2004/83/EC of 29 April 2004 on minimum standards for the qualification and status of third-country nationals or stateless persons as refugees or as persons who otherwise need international protection and the content of the protection granted;[2]

(g) 'long-term resident's EC residence permit' means a residence permit issued by the Member State concerned upon the acquisition of long-term resident status.

Article 3 Scope

1. This Directive applies to third-country nationals residing legally in the territory of a Member State.

2. This Directive does not apply to third-country nationals who:

   (a) reside in order to pursue studies or vocational training;

   (b) are authorised to reside in a Member State on the basis of temporary protection or have applied for authorisation to reside on that basis and are awaiting a decision on their status;

   (c) are authorised to reside in a Member State on the basis of a form of protection other than international protection or have applied for authorisation to reside on that basis and are awaiting a decision on their status;

* **Editor's Note:** As amended up to Directive 2011/51 (OJ 2011 L132/1).

[1] OJ L 251, 3.10.2003, p. 12.

[2] OJ L 304, 30.9.2004, p. 12.

(d) have applied for international protection and whose application has not yet given rise to a final decision;
(e) reside solely on temporary grounds such as au pair or seasonal worker, or as workers posted by a service provider for the purposes of cross-border provision of services, or as cross-border providers of services or in cases where their residence permit has been formally limited;
(f) enjoy a legal status governed by the Vienna Convention on Diplomatic Relations of 1961, the Vienna Convention on Consular Relations of 1963, the Convention of 1969 on Special Missions or the Vienna Convention on the Representation of States in their Relations with International Organisations of a Universal Character of 1975.

3. This Directive shall apply without prejudice to more favourable provisions of:
(a) bilateral and multilateral agreements between the Community or the Community and its Member States, on the one hand, and third countries, on the other;
(b) bilateral agreements already concluded between a Member State and a third country before the date of entry into force of this Directive;
(c) the European Convention on Establishment of 13 December 1955, the European Social Charter of 18 October 1961, the amended European Social Charter of 3 May 1987 and the European Convention on the Legal Status of Migrant Workers of 24 November 1977, paragraph 11 of the Schedule to the Convention Relating to the Status of Refugees of 28 July 1951, as amended by the Protocol signed in New York on 31 January 1967, and the European Agreement on Transfer of Responsibility for Refugees of 16 October 1980.

Chapter II Long-term resident status in a Member State

Article 4 Duration of residence

1. Member States shall grant long-term resident status to third-country nationals who have resided legally and continuously within its territory for five years immediately prior to the submission of the relevant application.

1a. Member States shall not grant long-term resident status on the basis of international protection in the event of the revocation of, ending of or refusal to renew international protection as laid down in Articles 14(3) and 19(3) of Directive 2004/83/EC.

2. Periods of residence for the reasons referred to in Article 3(2)(e) and (f) shall not be taken into account for the purposes of calculating the period referred to in paragraph 1.

Regarding the cases covered in Article 3(2)(a), where the third-country national concerned has acquired a title of residence which will enable him/her to be granted long-term resident status, only half of the periods of residence for study purposes or vocational training may be taken into account in the calculation of the period referred to in paragraph 1.

Regarding persons to whom international protection has been granted, at least half of the period between the date of the lodging of the application for international protection on the basis of which that international protection was granted and the date of the grant of the residence permit referred to in Article 24 of Directive 2004/83/EC, or the whole of that period if it exceeds 18 months, shall be taken into account in the calculation of the period referred to in paragraph 1.

3. Periods of absence from the territory of the Member State concerned shall not interrupt the period referred to in paragraph 1 and shall be taken into account for its calculation where they are shorter than six consecutive months and do not exceed in total 10 months within the period referred to in paragraph 1.

In cases of specific or exceptional reasons of a temporary nature and in accordance with their national law, Member States may accept that a longer period of absence than that which is referred to in the first subparagraph shall not interrupt the period referred to in paragraph 1. In such cases Member States shall not take into account the relevant period of absence in the calculation of the period referred to in paragraph 1.

By way of derogation from the second subparagraph, Member States may take into account in the calculation of the total period referred to in paragraph 1 periods of absence relating to secondment for employment purposes, including the provision of cross-border services.

Article 5 Conditions for acquiring long-term resident status

1. Member States shall require third-country nationals to provide evidence that they have, for themselves and for dependent family members:

(a) stable and regular resources which are sufficient to maintain himself/herself and the members of his/her family, without recourse to the social assistance system of the Member State concerned. Member States shall evaluate these resources by reference to their nature and regularity and may take into account the level of minimum wages and pensions prior to the application for long-term resident status;

(b) sickness insurance in respect of all risks normally covered for his/her own nationals in the Member State concerned.

2. Member States may require third-country nationals to comply with integration conditions, in accordance with national law.

Article 6 Public policy and public security

1. Member States may refuse to grant long-term resident status on grounds of public policy or public security.

When taking the relevant decision, the Member State shall consider the severity or type of offence against public policy or public security, or the danger that emanates from the person concerned, while also having proper regard to the duration of residence and to the existence of links with the country of residence.

2. The refusal referred to in paragraph 1 shall not be founded on economic considerations.

Article 7 Acquisition of long-term resident status

1. To acquire long-term resident status, the third-country national concerned shall lodge an application with the competent authorities of the Member State in which he/she resides. The application shall be accompanied by documentary evidence to be determined by national law that he/she meets the conditions set out in Articles 4 and 5 as well as, if required, by a valid travel document or its certified copy.

The evidence referred to in the first subparagraph may also include documentation with regard to appropriate accommodation.

2. The competent national authorities shall give the applicant written notification of the decision as soon as possible and in any event no later than six months from the date on which the application was lodged. Any such decision shall be notified to the third-country national concerned in accordance with the notification procedures under the relevant national legislation.

In exceptional circumstances linked to the complexity of the examination of the application, the time limit referred to in the first subparagraph may be extended.

In addition, the person concerned shall be informed about his/her rights and obligations under this Directive.

Any consequences of no decision being taken by the end of the period provided for in this provision shall be determined by national legislation of the relevant Member State.

3. If the conditions provided for by Articles 4 and 5 are met, and the person does not represent a threat within the meaning of Article 6, the Member State concerned shall grant the third-country national concerned long-term resident status.

Article 8 Long-term resident's EC residence permit

1. The status as long-term resident shall be permanent, subject to Article 9.

2. Member States shall issue a long-term resident's EC residence permit to long-term residents. The permit shall be valid at least for five years; it shall, upon application if required, be automatically renewable on expiry.

3. A long-term resident's EC residence permit may be issued in the form of a sticker or of a separate document. It shall be issued in accordance with the rules and standard model as set out in Council Regulation (EC) No 1030/2002 of 13 June 2002 laying down a uniform format for residence permits for third-country nationals.[3] Under the heading 'type of permit', the Member States shall enter 'long-term resident—EC'.

4. Where a Member State issues a long-term resident's EU residence permit to a third-country national to whom it granted international protection, it shall enter the following remark in that long-term resident's EU residence permit, under the heading 'Remarks': 'International protection granted by [name of the Member State] on [date]'.

5. Where a long-term resident's EU residence permit is issued by a second Member State to a third-country national who already has a long-term resident's EU residence permit issued by another Member State which contains the remark referred to in paragraph 4, the second Member State shall enter the same remark in the long-term resident's EU residence permit.

Before the second Member State enters the remark referred to in paragraph 4, it shall request the Member State mentioned in that remark to provide information as to whether the long-term resident is still a beneficiary of international protection. The Member State mentioned in the remark shall reply no later than 1 month after receiving the request for information. Where international protection has been withdrawn by a final decision, the second Member State shall not enter that remark.

6. Where, in accordance with the relevant international instruments or national law, responsibility for the international protection of the long-term resident was transferred to the second Member State after the long-term resident's EU residence permit referred to in paragraph 5 was issued, the second Member State shall amend accordingly the remark referred to in paragraph 4 no later than 3 months after the transfer.

Article 9 Withdrawal or loss of status

1. Long-term residents shall no longer be entitled to maintain long-term resident status in the following cases:

(a) detection of fraudulent acquisition of long-term resident status;

(b) adoption of an expulsion measure under the conditions provided for in Article 12;

(c) in the event of absence from the territory of the Community for a period of 12 consecutive months.

2. By way of derogation from paragraph 1(c), Member States may provide that absences exceeding 12 consecutive months or for specific or exceptional reasons shall not entail withdrawal or loss of status.

3. Member States may provide that the long-term resident shall no longer be entitled to maintain his/her long-term resident status in cases where he/she constitutes a threat to public policy, in consideration of the seriousness of the offences he/she committed, but such threat is not a reason for expulsion within the meaning of Article 12.

3a. Member States may withdraw the long-term resident status in the event of the revocation of, ending of or refusal to renew international protection as laid down in Articles 14(3) and 19(3) of Directive 2004/83/EC if the long-term resident status was obtained on the basis of international protection.

4. The long-term resident who has resided in another Member State in accordance with Chapter III shall no longer be entitled to maintain his/her long-term resident status acquired in the first Member State when such a status is granted in another Member State pursuant to Article 23.

In any case after six years of absence from the territory of the Member State that granted long-term resident status the person concerned shall no longer be entitled to maintain his/her long term resident status in the said Member State.

By way of derogation from the second subparagraph the Member State concerned may provide that for specific reasons the long-term resident shall maintain his/her status in the said Member State in case of absences for a period exceeding six years.

[3] OJ L 157, 15.6.2002, p. 1.

5. With regard to the cases referred to in paragraph 1(c) and in paragraph 4, Member States who have granted the status shall provide for a facilitated procedure for the re-acquisition of long-term resident status.

The said procedure shall apply in particular to the cases of persons that have resided in a second Member State on grounds of pursuit of studies.

The conditions and the procedure for the re-acquisition of long-term resident status shall be determined by national law.

6. The expiry of a long-term resident's EC residence permit shall in no case entail withdrawal or loss of long-term resident status.

7. Where the withdrawal or loss of long-term resident status does not lead to removal, the Member State shall authorise the person concerned to remain in its territory if he/she fulfils the conditions provided for in its national legislation and/or if he/she does not constitute a threat to public policy or public security.

Article 10 Procedural guarantees

1. Reasons shall be given for any decision rejecting an application for long-term resident status or withdrawing that status. Any such decision shall be notified to the third-country national concerned in accordance with the notification procedures under the relevant national legislation. The notification shall specify the redress procedures available and the time within which he/she may act.

2. Where an application for long-term resident status is rejected or that status is withdrawn or lost or the residence permit is not renewed, the person concerned shall have the right to mount a legal challenge in the Member State concerned.

Article 11 Equal treatment

1. Long-term residents shall enjoy equal treatment with nationals as regards:
   - (a) access to employment and self-employed activity, provided such activities do not entail even occasional involvement in the exercise of public authority, and conditions of employment and working conditions, including conditions regarding dismissal and remuneration;
   - (b) education and vocational training, including study grants in accordance with national law;
   - (c) recognition of professional diplomas, certificates and other qualifications, in accordance with the relevant national procedures;
   - (d) social security, social assistance and social protection as defined by national law;
   - (e) tax benefits;
   - (f) access to goods and services and the supply of goods and services made available to the public and to procedures for obtaining housing;
   - (g) freedom of association and affiliation and membership of an organisation representing workers or employers or of any organisation whose members are engaged in a specific occupation, including the benefits conferred by such organisations, without prejudice to the national provisions on public policy and public security;
   - (h) free access to the entire territory of the Member State concerned, within the limits provided for by the national legislation for reasons of security.

2. With respect to the provisions of paragraph 1, points (b), (d), (e), (f) and (g), the Member State concerned may restrict equal treatment to cases where the registered or usual place of residence of the long-term resident, or that of family members for whom he/she claims benefits, lies within the territory of the Member State concerned.

3. Member States may restrict equal treatment with nationals in the following cases:
   - (a) Member States may retain restrictions to access to employment or self-employed activities in cases where, in accordance with existing national or Community legislation, these activities are reserved to nationals, EU or EEA citizens;
   - (b) Member States may require proof of appropriate language proficiency for access to education and training. Access to university may be subject to the fulfilment of specific educational prerequisites.

4. Member States may limit equal treatment in respect of social assistance and social protection to core benefits.

4a. As far as the Member State which granted international protection is concerned, paragraphs 3 and 4 shall be without prejudice to Directive 2004/83/EC.

5. Member States may decide to grant access to additional benefits in the areas referred to in paragraph 1.

Member States may also decide to grant equal treatment with regard to areas not covered in paragraph 1.

Article 12 Protection against expulsion

1. Member States may take a decision to expel a long-term resident solely where he/she constitutes an actual and sufficiently serious threat to public policy or public security.

2. The decision referred to in paragraph 1 shall not be founded on economic considerations.

3. Before taking a decision to expel a long-term resident, Member States shall have regard to the following factors:

(a) the duration of residence in their territory;
(b) the age of the person concerned;
(c) the consequences for the person concerned and family members;
(d) links with the country of residence or the absence of links with the country of origin.

3a. Where a Member State decides to expel a long-term resident whose long-term resident's EU residence permit contains the remark referred to in Article 8(4), it shall request the Member State mentioned in that remark to confirm whether the person concerned is still a beneficiary of international protection in that Member State. The Member State mentioned in the remark shall reply no later than 1 month after receiving the request for information.

3b. If the long-term resident is still a beneficiary of international protection in the Member State mentioned in the remark, that person shall be expelled to that Member State, which shall, without prejudice to the applicable Union or national law and to the principle of family unity, immediately readmit, without formalities, that beneficiary and his/her family members.

3c. By way of derogation from paragraph 3b, the Member State which adopted the expulsion decision shall retain the right to remove, in accordance with its international obligations, the long-term resident to a country other than the Member State which granted international protection where that person fulfils the conditions specified in Article 21(2) of Directive 2004/83/EC.

4. Where an expulsion decision has been adopted, a judicial redress procedure shall be available to the long-term resident in the Member State concerned.

5. Legal aid shall be given to long-term residents lacking adequate resources, on the same terms as apply to nationals of the State where they reside.

6. This Article shall be without prejudice to Article 21(1) of Directive 2004/83/EC.

Article 13 More favourable national provisions

Member States may issue residence permits of permanent or unlimited validity on terms that are more favourable than those laid down by this Directive. Such residence permits shall not confer the right of residence in the other Member States as provided by Chapter III of this Directive.

Chapter III Residence in the other Member States

Article 14 Principle

1. A long-term resident shall acquire the right to reside in the territory of Member States other than the one which granted him/her the long-term residence status, for a period exceeding three months, provided that the conditions set out in this chapter are met.

2. A long-term resident may reside in a second Member State on the following grounds:

(a) exercise of an economic activity in an employed or self-employed capacity;

(b) pursuit of studies or vocational training;
(c) other purposes.

3. In cases of an economic activity in an employed or self-employed capacity referred to in paragraph 2(a), Member States may examine the situation of their labour market and apply their national procedures regarding the requirements for, respectively, filling a vacancy, or for exercising such activities.

For reasons of labour market policy, Member States may give preference to Union citizens, to third-country nationals, when provided for by Community legislation, as well as to third-country nationals who reside legally and receive unemployment benefits in the Member State concerned.

4. By way of derogation from the provisions of paragraph 1, Member States may limit the total number of persons entitled to be granted right of residence, provided that such limitations are already set out for the admission of third-country nationals in the existing legislation at the time of the adoption of this Directive.

5. This chapter does not concern the residence of long-term residents in the territory of the Member States:

(a) as employed workers posted by a service provider for the purposes of cross-border provision of services;
(b) as providers of cross-border services.

Member States may decide, in accordance with national law, the conditions under which long-term residents who wish to move to a second Member State with a view to exercising an economic activity as seasonal workers may reside in that Member State. Cross-border workers may also be subject to specific provisions of national law.

6. This Chapter is without prejudice to the relevant Community legislation on social security with regard to third-country nationals.

Article 15 Conditions for residence in a second Member State

1. As soon as possible and no later than three months after entering the territory of the second Member State, the long-term resident shall apply to the competent authorities of that Member State for a residence permit.

Member States may accept that the long-term resident submits the application for a residence permit to the competent authorities of the second Member State while still residing in the territory of the first Member State.

2. Member States may require the persons concerned to provide evidence that they have:

(a) stable and regular resources which are sufficient to maintain themselves and the members of their families, without recourse to the social assistance of the Member State concerned. For each of the categories referred to in Article 14(2), Member States shall evaluate these resources by reference to their nature and regularity and may take into account the level of minimum wages and pensions;
(b) sickness insurance covering all risks in the second Member State normally covered for its own nationals in the Member State concerned.

3. Member States may require third-country nationals to comply with integration measures, in accordance with national law.

This condition shall not apply where the third-country nationals concerned have been required to comply with integration conditions in order to be granted long-term resident status, in accordance with the provisions of Article 5(2).

Without prejudice to the second subparagraph, the persons concerned may be required to attend language courses.

4. The application shall be accompanied by documentary evidence, to be determined by national law, that the persons concerned meets the relevant conditions, as well as by their long-term resident permit and a valid travel document or their certified copies.

The evidence referred to in the first subparagraph may also include documentation with regard to appropriate accommodation.

In particular:

(a) in case of exercise of an economic activity the second Member State may require the persons concerned to provide evidence:

(i) if they are in an employed capacity, that they have an employment contract, a statement by the employer that they are hired or a proposal for an employment contract, under the conditions provided for by national legislation. Member States shall determine which of the said forms of evidence is required;

(ii) if they are in a self-employed capacity, that they have the appropriate funds which are needed, in accordance with national law, to exercise an economic activity in such capacity, presenting the necessary documents and permits;

(b) in case of study or vocational training the second Member State may require the persons concerned to provide evidence of enrolment in an accredited establishment in order to pursue studies or vocational training.

Article 16 Family members

1. When the long-term resident exercises his/her right of residence in a second Member State and when the family was already constituted in the first Member State, the members of his/her family, who fulfil the conditions referred to in Article 4(1) of Directive 2003/86/EC shall be authorised to accompany or to join the long-term resident.

2. When the long-term resident exercises his/her right of residence in a second Member State and when the family was already constituted in the first Member State, the members of his/her family, other than those referred to in Article 4(1) of Directive 2003/86/EC may be authorised to accompany or to join the long-term resident.

3. With respect to the submission of the application for a residence permit, the provisions of Article 15(1) apply.

4. The second Member State may require the family members concerned to present with their application for a residence permit:

(a) their long-term resident's EC residence permit or residence permit and a valid travel document or their certified copies;

(b) evidence that they have resided as members of the family of the long-term resident in the first Member State;

(c) evidence that they have stable and regular resources which are sufficient to maintain themselves without recourse to the social assistance of the Member State concerned or that the long-term resident has such resources and insurance for them, as well as sickness insurance covering all risks in the second Member State. Member States shall evaluate these resources by reference to their nature and regularity and may take into account the level of minimum wages and pensions.

5. Where the family was not already constituted in the first Member State, Directive 2003/86/EC shall apply.

Article 17 Public policy and public security

1. Member States may refuse applications for residence from long-term residents or their family members where the person concerned constitutes a threat to public policy or public security.

When taking the relevant decision, the Member State shall consider the severity or type of offence against public policy or public security committed by the long-term resident or his/her family member(s), or the danger that emanates from the person concerned.

2. The decision referred to in paragraph 1 shall not be based on economic considerations.

Article 18 Public health

1. Member States may refuse applications for residence from long-term residents or their family members where the person concerned constitutes a threat to public health.

2. The only diseases that may justify a refusal to allow entry or the right of residence in the territory of the second Member State shall be the diseases as defined by the relevant applicable instruments of the World Health Organisation's and such other infectious or contagious parasite-based

diseases as are the subject of protective provisions in relation to nationals in the host country. Member States shall not introduce new more restrictive provisions or practices.

3. Diseases contracted after the first residence permit was issued in the second Member State shall not justify a refusal to renew the permit or expulsion from the territory.

4. A Member State may require a medical examination, for persons to whom this Directive applies, in order to certify that they do not suffer from any of the diseases referred to in paragraph 2. Such medical examinations, which may be free of charge, shall not be performed on a systematic basis.

Article 19 Examination of applications and issue of a residence permit

1. The competent national authorities shall process applications within four months from the date that these have been lodged.

If an application is not accompanied by the documentary evidence listed in Articles 15 and 16, or in exceptional circumstances linked with the complexity of the examination of the application, the time limit referred to in the first subparagraph may be extended for a period not exceeding three months. In such cases the competent national authorities shall inform the applicant thereof.

2. If the conditions provided for in Articles 14, 15 and 16 are met, then, subject to the provisions relating to public policy, public security and public health in Articles 17 and 18, the second Member State shall issue the long-term resident with a renewable residence permit. This residence permit shall, upon application, if required, be renewable on expiry. The second Member State shall inform the first Member State of its decision.

3. The second Member State shall issue members of the long-term resident's family with renewable residence permits valid for the same period as the permit issued to the long-term resident.

Article 19a Amendments of long-term resident's EU residence permits

1. Where a long-term resident's EU residence permit contains the remark referred to in Article 8(4), and where, in accordance with the relevant international instruments or national law, responsibility for the international protection of the long-term resident is transferred to a second Member State before that Member State issues the long-term resident's EU residence permit referred to in Article 8(5), the second Member State shall ask the Member State which has issued the long-term resident's EU residence permit to amend that remark accordingly.

2. Where a long-term resident is granted international protection in the second Member State before that Member State issued the long-term resident's EU residence permit referred to in Article 8(5), that Member State shall ask the Member State which has issued the long-term resident's EU residence permit to amend it in order to enter the remark referred to in Article 8(4).

3. Following the request referred to in paragraphs 1 and 2, the Member State which has issued the long-term resident's EU residence permit shall issue the amended long-term resident's EU residence permit no later than 3 months after receiving the request from the second Member State.

Article 20 Procedural guarantees

1. Reasons shall be given for any decision rejecting an application for a residence permit. It shall be notified to the third-country national concerned in accordance with the notification procedures under the relevant national legislation. The notification shall specify the possible redress procedures available and the time limit for taking action.

Any consequences of no decision being taken by the end of the period referred to in Article 19(1) shall be determined by the national legislation of the relevant Member State.

2. Where an application for a residence permit is rejected, or the permit is not renewed or is withdrawn, the person concerned shall have the right to mount a legal challenge in the Member State concerned.

Article 21 Treatment granted in the second Member State

1. As soon as they have received the residence permit provided for by Article 19 in the second Member State, long-term residents shall in that Member State enjoy equal treatment in the areas and under the conditions referred to in Article 11.

2. Long-term residents shall have access to the labour market in accordance with the provisions of paragraph 1.

Member States may provide that the persons referred to in Article 14(2)(a) shall have restricted access to employed activities different than those for which they have been granted their residence permit under the conditions set by national legislation for a period not exceeding 12 months.

Member States may decide in accordance with national law the conditions under which the persons referred to in Article 14(2)(b) or (c) may have access to an employed or self-employed activity.

3. As soon as they have received the residence permit provided for by Article 19 in the second Member State, members of the family of the long-term resident shall in that Member State enjoy the rights listed in Article 14 of Directive 2003/86/EC.

Article 22 Withdrawal of residence permit and obligation to readmit

1. Until the third-country national has obtained long-term resident status, the second Member State may decide to refuse to renew or to withdraw the resident permit and to oblige the person concerned and his/her family members, in accordance with the procedures provided for by national law, including removal procedures, to leave its territory in the following cases:

(a) on grounds of public policy or public security as defined in Article 17;

(b) where the conditions provided for in Articles 14, 15 and 16 are no longer met;

(c) where the third-country national is not lawfully residing in the Member State concerned.

2. If the second Member State adopts one of the measures referred to in paragraph 1, the first Member State shall immediately readmit without formalities the long-term resident and his/her family members. The second Member State shall notify the first Member State of its decision.

3. Until the third-country national has obtained long-term resident status and without prejudice to the obligation to readmit referred to in paragraph 2, the second Member State may adopt a decision to remove the third-country national from the territory of the Union, in accordance with and under the guarantees of Article 12, on serious grounds of public policy or public security.

In such cases, when adopting the said decision the second Member State shall consult the first Member State.

When the second Member State adopts a decision to remove the third-country national concerned, it shall take all the appropriate measures to effectively implement it. In such cases the second Member State shall provide to the first Member State appropriate information with respect to the implementation of the removal decision.

3a. Unless, in the meantime, the international protection has been withdrawn or the person falls within one of the categories specified in Article 21(2) of Directive 2004/83/EC, paragraph 3 of this Article shall not apply to third-country nationals whose long-term resident's EU residence permit issued by the first Member State contains the remark referred to in Article 8(4) of this Directive.

This paragraph shall be without prejudice to Article 21(1) of Directive 2004/83/EC.

4. Removal decisions may not be accompanied by a permanent ban on residence in the cases referred to in paragraph 1(b) and (c).

5. The obligation to readmit referred to in paragraph 2 shall be without prejudice to the possibility of the long-term resident and his/her family members moving to a third Member State.

Article 23 Acquisition of long-term resident status in the second Member State

1. Upon application, the second Member State shall grant long-term residents the status provided for by Article 7, subject to the provisions of Articles 3, 4, 5 and 6. The second Member State shall notify its decision to the first Member State.

2. The procedure laid down in Article 7 shall apply to the presentation and examination of applications for long-term resident status in the second Member State. Article 8 shall apply for the issuance of the residence permit. Where the application is rejected, the procedural guarantees provided for by Article 10 shall apply.

Chapter IV Final provisions

Article 24 Report and rendez-vous clause

Periodically, and for the first time no later than 23 January 2011, the Commission shall report to the European Parliament and to the Council on the application of this Directive in the Member States and shall propose such amendments as may be necessary. These proposals for amendments shall be made by way of priority in relation to Articles 4, 5, 9, 11 and to Chapter III.

Article 25 Contact points

Member States shall appoint contact points who will be responsible for receiving and transmitting the information and documentation referred to in Articles 8, 12, 19, 19a, 22 and 23.

Member States shall provide appropriate cooperation in the exchange of the information and documentation referred to in the first paragraph.

Article 26 Transposition

Member States shall bring into force the laws, regulations and administrative provisions necessary to comply with this Directive by 23 January 2006 at the latest. They shall forthwith inform the Commission thereof.

When Member States adopt these measures, they shall contain a reference to this Directive or shall be accompanied by such reference on the occasion of their official publication. The methods of making such reference shall be laid down by Member States.

Article 27 Entry into force

This Directive shall enter into force on the day of its publication in the *Official Journal of the European Union*.

Article 28 Addressees

This Directive is addressed to the Member States in accordance with the Treaty establishing the European Community.

Done at Brussels, 25 November 2003.

Directive 2004/38/EC of the European Parliament and of the Council of 29 April 2004 on the right of citizens of the Union and their family members to move and reside freely within the territory of the Member States*

[OJ 2004 L158/77]

(Entry into force 30/4/2006 at which time Regulation (EEC) No 1612/68 is amended and Directives 64/221/EEC, 68/360/EEC, 72/194/EEC, 73/148/EEC, 75/34/EEC, 75/35/EEC, 90/364/EEC, 90/365/EEC and 93/96/EEC are repealed)

Chapter I General provisions

Article 1 Subject

This Directive lays down:

(a) the conditions governing the exercise of the right of free movement and residence within the territory of the Member States by Union citizens and their family members;

(b) the right of permanent residence in the territory of the Member States for Union citizens and their family members;

* **Editor's Note:** As corrected to OJ 2007 L204/28 and amended by Regulation 492/2011 (OJ 2011 L141/1).

(c) the limits placed on the rights set out in (a) and (b) on grounds of public policy, public security or public health.

Article 2 Definitions

For the purposes of this Directive:

(1) 'Union citizen' means any person having the nationality of a Member State;

(2) 'Family member' means:

(a) the spouse;

(b) the partner with whom the Union citizen has contracted a registered partnership, on the basis of the legislation of a Member State, if the legislation of the host Member State treats registered partnerships as equivalent to marriage and in accordance with the conditions laid down in the relevant legislation of the host Member State;

(c) the direct descendants who are under the age of 21 or are dependants and those of the spouse or partner as defined in point (b);

(d) the dependent direct relatives in the ascending line and those of the spouse or partner as defined in point (b);

(3) 'Host Member State' means the Member State to which a Union citizen moves in order to exercise his/her right of free movement and residence.

Article 3 Beneficiaries

1. This Directive shall apply to all Union citizens who move to or reside in a Member State other than that of which they are a national, and to their family members as defined in point 2 of Article 2 who accompany or join them.

2. Without prejudice to any right to free movement and residence the persons concerned may have in their own right, the host Member State shall, in accordance with its national legislation, facilitate entry and residence for the following persons:

(a) any other family members, irrespective of their nationality, not falling under the definition in point 2 of Article 2 who, in the country from which they have come, are dependants or members of the household of the Union citizen having the primary right of residence, or where serious health grounds strictly require the personal care of the family member by the Union citizen;

(b) the partner with whom the Union citizen has a durable relationship, duly attested. The host Member State shall undertake an extensive examination of the personal circumstances and shall justify any denial of entry or residence to these people.

Chapter II Right of exit and entry

Article 4 Right of exit

1. Without prejudice to the provisions on travel documents applicable to national border controls, all Union citizens with a valid identity card or passport and their family members who are not nationals of a Member State and who hold a valid passport shall have the right to leave the territory of a Member State to travel to another Member State.

2. No exit visa or equivalent formality may be imposed on the persons to whom paragraph 1 applies.

3. Member States shall, acting in accordance with their laws, issue to their own nationals, and renew, an identity card or passport stating their nationality.

4. The passport shall be valid at least for all Member States and for countries through which the holder must pass when travelling between Member States. Where the law of a Member State does not provide for identity cards to be issued, the period of validity of any passport on being issued or renewed shall be not less than five years.

Article 5 Right of entry

1. Without prejudice to the provisions on travel documents applicable to national border controls, Member States shall grant Union citizens leave to enter their territory with a valid identity

card or passport and shall grant family members who are not nationals of a Member State leave to enter their territory with a valid passport. No entry visa or equivalent formality may be imposed on Union citizens.

2. Family members who are not nationals of a Member State shall only be required to have an entry visa in accordance with Regulation (EC) No 539/2001 or, where appropriate, with national law. For the purposes of this Directive, possession of the valid residence card referred to in Article 10 shall exempt such family members from the visa requirement. Member States shall grant such persons every facility to obtain the necessary visas. Such visas shall be issued free of charge as soon as possible and on the basis of an accelerated procedure.

3. The host Member State shall not place an entry or exit stamp in the passport of family members who are not nationals of a Member State provided that they present the residence card provided for in Article 10.

4. Where a Union citizen, or a family member who is not a national of a Member State, does not have the necessary travel documents or, if required, the necessary visas, the Member State concerned shall, before turning them back, give such persons every reasonable opportunity to obtain the necessary documents or have them brought to them within a reasonable period of time or to corroborate or prove by other means that they are covered by the right of free movement and residence.

5. The Member State may require the person concerned to report his/her presence within its territory within a reasonable and non-discriminatory period of time. Failure to comply with this requirement may make the person concerned liable to proportionate and non-discriminatory sanctions.

Chapter III Right of residence

Article 6 Right of residence for up to three months

1. Union citizens shall have the right of residence on the territory of another Member State for a period of up to three months without any conditions or any formalities other than the requirement to hold a valid identity card or passport.

2. The provisions of paragraph 1 shall also apply to family members in possession of a valid passport who are not nationals of a Member State, accompanying or joining the Union citizen.

Article 7 Right of residence for more than three months

1. All Union citizens shall have the right of residence on the territory of another Member State for a period of longer than three months if they:

(a) are workers or self-employed persons in the host Member State; or

(b) have sufficient resources for themselves and their family members not to become a burden on the social assistance system of the host Member State during their period of residence and have comprehensive sickness insurance cover in the host Member State; or

(c) – are enrolled at a private or public establishment, accredited or financed by the host Member State on the basis of its legislation or administrative practice, for the principal purpose of following a course of study, including vocational training; and

– have comprehensive sickness insurance cover in the host Member State and assure the relevant national authority, by means of a declaration or by such equivalent means as they may choose, that they have sufficient resources for themselves and their family members not to become a burden on the social assistance system of the host Member State during their period of residence; or

(d) are family members accompanying or joining a Union citizen who satisfies the conditions referred to in points (a), (b) or (c).

2. The right of residence provided for in paragraph 1 shall extend to family members who are not nationals of a Member State, accompanying or joining the Union citizen in the host Member State, provided that such Union citizen satisfies the conditions referred to in paragraph 1(a), (b) or (c).

3. For the purposes of paragraph 1(a), a Union citizen who is no longer a worker or self-employed person shall retain the status of worker or self-employed person in the following circumstances:

(a) he/she is temporarily unable to work as the result of an illness or accident;

(b) he/she is in duly recorded involuntary unemployment after having been employed for more than one year and has registered as a job-seeker with the relevant employment office;

(c) he/she is in duly recorded involuntary unemployment after completing a fixed-term employment contract of less than a year or after having become involuntarily unemployed during the first twelve months and has registered as a job-seeker with the relevant employment office. In this case, the status of worker shall be retained for no less than six months;

(d) he/she embarks on vocational training. Unless he/she is involuntarily unemployed, the retention of the status of worker shall require the training to be related to the previous employment.

4. By way of derogation from paragraphs 1(d) and 2 above, only the spouse, the registered partner provided for in Article 2(2)(b) and dependent children shall have the right of residence as family members of a Union citizen meeting the conditions under 1(c) above. Article 3(2) shall apply to his/her dependent direct relatives in the ascending lines and those of his/her spouse or registered partner.

Article 8 Administrative formalities for Union citizens

1. Without prejudice to Article 5(5), for periods of residence longer than three months, the host Member State may require Union citizens to register with the relevant authorities.

2. The deadline for registration may not be less than three months from the date of arrival. A registration certificate shall be issued immediately, stating the name and address of the person registering and the date of the registration. Failure to comply with the registration requirement may render the person concerned liable to proportionate and non-discriminatory sanctions.

3. For the registration certificate to be issued, Member States may only require that

- Union citizens to whom point (a) of Article 7(1) applies present a valid identity card or passport, a confirmation of engagement from the employer or a certificate of employment, or proof that they are self-employed persons;
- Union citizens to whom point (b) of Article 7(1) applies present a valid identity card or passport and provide proof that they satisfy the conditions laid down therein;
- Union citizens to whom point (c) of Article 7(1) applies present a valid identity card or passport, provide proof of enrolment at an accredited establishment and of comprehensive sickness insurance cover and the declaration or equivalent means referred to in point (c) of Article 7(1). Member States may not require this declaration to refer to any specific amount of resources.

4. Member States may not lay down a fixed amount which they regard as 'sufficient resources', but they must take into account the personal situation of the person concerned. In all cases this amount shall not be higher than the threshold below which nationals of the host Member State become eligible for social assistance, or, where this criterion is not applicable, higher than the minimum social security pension paid by the host Member State.

5. For the registration certificate to be issued to family members of Union citizens, who are themselves Union citizens, Member States may require the following documents to be presented:

(a) a valid identity card or passport;

(b) a document attesting to the existence of a family relationship or of a registered partnership;

(c) where appropriate, the registration certificate of the Union citizen whom they are accompanying or joining;

(d) in cases falling under points (c) and (d) of Article 2(2), documentary evidence that the conditions laid down therein are met;

(e) in cases falling under Article 3(2)(a), a document issued by the relevant authority in the country of origin or country from which they are arriving certifying that they are dependants or members of the household of the Union citizen, or proof of the existence of serious health grounds which strictly require the personal care of the family member by the Union citizen;

(f) in cases falling under Article 3(2)(b), proof of the existence of a durable relationship with the Union citizen.

Article 9 Administrative formalities for family members who are not nationals of a Member State

1. Member States shall issue a residence card to family members of a Union citizen who are not nationals of a Member State, where the planned period of residence is for more than three months.

2. The deadline for submitting the residence card application may not be less than three months from the date of arrival.

3. Failure to comply with the requirement to apply for a residence card may make the person concerned liable to proportionate and non-discriminatory sanctions.

Article 10 Issue of residence cards

1. The right of residence of family members of a Union citizen who are not nationals of a Member State shall be evidenced by the issuing of a document called 'Residence card of a family member of a Union citizen' no later than six months from the date on which they submit the application. A certificate of application for the residence card shall be issued immediately.

2. For the residence card to be issued, Member States shall require presentation of the following documents:

(a) a valid passport;

(b) a document attesting to the existence of a family relationship or of a registered partnership;

(c) the registration certificate or, in the absence of a registration system, any other proof of residence in the host Member State of the Union citizen whom they are accompanying or joining;

(d) in cases falling under points (c) and (d) of Article 2(2), documentary evidence that the conditions laid down therein are met;

(e) in cases falling under Article 3(2)(a), a document issued by the relevant authority in the country of origin or country from which they are arriving certifying that they are dependants or members of the household of the Union citizen, or proof of the existence of serious health grounds which strictly require the personal care of the family member by the Union citizen;

(f) in cases falling under Article 3(2)(b), proof of the existence of a durable relationship with the Union citizen.

Article 11 Validity of the residence card

1. The residence card provided for by Article 10(1) shall be valid for five years from the date of issue or for the envisaged period of residence of the Union citizen, if this period is less than five years.

2. The validity of the residence card shall not be affected by temporary absences not exceeding six months a year, or by absences of a longer duration for compulsory military service or by one absence of a maximum of twelve consecutive months for important reasons such as pregnancy and childbirth, serious illness, study or vocational training, or a posting in another Member State or a third country.

Article 12 Retention of the right of residence by family members in the event of death or departure of the Union citizen

1. Without prejudice to the second subparagraph, the Union citizen's death or departure from the host Member State shall not affect the right of residence of his/her family members who are nationals of a Member State.

Before acquiring the right of permanent residence, the persons concerned must meet the conditions laid down in points (a), (b), (c) or (d) of Article 7(1).

2. Without prejudice to the second subparagraph, the Union citizen's death shall not entail loss of the right of residence of his/her family members who are not nationals of a Member State and who have been residing in the host Member State as family members for at least one year before the Union citizen's death.

Before acquiring the right of permanent residence, the right of residence of the persons concerned shall remain subject to the requirement that they are able to show that they are workers or self-employed persons or that they have sufficient resources for themselves and their family members not to become a burden on the social assistance system of the host Member State during their period of residence and have comprehensive sickness insurance cover in the host Member State, or that they are members of the family, already constituted in the host Member State, of a person satisfying these requirements. 'Sufficient resources' shall be as defined in Article 8(4).

Such family members shall retain their right of residence exclusively on a personal basis.

3. The Union citizen's departure from the host Member State or his/her death shall not entail loss of the right of residence of his/her children or of the parent who has actual custody of the children, irrespective of nationality, if the children reside in the host Member State and are enrolled at an educational establishment, for the purpose of studying there, until the completion of their studies.

Article 13 Retention of the right of residence by family members in the event of divorce, annulment of marriage or termination of registered partnership

1. Without prejudice to the second subparagraph, divorce, annulment of the Union citizen's marriage or termination of his/her registered partnership, as referred to in point 2(b) of Article 2 shall not affect the right of residence of his/her family members who are nationals of a Member State.

Before acquiring the right of permanent residence, the persons concerned must meet the conditions laid down in points (a), (b), (c) or (d) of Article 7(1).

2. Without prejudice to the second subparagraph, divorce, annulment of marriage or termination of the registered partnership referred to in point 2(b) of Article 2 shall not entail loss of the right of residence of a Union citizen's family members who are not nationals of a Member State where:

(a) prior to initiation of the divorce or annulment proceedings or termination of the registered partnership referred to in point 2(b) of Article 2, the marriage or registered partnership has lasted at least three years, including one year in the host Member State; or
(b) by agreement between the spouses or the partners referred to in point 2(b) of Article 2 or by court order, the spouse or partner who is not a national of a Member State has custody of the Union citizen's children; or
(c) this is warranted by particularly difficult circumstances, such as having been a victim of domestic violence while the marriage or registered partnership was subsisting; or
(d) by agreement between the spouses or partners referred to in point 2(b) of Article 2 or by court order, the spouse or partner who is not a national of a Member State has the right of access to a minor child, provided that the court has ruled that such access must be in the host Member State, and for as long as is required.

Before acquiring the right of permanent residence, the right of residence of the persons concerned shall remain subject to the requirement that they are able to show that they are workers or self-employed persons or that they have sufficient resources for themselves and their family members not to become a burden on the social assistance system of the host Member State during their period of residence and have comprehensive sickness insurance cover in the host Member State, or that they are members of the family, already constituted in the host Member State, of a person satisfying these requirements. 'Sufficient resources' shall be as defined in Article 8(4).

Such family members shall retain their right of residence exclusively on a personal basis.

Article 14 Retention of the right of residence

1. Union citizens and their family members shall have the right of residence provided for in Article 6, as long as they do not become an unreasonable burden on the social assistance system of the host Member State.

2. Union citizens and their family members shall have the right of residence provided for in Articles 7, 12 and 13 as long as they meet the conditions set out therein. In specific cases where there is a reasonable doubt as to whether a Union citizen or his/her family members satisfies the conditions set out in Articles 7, 12 and 13, Member States may verify if these conditions are fulfilled. This verification shall not be carried out systematically.

3. An expulsion measure shall not be the automatic consequence of a Union citizen's or his or her family member's recourse to the social assistance system of the host Member State.

4. By way of derogation from paragraphs 1 and 2 and without prejudice to the provisions of Chapter VI, an expulsion measure may in no case be adopted against Union citizens or their family members if:

(a) the Union citizens are workers or self-employed persons, or

(b) the Union citizens entered the territory of the host Member State in order to seek employment. In this case, the Union citizens and their family members may not be expelled for as long as the Union citizens can provide evidence that they are continuing to seek employment and that they have a genuine chance of being engaged.

Article 15 Procedural safeguards

1. The procedures provided for by Articles 30 and 31 shall apply by analogy to all decisions restricting free movement of Union citizens and their family members on grounds other than public policy, public security or public health.

2. Expiry of the identity card or passport on the basis of which the person concerned entered the host Member State and was issued with a registration certificate or residence card shall not constitute a ground for expulsion from the host Member State.

3. The host Member State may not impose a ban on entry in the context of an expulsion decision to which paragraph 1 applies.

Chapter IV Right of permanent residence

Section I Eligibility

Article 16 General rule for Union citizens and their family members

1. Union citizens who have resided legally for a continuous period of five years in the host Member State shall have the right of permanent residence there. This right shall not be subject to the conditions provided for in Chapter III.

2. Paragraph 1 shall apply also to family members who are not nationals of a Member State and have legally resided with the Union citizen in the host Member State for a continuous period of five years.

3. Continuity of residence shall not be affected by temporary absences not exceeding a total of six months a year, or by absences of a longer duration for compulsory military service, or by one absence of a maximum of twelve consecutive months for important reasons such as pregnancy and childbirth, serious illness, study or vocational training, or a posting in another Member State or a third country.

4. Once acquired, the right of permanent residence shall be lost only through absence from the host Member State for a period exceeding two consecutive years.

Article 17 Exemptions for persons no longer working in the host Member State and their family members

1. By way of derogation from Article 16, the right of permanent residence in the host Member State shall be enjoyed before completion of a continuous period of five years of residence by:

(a) workers or self-employed persons who, at the time they stop working, have reached the age laid down by the law of that Member State for entitlement to an old age pension or workers who cease paid employment to take early retirement, provided that they have been working in that Member State for at least the preceding twelve months and have resided there continuously for more than three years.

If the law of the host Member State does not grant the right to an old age pension to certain categories of self-employed persons, the age condition shall be deemed to have been met once the person concerned has reached the age of 60;

(b) workers or self-employed persons who have resided continuously in the host Member State for more than two years and stop working there as a result of permanent incapacity to work.

If such incapacity is the result of an accident at work or an occupational disease entitling the person concerned to a benefit payable in full or in part by an institution in the host Member State, no condition shall be imposed as to length of residence;

(c) workers or self-employed persons who, after three years of continuous employment and residence in the host Member State, work in an employed or self-employed capacity in another Member State, while retaining their place of residence in the host Member State, to which they return, as a rule, each day or at least once a week.

For the purposes of entitlement to the rights referred to in points (a) and (b), periods of employment spent in the Member State in which the person concerned is working shall be regarded as having been spent in the host Member State.

Periods of involuntary unemployment duly recorded by the relevant employment office, periods not worked for reasons not of the person's own making and absences from work or cessation of work due to illness or accident shall be regarded as periods of employment.

2. The conditions as to length of residence and employment laid down in point (a) of paragraph 1 and the condition as to length of residence laid down in point (b) of paragraph 1 shall not apply if the worker's or the self-employed person's spouse or partner as referred to in point 2(b) of Article 2 is a national of the host Member State or has lost the nationality of that Member State by marriage to that worker or self-employed person.

3. Irrespective of nationality, the family members of a worker or a self-employed person who are residing with him in the territory of the host Member State shall have the right of permanent residence in that Member State, if the worker or self-employed person has acquired himself the right of permanent residence in that Member State on the basis of paragraph 1.

4. If, however, the worker or self-employed person dies while still working but before acquiring permanent residence status in the host Member State on the basis of paragraph 1, his family members who are residing with him in the host Member State shall acquire the right of permanent residence there, on condition that:

(a) the worker or self-employed person had, at the time of death, resided continuously on the territory of that Member State for two years; or

(b) the death resulted from an accident at work or an occupational disease; or

(c) the surviving spouse lost the nationality of that Member State following marriage to the worker or self-employed person.

Article 18 Acquisition of the right of permanent residence by certain family members who are not nationals of a Member State

Without prejudice to Article 17, the family members of a Union citizen to whom Articles 12(2) and 13(2) apply, who satisfy the conditions laid down therein, shall acquire the right of permanent residence after residing legally for a period of five consecutive years in the host Member State.

Section II Administrative formalities

Article 19 Document certifying permanent residence for Union citizens

1. Upon application Member States shall issue Union citizens entitled to permanent residence, after having verified duration of residence, with a document certifying permanent residence.

2. The document certifying permanent residence shall be issued as soon as possible.

Article 20 Permanent residence card for family members who are not nationals of a Member State

1. Member States shall issue family members who are not nationals of a Member State entitled to permanent residence with a permanent residence card within six months of the submission of the application. The permanent residence card shall be renewable automatically every ten years.

2. The application for a permanent residence card shall be submitted before the residence card expires. Failure to comply with the requirement to apply for a permanent residence card may render the person concerned liable to proportionate and non-discriminatory sanctions.

3. Interruption in residence not exceeding two consecutive years shall not affect the validity of the permanent residence card.

Article 21 Continuity of residence

For the purposes of this Directive, continuity of residence may be attested by any means of proof in use in the host Member State. Continuity of residence is broken by any expulsion decision duly enforced against the person concerned.

Chapter V Provisions common to the right of residence and the right of permanent residence

Article 22 Territorial scope

The right of residence and the right of permanent residence shall cover the whole territory of the host Member State. Member States may impose territorial restrictions on the right of residence and the right of permanent residence only where the same restrictions apply to their own nationals.

Article 23 Related rights

Irrespective of nationality, the family members of a Union citizen who have the right of residence or the right of permanent residence in a Member State shall be entitled to take up employment or self-employment there.

Article 24 Equal treatment

1. Subject to such specific provisions as are expressly provided for in the Treaty and secondary law, all Union citizens residing on the basis of this Directive in the territory of the host Member State shall enjoy equal treatment with the nationals of that Member State within the scope of the Treaty. The benefit of this right shall be extended to family members who are not nationals of a Member State and who have the right of residence or permanent residence.

2. By way of derogation from paragraph 1, the host Member State shall not be obliged to confer entitlement to social assistance during the first three months of residence or, where appropriate, the longer period provided for in Article 14(4)(b), nor shall it be obliged, prior to acquisition of the right of permanent residence, to grant maintenance aid for studies, including vocational training, consisting in student grants or student loans to persons other than workers, self-employed persons, persons who retain such status and members of their families.

Article 25 General provisions concerning residence documents

1. Possession of a registration certificate as referred to in Article 8, of a document certifying permanent residence, of a certificate attesting submission of an application for a family member residence card, of a residence card or of a permanent residence card, may under no circumstances be made a precondition for the exercise of a right or the completion of an administrative formality, as entitlement to rights may be attested by any other means of proof.

2. All documents mentioned in paragraph 1 shall be issued free of charge or for a charge not exceeding that imposed on nationals for the issuing of similar documents.

Article 26 Checks

Member States may carry out checks on compliance with any requirement deriving from their national legislation for non-nationals always to carry their registration certificate or residence card, provided that the same requirement applies to their own nationals as regards their identity card. In the event of failure to comply with this requirement, Member States may impose the same sanctions as those imposed on their own nationals for failure to carry their identity card.

Chapter VI Restrictions on the right of entry and the right of residence on grounds of public policy, public security or public health

Article 27 General principles

1. Subject to the provisions of this Chapter, Member States may restrict the freedom of movement and residence of Union citizens and their family members, irrespective of nationality, on grounds of public policy, public security or public health. These grounds shall not be invoked to serve economic ends.

2. Measures taken on grounds of public policy or public security shall comply with the principle of proportionality and shall be based exclusively on the personal conduct of the individual concerned.

Previous criminal convictions shall not in themselves constitute grounds for taking such measures.

The personal conduct of the individual concerned must represent a genuine, present and sufficiently serious threat affecting one of the fundamental interests of society. Justifications that are isolated from the particulars of the case or that rely on considerations of general prevention shall not be accepted.

3. In order to ascertain whether the person concerned represents a danger for public policy or public security, when issuing the registration certificate or, in the absence of a registration system, not later than three months from the date of arrival of the person concerned on its territory or from the date of reporting his/her presence within the territory, as provided for in Article 5(5), or when issuing the residence card, the host Member State may, should it consider this essential, request the Member State of origin and, if need be, other Member States to provide information concerning any previous police record the person concerned may have. Such enquiries shall not be made as a matter of routine. The Member State consulted shall give its reply within two months.

4. The Member State which issued the passport or identity card shall allow the holder of the document who has been expelled on grounds of public policy, public security, or public health from another Member State to re-enter its territory without any formality even if the document is no longer valid or the nationality of the holder is in dispute.

Article 28 Protection against expulsion

1. Before taking an expulsion decision on grounds of public policy or public security, the host Member State shall take account of considerations such as how long the individual concerned has resided on its territory, his/her age, state of health, family and economic situation, social and cultural integration into the host Member State and the extent of his/her links with the country of origin.

2. The host Member State may not take an expulsion decision against Union citizens or their family members, irrespective of nationality, who have the right of permanent residence on its territory, except on serious grounds of public policy or public security.

3. An expulsion decision may not be taken against Union citizens, except if the decision is based on imperative grounds of public security, as defined by Member States, if they:

(a) have resided in the host Member State for the previous ten years; or
(b) are a minor, except if the expulsion is necessary for the best interests of the child, as provided for in the United Nations Convention on the Rights of the Child of 20 November 1989.

Article 29 Public health

1. The only diseases justifying measures restricting freedom of movement shall be the diseases with epidemic potential as defined by the relevant instruments of the World Health Organisation and other infectious diseases or contagious parasitic diseases if they are the subject of protection provisions applying to nationals of the host Member State.

2. Diseases occurring after a three-month period from the date of arrival shall not constitute grounds for expulsion from the territory.

3. Where there are serious indications that it is necessary, Member States may, within three months of the date of arrival, require persons entitled to the right of residence to undergo, free of charge, a medical examination to certify that they are not suffering from any of the conditions referred to in paragraph 1. Such medical examinations may not be required as a matter of routine.

Article 30 Notification of decisions

1. The persons concerned shall be notified in writing of any decision taken under Article 27(1), in such a way that they are able to comprehend its content and the implications for them.

2. The persons concerned shall be informed, precisely and in full, of the public policy, public security or public health grounds on which the decision taken in their case is based, unless this is contrary to the interests of State security.

3. The notification shall specify the court or administrative authority with which the person concerned may lodge an appeal, the time limit for the appeal and, where applicable, the time allowed for the person to leave the territory of the Member State. Save in duly substantiated cases of urgency, the time allowed to leave the territory shall be not less than one month from the date of notification.

Article 31 Procedural safeguards

1. The persons concerned shall have access to judicial and, where appropriate, administrative redress procedures in the host Member State to appeal against or seek review of any decision taken against them on the grounds of public policy, public security or public health.

2. Where the application for appeal against or judicial review of the expulsion decision is accompanied by an application for an interim order to suspend enforcement of that decision, actual removal from the territory may not take place until such time as the decision on the interim order has been taken, except:

- where the expulsion decision is based on a previous judicial decision; or
- where the persons concerned have had previous access to judicial review; or
- where the expulsion decision is based on imperative grounds of public security under Article 28(3).

3. The redress procedures shall allow for an examination of the legality of the decision, as well as of the facts and circumstances on which the proposed measure is based. They shall ensure that the decision is not disproportionate, particularly in view of the requirements laid down in Article 28.

4. Member States may exclude the individual concerned from their territory pending the redress procedure, but they may not prevent the individual from submitting his/her defence in person, except when his/her appearance may cause serious troubles to public policy or public security or when the appeal or judicial review concerns a denial of entry to the territory.

Article 32 Duration of exclusion orders

1. Persons excluded on grounds of public policy or public security may submit an application for lifting of the exclusion order after a reasonable period, depending on the circumstances, and in any event after three years from enforcement of the final exclusion order which has been validly adopted in accordance with Community law, by putting forward arguments to establish that there has been a material change in the circumstances which justified the decision ordering their exclusion.

The Member State concerned shall reach a decision on this application within six months of its submission.

2. The persons referred to in paragraph 1 shall have no right of entry to the territory of the Member State concerned while their application is being considered.

Article 33 Expulsion as a penalty or legal consequence

1. Expulsion orders may not be issued by the host Member State as a penalty or legal consequence of a custodial penalty, unless they conform to the requirements of Articles 27, 28 and 29.

2. If an expulsion order, as provided for in paragraph 1, is enforced more than two years after it was issued, the Member State shall check that the individual concerned is currently and genuinely a threat to public policy or public security and shall assess whether there has been any material change in the circumstances since the expulsion order was issued.

Chapter VII Final provisions

Article 34 Publicity

Member States shall disseminate information concerning the rights and obligations of Union citizens and their family members on the subjects covered by this Directive, particularly by means of awareness-raising campaigns conducted through national and local media and other means of communication.

Article 35 Abuse of rights

Member States may adopt the necessary measures to refuse, terminate or withdraw any right conferred by this Directive in the case of abuse of rights or fraud, such as marriages of convenience. Any such measure shall be proportionate and subject to the procedural safeguards provided for in Articles 30 and 31.

Article 36 Sanctions

Member States shall lay down provisions on the sanctions applicable to breaches of national rules adopted for the implementation of this Directive and shall take the measures required for their application. The sanctions laid down shall be effective and proportionate. Member States shall notify the Commission of these provisions not later than 30 April 2006 and as promptly as possible in the case of any subsequent changes.

Article 37 More favourable national provisions

The provisions of this Directive shall not affect any laws, regulations or administrative provisions laid down by a Member State which would be more favourable to the persons covered by this Directive.

Article 38 Repeals

(Paragraph 1 has been repealed.)

2. Directives 64/221/EEC, 68/360/EEC, 72/194/EEC, 73/148/EEC, 75/34/EEC, 75/35/EEC, 90/364/EEC, 90/365/EEC and 93/96/EEC shall be repealed with effect from 30 April 2006.

3. References made to the repealed provisions and Directives shall be construed as being made to this Directive.

Article 39 Report

No later than 30 April 2008 the Commission shall submit a report on the application of this Directive to the European Parliament and the Council, together with any necessary proposals, notably on the opportunity to extend the period of time during which Union citizens and their family members may reside in the territory of the host Member State without any conditions. The Member States shall provide the Commission with the information needed to produce the report.

Article 40 Transposition

1. Member States shall bring into force the laws, regulations and administrative provisions necessary to comply with this Directive by 30 April 2006.

When Member States adopt those measures, they shall contain a reference to this Directive or shall be accompanied by such a reference on the occasion of their official publication. The methods of making such reference shall be laid down by the Member States.

2. Member States shall communicate to the Commission the text of the provisions of national law which they adopt in the field covered by this Directive together with a table showing how the provisions of this Directive correspond to the national provisions adopted.

Article 41 Entry into force
This Directive shall enter into force on the day of its publication in the *Official Journal of the European Union*.

Article 42 Addressees
This Directive is addressed to the Member States.

Done at Brussels, 29 April 2004.

Directive 2005/36/EC of the European Parliament and of the Council of 7 September 2005 on the recognition of professional qualifications*

[OJ 2005 L255/22]

Title I General provisions

Article 1 Purpose
This Directive establishes rules according to which a Member State which makes access to or pursuit of a regulated profession in its territory contingent upon possession of specific professional qualifications (referred to hereinafter as the host Member State) shall recognise professional qualifications obtained in one or more other Member States (referred to hereinafter as the home Member State) and which allow the holder of the said qualifications to pursue the same profession there, for access to and pursuit of that profession. This Directive also establishes rules concerning partial access to a regulated profession and recognition of professional traineeships pursued in another Member State.

Article 2 Scope
1. This Directive shall apply to all nationals of a Member State wishing to pursue a regulated profession in a Member State, including those belonging to the liberal professions, other than that in which they obtained their professional qualifications, on either a self-employed or employed basis.

This Directive shall also apply to all nationals of a Member State who have pursued a professional traineeship outside the home Member State.

2. Each Member State may permit Member State nationals in possession of evidence of professional qualifications not obtained in a Member State to pursue a regulated profession within the meaning of Article 3(1)(a) on its territory in accordance with its rules. In the case of professions covered by Title III, Chapter III, this initial recognition shall respect the minimum training conditions laid down in that Chapter.

3. Where, for a given regulated profession, other specific arrangements directly related to the recognition of professional qualifications are established in a separate instrument of Community law, the corresponding provisions of this Directive shall not apply.

4. This Directive shall not apply to notaries who are appointed by an official act of government.

* **Editor's Note:** As amended following Bulgarian and Romanian entry to the EU (OJ 2006 L363/141) and corrected by OJ 2007 L271/18 and OJ 2008 L93/28. Further amended by OJ 2012 L180/9 (Regulation 632/2012), Directive 2013/25 (OJ 2013 L158/368), Directive 2013/55 (OJ 2013 L354/132) and Decision 2019/608 (OJ 2019 L104/1).

Article 3 Definitions

...

2. A profession practised by the members of an association or organisation listed in Annex I shall be treated as a regulated profession.

The purpose of the associations or organisations referred to in the first subparagraph is, in particular, to promote and maintain a high standard in the professional field concerned. To that end they are recognised in a special form by a Member State and award evidence of formal qualifications to their members, ensure that their members respect the rules of professional conduct which they prescribe, and confer on them the right to use a title or designatory letters or to benefit from a status corresponding to those formal qualifications.

On each occasion that a Member State grants recognition to an association or organisation referred to in the first subparagraph, it shall inform the Commission. The Commission shall examine whether that association or organisation fulfils the conditions provided for in the second subparagraph. In order to take due account of regulatory developments in Member States, the Commission shall be empowered to adopt delegated acts in accordance with Article 57c in order to update Annex I where the conditions provided for in the second subparagraph are satisfied.

Where the conditions provided for in the second subparagraph are not satisfied, the Commission shall adopt an implementing act in order to reject the requested update of Annex I.

3. Evidence of formal qualifications issued by a third country shall be regarded as evidence of formal qualifications if the holder has three years' professional experience in the profession concerned on the territory of the Member State which recognised that evidence of formal qualifications in accordance with Article 2(2), certified by that Member State.

Article 4 Effects of recognition

1. The recognition of professional qualifications by the host Member State shall allow beneficiaries to gain access in that Member State to the same profession as that for which they are qualified in the home Member State and to pursue it in the host Member State under the same conditions as its nationals.

2. For the purposes of this Directive, the profession which the applicant wishes to pursue in the host Member State is the same as that for which he is qualified in his home Member State if the activities covered are comparable.

3. By way of derogation from paragraph 1, partial access to a profession in the host Member State shall be granted under the conditions laid down in Article 4f.

... (4a to 4f)

Title II Free provision of services

Article 5 Principle of the free provision of services

1. Without prejudice to specific provisions of Community law, as well as to Articles 6 and 7 of this Directive, Member States shall not restrict, for any reason relating to professional qualifications, the free provision of services in another Member State:

(a) if the service provider is legally established in a Member State for the purpose of pursuing the same profession there (hereinafter referred to as the Member State of establishment), and

(b) where the service provider moves, if he has pursued that profession in one or several Member States for at least one year during the last 10 years preceding the provision of services when the profession is not regulated in the Member State of establishment. The condition of one year's pursuit shall not apply if the profession or the education and training leading to the profession is regulated.

2. The provisions of this title shall only apply where the service provider moves to the territory of the host Member State to pursue, on a temporary and occasional basis, the profession referred to in paragraph 1.

The temporary and occasional nature of the provision of services shall be assessed case by case, in particular in relation to its duration, its frequency, its regularity and its continuity.

3. Where a service provider moves, he shall be subject to professional rules of a professional, statutory or administrative nature which are directly linked to professional qualifications, such as the definition of the profession, the use of titles and serious professional malpractice which is directly and specifically linked to consumer protection and safety, as well as disciplinary provisions which are applicable in the host Member State to professionals who pursue the same profession in that Member State.

Article 6 Exemptions

Pursuant to Article 5(1), the host Member State shall exempt service providers established in another Member State from the requirements which it places on professionals established in its territory relating to:

(a) authorisation by, registration with or membership of a professional organisation or body. In order to facilitate the application of disciplinary provisions in force on their territory according to Article 5(3), Member States may provide either for automatic temporary registration with or for pro forma membership of such a professional organisation or body, provided that such registration or membership does not delay or complicate in any way the provision of services and does not entail any additional costs for the service provider. A copy of the declaration and, where applicable, of the renewal referred to in Article 7(1), accompanied, for professions which have implications for public health and safety referred to in Article 7(4) or which benefit from automatic recognition under Title III Chapter III, by a copy of the documents referred to in Article 7(2) shall be sent by the competent authority to the relevant professional organisation or body, and this shall constitute automatic temporary registration or pro forma membership for this purpose;

(b) registration with a public social security body for the purpose of settling accounts with an insurer relating to activities pursued for the benefit of insured persons.

The service provider shall, however, inform in advance or, in an urgent case, afterwards, the body referred to in point (b) of the services which he has provided.

Article 7 Declaration to be made in advance, if the service provider moves

1. Member States may require that, where the service provider first moves from one Member State to another in order to provide services, he shall inform the competent authority in the host Member State in a written declaration to be made in advance including the details of any insurance cover or other means of personal or collective protection with regard to professional liability. Such declaration shall be renewed once a year if the service provider intends to provide temporary or occasional services in that Member State during that year. The service provider may supply the declaration by any means.

2. Moreover, for the first provision of services or if there is a material change in the situation substantiated by the documents, Member States may require that the declaration be accompanied by the following documents:

(a) proof of the nationality of the service provider;

(b) an attestation certifying that the holder is legally established in a Member State for the purpose of pursuing the activities concerned and that he is not prohibited from practising, even temporarily, at the moment of delivering the attestation;

(c) evidence of professional qualifications;

(d) for cases referred to in point (b) of Article 5(1), any means of proof that the service provider has pursued the activity concerned for at least one year during the previous 10 years;

(e) for professions in the security sector, in the health sector and professions related to the education of minors, including in childcare and early childhood education, where the Member State so requires for its own nationals, an attestation confirming the absence of temporary or final suspensions from exercising the profession or of criminal convictions;

(f) for professions that have patient safety implications, a declaration about the applicant's knowledge of the language necessary for practising the profession in the host Member State;

(g) for professions covering the activities referred to in Article 16 and which were notified by a Member State in accordance with Article 59(2), a certificate concerning the nature and duration of the activity issued by the competent authority or body of the Member State where the service provider is established.

2a. Submission of a required declaration by the service provider in accordance with paragraph 1 shall entitle that service provider to have access to the service activity or to exercise that activity in the entire territory of the Member State concerned. A Member State may require additional information listed in paragraph 2 concerning the professional qualifications of the service provider if:

(a) the profession is regulated in parts of that Member State's territory in a different manner;

(b) such regulation is applicable also to all nationals of that Member State;

(c) the differences in such regulation are justified by overriding reasons of general interest relating to public health or safety of service recipients; and

(d) the Member State has no other means of obtaining such information.

3. The service shall be provided under the professional title of the Member State of establishment, in so far as such a title exists in that Member State for the professional activity in question. That title shall be indicated in the official language or one of the official languages of the Member State of establishment in such a way as to avoid any confusion with the professional title of the host Member State. Where no such professional title exists in the Member State of establishment, the service provider shall indicate his formal qualification in the official language or one of the official languages of that Member State. By way of exception, the service shall be provided under the professional title of the host Member State for cases referred to in Title III Chapter III.

4. For the first provision of services, in the case of regulated professions that have public health or safety implications which do not benefit from automatic recognition under Chapter II, III or IIIa of Title III, the competent authority of the host Member State may check the professional qualifications of the service provider prior to the first provision of services. Such a prior check shall be possible only where the purpose of the check is to avoid serious damage to the health or safety of the service recipient due to a lack of professional qualification of the service provider and where the check does not go beyond what is necessary for that purpose.

No later than one month after receipt of the declaration and accompanying documents, referred to in paragraphs 1 and 2, the competent authority shall inform the service provider of its decision:

(a) not to check his professional qualifications;

(b) having checked his professional qualifications:

(i) to require the service provider to take an aptitude test; or

(ii) to allow the provision of services.

Where there is a difficulty which would result in delay in taking a decision under the second subparagraph, the competent authority shall notify the service provider of the reason for the delay within the same deadline. The difficulty shall be solved within one month of that notification and the decision finalised within two months of resolution of the difficulty.

Where there is a substantial difference between the professional qualifications of the service provider and the training required in the host Member State, to the extent that that difference is such as to be harmful to public health or safety, and that it cannot be compensated by the service provider's professional experience or by knowledge, skills and competences acquired through lifelong learning formally validated to that end by a relevant body, the host Member State shall give that service provider the opportunity to show, by means of an aptitude test, as referred to in point (b) of the second subparagraph, that they have acquired the knowledge, skills or competence that were lacking. The host Member State shall take a decision on that basis on whether to allow the provision of services. In any case, it must be possible to provide the service within one month of the decision taken in accordance with the second subparagraph.

In the absence of a reaction of the competent authority within the deadlines set out in the second and third subparagraphs, the service may be provided.

In cases where professional qualifications have been verified under this paragraph, the service shall be provided under the professional title of the host Member State.

Article 8 Administrative cooperation

1. The competent authorities of the host Member State may ask the competent authorities of the Member State of establishment, in the event of justified doubts, to provide any information relevant to the legality of the service provider's establishment and good conduct, as well as the absence of any disciplinary or criminal sanctions of a professional nature. In the event that the competent authorities of the host Member State decide to check the service provider's professional qualifications, they may ask the competent authorities of the Member State of establishment for information about the service provider's training courses to the extent necessary to assess substantial differences likely to be harmful to public health or safety. The competent authorities of the Member State of establishment shall provide that information in accordance with Article 56. In the case of non-regulated professions in the home Member State, the assistance centres referred to in Article 57b may also provide such information.

2. The competent authorities shall ensure the exchange of all information necessary for complaints by a recipient of a service against a service provider to be correctly pursued. Recipients shall be informed of the outcome of the complaint.

Article 9 Information to be given to the recipients of the service

In cases where the service is provided under the professional title of the Member State of establishment or under the formal qualification of the service provider, in addition to the other requirements relating to information contained in Community law, the competent authorities of the host Member State may require the service provider to furnish the recipient of the service with any or all of the following information:

(a) if the service provider is registered in a commercial register or similar public register, the register in which he is registered, his registration number, or equivalent means of identification contained in that register;

(b) if the activity is subject to authorisation in the Member State of establishment, the name and address of the competent supervisory authority;

(c) any professional association or similar body with which the service provider is registered;

(d) the professional title or, where no such title exists, the formal qualification of the service provider and the Member State in which it was awarded;

(e) if the service provider performs an activity which is subject to VAT, the VAT identification number referred to in Article 22(1) of the sixth Council Directive 77/388/EEC of 17 May 1977 on the harmonisation of the laws of the Member States relating to turnover taxes—Common system of value added tax: uniform basis of assessment;[1]

(f) details of any insurance cover or other means of personal or collective protection with regard to professional liability.

Title III Freedom of establishment

Chapter I General system for the recognition of evidence of training

Article 10 Scope

This Chapter applies to all professions which are not covered by Chapters II and III of this Title and in the following cases in which the applicant, for specific and exceptional reasons, does not satisfy the conditions laid down in those Chapters:

(a) for activities listed in Annex IV, when the migrant does not meet the requirements set out in Articles 17, 18 and 19;

[1] OJ L 145, 13.6.1977, p. 1. Directive as last amended by Directive 2004/66/EC (OJ L 168, 1.5.2004, p. 35).

(b) for doctors with basic training, specialised doctors, nurses responsible for general care, dental practitioners, specialised dental practitioners, veterinary surgeons, midwives, pharmacists and architects, when the migrant does not meet the requirements of effective and lawful professional practice referred to in Articles 23, 27, 33, 37, 39, 43 and 49;
(c) for architects, when the migrant holds evidence of formal qualification not listed in Annex V, point 5.7;
(d) without prejudice to Articles 21(1), 23 and 27, for doctors, nurses, dental practitioners, veterinary surgeons, midwives, pharmacists and architects holding evidence of formal qualifications as a specialist, who must have taken part in the training leading to the possession of a title listed in Annex V, points 5.1.1, 5.2.2, 5.3.2, 5.4.2, 5.5.2, 5.6.2 and 5.7.1, and solely for the purpose of the recognition of the relevant specialty;
(e) for nurses responsible for general care and specialised nurses holding evidence of formal qualifications as a specialist who must have taken part in the training leading to the possession of a title listed in Annex V, point 5.2.2, when the migrant seeks recognition in another Member State where the relevant professional activities are pursued by specialised nurses without training as general care nurse;
(f) for specialised nurses without training as general care nurse, when the migrant seeks recognition in another Member State where the relevant professional activities are pursued by nurses responsible for general care, specialised nurses without training as general care nurse or specialised nurses holding evidence of formal qualifications as a specialist who must have taken part in the training leading to the possession of the titles listed in Annex V, point 5.2.2;
(g) for migrants meeting the requirements set out in Article 3(3).

Article 11 Levels of qualification

For the purposes of Article 13 and Article 14(6), professional qualifications shall be grouped under the following levels:

(a) an attestation of competence issued by a competent authority in the home Member State designated pursuant to legislative, regulatory or administrative provisions of that Member State, on the basis of:
  (i) either a training course not forming part of a certificate or diploma within the meaning of points (b), (c), (d) or (e), or a specific examination without prior training, or full-time pursuit of the profession in a Member State for three consecutive years or for an equivalent duration on a part-time basis during the previous 10 years,
  (ii) or general primary or secondary education, attesting that the holder has acquired general knowledge;
(b) a certificate attesting to a successful completion of a secondary course,
  (i) either general in character, supplemented by a course of study or professional training other than those referred to in point (c) and/or by the probationary or professional practice required in addition to that course,
  (ii) or technical or professional in character, supplemented where appropriate by a course of study or professional training as referred to in point (i), and/or by the probationary or professional practice required in addition to that course;
(c) a diploma certifying successful completion of
  (i) either training at post-secondary level other than that referred to in points (d) and (e) of a duration of at least one year or of an equivalent duration on a part-time basis, one of the conditions of entry of which is, as a general rule, the successful completion of the secondary course required to obtain entry to university or higher education or the completion of equivalent school education of the second secondary level, as well as the professional training which may be required in addition to that post-secondary course; or

(ii) regulated education and training or, in the case of regulated professions, vocational training with a special structure, with competences going beyond what is provided for in level b, equivalent to the level of training provided for under point (i), if such training provides a comparable professional standard and prepares the trainee for a comparable level of responsibilities and functions provided that the diploma is accompanied by a certificate from the home Member State;

(d) a diploma certifying that the holder has successfully completed training at post-secondary level of at least three and not more than four years' duration, or of an equivalent duration on a part-time basis, which may in addition be expressed with an equivalent number of ECTS credits, at a university or establishment of higher education or another establishment of equivalent level and, where appropriate, that he has successfully completed the professional training required in addition to the post-secondary course;

(e) a diploma certifying that the holder has successfully completed a post-secondary course of at least four years' duration, or of an equivalent duration on a part-time basis, which may in addition be expressed with an equivalent number of ECTS credits, at a university or establishment of higher education or another establishment of equivalent level and, where appropriate, that he has successfully completed the professional training required in addition to the post-secondary course.

Article 12 Equal treatment of qualifications

Any evidence of formal qualifications or set of evidence of formal qualifications issued by a competent authority in a Member State, certifying successful completion of training in the Union, on a full or part-time basis, within or outside formal programmes, which is recognised by that Member State as being of an equivalent level and which confers on the holder the same rights of access to or pursuit of a profession or prepares for the pursuit of that profession, shall be treated as evidence of formal qualifications referred to in Article 11, including the level in question.

Any professional qualification which, although not satisfying the requirements contained in the legislative, regulatory or administrative provisions in force in the home Member State for access to or the pursuit of a profession, confers on the holder acquired rights by virtue of these provisions, shall also be treated as such evidence of formal qualifications under the same conditions as set out in the first subparagraph. This applies in particular if the home Member State raises the level of training required for admission to a profession and for its exercise, and if an individual who has undergone former training, which does not meet the requirements of the new qualification, benefits from acquired rights by virtue of national legislative, regulatory or administrative provisions; in such case this former training is considered by the host Member State, for the purposes of the application of Article 13, as corresponding to the level of the new training.

Article 13 Conditions for recognition

1. If access to or pursuit of a regulated profession in a host Member State is contingent upon possession of specific professional qualifications, the competent authority of that Member State shall permit applicants to access and pursue that profession, under the same conditions as apply to its nationals, if they possess an attestation of competence or evidence of formal qualifications referred to in Article 11, required by another Member State in order to gain access to and pursue that profession on its territory.

Attestations of competence or evidence of formal qualifications shall be issued by a competent authority in a Member State, designated in accordance with the laws, regulations or administrative provisions of that Member State.

2. Access to, and pursuit of, a profession as described in paragraph 1 shall also be granted to applicants who have pursued the profession in question on a full-time basis for one year or for an equivalent overall duration on a part-time basis during the previous 10 years in another Member State which does not regulate that profession, and who possess one or more attestations of competence or evidence of formal qualifications issued by another Member State which does not regulate the profession.

Attestations of competence and evidence of formal qualifications shall satisfy the following conditions:

(a) they are issued by a competent authority in a Member State, designated in accordance with the laws, regulations or administrative provisions of that Member State;

(b) they attest that the holder has been prepared for the pursuit of the profession in question.

The one year of professional experience referred to in the first subparagraph may not, however, be required if the evidence of formal qualifications which the applicant possesses certifies regulated education and training.

3. The host Member State shall accept the level attested under Article 11 by the home Member State, as well as the certificate by which the home Member State certifies that regulated education and training or vocational training with a special structure referred to in point (c)(ii) of Article 11 is equivalent to the level provided for in point (c)(i) of Article 11.

4. By way of derogation from paragraphs 1 and 2 of this Article and from Article 14, the competent authority of the host Member State may refuse access to, and pursuit of, the profession to holders of an attestation of competence classified under point (a) of Article 11 where the national professional qualification required to exercise the profession on its territory is classified under point (e) of Article 11.

Article 14 Compensation measures

1. Article 13 shall not preclude the host Member State from requiring the applicant to complete an adaptation period of up to three years or to take an aptitude test if:

(a) the training the applicant has received covers substantially different matters than those covered by the evidence of formal qualifications required in the host Member State;

(b) the regulated profession in the host Member State comprises one or more regulated professional activities which do not exist in the corresponding profession in the applicant's home Member State, and the training required in the host Member State covers substantially different matters from those covered by the applicant's attestation of competence or evidence of formal qualifications.

2. If the host Member State makes use of the option provided for in paragraph 1, it must offer the applicant the choice between an adaptation period and an aptitude test.

Where a Member State considers, with respect to a given profession, that it is necessary to derogate from the requirement, set out in the previous subparagraph, that it give the applicant a choice between an adaptation period and an aptitude test, it shall inform the other Member States and the Commission in advance and provide sufficient justification for the derogation.

Where the Commission considers that the derogation referred to in the second subparagraph is inappropriate or that it is not in accordance with Union law, it shall adopt an implementing act, within three months of receiving all necessary information, to ask the relevant Member State to refrain from taking the envisaged measure. In the absence of a response from the Commission within that deadline, the derogation may be applied.

3. By way of derogation from the principle of the right of the applicant to choose, as laid down in paragraph 2, for professions whose pursuit requires precise knowledge of national law and in respect of which the provision of advice and/or assistance concerning national law is an essential and constant aspect of the professional activity, the host Member State may stipulate either an adaptation period or an aptitude test.

This applies also to the cases provided for in Article 10 points (b) and (c), in Article 10 point (d) concerning doctors and dental practitioners, in Article 10 point (f) when the migrant seeks recognition in another Member State where the relevant professional activities are pursued by nurses responsible for general care or specialised nurses holding evidence of formal qualifications as a specialist who must have taken part in the training leading to the possession of the titles listed in Annex V, point 5.2.2 and in Article 10 point (g).

In the cases covered by Article 10 point (a), the host Member State may require an adaptation period or an aptitude test if the migrant envisages pursuing professional activities in a self-employed capacity or as a manager of an undertaking which require the knowledge and the application of the specific national rules in force, provided that knowledge and application of those rules are required by the competent authorities of the host Member State for access to such activities by its own nationals.

By way of derogation from the principle of the right of the applicant to choose, as laid down in paragraph 2, the host Member State may stipulate either an adaptation period or an aptitude test in the case of:

(a) a holder of a professional qualification referred to in point (a) of Article 11, who applies for recognition of his professional qualifications where the national professional qualification required is classified under point (c) of Article 11; or

(b) a holder of a professional qualification referred to in point (b) of Article 11, who applies for recognition of his professional qualifications where the national professional qualification required is classified under point (d) or (e) of Article 11.

In the case of a holder of a professional qualification referred to in point (a) of Article 11 who applies for recognition of his professional qualifications where the national professional qualification required is classified under point (d) of Article 11, the host Member State may impose both an adaptation period and an aptitude test.

4. For the purposes of paragraphs 1 and 5, 'substantially different matters' means matters in respect of which knowledge, skills and competences acquired are essential for pursuing the profession and with regard to which the training received by the migrant shows significant differences in terms of content from the training required by the host Member State.

5. Paragraph 1 shall be applied with due regard to the principle of proportionality. In particular, if the host Member State intends to require the applicant to complete an adaptation period or take an aptitude test, it must first ascertain whether the knowledge, skills and competences acquired by the applicant in the course of his professional experience or through lifelong learning, and formally validated to that end by a relevant body, in any Member State or in a third country, is of such nature as to cover, in full or in part, the substantially different matters defined in paragraph 4.

6. The decision imposing an adaptation period or an aptitude test shall be duly justified. In particular, the applicant shall be provided with the following information:

(a) the level of the professional qualification required in the host Member State and the level of the professional qualification held by the applicant in accordance with the classification set out in Article 11; and

(b) the substantial differences referred to in paragraph 4 and the reasons for which those differences cannot be compensated by knowledge, skills and competences acquired in the course of professional experience or through lifelong learning formally validated to that end by a relevant body.

7. Member States shall ensure that an applicant has the possibility of taking the aptitude test referred to in paragraph 1 not later than six months after the initial decision imposing an aptitude test on the applicant.

Chapter II Recognition of professional experience

Article 16 Requirements regarding professional experience

If, in a Member State, access to or pursuit of one of the activities listed in Annex IV is contingent upon possession of general, commercial or professional knowledge and aptitudes, that Member State shall recognise previous pursuit of the activity in another Member State as sufficient proof of such knowledge and aptitudes. The activity must have been pursued in accordance with Articles 17, 18 and 19.

Chapter III Recognition on the basis of coordination of minimum training conditions

Section 1 General provisions

Article 21 Principle of automatic recognition

1. Each Member State shall recognise evidence of formal qualifications as doctor giving access to the professional activities of doctor with basic training and specialised doctor, as nurse responsible for general care, as dental practitioner, as specialised dental practitioner, as veterinary surgeon,

as pharmacist and as architect, listed in Annex V, points 5.1.1, 5.1.2, 5.2.2, 5.3.2, 5.3.3, 5.4.2, 5.6.2 and 5.7.1 respectively, which satisfy the minimum training conditions referred to in Articles 24, 25, 31, 34, 35, 38, 44 and 46 respectively, and shall, for the purposes of access to and pursuit of the professional activities, give such evidence the same effect on its territory as the evidence of formal qualifications which it itself issues.

Such evidence of formal qualifications must be issued by the competent bodies in the Member States and accompanied, where appropriate, by the certificates listed in Annex V, points 5.1.1, 5.1.2, 5.2.2, 5.3.2, 5.3.3, 5.4.2, 5.6.2 and 5.7.1 respectively.

The provisions of the first and second subparagraphs do not affect the acquired rights referred to in Articles 23, 27, 33, 37, 39 and 49.

2. Each Member State shall recognise, for the purpose of pursuing general medical practice in the framework of its national social security system, evidence of formal qualifications listed in Annex V, point 5.1.4 and issued to nationals of the Member States by the other Member States in accordance with the minimum training conditions laid down in Article 28.

The provisions of the previous subparagraph do not affect the acquired rights referred to in Article 30.

3. Each Member State shall recognise evidence of formal qualifications as a midwife, awarded to nationals of Member States by the other Member States, listed in Annex V, point 5.5.2, which complies with the minimum training conditions referred to in Article 40 and satisfies the criteria set out in Article 41, and shall, for the purposes of access to and pursuit of the professional activities, give such evidence the same effect on its territory as the evidence of formal qualifications which it itself issues. This provision does not affect the acquired rights referred to in Articles 23 and 43.

4. In respect of the operation of pharmacies that are not subject to territorial restrictions, a Member State may, by way of derogation, decide not to give effect to evidence of formal qualifications referred to in point 5.6.2 of Annex V, for the setting up of new pharmacies open to the public. For the purposes of this paragraph, pharmacies which have been open for less than three years shall also be considered as new pharmacies.

That derogation may not be applied in respect of pharmacists whose formal qualifications have already been recognised by the competent authorities of the host Member State for other purposes and who have been effectively and lawfully engaged in the professional activities of a pharmacist for at least three consecutive years in that Member State.

5. Evidence of formal qualifications as an architect referred to in Annex V, point 5.7.1, which is subject to automatic recognition pursuant to paragraph 1, proves completion of a course of training which began not earlier than during the academic reference year referred to in that Annex.

6. Each Member State shall make access to, and pursuit of, the professional activities of doctors, nurses responsible for general care, dental practitioners, veterinary surgeons, midwives and pharmacists subject to possession of evidence of formal qualifications referred to in points 5.1.1, 5.1.2, 5.1.4, 5.2.2, 5.3.2, 5.3.3, 5.4.2, 5.5.2 and 5.6.2 of Annex V respectively, attesting that the professional concerned, over the duration of his training, has acquired, as appropriate, the knowledge, skills and competences referred to in Articles 24(3), 31(6), 31(7), 34(3), 38(3), 40(3) and 44(3).

In order to take account of generally acknowledged scientific and technical progress, the Commission shall be empowered to adopt delegated acts in accordance with Article 57c to update the knowledge and skills referred to in Articles 24(3), 31(6), 34(3), 38(3), 40(3), 44(3) and 46(4) to reflect the evolution of Union law directly affecting the professionals concerned.

Such updates shall not entail an amendment of existing essential legislative principles in Member States regarding the structure of professions as regards training and conditions of access by natural persons. Such updates shall respect the responsibility of the Member States for the organisation of education systems, as set out in Article 165(1) of the Treaty on the Functioning of the European Union (TFEU).

...

Chapter IIIA Automatic recognition on the basis of common training principles

Article 49a Common training framework

1. For the purpose of this Article, 'common training framework' means a common set of minimum knowledge, skills and competences necessary for the pursuit of a specific profession. A common training framework shall not replace national training programmes unless a Member State decides otherwise under national law. For the purpose of access to and pursuit of a profession in Member States which regulate that profession, a Member State shall give evidence of professional qualifications acquired on the basis of such a framework the same effect in its territory as the evidence of formal qualifications which it itself issues, on condition that such framework fulfils the conditions laid down in paragraph 2.

2. A common training framework shall comply with the following conditions:

(a) the common training framework enables more professionals to move across Member States;

(b) the profession to which the common training framework applies is regulated, or the education and training leading to the profession is regulated in at least one third of the Member States;

(c) the common set of knowledge, skills and competences combines the knowledge, skills and competences required in the systems of education and training applicable in at least one third of the Member States; it shall be irrelevant whether the knowledge, skills and competences have been acquired as part of a general training course at a university or higher education institution or as part of a vocational training course;

(d) the common training framework shall be based on levels of the EQF, as defined in Annex II of the Recommendation of the European Parliament and of the Council of 23 April 2008 on the establishment of the European Qualifications Framework for lifelong learning;[2]

(e) the profession concerned is neither covered by another common training framework nor subject to automatic recognition under Chapter III of Title III;

(f) the common training framework has been prepared following a transparent due process, including the relevant stakeholders from Member States where the profession is not regulated;

(g) the common training framework permits nationals from any Member State to be eligible for acquiring the professional qualification under such framework without first being required to be a member of any professional organisation or to be registered with such organisation.

3. Representative professional organisations at Union level, as well as national professional organisations or competent authorities from at least one third of the Member States, may submit to the Commission suggestions for common training frameworks which meet the conditions laid down in paragraph 2.

4. The Commission shall be empowered to adopt delegated acts in accordance with Article 57c to establish a common training framework for a given profession based on the conditions laid down in paragraph 2 of this Article.

5. A Member State shall be exempted from the obligation of introducing the common training framework referred to in paragraph 4 on its territory and from the obligation of granting automatic recognition to the professional qualifications acquired under that common training framework if one of the following conditions is fulfilled:

(a) there are no education or training institutions available in its territory to offer such training for the profession concerned;

(b) the introduction of the common training framework would adversely affect the organisation of its system of education and professional training;

[2] OJ C 111, 6.5.2008, p. 1.

(c) there are substantial differences between the common training framework and the training required in its territory, which entail serious risks for public policy, public security, public health or for the safety of the service recipients or the protection of the environment.

6. Member States shall, within six months of the entry into force of the delegated act referred to in paragraph 4, notify to the Commission and to the other Member States:

(a) the national qualifications, and where applicable the national professional titles, that comply with the common training framework; or

(b) any use of the exemption referred to in paragraph 5, along with a justification of which conditions under that paragraph were fulfilled. The Commission may, within three months, request further clarification if it considers that a Member State has provided no or insufficient justification that one of these conditions has been fulfilled. The Member State shall reply within three months of any such request.

The Commission may adopt an implementing act to list the national professional qualifications and national professional titles benefiting from automatic recognition under the common training framework adopted in accordance with paragraph 4.

7. This Article also applies to specialties of a profession, provided such specialties concern professional activities the access to and the pursuit of which are regulated in Member States, where the profession is already subject to automatic recognition under Chapter III of Title III, but not the specialty concerned.

Article 49b Common training tests

1. For the purpose of this Article, a 'common training test' means a standardised aptitude test available across participating Member States and reserved to holders of a particular professional qualification. Passing such a test in a Member State shall entitle the holder of a particular professional qualification to pursue the profession in any host Member State concerned under the same conditions as the holders of professional qualifications acquired in that Member State.

2. The common training test shall comply with the following conditions:

(a) the common training test enables more professionals to move across Member States;

(b) the profession to which the common training test applies is regulated, or the education and training leading to the profession concerned is regulated in at least one third of the Member States;

(c) the common training test has been prepared following a transparent due process, including the relevant stakeholders from Member States where the profession is not regulated;

(d) the common training test permits nationals from any Member State to participate in such a test and in the practical organisation of such tests in Member States without first being required to be a member of any professional organisation or to be registered with such organisation.

3. Representative professional organisations at Union level, as well as national professional organisations or competent authorities from at least one third of the Member States, may submit to the Commission suggestions for common training tests which meet the conditions laid down in paragraph 2.

4. The Commission shall be empowered to adopt delegated acts in accordance with Article 57c to establish the contents of a common training test, and the conditions required for taking and passing the test.

5. A Member State shall be exempted from the obligation of organising the common training test referred to in paragraph 4 on its territory and from the obligation of granting automatic recognition to professionals who have passed the common training test if one of the following conditions is fulfilled:

(a) the profession concerned is not regulated on its territory;

(b) the contents of the common training test will not sufficiently mitigate serious risks for public health or the safety of the service recipients, which are relevant on its territory;

(c) the contents of the common training test would render access to the profession significantly less attractive compared to national requirements.

6. Member States shall, within six months of the entry into force of the delegated act referred to in paragraph 4, notify to the Commission and to the other Member States:

(a) the available capacity for organising such tests; or

(b) any use of the exemption referred to in paragraph 5, along with the justification of which conditions under that paragraph were fulfilled. The Commission may, within three months, request further clarification, if it considers that a Member State has provided no or insufficient justification that one of these conditions has been fulfilled. The Member State shall reply within three months of any such request.

The Commission may adopt an implementing act to list the Member States in which the common training tests adopted in accordance with paragraph 4 are to be organised, the frequency during a calendar year and other arrangements necessary for organising common training tests across Member States.

Chapter IV Common provisions on establishment

Article 50 Documentation and formalities

1. Where the competent authorities of the host Member State decide on an application for authorisation to pursue the regulated profession in question by virtue of this Title, those authorities may demand the documents and certificates listed in Annex VII.

The documents referred to in Annex VII, point 1(d), (e) and (f), shall not be more than three months old by the date on which they are submitted.

The Member States, bodies and other legal persons shall guarantee the confidentiality of the information which they receive.

2. In the event of justified doubts, the host Member State may require from the competent authorities of a Member State confirmation of the authenticity of the attestations and evidence of formal qualifications awarded in that other Member State, as well as, where applicable, confirmation of the fact that the beneficiary fulfils, for the professions referred to in Chapter III of this Title, the minimum training conditions set out respectively in Articles 24, 25, 28, 31, 34, 35, 38, 40, 44 and 46.

3. In cases of justified doubt, where evidence of formal qualifications, as defined in Article 3(1)(c), has been issued by a competent authority in a Member State and includes training received in whole or in part in an establishment legally established in the territory of another Member State, the host Member State shall be entitled to verify with the competent body in the Member State of origin of the award:

(a) whether the training course at the establishment which gave the training has been formally certified by the educational establishment based in the Member State of origin of the award;

(b) whether the evidence of formal qualifications issued is the same as that which would have been awarded if the course had been followed entirely in the Member State of origin of the award; and

(c) whether the evidence of formal qualifications confers the same professional rights in the territory of the Member State of origin of the award.

3a. In the event of justified doubts, the host Member State may require from the competent authorities of a Member State confirmation of the fact that the applicant is not suspended or prohibited from the pursuit of the profession as a result of serious professional misconduct or conviction of criminal offences relating to the pursuit of any of his professional activities.

3b. Exchange of information between competent authorities of different Member States under this Article shall take place via IMI.

4. Where a host Member State requires its nationals to swear a solemn oath or make a sworn statement in order to gain access to a regulated profession, and where the wording of that oath or

statement cannot be used by nationals of the other Member States, the host Member State shall ensure that the persons concerned can use an appropriate equivalent wording.

Article 51
Procedure for the mutual recognition of professional qualifications

1. The competent authority of the host Member State shall acknowledge receipt of the application within one month of receipt and inform the applicant of any missing document.

2. The procedure for examining an application for authorisation to practise a regulated profession must be completed as quickly as possible and lead to a duly substantiated decision by the competent authority in the host Member State in any case within three months after the date on which the applicant's complete file was submitted. However, this deadline may be extended by one month in cases falling under Chapters I and II of this Title.

3. The decision, or failure to reach a decision within the deadline, shall be subject to appeal under national law.

Article 52 Use of professional titles

1. If, in a host Member State, the use of a professional title relating to one of the activities of the profession in question is regulated, nationals of the other Member States who are authorised to practise a regulated profession on the basis of Title III shall use the professional title of the host Member State, which corresponds to that profession in that Member State, and make use of any associated initials.

2. Where a profession is regulated in the host Member State by an association or organisation within the meaning of Article 3(2), nationals of Member States shall not be authorised to use the professional title issued by that organisation or association, or its abbreviated form, unless they furnish proof that they are members of that association or organisation.

If the association or organisation makes membership contingent upon certain qualifications, it may do so, only under the conditions laid down in this Directive, in respect of nationals of other Member States who possess professional qualifications.

3. A Member State may not reserve the use of the professional title to the holders of professional qualifications if it has not notified the association or organisation to the Commission and to the other Member States in accordance with Article 3(2).

Title IV Detailed rules for pursuing the profession

Article 53 Knowledge of languages

1. Professionals benefiting from the recognition of professional qualifications shall have a knowledge of languages necessary for practising the profession in the host Member State.

2. A Member State shall ensure that any controls carried out by, or under the supervision of, the competent authority for controlling compliance with the obligation under paragraph 1 shall be limited to the knowledge of one official language of the host Member State, or one administrative language of the host Member State provided that it is also an official language of the Union.

3. Controls carried out in accordance with paragraph 2 may be imposed if the profession to be practised has patient safety implications. Controls may be imposed in respect of other professions in cases where there is a serious and concrete doubt about the sufficiency of the professional's language knowledge in respect of the professional activities that that professional intends to pursue.

Controls may be carried out only after the issuance of a European Professional Card in accordance with Article 4d or after the recognition of a professional qualification, as the case may be.

4. Any language controls shall be proportionate to the activity to be pursued. The professional concerned shall be allowed to appeal such controls under national law.

Article 54 Use of academic titles
Without prejudice to Articles 7 and 52, the host Member State shall ensure that the right shall be conferred on the persons concerned to use academic titles conferred on them in the home Member

State, and possibly an abbreviated form thereof, in the language of the home Member State. The host Member State may require that title to be followed by the name and address of the establishment or examining board which awarded it. Where an academic title of the home Member State is liable to be confused in the host Member State with a title which, in the latter Member State, requires supplementary training not acquired by the beneficiary, the host Member State may require the beneficiary to use the academic title of the home Member State in an appropriate form, to be laid down by the host Member State.

Article 55 Approval by health insurance funds

Without prejudice to Article 5(1) and Article 6, first subparagraph, point (b), Member States which require persons who acquired their professional qualifications in their territory to complete a preparatory period of in-service training and/or a period of professional experience in order to be approved by a health insurance fund, shall waive this obligation for the holders of evidence of professional qualifications of doctor and dental practitioner acquired in other Member States.

Article 55a Recognition of professional traineeship

1. If access to a regulated profession in the home Member State is contingent upon completion of a professional traineeship, the competent authority of the home Member State shall, when considering a request for authorisation to exercise the regulated profession, recognise professional traineeships carried out in another Member State provided the traineeship is in accordance with the published guidelines referred to in paragraph 2, and shall take into account professional traineeships carried out in a third country. However, Member States may, in national legislation, set a reasonable limit on the duration of the part of the professional traineeship which can be carried out abroad.

2. Recognition of the professional traineeship shall not replace any requirements in place to pass an examination in order to gain access to the profession in question. The competent authorities shall publish guidelines on the organisation and recognition of professional traineeships carried out in another Member State or in a third country, in particular on the role of the supervisor of the professional traineeship.

Title V Administrative cooperation and responsibility for implementation

Article 56 Competent authorities

1. The competent authorities of the host Member State and of the home Member State shall work in close collaboration and shall provide mutual assistance in order to facilitate application of this Directive. They shall ensure the confidentiality of the information which they exchange.

2. The competent authorities of the home and the host Member States shall exchange information regarding disciplinary action or criminal sanctions taken or any other serious, specific circumstances which are likely to have consequences for the pursuit of activities under this Directive. In so doing, they shall respect personal data protection rules provided for in Directives 95/46/EC and 2002/58/EC.

The home Member State shall examine the veracity of the circumstances and its authorities shall decide on the nature and scope of the investigations which need to be carried out and shall inform the host Member State of the conclusions which it draws from the information available to it.

2a. For the purposes of paragraphs 1 and 2, the competent authorities shall use IMI.

3. Each Member State shall, no later than 20 October 2007, designate the authorities and bodies competent to award or receive evidence of formal qualifications and other documents or information, and those competent to receive applications and take the decisions referred to in this Directive, and shall forthwith inform the other Member States and the Commission thereof.

4. Each Member State shall designate a coordinator for the activities of the competent authorities referred to in paragraph 1 and shall inform other Member States and the Commission thereof.

The coordinators' tasks shall be:

(a) to promote uniform application of this Directive;
(b) to collect all the information which is relevant for application of this Directive, such as on the conditions for access to regulated professions in the Member States;
(c) to examine suggestions for common training frameworks and common training tests;
(d) to exchange information and best practice for the purpose of optimising continuous professional development in Member States;
(e) to exchange information and best practice on the application of compensation measures referred to in Article 14.

For the purpose of carrying out the task set out in point (b) of this paragraph, the coordinators may solicit the help of the assistance centres referred to in Article 57b.

. . .

Done at Strasbourg, 7 September 2005.

Directive 2006/123/EC of the European Parliament and of the Council of 12 December 2006 on services in the internal market

[OJ 2006 L376/36]

Chapter I General provisions

Article 1 Subject matter

1. This Directive establishes general provisions facilitating the exercise of the freedom of establishment for service providers and the free movement of services, while maintaining a high quality of services.

2. This Directive does not deal with the liberalisation of services of general economic interest, reserved to public or private entities, nor with the privatisation of public entities providing services.

3. This Directive does not deal with the abolition of monopolies providing services nor with aids granted by Member States which are covered by Community rules on competition.

This Directive does not affect the freedom of Member States to define, in conformity with Community law, what they consider to be services of general economic interest, how those services should be organised and financed, in compliance with the State aid rules, and what specific obligations they should be subject to.

4. This Directive does not affect measures taken at Community level or at national level, in conformity with Community law, to protect or promote cultural or linguistic diversity or media pluralism.

5. This Directive does not affect Member States' rules of criminal law. However, Member States may not restrict the freedom to provide services by applying criminal law provisions which specifically regulate or affect access to or exercise of a service activity in circumvention of the rules laid down in this Directive.

6. This Directive does not affect labour law, that is any legal or contractual provision concerning employment conditions, working conditions, including health and safety at work and the relationship between employers and workers, which Member States apply in accordance with national law which respects Community law. Equally, this Directive does not affect the social security legislation of the Member States.

7. This Directive does not affect the exercise of fundamental rights as recognised in the Member States and by Community law. Nor does it affect the right to negotiate, conclude and enforce collective agreements and to take industrial action in accordance with national law and practices which respect Community law.

Article 2 Scope

1. This Directive shall apply to services supplied by providers established in a Member State.

2. This Directive shall not apply to the following activities:
   (a) non-economic services of general interest;
   (b) financial services, such as banking, credit, insurance and re-insurance, occupational or personal pensions, securities, investment funds, payment and investment advice, including the services listed in Annex I to Directive 2006/48/EC;
   (c) electronic communications services and networks, and associated facilities and services, with respect to matters covered by Directives 2002/19/EC, 2002/20/EC, 2002/21/EC, 2002/22/EC and 2002/58/EC;
   (d) services in the field of transport, including port services, falling within the scope of Title V of the Treaty;
   (e) services of temporary work agencies;
   (f) healthcare services whether or not they are provided via healthcare facilities, and regardless of the ways in which they are organised and financed at national level or whether they are public or private;
   (g) audiovisual services, including cinematographic services, whatever their mode of production, distribution and transmission, and radio broadcasting;
   (h) gambling activities which involve wagering a stake with pecuniary value in games of chance, including lotteries, gambling in casinos and betting transactions;
   (i) activities which are connected with the exercise of official authority as set out in Article 45 of the Treaty;
   (j) social services relating to social housing, childcare and support of families and persons permanently or temporarily in need which are provided by the State, by providers mandated by the State or by charities recognised as such by the State;
   (k) private security services;
   (l) services provided by notaries and bailiffs, who are appointed by an official act of government.

3. This Directive shall not apply to the field of taxation.

Article 3 Relationship with other provisions of Community law

1. If the provisions of this Directive conflict with a provision of another Community act governing specific aspects of access to or exercise of a service activity in specific sectors or for specific professions, the provision of the other Community act shall prevail and shall apply to those specific sectors or professions. These include:
   (a) Directive 96/71/EC;
   (b) Regulation (EEC) No 1408/71;
   (c) Council Directive 89/552/EEC of 3 October 1989 on the coordination of certain provisions laid down by law, regulation or administrative action in Member States concerning the pursuit of television broadcasting activities;[1]
   (d) Directive 2005/36/EC.

2. This Directive does not concern rules of private international law, in particular rules governing the law applicable to contractual and non contractual obligations, including those which guarantee that consumers benefit from the protection granted to them by the consumer protection rules laid down in the consumer legislation in force in their Member State.

3. Member States shall apply the provisions of this Directive in compliance with the rules of the Treaty on the right of establishment and the free movement of services.

Article 4 Definitions

For the purposes of this Directive, the following definitions shall apply:

1) 'service' means any self-employed economic activity, normally provided for remuneration, as referred to in Article 50 of the Treaty;

2) 'provider' means any natural person who is a national of a Member State, or any legal person as referred to in Article 48 of the Treaty and established in a Member State, who offers or provides a service;

[1] OJ L 298, 17.10.1989, p. 23. Directive as amended by Directive 97/36/EC of the European Parliament and of the Council (OJ L 202, 30.7.1997, p. 60).

3) 'recipient' means any natural person who is a national of a Member State or who benefits from rights conferred upon him by Community acts, or any legal person as referred to in Article 48 of the Treaty and established in a Member State, who, for professional or non-professional purposes, uses, or wishes to use, a service;

4) 'Member State of establishment' means the Member State in whose territory the provider of the service concerned is established;

5) 'establishment' means the actual pursuit of an economic activity, as referred to in Article 43 of the Treaty, by the provider for an indefinite period and through a stable infrastructure from where the business of providing services is actually carried out;

6) 'authorisation scheme' means any procedure under which a provider or recipient is in effect required to take steps in order to obtain from a competent authority a formal decision, or an implied decision, concerning access to a service activity or the exercise thereof;

7) 'requirement' means any obligation, prohibition, condition or limit provided for in the laws, regulations or administrative provisions of the Member States or in consequence of case-law, administrative practice, the rules of professional bodies, or the collective rules of professional associations or other professional organisations, adopted in the exercise of their legal autonomy; rules laid down in collective agreements negotiated by the social partners shall not as such be seen as requirements within the meaning of this Directive;

8) 'overriding reasons relating to the public interest' means reasons recognised as such in the case law of the Court of Justice, including the following grounds: public policy; public security; public safety; public health; preserving the financial equilibrium of the social security system; the protection of consumers, recipients of services and workers; fairness of trade transactions; combating fraud; the protection of the environment and the urban environment; the health of animals; intellectual property; the conservation of the national historic and artistic heritage; social policy objectives and cultural policy objectives;

9) 'competent authority' means any body or authority which has a supervisory or regulatory role in a Member State in relation to service activities, including, in particular, administrative authorities, including courts acting as such, professional bodies, and those professional associations or other professional organisations which, in the exercise of their legal autonomy, regulate in a collective manner access to service activities or the exercise thereof;

10) 'Member State where the service is provided' means the Member State where the service is supplied by a provider established in another Member State;

11) 'regulated profession' means a professional activity or a group of professional activities as referred to in Article 3(1)(a) of Directive 2005/36/EC;

12) 'commercial communication' means any form of communication designed to promote, directly or indirectly, the goods, services or image of an undertaking, organisation or person engaged in commercial, industrial or craft activity or practising a regulated profession. The following do not in themselves constitute commercial communications:

(a) information enabling direct access to the activity of the undertaking, organisation or person, including in particular a domain name or an electronic-mailing address;

(b) communications relating to the goods, services or image of the undertaking, organisation or person, compiled in an independent manner, particularly when provided for no financial consideration.

Chapter II Administrative simplification

Article 5 Simplification of procedures

1. Member States shall examine the procedures and formalities applicable to access to a service activity and to the exercise thereof. Where procedures and formalities examined under this paragraph are not sufficiently simple, Member States shall simplify them.

2. The Commission may introduce harmonised forms at Community level, in accordance with the procedure referred to in Article 40(2). These forms shall be equivalent to certificates, attestations and any other documents required of a provider.

3. Where Member States require a provider or recipient to supply a certificate, attestation or any other document proving that a requirement has been satisfied, they shall accept any document from another Member State which serves an equivalent purpose or from which it is clear that the requirement in question has been satisfied. They may not require a document from another Member State to be produced in its original form, or as a certified copy or as a certified translation, save in the cases provided for in other Community instruments or where such a requirement is justified by an overriding reason relating to the public interest, including public order and security.

The first subparagraph shall not affect the right of Member States to require non-certified translations of documents in one of their official languages.

4. Paragraph 3 shall not apply to the documents referred to in Article 7(2) and 50 of Directive 2005/36/EC, in Articles 45(3), 46, 49 and 50 of Directive 2004/18/EC of the European Parliament and of the Council of 31 March 2004 on the coordination of procedures for the award of public works contracts, public supply contracts and public service contracts,[2] in Article 3(2) of Directive 98/5/EC of the European Parliament and of the Council of 16 February 1998 to facilitate practice of the profession of lawyer on a permanent basis in a Member State other than that in which the qualification was obtained,[3] in the First Council Directive 68/151/EEC of 9 March 1968 on coordination of safeguards which, for the protection of the interests of members and others, are required by Member States of companies within the meaning of the second paragraph of Article 58 of the Treaty, with a view to making such safeguards equivalent throughout the Community[4] and in the Eleventh Council Directive 89/666/EEC of 21 December 1989 concerning disclosure requirements in respect of branches opened in a Member State by certain types of company governed by the law of another State.[5]

Article 6 Points of single contact

1. Member States shall ensure that it is possible for providers to complete the following procedures and formalities through points of single contact:

(a) all procedures and formalities needed for access to his service activities, in particular, all declarations, notifications or applications necessary for authorisation from the competent authorities, including applications for inclusion in a register, a roll or a database, or for registration with a professional body or association;

(b) any applications for authorisation needed to exercise his service activities.

2. The establishment of points of single contact shall be without prejudice to the allocation of functions and powers among the authorities within national systems.

Article 7 Right to information

1. Member States shall ensure that the following information is easily accessible to providers and recipients through the points of single contact:

(a) requirements applicable to providers established in their territory, in particular those requirements concerning the procedures and formalities to be completed in order to access and to exercise service activities;

(b) the contact details of the competent authorities enabling the latter to be contacted directly, including the details of those authorities responsible for matters concerning the exercise of service activities;

(c) the means of, and conditions for, accessing public registers and databases on providers and services;

(d) the means of redress which are generally available in the event of dispute between the competent authorities and the provider or the recipient, or between a provider and a recipient or between providers;

[2] OJ L 134, 30.4.2004, p. 114. Directive as last amended by Commission Regulation (EC) No 2083/2005 (OJ L 333, 20.12.2005, p. 28).

[3] OJ L 77, 14.3.1998, p. 36. Directive as amended by the Act of Accession.

[4] OJ L 65, 14.3.1968, p. 8. Directive as last amended by Directive/58/EC of the European Parliament and of the Council (OJ L 221, 4.9.2003, p. 13).

[5] OJ L 395, 30.12.1989, p. 36.

(e) the contact details of the associations or organisations, other than the competent authorities, from which providers or recipients may obtain practical assistance.

2. Member States shall ensure that it is possible for providers and recipients to receive, at their request, assistance from the competent authorities, consisting in information on the way in which the requirements referred to in point (a) of paragraph 1 are generally interpreted and applied. Where appropriate, such advice shall include a simple step-by-step guide. The information shall be provided in plain and intelligible language.

3. Member States shall ensure that the information and assistance referred to in paragraphs 1 and 2 are provided in a clear and unambiguous manner, that they are easily accessible at a distance and by electronic means and that they are kept up to date.

4. Member States shall ensure that the points of single contact and the competent authorities respond as quickly as possible to any request for information or assistance as referred to in paragraphs 1 and 2 and, in cases where the request is faulty or unfounded, inform the applicant accordingly without delay.

5. Member States and the Commission shall take accompanying measures in order to encourage points of single contact to make the information provided for in this Article available in other Community languages. This does not interfere with Member States' legislation on the use of languages.

6. The obligation for competent authorities to assist providers and recipients does not require those authorities to provide legal advice in individual cases but concerns only general information on the way in which requirements are usually interpreted or applied.

Article 8 Procedures by electronic means

1. Member States shall ensure that all procedures and formalities relating to access to a service activity and to the exercise thereof may be easily completed, at a distance and by electronic means, through the relevant point of single contact and with the relevant competent authorities.

2. Paragraph 1 shall not apply to the inspection of premises on which the service is provided or of equipment used by the provider or to physical examination of the capability or of the personal integrity of the provider or of his responsible staff.

3. The Commission shall, in accordance with the procedure referred to in Article 40(2), adopt detailed rules for the implementation of paragraph 1 of this Article with a view to facilitating the interoperability of information systems and use of procedures by electronic means between Member States, taking into account common standards developed at Community level.

Chapter III Freedom of establishment for providers

Section 1 Authorisations

Article 9 Authorisation schemes

1. Member States shall not make access to a service activity or the exercise thereof subject to an authorisation scheme unless the following conditions are satisfied:

(a) the authorisation scheme does not discriminate against the provider in question;

(b) the need for an authorisation scheme is justified by an overriding reason relating to the public interest;

(c) the objective pursued cannot be attained by means of a less restrictive measure, in particular because an a posteriori inspection would take place too late to be genuinely effective.

2. In the report referred to in Article 39(1), Member States shall identify their authorisation schemes and give reasons showing their compatibility with paragraph 1 of this Article.

3. This section shall not apply to those aspects of authorisation schemes which are governed directly or indirectly by other Community instruments.

Article 10 Conditions for the granting of authorisation

1. Authorisation schemes shall be based on criteria which preclude the competent authorities from exercising their power of assessment in an arbitrary manner.

2. The criteria referred to in paragraph 1 shall be:

(a) non-discriminatory;
(b) justified by an overriding reason relating to the public interest;
(c) proportionate to that public interest objective;
(d) clear and unambiguous;
(e) objective;
(f) made public in advance;
(g) transparent and accessible.

3. The conditions for granting authorisation for a new establishment shall not duplicate requirements and controls which are equivalent or essentially comparable as regards their purpose to which the provider is already subject in another Member State or in the same Member State. The liaison points referred to in Article 28(2) and the provider shall assist the competent authority by providing any necessary information regarding those requirements.

4. The authorisation shall enable the provider to have access to the service activity, or to exercise that activity, throughout the national territory, including by means of setting up agencies, subsidiaries, branches or offices, except where an authorisation for each individual establishment or a limitation of the authorisation to a certain part of the territory is justified by an overriding reason relating to the public interest.

5. The authorisation shall be granted as soon as it is established, in the light of an appropriate examination, that the conditions for authorisation have been met.

6. Except in the case of the granting of an authorisation, any decision from the competent authorities, including refusal or withdrawal of an authorisation, shall be fully reasoned and shall be open to challenge before the courts or other instances of appeal.

7. This Article shall not call into question the allocation of the competences, at local or regional level, of the Member States' authorities granting authorisations.

Article 11 Duration of authorisation

1. An authorisation granted to a provider shall not be for a limited period, except where:

(a) the authorisation is being automatically renewed or is subject only to the continued fulfilment of requirements;
(b) the number of available authorisations is limited by an overriding reason relating to the public interest; or
(c) a limited authorisation period can be justified by an overriding reason relating to the public interest.

2. Paragraph 1 shall not concern the maximum period before the end of which the provider must actually commence his activity after receiving authorisation.

3. Member States shall require a provider to inform the relevant point of single contact provided for in Article 6 of the following changes:

(a) the creation of subsidiaries whose activities fall within the scope of the authorisation scheme;
(b) changes in his situation which result in the conditions for authorisation no longer being met.

4. This Article shall be without prejudice to the Member States' ability to revoke authorisations, when the conditions for authorisation are no longer met.

Article 12 Selection from among several candidates

1. Where the number of authorisations available for a given activity is limited because of the scarcity of available natural resources or technical capacity, Member States shall apply a selection procedure to potential candidates which provides full guarantees of impartiality and transparency,

including, in particular, adequate publicity about the launch, conduct and completion of the procedure.

2. In the cases referred to in paragraph 1, authorisation shall be granted for an appropriate limited period and may not be open to automatic renewal nor confer any other advantage on the provider whose authorisation has just expired or on any person having any particular links with that provider.

3. Subject to paragraph 1 and to Articles 9 and 10, Member States may take into account, in establishing the rules for the selection procedure, considerations of public health, social policy objectives, the health and safety of employees or self-employed persons, the protection of the environment, the preservation of cultural heritage and other overriding reasons relating to the public interest, in conformity with Community law.

Article 13 Authorisation procedures

1. Authorisation procedures and formalities shall be clear, made public in advance and be such as to provide the applicants with a guarantee that their application will be dealt with objectively and impartially.

2. Authorisation procedures and formalities shall not be dissuasive and shall not unduly complicate or delay the provision of the service. They shall be easily accessible and any charges which the applicants may incur from their application shall be reasonable and proportionate to the cost of the authorisation procedures in question and shall not exceed the cost of the procedures.

3. Authorisation procedures and formalities shall provide applicants with a guarantee that their application will be processed as quickly as possible and, in any event, within a reasonable period which is fixed and made public in advance. The period shall run only from the time when all documentation has been submitted. When justified by the complexity of the issue, the time period may be extended once, by the competent authority, for a limited time. The extension and its duration shall be duly motivated and shall be notified to the applicant before the original period has expired.

4. Failing a response within the time period set or extended in accordance with paragraph 3, authorisation shall be deemed to have been granted. Different arrangements may nevertheless be put in place, where justified by overriding reasons relating to the public interest, including a legitimate interest of third parties.

5. All applications for authorisation shall be acknowledged as quickly as possible. The acknowledgement must specify the following:

(a) the period referred to in paragraph 3;
(b) the available means of redress;
(c) where applicable, a statement that in the absence of a response within the period specified, the authorisation shall be deemed to have been granted.

6. In the case of an incomplete application, the applicant shall be informed as quickly as possible of the need to supply any additional documentation, as well as of any possible effects on the period referred to in paragraph 3.

7. When a request is rejected because it fails to comply with the required procedures or formalities, the applicant shall be informed of the rejection as quickly as possible.

Section 2 Requirements prohibited or subject to evaluation

Article 14 Prohibited requirements

Member States shall not make access to, or the exercise of, a service activity in their territory subject to compliance with any of the following:

1) discriminatory requirements based directly or indirectly on nationality or, in the case of companies, the location of the registered office, including in particular:

(a) nationality requirements for the provider, his staff, persons holding the share capital or members of the provider's management or supervisory bodies;
(b) a requirement that the provider, his staff, persons holding the share capital or members of the provider's management or supervisory bodies be resident within the territory;

2) a prohibition on having an establishment in more than one Member State or on being entered in the registers or enrolled with professional bodies or associations of more than one Member State;

3) restrictions on the freedom of a provider to choose between a principal or a secondary establishment, in particular an obligation on the provider to have its principal establishment in their territory, or restrictions on the freedom to choose between establishment in the form of an agency, branch or subsidiary;

4) conditions of reciprocity with the Member State in which the provider already has an establishment, save in the case of conditions of reciprocity provided for in Community instruments concerning energy;

5) the case-by-case application of an economic test making the granting of authorisation subject to proof of the existence of an economic need or market demand, an assessment of the potential or current economic effects of the activity or an assessment of the appropriateness of the activity in relation to the economic planning objectives set by the competent authority; this prohibition shall not concern planning requirements which do not pursue economic aims but serve overriding reasons relating to the public interest;

6) the direct or indirect involvement of competing operators, including within consultative bodies, in the granting of authorisations or in the adoption of other decisions of the competent authorities, with the exception of professional bodies and associations or other organisations acting as the competent authority; this prohibition shall not concern the consultation of organisations, such as chambers of commerce or social partners, on matters other than individual applications for authorisation, or a consultation of the public at large;

7) an obligation to provide or participate in a financial guarantee or to take out insurance from a provider or body established in their territory. This shall not affect the possibility for Member States to require insurance or financial guarantees as such, nor shall it affect requirements relating to the participation in a collective compensation fund, for instance for members of professional bodies or organisations;

8) an obligation to have been pre-registered, for a given period, in the registers held in their territory or to have previously exercised the activity for a given period in their territory.

Article 15 Requirements to be evaluated

1. Member States shall examine whether, under their legal system, any of the requirements listed in paragraph 2 are imposed and shall ensure that any such requirements are compatible with the conditions laid down in paragraph 3. Member States shall adapt their laws, regulations or administrative provisions so as to make them compatible with those conditions.

2. Member States shall examine whether their legal system makes access to a service activity or the exercise of it subject to compliance with any of the following non-discriminatory requirements:

(a) quantitative or territorial restrictions, in particular in the form of limits fixed according to population or of a minimum geographical distance between providers;
(b) an obligation on a provider to take a specific legal form;
(c) requirements which relate to the shareholding of a company;
(d) requirements, other than those concerning matters covered by Directive 2005/36/EC or provided for in other Community instruments, which reserve access to the service activity in question to particular providers by virtue of the specific nature of the activity;
(e) a ban on having more than one establishment in the territory of the same State;
(f) requirements fixing a minimum number of employees;
(g) fixed minimum and/or maximum tariffs with which the provider must comply;
(h) an obligation on the provider to supply other specific services jointly with his service.

3. Member States shall verify that the requirements referred to in paragraph 2 satisfy the following conditions:

(a) non-discrimination: requirements must be neither directly nor indirectly discriminatory according to nationality nor, with regard to companies, according to the location of the registered office;

(b) necessity: requirements must be justified by an overriding reason relating to the public interest;
(c) proportionality: requirements must be suitable for securing the attainment of the objective pursued; they must not go beyond what is necessary to attain that objective and it must not be possible to replace those requirements with other, less restrictive measures which attain the same result.

4. Paragraphs 1, 2 and 3 shall apply to legislation in the field of services of general economic interest only insofar as the application of these paragraphs does not obstruct the performance, in law or in fact, of the particular task assigned to them.

5. In the mutual evaluation report provided for in Article 39(1), Member States shall specify the following:

(a) the requirements that they intend to maintain and the reasons why they consider that those requirements comply with the conditions set out in paragraph 3;
(b) the requirements which have been abolished or made less stringent.

6. From 28 December 2006 Member States shall not introduce any new requirement of a kind listed in paragraph 2, unless that requirement satisfies the conditions laid down in paragraph 3.

7. Member States shall notify the Commission of any new laws, regulations or administrative provisions which set requirements as referred to in paragraph 6, together with the reasons for those requirements. The Commission shall communicate the provisions concerned to the other Member States. Such notification shall not prevent Member States from adopting the provisions in question.

Within a period of 3 months from the date of receipt of the notification, the Commission shall examine the compatibility of any new requirements with Community law and, where appropriate, shall adopt a decision requesting the Member State in question to refrain from adopting them or to abolish them.

The notification of a draft national law in accordance with Directive 98/34/EC shall fulfil the obligation of notification provided for in this Directive.

Chapter IV Free movement of services

Section 1 Freedom to provide services and related derogations

Article 16 Freedom to provide services

1. Member States shall respect the right of providers to provide services in a Member State other than that in which they are established.

The Member State in which the service is provided shall ensure free access to and free exercise of a service activity within its territory.

Member States shall not make access to or exercise of a service activity in their territory subject to compliance with any requirements which do not respect the following principles:

(a) non-discrimination: the requirement may be neither directly nor indirectly discriminatory with regard to nationality or, in the case of legal persons, with regard to the Member State in which they are established;
(b) necessity: the requirement must be justified for reasons of public policy, public security, public health or the protection of the environment;
(c) proportionality: the requirement must be suitable for attaining the objective pursued, and must not go beyond what is necessary to attain that objective.

2. Member States may not restrict the freedom to provide services in the case of a provider established in another Member State by imposing any of the following requirements:

(a) an obligation on the provider to have an establishment in their territory;
(b) an obligation on the provider to obtain an authorisation from their competent authorities including entry in a register or registration with a professional body or association in their territory, except where provided for in this Directive or other instruments of Community law;

(c) a ban on the provider setting up a certain form or type of infrastructure in their territory, including an office or chambers, which the provider needs in order to supply the services in question;
(d) the application of specific contractual arrangements between the provider and the recipient which prevent or restrict service provision by the self-employed;
(e) an obligation on the provider to possess an identity document issued by its competent authorities specific to the exercise of a service activity;
(f) requirements, except for those necessary for health and safety at work, which affect the use of equipment and material which are an integral part of the service provided;
(g) restrictions on the freedom to provide the services referred to in Article 19.

3. The Member State to which the provider moves shall not be prevented from imposing requirements with regard to the provision of a service activity, where they are justified for reasons of public policy, public security, public health or the protection of the environment and in accordance with paragraph 1. Nor shall that Member State be prevented from applying, in accordance with Community law, its rules on employment conditions, including those laid down in collective agreements.

4. By 28 December 2011 the Commission shall, after consultation of the Member States and the social partners at Community level, submit to the European Parliament and the Council a report on the application of this Article, in which it shall consider the need to propose harmonisation measures regarding service activities covered by this Directive.

Article 17 Additional derogations from the freedom to provide services

Article 16 shall not apply to:

1) services of general economic interest which are provided in another Member State, inter alia:
(a) in the postal sector, services covered by Directive 97/67/EC of the European Parliament and of the Council of 15 December 1997 on common rules for the development of the internal market of Community postal services and the improvement of quality of service;[6]
(b) in the electricity sector, services covered by Directive/54/EC[7] of the European Parliament and of the Council of 26 June concerning common rules for the internal market in electricity;
(c) in the gas sector, services covered by Directive/55/EC of the European Parliament and of the Council of 26 June concerning common rules for the internal market in natural gas;[8]
(d) water distribution and supply services and waste water services;
(e) treatment of waste;

2) matters covered by Directive 96/71/EC;

3) matters covered by Directive 95/46/EC of the European Parliament and of the Council of 24 October 1995 on the protection of individuals with regard to the processing of personal data and on the free movement of such data;[9]

4) matters covered by Council Directive 77/249/EEC of 22 March 1977 to facilitate the effective exercise by lawyers of freedom to provide services;[10]

5) the activity of judicial recovery of debts;

6) matters covered by Title II of Directive 2005/36/EC, as well as requirements in the Member State where the service is provided which reserve an activity to a particular profession;

7) matters covered by Regulation (EEC) No 1408/71;

[6] 6 OJ L 15, 21.1.1998, p. 14. Directive as last amended by Regulation (EC) No 1882/2003 (OJ L 284, 31.10.2003, p. 1).
[7] OJ L 176, 15.7.2003, p. 37. Directive as last amended by Commission Decision 2006/653/EC (OJ L 270, 29.9.2006, p. 72).
[8] OJ L 176, 15.7.2003, p. 57.
[9] OJ L 281, 23.11.1995, p. 31. Directive as amended by Regulation (EC) No 1882/2003.
[10] OJ L 78, 26.3.1977, p. 17. Directive as last amended by the Act of Accession.

8) as regards administrative formalities concerning the free movement of persons and their residence, matters covered by the provisions of Directive 2004/38/EC that lay down administrative formalities of the competent authorities of the Member State where the service is provided with which beneficiaries must comply;

9) as regards third country nationals who move to another Member State in the context of the provision of a service, the possibility for Member States to require visa or residence permits for third country nationals who are not covered by the mutual recognition regime provided for in Article 21 of the Convention implementing the Schengen Agreement of 14 June 1985 on the gradual abolition of checks at the common borders[11] or the possibility to oblige third country nationals to report to the competent authorities of the Member State in which the service is provided on or after their entry;

10) as regards the shipment of waste, matters covered by Council Regulation (EEC) No 259/93 of 1 February 1993 on the supervision and control of shipments of waste within, into and out of the European Community;[12]

11) copyright, neighbouring rights and rights covered by Council Directive 87/54/EEC of 16 December 1986 on the legal protection of topographies of semiconductor products[13] and by Directive 96/9/EC of the European Parliament and of the Council of 11 March 1996 on the legal protection of databases,[14] as well as industrial property rights;

12) acts requiring by law the involvement of a notary;

13) matters covered by Directive 2006/43/EC of the European Parliament and of the Council of 17 May 2006 on statutory audit of annual accounts and consolidated accounts;[15]

14) the registration of vehicles leased in another Member State;

15) provisions regarding contractual and non-contractual obligations, including the form of contracts, determined pursuant to the rules of private international law.

Article 18 Case-by-case derogations

1. By way of derogation from Article 16, and in exceptional circumstances only, a Member State may, in respect of a provider established in another Member State, take measures relating to the safety of services.

2. The measures provided for in paragraph 1 may be taken only if the mutual assistance procedure laid down in Article 35 is complied with and the following conditions are fulfilled:

(a) the national provisions in accordance with which the measure is taken have not been subject to Community harmonisation in the field of the safety of services;

(b) the measures provide for a higher level of protection of the recipient than would be the case in a measure taken by the Member State of establishment in accordance with its national provisions;

(c) the Member State of establishment has not taken any measures or has taken measures which are insufficient as compared with those referred to in Article 35(2);

(d) the measures are proportionate.

3. Paragraphs 1 and 2 shall be without prejudice to provisions, laid down in Community instruments, which guarantee the freedom to provide services or which allow derogations therefrom.

Section 2 Rights of recipients of services

Article 19 Prohibited restrictions

Member States may not impose on a recipient requirements which restrict the use of a service supplied by a provider established in another Member State, in particular the following requirements:

(a) an obligation to obtain authorisation from or to make a declaration to their competent authorities;

[11] OJ L 239, 22.9.2000, p. 19. Convention as last amended by Regulation (EC) No 1160/2005 of the European Parliament and of the Council (OJ L 191, 22.7.2005, p. 18).

[12] OJ L 30, 6.2.1993, p. 1. Regulation as last amended by Commission Regulation (EC) No 2557/2001 (OJ L 349, 31.12.2001, p. 1).

[13] OJ L 24, 27.1.1987, p. 36. [14] OJ L 77, 27.3.1996, p. 20. [15] OJ L 157, 9.6.2006, p. 87.

(b) discriminatory limits on the grant of financial assistance by reason of the fact that the provider is established in another Member State or by reason of the location of the place at which the service is provided.

Article 20 Non-discrimination

1. Member States shall ensure that the recipient is not made subject to discriminatory requirements based on his nationality or place of residence.

2. Member States shall ensure that the general conditions of access to a service, which are made available to the public at large by the provider, do not contain discriminatory provisions relating to the nationality or place of residence of the recipient, but without precluding the possibility of providing for differences in the conditions of access where those differences are directly justified by objective criteria.

Article 21 Assistance for recipients

1. Member States shall ensure that recipients can obtain, in their Member State of residence, the following information:

(a) general information on the requirements applicable in other Member States relating to access to, and exercise of, service activities, in particular those relating to consumer protection;

(b) general information on the means of redress available in the case of a dispute between a provider and a recipient;

(c) the contact details of associations or organisations, including the centres of the European Consumer Centres Network, from which providers or recipients may obtain practical assistance.

Where appropriate, advice from the competent authorities shall include a simple step-by-step guide. Information and assistance shall be provided in a clear and unambiguous manner, shall be easily accessible at a distance, including by electronic means, and shall be kept up to date.

2. Member States may confer responsibility for the task referred to in paragraph 1 on points of single contact or on any other body, such as the centres of the European Consumer Centres Network, consumer associations or Euro Info Centres.

Member States shall communicate to the Commission the names and contact details of the designated bodies. The Commission shall transmit them to all Member States.

3. In fulfilment of the requirements set out in paragraphs 1 and 2, the body approached by the recipient shall, if necessary, contact the relevant body for the Member State concerned. The latter shall send the information requested as soon as possible to the requesting body which shall forward the information to the recipient. Member States shall ensure that those bodies give each other mutual assistance and shall put in place all possible measures for effective cooperation. Together with the Commission, Member States shall put in place practical arrangements necessary for the implementation of paragraph 1.

4. The Commission shall, in accordance with the procedure referred to in Article 40(2), adopt measures for the implementation of paragraphs 1, 2 and 3 of this Article, specifying the technical mechanisms for the exchange of information between the bodies of the various Member States and, in particular, the interoperability of information systems, taking into account common standards.

Chapter V Quality of services

Article 22 Information on providers and their services

1. Member States shall ensure that providers make the following information available to the recipient:

(a) the name of the provider, his legal status and form, the geographic address at which he is established and details enabling him to be contacted rapidly and communicated with directly and, as the case may be, by electronic means;

(b) where the provider is registered in a trade or other similar public register, the name of that register and the provider's registration number, or equivalent means of identification in that register;
(c) where the activity is subject to an authorisation scheme, the particulars of the relevant competent authority or the single point of contact;
(d) where the provider exercises an activity which is subject to VAT, the identification number referred to in Article 22(1) of Sixth Council Directive 77/388/EEC of 17 May 1977 on the harmonisation of the laws of the Member States relating to turnover taxes—Common system of value added tax: uniform basis of assessment;[16]
(e) in the case of the regulated professions, any professional body or similar institution with which the provider is registered, the professional title and the Member State in which that title has been granted;
(f) the general conditions and clauses, if any, used by the provider;
(g) the existence of contractual clauses, if any, used by the provider concerning the law applicable to the contract and/or the competent courts;
(h) the existence of an after-sales guarantee, if any, not imposed by law;
(i) the price of the service, where a price is pre-determined by the provider for a given type of service;
(j) the main features of the service, if not already apparent from the context;
(k) the insurance or guarantees referred to in Article 23(1), and in particular the contact details of the insurer or guarantor and the territorial coverage.

2. Member States shall ensure that the information referred to in paragraph 1, according to the provider's preference:
(a) is supplied by the provider on his own initiative;
(b) is easily accessible to the recipient at the place where the service is provided or the contract concluded;
(c) can be easily accessed by the recipient electronically by means of an address supplied by the provider;
(d) appears in any information documents supplied to the recipient by the provider which set out a detailed description of the service he provides.

3. Member States shall ensure that, at the recipient's request, providers supply the following additional information:
(a) where the price is not pre-determined by the provider for a given type of service, the price of the service or, if an exact price cannot be given, the method for calculating the price so that it can be checked by the recipient, or a sufficiently detailed estimate;
(b) as regards the regulated professions, a reference to the professional rules applicable in the Member State of establishment and how to access them;
(c) information on their multidisciplinary activities and partnerships which are directly linked to the service in question and on the measures taken to avoid conflicts of interest. That information shall be included in any information document in which providers give a detailed description of their services;
(d) any codes of conduct to which the provider is subject and the address at which these codes may be consulted by electronic means, specifying the language version available;
(e) where a provider is subject to a code of conduct, or member of a trade association or professional body which provides for recourse to a non-judicial means of dispute settlement, information in this respect. The provider shall specify how to access detailed information on the characteristics of, and conditions for, the use of non-judicial means of dispute settlement.

[16] OJ L 145, 13.6.1977, p. 1. Directive as last amended by Directive 2006/18/EC (OJ L 51, 22.2.2006, p. 12).

4. Member States shall ensure that the information which a provider must supply in accordance with this Chapter is made available or communicated in a clear and unambiguous manner, and in good time before conclusion of the contract or, where there is no written contract, before the service is provided.

5. The information requirements laid down in this Chapter are in addition to requirements already provided for in Community law and do not prevent Member States from imposing additional information requirements applicable to providers established in their territory.

6. The Commission may, in accordance with the procedure referred to in Article 40(2), specify the content of the information provided for in paragraphs 1 and 3 of this Article according to the specific nature of certain activities and may specify the practical means of implementing paragraph 2 of this Article.

Article 23 Professional liability insurance and guarantees

1. Member States may ensure that providers whose services present a direct and particular risk to the health or safety of the recipient or a third person, or to the financial security of the recipient, subscribe to professional liability insurance appropriate to the nature and extent of the risk, or provide a guarantee or similar arrangement which is equivalent or essentially comparable as regards its purpose.

2. When a provider establishes himself in their territory, Member States may not require professional liability insurance or a guarantee from the provider where he is already covered by a guarantee which is equivalent, or essentially comparable with regard to its purpose and the cover it provides in terms of the insured risk, the insured sum or a ceiling for the guarantee and possible exclusions from the cover, in another Member State in which the provider is already established. Where equivalence is only partial, Member States may require a supplementary guarantee to cover those aspects not already covered.

When a Member State requires a provider established in its territory to subscribe to professional liability insurance or to provide another guarantee, that Member State shall accept as sufficient evidence attestations of such insurance cover issued by credit institutions and insurers established in other Member States.

3. Paragraphs 1 and 2 shall not affect professional insurance or guarantee arrangements provided for in other Community instruments.

4. For the implementation of paragraph 1, the Commission may, in accordance with the regulatory procedure referred to in Article 40(2), establish a list of services which exhibit the characteristics referred to in paragraph 1 of this Article. The Commission may also, in accordance with the procedure referred to in Article 40(3), adopt measures designed to amend non-essential elements of this Directive by supplementing it by establishing common criteria for defining, for the purposes of the insurance or guarantees referred to in paragraph 1 of this Article, what is appropriate to the nature and extent of the risk.

5. For the purpose of this Article

- 'direct and particular risk' means a risk arising directly from the provision of the service,
- 'health and safety' means, in relation to a recipient or a third person, the prevention of death or serious personal injury,
- 'financial security' means, in relation to a recipient, the prevention of substantial losses of money or of value of property,
- 'professional liability insurance' means insurance taken out by a provider in respect of potential liabilities to recipients and, where applicable, third parties arising out of the provision of the service.

Article 24 Commercial communications by the regulated professions

1. Member States shall remove all total prohibitions on commercial communications by the regulated professions.

2. Member States shall ensure that commercial communications by the regulated professions comply with professional rules, in conformity with Community law, which relate, in particular, to

the independence, dignity and integrity of the profession, as well as to professional secrecy, in a manner consistent with the specific nature of each profession. Professional rules on commercial communications shall be non-discriminatory, justified by an overriding reason relating to the public interest and proportionate.

Article 25 Multidisciplinary activities

1. Member States shall ensure that providers are not made subject to requirements which oblige them to exercise a given specific activity exclusively or which restrict the exercise jointly or in partnership of different activities.

However, the following providers may be made subject to such requirements:

(a) the regulated professions, in so far as is justified in order to guarantee compliance with the rules governing professional ethics and conduct, which vary according to the specific nature of each profession, and is necessary in order to ensure their independence and impartiality;

(b) providers of certification, accreditation, technical monitoring, test or trial services, in so far as is justified in order to ensure their independence and impartiality.

2. Where multidisciplinary activities between providers referred to in points (a) and (b) of paragraph 1 are authorised, Member States shall ensure the following:

(a) that conflicts of interest and incompatibilities between certain activities are prevented;

(b) that the independence and impartiality required for certain activities is secured;

(c) that the rules governing professional ethics and conduct for different activities are compatible with one another, especially as regards matters of professional secrecy.

3. In the report referred to in Article 39(1), Member States shall indicate which providers are subject to the requirements laid down in paragraph 1 of this Article, the content of those requirements and the reasons for which they consider them to be justified.

Article 26 Policy on quality of services

1. Member States shall, in cooperation with the Commission, take accompanying measures to encourage providers to take action on a voluntary basis in order to ensure the quality of service provision, in particular through use of one of the following methods:

(a) certification or assessment of their activities by independent or accredited bodies;

(b) drawing up their own quality charter or participation in quality charters or labels drawn up by professional bodies at Community level.

2. Member States shall ensure that information on the significance of certain labels and the criteria for applying labels and other quality marks relating to services can be easily accessed by providers and recipients.

3. Member States shall, in cooperation with the Commission, take accompanying measures to encourage professional bodies, as well as chambers of commerce and craft associations and consumer associations, in their territory to cooperate at Community level in order to promote the quality of service provision, especially by making it easier to assess the competence of a provider.

4. Member States shall, in cooperation with the Commission, take accompanying measures to encourage the development of independent assessments, notably by consumer associations, in relation to the quality and defects of service provision, and, in particular, the development at Community level of comparative trials or testing and the communication of the results.

5. Member States, in cooperation with the Commission, shall encourage the development of voluntary European standards with the aim of facilitating compatibility between services supplied by providers in different Member States, information to the recipient and the quality of service provision.

Article 27 Settlement of disputes

1. Member States shall take the general measures necessary to ensure that providers supply contact details, in particular a postal address, fax number or e-mail address and telephone number to which all recipients, including those resident in another Member State, can send a complaint or a

request for information about the service provided. Providers shall supply their legal address if this is not their usual address for correspondence.

Member States shall take the general measures necessary to ensure that providers respond to the complaints referred to in the first subparagraph in the shortest possible time and make their best efforts to find a satisfactory solution.

2. Member States shall take the general measures necessary to ensure that providers are obliged to demonstrate compliance with the obligations laid down in this Directive as to the provision of information and to demonstrate that the information is accurate.

3. Where a financial guarantee is required for compliance with a judicial decision, Member States shall recognise equivalent guarantees lodged with a credit institution or insurer established in another Member State. Such credit institutions must be authorised in a Member State in accordance with Directive 2006/48/EC and such insurers in accordance, as appropriate, with First Council Directive 73/239/EEC of 24 July 1973 on the coordination of laws, regulations and administrative provisions relating to the taking-up and pursuit of the business of direct insurance other than life assurance[17] and Directive 2002/83/EC of the European Parliament and of the Council of 5 November 2002 concerning life assurance.[18]

4. Member States shall take the general measures necessary to ensure that providers who are subject to a code of conduct, or are members of a trade association or professional body, which provides for recourse to a non-judicial means of dispute settlement inform the recipient thereof and mention that fact in any document which presents their services in detail, specifying how to access detailed information on the characteristics of, and conditions for, the use of such a mechanism.

Chapter VI Administrative cooperation

Article 28 Mutual assistance—general obligations

1. Member States shall give each other mutual assistance, and shall put in place measures for effective cooperation with one another, in order to ensure the supervision of providers and the services they provide.

2. For the purposes of this Chapter, Member States shall designate one or more liaison points, the contact details of which shall be communicated to the other Member States and the Commission. The Commission shall publish and regularly update the list of liaison points.

3. Information requests and requests to carry out any checks, inspections and investigations under this Chapter shall be duly motivated, in particular by specifying the reason for the request. Information exchanged shall be used only in respect of the matter for which it was requested.

4. In the event of receiving a request for assistance from competent authorities in another Member State, Member States shall ensure that providers established in their territory supply their competent authorities with all the information necessary for supervising their activities in compliance with their national laws.

5. In the event of difficulty in meeting a request for information or in carrying out checks, inspections or investigations, the Member State in question shall rapidly inform the requesting Member State with a view to finding a solution.

6. Member States shall supply the information requested by other Member States or the Commission by electronic means and within the shortest possible period of time.

7. Member States shall ensure that registers in which providers have been entered, and which may be consulted by the competent authorities in their territory, may also be consulted, in accordance with the same conditions, by the equivalent competent authorities of the other Member States.

[17] OJ L 228, 16.8.1973, p. 3. Directive as last amended by Directive 2005/68/EC of the European Parliament and of the Council (OJ L 323, 9.12.2005, p. 1).

[18] OJ L 345, 19.12.2002, p. 1. Directive as last amended by Directive 2005/68/EC.

8. Member States shall communicate to the Commission information on cases where other Member States do not fulfil their obligation of mutual assistance. Where necessary, the Commission shall take appropriate steps, including proceedings provided for in Article 226 of the Treaty, in order to ensure that the Member States concerned comply with their obligation of mutual assistance. The Commission shall periodically inform Member States about the functioning of the mutual assistance provisions.

Article 29 Mutual assistance—general obligations for the Member State of establishment

1. With respect to providers providing services in another Member State, the Member State of establishment shall supply information on providers established in its territory when requested to do so by another Member State and, in particular, confirmation that a provider is established in its territory and, to its knowledge, is not exercising his activities in an unlawful manner.

2. The Member State of establishment shall undertake the checks, inspections and investigations requested by another Member State and shall inform the latter of the results and, as the case may be, of the measures taken. In so doing, the competent authorities shall act to the extent permitted by the powers vested in them in their Member State. The competent authorities can decide on the most appropriate measures to be taken in each individual case in order to meet the request by another Member State.

3. Upon gaining actual knowledge of any conduct or specific acts by a provider established in its territory which provides services in other Member States, that, to its knowledge, could cause serious damage to the health or safety of persons or to the environment, the Member State of establishment shall inform all other Member States and the Commission within the shortest possible period of time.

Article 30 Supervision by the Member State of establishment in the event of the temporary movement of a provider to another Member State

1. With respect to cases not covered by Article 31(1), the Member State of establishment shall ensure that compliance with its requirements is supervised in conformity with the powers of supervision provided for in its national law, in particular through supervisory measures at the place of establishment of the provider.

2. The Member State of establishment shall not refrain from taking supervisory or enforcement measures in its territory on the grounds that the service has been provided or caused damage in another Member State.

3. The obligation laid down in paragraph 1 shall not entail a duty on the part of the Member State of establishment to carry out factual checks and controls in the territory of the Member State where the service is provided. Such checks and controls shall be carried out by the authorities of the Member State where the provider is temporarily operating at the request of the authorities of the Member State of establishment, in accordance with Article 31.

Article 31 Supervision by the Member State where the service is provided in the event of the temporary movement of the provider

1. With respect to national requirements which may be imposed pursuant to Articles 16 or 17, the Member State where the service is provided is responsible for the supervision of the activity of the provider in its territory. In conformity with Community law, the Member State where the service is provided:

(a) shall take all measures necessary to ensure the provider complies with those requirements as regards the access to and the exercise of the activity;

(b) shall carry out the checks, inspections and investigations necessary to supervise the service provided.

2. With respect to requirements other than those referred to in paragraph 1, where a provider moves temporarily to another Member State in order to provide a service without being established there, the competent authorities of that Member State shall participate in the supervision of the provider in accordance with paragraphs 3 and 4.

3. At the request of the Member State of establishment, the competent authorities of the Member State where the service is provided shall carry out any checks, inspections and investigations necessary for ensuring the effective supervision by the Member State of establishment. In so doing, the competent authorities shall act to the extent permitted by the powers vested in them in their Member State. The competent authorities may decide on the most appropriate measures to be taken in each individual case in order to meet the request by the Member State of establishment.

4. On their own initiative, the competent authorities of the Member State where the service is provided may conduct checks, inspections and investigations on the spot, provided that those checks, inspections or investigations are not discriminatory, are not motivated by the fact that the provider is established in another Member State and are proportionate.

Article 32 Alert mechanism

1. Where a Member State becomes aware of serious specific acts or circumstances relating to a service activity that could cause serious damage to the health or safety of persons or to the environment in its territory or in the territory of other Member States, that Member State shall inform the Member State of establishment, the other Member States concerned and the Commission within the shortest possible period of time.

2. The Commission shall promote and take part in the operation of a European network of Member States' authorities in order to implement paragraph 1.

3. The Commission shall adopt and regularly update, in accordance with the procedure referred to in Article 40(2), detailed rules concerning the management of the network referred to in paragraph 2 of this Article.

Done at Strasbourg, 12 December 2006.

Regulation (EU) No 492/2011 of the European Parliament and of the Council of 5 April 2011 on freedom of movement for workers within the Union*

[OJ 2011 L141/1]

Chapter I Employment, equal treatment and workers' families

Section 1 Eligibility for employment

Article 1

1. Any national of a Member State shall, irrespective of his place of residence, have the right to take up an activity as an employed person, and to pursue such activity, within the territory of another Member State in accordance with the provisions laid down by law, regulation or administrative action governing the employment of nationals of that State.

2. He shall, in particular, have the right to take up available employment in the territory of another Member State with the same priority as nationals of that State.

Article 2

Any national of a Member State and any employer pursuing an activity in the territory of a Member State may exchange their applications for and offers of employment, and may conclude and perform contracts of employment in accordance with the provisions in force laid down by law, regulation or administrative action, without any discrimination resulting therefrom.

* **Editor's Note:** As amended by Directive 2016/589 (OJ 2016 L107/1) and Regulation 1149/2019 (OJ 2019 L186/21).

Article 3

1. Under this Regulation, provisions laid down by law, regulation or administrative action or administrative practices of a Member State shall not apply:

(a) where they limit application for and offers of employment, or the right of foreign nationals to take up and pursue employment or subject these to conditions not applicable in respect of their own nationals; or

(b) where, though applicable irrespective of nationality, their exclusive or principal aim or effect is to keep nationals of other Member States away from the employment offered.

The first subparagraph shall not apply to conditions relating to linguistic knowledge required by reason of the nature of the post to be filled.

2. There shall be included in particular among the provisions or practices of a Member State referred to in the first subparagraph of paragraph 1 those which:

(a) prescribe a special recruitment procedure for foreign nationals;

(b) limit or restrict the advertising of vacancies in the press or through any other medium or subject it to conditions other than those applicable in respect of employers pursuing their activities in the territory of that Member State;

(c) subject eligibility for employment to conditions of registration with employment offices or impede recruitment of individual workers, where persons who do not reside in the territory of that State are concerned.

Article 4

1. Provisions laid down by law, regulation or administrative action of the Member States which restrict by number or percentage the employment of foreign nationals in any undertaking, branch of activity or region, or at a national level, shall not apply to nationals of the other Member States.

2. When in a Member State the granting of any benefit to undertakings is subject to a minimum percentage of national workers being employed, nationals of the other Member States shall be counted as national workers, subject to Directive 2005/36/EC of the European Parliament and of the Council of 7 September 2005 on the recognition of professional qualifications.[1]

Article 5

A national of a Member State who seeks employment in the territory of another Member State shall receive the same assistance there as that afforded by the employment offices in that State to their own nationals seeking employment.

Article 6

1. The engagement and recruitment of a national of one Member State for a post in another Member State shall not depend on medical, vocational or other criteria which are discriminatory on grounds of nationality by comparison with those applied to nationals of the other Member State who wish to pursue the same activity.

2. A national who holds an offer in his name from an employer in a Member State other than that of which he is a national may have to undergo a vocational test, if the employer expressly requests this when making his offer of employment.

Section 2 Employment and equality of treatment

Article 7

1. A worker who is a national of a Member State may not, in the territory of another Member State, be treated differently from national workers by reason of his nationality in respect of any conditions of employment and work, in particular as regards remuneration, dismissal, and, should he become unemployed, reinstatement or re-employment.

2. He shall enjoy the same social and tax advantages as national workers.

3. He shall also, by virtue of the same right and under the same conditions as national workers, have access to training in vocational schools and retraining centres.

[1] OJ L 255, 30.9.2005, p. 22.

4. Any clause of a collective or individual agreement or of any other collective regulation concerning eligibility for employment, remuneration and other conditions of work or dismissal shall be null and void in so far as it lays down or authorises discriminatory conditions in respect of workers who are nationals of the other Member States.

Article 8

A worker who is a national of a Member State and who is employed in the territory of another Member State shall enjoy equality of treatment as regards membership of trade unions and the exercise of rights attaching thereto, including the right to vote and to be eligible for the administration or management posts of a trade union. He may be excluded from taking part in the management of bodies governed by public law and from holding an office governed by public law. Furthermore, he shall have the right of eligibility for workers' representative bodies in the undertaking.

The first paragraph of this Article shall not affect laws or regulations in certain Member States which grant more extensive rights to workers coming from the other Member States.

Article 9

1. A worker who is a national of a Member State and who is employed in the territory of another Member State shall enjoy all the rights and benefits accorded to national workers in matters of housing, including ownership of the housing he needs.

2. A worker referred to in paragraph 1 may, with the same right as nationals, put his name down on the housing lists in the region in which he is employed, where such lists exist, and shall enjoy the resultant benefits and priorities.

If his family has remained in the country whence he came, they shall be considered for this purpose as residing in the said region, where national workers benefit from a similar presumption.

Section 3 Workers' families

Article 10

The children of a national of a Member State who is or has been employed in the territory of another Member State shall be admitted to that State's general educational, apprenticeship and vocational training courses under the same conditions as the nationals of that State, if such children are residing in its territory.

Member States shall encourage all efforts to enable such children to attend these courses under the best possible conditions.

Done at Strasbourg, 5 April 2011.

Social policy: equal pay and treatment

Council Directive of 19 December 1978 on the progressive implementation of the principle of equal treatment for men and women in matters of social security (79/7/EEC)

[OJ 1979 L6/24]

Article 1

The purpose of this Directive is the progressive implementation, in the field of social security and other elements of social protection provided for in Article 3, of the principle of equal treatment for men and women in matters of social security, hereinafter referred to as 'the principle of equal treatment'.

Article 2

This Directive shall apply to the working population—including self-employed persons, workers and self-employed persons whose activity is interrupted by illness, accident or involuntary unemployment and persons seeking employment—and to retired or invalided workers and self-employed persons.

Article 3

1. This Directive shall apply to:
   (a) statutory schemes which provide protection against the following risks:
   - sickness,
   - invalidity,
   - old age,
   - accidents at work and occupational diseases,
   - unemployment;

   (b) social assistance, in so far as it is intended to supplement or replace the schemes referred to in (a).

2. This Directive shall not apply to the provisions concerning survivors' benefits nor to those concerning family benefits, except in the case of family benefits granted by way of increases of benefits due in respect of the risks referred to in paragraph 1(a).

3. With a view to ensuring implementation of the principle of equal treatment in occupational schemes, the Council, acting on a proposal from the Commission, will adopt provisions defining its substance, its scope and the arrangements for its application.

Article 4

1. The principle of equal treatment means that there shall be no discrimination whatsoever on ground of sex either directly, or indirectly by reference in particular to marital or family status, in particular as concerns:
   - the scope of the schemes and the conditions of access thereto,
   - the obligation to contribute and the calculation of contributions,
   - the calculation of benefits including increases due in respect of a spouse and for dependants and the conditions governing the duration and retention of entitlement to benefits.

2. The principle of equal treatment shall be without prejudice to the provisions relating to the protection of women on the grounds of maternity.

Article 5

Member States shall take the measures necessary to ensure that any laws, regulations and administrative provisions contrary to the principle of equal treatment are abolished.

Article 6

Member States shall introduce into their national legal systems such measures as are necessary to enable all persons who consider themselves wronged by failure to apply the principle of equal treatment to pursue their claims by judicial process, possibly after recourse to other competent authorities.

Article 7

1. This Directive shall be without prejudice to the right of Member States to exclude from its scope:
   (a) the determination of pensionable age for the purposes of granting old-age and retirement pensions and the possible consequences thereof for other benefits;
   (b) advantages in respect of old-age pension schemes granted to persons who have brought up children; the acquisition of benefit entitlements following periods of interruption of employment due to the bringing up of children;
   (c) the granting of old-age or invalidity benefit entitlements by virtue of the derived entitlements of a wife;

(d) the granting of increases of long-term invalidity, old-age, accidents at work and occupational disease benefits for a dependent wife;

(e) the consequences of the exercise, before the adoption of this Directive, of a right of option not to acquire rights or incur obligations under a statutory scheme.

2. Member States shall periodically examine matters excluded under paragraph 1 in order to ascertain, in the light of social developments in the matter concerned, whether there is justification for maintaining the exclusions concerned.

Article 8

1. Member States shall bring into force the laws, regulations and administrative provisions necessary to comply with this Directive within six years of its notification. They shall immediately inform the Commission thereof.

2. Member States shall communicate to the Commission the text of laws, regulations and administrative provisions which they adopt in the field covered by this Directive, including measures adopted pursuant to Article 7(2).

They shall inform the Commission of their reasons for maintaining any existing provisions on the matters referred to in Article 7(1) and of the possibilities for reviewing them at a later date.

Article 9

Within seven years of notification of this Directive, Member States shall forward all information necessary to the Commission to enable it to draw up a report on the application of this Directive for submission to the Council and to propose such further measures as may be required for the implementation of the principle of equal treatment.

Article 10

This Directive is addressed to the Member States.

Done at Brussels, 19 December 1978.

Council Directive 86/613 was repealed with effect from 5 August 2012 and replaced by Directive 2010/41 reproduced at the end of this section

Council Directive 2000/43/EC of 29 June 2000 implementing the principle of equal treatment between persons irrespective of racial or ethnic origin

[OJ 2000 L180/22]

Chapter I General provisions

Article 1 Purpose

The purpose of this Directive is to lay down a framework for combating discrimination on the grounds of racial or ethnic origin, with a view to putting into effect in the Member States the principle of equal treatment.

Article 2 Concept of discrimination

1. For the purposes of this Directive, the principle of equal treatment shall mean that there shall be no direct or indirect discrimination based on racial or ethnic origin.

2. For the purposes of paragraph 1:

(a) direct discrimination shall be taken to occur where one person is treated less favourably than another is, has been or would be treated in a comparable situation on grounds of racial or ethnic origin;

(b) indirect discrimination shall be taken to occur where an apparently neutral provision, criterion or practice would put persons of a racial or ethnic origin at a particular disadvantage compared with other persons, unless that provision, criterion or practice is objectively justified by a legitimate aim and the means of achieving that aim are appropriate and necessary.

3. Harassment shall be deemed to be discrimination within the meaning of paragraph 1, when an unwanted conduct related to racial or ethnic origin takes place with the purpose or effect of violating the dignity of a person and of creating an intimidating, hostile, degrading, humiliating or offensive environment. In this context, the concept of harassment may be defined in accordance with the national laws and practice of the Member States.

4. An instruction to discriminate against persons on grounds of racial or ethnic origin shall be deemed to be discrimination within the meaning of paragraph 1.

Article 3 Scope

1. Within the limits of the powers conferred upon the Community, this Directive shall apply to all persons, as regards both the public and private sectors, including public bodies, in relation to:

(a) conditions for access to employment, to self-employment and to occupation, including selection criteria and recruitment conditions, whatever the branch of activity and at all levels of the professional hierarchy, including promotion;
(b) access to all types and to all levels of vocational guidance, vocational training, advanced vocational training and retraining, including practical work experience;
(c) employment and working conditions, including dismissals and pay;
(d) membership of and involvement in an organisation of workers or employers, or any organisation whose members carry on a particular profession, including the benefits provided for by such organisations;
(e) social protection, including social security and healthcare;
(f) social advantages;
(g) education;
(h) access to and supply of goods and services which are available to the public, including housing.

2. This Directive does not cover difference of treatment based on nationality and is without prejudice to provisions and conditions relating to the entry into and residence of third-country nationals and stateless persons on the territory of Member States, and to any treatment which arises from the legal status of the third-country nationals and stateless persons concerned.

Article 4 Genuine and determining occupational requirements

Notwithstanding Article 2(1) and (2), Member States may provide that a difference of treatment which is based on a characteristic related to racial or ethnic origin shall not constitute discrimination where, by reason of the nature of the particular occupational activities concerned or of the context in which they are carried out, such a characteristic constitutes a genuine and determining occupational requirement, provided that the objective is legitimate and the requirement is proportionate.

Article 5 Positive action

With a view to ensuring full equality in practice, the principle of equal treatment shall not prevent any Member State from maintaining or adopting specific measures to prevent or compensate for disadvantages linked to racial or ethnic origin.

Article 6 Minimum requirements

1. Member States may introduce or maintain provisions which are more favourable to the protection of the principle of equal treatment than those laid down in this Directive.

2. The implementation of this Directive shall under no circumstances constitute grounds for a reduction in the level of protection against discrimination already afforded by Member States in the fields covered by this Directive.

Chapter II Remedies and enforcement

Article 7 Defence of rights

1. Member States shall ensure that judicial and/or administrative procedures, including where they deem it appropriate conciliation procedures, for the enforcement of obligations under this Directive are available to all persons who consider themselves wronged by failure to apply the principle of equal treatment to them, even after the relationship in which the discrimination is alleged to have occurred has ended.

2. Member States shall ensure that associations, organisations or other legal entities, which have, in accordance with the criteria laid down by their national law, a legitimate interest in ensuring that the provisions of this Directive are complied with, may engage, either on behalf or in support of the complainant, with his or her approval, in any judicial and/or administrative procedure provided for the enforcement of obligations under this Directive.

3. Paragraphs 1 and 2 are without prejudice to national rules relating to time limits for bringing actions as regards the principle of equality of treatment.

Article 8 Burden of proof

1. Member States shall take such measures as are necessary, in accordance with their national judicial systems, to ensure that, when persons who consider themselves wronged because the principle of equal treatment has not been applied to them establish, before a court or other competent authority, facts from which it may be presumed that there has been direct or indirect discrimination, it shall be for the respondent to prove that there has been no breach of the principle of equal treatment.

2. Paragraph 1 shall not prevent Member States from introducing rules of evidence which are more favourable to plaintiffs.

3. Paragraph 1 shall not apply to criminal procedures.

4. Paragraphs 1, 2 and 3 shall also apply to any proceedings brought in accordance with Article 7(2).

5. Member States need not apply paragraph 1 to proceedings in which it is for the court or competent body to investigate the facts of the case.

Article 9 Victimisation

Member States shall introduce into their national legal systems such measures as are necessary to protect individuals from any adverse treatment or adverse consequence as a reaction to a complaint or to proceedings aimed at enforcing compliance with the principle of equal treatment.

Article 10 Dissemination of information

Member States shall take care that the provisions adopted pursuant to this Directive, together with the relevant provisions already in force, are brought to the attention of the persons concerned by all appropriate means throughout their territory.

Article 11 Social dialogue

1. Member States shall, in accordance with national traditions and practice, take adequate measures to promote the social dialogue between the two sides of industry with a view to fostering equal treatment, including through the monitoring of workplace practices, collective agreements, codes of conduct, research or exchange of experiences and good practices.

2. Where consistent with national traditions and practice, Member States shall encourage the two sides of the industry without prejudice to their autonomy to conclude, at the appropriate level, agreements laying down anti-discrimination rules in the fields referred to in Article 3 which fall within the scope of collective bargaining. These agreements shall respect the minimum requirements laid down by this Directive and the relevant national implementing measures.

Article 12 Dialogue with non-governmental organisations

Member States shall encourage dialogue with appropriate non-governmental organisations which have, in accordance with their national law and practice, a legitimate interest in contributing to the fight against discrimination on grounds of racial and ethnic origin with a view to promoting the principle of equal treatment.

Chapter III Bodies for the promotion of equal treatment

Article 13

1. Member States shall designate a body or bodies for the promotion of equal treatment of all persons without discrimination on the grounds of racial or ethnic origin. These bodies may form part of agencies charged at national level with the defence of human rights or the safeguard of individuals' rights.

2. Member States shall ensure that the competences of these bodies include:

- without prejudice to the right of victims and of associations, organisations or other legal entities referred to in Article 7(2), providing independent assistance to victims of discrimination in pursuing their complaints about discrimination,
- conducting independent surveys concerning discrimination,
- publishing independent reports and making recommendations on any issue relating to such discrimination.

Chapter IV Final provisions

Article 14 Compliance

Member States shall take the necessary measures to ensure that:

(a) any laws, regulations and administrative provisions contrary to the principle of equal treatment are abolished;

(b) any provisions contrary to the principle of equal treatment which are included in individual or collective contracts or agreements, internal rules of undertakings, rules governing profit-making or non-profit-making associations, and rules governing the independent professions and workers' and employers' organisations, are or may be declared, null and void or are amended.

Article 15 Sanctions

Member States shall lay down the rules on sanctions applicable to infringements of the national provisions adopted pursuant to this Directive and shall take all measures necessary to ensure that they are applied. The sanctions, which may comprise the payment of compensation to the victim, must be effective, proportionate and dissuasive. The Member States shall notify those provisions to the Commission by 19 July 2003 at the latest and shall notify it without delay of any subsequent amendment affecting them.

Article 16 Implementation

Member States shall adopt the laws, regulations and administrative provisions necessary to comply with this Directive by 19 July 2003 or may entrust management and labour, at their joint request, with the implementation of this Directive as regards provisions falling within the scope of collective agreements. In such cases, Member States shall ensure that by 19 July 2003, management and labour introduce the necessary measures by agreement, Member States being required to take any necessary measures to enable them at any time to be in a position to guarantee the results imposed by this Directive. They shall forthwith inform the Commission thereof.

When Member States adopt these measures, they shall contain a reference to this Directive or be accompanied by such a reference on the occasion of their official publication. The methods of making such a reference shall be laid down by the Member States.

Article 17 Report

1. Member States shall communicate to the Commission by 19 July 2005, and every five years thereafter, all the information necessary for the Commission to draw up a report to the European Parliament and the Council on the application of this Directive.

2. The Commission's report shall take into account, as appropriate, the views of the European Monitoring Centre on Racism and Xenophobia, as well as the viewpoints of the social partners and relevant non-governmental organisations. In accordance with the principle of gender mainstreaming, this report shall, inter alia, provide an assessment of the impact of the measures taken on women and men. In the light of the information received, this report shall include, if necessary, proposals to revise and update this Directive.

Article 18 Entry into force

This Directive shall enter into force on the day of its publication in the *Official Journal of the European Communities*.

Article 19 Addressees

This Directive is addressed to the Member States.

Done at Luxembourg, 29 June 2000.

Council Directive 2000/78/EC of 27 November 2000 establishing a general framework for equal treatment in employment and occupation

[OJ 2000 L303/16]

Chapter I General provisions

Article 1 Purpose

The purpose of this Directive is to lay down a general framework for combating discrimination on the grounds of religion or belief, disability, age or sexual orientation as regards employment and occupation, with a view to putting into effect in the Member States the principle of equal treatment.

Article 2 Concept of discrimination

1. For the purposes of this Directive, the 'principle of equal treatment' shall mean that there shall be no direct or indirect discrimination whatsoever on any of the grounds referred to in Article 1.

2. For the purposes of paragraph 1:
   (a) direct discrimination shall be taken to occur where one person is treated less favourably than another is, has been or would be treated in a comparable situation, on any of the grounds referred to in Article 1;
   (b) indirect discrimination shall be taken to occur where an apparently neutral provision, criterion or practice would put persons having a particular religion or belief, a particular disability, a particular age, or a particular sexual orientation at a particular disadvantage compared with other persons unless:
      (i) that provision, criterion or practice is objectively justified by a legitimate aim and the means of achieving that aim are appropriate and necessary, or
      (ii) as regards persons with a particular disability, the employer or any person or organisation to whom this Directive applies, is obliged, under national legislation, to take appropriate measures in line with the principles contained in Article 5 in order to eliminate disadvantages entailed by such provision, criterion or practice.

3. Harassment shall be deemed to be a form of discrimination within the meaning of paragraph 1, when unwanted conduct related to any of the grounds referred to in Article 1 takes place with the purpose or effect of violating the dignity of a person and of creating an intimidating, hostile, degrading, humiliating or offensive environment. In this context, the concept of harassment may be defined in accordance with the national laws and practice of the Member States.

4. An instruction to discriminate against persons on any of the grounds referred to in Article 1 shall be deemed to be discrimination within the meaning of paragraph 1.

5. This Directive shall be without prejudice to measures laid down by national law which, in a democratic society, are necessary for public security, for the maintenance of public order and the prevention of criminal offences, for the protection of health and for the protection of the rights and freedoms of others.

Article 3 Scope

1. Within the limits of the areas of competence conferred on the Community, this Directive shall apply to all persons, as regards both the public and private sectors, including public bodies, in relation to:

(a) conditions for access to employment, to self-employment or to occupation, including selection criteria and recruitment conditions, whatever the branch of activity and at all levels of the professional hierarchy, including promotion;

(b) access to all types and to all levels of vocational guidance, vocational training, advanced vocational training and retraining, including practical work experience;

(c) employment and working conditions, including dismissals and pay;

(d) membership of, and involvement in, an organisation of workers or employers, or any organisation whose members carry on a particular profession, including the benefits provided for by such organisations.

2. This Directive does not cover differences of treatment based on nationality and is without prejudice to provisions and conditions relating to the entry into and residence of third-country nationals and stateless persons in the territory of Member States, and to any treatment which arises from the legal status of the third-country nationals and stateless persons concerned.

3. This Directive does not apply to payments of any kind made by state schemes or similar, including state social security or social protection schemes.

4. Member States may provide that this Directive, in so far as it relates to discrimination on the grounds of disability and age, shall not apply to the armed forces.

Article 4 Occupational requirements

1. Notwithstanding Article 2(1) and (2), Member States may provide that a difference of treatment which is based on a characteristic related to any of the grounds referred to in Article 1 shall not constitute discrimination where, by reason of the nature of the particular occupational activities concerned or of the context in which they are carried out, such a characteristic constitutes a genuine and determining occupational requirement, provided that the objective is legitimate and the requirement is proportionate.

2. Member States may maintain national legislation in force at the date of adoption of this Directive or provide for future legislation incorporating national practices existing at the date of adoption of this Directive pursuant to which, in the case of occupational activities within churches and other public or private organisations the ethos of which is based on religion or belief, a difference of treatment based on a person's religion or belief shall not constitute discrimination where, by reason of the nature of these activities or of the context in which they are carried out, a person's religion or belief constitute a genuine, legitimate and justified occupational requirement, having regard to the organisation's ethos. This difference of treatment shall be implemented taking account of Member States' constitutional provisions and principles, as well as the general principles of Community law, and should not justify discrimination on another ground.

Provided that its provisions are otherwise complied with, this Directive shall thus not prejudice the right of churches and other public or private organisations, the ethos of which is based on religion or belief, acting in conformity with national constitutions and laws, to require individuals working for them to act in good faith and with loyalty to the organisation's ethos.

Article 5 Reasonable accommodation for disabled persons

In order to guarantee compliance with the principle of equal treatment in relation to persons with disabilities, reasonable accommodation shall be provided. This means that employers shall take appropriate measures, where needed in a particular case, to enable a person with a disability to have access to, participate in, or advance in employment, or to undergo training, unless such measures would impose a disproportionate burden on the employer. This burden shall not be disproportionate when it is sufficiently remedied by measures existing within the framework of the disability policy of the Member State concerned.

Article 6 Justification of differences of treatment on grounds of age

1. Notwithstanding Article 2(2), Member States may provide that differences of treatment on grounds of age shall not constitute discrimination, if, within the context of national law, they are objectively and reasonably justified by a legitimate aim, including legitimate employment policy, labour market and vocational training objectives, and if the means of achieving that aim are appropriate and necessary.

Such differences of treatment may include, among others:

(a) the setting of special conditions on access to employment and vocational training, employment and occupation, including dismissal and remuneration conditions, for young people, older workers and persons with caring responsibilities in order to promote their vocational integration or ensure their protection;

(b) the fixing of minimum conditions of age, professional experience or seniority in service for access to employment or to certain advantages linked to employment;

(c) the fixing of a maximum age for recruitment which is based on the training requirements of the post in question or the need for a reasonable period of employment before retirement.

2. Notwithstanding Article 2(2), Member States may provide that the fixing for occupational social security schemes of ages for admission or entitlement to retirement or invalidity benefits, including the fixing under those schemes of different ages for employees or groups or categories of employees, and the use, in the context of such schemes, of age criteria in actuarial calculations, does not constitute discrimination on the grounds of age, provided this does not result in discrimination on the grounds of sex.

Article 7 Positive action

1. With a view to ensuring full equality in practice, the principle of equal treatment shall not prevent any Member State from maintaining or adopting specific measures to prevent or compensate for disadvantages linked to any of the grounds referred to in Article 1.

2. With regard to disabled persons, the principle of equal treatment shall be without prejudice to the right of Member States to maintain or adopt provisions on the protection of health and safety at work or to measures aimed at creating or maintaining provisions or facilities for safeguarding or promoting their integration into the working environment.

Article 8 Minimum requirements

1. Member States may introduce or maintain provisions which are more favourable to the protection of the principle of equal treatment than those laid down in this Directive.

2. The implementation of this Directive shall under no circumstances constitute grounds for a reduction in the level of protection against discrimination already afforded by Member States in the fields covered by this Directive.

Chapter II Remedies and enforcement

Article 9 Defence of rights

1. Member States shall ensure that judicial and/or administrative procedures, including where they deem it appropriate conciliation procedures, for the enforcement of obligations under this Directive are available to all persons who consider themselves wronged by failure to apply the principle of equal treatment to them, even after the relationship in which the discrimination is alleged to have occurred has ended.

2. Member States shall ensure that associations, organisations or other legal entities which have, in accordance with the criteria laid down by their national law, a legitimate interest in

ensuring that the provisions of this Directive are complied with, may engage, either on behalf or in support of the complainant, with his or her approval, in any judicial and/or administrative procedure provided for the enforcement of obligations under this Directive.

3. Paragraphs 1 and 2 are without prejudice to national rules relating to time limits for bringing actions as regards the principle of equality of treatment.

Article 10 Burden of proof

1. Member States shall take such measures as are necessary, in accordance with their national judicial systems, to ensure that, when persons who consider themselves wronged because the principle of equal treatment has not been applied to them establish, before a court or other competent authority, facts from which it may be presumed that there has been direct or indirect discrimination, it shall be for the respondent to prove that there has been no breach of the principle of equal treatment.

2. Paragraph 1 shall not prevent Member States from introducing rules of evidence which are more favourable to plaintiffs.

3. Paragraph 1 shall not apply to criminal procedures.

4. Paragraphs 1, 2 and 3 shall also apply to any legal proceedings commenced in accordance with Article 9(2).

5. Member States need not apply paragraph 1 to proceedings in which it is for the court or competent body to investigate the facts of the case.

Article 11 Victimisation

Member States shall introduce into their national legal systems such measures as are necessary to protect employees against dismissal or other adverse treatment by the employer as a reaction to a complaint within the undertaking or to any legal proceedings aimed at enforcing compliance with the principle of equal treatment.

Done at Brussels, 27 November 2000.

Council Directive 2004/113/EC of 13 December 2004 implementing the principle of equal treatment between men and women in the access to and supply of goods and services

[OJ 2004 L373/37]

Chapter I General provisions

Article 1 Purpose

The purpose of this Directive is to lay down a framework for combating discrimination based on sex in access to and supply of goods and services, with a view to putting into effect in the Member States the principle of equal treatment between men and women.

Article 2 Definitions

For the purposes of this Directive, the following definitions shall apply:

(a) direct discrimination: where one person is treated less favourably, on grounds of sex, than another is, has been or would be treated in a comparable situation;

(b) indirect discrimination: where an apparently neutral provision, criterion or practice would put persons of one sex at a particular disadvantage compared with persons of the other sex, unless that provision, criterion or practice is objectively justified by a legitimate aim and the means of achieving that aim are appropriate and necessary;

(c) harassment: where an unwanted conduct related to the sex of a person occurs with the purpose or effect of violating the dignity of a person and of creating an intimidating, hostile, degrading, humiliating or offensive environment;

(d) sexual harassment: where any form of unwanted physical, verbal, non-verbal or physical conduct of a sexual nature occurs, with the purpose or effect of violating the dignity of a person, in particular when creating an intimidating, hostile, degrading, humiliating or offensive environment.

Article 3 Scope

1. Within the limits of the powers conferred upon the Community, this Directive shall apply to all persons who provide goods and services, which are available to the public irrespective of the person concerned as regards both the public and private sectors, including public bodies, and which are offered outside the area of private and family life and the transactions carried out in this context.

2. This Directive does not prejudice the individual's freedom to choose a contractual partner as long as an individual's choice of contractual partner is not based on that person's sex.

3. This Directive shall not apply to the content of media and advertising nor to education.

4. This Directive shall not apply to matters of employment and occupation. This Directive shall not apply to matters of self-employment, insofar as these matters are covered by other Community legislative acts.

Article 4 Principle of equal treatment

1. For the purposes of this Directive, the principle of equal treatment between men and women shall mean that

(a) there shall be no direct discrimination based on sex, including less favourable treatment of women for reasons of pregnancy and maternity;

(b) there shall be no indirect discrimination based on sex.

2. This Directive shall be without prejudice to more favourable provisions concerning the protection of women as regards pregnancy and maternity.

3. Harassment and sexual harassment within the meaning of this Directive shall be deemed to be discrimination on the grounds of sex and therefore prohibited. A person's rejection of, or submission to, such conduct may not be used as a basis for a decision affecting that person.

4. Instruction to direct or indirect discrimination on the grounds of sex shall be deemed to be discrimination within the meaning of this Directive.

5. This Directive shall not preclude differences in treatment, if the provision of the goods and services exclusively or primarily to members of one sex is justified by a legitimate aim and the means of achieving that aim are appropriate and necessary.

Article 5 Actuarial factors

1. Member States shall ensure that in all new contracts concluded after 21 December 2007 at the latest, the use of sex as a factor in the calculation of premiums and benefits for the purposes of insurance and related financial services shall not result in differences in individuals' premiums and benefits.

2. Notwithstanding paragraph 1, Member States may decide before 21 December 2007 to permit proportionate differences in individuals' premiums and benefits where the use of sex is a determining factor in the assessment of risk based on relevant and accurate actuarial and statistical data. The Member States concerned shall inform the Commission and ensure that accurate data relevant to the use of sex as a determining actuarial factor are compiled, published and regularly updated. These Member States shall review their decision five years after 21 December 2007, taking into account the Commission report referred to in Article 16, and shall forward the results of this review to the Commission.

3. In any event, costs related to pregnancy and maternity shall not result in differences in individuals' premiums and benefits. Member States may defer implementation of the measures necessary to comply with this paragraph until two years after 21 December 2007 at the latest. In that case the Member States concerned shall immediately inform the Commission.

Article 6 Positive action

With a view to ensuring full equality in practice between men and women, the principle of equal treatment shall not prevent any Member State from maintaining or adopting specific measures to prevent or compensate for disadvantages linked to sex.

Article 7 Minimum requirements

1. Member States may introduce or maintain provisions which are more favourable to the protection of the principle of equal treatment between men and women than those laid down in this Directive.

2. The implementation of this Directive shall in no circumstances constitute grounds for a reduction in the level of protection against discrimination already afforded by Member States in the fields covered by this Directive.

Chapter II Remedies and enforcement

Article 8 Defence of rights

1. Member States shall ensure that judicial and/or administrative procedures, including where they deem it appropriate conciliation procedures, for the enforcement of the obligations under this Directive are available to all persons who consider themselves wronged by failure to apply the principle of equal treatment to them, even after the relationship in which the discrimination is alleged to have occurred has ended.

2. Member States shall introduce into their national legal systems such measures as are necessary to ensure real and effective compensation or reparation, as the Member States so determine, for the loss and damage sustained by a person injured as a result of discrimination within the meaning of this Directive, in a way which is dissuasive and proportionate to the damage suffered. The fixing of a prior upper limit shall not restrict such compensation or reparation.

3. Member States shall ensure that associations, organisations or other legal entities, which have, in accordance with the criteria laid down by their national law, a legitimate interest in ensuring that the provisions of this Directive are complied with, may engage, on behalf or in support of the complainant, with his or her approval, in any judicial and/or administrative procedure provided for the enforcement of obligations under this Directive.

4. Paragraphs 1 and 3 shall be without prejudice to national rules on time limits for bringing actions relating to the principle of equal treatment.

Article 9 Burden of proof

1. Member States shall take such measures as are necessary, in accordance with their national judicial systems, to ensure that, when persons who consider themselves wronged because the principle of equal treatment has not been applied to them establish, before a court or other competent authority, facts from which it may be presumed that there has been direct or indirect discrimination, it shall be for the respondent to prove that there has been no breach of the principle of equal treatment.

2. Paragraph 1 shall not prevent Member States from introducing rules of evidence, which are more favourable to plaintiffs.

3. Paragraph 1 shall not apply to criminal procedures.

4. Paragraphs 1, 2 and 3 shall also apply to any proceedings brought in accordance with Article 8(3).

5. Member States need not apply paragraph 1 to proceedings in which it is for the court or other competent authority to investigate the facts of the case.

Article 10 Victimisation

Member States shall introduce into their national legal systems such measures as are necessary to protect persons from any adverse treatment or adverse consequence as a reaction to a complaint or to legal proceedings aimed at enforcing compliance with the principle of equal treatment.

Article 11 Dialogue with relevant stakeholders

With a view to promoting the principle of equal treatment, Member States shall encourage dialogue with relevant stakeholders which have, in accordance with national law and practice, a legitimate interest in contributing to the fight against discrimination on grounds of sex in the area of access to and supply of goods and services.

Chapter III Bodies for the promotion of equal treatment

Article 12

1. Member States shall designate and make the necessary arrangements for a body or bodies for the promotion, analysis, monitoring and support of equal treatment of all persons without discrimination on the grounds of sex. These bodies may form part of agencies charged at national level with the defence of human rights or the safeguard of individuals' rights, or the implementation of the principle of equal treatment.

2. Member States shall ensure that the competencies of the bodies referred to in paragraph 1 include:

(a) without prejudice to the rights of victims and of associations, organisations or other legal entities referred to in Article 8(3), providing independent assistance to victims of discrimination in pursuing their complaints about discrimination;
(b) conducting independent surveys concerning discrimination;
(c) publishing independent reports and making recommendations on any issue relating to such discrimination.

Chapter IV Final provisions

Article 13 Compliance

Member States shall take the necessary measures to ensure that the principle of equal treatment is respected in relation to the access to and supply of goods and services within the scope of this Directive, and in particular that:

(a) any laws, regulations and administrative provisions contrary to the principle of equal treatment are abolished;
(b) any contractual provisions, internal rules of undertakings, and rules governing profit-making or non-profit-making associations contrary to the principle of equal treatment are, or may be, declared null and void or are amended.

Article 14 Penalties

Member States shall lay down the rules on penalties applicable to infringements of the national provisions adopted pursuant to this Directive and shall take all measures necessary to ensure that they are applied. The penalties, which may comprise the payment of compensation to the victim, shall be effective, proportionate and dissuasive. Member States shall notify those provisions to the Commission by 21 December 2007 at the latest and shall notify it without delay of any subsequent amendment affecting them.

Article 15 Dissemination of information

Member States shall take care that the provisions adopted pursuant to this Directive, together with the relevant provisions already in force, are brought to the attention of the persons concerned by all appropriate means throughout their territory.

Article 16 Reports

1. Member States shall communicate all available information concerning the application of this Directive to the Commission, by 21 December 2009. and every five years thereafter. The Commission shall draw up a summary report, which shall include a review of the current practices of Member States in relation to Article 5 with regard to the use of sex as a factor in the calculation of premiums and benefits. It shall submit this report to the European Parliament and to the Council no later 21 December 2010. Where appropriate, the Commission shall accompany its report with proposals to modify the Directive.

2. The Commission's report shall take into account the viewpoints of relevant stakeholders.

Article 17 Transposition

1. Member States shall bring into force the laws, regulations and administrative provisions necessary to comply with this Directive by 21 December 2007 at the latest. They shall forthwith

communicate to the Commission the text of those provisions. When Member States adopt these measures, they shall contain a reference to this Directive or be accompanied by such a reference on the occasion of their official publication. The methods of making such publication of reference shall be laid down by the Member States.

2. Member States shall communicate to the Commission the text of the main provisions of national law which they adopt in the field covered by this Directive.

Article 18 Entry into force

This Directive shall enter into force on the day of its publication in the *Official Journal of the European Union.*

Article 19 Addressees

This Directive is addressed to the Member States.

Done at Brussels, 13 December 2004.

Directive 2006/54/EC of the European Parliament and of the Council of 5 July 2006 on the implementation of the principle of equal opportunities and equal treatment of men and women in matters of employment and occupation (recast)

[OJ 2006 L204/23]

Title I General provisions

Article 1 Purpose

The purpose of this Directive is to ensure the implementation of the principle of equal opportunities and equal treatment of men and women in matters of employment and occupation.

To that end, it contains provisions to implement the principle of equal treatment in relation to:

(a) access to employment, including promotion, and to vocational training;
(b) working conditions, including pay;
(c) occupational social security schemes.

It also contains provisions to ensure that such implementation is made more effective by the establishment of appropriate procedures.

Article 2 Definitions

1. For the purposes of this Directive, the following definitions shall apply:

(a) 'direct discrimination': where one person is treated less favourably on grounds of sex than another is, has been or would be treated in a comparable situation;
(b) 'indirect discrimination': where an apparently neutral provision, criterion or practice would put persons of one sex at a particular disadvantage compared with persons of the other sex, unless that provision, criterion or practice is objectively justified by a legitimate aim, and the means of achieving that aim are appropriate and necessary;
(c) 'harassment': where unwanted conduct related to the sex of a person occurs with the purpose or effect of violating the dignity of a person, and of creating an intimidating, hostile, degrading, humiliating or offensive environment;
(d) 'sexual harassment': where any form of unwanted verbal, non-verbal or physical conduct of a sexual nature occurs, with the purpose or effect of violating the dignity of a person, in particular when creating an intimidating, hostile, degrading, humiliating or offensive environment;
(e) 'pay': the ordinary basic or minimum wage or salary and any other consideration, whether in cash or in kind, which the worker receives directly or indirectly, in respect of his/her employment from his/her employer;

(f) 'occupational social security schemes': schemes not governed by Council Directive 79/7/EEC of 19 December 1978 on the progressive implementation of the principle of equal treatment for men and women in matters of social security[1] whose purpose is to provide workers, whether employees or self-employed, in an undertaking or group of undertakings, area of economic activity, occupational sector or group of sectors with benefits intended to supplement the benefits provided by statutory social security schemes or to replace them, whether membership of such schemes is compulsory or optional.

2. For the purposes of this Directive, discrimination includes:
 (a) harassment and sexual harassment, as well as any less favourable treatment based on a person's rejection of or submission to such conduct;
 (b) instruction to discriminate against persons on grounds of sex;
 (c) any less favourable treatment of a woman related to pregnancy or maternity leave within the meaning of Directive 92/85/EEC.

Article 3 Positive action

Member States may maintain or adopt measures within the meaning of Article 141(4) of the Treaty with a view to ensuring full equality in practice between men and women in working life.

Title II Specific provisions

Chapter 1 Equal pay

Article 4 Prohibition of discrimination

For the same work or for work to which equal value is attributed, direct and indirect discrimination on grounds of sex with regard to all aspects and conditions of remuneration shall be eliminated.

In particular, where a job classification system is used for determining pay, it shall be based on the same criteria for both men and women and so drawn up as to exclude any discrimination on grounds of sex.

Chapter 2 Equal treatment in occupational social security schemes

Article 5 Prohibition of discrimination

Without prejudice to Article 4, there shall be no direct or indirect discrimination on grounds of sex in occupational social security schemes, in particular as regards:
 (a) the scope of such schemes and the conditions of access to them;
 (b) the obligation to contribute and the calculation of contributions;
 (c) the calculation of benefits, including supplementary benefits due in respect of a spouse or dependants, and the conditions governing the duration and retention of entitlement to benefits.

Article 6 Personal scope

This Chapter shall apply to members of the working population, including self-employed persons, persons whose activity is interrupted by illness, maternity, accident or involuntary unemployment and persons seeking employment and to retired and disabled workers, and to those claiming under them, in accordance with national law and/or practice.

Article 7 Material scope

1. This Chapter applies to:
 (a) occupational social security schemes which provide protection against the following risks:
  (i) sickness,
  (ii) invalidity,

[1] OJ L 6, 10.1.1979, p. 24.

(iii) old age, including early retirement,
(iv) industrial accidents and occupational diseases,
(v) unemployment;

(b) occupational social security schemes which provide for other social benefits, in cash or in kind, and in particular survivors' benefits and family allowances, if such benefits constitute a consideration paid by the employer to the worker by reason of the latter's employment.

2. This Chapter also applies to pension schemes for a particular category of worker such as that of public servants if the benefits payable under the scheme are paid by reason of the employment relationship with the public employer. The fact that such a scheme forms part of a general statutory scheme shall be without prejudice in that respect.

Article 8 Exclusions from the material scope

1. This Chapter does not apply to:

(a) individual contracts for self-employed persons;
(b) single-member schemes for self-employed persons;
(c) insurance contracts to which the employer is not a party, in the case of workers;
(d) optional provisions of occupational social security schemes offered to participants individually to guarantee them:
    (i) either additional benefits,
    (ii) or a choice of date on which the normal benefits for self-employed persons will start, or a choice between several benefits;
(e) occupational social security schemes in so far as benefits are financed by contributions paid by workers on a voluntary basis.

2. This Chapter does not preclude an employer granting to persons who have already reached the retirement age for the purposes of granting a pension by virtue of an occupational social security scheme, but who have not yet reached the retirement age for the purposes of granting a statutory retirement pension, a pension supplement, the aim of which is to make equal or more nearly equal the overall amount of benefit paid to these persons in relation to the amount paid to persons of the other sex in the same situation who have already reached the statutory retirement age, until the persons benefiting from the supplement reach the statutory retirement age.

Article 9 Examples of discrimination

1. Provisions contrary to the principle of equal treatment shall include those based on sex, either directly or indirectly, for:

(a) determining the persons who may participate in an occupational social security scheme;
(b) fixing the compulsory or optional nature of participation in an occupational social security scheme;
(c) laying down different rules as regards the age of entry into the scheme or the minimum period of employment or membership of the scheme required to obtain the benefits thereof;
(d) laying down different rules, except as provided for in points (h) and (j), for the reimbursement of contributions when a worker leaves a scheme without having fulfilled the conditions guaranteeing a deferred right to long-term benefits;
(e) setting different conditions for the granting of benefits or restricting such benefits to workers of one or other of the sexes;
(f) fixing different retirement ages;
(g) suspending the retention or acquisition of rights during periods of maternity leave or leave for family reasons which are granted by law or agreement and are paid by the employer;
(h) setting different levels of benefit, except in so far as may be necessary to take account of actuarial calculation factors which differ according to sex in the case of defined-contribution schemes; in the case of funded defined-benefit schemes, certain elements may be unequal

where the inequality of the amounts results from the effects of the use of actuarial factors differing according to sex at the time when the scheme's funding is implemented;

(i) setting different levels for workers' contributions;

(j) setting different levels for employers' contributions, except:

(i) in the case of defined-contribution schemes if the aim is to equalise the amount of the final benefits or to make them more nearly equal for both sexes,

(ii) in the case of funded defined-benefit schemes where the employer's contributions are intended to ensure the adequacy of the funds necessary to cover the cost of the benefits defined;

(k) laying down different standards or standards applicable only to workers of a specified sex, except as provided for in points (h) and (j), as regards the guarantee or retention of entitlement to deferred benefits when a worker leaves a scheme.

2. Where the granting of benefits within the scope of this Chapter is left to the discretion of the scheme's management bodies, the latter shall comply with the principle of equal treatment.

Chapter 3 Equal treatment as regards access to employment, vocational training and promotion and working conditions

Article 14 Prohibition of discrimination

1. There shall be no direct or indirect discrimination on grounds of sex in the public or private sectors, including public bodies, in relation to:

(a) conditions for access to employment, to self-employment or to occupation, including selection criteria and recruitment conditions, whatever the branch of activity and at all levels of the professional hierarchy, including promotion;

(b) access to all types and to all levels of vocational guidance, vocational training, advanced vocational training and retraining, including practical work experience;

(c) employment and working conditions, including dismissals, as well as pay as provided for in Article 141 of the Treaty;

(d) membership of, and involvement in, an organisation of workers or employers, or any organisation whose members carry on a particular profession, including the benefits provided for by such organisations.

2. Member States may provide, as regards access to employment including the training leading thereto, that a difference of treatment which is based on a characteristic related to sex shall not constitute discrimination where, by reason of the nature of the particular occupational activities concerned or of the context in which they are carried out, such a characteristic constitutes a genuine and determining occupational requirement, provided that its objective is legitimate and the requirement is proportionate.

Article 15 Return from maternity leave

A woman on maternity leave shall be entitled, after the end of her period of maternity leave, to return to her job or to an equivalent post on terms and conditions which are no less favourable to her and to benefit from any improvement in working conditions to which she would have been entitled during her absence.

Article 16 Paternity and adoption leave

This Directive is without prejudice to the right of Member States to recognise distinct rights to paternity and/or adoption leave. Those Member States which recognise such rights shall take the necessary measures to protect working men and women against dismissal due to exercising those rights and ensure that, at the end of such leave, they are entitled to return to their jobs or to equivalent posts on terms and conditions which are no less favourable to them, and to benefit from any improvement in working conditions to which they would have been entitled during their absence.

Title III Horizontal provisions

Chapter 1 Remedies and enforcement

Section 1 Remedies

Article 17 Defence of rights

1. Member States shall ensure that, after possible recourse to other competent authorities including where they deem it appropriate conciliation procedures, judicial procedures for the enforcement of obligations under this Directive are available to all persons who consider themselves wronged by failure to apply the principle of equal treatment to them, even after the relationship in which the discrimination is alleged to have occurred has ended.

2. Member States shall ensure that associations, organisations or other legal entities which have, in accordance with the criteria laid down by their national law, a legitimate interest in ensuring that the provisions of this Directive are complied with, may engage, either on behalf or in support of the complainant, with his/her approval, in any judicial and/or administrative procedure provided for the enforcement of obligations under this Directive.

3. Paragraphs 1 and 2 are without prejudice to national rules relating to time limits for bringing actions as regards the principle of equal treatment.

Article 18 Compensation or reparation

Member States shall introduce into their national legal systems such measures as are necessary to ensure real and effective compensation or reparation as the Member States so determine for the loss and damage sustained by a person injured as a result of discrimination on grounds of sex, in a way which is dissuasive and proportionate to the damage suffered. Such compensation or reparation may not be restricted by the fixing of a prior upper limit, except in cases where the employer can prove that the only damage suffered by an applicant as a result of discrimination within the meaning of this Directive is the refusal to take his/her job application into consideration.

Section 2 Burden of proof

Article 19 Burden of proof

1. Member States shall take such measures as are necessary, in accordance with their national judicial systems, to ensure that, when persons who consider themselves wronged because the principle of equal treatment has not been applied to them establish, before a court or other competent authority, facts from which it may be presumed that there has been direct or indirect discrimination, it shall be for the respondent to prove that there has been no breach of the principle of equal treatment.

2. Paragraph 1 shall not prevent Member States from introducing rules of evidence which are more favourable to plaintiffs.

3. Member States need not apply paragraph 1 to proceedings in which it is for the court or competent body to investigate the facts of the case.

4. Paragraphs 1, 2 and 3 shall also apply to:
   - (a) the situations covered by Article 141 of the Treaty and, insofar as discrimination based on sex is concerned, by Directives 92/85/EEC and 96/34/EC;
   - (b) any civil or administrative procedure concerning the public or private sector which provides for means of redress under national law pursuant to the measures referred to in (a) with the exception of out-of-court procedures of a voluntary nature or provided for in national law.

5. This Article shall not apply to criminal procedures, unless otherwise provided by the Member States.

Chapter 3 General horizontal provisions

Article 23 Compliance

Member States shall take all necessary measures to ensure that:

(a) any laws, regulations and administrative provisions contrary to the principle of equal treatment are abolished;

(b) provisions contrary to the principle of equal treatment in individual or collective contracts or agreements, internal rules of undertakings or rules governing the independent occupations and professions and workers' and employers' organisations or any other arrangements shall be, or may be, declared null and void or are amended;

(c) occupational social security schemes containing such provisions may not be approved or extended by administrative measures.

Article 24 Victimisation

Member States shall introduce into their national legal systems such measures as are necessary to protect employees, including those who are employees' representatives provided for by national laws and/or practices, against dismissal or other adverse treatment by the employer as a reaction to a complaint within the undertaking or to any legal proceedings aimed at enforcing compliance with the principle of equal treatment.

Article 25 Penalties

Member States shall lay down the rules on penalties applicable to infringements of the national provisions adopted pursuant to this Directive, and shall take all measures necessary to ensure that they are applied. The penalties, which may comprise the payment of compensation to the victim, must be effective, proportionate and dissuasive. The Member States shall notify those provisions to the Commission by 5 October 2005 at the latest and shall notify it without delay of any subsequent amendment affecting them.

Article 26 Prevention of discrimination

Member States shall encourage, in accordance with national law, collective agreements or practice, employers and those responsible for access to vocational training to take effective measures to prevent all forms of discrimination on grounds of sex, in particular harassment and sexual harassment in the workplace, in access to employment, vocational training and promotion.

Article 27 Minimum requirements

1. Member States may introduce or maintain provisions which are more favourable to the protection of the principle of equal treatment than those laid down in this Directive.

2. Implementation of this Directive shall under no circumstances be sufficient grounds for a reduction in the level of protection of workers in the areas to which it applies, without prejudice to the Member States' right to respond to changes in the situation by introducing laws, regulations and administrative provisions which differ from those in force on the notification of this Directive, provided that the provisions of this Directive are complied with.

Article 28 Relationship to Community and national provisions

1. This Directive shall be without prejudice to provisions concerning the protection of women, particularly as regards pregnancy and maternity.

2. This Directive shall be without prejudice to the provisions of Directive 96/34/EC and Directive 92/85/EEC.

Article 29 Gender mainstreaming

Member States shall actively take into account the objective of equality between men and women when formulating and implementing laws, regulations, administrative provisions, policies and activities in the areas referred to in this Directive.

Article 30 Dissemination of information

Member States shall ensure that measures taken pursuant to this Directive, together with the provisions already in force, are brought to the attention of all the persons concerned by all suitable means and, where appropriate, at the workplace.

Done at Strasbourg, 5 July 2006.

Directive 2010/41/EU of the European Parliament and of the Council of 7 July 2010 on the application of the principle of equal treatment between men and women engaged in an activity in a self-employed capacity

[OJ 2010 L180/1]

Article 1 Subject matter

1. This Directive lays down a framework for putting into effect in the Member States the principle of equal treatment between men and women engaged in an activity in a self-employed capacity, or contributing to the pursuit of such an activity, as regards those aspects not covered by Directives 2006/54/EC and 79/7/EEC.

2. The implementation of the principle of equal treatment between men and women in the access to and supply of goods and services remains covered by Directive 2004/113/EC.

Article 2 Scope

This Directive covers:

(a) self-employed workers, namely all persons pursuing a gainful activity for their own account, under the conditions laid down by national law;

(b) the spouses of self-employed workers or, when and in so far as recognised by national law, the life partners of self-employed workers, not being employees or business partners, where they habitually, under the conditions laid down by national law, participate in the activities of the self-employed worker and perform the same tasks or ancillary tasks.

Article 3 Definitions

For the purposes of this Directive, the following definitions shall apply:

(a) 'direct discrimination': where one person is treated less favourably on grounds of sex than another is, has been or would be, treated in a comparable situation;

(b) 'indirect discrimination': where an apparently neutral provision, criterion or practice would put persons of one sex at a particular disadvantage compared with persons of the other sex, unless that provision, criterion or practice is objectively justified by a legitimate aim, and the means of achieving that aim are appropriate and necessary;

(c) 'harassment': where unwanted conduct related to the sex of a person occurs with the purpose, or effect, of violating the dignity of that person, and of creating an intimidating, hostile, degrading, humiliating or offensive environment;

(d) 'sexual harassment': where any form of unwanted verbal, non-verbal, or physical, conduct of a sexual nature occurs, with the purpose or effect of violating the dignity of a person, in particular when creating an intimidating, hostile, degrading, humiliating or offensive environment.

Article 4 Principle of equal treatment

1. The principle of equal treatment means that there shall be no discrimination whatsoever on grounds of sex in the public or private sectors, either directly or indirectly, for instance in relation to

the establishment, equipment or extension of a business or the launching or extension of any other form of self-employed activity.

2. In the areas covered by paragraph 1, harassment and sexual harassment shall be deemed to be discrimination on grounds of sex and therefore prohibited. A person's rejection of, or submission to, such conduct may not be used as a basis for a decision affecting that person.

3. In the areas covered by paragraph 1, an instruction to discriminate against persons on grounds of sex shall be deemed to be discrimination.

Article 5 Positive action

Member States may maintain or adopt measures within the meaning of Article 157(4) of the Treaty on the Functioning of the European Union with a view to ensuring full equality in practice between men and women in working life, for instance aimed at promoting entrepreneurship initiatives among women.

Article 6 Establishment of a company

Without prejudice to the specific conditions for access to certain activities which apply equally to both sexes, the Member States shall take the measures necessary to ensure that the conditions for the establishment of a company between spouses, or between life partners when and in so far as recognised by national law, are not more restrictive than the conditions for the establishment of a company between other persons.

Article 7 Social protection

1. Where a system for social protection for self-employed workers exists in a Member State, that Member State shall take the necessary measures to ensure that spouses and life partners referred to in Article 2(b) can benefit from a social protection in accordance with national law.

2. The Member States may decide whether the social protection referred to in paragraph 1 is implemented on a mandatory or voluntary basis.

Article 8 Maternity benefits

1. The Member States shall take the necessary measures to ensure that female self-employed workers and female spouses and life partners referred to in Article 2 may, in accordance with national law, be granted a sufficient maternity allowance enabling interruptions in their occupational activity owing to pregnancy or motherhood for at least 14 weeks.

2. The Member States may decide whether the maternity allowance referred to in paragraph 1 is granted on a mandatory or voluntary basis.

3. The allowance referred to in paragraph 1 shall be deemed sufficient if it guarantees an income at least equivalent to:

(a) the allowance which the person concerned would receive in the event of a break in her activities on grounds connected with her state of health and/or;

(b) the average loss of income or profit in relation to a comparable preceding period subject to any ceiling laid down under national law and/or;

(c) any other family related allowance established by national law, subject to any ceiling laid down under national law.

4. The Member States shall take the necessary measures to ensure that female self-employed workers and female spouses and life partners referred to in Article 2 have access to any existing services supplying temporary replacements or to any existing national social services. The Member States may provide that access to those services is an alternative to or a part of the allowance referred to in paragraph 1 of this Article.

Article 9 Defence of rights

1. The Member States shall ensure that judicial or administrative proceedings, including, where Member States consider it appropriate, conciliation procedures, for the enforcement of the obligations under this Directive are available to all persons who consider they have sustained loss

or damage as a result of a failure to apply the principle of equal treatment to them, even after the relationship in which the discrimination is alleged to have occurred has ended.

2. The Member States shall ensure that associations, organisations and other legal entities which have, in accordance with the criteria laid down by their national law, a legitimate interest in ensuring that this Directive is complied with may engage, either on behalf or in support of the complainant, with his or her approval, in any judicial or administrative proceedings provided for the enforcement of obligations under this Directive.

3. Paragraphs 1 and 2 shall be without prejudice to national rules on time limits for bringing actions relating to the principle of equal treatment.

Article 10 Compensation or reparation

The Member States shall introduce such measures into their national legal systems as are necessary to ensure real and effective compensation or reparation, as Member States so determine, for the loss or damage sustained by a person as a result of discrimination on grounds of sex, such compensation or reparation being dissuasive and proportionate to the loss or damage suffered. Such compensation or reparation shall not be limited by the fixing of a prior upper limit.

Article 11 Equality bodies

1. The Member States shall take the necessary measures to ensure that the body or bodies designated in accordance with Article 20 of Directive 2006/54/EC are also competent for the promotion, analysis, monitoring and support of equal treatment of all persons covered by this Directive without discrimination on grounds of sex.

2. The Member States shall ensure that the tasks of the bodies referred to in paragraph 1 include:

(a) providing independent assistance to victims of discrimination in pursuing their complaints of discrimination, without prejudice to the rights of victims and of associations, organisations and other legal entities referred to in Article 9(2);

(b) conducting independent surveys on discrimination;

(c) publishing independent reports and making recommendations on any issue relating to such discrimination;

(d) exchanging, at the appropriate level, the information available with the corresponding European bodies, such as the European Institute for Gender Equality.

Article 12 Gender mainstreaming

The Member States shall actively take into account the objective of equality between men and women when formulating and implementing laws, regulations, administrative provisions, policies and activities in the areas referred to in this Directive.

Article 13 Dissemination of information

The Member States shall ensure that the provisions adopted pursuant to this Directive, together with the relevant provisions already in force, are brought by all appropriate means to the attention of the persons concerned throughout their territory.

Article 14 Level of protection

The Member States may introduce or maintain provisions which are more favourable to the protection of the principle of equal treatment between men and women than those laid down in this Directive.

The implementation of this Directive shall under no circumstances constitute grounds for a reduction in the level of protection against discrimination already afforded by Member States in the fields covered by this Directive.

Done at Strasbourg, 7 July 2010.

Social policy: worker protection

Council Directive 2001/23/EC of 12 March 2001 on the approximation of the laws of the Member States relating to the safeguarding of employees' rights in the event of transfers of undertakings, businesses or parts of undertakings or businesses*

[OJ 2001 L82/16]

Chapter I Scope and definitions

Article 1

1. (a) This Directive shall apply to any transfer of an undertaking, business, or part of an undertaking or business to another employer as a result of a legal transfer or merger.
   (b) Subject to subparagraph (a) and the following provisions of this Article, there is a transfer within the meaning of this Directive where there is a transfer of an economic entity which retains its identity, meaning an organised grouping of resources which has the objective of pursuing an economic activity, whether or not that activity is central or ancillary.
   (c) This Directive shall apply to public and private undertakings engaged in economic activities whether or not they are operating for gain. An administrative reorganisation of public administrative authorities, or the transfer of administrative functions between public administrative authorities, is not a transfer within the meaning of this Directive.

2. This Directive shall apply where and in so far as the undertaking, business or part of the undertaking or business to be transferred is situated within the territorial scope of the Treaty.

3. This Directive shall apply to a transfer of a seagoing vessel that is part of a transfer of an undertaking, business or part of an undertaking or business within the meaning of paragraphs 1 and 2, provided that the transferee is situated, or the transferred undertaking, business, or part of an undertaking or business remains, within the territorial scope of the Treaty.

This Directive shall not apply where the object of the transfer consists exclusively of one or more seagoing vessels.

Chapter II Safeguarding of employees' rights

Article 3

1. The transferor's rights and obligations arising from a contract of employment or from an employment relationship existing on the date of a transfer shall, by reason of such transfer, be transferred to the transferee.

Member States may provide that, after the date of transfer, the transferor and the transferee shall be jointly and severally liable in respect of obligations which arose before the date of transfer from a contract of employment or an employment relationship existing on the date of the transfer.

2. Member States may adopt appropriate measures to ensure that the transferor notifies the transferee of all the rights and obligations which will be transferred to the transferee under this

* **Editor's Note:** This Directive repeals and replaces Council Directive 77/187/EEC (OJ L61, 5.3.1977, p. 26) and Council Directive 98/50/EC (OJ L201, 17.7.1998, p. 88). As amended by Directive 2015/1794 (OJ 2015 L263/1). As corrected to OJ 2015 L181/84.

Article, so far as those rights and obligations are or ought to have been known to the transferor at the time of the transfer. A failure by the transferor to notify the transferee of any such right or obligation shall not affect the transfer of that right or obligation and the rights of any employees against the transferee and/or transferor in respect of that right or obligation.

3. Following the transfer, the transferee shall continue to observe the terms and conditions agreed in any collective agreement on the same terms applicable to the transferor under that agreement, until the date of termination or expiry of the collective agreement or the entry into force or application of another collective agreement. Member States may limit the period for observing such terms and conditions with the proviso that it shall not be less than one year.

4. (a) Unless Member States provide otherwise, paragraphs 1 and 3 shall not apply in relation to employees' rights to old-age, invalidity or survivors' benefits under supplementary company or intercompany pension schemes outside the statutory social security schemes in Member States.

(b) Even where they do not provide in accordance with sub-paragraph (a) that paragraphs 1 and 3 apply in relation to such rights, Member States shall adopt the measures necessary to protect the interests of employees and of persons no longer employed in the transferor's business at the time of the transfer in respect of rights conferring on them immediate or prospective entitlement to old age benefits, including survivors' benefits, under supplementary schemes referred to in subparagraph (a).

Article 4

1. The transfer of the undertaking, business or part of the undertaking or business shall not in itself constitute grounds for dismissal by the transferor or the transferee. This provision shall not stand in the way of dismissals that may take place for economic, technical or organisational reasons entailing changes in the workforce. Member States may provide that the first sub-paragraph shall not apply to certain specific categories of employees who are not covered by the laws or practice of the Member States in respect of protection against dismissal.

2. If the contract of employment or the employment relationship is terminated because the transfer involves a substantial change in working conditions to the detriment of the employee, the employer shall be regarded as having been responsible for termination of the contract of employment or of the employment relationship.

Article 5

1. Unless Member States provide otherwise, Articles 3 and 4 shall not apply to any transfer of an undertaking, business or part of an undertaking or business where the transferor is the subject of bankruptcy proceedings or any analogous insolvency proceedings which have been instituted with a view to the liquidation of the assets of the transferor and are under the supervision of a competent public authority (which may be an insolvency practitioner authorised by a competent public authority).

2. Where Articles 3 and 4 apply to a transfer during insolvency proceedings which have been opened in relation to a transferor (whether or not those proceedings have been instituted with a view to the liquidation of the assets of the transferor) and provided that such proceedings are under the supervision of a competent public authority (which may be an insolvency practitioner determined by national law) a Member State may provide that:

(a) notwithstanding Article 3(1), the transferor's debts arising from any contracts of employment or employment relationships and payable before the transfer or before the opening of the insolvency proceedings shall not be transferred to the transferee, provided that such proceedings give rise, under the law of that Member State, to protection at least equivalent to that provided for in situations covered by Council Directive 80/987/EEC of 20 October 1980 on the approximation of the laws of the Member States relating to the protection of employees in the event of the insolvency of their employer,[1] and, or alternatively, that,

(b) the transferee, transferor or person or persons exercising the transferor's functions, on the one hand, and the representatives of the employees on the other hand may agree alterations, in so far as current law or practice permits, to the employees' terms and

[1] OJ L 283, 20.10.1980, p. 23. Directive as last amended by the 1994 Act of Accession.

conditions of employment designed to safeguard employment opportunities by ensuring the survival of the undertaking, business or part of the undertaking or business.

3. A Member State may apply paragraph 20(b) to any transfers where the transferor is in a situation of serious economic crisis, as defined by national law, provided that the situation is declared by a competent public authority and open to judicial supervision, on condition that such provisions already existed in national law on 17 July 1998.

The Commission shall present a report on the effects of this provision before 17 July 2003 and shall submit any appropriate proposals to the Council.

4. Member States shall take appropriate measures with a view to preventing misuse of insolvency proceedings in such a way as to deprive employees of the rights provided for in this Directive.

Article 6

1. If the undertaking, business or part of an undertaking or business preserves its autonomy, the status and function of the representatives or of the representation of the employees affected by the transfer shall be preserved on the same terms and subject to the same conditions as existed before the date of the transfer by virtue of law, regulation, administrative provision or agreement, provided that the conditions necessary for the constitution of the employee's representation are fulfilled.

The first subparagraph shall not apply if, under the laws, regulations, administrative provisions or practice in the Member States, or by agreement with the representatives of the employees, the conditions necessary for the reappointment of the representatives of the employees or for the reconstitution of the representation of the employees are fulfilled.

Where the transferor is the subject of bankruptcy proceedings or any analogous insolvency proceedings which have been instituted with a view to the liquidation of the assets of the transferor and are under the supervision of a competent public authority (which may be an insolvency practitioner authorised by a competent public authority), Member States may take the necessary measures to ensure that the transferred employees are properly represented until the new election or designation of representatives of the employees.

If the undertaking, business or part of an undertaking or business does not preserve its autonomy, the Member States shall take the necessary measures to ensure that the employees transferred who were represented before the transfer continue to be properly represented during the period necessary for the reconstitution or reappointment of the representation of employees in accordance with national law or practice.

2. If the term of office of the representatives of the employees affected by the transfer expires as a result of the transfer, the representatives shall continue to enjoy the protection provided by the laws, regulations, administrative provisions or practice of the Member States.

Done at Brussels, 12 March 2001.

Council Directive 92/85/EEC of 19 October 1992 on the introduction of measures to encourage improvements in the safety and health at work of pregnant workers and workers who have recently given birth or are breastfeeding (tenth individual Directive within the meaning of Article 16(1) of Directive 89/391/EEC)*

[OJ 1992 L348/1]

Section I Purpose and definitions

Article 1 Purpose

1. The purpose of this Directive, which is the tenth individual Directive within the meaning of Article 16(1) of Directive 89/391/EEC, is to implement measures to encourage improvements in the

* **Editor's Note:** As amended by Directive 2007/30 (OJ 2007 L165/21) and Directive 2014/27 (OJ 2014 L65/7).

safety and health at work of pregnant workers and workers who have recently given birth or who are breastfeeding.

2. The provisions of Directive 89/391/EEC, except for Article 2(2) thereof, shall apply in full to the whole area covered by paragraph 1, without prejudice to any more stringent and/or specific provisions contained in this Directive.

3. This Directive may not have the effect of reducing the level of protection afforded to pregnant workers, workers who have recently given birth or who are breastfeeding as compared with the situation which exists in each Member State on the date on which this Directive is adopted.

Article 2 Definitions

For the purposes of this Directive:

(a) *pregnant worker* shall mean a pregnant worker who informs her employer of her condition, in accordance with national legislation and/or national practice;

(b) *worker who has recently given birth* shall mean a worker who has recently given birth within the meaning of national legislation and/or national practice and who informs her employer of her condition, in accordance with that legislation and/or practice;

(c) *worker who is breastfeeding* shall mean a worker who is breastfeeding within the meaning of national legislation and/or national practice and who informs her employer of her condition, in accordance with that legislation and/or practice.

Section II General provisions

Article 7 Night work

1. Member States shall take the necessary measures to ensure that workers referred to in Article 2 are not obliged to perform night work during their pregnancy and for a period following childbirth which shall be determined by the national authority competent for safety and health, subject to submission, in accordance with the procedures laid down by the Member States, of a medical certificate stating that this is necessary for the safety or health of the worker concerned.

2. The measures referred to in paragraph 1 must entail the possibility, in accordance with national legislation and/or national practice, of:

(a) transfer to daytime work; or

(b) leave from work or extension of maternity leave where such a transfer is not technically and/or objectively feasible or cannot reasonably be required on duly substantiated grounds.

Article 8 Maternity leave

1. Member States shall take the necessary measures to ensure that workers within the meaning of Article 2 are entitled to a continuous period of maternity leave of at least 14 weeks allocated before and/or after confinement in accordance with national legislation and/or practice.

2. The maternity leave stipulated in paragraph 1 must include compulsory maternity leave of at least two weeks allocated before and/or after confinement in accordance with national legislation and/or practice.

Article 10 Prohibition of dismissal

In order to guarantee workers, within the meaning of Article 2, the exercise of their health and safety protection rights as recognised under this Article, it will be provided that:

1. Member States shall take the necessary measures to prohibit the dismissal of workers, within the meaning of Article 2, during the period from the beginning of their pregnancy to the end of the maternity leave referred to in Article 8(1), save in exceptional cases not connected with their condition which are permitted under national legislation and/or practice and, where applicable, provided that the competent authority has given its consent;

2. if a worker, within the meaning of Article 2, is dismissed during the period referred to in point 1, the employer must cite duly substantiated grounds for her dismissal in writing;

3. Member States shall take the necessary measures to protect workers, within the meaning of Article 2, from consequences of dismissal which is unlawful by virtue of point 1.

Article 11 Employment rights

In order to guarantee workers within the meaning of Article 2 the exercise of their health and safety protection rights as recognised in this Article, it shall be provided that:

1. in the cases referred to in Articles 5, 6 and 7, the employment rights relating to the employment contract, including the maintenance of a payment to, and/or entitlement to an adequate allowance for, workers within the meaning of Article 2, must be ensured in accordance with national legislation and/or national practice;

2. in the case referred to in Article 8, the following must be ensured:
   (a) the rights connected with the employment contract of workers within the meaning of Article 2, other than those referred to in point (b) below;
   (b) maintenance of a payment to, and/or entitlement to an adequate allowance for, workers within the meaning of Article 2;

3. the allowance referred to in point 2(b) shall be deemed adequate if it guarantees income at least equivalent to that which the worker concerned would receive in the event of a break in her activities on grounds connected with her state of health, subject to any ceiling laid down under national legislation;

4. Member States may make entitlement to pay or the allowance referred to in points 1 and 2(b) conditional upon the worker concerned fulfilling the conditions of eligibility for such benefits laid down under national legislation.

These conditions may under no circumstances provide for periods of previous employment in excess of 12 months immediately prior to the presumed date of confinement.

Article 12 Defence of rights

Member States shall introduce into their national legal systems such measures as are necessary to enable all workers who should themselves wronged by failure to comply with the obligations arising from the Directive to pursue their claims by judicial process (and/or, in accordance with national laws and/or practice) by recourse to other competent authorities.

. . .

Done at Luxembourg, 19 October 1992.

Council Directive 98/59/EC of 20 July 1998 on the approximation of the laws of the Member States relating to collective redundancies*

[OJ 1998 L225/16]

Section I Definitions and scope

Article 1

1. For the purposes of this Directive:
   (a) 'collective redundancies' means dismissals effected by an employer for one or more reasons not related to the individual workers concerned where, according to the choice of the Member States, the number of redundancies is:
   (i) either, over a period of 30 days:
      – at least 10 in establishments normally employing more than 20 and less than 100 workers,

* **Editor's Note:** This repeals Directive 75/129 as amended by Directive 92/56. As corrected by OJ 2007 L59/84. As further amended by Directive 2015/1794 (OJ 2015 L263/1).

- at least 10% of the number of workers in establishments normally employing at least 100 but less than 300 workers,
- at least 30 in establishments normally employing 300 workers or more,

(ii) or, over a period of 90 days, at least 20, whatever the number of workers normally employed in the establishments in question;

(b) 'workers' representatives means the workers' representatives provided for by the laws or practices of the Member States.

For the purpose of calculating the number of redundancies provided for in the first subparagraph of point (a), terminations of an employment contract which occur on the employer's initiative for one or more reasons not related to the individual workers concerned shall be assimilated to redundancies, provided that there are at least five redundancies.

2. This Directive shall not apply to:

(a) collective redundancies effected under contracts of employment concluded for limited periods of time or for specific tasks except where such redundancies take place prior to the date of expiry or the completion of such contracts;

(b) workers employed by public administrative bodies or by establishments governed by public law (or, in Member States where this concept is unknown, by equivalent bodies);

Section II Information and consultation

Article 2

1. Where an employer is contemplating collective redundancies, he shall begin consultations with the workers' representatives in good time with a view to reaching an agreement.

2. These consultations shall, at least, cover ways and means of avoiding collective redundancies or reducing the number of workers affected, and of mitigating the consequences by recourse to accompanying social measures aimed, *inter alia*, at aid for redeploying or retraining workers made redundant.

Member States may provide that the workers' representatives may call on the services of experts in accordance with national legislation and/or practice.

3. To enable workers' representatives to make constructive proposals, the employers shall in good time during the course of the consultations:

(a) supply them with all relevant information and

(b) in any event notify them in writing of:

(i) the reasons for the projected redundancies;

(ii) the number of categories of workers to be made redundant;

(iii) the number and categories of workers normally employed;

(iv) the period over which the projected redundancies are to be effected;

(v) the criteria proposed for the selection of the workers to be made redundant in so far as national legislation and/or practice confers the power therefore upon the employer;

(vi) the method for calculating any redundancy payments other than those arising out of national legislation and/or practice.

The employer shall forward to the competent public authority a copy of, at least, the elements of the written communication which are provided for in the first subparagraph, point (b), subpoints (i) to (v).

4. The obligations laid down in paragraphs 1, 2 and 3 shall apply irrespective of whether the decision regarding collective redundancies is being taken by the employer or by an undertaking controlling the employer.

In considering alleged breaches of the information, consultation and notification requirements laid down by this Directive, account shall not be taken of any defence on the part of the employer on the ground that the necessary information has not been provided to the employer by the undertaking which took the decision leading to collective redundancies.

Section III Procedure for collective redundancies

Article 3

1. Employers shall notify the competent public authority in writing of any projected collective redundancies.

However, Member States may provide that in the case of planned collective redundancies arising from termination of the establishment's activities as a result of a judicial decision, the employer shall be obliged to notify the competent public authority in writing only if the latter so requests.

This notification shall contain all relevant information concerning the projected collective redundancies and the consultations with workers' representatives provided for in Article 2, and particularly the reasons for the redundancies, the number of workers to be made redundant, the number of workers normally employed and the period over which the redundancies are to be effected.

Where the projected collective redundancy concerns members of the crew of a seagoing vessel, the employer shall notify the competent authority of the State of the flag which the vessel flies.

2. Employers shall forward to the workers' representatives a copy of the notification provided for in paragraph 1.

The workers' representatives may send any comments they may have to the competent public authority.

Article 4

1. Projected collective redundancies notified to the competent public authority shall take effect not earlier than 30 days after the notification referred to in Article 3(1) without prejudice to any provisions governing individual rights with regard to notice of dismissal.

Member States may grant the competent public authority the power to reduce the period provided for in the preceding subparagraph.

2. The period provided for in paragraph 1 shall be used by the competent public authority to seek solutions to the problems raised by the projected collective redundancies.

3. Where the initial period provided for in paragraph 1 is shorter than 60 days, Member States may grant the competent public authority the power to extend the initial period to 60 days following notification where the problems raised by the projected collective redundancies are not likely to be solved within the initial period.

Member States may grant the competent public authority wider powers of extension. The employer must be informed of the extension and the grounds for it before expiry of the initial period provided for in paragraph 1.

4. Member States need not apply this Article to collective redundancies arising from termination of the establishment's activities where this is the result of a judicial decision.

Section IV Final provisions

Article 5

This Directive shall not affect the right of Member States to apply or to introduce laws, regulations or administrative provisions which are more favourable to workers or to promote or to allow the application of collective agreements more favourable to workers.

Article 6

Member States shall ensure that judicial and/or administrative procedures for the enforcement of obligations under this Directive are available to the workers' representatives and/or workers.

Article 7

Member States shall forward to the Commission the text of any fundamental provisions of national law already adopted or being adopted in the area governed by this Directive.

Article 8

1. The Directives listed in Annex I, Part A, are hereby repealed without prejudice to the obligations of the Member States concerning the deadlines for transposition of the said Directive set out in Annex I, Part B.

2. References to the repealed Directives shall be construed as references to this Directive and shall be read in accordance with the correlation table in Annex II.

Article 9

This Directive shall enter into force on the 20th day following its publication in the *Official Journal of the European Communities*.

Article 10

This Directive is addressed to the Member States.

Done at Brussels, 20 July 1998.

Directive 2003/88/EC of the European Parliament and of the Council of 4 November 2003 concerning certain aspects of the organisation of working time*

[OJ 2003 L299/9]

Chapter 1 Scope and definitions

Article 1 Purpose and scope

1. This Directive lays down minimum safety and health requirements for the organisation of working time.

2. This Directive applies to:

(a) minimum periods of daily rest, weekly rest and annual leave, to breaks and maximum weekly working time; and

(b) certain aspects of night work, shift work and patterns of work.

3. This Directive shall apply to all sectors of activity, both public and private, within the meaning of Article 2 of Directive 89/391/EEC, without prejudice to Articles 14, 17, 18 and 19 of this Directive.

This Directive shall not apply to seafarers, as defined in Directive 1999/63/EC without prejudice to Article 2(8) of this Directive.

4. The provisions of Directive 89/391/EEC are fully applicable to the matters referred to in paragraph 2, without prejudice to more stringent and/or specific provisions contained in this Directive.

Article 2 Definitions

For the purposes of this Directive, the following definitions shall apply:

1. 'working time' means any period during which the worker is working, at the employer's disposal and carrying out his activity or duties, in accordance with national laws and/or practice;

2. 'rest period' means any period which is not working time;

3. 'night time' means any period of not less than seven hours, as defined by national law, and which must include, in any case, the period between midnight and 5.00;

4. 'night worker' means:

(a) on the one hand, any worker, who, during night time, works at least three hours of his daily working time as a normal course; and

(b) on the other hand, any worker who is likely during night time to work a certain proportion of his annual working time, as defined at the choice of the Member State concerned:

(i) by national legislation, following consultation with the two sides of industry; or

(ii) by collective agreements or agreements concluded between the two sides of industry at national or regional level;

* **Editor's Note:** This Directive repeals and replaces Directives 93/104 and 2000/34.

5. 'shift work' means any method of organising work in shifts whereby workers succeed each other at the same work stations according to a certain pattern, including a rotating pattern, and which may be continuous or discontinuous, entailing the need for workers to work at different times over a given period of days or weeks;

6. 'shift worker' means any worker whose work schedule is part of shift work;

7. 'mobile worker' means any worker employed as a member of travelling or flying personnel by an undertaking which operates transport services for passengers or goods by road, air or inland waterway;

8. 'offshore work' means work performed mainly on or from offshore installations (including drilling rigs), directly or indirectly in connection with the exploration, extraction or exploitation of mineral resources, including hydrocarbons, and diving in connection with such activities, whether performed from an offshore installation or a vessel;

9. 'adequate rest' means that workers have regular rest periods, the duration of which is expressed in units of time and which are sufficiently long and continuous to ensure that, as a result of fatigue or other irregular working patterns, they do not cause injury to themselves, to fellow workers or to others and that they do not damage their health, either in the short term or in the longer term.

Chapter 2 Minimum rest periods—Other aspects of the organisation of working time

Article 3 Daily rest

Member States shall take the measures necessary to ensure that every worker is entitled to a minimum daily rest period of 11 consecutive hours per 24-hour period.

Article 4 Breaks

Member States shall take the measures necessary to ensure that, where the working day is longer than six hours, every worker is entitled to a rest break, the details of which, including duration and the terms on which it is granted, shall be laid down in collective agreements or agreements between the two sides of industry or, failing that, by national legislation.

Article 5 Weekly rest period

Member States shall take the measures necessary to ensure that, per each seven-day period, every worker is entitled to a minimum uninterrupted rest period of 24 hours plus the 11 hours' daily rest referred to in Article 3.

If objective, technical or work organisation conditions so justify, a minimum rest period of 24 hours may be applied.

Article 6 Maximum weekly working time

Member States shall take the measures necessary to ensure that, in keeping with the need to protect the safety and health of workers:

(a) the period of weekly working time is limited by means of laws, regulations or administrative provisions or by collective agreements or agreements between the two sides of industry;

(b) the average working time for each seven-day period, including overtime, does not exceed 48 hours.

Article 7 Annual leave

1. Member States shall take the measures necessary to ensure that every worker is entitled to paid annual leave of at least four weeks in accordance with the conditions for entitlement to, and granting of, such leave laid down by national legislation and/or practice.

2. The minimum period of paid annual leave may not be replaced by an allowance in lieu, except where the employment relationship is terminated.

Chapter 3 Night work—Shift work—Patterns of work

Article 8 Length of night work

Member States shall take the measures necessary to ensure that:

(a) normal hours of work for night workers do not exceed an average of eight hours in any 24-hour period;

(b) night workers whose work involves special hazards or heavy physical or mental strain do not work more than eight hours in any period of 24 hours during which they perform night work.

For the purposes of point (b), work involving special hazards or heavy physical or mental strain shall be defined by national legislation and/or practice or by collective agreements or agreements concluded between the two sides of industry, taking account of the specific effects and hazards of night work.

Article 9 Health assessment and transfer of night workers to day work

1. Member States shall take the measures necessary to ensure that:

(a) night workers are entitled to a free health assessment before their assignment and thereafter at regular intervals;

(b) night workers suffering from health problems recognised as being connected with the fact that they perform night work are transferred whenever possible to day work to which they are suited.

2. The free health assessment referred to in paragraph 1(a) must comply with medical confidentiality.

3. The free health assessment referred to in paragraph 1(a) may be conducted within the national health system.

Article 10 Guarantees for night-time working

Member States may make the work of certain categories of night workers subject to certain guarantees, under conditions laid down by national legislation and/or practice, in the case of workers who incur risks to their safety or health linked to night-time working.

Article 11 Notification of regular use of night workers

Member States shall take the measures necessary to ensure that an employer who regularly uses night workers brings this information to the attention of the competent authorities if they so request.

Article 12 Safety and health protection

Member States shall take the measures necessary to ensure that:

(a) night workers and shift workers have safety and health protection appropriate to the nature of their work;

(b) appropriate protection and prevention services or facilities with regard to the safety and health of night workers and shift workers are equivalent to those applicable to other workers and are available at all times.

Article 13 Pattern of work

Member States shall take the measures necessary to ensure that an employer who intends to organise work according to a certain pattern takes account of the general principle of adapting work to the worker, with a view, in particular, to alleviating monotonous work and work at a predetermined work-rate, depending on the type of activity, and of safety and health requirements, especially as regards breaks during working time.

Done at Brussels, 4 November 2003.

Competition

Regulation No 17—First Regulation implementing Articles 81 and 82 of the Treaty*

[OJ Sp. Ed. 1962, No 204/62, p. 87]

Article 8 Duration and revocation of decisions under Article 85(3)

3. The Commission may revoke or amend its decision or prohibit specified acts by the parties:
   (a) where there has been a change in any of the facts which were basic to the making of the decision;
   (b) where the parties commit a breach of any obligation attached to the decision;
   (c) where the decision is based on incorrect information or was induced by deceit;
   (d) where the parties abuse the exemption from the provisions of Article 85(1) of the Treaty granted to them by the decision.

In cases to which subparagraphs (b), (c) or (d) apply, the decision may be revoked with retroactive effect.

Commission Notice on agreements of minor importance which do not appreciably restrict competition under Article 101(1) of the Treaty on the Functioning of the European Union (De Minimis Notice)

[OJ 2014 C291/01]

I

1. Article 101(1) of the Treaty on the Functioning of the European Union prohibits agreements between undertakings which may affect trade between Member States and which have as their object or effect the prevention, restriction or distortion of competition within the internal market. The Court of Justice of the European Union has clarified that that provision is not applicable where the impact of the agreement on trade between Member States or on competition is not appreciable.[1]

2. The Court of Justice has also clarified that an agreement which may affect trade between Member States and which has as its object the prevention, restriction or distortion of competition within the internal market constitutes, by its nature and independently of any concrete effects that it may have, an appreciable restriction of competition.[2] This Notice therefore does not cover agreements which have as their object the prevention, restriction or distortion of competition within the internal market.

3. In this Notice the Commission indicates, with the help of market share thresholds, the circumstances in which it considers that agreements which may have as their effect the prevention, restriction or distortion of competition within the internal market do not constitute an appreciable restriction of competition under Article 101 of the Treaty. This negative definition of

* **Editor's Note:** Following the entry into force of Regulation No 1/2003, included below, Article 8(3) is the only Article which remains, temporarily, in force. To those who continue to question the inclusion of this foundational piece of legislation or believe Regulation 17 to be long dead, I can assure you the reports of its death are greatly exaggerated! This was still the case as of 22 March 2023. See 31962R0017, http://data.europa.eu/eli/reg/1962/17/oj or http://data.europa.eu/eli/reg/1962/17/2004-05-01.

1 See Case C-226/11 *Expedia*, not yet reported, paragraphs 16 and 17.

2 See Case C-226/11 *Expedia*, in particular paragraphs 35, 36 and 37.

appreciability does not imply that agreements between undertakings which exceed the thresholds set out in this Notice constitute an appreciable restriction of competition. Such agreements may still have only a negligible effect on competition and may therefore not be prohibited by Article 101(1) of the Treaty.[3]

4. Agreements may also fall outside Article 101(1) of the Treaty because they are not capable of appreciably affecting trade between Member States. This Notice does not indicate what constitutes an appreciable effect on trade between Member States. Guidance to that effect is to be found in the Commission's Notice on effect on trade,[4] in which the Commission quantifies, with the help of the combination of a 5 % market share threshold and a EUR 40 million turnover threshold, which agreements are in principle not capable of appreciably affecting trade between Member States.[5] Such agreements normally fall outside Article 101(1) of the Treaty even if they have as their object the prevention, restriction or distortion of competition.

5. In cases covered by this Notice, the Commission will not institute proceedings either upon a complaint or on its own initiative. In addition, where the Commission has instituted proceedings but undertakings can demonstrate that they have assumed in good faith that the market shares mentioned in points 8, 9, 10 and 11 were not exceeded, the Commission will not impose fines. Although not binding on them, this Notice is also intended to give guidance to the courts and competition authorities of the Member States in their application of Article 101 of the Treaty.[6]

6. The principles set out in this Notice also apply to decisions by associations of undertakings and to concerted practices.

7. This Notice is without prejudice to any interpretation of Article 101 of the Treaty which may be given by the Court of Justice of the European Union.

II

8. The Commission holds the view that agreements between undertakings which may affect trade between Member States and which may have as their effect the prevention, restriction or distortion of competition within the internal market, do not appreciably restrict competition within the meaning of Article 101(1) of the Treaty:

(a) if the aggregate market share held by the parties to the agreement does not exceed 10 % on any of the relevant markets affected by the agreement, where the agreement is made between undertakings which are actual or potential competitors on any of those markets (agreements between competitors);[7] or

(b) if the market share held by each of the parties to the agreement does not exceed 15 % on any of the relevant markets affected by the agreement, where the agreement is made between undertakings which are not actual or potential competitors on any of those markets (agreements between non-competitors).

9. In cases where it is difficult to classify the agreement as either an agreement between competitors or an agreement between non-competitors the 10 % threshold is applicable.

[3] See, for instance, Joined Cases C-215/96 and C-216/96 *Bagnasco and Others* [1999] ECR I-135, paragraphs 34 and 35.

[4] Commission Notice—Guidelines on the effect on trade concept contained in Articles 81and 82 of the Treaty (OJ C 101, 27.4.2004, p. 81), in particular points 44 to 57.

[5] It should be noted that agreements between small and medium sized undertakings (SMEs), as defined in the Commission Recommendation of 6 May 2003 concerning the definition of micro, small and medium-sized enterprises or any future recommendation replacing it (OJ L 124, 20.5.2003, p. 36), are also not normally capable of affecting trade between Member States. See in particular point 50 of the Notice on effect of trade.

[6] In particular, in order to determine whether or not a restriction of competition is appreciable, the competition authorities and the courts of Member States may take into account the thresholds established in this Notice but are not required to do so. See Case C-226/11 Expedia, paragraph 31.

[7] On the definition of actual or potential competitors, see the Communication from the Commission—Guidelines on the applicability of Article 101 of the Treaty on the Functioning of the European Union to horizontal cooperation agreements (OJ C 11, 14.1.2011, p. 1), point 10. Two undertakings are treated as actual competitors if they are active on the same relevant market. An undertaking is treated as a potential competitor of another undertaking if, in the absence of the agreement, in case of a small but permanent increase in relative prices it is likely that the former, within a short period of time, would undertake the necessary additional investments or other necessary switching costs to enter the relevant market on which the latter is active.

10. Where, in a relevant market, competition is restricted by the cumulative effect of agreements for the sale of goods or services entered into by different suppliers or distributors (cumulative foreclosure effect of parallel networks of agreements having similar effects on the market), the market share thresholds set out in point 8 and 9 are reduced to 5 %, both for agreements between competitors and for agreements between non-competitors. Individual suppliers or distributors with a market share not exceeding 5 %, are in general not considered to contribute significantly to a cumulative foreclosure effect.[8] A cumulative foreclosure effect is unlikely to exist if less than 30 % of the relevant market is covered by parallel (networks of) agreements having similar effects.

11. The Commission also holds the view that agreements do not appreciably restrict competition if the market shares of the parties to the agreement do not exceed the thresholds of respectively 10 %, 15 % and 5 % set out in points 8, 9 and 10 during two successive calendar years by more than 2 percentage points.

12. In order to calculate the market share, it is necessary to determine the relevant market. This consists of the relevant product market and the relevant geographic market. When defining the relevant market, reference should be had to the Notice on the definition of the relevant market.[9] The market shares are to be calculated on the basis of sales value data or, where appropriate, purchase value data. If value data are not available, estimates based on other reliable market information, including volume data, may be used.

13. In view of the clarification of the Court of Justice referred to in point 2, this Notice does not cover agreements which have as their object the prevention, restriction or distortion of competition within the internal market. The Commission will thus not apply the safe harbour created by the market share thresholds set out in points 8, 9, 10 and 11 to such agreements.[10] For instance, as regards agreements between competitors, the Commission will not apply the principles set out in this Notice to, in particular, agreements containing restrictions which, directly or indirectly, have as their object: a) the fixing of prices when selling products to third parties; b) the limitation of output or sales; or c) the allocation of markets or customers. Likewise, the Commission will not apply the safe harbour created by those market share thresholds to agreements containing any of the restrictions that are listed as hardcore restrictions in any current or future Commission block exemption regulation,[11] which are considered by the Commission to generally constitute restrictions by object.

14. The safe harbour created by the market share thresholds set out in points 8, 9, 10 and 11 is particularly relevant for categories of agreements not covered by any Commission block exemption regulation.[12] The safe harbour is also relevant for agreements covered by a Commission block exemption regulation to the extent that those agreements contain a so-called excluded restriction, that is a restriction not listed as a hardcore restriction but nonetheless not covered by the Commission block exemption regulation.[13]

[8] See also the Guidelines on Vertical Restraints (OJ C 130, 19.5.2010, p. 1, in particular points 76, 134 and 179. While in the Guidelines on Vertical Restraints in relation to certain restrictions reference is made not only to the total but also to the tied market share of a particular supplier or buyer, in this Notice all market share thresholds refer to total market shares.

[9] Notice on the definition of the relevant market for the purposes of Community competition law (OJ C 372, 9.12.1997, p. 5).

[10] For these agreements, the Commission will exercise its discretion in deciding whether or not to institute proceedings.

[11] For supply and distribution agreements between non-competitors see in particular Article 4 of Commission Regulation (EU) No 330/2010 of 20 April 2010 on the application of Article 101(3) of the Treaty on the Functioning of the European Union to categories of vertical agreements and concerted practices (OJ L 102, 23.4.2010, p. 1) and for licensing agreements between non-competitors see in particular Article 4(2) of Commission Regulation (EU) No 316/2014 of 21 March 2014 on the application of Article 101(3) of the Treaty on the Functioning of the European Union to categories of technology transfer agreements (OJ L 93, 28.3.2014, p. 17). For agreements between competitors see in particular Article 5 of Commission Regulation (EU) No 1217/2010 of 14 December 2010 on the application of Article 101(3) of the Treaty on the Functioning of the European Union to certain categories of research and development agreements (OJ L 335, 18.12.2010, p. 36), and Article 4 of Commission Regulation (EU) No 1218/2010 of 14 December 2010 on the application of Article 101(3) of the Treaty on the Functioning of the European Union to certain categories of specialisation agreements (OJ L 335, 18.12.2010, p. 43) as well as Article 4(1) of Regulation (EU) No 316/2014.

[12] For instance, trade mark licence agreements and most types of agreements between competitors, with the exception of research and development agreements and specialisation agreements, are not covered by any block exemption regulation.

[13] For excluded restrictions see in particular Article 5 of Regulation (EU) No 330/2010, Article 5 of Regulation (EU) No 316/2014 and Article 6 of Regulation (EU) No 1217/2010.

15. For the purpose of this Notice, the terms 'undertaking', 'party to the agreement', 'distributor' and 'supplier' include their respective connected undertakings.

16. For the purpose of the Notice 'connected undertakings' are:

(a) undertakings in which a party to the agreement, directly or indirectly:
   i. has the power to exercise more than half the voting rights, or
   ii. has the power to appoint more than half the members of the supervisory board, board of management or bodies legally representing the undertaking, or
   iii. has the right to manage the undertaking's affairs;

(b) undertakings which directly or indirectly have, over a party to the agreement, the rights or powers listed in (a);

(c) undertakings in which an undertaking referred to in (b) has, directly or indirectly, the rights or powers listed in (a);

(d) undertakings in which a party to the agreement together with one or more of the undertakings referred to in (a), (b) or (c), or in which two or more of the latter undertakings, jointly have the rights or powers listed in (a);

(e) undertakings in which the rights or the powers listed in (a) are jointly held by:
   i. parties to the agreement or their respective connected undertakings referred to in (a) to (d), or
   ii. one or more of the parties to the agreement or one or more of their connected undertakings referred to in (a) to (d) and one or more third parties.

17. For the purposes of point (e) in point 16, the market share held by these jointly held undertakings is apportioned equally to each undertaking having the rights or the powers listed in point (a) in point 16.

Commission Notice on the definition of relevant market for the purposes of Community competition law (97/C 372/03)*

[OJ 1997 C372/5]

I. INTRODUCTION

1. The purpose of this notice is to provide guidance as to how the Commission applies the concept of relevant product and geographic market in its ongoing enforcement of Community competition law, in particular the application of Council Regulation No 17 and (EEC) No 4064/89, their equivalents in other sectoral applications such as transport, coal and steel, and agriculture, and the relevant provisions of the EEA Agreement.[1] Throughout this notice, references to Articles 85 and 86 of the Treaty and to merger control are to be understood as referring to the equivalent provisions in the EEA Agreement and the ECSC Treaty.

2. Market definition is a tool to identify and define the boundaries of competition between firms. It serves to establish the framework within which competition policy is applied by the Commission. The main purpose of market definition is to identify in a systematic way the competitive constraints that the undertakings involved[2] face. The objective of defining a market in both its product and geographic dimension is to identify those actual competitors of the undertakings involved that are

* **Editor's Note:** https://ec.europa.eu/competition/antitrust/legislation/market.html. All the Commission Competition antitrust notices can be found here: https://ec.europa.eu/competition-policy/antitrust/legislation/legislation-notices_en.

[1] The focus of assessment in State aid cases is the aid recipient and the industry/sector concerned rather than identification of competitive constraints faced by the aid recipient. When consideration of market power and therefore of the relevant market are raised in any particular case, elements of the approach outlined here might serve as a basis for the assessment of State aid cases.

[2] For the purposes of this notice, the undertakings involved will be, in the case of a concentration, the parties to the concentration; in investigations within the meaning of Article 86 of the Treaty, the undertaking being investigated or the complainants; for investigations within the meaning of Article 85, the parties to the Agreement.

capable of constraining those undertakings' behaviour and of preventing them from behaving independently of effective competitive pressure. It is from this perspective that the market definition makes it possible *inter alia* to calculate market shares that would convey meaningful information regarding market power for the purposes of assessing dominance or for the purposes of applying Article 85.

3. It follows from point 2 that the concept of 'relevant market' is different from other definitions of market often used in other contexts. For instance, companies often use the term 'market' to refer to the area where it sells its products or to refer broadly to the industry or sector where it belongs.

4. The definition of the relevant market in both its product and its geographic dimensions often has a decisive influence on the assessment of a competition case. By rendering public the procedures which the Commission follows when considering market definition and by indicating the criteria and evidence on which it relies to reach a decision, the Commission expects to increase the transparency of its policy and decision-making in the area of competition policy.

5. Increased transparency will also result in companies and their advisers being able to better anticipate the possibility that the Commission may raise competition concerns in an individual case. Companies could, therefore, take such a possibility into account in their own internal decision-making when contemplating, for instance, acquisitions, the creation of joint ventures, or the establishment of certain agreements. It is also intended that companies should be in a better position to understand what sort of information the Commission considers relevant for the purposes of market definition.

6. The Commission's interpretation of 'relevant market' is without prejudice to the interpretation which may be given by the Court of Justice or the Court of First Instance of the European Communities.

II. DEFINITION OF RELEVANT MARKET

Definition of relevant product market and relevant geographic market

7. The Regulations based on Article 85 and 86 of the Treaty, in particular in section 6 of Form A/B with respect to Regulation No 17, as well as in section 6 of Form CO with respect to Regulation (EEC) No 4064/89 on the control of concentrations having a Community dimension have laid down the following definitions, 'Relevant product markets' are defined as follows:

'A relevant product market comprises all those products and/or services which are regarded as interchangeable or substitutable by the consumer, by reason of the products' characteristics, their prices and their intended use'.

8. 'Relevant geographic markets' are defined as follows:

'The relevant geographic market comprises the area in which the undertakings concerned are involved in the supply and demand of products or services, in which the conditions of competition are sufficiently homogeneous and which can be distinguished from neighbouring areas because the conditions of competition are appreciably different in those area'.

9. The relevant market within which to assess a given competition issue is therefore established by the combination of the product and geographic markets. The Commission interprets the definitions in paragraphs 7 and 8 (which reflect the case-law of the Court of Justice and the Court of First Instance as well as its own decision-making practice) according to the orientations defined in this notice.

Concept of relevant market and objectives of Community competition policy

10. The concept of relevant market is closely related to the objectives pursued under Community competition policy. For example, under the Community's merger control, the objective in controlling structural changes in the supply of a product/service is to prevent the creation or reinforcement of a dominant position as a result of which effective competition would be significantly impeded in a substantial part of the common market. Under the Community's competition rules, a dominant position is such that a firm or group of firms would be in a position to behave to an appreciable extent

independently of its competitors, customers and ultimately of its consumers.[3] Such a position would usually arise when a firm or group of firms accounted for a large share of the supply in any given market, provided that other factors analysed in the assessment (such as entry barriers, customers' capacity to react, etc.) point in the same direction.

11. The same approach is followed by the Commission in its application of Article 86 of the Treaty to firms that enjoy a single or collective dominant position. Within the meaning of Regulation No 17, the Commission has the power to investigate and bring to an end abuses of such a dominant position, which must also be defined by reference to the relevant market. Markets may also need to be defined in the application of Article 85 of the Treaty, in particular, in determining whether an appreciable restriction of competition exists or in establishing if the condition pursuant to Article 85(3)(b) for an exemption from the application of Article 85(1) is met.

12. The criteria for defining the relevant market are applied generally for the analysis of certain types of behaviour in the market and for the analysis of structural changes in the supply of products. This methodology, though, might lead to different results depending on the nature of the competition issue being examined. For instance, the scope of the geographic market might be different when analysing a concentration, where the analysis is essentially prospective, from an analysis of past behaviour. The different time horizon considered in each case might lead to the result that different geographic markets are defined for the same products depending on whether the Commission is examining a change in the structure of supply, such as a concentration or a cooperative joint venture, or examining issues relating to certain past behaviour.

Basic principles for market definition

Competitive constraints

13. Firms are subject to three main sources or competitive constraints: demand substitutability, supply substitutability and potential competition. From an economic point of view, for the definition of the relevant market, demand substitution constitutes the most immediate and effective disciplinary force on the suppliers of a given product, in particular in relation to their pricing decisions. A firm or a group of firms cannot have a significant impact on the prevailing conditions of sale, such as prices, if its customers are in a position to switch easily to available substitute products or to suppliers located elsewhere. Basically, the exercise of market definition consists in identifying the effective alternative sources of supply for the customers of the undertakings involved, in terms both of products/services and of geographic location of suppliers.

14. The competitive constraints arising from supply side substitutability other then those described in paragraphs 20 to 23 and from potential competition are in general less immediate and in any case require an analysis of additional factors. As a result such constraints are taken into account at the assessment stage of competition analysis.

Demand substitution

15. The assessment of demand substitution entails a determination of the range of products which are viewed as substitutes by the consumer. One way of making this determination can be viewed as a speculative experiment, postulating a hypothetical small, lasting change in relative prices and evaluating the likely reactions of customers to that increase. The exercise of market definition focuses on prices for operational and practical purposes, and more precisely on demand substitution arising from small, permanent changes in relative prices. This concept can provide clear indications as to the evidence that is relevant in defining markets.

16. Conceptually, this approach means that, starting from the type of products that the undertakings involved sell and the area in which they sell them, additional products and areas will be included in, or excluded from, the market definition depending on whether competition from these other products and areas affect or restrain sufficiently the pricing of the parties' products in the short term.

[3] Definition given by the Court of Justice in its judgment of 13 February 1979 in Case 85/76, Hoffmann-La Roche [1979] ECR 461, and confirmed in subsequent judgments.

17. The question to be answered is whether the parties' customers would switch to readily available substitutes or to suppliers located elsewhere in response to a hypothetical small (in the range 5% to 10%) but permanent relative price increase in the products and areas being considered. If substitution were enough to make the price increase unprofitable because of the resulting loss of sales, additional substitutes and areas are included in the relevant market. This would be done until the set of products and geographical areas is such that small, permanent increases in relative prices would be profitable. The equivalent analysis is applicable in cases concerning the concentration of buying power, where the starting point would then be the supplier and the price test serves to identify the alternative distribution channels or outlets for the supplier's products. In the application of these principles, careful account should be taken of certain particular situations as described within paragraphs 56 and 58.

18. A practical example of this test can be provided by its application to a merger of, for instance, soft-drink bottlers. An issue to examine in such a case would be to decide whether different flavours of soft drinks belong to the same market. In practice, the question to address would be whether consumers of flavour A would switch to other flavours when confronted with a permanent price increase of 5% to 10% for flavour A. If a sufficient number of consumers would switch to, say, flavour B, to such an extent that the price increase for flavour A would not be profitable owing to the resulting loss of sales, then the market would comprise at least flavours A and B. The process would have to be extended in addition to other available flavours until a set of products is identified for which a price rise would not induce a sufficient substitution in demand.

19. Generally, and in particular for the analysis of merger cases, the price to take into account will be the prevailing market price. This may not be the case where the prevailing price has been determined in the absence of sufficient competition. In particular for the investigation of abuses of dominant positions, the fact that the prevailing price might already have been substantially increased will be taken into account.

Supply substitution

20. Supply-side substitutability may also be taken into account when defining markets in those situations in which its effects are equivalent to those of demand substitution in terms of effectiveness and immediacy. This means that suppliers are able to switch production to the relevant products and market them in the short term[4] without incurring significant additional costs or risks in response to small and permanent changes in relative prices. When these conditions are met, the additional production that is put on the market will have a disciplinary effect on the competitive behaviour of the companies involved. Such an impact in terms of effectiveness and immediacy is equivalent to the demand substitution effect.

21. These situations typically arise when companies market a wide range of qualities or grades of one product; even if, for a given final customer or group of consumers, the different qualities are not substitutable, the different qualities will be grouped into one product market, provided that most of the suppliers are able to offer and sell the various qualities immediately and without the significant increases in costs described above. In such cases, the relevant product market will encompass all products that are substitutable in demand and supply, and the current sales of those products will be aggregated so as to give the total value or volume of the market. The same reasoning may lead to group different geographic areas.

22. A practical example of the approach to supply-side substitutability when defining product markets is to be found in the case of paper. Paper is usually supplied in a range of different qualities, from standard writing paper to high quality papers to be used, for instance, to publish art books. From a demand point of view, different qualities of paper cannot be used for any given use, i.e. an art book or a high quality publication cannot be based on lower quality papers. However, paper plants are prepared to manufacture the different qualities, and production can be adjusted with negligible costs and in a short time-frame. In the absence of particular difficulties in distribution,

[4] That is such a period that does not entail a significant adjustment of existing tangible and intangible assets (see paragraph 23).

paper manufacturers are able therefore, to compete for orders of the various qualities, in particular if orders are placed with sufficient lead time to allow for modification of production plans. Under such circumstances, the Commission would not define a separate market for each quality of paper and its respective use. The various qualities of paper are included in the relevant market, and their sales added up to estimate total market value and volume.

23. When supply-side substitutability would entail the need to adjust significantly existing tangible and intangible assets, additional investments, strategic decisions or time delays, it will not be considered at the stage of market definition. Examples where supply-side substitution did not induce the Commission to enlarge the market are offered in the area of consumer products, in particular for branded beverages. Although bottling plants may in principle bottle different beverages, there are costs and lead times involved (in terms of advertising, product testing and distribution) before the products can actually be sold. In these cases, the effects of supply-side substitutability and other forms of potential competition would then be examined at a later stage.

Potential competition

24. The third source of competitive constraint, potential competition, is not taken into account when defining markets, since the conditions under which potential competition will actually represent an effective competitive constraint depend on the analysis of specific factors and circumstances related to the conditions of entry. If required, this analysis is only carried out at a subsequent stage, in general once the position of the companies involved in the relevant market has already been ascertained, and when such position gives rise to concerns from a competition point of view.

III. EVIDENCE RELIED ON TO DEFINE RELEVANT MARKETS

The process of defining the relevant market in practice

Product dimension

25. There is a range of evidence permitting an assessment of the extent to which substitution would take place. In individual cases, certain types of evidence will be determinant, depending very much on the characteristics and specificity of the industry and products or services that are being examined. The same type of evidence may be of no importance in other cases. In most cases, a decision will have to be based on the consideration of a number of criteria and different items of evidence. The Commission follows an open approach to empirical evidence, aimed at making an effective use of all available information which may be relevant in individual cases. The Commission does not follow a rigid hierarchy of different sources of information or types of evidence.

26. The process of defining relevant markets may be summarized as follows: on the basis of the preliminary information available or information submitted by the undertakings involved, the Commission will usually be in a position to broadly establish the possible relevant markets within which, for instance, a concentration or a restriction of competition has to be assessed. In general, and for all practical purposes when handling individual cases, the question will usually be to decide on a few alternative possible relevant markets. For instance, with respect to the product market, the issue will often be to establish whether product A and product B belong or do not belong to the same product market. it is often the case that the inclusion of product B would be enough to remove any competition concerns.

27. In such situations it is not necessary to consider whether the market includes additional products, or to reach a definitive conclusion on the precise product market. If under the conceivable alternative market definitions the operation in question does not raise competition concerns, the question of market definition will be left open, reducing thereby the burden on companies to supply information.

Geographic dimension

28. The Commission's approach to geographic market definition might be summarized as follows: it will take a preliminary view of the scope of the geographic market on the basis of broad indications as to the distribution of market shares between the parties and their competitors, as well as a preliminary analysis of pricing and price differences at national and Community or EEA level. This initial view is used basically as a working hypothesis to focus the Commission's enquiries for the purposes of arriving at a precise geographic market definition.

29. The reasons behind any particular configuration of prices and market shares need to be explored. Companies might enjoy high market shares in their domestic markets just because of the weight of the past, and conversely, a homogeneous presence of companies throughout the EEA might be consistent with national or regional geographic markets. The initial working hypothesis will therefore be checked against an analysis of demand characteristics (importance of national or local preferences, current patterns of purchases of customers, product differentiation/brands, other) in order to establish whether companies in different areas do indeed constitute a real alternative source of supply for consumers. The theoretical experiment is again based on substitution arising from changes in relative prices, and the question to answer is again whether the customers of the parties would switch their orders to companies located elsewhere in the short term and at a negligible cost.

30. If necessary, a further check on supply factors will be carried out to ensure that those companies located in differing areas do not face impediments in developing their sales on competitive terms throughout the whole geographic market. This analysis will include an examination of requirements for a local presence in order to sell in that area the conditions of access to distribution channels, costs associated with setting up a distribution network, and the presence or absence of regulatory barriers arising from public procurement, price regulations, quotas and tariffs limiting trade or production, technical standards, monopolies, freedom of establishment, requirements for administrative authorizations, packaging regulations, etc. In short, the Commission will identify possible obstacles and barriers isolating companies located in a given area from the competitive pressure of companies located outside that area, so as to determine the precise degree of market interpenetration at national, European or global level.

31. The actual pattern and evolution of trade flows offers useful supplementary indications as to the economic importance of each demand or supply factor mentioned above, and the extent to which they may or may not constitute actual barriers creating different geographic markets. The analysis of trade flows will generally address the question of transport costs and the extent to which these may hinder trade between different areas, having regard to plant location, costs of production and relative price levels.

Market integration in the Community

32. Finally, the Commission also takes into account the continuing process of market integration, in particular in the Community, when defining geographic markets, especially in the area of concentrations and structural joint ventures. The measures adopted and implemented in the internal market programme to remove barriers to trade and further integrate the Community markets cannot be ignored when assessing the effects on competition of a concentration or a structural joint venture. A situation where national markets have been artificially isolated from each other because of the existence of legislative barriers that have now been removed will generally lead to a cautious assessment of past evidence regarding prices, market shares or trade patterns. A process of market integration that would, in the short term, lead to wider geographic markets may therefore be taken into consideration when defining the geographic market for the purposes of assessing concentrations and joint ventures.

The process of gathering evidence

33. When a precise market definition is deemed necessary, the Commission will often contact the main customers and the main companies in the industry to enquire into their views about the boundaries of product and geographic markets and to obtain the necessary factual evidence to reach a conclusion. The Commission might also contact the relevant professional associations, and

companies active in upstream markets, so as to be able to define, in so far as necessary, separate product and geographic markets, for different levels of production or distribution of the products/services in question. It might also request additional information to the undertakings involved.

34. Where appropriate, the Commission will address written requests for information to the market players mentioned above. These requests will usually include questions relating to the perceptions of companies about reactions to hypothetical price increases and their views of the boundaries of the relevant market. They will also ask for provision of the factual information the Commission deems necessary to reach a conclusion on the extent of the relevant market. The Commission might also discuss with marketing directors or other officers of those companies to gain a better understanding on how negotiations between suppliers and customers take place and better understand issues relating to the definition of the relevant market. Where appropriate, they might also carry out visits or inspections to the premises of the parties, their customers and/or their competitors, in order to better understand how products are manufactured and sold.

35. The type of evidence relevant to reach a conclusion as to the product market can be categorized as follows:

Evidence to define markets—product dimension

36. An analysis of the product characteristics and its intended use allows the Commission, as a first step, to limit the field of investigation of possible substitutes. However, product characteristics and intended use are insufficient to show whether two products are demand substitutes. Functional interchangeability or similarity in characteristics may not, in themselves, provide sufficient criteria, because the responsiveness of customers to relative price changes may be determined by other considerations as well. For example, there may be different competitive constraints in the original equipment market for car components and in spare parts, thereby leading to a separate delineation of two relevant markets. Conversely, differences in product characteristics are not in themselves sufficient to exclude demand substitutability, since this will depend to a large extent on how customers value different characteristics.

37. The type of evidence the Commission considers relevant to assess whether two products are demand substitutes can be categorized as follows:

38. *Evidence of substitution in the recent past*. In certain cases, it is possible to analyse evidence relating to recent past events or shocks in the market that offer actual examples of substitution between two products. When available, this sort of information will normally be fundamental for market definition. If there have been changes in relative prices in the past (all else being equal), the reactions in terms of quantities demanded will be determinant in establishing substitutability. Launches of new products in the past can also offer useful information, when it is possible to precisely analyse which products have lost sales to the new product.

39. There are a number of *quantitative* tests that have specifically been designed for the purpose of delineating markets. These tests consist of various econometric and statistical approaches estimates of elasticities and cross-price elasticities[5] for the demand of a product, tests based on similarity of price movements over time, the analysis of causality between price series and similarity of price levels and/or their convergence. The Commission takes into account the available quantitative evidence capable of withstanding rigorous scrutiny for the purposes of establishing patterns of substitution in the past.

40. *Views of customers and competitors*. The Commission often contacts the main customers and competitors of the companies involved in its enquiries, to gather their views on the boundaries of the product market as well as most of the factual information it requires to reach a conclusion on the scope of the market. Reasoned answers of customers and competitors as to what would happen if relative prices for the candidate products were to increase in the candidate geographic area by a

[5] Own-price elasticity of demand for product X is a measure of the responsiveness of demand for X to percentage change in its own price. Cross-price elasticity between products X and Y is the responsiveness of demand for product X to percentage change in the price of product Y.

small amount (for instance of 5% to 10%) are taken into account when they are sufficiently backed by factual evidence.

41. *Consumer preferences*. In the case of consumer goods, it may be difficult for the Commission to gather the direct views of end consumers about substitute products. *Marketing studies* that companies have commissioned in the past and that are used by companies in their own decision-making as to pricing of their products and/or marketing actions may provide useful information for the Commission's delineation of the relevant market. Consumer surveys on usage patterns and attitudes, data from consumer's purchasing patterns, the views expressed by retailers and more generally, market research studies submitted by the parties and their competitors are taken into account to establish whether an economically significant proportion of consumers consider two products as substitutable, also taking into account the importance of brands for the products in question. The methodology followed in consumer surveys carried out *ad hoc* by the undertakings involved or their competitors for the purposes of a merger procedure or a procedure pursuant to Regulation No 17 will usually be scrutinized with utmost care. Unlike pre-existing studies, they have not been prepared in the normal course of business for the adoption of business decisions.

42. *Barriers and costs associated with switching demand to potential substitutes*. There are a number of barriers and costs that might prevent the Commission from considering two *prima facie* demand substitutes as belonging to one single product market. It is not possible to provide an exhaustive list of all the possible barriers to substitution and of switching costs. These barriers or obstacles might have a wide range of origins, and in its decisions, the Commission has been confronted with regulatory barriers or other forms of State intervention, constraints arising in downstream markets, need to incur specific capital investment or loss in current output in order to switch to alternative inputs, the location of customers, specific investment in production process, learning and human capital investment, retooling costs or other investments, uncertainty about quality and reputation of unknown suppliers, and others.

43. *Different categories of customers and price discrimination*. The extent of the product market might be narrowed in the presence of distinct groups of customers. A distinct group of customers for the relevant product may constitute a narrower, distinct market when such a group could be subject to price discrimination. This will usually be the case when two conditions are met: (a) it is possible to identify clearly which group an individual customer belongs to at the moment of selling the relevant products to him, and (b) trade among customers or arbitrage by third parties should not be feasible.

Evidence for defining markets—geographic dimension

44. The type of evidence the Commission considers relevant to reach a conclusion as to the geographic market can be categorized as follows:

45. *Past evidence of diversion of orders to other areas*. In certain cases, evidence on changes in prices between different areas and consequent reactions by customers might be available. Generally, the same quantitative tests used for product market definition might as well be used in geographic market definition, bearing in mind that international comparisons of prices might be more complex due to a number of factors such as exchange rate movements, taxation and product differentiation.

46. *Basic demand characteristics*. The nature of demand for the relevant product may in itself determine the scope of the geographical market. Factors such as national preferences or preferences for national brands, language, culture and life style, and the need for a local presence have a strong potential to limit the geographic scope of competition.

47. *Views of customers and competitors*. Where appropriate, the Commission will contact the main customers and competitors of the parties in its enquiries, to gather their views on the boundaries of the geographic market as well as most of the factual information it requires to reach a conclusion on the scope of the market when they are sufficiently backed by factual evidence.

48. *Current geographic pattern of purchases*. An examination of the customers' current geographic pattern of purchases provides useful evidence as to the possible scope of the geographic market. When customers purchase from companies located anywhere in the Community or the EEA

on similar terms, or they procure their supplies through effective tendering procedures in which companies from anywhere in the Community or the EEA submit bids, usually the geographic market will be considered to be Community-wide.

49. *Trade flows/pattern of shipments.* When the number of customers is so large that it is not possible to obtain through them a clear picture of geographic purchasing patterns, information on trade flows might be used alternatively, provided that the trade statistics are available with a sufficient degree of detail for the relevant products. Trade flows, and above all, the rationale behind trade flows provide useful insights and information for the purpose of establishing the scope of the geographic market but are not in themselves conclusive.

50. *Barriers and switching costs associated to divert orders to companies located in other areas.* The absence of trans-border purchases or trade flows, for instance, does not necessarily mean that the market is at most national in scope. Still, barriers isolating the national market have to identified before it is concluded that the relevant geographic market in such a case is national. Perhaps the clearest obstacle for a customer to divert its orders to other areas is the impact of transport costs and transport restrictions arising from legislation or from the nature of the relevant products. The impact of transport costs will usually limit the scope of the geographic market for bulky, low-value products, bearing in mind that a transport disadvantage might also be compensated by a comparative advantage in other costs (labour costs or raw materials). Access to distribution in a given area, regulatory barriers still existing in certain sectors, quotas and custom tariffs might also constitute barriers isolating a geographic area from the competitive pressure of companies located outside that area. Significant switching costs in procuring supplies from companies located in other countries constitute additional sources of such barriers.

51. On the basis of the evidence gathered, the Commission will then define a geographic market that could range from a local dimension to a global one, and there are examples of both local and global markets in past decisions of the Commission.

52. The paragraphs above describe the different factors which might be relevant to define markets. This does not imply that in each individual case it will be necessary to obtain evidence and assess each of these factors. Often in practice the evidence provided by a subset of these factors will be sufficient to reach a conclusion, as shown in the past decisional practice of the Commission.

IV. CALCULATION OF MARKET SHARE

53. The definition of the relevant market in both its product and geographic dimensions allows the identification the suppliers and the customers/consumers active on that market. On that basis, a total market size and market shares for each supplier can be calculated on the basis of their sales of the relevant products in the relevant area. In practice, the total market size and market shares are often available from market sources, i.e. companies' estimates, studies commissioned from industry consultants and/or trade associations. When this is not the case, or when available estimates are not reliable, the Commission will usually ask each supplier in the relevant market to provide its own sales in order to calculate total market size and market shares.

54. If sales are usually the reference to calculate market shares, there are nevertheless other indications that, depending on the specific products or industry in question, can offer useful information such as, in particular, capacity, the number of players in bidding markets, units of fleet as in aerospace, or the reserves held in the case of sectors such as mining.

55. As a rule of thumb, both volume sales and value sales provide useful information. In cases of differentiated products, sales in value and their associated market share will usually be considered to better reflect the relative position and strength of each supplier.

V. ADDITIONAL CONSIDERATIONS

56. There are certain areas where the application of the principles above has to be undertaken with care. This is the case when considering primary and secondary markets, in particular, when the

behaviour of undertakings at a point in time has to be analysed pursuant to Article 86. The method of defining markets in these cases is the same, i.e. assessing the responses of customers based on their purchasing decisions to relative price changes, but taking into account as well, constraints on substitution imposed by conditions in the connected markets. A narrow definition of market for secondary products, for instance, spare parts, may result when compatibility with the primary product is important. Problems of finding compatible secondary products together with the existence of high prices and a long lifetime of the primary products may render relative price increases of secondary products profitable. A different market definition may result if significant substitution between secondary products is possible or if the characteristics of the primary products make quick and direct consumer responses to relative price increases of the secondary products feasible.

57. In certain cases, the existence of chains of substitution might lead to the definition of a relevant market where products or areas at the extreme of the market are not directly substitutable. An example might be provided by the geographic dimension of a product with significant transport costs. In such cases, deliveries from a given plant are limited to a certain area around each plant by the impact of transport costs. In principle, such an area could constitute the relevant geographic market. However, if the distribution of plants is such that there are considerable overlaps between the areas around different plants, it is possible that the pricing of those products will be constrained by a chain substitution effect, and lead to the definition of a broader geographic market. The same reasoning may apply if product B is a demand substitute for products A and C. Even if products A and C are not direct demand substitutes, they might be found to be in the same relevant product market since their respective pricing might be constrained by substitution to B.

58. From a practical perspective, the concept of chains of substitution has to be corroborated by actual evidence, for instance related to price interdependence at the extremes of the chains of substitution, in order to lead to an extension of the relevant market in an individual case. Price levels at the extremes of the chains would have to be of the same magnitude as well.

Council Regulation (EC) No 1/2003 of 16 December 2002 on the implementation of the rules on competition laid down in Articles 81 and 82 of the Treaty*

[OJ 2003 L1/1]

Chapter I Principles

Article 1 Application of Articles 81 and 82 of the Treaty

1. Agreements, decisions and concerted practices caught by Article 81(1) of the Treaty which do not satisfy the conditions of Article 81(3) of the Treaty shall be prohibited, no prior decision to that effect being required.

2. Agreements, decisions and concerted practices caught by Article 81(1) of the Treaty which satisfy the conditions of Article 81(3) of the Treaty shall not be prohibited, no prior decision to that effect being required.

3. The abuse of a dominant position referred to in Article 82 of the Treaty shall be prohibited, no prior decision to that effect being required.

Article 2 Burden of proof

In any national or Community proceedings for the application of Articles 81 and 82 of the Treaty, the burden of proving an infringement of Article 81(1) or of Article 82 of the Treaty shall rest on the

* **Editor's Note:** This Regulation replaced Regulation 17 with effect from 1 May 2004, with the exception of Art 8 which remains in force. As amended by Regulation 411/2004 (OJ 2004 L68/1), Regulation 1419/2006 (OJ 2006 L269/1) and Regulations 169, 246 and 487/2009 (OJ 2009 L61/1, L79/1 and L148/1).

party or the authority alleging the infringement. The undertaking or association of undertakings claiming the benefit of Article 81(3) of the Treaty shall bear the burden of proving that the conditions of that paragraph are fulfilled.

Article 3 Relationship between Articles 81 and 82 of the Treaty and national competition laws

1. Where the competition authorities of the Member States or national courts apply national competition law to agreements, decisions by associations of undertakings or concerted practices within the meaning of Article 81(1) of the Treaty which may affect trade between Member States within the meaning of that provision, they shall also apply Article 81 of the Treaty to such agreements, decisions or concerted practices. Where the competition authorities of the Member States or national courts apply national competition law to any abuse prohibited by Article 82 of the Treaty, they shall also apply Article 82 of the Treaty.

2. The application of national competition law may not lead to the prohibition of agreements, decisions by associations of undertakings or concerted practices which may affect trade between Member States but which do not restrict competition within the meaning of Article 81(1) of the Treaty, or which fulfil the conditions of Article 81(3) of the Treaty or which are covered by a Regulation for the application of Article 81(3) of the Treaty. Member States shall not under this Regulation be precluded from adopting and applying on their territory stricter national laws which prohibit or sanction unilateral conduct engaged in by undertakings.

3. Without prejudice to general principles and other provisions of Community law, paragraphs 1 and 2 do not apply when the competition authorities and the courts of the Member States apply national merger control laws nor do they preclude the application of provisions of national law that predominantly pursue an objective different from that pursued by Articles 81 and 82 of the Treaty.

Chapter II Powers

Article 4 Powers of the Commission

For the purpose of applying Articles 81 and 82 of the Treaty, the Commission shall have the powers provided for by this Regulation.

Article 5 Powers of the competition authorities of the Member States

The competition authorities of the Member States shall have the power to apply Articles 81 and 82 of the Treaty in individual cases. For this purpose, acting on their own initiative or on a complaint, they may take the following decisions:

- requiring that an infringement be brought to an end,
- ordering interim measures,
- accepting commitments,
- imposing fines, periodic penalty payments or any other penalty provided for in their national law.

Where on the basis of the information in their possession the conditions for prohibition are not met they may likewise decide that there are no grounds for action on their part.

Article 6 Powers of the national courts

National courts shall have the power to apply Articles 81 and 82 of the Treaty.

Chapter III Commission decisions

Article 7 Finding and termination of infringement

1. Where the Commission, acting on a complaint or on its own initiative, finds that there is an infringement of Article 81 or of Article 82 of the Treaty, it may by decision require the undertakings and associations of undertakings concerned to bring such infringement to an end. For this purpose, it may impose on them any behavioural or structural remedies which are proportionate to the infringement committed and necessary to bring the infringement effectively to an end. Structural

remedies can only be imposed either where there is no equally effective behavioural remedy or where any equally effective behavioural remedy would be more burdensome for the undertaking concerned than the structural remedy. If the Commission has a legitimate interest in doing so, it may also find that an infringement has been committed in the past.

2. Those entitled to lodge a complaint for the purposes of paragraph 1 are natural or legal persons who can show a legitimate interest and Member States.

Article 8 Interim measures

1. In cases of urgency due to the risk of serious and irreparable damage to competition, the Commission, acting on its own initiative may by decision, on the basis of a prima facie finding of infringement, order interim measures.

2. A decision under paragraph 1 shall apply for a specified period of time and may be renewed in so far this is necessary and appropriate.

Article 9 Commitments

1. Where the Commission intends to adopt a decision requiring that an infringement be brought to an end and the undertakings concerned offer commitments to meet the concerns expressed to them by the Commission in its preliminary assessment, the Commission may by decision make those commitments binding on the undertakings. Such a decision may be adopted for a specified period and shall conclude that there are no longer grounds for action by the Commission.

2. The Commission may, upon request or on its own initiative, reopen the proceedings:

(a) where there has been a material change in any of the facts on which the decision was based;

(b) where the undertakings concerned act contrary to their commitments; or

(c) where the decision was based on incomplete, incorrect or misleading information provided by the parties.

Article 10 Finding of inapplicability

Where the Community public interest relating to the application of Articles 81 and 82 of the Treaty so requires, the Commission, acting on its own initiative, may by decision find that Article 81 of the Treaty is not applicable to an agreement, a decision by an association of undertakings or a concerted practice, either because the conditions of Article 81(1) of the Treaty are not fulfilled, or because the conditions of Article 81(3) of the Treaty are satisfied.

The Commission may likewise make such a finding with reference to Article 82 of the Treaty.

Chapter IV Cooperation

Article 11

Cooperation between the Commission and the competition authorities of the Member States

1. The Commission and the competition authorities of the Member States shall apply the Community competition rules in close cooperation.

2. The Commission shall transmit to the competition authorities of the Member States copies of the most important documents it has collected with a view to applying Articles 7, 8, 9, 10 and Article 29(1). At the request of the competition authority of a Member State, the Commission shall provide it with a copy of other existing documents necessary for the assessment of the case.

3. The competition authorities of the Member States shall, when acting under Article 81 or Article 82 of the Treaty, inform the Commission in writing before or without delay after commencing the first formal investigative measure. This information may also be made available to the competition authorities of the other Member States.

4. No later than 30 days before the adoption of a decision requiring that an infringement be brought to an end, accepting commitments or withdrawing the benefit of a block exemption Regulation, the competition authorities of the Member States shall inform the Commission. To that effect, they shall provide the Commission with a summary of the case, the envisaged decision or, in

the absence thereof, any other document indicating the proposed course of action. This information may also be made available to the competition authorities of the other Member States. At the request of the Commission, the acting competition authority shall make available to the Commission other documents it holds which are necessary for the assessment of the case. The information supplied to the Commission may be made available to the competition authorities of the other Member States. National competition authorities may also exchange between themselves information necessary for the assessment of a case that they are dealing with under Article 81 or Article 82 of the Treaty.

5. The competition authorities of the Member States may consult the Commission on any case involving the application of Community law.

6. The initiation by the Commission of proceedings for the adoption of a decision under Chapter III shall relieve the competition authorities of the Member States of their competence to apply Articles 81 and 82 of the Treaty. If a competition authority of a Member State is already acting on a case, the Commission shall only initiate proceedings after consulting with that national competition authority.

Article 12 Exchange of information

1. For the purpose of applying Articles 81 and 82 of the Treaty the Commission and the competition authorities of the Member States shall have the power to provide one another with and use in evidence any matter of fact or of law, including confidential information.

2. Information exchanged shall only be used in evidence for the purpose of applying Article 81 or Article 82 of the Treaty and in respect of the subject-matter for which it was collected by the transmitting authority. However, where national competition law is applied in the same case and in parallel to Community competition law and does not lead to a different outcome, information exchanged under this Article may also be used for the application of national competition law.

3. Information exchanged pursuant to paragraph 1 can only be used in evidence to impose sanctions on natural persons where:

- the law of the transmitting authority foresees sanctions of a similar kind in relation to an infringement of Article 81 or Article 82 of the Treaty or, in the absence thereof,
- the information has been collected in a way which respects the same level of protection of the rights of defence of natural persons as provided for under the national rules of the receiving authority. However, in this case, the information exchanged cannot be used by the receiving authority to impose custodial sanctions.

Article 13 Suspension or termination of proceedings

1. Where competition authorities of two or more Member States have received a complaint or are acting on their own initiative under Article 81 or Article 82 of the Treaty against the same agreement, decision of an association or practice, the fact that one authority is dealing with the case shall be sufficient grounds for the others to suspend the proceedings before them or to reject the complaint. The Commission may likewise reject a complaint on the ground that a competition authority of a Member State is dealing with the case.

2. Where a competition authority of a Member State or the Commission has received a complaint against an agreement, decision of an association or practice which has already been dealt with by another competition authority, it may reject it.

Article 15 Cooperation with national courts

1. In proceedings for the application of Article 81 or Article 82 of the Treaty, courts of the Member States may ask the Commission to transmit to them information in its possession or its opinion on questions concerning the application of the Community competition rules.

2. Member States shall forward to the Commission a copy of any written judgment of national courts deciding on the application of Article 81 or Article 82 of the Treaty. Such copy shall be forwarded without delay after the full written judgment is notified to the parties.

3. Competition authorities of the Member States, acting on their own initiative, may submit written observations to the national courts of their Member State on issues relating to the application

of Article 81 or Article 82 of the Treaty. With the permission of the court in question, they may also submit oral observations to the national courts of their Member State. Where the coherent application of Article 81 or Article 82 of the Treaty so requires, the Commission, acting on its own initiative, may submit written observations to courts of the Member States. With the permission of the court in question, it may also make oral observations.

For the purpose of the preparation of their observations only, the competition authorities of the Member States and the Commission may request the relevant court of the Member State to transmit or ensure the transmission to them of any documents necessary for the assessment of the case.

4. This Article is without prejudice to wider powers to make observations before courts conferred on competition authorities of the Member States under the law of their Member State.

Article 16 Uniform application of Community competition law

1. When national courts rule on agreements, decisions or practices under Article 81 or Article 82 of the Treaty which are already the subject of a Commission decision, they cannot take decisions running counter to the decision adopted by the Commission. They must also avoid giving decisions which would conflict with a decision contemplated by the Commission in proceedings it has initiated. To that effect, the national court may assess whether it is necessary to stay its proceedings. This obligation is without prejudice to the rights and obligations under Article 234 of the Treaty.

2. When competition authorities of the Member States rule on agreements, decisions or practices under Article 81 or Article 82 of the Treaty which are already the subject of a Commission decision, they cannot take decisions which would run counter to the decision adopted by the Commission.

Chapter V Powers of investigation

Article 17 Investigations into sectors of the economy and into types of agreements

1. Where the trend of trade between Member States, the rigidity of prices or other circumstances suggest that competition may be restricted or distorted within the common market, the Commission may conduct its inquiry into a particular sector of the economy or into a particular type of agreements across various sectors. In the course of that inquiry, the Commission may request the undertakings or associations of undertakings concerned to supply the information necessary for giving effect to Articles 81 and 82 of the Treaty and may carry out any inspections necessary for that purpose.

The Commission may in particular request the undertakings or associations of undertakings concerned to communicate to it all agreements, decisions and concerted practices.

The Commission may publish a report on the results of its inquiry into particular sectors of the economy or particular types of agreements across various sectors and invite comments from interested parties.

2. Articles 14, 18, 19, 20, 22, 23 and 24 shall apply *mutatis mutandis*.

Article 18 Requests for information

1. In order to carry out the duties assigned to it by this Regulation, the Commission may, by simple request or by decision, require undertakings and associations of undertakings to provide all necessary information.

2. When sending a simple request for information to an undertaking or association of undertakings, the Commission shall state the legal basis and the purpose of the request, specify what information is required and fix the time-limit within which the information is to be provided, and the penalties provided for in Article 23 for supplying incorrect or misleading information.

3. Where the Commission requires undertakings and associations of undertakings to supply information by decision, it shall state the legal basis and the purpose of the request, specify what information is required and fix the time-limit within which it is to be provided. It shall also indicate the penalties provided for in Article 23 and indicate or impose the penalties provided for in Article 24. It shall further indicate the right to have the decision reviewed by the Court of Justice.

4. The owners of the undertakings or their representatives and, in the case of legal persons, companies or firms, or associations having no legal personality, the persons authorised to represent them by law or by their constitution shall supply the information requested on behalf of the undertaking or the association of undertakings concerned. Lawyers duly authorised to act may supply the information on behalf of their clients. The latter shall remain fully responsible if the information supplied is incomplete, incorrect or misleading.

5. The Commission shall without delay forward a copy of the simple request or of the decision to the competition authority of the Member State in whose territory the seat of the undertaking or association of undertakings is situated and the competition authority of the Member State whose territory is affected.

6. At the request of the Commission the governments and competition authorities of the Member States shall provide the Commission with all necessary information to carry out the duties assigned to it by this Regulation.

Article 19 Power to take statements

1. In order to carry out the duties assigned to it by this Regulation, the Commission may interview any natural or legal person who consents to be interviewed for the purpose of collecting information relating to the subject-matter of an investigation.

2. Where an interview pursuant to paragraph 1 is conducted in the premises of an undertaking, the Commission shall inform the competition authority of the Member State in whose territory the interview takes place. If so requested by the competition authority of that Member State, its officials may assist the officials and other accompanying persons authorised by the Commission to conduct the interview.

Article 20 The Commission's powers of inspection

1. In order to carry out the duties assigned to it by this Regulation, the Commission may conduct all necessary inspections of undertakings and associations of undertakings.

2. The officials and other accompanying persons authorised by the Commission to conduct an inspection are empowered:

(a) to enter any premises, land and means of transport of undertakings and associations of undertakings;

(b) to examine the books and other records related to the business, irrespective of the medium on which they are stored;

(c) to take or obtain in any form copies of or extracts from such books or records;

(d) to seal any business premises and books or records for the period and to the extent necessary for the inspection;

(e) to ask any representative or member of staff of the undertaking or association of undertakings for explanations on facts or documents relating to the subject-matter and purpose of the inspection and to record the answers.

3. The officials and other accompanying persons authorised by the Commission to conduct an inspection shall exercise their powers upon production of a written authorisation specifying the subject matter and purpose of the inspection and the penalties provided for in Article 23 in case the production of the required books or other records related to the business is incomplete or where the answers to questions asked under paragraph 2 of the present Article are incorrect or misleading. In good time before the inspection, the Commission shall give notice of the inspection to the competition authority of the Member State in whose territory it is to be conducted.

4. Undertakings and associations of undertakings are required to submit to inspections ordered by decision of the Commission. The decision shall specify the subject matter and purpose of the inspection, appoint the date on which it is to begin and indicate the penalties provided for in Articles 23 and 24 and the right to have the decision reviewed by the Court of Justice. The Commission shall take such decisions after consulting the competition authority of the Member State in whose territory the inspection is to be conducted.

5. Officials of as well as those authorised or appointed by the competition authority of the Member State in whose territory the inspection is to be conducted shall, at the request of that authority or of the Commission, actively assist the officials and other accompanying persons authorised by the Commission. To this end, they shall enjoy the powers specified in paragraph 2.

6. Where the officials and other accompanying persons authorised by the Commission find that an undertaking opposes an inspection ordered pursuant to this Article, the Member State concerned shall afford them the necessary assistance, requesting where appropriate the assistance of the police or of an equivalent enforcement authority, so as to enable them to conduct their inspection.

7. If the assistance provided for in paragraph 6 requires authorisation from a judicial authority according to national rules, such authorisation shall be applied for. Such authorisation may also be applied for as a precautionary measure.

8. Where authorisation as referred to in paragraph 7 is applied for, the national judicial authority shall control that the Commission decision is authentic and that the coercive measures envisaged are neither arbitrary nor excessive having regard to the subject matter of the inspection. In its control of the proportionality of the coercive measures, the national judicial authority may ask the Commission, directly or through the Member State competition authority, for detailed explanations in particular on the grounds the Commission has for suspecting infringement of Articles 81 and 82 of the Treaty, as well as on the seriousness of the suspected infringement and on the nature of the involvement of the undertaking concerned. However, the national judicial authority may not call into question the necessity for the inspection nor demand that it be provided with the information in the Commission's file. The lawfulness of the Commission decision shall be subject to review only by the Court of Justice.

Article 21 Inspection of other premises

1. If a reasonable suspicion exists that books or other records related to the business and to the subject-matter of the inspection, which may be relevant to prove a serious violation of Article 81 or Article 82 of the Treaty, are being kept in any other premises, land and means of transport, including the homes of directors, managers and other members of staff of the undertakings and associations of undertakings concerned, the Commission can by decision order an inspection to be conducted in such other premises, land and means of transport.

2. The decision shall specify the subject matter and purpose of the inspection, appoint the date on which it is to begin and indicate the right to have the decision reviewed by the Court of Justice. It shall in particular state the reasons that have led the Commission to conclude that a suspicion in the sense of paragraph 1 exists. The Commission shall take such decisions after consulting the competition authority of the Member State in whose territory the inspection is to be conducted.

3. A decision adopted pursuant to paragraph 1 cannot be executed without prior authorisation from the national judicial authority of the Member State concerned. The national judicial authority shall control that the Commission decision is authentic and that the coercive measures envisaged are neither arbitrary nor excessive having regard in particular to the seriousness of the suspected infringement, to the importance of the evidence sought, to the involvement of the undertaking concerned and to the reasonable likelihood that business books and records relating to the subject matter of the inspection are kept in the premises for which the authorisation is requested. The national judicial authority may ask the Commission, directly or through the Member State competition authority, for detailed explanations on those elements which are necessary to allow its control of the proportionality of the coercive measures envisaged.

However, the national judicial authority may not call into question the necessity for the inspection nor demand that it be provided with information in the Commission's file. The lawfulness of the Commission decision shall be subject to review only by the Court of Justice.

4. The officials and other accompanying persons authorised by the Commission to conduct an inspection ordered in accordance with paragraph 1 of this Article shall have the powers set out in Article 20(2)(a), (b) and (c). Article 20(5) and (6) shall apply *mutatis mutandis*.

Article 22 Investigations by competition authorities of Member States

1. The competition authority of a Member State may in its own territory carry out any inspection or other fact-finding measure under its national law on behalf and for the account of the competition authority of another Member State in order to establish whether there has been an infringement of Article 81 or Article 82 of the Treaty. Any exchange and use of the information collected shall be carried out in accordance with Article 12.

2. At the request of the Commission, the competition authorities of the Member States shall undertake the inspections which the Commission considers to be necessary under Article 20(1) or which it has ordered by decision pursuant to Article 20(4). The officials of the competition authorities of the Member States who are responsible for conducting these inspections as well as those authorised or appointed by them shall exercise their powers in accordance with their national law.

If so requested by the Commission or by the competition authority of the Member State in whose territory the inspection is to be conducted, officials and other accompanying persons authorised by the Commission may assist the officials of the authority concerned.

Chapter VI Penalties

Article 23 Fines

1. The Commission may by decision impose on undertakings and associations of undertakings fines not exceeding 1% of the total turnover in the preceding business year where, intentionally or negligently:

(a) they supply incorrect or misleading information in response to a request made pursuant to Article 17 or Article 18(2);

(b) in response to a request made by decision adopted pursuant to Article 17 or Article 18(3), they supply incorrect, incomplete or misleading information or do not supply information within the required time-limit;

(c) they produce the required books or other records related to the business in incomplete form during inspections under Article 20 or refuse to submit to inspections ordered by a decision adopted pursuant to Article 20(4);

(d) in response to a question asked in accordance with Article 20(2)(e),
- they give an incorrect or misleading answer,
- they fail to rectify within a time-limit set by the Commission an incorrect, incomplete or misleading answer given by a member of staff, or
- they fail or refuse to provide a complete answer on facts relating to the subject-matter and purpose of an inspection ordered by a decision adopted pursuant to Article 20(4);

(e) seals affixed in accordance with Article 20(2)(d) by officials or other accompanying persons authorised by the Commission have been broken.

2. The Commission may by decision impose fines on undertakings and associations of undertakings where, either intentionally or negligently:

(a) they infringe Article 81 or Article 82 of the Treaty; or

(b) they contravene a decision ordering interim measures under Article 8; or

(c) they fail to comply with a commitment made binding by a decision pursuant to Article 9.

For each undertaking and association of undertakings participating in the infringement, the fine shall not exceed 10% of its total turnover in the preceding business year.

Where the infringement of an association relates to the activities of its members, the fine shall not exceed 10% of the sum of the total turnover of each member active on the market affected by the infringement of the association.

3. In fixing the amount of the fine, regard shall be had both to the gravity and to the duration of the infringement.

4. When a fine is imposed on an association of undertakings taking account of the turnover of its members and the association is not solvent, the association is obliged to call for contributions from its members to cover the amount of the fine.

Where such contributions have not been made to the association within a time-limit fixed by the Commission, the Commission may require payment of the fine directly by any of the undertakings whose representatives were members of the decision-making bodies concerned of the association.

After the Commission has required payment under the second subparagraph, where necessary to ensure full payment of the fine, the Commission may require payment of the balance by any of the members of the association which were active on the market on which the infringement occurred.

However, the Commission shall not require payment under the second or the third subparagraph from undertakings which show that they have not implemented the infringing decision of the association and either were not aware of its existence or have actively distanced themselves from it before the Commission started investigating the case.

The financial liability of each undertaking in respect of the payment of the fine shall not exceed 10% of its total turnover in the preceding business year.

5. Decisions taken pursuant to paragraphs 1 and 2 shall not be of a criminal law nature.

Article 24 Periodic penalty payments

1. The Commission may, by decision, impose on undertakings or associations of undertakings periodic penalty payments not exceeding 5% of the average daily turnover in the preceding business year per day and calculated from the date appointed by the decision, in order to compel them:

(a) to put an end to an infringement of Article 81 or Article 82 of the Treaty, in accordance with a decision taken pursuant to Article 7;

(b) to comply with a decision ordering interim measures taken pursuant to Article 8;

(c) to comply with a commitment made binding by a decision pursuant to Article 9;

(d) to supply complete and correct information which it has requested by decision taken pursuant to Article 17 or Article 18(3);

(e) to submit to an inspection which it has ordered by decision taken pursuant to Article 20(4).

2. Where the undertakings or associations of undertakings have satisfied the obligation which the periodic penalty payment was intended to enforce, the Commission may fix the definitive amount of the periodic penalty payment at a figure lower than that which would arise under the original decision. Article 23(4) shall apply correspondingly.

Chapter VIII Hearings and professional secrecy

Article 27 Hearing of the parties, complainants and others

1. Before taking decisions as provided for in Articles 7, 8, 23 and Article 24(2), the Commission shall give the undertakings or associations of undertakings which are the subject of the proceedings conducted by the Commission the opportunity of being heard on the matters to which the Commission has taken objection. The Commission shall base its decisions only on objections on which the parties concerned have been able to comment. Complainants shall be associated closely with the proceedings.

2. The rights of defence of the parties concerned shall be fully respected in the proceedings. They shall be entitled to have access to the Commission's file, subject to the legitimate interest of undertakings in the protection of their business secrets. The right of access to the file shall not extend to confidential information and internal documents of the Commission or the competition authorities of the Member States. In particular, the right of access shall not extend to correspondence between the Commission and the competition authorities of the Member States, or between the latter, including documents drawn up pursuant to Articles 11 and 14. Nothing in this paragraph shall prevent the Commission from disclosing and using information necessary to prove an infringement.

3. If the Commission considers it necessary, it may also hear other natural or legal persons. Applications to be heard on the part of such persons shall, where they show a sufficient interest, be

granted. The competition authorities of the Member States may also ask the Commission to hear other natural or legal persons.

4. Where the Commission intends to adopt a decision pursuant to Article 9 or Article 10, it shall publish a concise summary of the case and the main content of the commitments or of the proposed course of action. Interested third parties may submit their observations within a time limit which is fixed by the Commission in its publication and which may not be less than one month. Publication shall have regard to the legitimate interest of undertakings in the protection of their business secrets.

Article 28 Professional secrecy

1. Without prejudice to Articles 12 and 15, information collected pursuant to Articles 17 to 22 shall be used only for the purpose for which it was acquired.

2. Without prejudice to the exchange and to the use of information foreseen in Articles 11, 12, 14, 15 and 27, the Commission and the competition authorities of the Member States, their officials, servants and other persons working under the supervision of these authorities as well as officials and civil servants of other authorities of the Member States shall not disclose information acquired or exchanged by them pursuant to this Regulation and of the kind covered by the obligation of professional secrecy. This obligation also applies to all representatives and experts of Member States attending meetings of the Advisory Committee pursuant to Article 14.

Done at Brussels, 16 December 2002.

Council Regulation (EC) No 139/2004 of 20 January 2004 on the control of concentrations between undertakings (the EC Merger Regulation)*

[OJ 2004 L24/22]

Article 1 Scope

1. Without prejudice to Article 4(5) and Article 22, this Regulation shall apply to all concentrations with a Community dimension as defined in this Article.

2. A concentration has a Community dimension where:

(a) the combined aggregate worldwide turnover of all the undertakings concerned is more than EUR 5000 million; and

(b) the aggregate Community-wide turnover of each of at least two of the undertakings concerned is more than EUR 250 million,

unless each of the undertakings concerned achieves more than two-thirds of its aggregate Community-wide turnover within one and the same Member State.

3. A concentration that does not meet the thresholds laid down in paragraph 2 has a Community dimension where:

(a) the combined aggregate worldwide turnover of all the undertakings concerned is more than EUR 2500 million;

(b) in each of at least three Member States, the combined aggregate turnover of all the undertakings concerned is more than EUR 100 million;

(c) in each of at least three Member States included for the purpose of point (b), the aggregate turnover of each of at least two of the undertakings concerned is more than EUR 25 million; and

(d) the aggregate Community-wide turnover of each of at least two of the undertakings concerned is more than EUR 100 million,

unless each of the undertakings concerned achieves more than two-thirds of its aggregate Community-wide turnover within one and the same Member State.

* **Editor's Note:** This Regulation replaces and repeals Regulations 4064/89 and 1310/97.

4. On the basis of statistical data that may be regularly provided by the Member States, the Commission shall report to the Council on the operation of the thresholds and criteria set out in paragraphs 2 and 3 by 1 July 2009 and may present proposals pursuant to paragraph 5.

5. Following the report referred to in paragraph 4 and on a proposal from the Commission, the Council, acting by a qualified majority, may revise the thresholds and criteria mentioned in paragraph 3.

Article 2 Appraisal of concentrations

1. Concentrations within the scope of this Regulation shall be appraised in accordance with the objectives of this Regulation and the following provisions with a view to establishing whether or not they are compatible with the common market.

In making this appraisal, the Commission shall take into account:

(a) the need to maintain and develop effective competition within the common market in view of, among other things, the structure of all the markets concerned and the actual or potential competition from undertakings located either within or outwith the Community;

(b) the market position of the undertakings concerned and their economic and financial power, the alternatives available to suppliers and users, their access to supplies or markets, any legal or other barriers to entry, supply and demand trends for the relevant goods and services, the interests of the intermediate and ultimate consumers, and the development of technical and economic progress provided that it is to consumers' advantage and does not form an obstacle to competition.

2. A concentration which would not significantly impede effective competition in the common market or in a substantial part of it, in particular as a result of the creation or strengthening of a dominant position, shall be declared compatible with the common market.

3. A concentration which would significantly impede effective competition, in the common market or in a substantial part of it, in particular as a result of the creation or strengthening of a dominant position, shall be declared incompatible with the common market.

4. To the extent that the creation of a joint venture constituting a concentration pursuant to Article 3 has as its object or effect the coordination of the competitive behaviour of undertakings that remain independent, such coordination shall be appraised in accordance with the criteria of a Article 81(1) and (3) of the Treaty, with a view to establishing whether or not the operation is compatible with the common market.

5. In making this appraisal, the Commission shall take into account in particular:

- whether two or more parent companies retain, to a significant extent, activities in the same market as the joint venture or in a market which is downstream or upstream from that of the joint venture or in a neighbouring market closely related to this market,
- whether the coordination which is the direct consequence of the creation of the joint venture affords the undertakings concerned the possibility of eliminating competition in respect of a substantial part of the products or services in question.

Article 3 Definition of concentration

1. A concentration shall be deemed to arise where a change of control on a lasting basis results from:

(a) the merger of two or more previously independent undertakings or parts of undertakings, or

(b) the acquisition, by one or more persons already controlling at least one undertaking, or by one or more undertakings, whether by purchase of securities or assets, by contract or by any other means, of direct or indirect control of the whole or parts of one or more other undertakings.

2. Control shall be constituted by rights, contracts or any other means which, either separately or in combination and having regard to the considerations of fact or law involved, confer the possibility of exercising decisive influence on an undertaking, in particular by:

(a) ownership or the right to use all or part of the assets of an undertaking;

(b) rights or contracts which confer decisive influence on the composition, voting or decisions of the organs of an undertaking.

3. Control is acquired by persons or undertakings which:
   (a) are holders of the rights or entitled to rights under the contracts concerned; or
   (b) while not being holders of such rights or entitled to rights under such contracts, have the power to exercise the rights deriving therefrom.

4. The creation of a joint venture performing on a lasting basis all the functions of an autonomous economic entity shall constitute a concentration within the meaning of paragraph 1(b).

5. A concentration shall not be deemed to arise where:
   (a) credit institutions or other financial institutions or insurance companies, the normal activities of which include transactions and dealing in securities for their own account or for the account of others, hold on a temporary basis securities which they have acquired in an undertaking with a view to reselling them, provided that they do not exercise voting rights in respect of those securities with a view to determining the competitive behaviour of that undertaking or provided that they exercise such voting rights only with a view to preparing the disposal of all or part of that undertaking or of its assets or the disposal of those securities and that any such disposal takes place within one year of the date of acquisition; that period may be extended by the Commission on request where such institutions or companies can show that the disposal was not reasonably possible within the period set;
   (b) control is acquired by an office-holder according to the law of a Member State relating to liquidation, winding up, insolvency, cessation of payments, compositions or analogous proceedings;
   (c) the operations referred to in paragraph 1(b) are carried out by the financial holding companies referred to in Article 5(3) of Fourth Council Directive 78/660/EEC of 25 July 1978 based on Article 54(3)(g) of the Treaty on the annual accounts of certain types of companies[1] provided however that the voting rights in respect of the holding are exercised, in particular in relation to the appointment of members of the management and supervisory bodies of the undertakings in which they have holdings, only to maintain the full value of those investments and not to determine directly or indirectly the competitive conduct of those undertakings.

Article 4 Prior notification of concentrations and pre-notification referral at the request of the notifying parties

1. Concentrations with a Community dimension defined in this Regulation shall be notified to the Commission prior to their implementation and following the conclusion of the agreement, the announcement of the public bid, or the acquisition of a controlling interest.

Notification may also be made where the undertakings concerned demonstrate to the Commission a good faith intention to conclude an agreement or, in the case of a public bid, where they have publicly announced an intention to make such a bid, provided that the intended agreement or bid would result in a concentration with a Community dimension.

For the purposes of this Regulation, the term 'notified concentration' shall also cover intended concentrations notified pursuant to the second subparagraph. For the purposes of paragraphs 4 and 5 of this Article, the term 'concentration' includes intended concentrations within the meaning of the second subparagraph.

2. A concentration which consists of a merger within the meaning of Article 3(1)(a) or in the acquisition of joint control within the meaning of Article 3(1)(b) shall be notified jointly by the parties to the merger or by those acquiring joint control as the case may be. In all other cases, the notification shall be effected by the person or undertaking acquiring control of the whole or parts of one or more undertakings.

3. Where the Commission finds that a notified concentration falls within the scope of this Regulation, it shall publish the fact of the notification, at the same time indicating the names of the

[1] OJ L 222, 14.8.1978, p. 11. Directive as last amended by Directive 2003/51/EC of the European Parliament and of the Council (OJ L 178, 17.7.2003, p. 16).

undertakings concerned, their country of origin, the nature of the concentration and the economic sectors involved. The Commission shall take account of the legitimate interest of undertakings in the protection of their business secrets.

4. Prior to the notification of a concentration within the meaning of paragraph 1, the persons or undertakings referred to in paragraph 2 may inform the Commission, by means of a reasoned submission, that the concentration may significantly affect competition in a market within a Member State which presents all the characteristics of a distinct market and should therefore be examined, in whole or in part, by that Member State.

The Commission shall transmit this submission to all Member States without delay. The Member State referred to in the reasoned submission shall, within 15 working days of receiving the submission, express its agreement or disagreement as regards the request to refer the case. Where that Member State takes no such decision within this period, it shall be deemed to have agreed.

Unless that Member State disagrees, the Commission, where it considers that such a distinct market exists, and that competition in that market may be significantly affected by the concentration, may decide to refer the whole or part of the case to the competent authorities of that Member State with a view to the application of that State's national competition law.

The decision whether or not to refer the case in accordance with the third subparagraph shall be taken within 25 working days starting from the receipt of the reasoned submission by the Commission. The Commission shall inform the other Member States and the persons or undertakings concerned of its decision. If the Commission does not take a decision within this period, it shall be deemed to have adopted a decision to refer the case in accordance with the submission made by the persons or undertakings concerned.

If the Commission decides, or is deemed to have decided, pursuant to the third and fourth subparagraphs, to refer the whole of the case, no notification shall be made pursuant to paragraph 1 and national competition law shall apply. Article 9(6) to (9) shall apply *mutatis mutandis*.

5. With regard to a concentration as defined in Article 3 which does not have a Community dimension within the meaning of Article 1 and which is capable of being reviewed under the national competition laws of at least three Member States, the persons or undertakings referred to in paragraph 2 may, before any notification to the competent authorities, inform the Commission by means of a reasoned submission that the concentration should be examined by the Commission.

The Commission shall transmit this submission to all Member States without delay.

Any Member State competent to examine the concentration under its national competition law may, within 15 working days of receiving the reasoned submission, express its disagreement as regards the request to refer the case.

Where at least one such Member State has expressed its disagreement in accordance with the third subparagraph within the period of 15 working days, the case shall not be referred. The Commission shall, without delay, inform all Member States and the persons or undertakings concerned of any such expression of disagreement.

Where no Member State has expressed its disagreement in accordance with the third subparagraph within the period of 15 working days, the concentration shall be deemed to have a Community dimension and shall be notified to the Commission in accordance with paragraphs 1 and 2. In such situations, no Member State shall apply its national competition law to the concentration.

6. The Commission shall report to the Council on the operation of paragraphs 4 and 5 by 1 July 2009. Following this report and on a proposal from the Commission, the Council, acting by a qualified majority, may revise paragraphs 4 and 5.

Article 5 Calculation of turnover

1. Aggregate turnover within the meaning of this Regulation shall comprise the amounts derived by the undertakings concerned in the preceding financial year from the sale of products and the provision of services falling within the undertakings' ordinary activities after deduction of sales rebates and of value added tax and other taxes directly related to turnover. The aggregate turnover of an undertaking concerned shall not include the sale of products or the provision of services between any of the undertakings referred to in paragraph 4.

Turnover, in the Community or in a Member State, shall comprise products sold and services provided to undertakings or consumers, in the Community or in that Member State as the case may be.

2. By way of derogation from paragraph 1, where the concentration consists of the acquisition of parts, whether or not constituted as legal entities, of one or more undertakings, only the turnover relating to the parts which are the subject of the concentration shall be taken into account with regard to the seller or sellers.

However, two or more transactions within the meaning of the first subparagraph which take place within a two-year period between the same persons or undertakings shall be treated as one and the same concentration arising on the date of the last transaction.

3. In place of turnover the following shall be used:

(a) for credit institutions and other financial institutions, the sum of the following income items as defined in Council Directive 86/635/EEC,[2] after deduction of value added tax and other taxes directly related to those items, where appropriate:

(i) interest income and similar income;

(ii) income from securities:

- income from shares and other variable yield securities,
- income from participating interests,
- income from shares in affiliated undertakings;

(iii) commissions receivable;

(iv) net profit on financial operations;

(v) other operating income.

The turnover of a credit or financial institution in the Community or in a Member State shall comprise the income items, as defined above, which are received by the branch or division of that institution established in the Community or in the Member State in question, as the case may be;

(b) for insurance undertakings, the value of gross premiums written which shall comprise all amounts received and receivable in respect of insurance contracts issued by or on behalf of the insurance undertakings, including also outgoing reinsurance premiums, and after deduction of taxes and parafiscal contributions or levies charged by reference to the amounts of individual premiums or the total volume of premiums; as regards Article 1(2)(b) and (3)(b), (c) and (d) and the final part of Article 1(2) and (3), gross premiums received from Community residents and from residents of one Member State respectively shall be taken into account.

4. Without prejudice to paragraph 2, the aggregate turnover of an undertaking concerned within the meaning of this Regulation shall be calculated by adding together the respective turnovers of the following:

(a) the undertaking concerned;

(b) those undertakings in which the undertaking concerned, directly or indirectly:

(i) owns more than half the capital or business assets, or

(ii) has the power to exercise more than half the voting rights, or

(iii) has the power to appoint more than half the members of the supervisory board, the administrative board or bodies legally representing the undertakings, or

(iv) has the right to manage the undertakings' affairs;

(c) those undertakings which have in the undertaking concerned the rights or powers listed in (b);

(d) those undertakings in which an undertaking as referred to in (c) has the rights or powers listed in (b);

(e) those undertakings in which two or more undertakings as referred to in (a) to (d) jointly have the rights or powers listed in (b).

[2] OJ L 372, 31.12.1986, p. 1. Directive as last amended by Directive 2003/51/EC of the European Parliament and of the Council.

5. Where undertakings concerned by the concentration jointly have the rights or powers listed in paragraph 4(b), in calculating the aggregate turnover of the undertakings concerned for the purposes of this Regulation:

(a) no account shall be taken of the turnover resulting from the sale of products or the provision of services between the joint undertaking and each of the undertakings concerned or any other undertaking connected with any one of them, as set out in paragraph 4(b) to (e);

(b) account shall be taken of the turnover resulting from the sale of products and the provision of services between the joint undertaking and any third undertakings. This turnover shall be apportioned equally amongst the undertakings concerned.

Article 6 Examination of the notification and initiation of proceedings

1. The Commission shall examine the notification as soon as it is received.

(a) Where it concludes that the concentration notified does not fall within the scope of this Regulation, it shall record that finding by means of a decision.

(b) Where it finds that the concentration notified, although falling within the scope of this Regulation, does not raise serious doubts as to its compatibility with the common market, it shall decide not to oppose it and shall declare that it is compatible with the common market.

A decision declaring a concentration compatible shall be deemed to cover restrictions directly related and necessary to the implementation of the concentration.

(c) Without prejudice to paragraph 2, where the Commission finds that the concentration notified falls within the scope of this Regulation and raises serious doubts as to its compatibility with the common market, it shall decide to initiate proceedings. Without prejudice to Article 9, such proceedings shall be closed by means of a decision as provided for in Article 8(1) to (4), unless the undertakings concerned have demonstrated to the satisfaction of the Commission that they have abandoned the concentration.

2. Where the Commission finds that, following modification by the undertakings concerned, a notified concentration no longer raises serious doubts within the meaning of paragraph 1(c), it shall declare the concentration compatible with the common market pursuant to paragraph 1(b).

The Commission may attach to its decision under paragraph 1(b) conditions and obligations intended to ensure that the undertakings concerned comply with the commitments they have entered into vis-à-vis the Commission with a view to rendering the concentration compatible with the common market.

3. The Commission may revoke the decision it took pursuant to paragraph 1(a) or (b) where:

(a) the decision is based on incorrect information for which one of the undertakings is responsible or where it has been obtained by deceit,

or

(b) the undertakings concerned commit a breach of an obligation attached to the decision.

4. In the cases referred to in paragraph 3, the Commission may take a decision under paragraph 1, without being bound by the time limits referred to in Article 10(1).

5. The Commission shall notify its decision to the undertakings concerned and the competent authorities of the Member States without delay.

Article 7 Suspension of concentrations

1. A concentration with a Community dimension as defined in Article 1, or which is to be examined by the Commission pursuant to Article 4(5), shall not be implemented either before its notification or until it has been declared compatible with the common market pursuant to a decision under Articles 6(1)(b), 8(1) or 8(2), or on the basis of a presumption according to Article 10(6).

2. Paragraph 1 shall not prevent the implementation of a public bid or of a series of transactions in securities including those convertible into other securities admitted to trading on a market such as a stock exchange, by which control within the meaning of Article 3 is acquired from various sellers, provided that:

(a) the concentration is notified to the Commission pursuant to Article 4 without delay; and

(b) the acquirer does not exercise the voting rights attached to the securities in question or does so only to maintain the full value of its investments based on a derogation granted by the Commission under paragraph 3.

3. The Commission may, on request, grant a derogation from the obligations imposed in paragraphs 1 or 2. The request to grant a derogation must be reasoned. In deciding on the request, the Commission shall take into account inter alia the effects of the suspension on one or more undertakings concerned by the concentration or on a third party and the threat to competition posed by the concentration. Such a derogation may be made subject to conditions and obligations in order to ensure conditions of effective competition. A derogation may be applied for and granted at any time, be it before notification or after the transaction.

4. The validity of any transaction carried out in contravention of paragraph 1 shall be dependent on a decision pursuant to Article 6(1)(b) or Article 8(1), (2) or (3) or on a presumption pursuant to Article 10(6).

This Article shall, however, have no effect on the validity of transactions in securities including those convertible into other securities admitted to trading on a market such as a stock exchange, unless the buyer and seller knew or ought to have known that the transaction was carried out in contravention of paragraph 1.

Article 8 Powers of decision of the Commission

1. Where the Commission finds that a notified concentration fulfils the criterion laid down in Article 2(2) and, in the cases referred to in Article 2(4), the criteria laid down in Article 81(3) of the Treaty, it shall issue a decision declaring the concentration compatible with the common market.

A decision declaring a concentration compatible shall be deemed to cover restrictions directly related and necessary to the implementation of the concentration.

2. Where the Commission finds that, following modification by the undertakings concerned, a notified concentration fulfils the criterion laid down in Article 2(2) and, in the cases referred to in Article 2(4), the criteria laid down in Article 81(3) of the Treaty, it shall issue a decision declaring the concentration compatible with the common market.

The Commission may attach to its decision conditions and obligations intended to ensure that the undertakings concerned comply with the commitments they have entered into vis-à-vis the Commission with a view to rendering the concentration compatible with the common market. A decision declaring a concentration compatible shall be deemed to cover restrictions directly related and necessary to the implementation of the concentration.

3. Where the Commission finds that a concentration fulfils the criterion defined in Article 2(3) or, in the cases referred to in Article 2(4), does not fulfil the criteria laid down in Article 81(3) of the Treaty, it shall issue a decision declaring that the concentration is incompatible with the common market.

4. Where the Commission finds that a concentration:

(a) has already been implemented and that concentration has been declared incompatible with the common market, or

(b) has been implemented in contravention of a condition attached to a decision taken under paragraph 2, which has found that, in the absence of the condition, the concentration would fulfil the criterion laid down in Article 2(3) or, in the cases referred to in Article 2(4), would not fulfil the criteria laid down in Article 81(3) of the Treaty, the Commission may:

- require the undertakings concerned to dissolve the concentration, in particular through the dissolution of the merger or the disposal of all the shares or assets acquired, so as to restore the situation prevailing prior to the implementation of the concentration; in circumstances where restoration of the situation prevailing before the implementation of the concentration is not possible through dissolution of the concentration, the Commission may take any other measure appropriate to achieve such restoration as far as possible,

– order any other appropriate measure to ensure that the undertakings concerned dissolve the concentration or take other restorative measures as required in its decision.

In cases falling within point (a) of the first subparagraph, the measures referred to in that subparagraph may be imposed either in a decision pursuant to paragraph 3 or by separate decision.

5. The Commission may take interim measures appropriate to restore or maintain conditions of effective competition where a concentration:

(a) has been implemented in contravention of Article 7, and a decision as to the compatibility of the concentration with the common market has not yet been taken;

(b) has been implemented in contravention of a condition attached to a decision under Article 6(1)(b) or paragraph 2 of this Article;

(c) has already been implemented and is declared incompatible with the common market.

6. The Commission may revoke the decision it has taken pursuant to paragraphs 1 or 2 where:

(a) the declaration of compatibility is based on incorrect information for which one of the undertakings is responsible or where it has been obtained by deceit; or

(b) the undertakings concerned commit a breach of an obligation attached to the decision.

7. The Commission may take a decision pursuant to paragraphs 1 to 3 without being bound by the time limits referred to in Article 10(3), in cases where:

(a) it finds that a concentration has been implemented

(i) in contravention of a condition attached to a decision under Article 6(1)(b), or

(ii) in contravention of a condition attached to a decision taken under paragraph 2 and in accordance with Article 10(2), which has found that, in the absence of the condition, the concentration would raise serious doubts as to its compatibility with the common market; or

(b) a decision has been revoked pursuant to paragraph 6.

8. The Commission shall notify its decision to the undertakings concerned and the competent authorities of the Member States without delay.

Article 9 Referral to the competent authorities of the Member States

1. The Commission may, by means of a decision notified without delay to the undertakings concerned and the competent authorities of the other Member States, refer a notified concentration to the competent authorities of the Member State concerned in the following circumstances.

2. Within 15 working days of the date of receipt of the copy of the notification, a Member State, on its own initiative or upon the invitation of the Commission, may inform the Commission, which shall inform the undertakings concerned, that:

(a) a concentration threatens to affect significantly competition in a market within that Member State, which presents all the characteristics of a distinct market, or

(b) a concentration affects competition in a market within that Member State, which presents all the characteristics of a distinct market and which does not constitute a substantial part of the common market.

3. If the Commission considers that, having regard to the market for the products or services in question and the geographical reference market within the meaning of paragraph 7, there is such a distinct market and that such a threat exists, either:

(a) it shall itself deal with the case in accordance with this Regulation; or

(b) it shall refer the whole or part of the case to the competent authorities of the Member State concerned with a view to the application of that State's national competition law.

If, however, the Commission considers that such a distinct market or threat does not exist, it shall adopt a decision to that effect which it shall address to the Member State concerned, and shall itself deal with the case in accordance with this Regulation.

In cases where a Member State informs the Commission pursuant to paragraph 2(b) that a concentration affects competition in a distinct market within its territory that does not form a substantial part of the common market, the Commission shall refer the whole or part of the case relating to the distinct market concerned, if it considers that such a distinct market is affected.

4. A decision to refer or not to refer pursuant to paragraph 3 shall be taken:
   (a) as a general rule within the period provided for in Article 10(1), second subparagraph, where the Commission, pursuant to Article 6(1)(b), has not initiated proceedings; or
   (b) within 65 working days at most of the notification of the concentration concerned where the Commission has initiated proceedings under Article 6(1)(c), without taking the preparatory steps in order to adopt the necessary measures under Article 8(2), (3) or (4) to maintain or restore effective competition on the market concerned.

5. If within the 65 working days referred to in paragraph 4(b) the Commission, despite a reminder from the Member State concerned, has not taken a decision on referral in accordance with paragraph 3 nor has taken the preparatory steps referred to in paragraph 4(b), it shall be deemed to have taken a decision to refer the case to the Member State concerned in accordance with paragraph 3(b).

6. The competent authority of the Member State concerned shall decide upon the case without undue delay.

Within 45 working days after the Commission's referral, the competent authority of the Member State concerned shall inform the undertakings concerned of the result of the preliminary competition assessment and what further action, if any, it proposes to take. The Member State concerned may exceptionally suspend this time limit where necessary information has not been provided to it by the undertakings concerned as provided for by its national competition law.

Where a notification is requested under national law, the period of 45 working days shall begin on the working day following that of the receipt of a complete notification by the competent authority of that Member State.

7. The geographical reference market shall consist of the area in which the undertakings concerned are involved in the supply and demand of products or services, in which the conditions of competition are sufficiently homogeneous and which can be distinguished from neighbouring areas because, in particular, conditions of competition are appreciably different in those areas. This assessment should take account in particular of the nature and characteristics of the products or services concerned, of the existence of entry barriers or of consumer preferences, of appreciable differences of the undertakings' market shares between the area concerned and neighbouring areas or of substantial price differences.

8. In applying the provisions of this Article, the Member State concerned may take only the measures strictly necessary to safeguard or restore effective competition on the market concerned.

9. In accordance with the relevant provisions of the Treaty, any Member State may appeal to the Court of Justice, and in particular request the application of Article 243 of the Treaty, for the purpose of applying its national competition law.

Article 10 Time limits for initiating proceedings and for decisions

1. Without prejudice to Article 6(4), the decisions referred to in Article 6(1) shall be taken within 25 working days at most. That period shall begin on the working day following that of the receipt of a notification or, if the information to be supplied with the notification is incomplete, on the working day following that of the receipt of the complete information. That period shall be increased to 35 working days where the Commission receives a request from a Member State in accordance with Article 9(2) or where, the undertakings concerned offer commitments pursuant to Article 6(2) with a view to rendering the concentration compatible with the common market.

2. Decisions pursuant to Article 8(1) or (2) concerning notified concentrations shall be taken as soon as it appears that the serious doubts referred to in Article 6(1)(c) have been removed, particularly as a result of modifications made by the undertakings concerned, and at the latest by the time limit laid down in paragraph 3.

3. Without prejudice to Article 8(7), decisions pursuant to Article 8(1) to (3) concerning notified concentrations shall be taken within not more than 90 working days of the date on which the proceedings are initiated. That period shall be increased to 105 working days where the undertakings concerned offer commitments pursuant to Article 8(2), second subparagraph, with a view to

rendering the concentration compatible with the common market, unless these commitments have been offered less than 55 working days after the initiation of proceedings. The periods set by the first subparagraph shall likewise be extended if the notifying parties make a request to that effect not later than 15 working days after the initiation of proceedings pursuant to Article 6 (1)(c). The notifying parties may make only one such request. Likewise, at any time following the initiation of proceedings, the periods set by the first subparagraph may be extended by the Commission with the agreement of the notifying parties. The total duration of any extension or extensions effected pursuant to this subparagraph shall not exceed 20 working days.

4. The periods set by paragraphs 1 and 3 shall exceptionally be suspended where, owing to circumstances for which one of the undertakings involved in the concentration is responsible, the Commission has had to request information by decision pursuant to Article 11 or to order an inspection by decision pursuant to Article 13.

The first subparagraph shall also apply to the period referred to in Article 9(4)(b).

5. Where the Court of Justice gives a judgment which annuls the whole or part of a Commission decision which is subject to a time limit set by this Article, the concentration shall be re-examined by the Commission with a view to adopting a decision pursuant to Article 6(1).

The concentration shall be re-examined in the light of current market conditions.

The notifying parties shall submit a new notification or supplement the original notification, without delay, where the original notification becomes incomplete by reason of intervening changes in market conditions or in the information provided. Where there are no such changes, the parties shall certify this fact without delay.

The periods laid down in paragraph 1 shall start on the working day following that of the receipt of complete information in a new notification, a supplemented notification, or a certification within the meaning of the third subparagraph.

The second and third subparagraphs shall also apply in the cases referred to in Article 6(4) and Article 8(7).

6. Where the Commission has not taken a decision in accordance with Article 6(1)(b), (c), 8(1), (2) or (3) within the time limits set in paragraphs 1 and 3 respectively, the concentration shall be deemed to have been declared compatible with the common market, without prejudice to Article 9.

Article 11 Requests for information

1. In order to carry out the duties assigned to it by this Regulation, the Commission may, by simple request or by decision, require the persons referred to in Article 3(1)(b), as well as undertakings and associations of undertakings, to provide all necessary information.

2. When sending a simple request for information to a person, an undertaking or an association of undertakings, the Commission shall state the legal basis and the purpose of the request, specify what information is required and fix the time limit within which the information is to be provided, as well as the penalties provided for in Article 14 for supplying incorrect or misleading information.

3. Where the Commission requires a person, an undertaking or an association of undertakings to supply information by decision, it shall state the legal basis and the purpose of the request, specify what information is required and fix the time limit within which it is to be provided. It shall also indicate the penalties provided for in Article 14 and indicate or impose the penalties provided for in Article 15. It shall further indicate the right to have the decision reviewed by the Court of Justice.

4. The owners of the undertakings or their representatives and, in the case of legal persons, companies or firms, or associations having no legal personality, the persons authorised to represent them by law or by their constitution, shall supply the information requested on behalf of the undertaking concerned. Persons duly authorised to act may supply the information on behalf of their clients. The latter shall remain fully responsible if the information supplied is incomplete, incorrect or misleading.

5. The Commission shall without delay forward a copy of any decision taken pursuant to paragraph 3 to the competent authorities of the Member State in whose territory the residence of the

person or the seat of the undertaking or association of undertakings is situated, and to the competent authority of the Member State whose territory is affected. At the specific request of the competent authority of a Member State, the Commission shall also forward to that authority copies of simple requests for information relating to a notified concentration.

6. At the request of the Commission, the governments and competent authorities of the Member States shall provide the Commission with all necessary information to carry out the duties assigned to it by this Regulation.

7. In order to carry out the duties assigned to it by this Regulation, the Commission may interview any natural or legal person who consents to be interviewed for the purpose of collecting information relating to the subject matter of an investigation. At the beginning of the interview, which may be conducted by telephone or other electronic means, the Commission shall state the legal basis and the purpose of the interview.

Where an interview is not conducted on the premises of the Commission or by telephone or other electronic means, the Commission shall inform in advance the competent authority of the Member State in whose territory the interview takes place. If the competent authority of that Member State so requests, officials of that authority may assist the officials and other persons authorised by the Commission to conduct the interview.

Article 12 Inspections by the authorities of the Member States

1. At the request of the Commission, the competent authorities of the Member States shall undertake the inspections which the Commission considers to be necessary under Article 13(1), or which it has ordered by decision pursuant to Article 13(4). The officials of the competent authorities of the Member States who are responsible for conducting these inspections as well as those authorised or appointed by them shall exercise their powers in accordance with their national law.

2. If so requested by the Commission or by the competent authority of the Member State within whose territory the inspection is to be conducted, officials and other accompanying persons authorised by the Commission may assist the officials of the authority concerned.

Article 13 The Commission's powers of inspection

1. In order to carry out the duties assigned to it by this Regulation, the Commission may conduct all necessary inspections of undertakings and associations of undertakings.

2. The officials and other accompanying persons authorised by the Commission to conduct an inspection shall have the power:

(a) to enter any premises, land and means of transport of undertakings and associations of undertakings;
(b) to examine the books and other records related to the business, irrespective of the medium on which they are stored;
(c) to take or obtain in any form copies of or extracts from such books or records;
(d) to seal any business premises and books or records for the period and to the extent necessary for the inspection;
(e) to ask any representative or member of staff of the undertaking or association of undertakings for explanations on facts or documents relating to the subject matter and purpose of the inspection and to record the answers.

3. Officials and other accompanying persons authorised by the Commission to conduct an inspection shall exercise their powers upon production of a written authorisation specifying the subject matter and purpose of the inspection and the penalties provided for in Article 14, in the production of the required books or other records related to the business which is incomplete or where answers to questions asked under paragraph 2 of this Article are incorrect or misleading. In good time before the inspection, the Commission shall give notice of the inspection to the competent authority of the Member State in whose territory the inspection is to be conducted.

4. Undertakings and associations of undertakings are required to submit to inspections ordered by decision of the Commission. The decision shall specify the subject matter and purpose of the inspection, appoint the date on which it is to begin and indicate the penalties provided for in Articles 14 and 15 and the right to have the decision reviewed by the Court of Justice. The Commission shall take such decisions after consulting the competent authority of the Member State in whose territory the inspection is to be conducted.

5. Officials of, and those authorised or appointed by, the competent authority of the Member State in whose territory the inspection is to be conducted shall, at the request of that authority or of the Commission, actively assist the officials and other accompanying persons authorised by the Commission. To this end, they shall enjoy the powers specified in paragraph 2.

6. Where the officials and other accompanying persons authorised by the Commission find that an undertaking opposes an inspection, including the sealing of business premises, books or records, ordered pursuant to this Article, the Member State concerned shall afford them the necessary assistance, requesting where appropriate the assistance of the police or of an equivalent enforcement authority, so as to enable them to conduct their inspection.

7. If the assistance provided for in paragraph 6 requires authorisation from a judicial authority according to national rules, such authorisation shall be applied for. Such authorisation may also be applied for as a precautionary measure.

8. Where authorisation as referred to in paragraph 7 is applied for, the national judicial authority shall ensure that the Commission decision is authentic and that the coercive measures envisaged are neither arbitrary nor excessive having regard to the subject matter of the inspection. In its control of proportionality of the coercive measures, the national judicial authority may ask the Commission, directly or through the competent authority of that Member State, for detailed explanations relating to the subject matter of the inspection. However, the national judicial authority may not call into question the necessity for the inspection nor demand that it be provided with the information in the Commission's file. The lawfulness of the Commission's decision shall be subject to review only by the Court of Justice.

Article 14 Fines

1. The Commission may by decision impose on the persons referred to in Article 3(1)b, undertakings or associations of undertakings, fines not exceeding 1% of the aggregate turnover of the undertaking or association of undertakings concerned within the meaning of Article 5 where, intentionally or negligently:

(a) they supply incorrect or misleading information in a submission, certification, notification or supplement thereto, pursuant to Article 4, Article 10(5) or Article 22(3);

(b) they supply incorrect or misleading information in response to a request made pursuant to Article 11(2);

(c) in response to a request made by decision adopted pursuant to Article 11(3), they supply incorrect, incomplete or misleading information or do not supply information within the required time limit;

(d) they produce the required books or other records related to the business in incomplete form during inspections under Article 13, or refuse to submit to an inspection ordered by decision taken pursuant to Article 13(4);

(e) in response to a question asked in accordance with Article 13(2)(e),
- they give an incorrect or misleading answer,
- they fail to rectify within a time limit set by the Commission an incorrect, incomplete or misleading answer given by a member of staff, or
- they fail or refuse to provide a complete answer on facts relating to the subject matter and purpose of an inspection ordered by a decision adopted pursuant to Article 13(4);

(f) seals affixed by officials or other accompanying persons authorised by the Commission in accordance with Article 13(2)(d) have been broken.

2. The Commission may by decision impose fines not exceeding 10% of the aggregate turnover of the undertaking concerned within the meaning of Article 5 on the persons referred to in Article 3(1)b or the undertakings concerned where, either intentionally or negligently, they:

(a) fail to notify a concentration in accordance with Articles 4 or 22(3) prior to its implementation, unless they are expressly authorised to do so by Article 7(2) or by a decision taken pursuant to Article 7(3);

(b) implement a concentration in breach of Article 7;

(c) implement a concentration declared incompatible with the common market by decision pursuant to Article 8(3) or do not comply with any measure ordered by decision pursuant to Article 8(4) or (5);

(d) fail to comply with a condition or an obligation imposed by decision pursuant to Articles 6(1)(b), Article 7(3) or Article 8(2), second subparagraph.

3. In fixing the amount of the fine, regard shall be had to the nature, gravity and duration of the infringement.

4. Decisions taken pursuant to paragraphs 1, 2 and 3 shall not be of a criminal law nature.

Article 15 Periodic penalty payments

1. The Commission may by decision impose on the persons referred to in Article 3(1)b, undertakings or associations of undertakings, periodic penalty payments not exceeding 5% of the average daily aggregate turnover of the undertaking or association of undertakings concerned within the meaning of Article 5 for each working day of delay, calculated from the date set in the decision, in order to compel them:

(a) to supply complete and correct information which it has requested by decision taken pursuant to Article 11(3);

(b) to submit to an inspection which it has ordered by decision taken pursuant to Article 13(4);

(c) to comply with an obligation imposed by decision pursuant to Article 6(1)(b), Article 7(3) or Article 8(2), second subparagraph; or;

(d) to comply with any measures ordered by decision pursuant to Article 8(4) or (5).

2. Where the persons referred to in Article 3(1)(b), undertakings or associations of undertakings have satisfied the obligation which the periodic penalty payment was intended to enforce, the Commission may fix the definitive amount of the periodic penalty payments at a figure lower than that which would arise under the original decision.

Article 16 Review by the Court of Justice

The Court of Justice shall have unlimited jurisdiction within the meaning of Article 229 of the Treaty to review decisions whereby the Commission has fixed a fine or periodic penalty payments; it may cancel, reduce or increase the fine or periodic penalty payment imposed.

Article 17 Professional secrecy

1. Information acquired as a result of the application of this Regulation shall be used only for the purposes of the relevant request, investigation or hearing.

2. Without prejudice to Article 4(3), Articles 18 and 20, the Commission and the competent authorities of the Member States, their officials and other servants and other persons working under the supervision of these authorities as well as officials and civil servants of other authorities of the Member States shall not disclose information they have acquired through the application of this Regulation of the kind covered by the obligation of professional secrecy.

3. Paragraphs 1 and 2 shall not prevent publication of general information or of surveys which do not contain information relating to particular undertakings or associations of undertakings.

Done at Brussels, 20 January 2004.

Commission Regulation (EC) No 773/2004 of 7 April 2004 relating to the conduct of proceedings by the Commission pursuant to Articles 81 and 82 of the EC Treaty*

[OJ 2004 L123/18]

Chapter I Scope

Article 1 Subject-matter and scope

This regulation applies to proceedings conducted by the Commission for the application of Articles 81 and 82 of the Treaty.

Chapter II Initiation of proceedings

Article 2 Initiation of proceedings

1. The Commission may decide to initiate proceedings with a view to adopting a decision pursuant to Chapter III of Regulation (EC) No 1/2003 at any point in time, but no later than the date on which it issues a preliminary assessment as referred to in Article 9(1) of that Regulation, a statement of objections or a request for the parties to express their interest in engaging in settlement discussions, or the date on which a notice pursuant to Article 27(4) of that Regulation is published, whichever is the earlier.

2. The Commission may make public the initiation of proceedings, in any appropriate way. Before doing so, it shall inform the parties concerned.

3. The Commission may exercise its powers of investigation pursuant to Chapter V of Regulation (EC) No 1/2003 before initiating proceedings.

4. The Commission may reject a complaint pursuant to Article 7 of Regulation (EC) No 1/2003 without initiating proceedings.

Chapter III Investigations by the Commission

Article 3 Power to take statements

1. Where the Commission interviews a person with his consent in accordance with Article 19 of Regulation (EC) No 1/2003, it shall, at the beginning of the interview, state the legal basis and the purpose of the interview, and recall its voluntary nature. It shall also inform the person interviewed of its intention to make a record of the interview.

2. The interview may be conducted by any means including by telephone or electronic means.

3. The Commission may record the statements made by the persons interviewed in any form.

A copy of any recording shall be made available to the person interviewed for approval. Where necessary, the Commission shall set a time-limit within which the person interviewed may communicate to it any correction to be made to the statement.

Article 4 Oral questions during inspections

1. When, pursuant to Article 20(2)(e) of Regulation (EC) No 1/2003, officials or other accompanying persons authorised by the Commission ask representatives or members of staff of an undertaking or of an association of undertakings for explanations, the explanations given may be recorded in any form.

2. A copy of any recording made pursuant to paragraph 1 shall be made available to the undertaking or association of undertakings concerned after the inspection.

3. In cases where a member of staff of an undertaking or of an association of undertakings who is not or was not authorised by the undertaking or by the association of undertakings

* **Editor's Note:** Read now Articles 101 and 102 TFEU. As amended by Regulations 1792/2006 (OJ 2006 L362/1) 622/2008 (OJ 2008 L171/3), 519/2013 (OJ 2013 L158/74) and 2015/1348 (OJ 2015 L208/3).

to provide explanations on behalf of the undertaking or association of undertakings has been asked for explanations, the Commission shall set a time-limit within which the undertaking or the association of undertakings may communicate to the Commission any rectification, amendment or supplement to the explanations given by such member of staff. The rectification, amendment or supplement shall be added to the explanations as recorded pursuant to paragraph 1.

Article 4a The Commission's Leniency Programme

1. The Commission may set the requirements and cooperation conditions under which it may reward undertakings that are or have been party to secret cartels, for their cooperation in disclosing the cartel and facilitating the establishment of an infringement, with immunity from fines or a reduction in fines which would otherwise be imposed under Article 23(2) of Regulation (EC) No 1/2003 (the Commission leniency programme).

Immunity from fines may be granted to the undertaking that is the first to submit evidence which in the Commission's view would enable it to carry out a targeted inspection or find an infringement of Article 101 of the Treaty in connection with the alleged cartel. A reduction in fines may be granted to undertakings which provide the Commission with evidence of the alleged infringement which represents significant added value with respect to the evidence already in the Commission's possession.

The Commission will only grant immunity from or a reduction of the fine under its leniency programme if, at the end of the administrative proceedings, the undertaking has met the requirements and cooperation conditions set out in the leniency programme. Those may cover, among others, the type of information and evidence the undertakings are required to submit and the further cooperation expected from the undertakings during the administrative proceedings.

2. In order to qualify for immunity from or reduction of the fine which would otherwise be imposed, undertakings shall provide the Commission with voluntary presentations of their knowledge of a secret cartel and their role therein, which may be also in the form of voluntary presentations of the knowledge of former or current employees or representatives of the undertaking (leniency corporate statements). Such leniency corporate statements shall be drawn up specifically for submission to the Commission with a view to obtaining immunity from or reduction of fines under the Commission's leniency programme.

3. The Commission will offer parties appropriate methods of providing leniency corporate statements other than by written submission, including orally. Oral corporate statements may be recorded and transcribed at the Commission's premises. The undertaking shall be granted an opportunity to check the technical accuracy of the recording of its oral statement at the Commission's premises, and, where necessary, to correct the substance of the statement without delay. The rules in this Regulation on leniency corporate statements shall apply to such statements irrespective of the medium on which they are stored. Pre-existing information, i.e. evidence that exists irrespective of the Commission proceedings and that is submitted to the Commission by an undertaking in the context of its application for immunity from or reduction of the fine, is not part of a leniency corporate statement.

Chapter IV Handling of complaints

Article 5 Admissibility of complaints

1. Natural and legal persons shall show a legitimate interest in order to be entitled to lodge a complaint for the purposes of Article 7 of Regulation (EC) No 1/2003.

Such complaints shall contain the information required by Form C, as set out in the Annex. The Commission may dispense with this obligation as regards part of the information, including documents, required by Form C.

2. Three paper copies as well as, if possible, an electronic copy of the complaint shall be submitted to the Commission. The complainant shall also submit a non-confidential version of the complaint, if confidentiality is claimed for any part of the complaint.

3. Complaints shall be submitted in one of the official languages of the Community.

Article 6 Participation of complainants in proceedings

1. Where the Commission issues a statement of objections relating to a matter in respect of which it has received a complaint, it shall provide the complainant with a copy of the non-confidential version of the statement of objections, except in cases where the settlement procedure applies, where it shall inform the complainant in writing of the nature and subject matter of the procedure. The Commission shall also set a time limit within which the complainant may make known its views in writing.

2. The Commission may, where appropriate, afford complainants the opportunity of expressing their views at the oral hearing of the parties to which a statement of objections has been issued, if complainants so request in their written comments.

Article 7 Rejection of complaints

1. Where the Commission considers that on the basis of the information in its possession there are insufficient grounds for acting on a complaint, it shall inform the complainant of its reasons and set a time-limit within which the complainant may make known its views in writing. The Commission shall not be obliged to take into account any further written submission received after the expiry of that time-limit.

2. If the complainant makes known its views within the time-limit set by the Commission and the written submissions made by the complainant do not lead to a different assessment of the complaint, the Commission shall reject the complaint by decision.

3. If the complainant fails to make known its views within the time-limit set by the Commission, the complaint shall be deemed to have been withdrawn.

Article 8 Access to information

1. Where the Commission has informed the complainant of its intention to reject a complaint pursuant to Article 7(1) the complainant may request access to the documents on which the Commission bases its provisional assessment. For this purpose, the complainant may however not have access to business secrets and other confidential information belonging to other parties involved in the proceedings.

Article 9 Rejections of complaints pursuant to Article 13 of Regulation (EC) No 1/2003

Where the Commission rejects a complaint pursuant to Article 13 of Regulation (EC) No 1/2003, it shall inform the complainant without delay of the national competition authority which is dealing or has already dealt with the case.

Chapter V Exercise of the right to be heard

Article 10 Statement of objections and reply

1. The Commission shall inform the parties concerned of the objections raised against them. The statement of objections shall be notified in writing to each of the parties against whom objections are raised.

2. The Commission shall, when notifying the statement of objections to the parties concerned, set a time-limit within which these parties may inform it in writing of their views. The Commission shall not be obliged to take into account written submissions received after the expiry of that time-limit.

3. The parties may, in their written submissions, set out all facts known to them which are relevant to their defence against the objections raised by the Commission. They shall attach any relevant documents as proof of the facts set out. They shall provide a paper original as well as an electronic copy or, where they do not provide an electronic copy, 31 paper copies of their submission and of the documents attached to it. They may propose that the Commission hear persons who may corroborate the facts set out in their submission.

Article 10a Settlement procedure in cartel cases

1. After the initiation of proceedings pursuant to Article 11(6) of Regulation (EC) No 1/2003, the Commission may set a time limit within which the parties may indicate in writing that they are prepared to engage in settlement discussions with a view to possibly introducing settlement submissions. The Commission shall not be obliged to take into account replies received after the expiry of that time limit.

If two or more parties within the same undertaking indicate their willingness to engage in settlement discussions pursuant to the first subparagraph, they shall appoint a joint representation to engage in discussions with the Commission on their behalf. When setting the time limit referred to in the first subparagraph, the Commission shall indicate to the relevant parties that they are identified within the same undertaking, for the sole purpose of enabling them to comply with this provision.

2. Parties taking part in settlement discussions may be informed by the Commission of:

(a) the objections it envisages to raise against them;

(b) the evidence used to determine the envisaged objections;

(c) non-confidential versions of any specified accessible document listed in the case file at that point in time, in so far as a request by the party is justified for the purpose of enabling the party to ascertain its position regarding a time period or any other particular aspect of the cartel; and

(d) the range of potential fines.

This information shall be confidential vis-à-vis third parties, save where the Commission has given a prior explicit authorisation for disclosure.

Should settlement discussions progress, the Commission may set a time limit within which the parties may commit to follow the settlement procedure by introducing settlement submissions reflecting the results of the settlement discussions and acknowledging their participation in an infringement of Article 101 of the Treaty as well as their liability. These settlement submissions shall be specifically drawn up by the undertakings concerned as a formal request to the Commission to adopt any decision in their case following the settlement procedure. Before the Commission sets a time limit for the introduction of settlement submissions, the parties concerned shall be entitled to have the information specified in the first subparagraph, disclosed to them, upon request, in a timely manner. The Commission shall not be obliged to take into account settlement submissions received after the expiry of that time limit. The Commission will offer parties appropriate methods of providing settlement submissions other than by written submission, including orally. Oral settlement submissions may be recorded and transcribed at the Commission's premises. The undertaking shall be granted an opportunity to check the technical accuracy of the recording of its oral submission at the Commission's premises, and, where necessary, to correct the substance of their submission without delay. The rules in this Regulation on settlement submissions shall apply to settlement submissions irrespective of the medium on which they are stored.

3. When the statement of objections notified to the parties reflects the contents of their settlement submissions, the written reply to the statement of objections by the parties concerned shall, within a time limit set by the Commission, confirm that the statement of objections addressed to them reflects the contents of their settlement submissions. The Commission may then proceed to the adoption of a Decision pursuant to Article 7 and Article 23 of Regulation (EC) No 1/2003 after consultation of the Advisory Committee on Restrictive Practices and Dominant Positions pursuant to Article 14 of Regulation (EC) No 1/2003.

4. The Commission may decide at any time during the procedure to discontinue settlement discussions altogether in a specific case or with respect to one or more of the parties involved, if it considers that procedural efficiencies are not likely to be achieved.

Article 11 Right to be heard

1. The Commission shall give the parties to whom it addresses a statement of objections the opportunity to be heard before consulting the Advisory Committee referred to in Article 14(1) of Regulation (EC) No 1/2003.

2. The Commission shall, in its decisions, deal only with objections in respect of which the parties referred to in paragraph 1 have been able to comment.

Article 12 Right to an oral hearing

1. The Commission shall give the parties to whom it addresses a statement of objections the opportunity to develop their arguments at an oral hearing, if they so request in their written submissions.

2. However, when introducing their settlement submissions the parties shall confirm to the Commission that they would only require having the opportunity to develop their arguments at an oral hearing, if the statement of objections does not reflect the contents of their settlement submissions.

Article 13 Hearing of other persons

1. If natural or legal persons other than those referred to in Articles 5 and 11 apply to be heard and show a sufficient interest, the Commission shall inform them in writing of the nature and subject matter of the procedure and shall set a time-limit within which they may make known their views in writing.

2. The Commission may, where appropriate, invite persons referred to in paragraph 1 to develop their arguments at the oral hearing of the parties to whom a statement of objections has been addressed, if the persons referred to in paragraph 1 so request in their written comments.

3. The Commission may invite any other person to express its views in writing and to attend the oral hearing of the parties to whom a statement of objections has been addressed. The Commission may also invite such persons to express their views at that oral hearing.

Article 14 Conduct of oral hearings

1. Hearings shall be conducted by a Hearing Officer in full independence.

2. The Commission shall invite the persons to be heard to attend the oral hearing on such date as it shall determine.

3. The Commission shall invite the competition authorities of the Member States to take part in the oral hearing. It may likewise invite officials and civil servants of other authorities of the Member States.

4. Persons invited to attend shall either appear in person or be represented by legal representatives or by representatives authorised by their constitution as appropriate. Undertakings and associations of undertakings may also be represented by a duly authorised agent appointed from among their permanent staff.

5. Persons heard by the Commission may be assisted by their lawyers or other qualified persons admitted by the Hearing Officer.

6. Oral hearings shall not be public. Each person may be heard separately or in the presence of other persons invited to attend, having regard to the legitimate interest of the undertakings in the protection of their business secrets and other confidential information.

7. The Hearing Officer may allow the parties to whom a statement of objections has been addressed, the complainants, other persons invited to the hearing, the Commission services and the authorities of the Member States to ask questions during the hearing.

8. The statements made by each person heard shall be recorded. Upon request, the recording of the hearing shall be made available to the persons who attended the hearing. Regard shall be had to the legitimate interest of the parties in the protection of their business secrets and other confidential information.

Done at Brussels, 7 April 2004.

Commission Regulation (EU) 2022/720 of 01 May 2022 on the application of Article 101(3) of the Treaty on the Functioning of the European Union to categories of vertical agreements and concerted practices

[OJ 2022 L134/4]

Article 1 Definitions

1. For the purposes of this Regulation, the following definitions shall apply:
   (a) 'vertical agreement' means an agreement or concerted practice between two or more undertakings, each of which operates, for the purposes of the agreement or the concerted practice, at a different level of the production or distribution chain, and relating to the conditions under which the parties may purchase, sell or resell certain goods or services;
   (b) 'vertical restraint' means a restriction of competition in a vertical agreement falling within the scope of Article 101(1) of the Treaty;
   (c) 'competing undertaking' means an actual or potential competitor; 'actual competitor' means an undertaking that is active on the same relevant market; 'potential competitor' means an undertaking that, in the absence of the vertical agreement, would, on realistic grounds and not just as a mere theoretical possibility, be likely, within a short period of time, to make the necessary additional investments or incur other necessary costs to enter the relevant market;
   (d) 'supplier' includes an undertaking that provides online intermediation services;
   (e) 'online intermediation services' means information society services within the meaning of Article 1(1), point (b), of Directive (EU) 2015/1535 of the European Parliament and of the Council which allow undertakings to offer goods or services:
      (i) to other undertakings, with a view to facilitating the initiating of direct transactions between those undertakings, or
      (ii) to final consumers, with a view to facilitating the initiating of direct transactions between those undertakings and final consumers,
   irrespective of whether and where the transactions are ultimately concluded;
   (f) 'non-compete obligation' means any direct or indirect obligation causing the buyer not to manufacture, purchase, sell or resell goods or services which compete with the contract goods or services, or any direct or indirect obligation on the buyer to purchase from the supplier or from another undertaking designated by the supplier more than 80% of the buyer's total purchases of the contract goods or services and their substitutes on the relevant market, calculated on the basis of the value or, where such is standard industry practice, the volume of its purchases in the preceding calendar year;
   (g) 'selective distribution system' means a distribution system where the supplier undertakes to sell the contract goods or services, either directly or indirectly, only to distributors selected on the basis of specified criteria and where these distributors undertake not to sell such goods or services to unauthorised distributors within the territory reserved by the supplier to operate that system;
   (h) 'exclusive distribution system' means a distribution system where the supplier allocates a territory or group of customers exclusively to itself or to a maximum of five buyers and restricts all its other buyers from actively selling into the exclusive territory or to the exclusive customer group;
   (i) 'intellectual property rights' includes industrial property rights, know-how, copyright and neighbouring rights;

(j) 'know-how' means a package of non-patented practical information, resulting from experience and testing by the supplier, which is secret, substantial and identified; 'secret' means that the know-how is not generally known or easily accessible; 'substantial' means that the know-how is significant and useful to the buyer for the use, sale or resale of the contract goods or services; 'identified' means that the know-how is described in a sufficiently comprehensive manner so as to make it possible to verify that it fulfils the criteria of secrecy and substantiality;

(k) 'buyer' includes an undertaking which, under an agreement falling within Article 101(1) of the Treaty, sells goods or services on behalf of another undertaking;

(l) 'active sales' means actively targeting customers by visits, letters, emails, calls or other means of direct communication or through targeted advertising and promotion, offline or online, for instance by means of print or digital media, including online media, price comparison services or advertising on search engines targeting customers in particular territories or customer groups, operating a website with a top-level domain corresponding to particular territories, or offering on a website languages that are commonly used in particular territories, where such languages are different from the ones commonly used in the territory in which the buyer is established;

(m) 'passive sales' means sales made in response to unsolicited requests from individual customers, including delivery of goods or services to the customer, without the sale having been initiated by actively targeting the particular customer, customer group or territory, and including sales resulting from participating in public procurement or responding to private invitations to tender.

2. For the purposes of this Regulation, the terms 'undertaking', 'supplier' and 'buyer' shall include their respective connected undertakings.

'Connected undertakings' means:

(a) undertakings in which a party to the agreement, directly or indirectly:
  (i) has the power to exercise more than half the voting rights, or
  (ii) has the power to appoint more than half the members of the supervisory board, board of management or bodies legally representing the undertaking, or

(b) undertakings which directly or indirectly have, over a party to the agreement, the rights or powers listed in point (a); or

(c) undertakings in which an undertaking referred to in point (b) has, directly or indirectly, the rights or powers listed in point (a); or

(d) undertakings in which a party to the agreement together with one or more of the undertakings referred to in points (a), (b) or (c), or in which two or more of the latter undertakings, jointly have the rights or powers listed in point (a); or

(e) undertakings in which the rights or the powers listed in point (a) are jointly held by:
  (i) parties to the agreement or their respective connected undertakings referred to in points (a) to (d), or
  (ii) one or more of the parties to the agreement or one or more of their connected undertakings referred to in points (a) to (d) and one or more third parties.

Article 2 Exemption

1. Pursuant to Article 101(3) of the Treaty and subject to the provisions of this Regulation, it is hereby declared that Article 101(1) of the Treaty shall not apply to vertical agreements. This exemption shall apply to the extent that such agreements contain vertical restraints.

2. The exemption provided for in paragraph 1 shall apply to vertical agreements entered into between an association of undertakings and an individual member, or between such an association and an individual supplier, only if all the members of the association are retailers of goods and if no individual member of the association, together with its connected undertakings, has a total annual turnover exceeding EUR 50 million. Vertical agreements entered into by such associations shall be covered by this Regulation without prejudice to the application of Article 101 of the Treaty to

horizontal agreements concluded between the members of the association or decisions adopted by the association.

3. The exemption provided for in paragraph 1 shall apply to vertical agreements containing provisions which relate to the assignment to the buyer or use by the buyer of intellectual property rights, provided that those provisions do not constitute the primary object of such agreements and are directly related to the use, sale or resale of goods or services by the buyer or its customers. The exemption applies on the condition that, in relation to the contract goods or services, those provisions do not contain restrictions of competition having the same object as vertical restraints which are not exempted under this Regulation.

4. The exemption provided for in paragraph 1 shall not apply to vertical agreements entered into between competing undertakings. However, that exemption shall apply where competing undertakings enter into a non-reciprocal vertical agreement and one of the following applies:

(a) the supplier is active at an upstream level as a manufacturer, importer, or wholesaler and at a downstream level as an importer, wholesaler, or retailer of goods, while the buyer is an importer, wholesaler, or retailer at the downstream level and not a competing undertaking at the upstream level where it buys the contract goods; or

(b) the supplier is a provider of services at several levels of trade, while the buyer provides its services at the retail level and is not a competing undertaking at the level of trade where it purchases the contract services.

5. The exceptions set out in paragraph 4, points (a) and (b) shall not apply to the exchange of information between the supplier and the buyer that is either not directly related to the implementation of the vertical agreement or is not necessary to improve the production or distribution of the contract goods or services, or which fulfils neither of those two conditions.

6. The exceptions set out in paragraph 4, points (a) and (b) shall not apply to vertical agreements relating to the provision of online intermediation services where the provider of the online intermediation services is a competing undertaking on the relevant market for the sale of the intermediated goods or services.

7. This Regulation shall not apply to vertical agreements the subject matter of which falls within the scope of any other block exemption regulation, unless otherwise provided for in such a regulation.

Article 3 Market share threshold

1. The exemption provided for in Article 2 shall apply on condition that the market share held by the supplier does not exceed 30% of the relevant market on which it sells the contract goods or services and the market share held by the buyer does not exceed 30% of the relevant market on which it purchases the contract goods or services.

2. For the purposes of paragraph 1, where in a multi-party agreement an undertaking buys the contract goods or services from one undertaking that is a party to the agreement and sells the contract goods or services to another undertaking that is also a party to the agreement, the market share of the first undertaking must respect the market share threshold provided for in that paragraph both as a buyer and a supplier in order for the exemption provided for in Article 2 to apply.

Article 4 Restrictions that remove the benefit of the block exemption – hardcore restrictions

The exemption provided for in Article 2 shall not apply to vertical agreements which, directly or indirectly, in isolation or in combination with other factors under the control of the parties, have as their object:

(a) the restriction of the buyer's ability to determine its sale price, without prejudice to the possibility of the supplier to impose a maximum sale price or recommend a sale price, provided that they do not amount to a fixed or minimum sale price as a result of pressure from, or incentives offered by, any of the parties;

(b) where the supplier operates an exclusive distribution system, the restriction of the territory into which, or of the customers to whom, the exclusive distributor may actively or passively sell the contract goods or services, except:
   (i) the restriction of active sales by the exclusive distributor and its direct customers, into a territory or to a customer group reserved to the supplier or allocated by the supplier exclusively to a maximum of five other exclusive distributors;
   (ii) the restriction of active or passive sales by the exclusive distributor and its customers to unauthorised distributors located in a territory where the supplier operates a selective distribution system for the contract goods or services;
   (iii) the restriction of the exclusive distributor's place of establishment;
   (iv) the restriction of active or passive sales to end users by an exclusive distributor operating at the wholesale level of trade;
   (v) the restriction of the exclusive distributor's ability to actively or passively sell components, supplied for the purposes of incorporation, to customers who would use them to manufacture the same type of goods as those produced by the supplier;

(c) where the supplier operates a selective distribution system,
   (i) the restriction of the territory into which, or of the customers to whom, the members of the selective distribution system may actively or passively sell the contract goods or services, except:
      (1) the restriction of active sales by the members of the selective distribution system and their direct customers, into a territory or to a customer group reserved to the supplier or allocated by the supplier exclusively to a maximum of five exclusive distributors;
      (2) the restriction of active or passive sales by the members of the selective distribution system and their customers to unauthorised distributors located within the territory where the selective distribution system is operated;
      (3) the restriction of the place of establishment of the members of the selective distribution system;
      (4) the restriction of active or passive sales to end users by members of the selective distribution system operating at the wholesale level of trade;
      (5) the restriction of the ability to actively or passively sell components, supplied for the purposes of incorporation, to customers who would use them to manufacture the same type of goods as those produced by the supplier;
   (ii) the restriction of cross-supplies between the members of the selective distribution system operating at the same or different levels of trade;
   (iii) the restriction of active or passive sales to end users by members of the selective distribution system operating at the retail level of trade, without prejudice to points (c)(i)(1) and (3);

(d) where the supplier operates neither an exclusive distribution system nor a selective distribution system, the restriction of the territory into which, or of the customers to whom, the buyer may actively or passively sell the contract goods or services, except:
   (i) the restriction of active sales by the buyer and its direct customers into a territory or to a customer group reserved to the supplier or allocated by the supplier exclusively to a maximum of five exclusive distributors;
   (ii) the restriction of active or passive sales by the buyer and its customers to unauthorised distributors located in a territory where the supplier operates a selective distribution system for the contract goods or services;
   (iii) the restriction of the buyer's place of establishment;
   (iv) the restriction of active or passive sales to end users by a buyer operating at the wholesale level of trade;
   (v) the restriction of the buyer's ability to actively or passively sell components, supplied for the purposes of incorporation, to customers who would use them to manufacture the same type of goods as those produced by the supplier;

(e) the prevention of the effective use of the internet by the buyer or its customers to sell the contract goods or services, as it restricts the territory into which or the customers to whom the contract goods or services may be sold within the meaning of points (b), (c) or (d), without prejudice to the possibility of imposing on the buyer:
  (i) other restrictions of online sales; or
  (ii) restrictions of online advertising that do not have the object of preventing the use of an entire online advertising channel;

(f) the restriction, agreed between a supplier of components and a buyer who incorporates those components, of the supplier's ability to sell the components as spare parts to end users or to repairers, wholesalers or other service providers not entrusted by the buyer with the repair or servicing of its goods.

Article 5 Excluded restrictions

1. The exemption provided for in Article 2 shall not apply to the following obligations contained in vertical agreements:

(a) any direct or indirect non-compete obligation, the duration of which is indefinite or exceeds 5 years;

(b) any direct or indirect obligation causing the buyer, after termination of the agreement, not to manufacture, purchase, sell or resell goods or services;

(c) any direct or indirect obligation causing the members of a selective distribution system not to sell the brands of particular competing suppliers;

(d) any direct or indirect obligation causing a buyer of online intermediation services not to offer, sell or resell goods or services to end users under more favourable conditions via competing online intermediation services;

2. By way of derogation from paragraph 1, point (a), the time limitation of five years shall not apply where the contract goods or services are sold by the buyer from premises and land owned by the supplier or leased by the supplier from third parties not connected with the buyer, provided that the duration of the non-compete obligation does not exceed the period of occupancy of the premises and land by the buyer.

3. By way of derogation from paragraph 1, point (b), the exemption provided for in Article 2 shall apply to any direct or indirect obligation causing the buyer, after termination of the agreement, not to manufacture, purchase, sell or resell goods or services where all of the following conditions are fulfilled:

(a) the obligation relates to goods or services which compete with the contract goods or services;

(b) the obligation is limited to the premises and land from which the buyer has operated during the contract period;

(c) the obligation is indispensable to protect know-how transferred by the supplier to the buyer;

(d) the duration of the obligation is limited to a period of one year after termination of the agreement.

Paragraph 1, point (b) shall be without prejudice to the possibility of imposing a restriction which is unlimited in time on the use and disclosure of know-how which has not entered the public domain.

Article 6 Withdrawal in individual cases

1. The Commission may withdraw the benefit of this Regulation, pursuant to Article 29(1) of Regulation (EC) No 1/2003, where it finds in any particular case that a vertical agreement to which the exemption provided for in Article 2 of this Regulation applies nevertheless has effects which are incompatible with Article 101(3) of the Treaty. Such effects may occur, for example, where the relevant market for the supply of online intermediation services is highly concentrated and competition between the providers of such services is restricted by the cumulative effect of parallel networks of

similar agreements that restrict buyers of the online intermediation services from offering, selling or reselling goods or services to end users under more favourable conditions on their direct sales channels.

2. The competition authority of a Member State may withdraw the benefit of this Regulation where the conditions of Article 29(2) of Regulation (EC) No 1/2003 are fulfilled.

Article 7 Non-application of this Regulation

Pursuant to Article 1a of Regulation No 19/65/EEC, the Commission may by regulation declare that, where parallel networks of similar vertical restraints cover more than 50% of a relevant market, this Regulation shall not apply to vertical agreements containing specific restraints relating to that market.

Article 8 Application of the market share threshold

For the purposes of applying the market share thresholds provided for in Article 3 the following rules shall apply:

(a) the market share of the supplier shall be calculated on the basis of market sales value data and the market share of the buyer shall be calculated on the basis of market purchase value data. If market sales value or market purchase value data are not available, estimates based on other reliable market information, including market sales and purchase volumes, may be used to establish the market share of the undertaking concerned;

(b) the market shares shall be calculated on the basis of data relating to the preceding calendar year;

(c) the market share of the supplier shall include any goods or services supplied to vertically integrated distributors for the purposes of sale;

(d) if a market share is initially not more than 30%, but subsequently rises above that level, the exemption provided for in Article 2 shall continue to apply for a period of two consecutive calendar years following the year in which the 30% threshold was first exceeded;

(e) the market share held by the undertakings referred to in Article 1(2), second subparagraph, point (e) shall be apportioned equally to each undertaking having the rights or the powers listed in point (a) of that subparagraph.

Article 9 Application of the turnover threshold

1. For the purpose of calculating total annual turnover within the meaning of Article 2(2), the turnover achieved during the previous financial year by the relevant party to the vertical agreement and the turnover achieved by its connected undertakings in respect of all goods and services, excluding all taxes and other duties, shall be added together. For this purpose, no account shall be taken of dealings between the party to the vertical agreement and its connected undertakings or between its connected undertakings.

2. The exemption provided for in Article 2 shall remain applicable where, for any period of two consecutive financial years, the total annual turnover threshold is exceeded by no more than 10%.

Article 10 Transitional period

The prohibition laid down in Article 101(1) of the Treaty shall not apply during the period from 1 June 2022 to 31 May 2023 in respect of agreements already in force on 31 May 2022 which do not satisfy the conditions for exemption provided for in this Regulation but which, on 31 May 2022, satisfied the conditions for exemption provided for in Regulation (EU) No 330/2010.

Article 11 Period of validity

This Regulation shall enter into force on 1 June 2022.

It shall expire on 31 May 2034.

This Regulation shall be binding in its entirety and directly applicable in all Member States.

Done at Brussels, 10 May 2022

Commission notice—Summary of: Guidelines on the effect on trade concept contained in Articles 101 and 102 of the Treaty on the Functioning of the European Union (TFEU)*

Guidelines on the effect on trade concept

SUMMARY OF:

Guidelines on the effect on trade concept contained in Articles 101 and 102 of the Treaty on the Functioning of the European Union (TFEU)

WHAT IS THE AIM OF THE GUIDELINES?

- Article 101 TFEU (ex Article 81 of the Treaty establishing the European Community (TEC)) bans cartels and behaviour that prevents, restricts or distorts competition (vertical and horizontal agreements) with certain exceptions (specified under Article 101(3)).
- Article 102 TFEU (ex Article 82 of the Treaty establishing the European Community (TEC)) outlaws abuses by companies with a dominant position.
- The two articles apply only when it can be established that agreements and practices are capable of appreciably affecting trade between EU countries.
- These European Commission guidelines seek to explain and set out the methodology for applying the concept of the effect on trade between EU countries with regard to competition cases, thus reflecting case law handed down by the Court of Justice of the European Union.

Key points

- In the case of Article 101 TFEU, if the agreement as a whole is capable of affecting trade between EU countries, the entire agreement is subject to EU law, including any parts of the agreement that individually do not affect trade between EU countries. In cases where the contractual relations between the same parties cover several activities, these activities must, in order to form part of the same agreement, be directly linked and form an integral part of the same overall business arrangement. If not, each activity constitutes a separate agreement.
- In the case of Article 102 TFEU, it is the abuse that must affect trade between EU countries. Conduct that forms part of an overall strategy pursued by the dominant firm must be assessed in terms of its overall impact. Where a dominant firm adopts various practices in pursuit of the same aim (e.g. seeking to eliminate or foreclose competitors), for Article 102 TFEU to be applicable to all the practices forming part of this overall strategy, it is sufficient that at least one of these practices is capable of affecting trade between EU countries.
- The guidelines focus on 3 main aspects and seek to clarify:
  - the concept of trade between EU countries as not being restricted to traditional exchanges of goods and services across borders. It is a wider concept, covering all cross-border economic activity including establishment. The concept implies that there must be an impact on cross-border economic activity involving at least (parts of) 2 EU countries;
  - the meaning of the words 'may affect' which define the nature of the required impact on trade between EU countries. According to the standard test developed by the Court of Justice, it must be possible to anticipate with a sufficient degree of probability, on the basis of a set of objective factors of law or fact, that the agreement or practice may have an influence, direct or indirect, actual or potential, on the pattern of trade between EU

* **Editor's Note:** This is a very short summary only of the c. 15-page full document, reviewed to 29 May 2020. Summary: Document 52004XC0427(06), https://eur-lex.europa.eu/LexUriServ/LexUriServ.do?uri=CELEX:52004XC0427(06):EN:HTML; Full document: OJ 2004 C101/81-96, https://ec.europa.eu/competition/antitrust/legislation/trade.html.

countries. In cases where the agreement or practice is liable to affect the competitive structure inside the EU, EU law jurisdiction is established;
- the notion of 'appreciability': the effect on trade criterion incorporates a quantitative element, limiting EU law jurisdiction to agreements and practices that are capable of having effects of a certain magnitude. Appreciability can be assessed in particular by reference to the position and the importance of the relevant firms on the market for the products concerned. This assessment depends on the circumstances of each individual case, in particular the nature of the agreement and practice, the nature of the products covered and the market position of the firms concerned.

- The Commission considers that in principle agreements are not capable of appreciably affecting trade between EU countries when 2 conditions are simultaneously satisfied:
  - the aggregate market share of the parties within the relevant market in the EU does not exceed 5%; and
  - in the case of horizontal agreements, the aggregate annual turnover of the firms in the products concerned does not exceed €40 million. In the case of vertical agreements, the aggregate turnover of the supplier in the products covered concerned does not exceed €40 million.
- The guidelines include an analysis of various forms of agreements and practices providing an indication of how the trade effect concept should be applied in practice.
- The effect of trade criterion is an autonomous EU law jurisdictional criterion. It must be assessed separately in each case and is a distinct assessment from that of the restriction of competition.

From when do the guidelines apply?

They have applied since 27 April 2004.

2006 Commission Notice on Immunity from fines and reduction of fines in cartel cases*

[OJ 2006 C298/11]

I. INTRODUCTION

(1) This notice sets out the framework for rewarding cooperation in the Commission investigation by undertakings which are or have been party to secret cartels affecting the Community. Cartels are agreements and/or concerted practices between two or more competitors aimed at coordinating their competitive behaviour on the market and/or influencing the relevant parameters of competition through practices such as the fixing of purchase or selling prices or other trading conditions, the allocation of production or sales quotas, the sharing of markets including bid-rigging, restrictions of imports or exports and/or anti-competitive actions against other competitors. Such practices are among the most serious violations of Article 81 EC.[1]

(2) By artificially limiting the competition that would normally prevail between them, undertakings avoid exactly those pressures that lead them to innovate, both in terms of product development and the introduction of more efficient production methods. Such practices also lead to more expensive raw materials and components for the Community companies that purchase from such producers. They ultimately result in artificial prices and reduced choice for the consumer. In the long term, they lead to a loss of competitiveness and reduced employment opportunities.

* **Editor's Note:** Known as the Leniency Notice: As amended by Commission Communication (OJ 2015 C256/01) https://eur-lex.europa.eu/legal-content/EN/TXT/?uri=CELEX:02006XC1208(04)-20150805, https://ec.europa.eu/competition/cartels/legislation/leniency_legislation.html.

[1] Reference in this text to Article 81 EC also covers Article 53 EEA when applied by the Commission according to the rules laid down in Article 56 of the EEA Agreement.

(3) By their very nature, secret cartels are often difficult to detect and investigate without the co-operation of undertakings or individuals implicated in them. Therefore, the Commission considers that it is in the Community interest to reward undertakings involved in this type of illegal practices which are willing to put an end to their participation and co-operate in the Commission's investigation, independently of the rest of the undertakings involved in the cartel. The interests of consumers and citizens in ensuring that secret cartels are detected and punished outweigh the interest in fining those undertakings that enable the Commission to detect and prohibit such practices.

(4) The Commission considers that the collaboration of an undertaking in the detection of the existence of a cartel has an intrinsic value. A decisive contribution to the opening of an investigation or to the finding of an infringement may justify the granting of immunity from any fine to the undertaking in question, on condition that certain additional requirements are fulfilled.

(5) Moreover, co-operation by one or more undertakings may justify a reduction of a fine by the Commission. Any reduction of a fine must reflect an undertaking's actual contribution, in terms of quality and timing, to the Commission's establishment of the infringement. Reductions are to be limited to those undertakings that provide the Commission with evidence that adds significant value to that already in the Commission's possession.

(6) In addition to submitting pre-existing documents, undertakings may provide the Commission with voluntary presentations of their knowledge of a cartel and their role therein prepared specially to be submitted under this leniency programme. These initiatives have proved to be useful for the effective investigation and termination of cartel infringements and they should not be discouraged by discovery orders issued in civil litigation. Potential leniency applicants might be dissuaded from cooperating with the Commission under this Notice if this could impair their position in civil proceedings, as compared to companies who do not cooperate. Such undesirable effect would significantly harm the public interest in ensuring effective public enforcement of Article 81 EC in cartel cases and thus its subsequent or parallel effective private enforcement.

(7) The supervisory task conferred on the Commission by the Treaty in competition matters does not only include the duty to investigate and punish individual infringements, but also encompasses the duty to pursue a general policy. The protection of corporate statements in the public interest is not a bar to their disclosure to other addressees of the statement of objections in order to safeguard their rights of defence in the procedure before the Commission, to the extent that it is technically possible to combine both interests by rendering corporate statements accessible only at the Commission premises and normally on a single occasion following the formal notification of the objections. Moreover, the Commission will process personal data in the context of this notice in conformity with its obligations under Regulation (EC) No 45/2001.[2]

II. IMMUNITY FROM FINES

A. Requirements to qualify for immunity from fines

(8) The Commission will grant immunity from any fine which would otherwise have been imposed to an undertaking disclosing its participation in an alleged cartel affecting the Community if that undertaking is the first to submit information and evidence which in the Commission's view will enable it to:

(a) carry out a targeted inspection in connection with the alleged cartel;[3] or

(b) find an infringement of Article 81 EC in connection with the alleged cartel.

(9) For the Commission to be able to carry out a targeted inspection within the meaning of point (8)(a), the undertaking must provide the Commission with the information and evidence listed below, to the extent that this, in the Commission's view, would not jeopardize the inspections:

[2] OJ L 8, 12.1.2001, p. 1.

[3] The assessment of the threshold will have to be carried out ex ante, i.e. without taking into account whether a given inspection has or has not been successful or whether or not an inspection has or has not been carried out. The assessment will be made exclusively on the basis of the type and the quality of the information submitted by the applicant.

(a) A corporate statement[4] which includes, in so far as it is known to the applicant at the time of the submission:
- A detailed description of the alleged cartel arrangement, including for instance its aims, activities and functioning; the product or service concerned, the geographic scope, the duration of and the estimated market volumes affected by the alleged cartel; the specific dates, locations, content of and participants in alleged cartel contacts, and all relevant explanations in connection with the pieces of evidence provided in support of the application.
- The name and address of the legal entity submitting the immunity application as well as the names and addresses of all the other undertakings that participate(d) in the alleged cartel;
- The names, positions, office locations and, where necessary, home addresses of all individuals who, to the applicant's knowledge, are or have been involved in the alleged cartel, including those individuals which have been involved on the applicant's behalf;
- Information on which other competition authorities, inside or outside the EU, have been approached or are intended to be approached in relation to the alleged cartel; and

(b) Other evidence relating to the alleged cartel in possession of the applicant or available to it at the time of the submission, including in particular any evidence contemporaneous to the infringement.

(10) Immunity pursuant to point (8)(a) will not be granted if, at the time of the submission, the Commission had already sufficient evidence to adopt a decision to carry out an inspection in connection with the alleged cartel or had already carried out such an inspection.

(11) Immunity pursuant to point (8)(b) will only be granted on the cumulative conditions that the Commission did not have, at the time of the submission, sufficient evidence to find an infringement of Article 81 EC in connection with the alleged cartel and that no undertaking had been granted conditional immunity from fines under point (8)(a) in connection with the alleged cartel. In order to qualify, an undertaking must be the first to provide contemporaneous, incriminating evidence of the alleged cartel as well as a corporate statement containing the kind of information specified in point (9)(a), which would enable the Commission to find an infringement of Article 81 EC.

(12) In addition to the conditions set out in points (8)(a), (9) and (10) or in points (8)(b) and 11, all the following conditions must be met in any case to qualify for any immunity from a fine:

(a) The undertaking cooperates genuinely,[5] fully, on a continuous basis and expeditiously from the time it submits its application throughout the Commission's administrative procedure. This includes:
- providing the Commission promptly with all relevant information and evidence relating to the alleged cartel that comes into its possession or is available to it;
- remaining at the Commission's disposal to answer promptly to any request that may contribute to the establishment of the facts;
- making current (and, if possible, former) employees and directors available for interviews with the Commission;
- not destroying, falsifying or concealing relevant information or evidence relating to the alleged cartel; and
- not disclosing the fact or any of the content of its application before the Commission has issued a statement of objections in the case, unless otherwise agreed;

(b) The undertaking ended its involvement in the alleged cartel immediately following its application, except for what would, in the Commission's view, be reasonably necessary to preserve the integrity of the inspections;

[4] Corporate statements may take the form of written documents signed by or on behalf of the undertaking or be made orally.

[5] This requires in particular that the applicant provides accurate, not misleading, and complete information. Cfr judgement of the European Court of Justice of 29 June 2006 in case C-301/04 P, Commission v SGL Carbon AG a.o., at paragraphs 68–70, and judgement of the European Court of Justice of 28 June 2005 in cases C-189/02 P, C-202/02 P, C-205/02 P, C-208/02 P and C-213/02 P, Dansk Rorindustri A/S a.o. v Commission, at paragraphs 395–399.

(c) When contemplating making its application to the Commission, the undertaking must not have destroyed, falsified or concealed evidence of the alleged cartel nor disclosed the fact or any of the content of its contemplated application, except to other competition authorities.

(13) An undertaking which took steps to coerce other undertakings to join the cartel or to remain in it is not eligible for immunity from fines. It may still qualify for a reduction of fines if it fulfils the relevant requirements and meets all the conditions therefor.

B. Procedure

(14) An undertaking wishing to apply for immunity from fines should contact the Commission's Directorate General for Competition. The undertaking may either initially apply for a marker or immediately proceed to make a formal application to the Commission for immunity from fines in order to meet the conditions in points (8)(a) or (8)(b), as appropriate. The Commission may disregard any application for immunity from fines on the ground that it has been submitted after the statement of objections has been issued.

(15) The Commission services may grant a marker protecting an immunity applicant's place in the queue for a period to be specified on a case-by-case basis in order to allow for the gathering of the necessary information and evidence. To be eligible to secure a marker, the applicant must provide the Commission with information concerning its name and address, the parties to the alleged cartel, the affected product(s) and territory(-ies), the estimated duration of the alleged cartel and the nature of the alleged cartel conduct. The applicant should also inform the Commission on other past or possible future leniency applications to other authorities in relation to the alleged cartel and justify its request for a marker. Where a marker is granted, the Commission services determine the period within which the applicant has to perfect the marker by submitting the information and evidence required to meet the relevant threshold for immunity. Undertakings which have been granted a marker cannot perfect it by making a formal application in hypothetical terms. If the applicant perfects the marker within the period set by the Commission services, the information and evidence provided will be deemed to have been submitted on the date when the marker was granted.

(16) An undertaking making a formal immunity application to the Commission must:

(a) provide the Commission with all information and evidence relating to the alleged cartel available to it, as specified in points (8) and (9), including corporate statements; or

(b) initially present this information and evidence in hypothetical terms, in which case the undertaking must present a detailed descriptive list of the evidence it proposes to disclose at a later agreed date. This list should accurately reflect the nature and content of the evidence, whilst safeguarding the hypothetical nature of its disclosure. Copies of documents, from which sensitive parts have been removed, may be used to illustrate the nature and content of the evidence. The name of the applying undertaking and of other undertakings involved in the alleged cartel need not be disclosed until the evidence described in its application is submitted. However, the product or service concerned by the alleged cartel, the geographic scope of the alleged cartel and the estimated duration must be clearly identified.

(17) If requested, the Directorate General for Competition will provide an acknowledgement of receipt of the undertaking's application for immunity from fines, confirming the date and, where appropriate, time of the application.

(18) Once the Commission has received the information and evidence submitted by the undertaking under point (16)(a) and has verified that it meets the conditions set out in points (8)(a) or (8)(b), as appropriate, it will grant the undertaking conditional immunity from fines in writing.

(19) If the undertaking has presented information and evidence in hypothetical terms, the Commission will verify that the nature and content of the evidence described in the detailed list referred to in point (16)(b) will meet the conditions set out in points (8)(a) or (8)(b), as appropriate, and inform the undertaking accordingly. Following the disclosure of the evidence no later than on the date agreed and having verified that it corresponds to the description made in the list, the Commission will grant the undertaking conditional immunity from fines in writing.

(20) If it becomes apparent that immunity is not available or that the undertaking failed to meet the conditions set out in points (8)(a) or (8)(b), as appropriate, the Commission will inform the undertaking in writing. In such case, the undertaking may withdraw the evidence disclosed for the purposes of its immunity application or request the Commission to consider it under section III of this notice. This does not prevent the Commission from using its normal powers of investigation in order to obtain the information.

(21) The Commission will not consider other applications for immunity from fines before it has taken a position on an existing application in relation to the same alleged infringement, irrespective of whether the immunity application is presented formally or by requesting a marker.

(22) If at the end of the administrative procedure, the undertaking has met the conditions set out in point (12), the Commission will grant it immunity from fines in the relevant decision. If at the end of the administrative procedure, the undertaking has not met the conditions set out in point (12), the undertaking will not benefit from any favorable treatment under this Notice. If the Commission, after having granted conditional immunity ultimately finds that the immunity applicant has acted as a coercer, it will withhold immunity.

III. REDUCTION OF A FINE

A. Requirements to qualify for reduction of a fine

(23) Undertakings disclosing their participation in an alleged cartel affecting the Community that do not meet the conditions under section II above may be eligible to benefit from a reduction of any fine that would otherwise have been imposed.

(24) In order to qualify, an undertaking must provide the Commission with evidence of the alleged infringement which represents significant added value with respect to the evidence already in the Commission's possession and must meet the cumulative conditions set out in points (12)(a) to (12)(c) above.

(25) The concept of 'added value' refers to the extent to which the evidence provided strengthens, by its very nature and/or its level of detail, the Commission's ability to prove the alleged cartel. In this assessment, the Commission will generally consider written evidence originating from the period of time to which the facts pertain to have a greater value than evidence subsequently established. Incriminating evidence directly relevant to the facts in question will generally be considered to have a greater value than that with only indirect relevance. Similarly, the degree of corroboration from other sources required for the evidence submitted to be relied upon against other undertakings involved in the case will have an impact on the value of that evidence, so that compelling evidence will be attributed a greater value than evidence such as statements which require corroboration if contested.

(26) The Commission will determine in any final decision adopted at the end of the administrative procedure the level of reduction an undertaking will benefit from, relative to the fine which would otherwise be imposed. For the:

- first undertaking to provide significant added value: a reduction of 30–50%,
- second undertaking to provide significant added value: a reduction of 20–30%,
- subsequent undertakings that provide significant added value: a reduction of up to 20%.

In order to determine the level of reduction within each of these bands, the Commission will take into account the time at which the evidence fulfilling the condition in point (24) was submitted and the extent to which it represents added value.

If the applicant for a reduction of a fine is the first to submit compelling evidence in the sense of point (25) which the Commission uses to establish additional facts increasing the gravity or the duration of the infringement, the Commission will not take such additional facts into account when setting any fine to be imposed on the undertaking which provided this evidence.

B. Procedure

(27) An undertaking wishing to benefit from a reduction of a fine must make a formal application to the Commission and it must present it with sufficient evidence of the alleged cartel to qualify

for a reduction of a fine in accordance with point (24) of this Notice. Any voluntary submission of evidence to the Commission which the undertaking that submits it wishes to be considered for the beneficial treatment of section III of this Notice must be clearly identified at the time of its submission as being part of a formal application for a reduction of a fine.

(28) If requested, the Directorate General for Competition will provide an acknowledgement of receipt of the undertaking's application for a reduction of a fine and of any subsequent submissions of evidence, confirming the date and, where appropriate, time of each submission. The Commission will not take any position on an application for a reduction of a fine before it has taken a position on any existing applications for conditional immunity from fines in relation to the same alleged cartel.

(29) If the Commission comes to the preliminary conclusion that the evidence submitted by the undertaking constitutes significant added value within the meaning of points (24) and (25), and that the undertaking has met the conditions of points (12) and (27), it will inform the undertaking in writing, no later than the date on which a statement of objections is notified, of its intention to apply a reduction of a fine within a specified band as provided in point (26). The Commission will also, within the same time frame, inform the undertaking in writing if it comes to the preliminary conclusion that the undertaking does not qualify for a reduction of a fine. The Commission may disregard any application for a reduction of fines on the grounds that it has been submitted after the statement of objections has been issued.

(30) The Commission will evaluate the final position of each undertaking which filed an application for a reduction of a fine at the end of the administrative procedure in any decision adopted. The Commission will determine in any such final decision:

(a) whether the evidence provided by an undertaking represented significant added value with respect to the evidence in the Commission's possession at that same time;
(b) whether the conditions set out in points (12)(a) to (12)(c) above have been met;
(c) the exact level of reduction an undertaking will benefit from within the bands specified in point (26).

If the Commission finds that the undertaking has not met the conditions set out in point (12), the undertaking will not benefit from any favourable treatment under this Notice.

IV. CORPORATE STATEMENTS MADE TO QUALIFY UNDER THIS NOTICE

(31) A corporate statement is a voluntary presentation by or on behalf of an undertaking to the Commission of the undertaking's knowledge of a cartel and its role therein prepared specially to be submitted under this Notice. Any statement made vis-à-vis the Commission in relation to this notice, forms part of the Commission's file and can thus be used in evidence.

(32) Upon the applicant's request, the Commission may accept that corporate statements be provided orally unless the applicant has already disclosed the content of the corporate statement to third parties. Oral corporate statements will be recorded and transcribed at the Commission's premises. In accordance with Article 19 of Council Regulation (EC) No 1/2003[6] and Articles 3 and 17 of Commission Regulation (EC) No 773/2004,[7] undertakings making oral corporate statements will be granted the opportunity to check the technical accuracy of the recording, which will be available at the Commission's premises and to correct the substance of their oral statements within a given time limit. Undertakings may waive these rights within the said time-limit, in which case the recording will from that moment on be deemed to have been approved. Following the explicit or implicit approval of the oral statement or the submission of any corrections to it, the undertaking

[6] OJ L 1, 4.1.2003, p. 1.
[7] OJ L 123, 27.4.2004, p. 18.

shall listen to the recordings at the Commission's premises and check the accuracy of the transcript within a given time limit. Non-compliance with the last requirement may lead to the loss of any beneficial treatment under this Notice.

(33) Access to corporate statements is only granted to the addressees of a statement of objections, provided that they commit,—together with the legal counsels getting access on their behalf—, not to make any copy by mechanical or electronic means of any information in the corporate statement to which access is being granted and to ensure that the information to be obtained from the corporate statement will solely be used for the purposes mentioned below. Other parties such as complainants will not be granted access to corporate statements. The Commission considers that this specific protection of a corporate statement is not justified as from the moment when the applicant discloses to third parties the content thereof.

(34) In accordance with the Commission Notice on rules for access to the Commission file,[8] access to the file is only granted to the addressees of a statement of objections on the condition that the information thereby obtained may only be used for the purposes of judicial or administrative proceedings for the application of the Union competition rules. Any failure during the proceedings to comply with the provisions of Regulation (EC) No 773/2004[9] on the use of information obtained through access to the file may be regarded as lack of cooperation within the meaning of points (12) and (27) of this Notice. Under certain circumstances it is subject to penalties to be laid down under national law.[10] Moreover, if any such use is made after the Commission has already adopted a prohibition decision in the proceedings, the Commission may, in addition to applicable penalties under national law, in any legal proceedings before the Union Courts, ask the Court to increase the fine in respect of the responsible undertaking. Should any of the above limitations to the use of information be breached, at any point in time, with the involvement of an outside counsel, the Commission may report the incident to the bar of that counsel, with a view to disciplinary action.

(35) Corporate statements made under the present Notice will only be transmitted to the competition authorities of the Member States pursuant to Article 12 of Regulation No 1/2003, provided that the conditions set out in the Network Notice[11] are met and provided that the level of protection against disclosure awarded by the receiving competition authority is equivalent to the one conferred by the Commission.

(35a) In line with paragraph 26a of the Commission Notice on the co-operation between the Commission and the courts of the EU Member States in the application of Articles 101 and 102 of the Treaty, the Commission will not at any time transmit leniency corporate statements to national courts for use in actions for damages for breaches of those Treaty provisions.[12] This paragraph is without prejudice to the situation referred to in Article 6(7) of Directive 2014/104/EU.

V. GENERAL CONSIDERATIONS

(36) The Commission will not take a position on whether or not to grant conditional immunity, or otherwise on whether or not to reward any application, if it becomes apparent that the application concerns infringements covered by the five years limitation period for the imposition of penalties stipulated in Article 25(1)(b) of Regulation 1/2003, as such applications would be devoid of purpose.

[8] OJ C 325, 22.12.2005, p. 7.

[9] Article 16a of Regulation (EC) No 773/2004, as amended by Commission Regulation (EU) 2015/1348 (OJ L 208, 5.8.2015, p. 3).

[10] Articles 7 and 8 of Directive 2014/104/EU of the European Parliament and of the Council of 26 November 2014 on certain rules-governing actions for damages under national law for infringements of the competition law provisions of the Member States and of the European Union (OJ L 349, 5.12.2014, p. 1).

[11] Commission Notice on cooperation within the Network of Competition Authorities, OJ C 101, 27.4.2004, p. 43.

[12] Commission Notice on the co-operation between the Commission and the courts of the EU Member States in the application of Articles 101 and 102 TFEU (OJ C 101, 27.4.2004, p. 54), as amended by the Communication from the Commission on Amendments to the Commission Notice on the cooperation between the Commission and courts of the EU Member States in the application of Articles 81 and 82 EC (OJ C 256, 5.8.2015, p. 5).

(37) From the date of its publication in the Official Journal, this notice replaces the 2002 Commission notice on immunity from fines and reduction of fines in cartel cases for all cases in which no undertaking has contacted the Commission in order to take advantage of the favourable treatment set out in that notice. However, points (31) to (35) of the current notice will be applied from the moment of its publication to all pending and new applications for immunity from fines or reduction of fines.

(38) The Commission is aware that this notice will create legitimate expectations on which undertakings may rely when disclosing the existence of a cartel to the Commission.

(39) In line with the Commission's practice, the fact that an undertaking cooperated with the Commission during its administrative procedure will be indicated in any decision, so as to explain the reason for the immunity or reduction of the fine. The fact that immunity or reduction in respect of fines is granted cannot protect an undertaking from the civil law consequences of its participation in an infringement of Article 81 EC.

(40) The Commission considers that normally public disclosure of documents and written or recorded statements received in the context of this notice would undermine certain public or private interests, for example the protection of the purpose of inspections and investigations, within the meaning of Article 4 of Regulation (EC) No 1049/2001,[13] even after the decision has been taken.

[13] OJ L 145, 31.5.2001, p. 43.

Part III

UK Brexit-Related Legislation

European Communities Act 1972*

(1972 c. 68)

1.—(1) This Act may be cited as the European Communities Act 1972.

2 General implementation of Treaties**

2.—(1) All such rights, powers, liabilities, obligations and restrictions from time to time created or arising by or under the Treaties, and all such remedies and procedures from time to time provided for by or under the Treaties, as in accordance with the Treaties are without further enactment to be given legal effect or used in the United Kingdom shall be recognised and available in law, and be enforced, allowed and followed accordingly; and the expression 'enforceable EU right' and similar expressions shall be read as referring to one to which this subsection applies.

(2) Subject to Schedule 2 to this Act, at any time after its passing Her Majesty may by Order in Council, and any designated Minister or department may by order, rules, regulations or scheme, make provision—

(a) for the purpose of implementing any EU obligation of the United Kingdom, or enabling any such obligation to be implemented, or of enabling any rights enjoyed or to be enjoyed by the United Kingdom under or by virtue of the Treaties to be exercised; or

(b) for the purpose of dealing with matters arising out of or related to any such obligation or rights or the coming into force, or the operation from time to time, of subsection (1) above;

and in the exercise of any statutory power or duty, including any power to give directions or to legislate by means of orders, rules, regulations or other subordinate instrument, the person entrusted with the power or duty may have regard to the objects of the EU and to any such obligation or rights as aforesaid.

In this subsection 'designated Minister or department' means such Minister of the Crown or government department as may from time to time be designated by Order in Council in relation to any matter or for any purpose, but subject to such restrictions or conditions (if any) as may be specified by the Order in Council.

* **Editor's Note:** Only s. 2 is retained as it is the only significant element of the Act still relevant following the amended European Union (Withdrawal) Act 2018, the European Union (Withdrawal Agreement) Act 2020, and Retained EU Law (Revocation and Reform) Bill (REUL) 2023. The Schedules have not been retained.

** **Editor's Note:** Section 2(2)(a)(b) excluded (N.I.) by Northern Ireland Constitution Act 1973 (c. 36, SIF 29:3), s. 2(2), Sch. 2 para. 3. Reference in s. 2(5) to 'that subsection' means s. 2(2) of this Act. Reference to a Minister of the Government of Northern Ireland to be construed, as respects the discharge of functions, as a reference to the head of a Northern Ireland department: Northern Ireland Constitution Act 1973 (c. 36, SIF 29:3), Sch. 5 para. 7(2).

European Union (Withdrawal) Act 2018*

(2018 c. 16)

(Contents omitted.)

An Act to repeal the European Communities Act 1972 and make other provision in connection with the withdrawal of the United Kingdom from the EU. [26th June 2018]

BE IT ENACTED by the Queen's most Excellent Majesty, by and with the advice and consent of the Lords Spiritual and Temporal, and Commons, in this present Parliament assembled, and by the authority of the same, as follows:—

Repeal of the ECA

1 Repeal of the European Communities Act 1972

The European Communities Act 1972 is repealed on exit day.

1A Saving for ECA for implementation period

(1) Subsections (2) to (4) have effect despite the repeal of the European Communities Act 1972 on exit day by section 1.

(2) The European Communities Act 1972, as it has effect in domestic law or the law of a relevant territory immediately before exit day, continues to have effect in domestic law or the law of the relevant territory on and after exit day so far as provided by subsections (3) to (5).

(3) The Act of 1972 has effect on and after exit day as if—

(a) the definitions of 'the Treaties' and 'the EU Treaties' given by section 1(2) to (4) (interpretation)—

(i) included Part 4 of the withdrawal agreement (implementation period), other than that Part so far as it relates to, or could be applied in relation to, the Common Foreign and Security Policy, but

(ii) were otherwise limited to anything which falls within those definitions as at immediately before exit day so far as it is not excluded by regulations made on or after exit day by a Minister of the Crown under this sub-paragraph,

(b) the reference in section 2(2) to the objects of the EU were a reference to those objects so far as they are applicable to and in the United Kingdom by virtue of Part 4 of the withdrawal agreement,

(c) section 2(3) (payment of EU costs etc.) were omitted,

(d) in section 3 (decisions on, and proof of, EU Treaties and EU instruments etc.)—

(i) the references to the Treaties in subsections (1) and (2) included the withdrawal agreement, and

(ii) the words in brackets in subsection (1) only applied so far as they are in accordance with Part 4 of the withdrawal agreement,

(e) references in sections 5 and 6 (customs duties and common agricultural policy) to the common customs tariff of the EU, directly applicable EU provision, the exclusion of customs duties, EU arrangements and agricultural levies of the EU were to such things so far as they are applicable to and in the United Kingdom by virtue of Part 4 of the withdrawal agreement, and

(f) in Part 2 of Schedule 1 (general definitions in relation to the EU)—

* **Editor's Note:** The European Union (Withdrawal Agreement) Act 2020 and now the Retained EU Law (Revocation and Reform) Bill (REUL) 2023 significantly modify and amend the EUWA 2018. The former amendments have been made, the latter are noted.

(i) in the definition of 'EU customs duty', the reference to directly applicable EU provision were to such provision so far as it is applicable to and in the United Kingdom by virtue of Part 4 of the withdrawal agreement, and
(ii) in the definition of 'Member' in the expression 'member State', after 'EU' there were inserted 'and for the purposes of this expression the United Kingdom is to be treated as if it were a member of the EU during the implementation period (within the meaning given by section 1A(6) of the European Union (Withdrawal) Act 2018)'.

(4) In this section 'relevant territory' means the Isle of Man, any of the Channel Islands or Gibraltar.

(5) Subsections (1) to (4) are repealed on IP completion day.

(6) In this Act—

'the implementation period' means the transition or implementation period provided for by Part 4 of the withdrawal agreement and beginning with exit day and ending on IP completion day;

'IP completion day' (and related expressions) have the same meaning as in the European Union (Withdrawal Agreement) Act 2020 (see section 39(1) to (5) of that Act);

'withdrawal agreement' has the same meaning as in that Act (see section 39(1) and (6) of that Act).

(7) In this Act—
(a) references to the European Communities Act 1972 are to be read, so far as the context permits or requires, as being or (as the case may be) including references to that Act as it continues to have effect by virtue of subsections (2) to (4) above, and
(b) references to any Part of the withdrawal agreement or the EEA EFTA separation agreement include references to any other provisions of that agreement so far as applying to that Part.

*Retention of existing EU law**

2 Saving for EU-derived domestic legislation

(1) EU-derived domestic legislation, as it has effect in domestic law immediately before IP completion day, continues to have effect in domestic law on and after IP completion day.

(2) This section is subject to section 5 and Schedule 1 (exceptions to savings and incorporation and section 5A (savings and incorporation: supplementary)).

3 Incorporation of direct EU legislation

(1) Direct EU legislation, so far as operative immediately before IP completion day, forms part of domestic law on and after IP completion day.

(2) In this Act 'direct EU legislation' means—
(a) any EU regulation, EU decision or EU tertiary legislation, as it has effect in EU law immediately before IP completion day and so far as—
(ai) it is applicable to and in the United Kingdom by virtue of Part 4 of the withdrawal agreement,
(bi) it neither has effect nor is to have effect by virtue of section 7A or 7B,
(i) it is not an exempt EU instrument (for which see section 20(1) and Schedule 6) and,
(ii) its effect is not reproduced in an enactment to which section 2(1) applies,
(b) any Annex to the EEA agreement, as it has effect in EU law immediately before IP completion day and so far as—
(ai) it is applicable to and in the United Kingdom by virtue of Part 4 of the withdrawal agreement,
(bi) it neither has effect nor is to have effect by virtue of section 7A or 7B,
(i) it refers to, or contains adaptations of, anything falling within paragraph (a), and
(ii) its effect is not reproduced in an enactment to which section 2(1) applies, or

* **Editor's Note:** The sections in this part of the Act will be subject to change by the REUL Act when it enters into force.

(c) Protocol 1 to the EEA agreement (which contains horizontal adaptations that apply in relation to EU instruments referred to in the Annexes to that agreement), as it has effect in EU law immediately before IP completion day and so far as—

(i) it is applicable to and in the United Kingdom by virtue of Part 4 of the withdrawal agreement, and

(ii) it neither has effect nor is to have effect by virtue of section 7A or 7B.

(3) For the purposes of this Act, any direct EU legislation is operative immediately before IP completion day if—

(a) in the case of anything which comes into force at a particular time and is stated to apply from a later time, it is in force and applies immediately before IP completion day,

(b) in the case of a decision which specifies to whom it is addressed, it has been notified to that person before IP completion day, and

(c) in any other case, it is in force immediately before IP completion day.

(4) This section—

(a) brings into domestic law any direct EU legislation only in the form of the English language version of that legislation, and

(b) does not apply to any such legislation for which there is no such version, but paragraph (a) does not affect the use of the other language versions of that legislation for the purposes of interpreting it.

(5) This section is subject to section 5 and Schedule 1 (exceptions to savings and incorporation) and section 5A (savings and incorporation: supplementary).

4 Saving for rights etc. under section 2(1) of the ECA*

(1) Any rights, powers, liabilities, obligations, restrictions, remedies and procedures which, immediately before IP completion day—

(a) are recognised and available in domestic law by virtue of section 2(1) of the European Communities Act 1972, and

(b) are enforced, allowed and followed accordingly,

continue on and after IP completion day to be recognised and available in domestic law (and to be enforced, allowed and followed accordingly).

(2) Subsection (1) does not apply to any rights, powers, liabilities, obligations, restrictions, remedies or procedures so far as they—

(a) form part of domestic law by virtue of section 3,

(aa) are, or are to be, recognised and available in domestic law (and enforced, allowed and followed accordingly) by virtue of section 7A or 7B, or

(b) arise under an EU directive (including as applied by the EEA agreement) and are not of a kind recognised by the European Court or any court or tribunal in the United Kingdom in a case decided before IP completion day (whether or not as an essential part of the decision in the case).

(3) This section is subject to section 5 and Schedule 1 (exceptions to savings and incorporation) and section 5A (savings and incorporation: supplementary).

5 Exceptions to savings and incorporation**

(1) The principle of the supremacy of EU law does not apply to any enactment or rule of law passed or made on or after IP completion day.

(2) Accordingly, the principle of the supremacy of EU law continues to apply on or after IP completion day so far as relevant to the interpretation, disapplication or quashing of any enactment or rule of law passed or made before IP completion day.

* **Editor's Note:** To be repealed at end of 2023 by REUL s. 4

** **Editor's Note:** Subject to amendment at end of 2023 by the Retained EU Law (Revocation and Reform) (REUL) Bill when enacted.

(3) Subsection (1) does not prevent the principle of the supremacy of EU law from applying to a modification made on or after IP completion day of any enactment or rule of law passed or made before IP completion day if the application of the principle is consistent with the intention of the modification.

(4) The Charter of Fundamental Rights is not part of domestic law on or after IP completion day.

(5) Subsection (4) does not affect the retention in domestic law on or after IP completion day in accordance with this Act of any fundamental rights or principles which exist irrespective of the Charter (and references to the Charter in any case law are, so far as necessary for this purpose, to be read as if they were references to any corresponding retained fundamental rights or principles).

(6) Schedule 1 (which makes further provision about exceptions to savings and incorporation) has effect.

(7) Subsections (1) to (6) and Schedule 1 are subject to relevant separation agreement law (for which see section 7C).

5A Savings and incorporation: supplementary

The fact that anything which continues to be, or forms part of, domestic law on or after IP completion day by virtue of section 2, 3 or 4 has an effect immediately before IP completion day which is time-limited by reference to the implementation period does not prevent it from having an indefinite effect on and after IP completion day by virtue of section 2, 3 or 4.

6 Interpretation of retained EU law*

(1) A court or tribunal—

(a) is not bound by any principles laid down, or any decisions made, on or after IP completion day by the European Court, and

(b) cannot refer any matter to the European Court on or after IP completion day.

(2) Subject to this and subsections (3) to (6), a court or tribunal may have regard to anything done on or after IP completion day by the European Court, another EU entity or the EU so far as it is relevant to any matter before the court or tribunal.

(3) Any question as to the validity, meaning or effect of any retained EU law is to be decided, so far as that law is unmodified on or after IP completion day and so far as they are relevant to it—

(a) in accordance with any retained case law and any retained general principles of EU law, and

(b) having regard (among other things) to the limits, immediately before IP completion day, of EU competences.

(4) But—

(a) the Supreme Court is not bound by any retained EU case law,

(b) the High Court of Justiciary is not bound by any retained EU case law when—

(i) sitting as a court of appeal otherwise than in relation to a compatibility issue (within the meaning given by section 288ZA(2) of the Criminal Procedure (Scotland) Act 1995) or a devolution issue (within the meaning given by paragraph 1 of Schedule 6 to the Scotland Act 1998), or

(ii) sitting on a reference under section 123(1) of the Criminal Procedure (Scotland) Act 1995, (ba) a relevant court or relevant tribunal is not bound by any retained EU case law so far as is provided for by regulations under subsection (5A), and

(c) no court or tribunal is bound by any retained domestic case law that it would not otherwise be bound by.

(5) In deciding whether to depart from any retained EU case law by virtue of subsection (4)(a) or (b), the Supreme Court or the High Court of Justiciary must apply the same test as it would apply in deciding whether to depart from its own case law.

* **Editor's Note:** Subject to amendment at end of 2023 by the Retained EU Law (Revocation and Reform) (REUL) Bill when enacted.

(5A) A Minister of the Crown may by regulations provide for—

(a) a court or tribunal to be a relevant court or (as the case may be) a relevant tribunal for the purposes of this section,

(b) the extent to which, or circumstances in which, a relevant court or relevant tribunal is not to be bound by retained EU case law,

(c) the test which a relevant court or relevant tribunal must apply in deciding whether to depart from any retained EU case law, or

(d) considerations which are to be relevant to—

(i) the Supreme Court or the High Court of Justiciary in applying the test mentioned in subsection (5), or

(ii) a relevant court or relevant tribunal in applying any test provided for by virtue of paragraph (c) above.

(5B) Regulations under subsection (5A) may (among other things) provide for—

(a) the High Court of Justiciary to be a relevant court when sitting otherwise than as mentioned in subsection (4)(b)(i) and (ii),

(b) the extent to which, or circumstances in which, a relevant court or relevant tribunal not being bound by retained EU case law includes (or does not include) that court or tribunal not being bound by retained domestic case law which relates to retained EU case law,

(c) other matters arising in relation to retained domestic case law which relates to retained EU case law (including by making provision of a kind which could be made in relation to retained EU case law), or

(d) the test mentioned in paragraph (c) of subsection (5A) or the considerations mentioned in paragraph (d) of that subsection to be determined (whether with or without the consent of a Minister of the Crown) by a person mentioned in subsection (5C)(a) to (e) or by more than one of those persons acting jointly.

(5C) Before making regulations under subsection (5A), a Minister of the Crown must consult—

(a) the President of the Supreme Court,

(b) the Lord Chief Justice of England and Wales,

(c) the Lord President of the Court of Session,

(d) the Lord Chief Justice of Northern Ireland,

(e) the Senior President of Tribunals, and

(f) such other persons as the Minister of the Crown considers appropriate.

(5D) No regulations may be made under subsection (5A) after IP completion day.

(6) Subsection (3) does not prevent the validity, meaning or effect of any retained EU law which has been modified on or after IP completion day from being decided as provided for in that subsection if doing so is consistent with the intention of the modifications.

(6A) Subsections (1) to (6) are subject to relevant separation agreement law (for which see section 7C).

(7) In this Act—

'retained case law' means—

(a) retained domestic case law, and

(b) retained EU case law;

'retained domestic case law' means any principles laid down by, and any decisions of, a court or tribunal in the United Kingdom, as they have effect immediately before IP completion day and so far as they—

(a) relate to anything to which section 2, 3 or 4 applies, and

(b) are not excluded by section 5 or Schedule 1,

(as those principles and decisions are modified by or under this Act or by other domestic law from time to time);

'retained EU case law' means any principles laid down by, and any decisions of, the European Court, as they have effect in EU law immediately before IP completion day and so far as they—

(a) relate to anything to which section 2, 3 or 4 applies, and

(b) are not excluded by section 5 or Schedule 1,

(as those principles and decisions are modified by or under this Act or by other domestic law from time to time);

'retained EU law' means anything which, on or after IP completion day, continues to be, or forms part of, domestic law by virtue of section 2, 3 or 4 or subsection (3) or (6) above (as that body of law is added to or otherwise modified by or under this Act or by other domestic law from time to time);

'retained general principles of EU law' means the general principles of EU law, as they have effect in EU law immediately before IP completion day and so far as they—

(a) relate to anything to which section 2, 3 or 4 applies, and

(b) are not excluded by section 5 or Schedule 1,

(as those principles are modified by or under this Act or by other domestic law from time to time).

7 Status of retained EU law*

(1) Anything which—

(a) was, immediately before exit day, primary legislation of a particular kind, subordinate legislation of a particular kind or another enactment of a particular kind, and

(b) continues to be domestic law on and after exit day by virtue of section 1A(2) or 1B(2),

continues to be domestic law as an enactment of the same kind.

(1A) Anything which—

(a) was, immediately before IP completion day, primary legislation of a particular kind, subordinate legislation of a particular kind or another enactment of a particular kind, and

(b) continues to be domestic law on and after IP completion day by virtue of section 2,

continues to be domestic law as an enactment of the same kind.

(2) Retained direct principal EU legislation cannot be modified by any primary or subordinate legislation other than—

(a) an Act of Parliament,

(b) any other primary legislation (so far as it has the power to make such a modification), or

(c) any subordinate legislation so far as it is made under a power which permits such a modification by virtue of—

(i) paragraph 3, 5(3)(a) or (4)(a), 8(3), 10(3)(a) or (4)(a), 11(2)(a) or 12(3) of Schedule 8,

(ii) any other provision made by or under this Act,

(iii) any provision made by or under an Act of Parliament passed before, and in the same Session as, this Act, or

(iv) any provision made on or after the passing of this Act by or under primary legislation.

(3) Retained direct minor EU legislation cannot be modified by any primary or subordinate legislation other than—

(a) an Act of Parliament,

(b) any other primary legislation (so far as it has the power to make such a modification), or

(c) any subordinate legislation so far as it is made under a power which permits such a modification by virtue of—

(i) paragraph 3, 5(2) or (4)(a), 8(3), 10(2) or (4)(a) or 12(3) of Schedule 8,

(ii) any other provision made by or under this Act,

(iii) any provision made by or under an Act of Parliament passed before, and in the same Session as, this Act, or

(iv) any provision made on or after the passing of this Act by or under primary legislation.

(4) Anything which is retained EU law by virtue of section 4 cannot be modified by any primary or subordinate legislation other than—

(a) an Act of Parliament,

(b) any other primary legislation (so far as it has the power to make such a modification), or

* **Editor's Note:** Subject to amendment at end of 2023 by the Retained EU Law (Revocation and Reform) (REUL) Bill when enacted.

(c) any subordinate legislation so far as it is made under a power which permits such a modification by virtue of—
(i) paragraph 3, 5(3)(b) or (4)(b), 8(3), 10(3)(b) or (4)(b), 11(2)(b) or 12(3) of Schedule 8,
(ii) any other provision made by or under this Act,
(iii) any provision made by or under an Act of Parliament passed before, and in the same Session as, this Act, or
(iv) any provision made on or after the passing of this Act by or under primary legislation.

(5) For other provisions about the status of retained EU law, see—
(a) section 5(1) to (3) and (7) (status of retained EU law in relation to other enactments or rules of law),
(b) section 6 (status of retained case law and retained general principles of EU law),
(ba) section 7C (status of case law of European Court etc in relation to retained EU law which is relevant separation agreement law),
(c) section 15(2) and Part 2 of Schedule 5 (status of retained EU law for the purposes of the rules of evidence),
(d) paragraphs 13 to 16 of Schedule 8 (affirmative and enhanced scrutiny procedure for, and information about, instruments which amend or revoke subordinate legislation under section 2(2) of the European Communities Act 1972 including subordinate legislation implementing EU directives),
(e) paragraphs 19 and 20 of that Schedule (status of certain retained direct EU legislation for the purposes of the Interpretation Act 1978), and
(f) paragraph 30 of that Schedule (status of retained direct EU legislation for the purposes of the Human Rights Act 1998).

(6) In this Act—

'retained direct minor EU legislation' means any retained direct EU legislation which is not retained direct principal EU legislation;

'retained direct principal EU legislation' means—
(a) any EU regulation so far as it—
(i) forms part of domestic law on and after IP completion day by virtue of section 3, and
(ii) was not EU tertiary legislation immediately before IP completion day, or
(b) any Annex to the EEA agreement so far as it—
(i) forms part of domestic law on and after IP completion day by virtue of section 3, and
(ii) refers to, or contains adaptations of, any EU regulation so far as it falls within paragraph (a),

(as modified by or under this Act or by other domestic law from time to time).

Further aspects of withdrawal

7A General implementation of remainder of withdrawal agreement

(1) Subsection (2) applies to—
(a) all such rights, powers, liabilities, obligations and restrictions from time to time created or arising by or under the withdrawal agreement, and
(b) all such remedies and procedures from time to time provided for by or under the withdrawal agreement, as in accordance with the withdrawal agreement are without further enactment to be given legal effect or used in the United Kingdom.

(2) The rights, powers, liabilities, obligations, restrictions, remedies and procedures concerned are to be—
(a) recognised and available in domestic law, and
(b) enforced, allowed and followed accordingly.

(3) Every enactment (including an enactment contained in this Act) is to be read and has effect subject to subsection (2).

(4) This section does not apply in relation to Part 4 of the withdrawal agreement so far as section 2(1) of the European Communities Act 1972 applies in relation to that Part.

(5) See also (among other things)—
- (a) Part 3 of the European Union (Withdrawal Agreement) Act 2020 (further provision about citizens' rights),
- (b) section 20 of that Act (financial provision),
- (c) section 7C of this Act (interpretation of law relating to withdrawal agreement etc),
- (d) section 8B of this Act (power in connection with certain other separation issues),
- (e) section 8C of this Act (power in connection with the Protocol on Ireland/Northern Ireland in withdrawal agreement), and
- (f) Parts 1B and 1C of Schedule 2 to this Act (powers involving devolved authorities in connection with certain other separation issues and the Ireland/Northern Ireland Protocol).

7B General implementation of EEA EFTA and Swiss agreements

(1) Subsection (2) applies to all such rights, powers, liabilities, obligations, restrictions, remedies and procedures as—
- (a) would from time to time be created or arise, or (in the case of remedies or procedures) be provided for, by or under the EEA EFTA separation agreement or the Swiss citizens' rights agreement, and
- (b) would, in accordance with Article 4(1) of the withdrawal agreement, be required to be given legal effect or used in the United Kingdom without further enactment,

if that Article were to apply in relation to the EEA EFTA separation agreement and the Swiss citizens' rights agreement, those agreements were part of EU law and the relevant EEA states and Switzerland were member States.

(2) The rights, powers, liabilities, obligations, restrictions, remedies and procedures concerned are to be—
- (a) recognised and available in domestic law, and
- (b) enforced, allowed and followed accordingly.

(3) Every enactment (other than section 7A but otherwise including an enactment contained in this Act) is to be read and has effect subject to subsection (2).

(4) See also (among other things)—
- (a) Part 3 of the European Union (Withdrawal Agreement) Act 2020 (further provision about citizens' rights),
- (b) section 7C of this Act (interpretation of law relating to the EEA EFTA separation agreement and the Swiss citizens' rights agreement etc),
- (c) section 8B of this Act (power in connection with certain other separation issues), and
- (d) Part 1B of Schedule 2 to this Act (powers involving devolved authorities in connection with certain other separation issues).

(5) In this section 'the relevant EEA states' means Norway, Iceland and Liechtenstein

(6) In this Act 'EEA EFTA separation agreement' and 'Swiss citizens' rights agreement' have the same meanings as in the European Union (Withdrawal Agreement) Act 2020 (see section 39(1) of that Act).

7C Interpretation of relevant separation agreement law

(1) Any question as to the validity, meaning or effect of any relevant separation agreement law is to be decided, so far as they are applicable—
- (a) in accordance with the withdrawal agreement, the EEA EFTA separation agreement and the Swiss citizens' rights agreement, and
- (b) having regard (among other things) to the desirability of ensuring that, where one of those agreements makes provision which corresponds to provision made by another of those agreements, the effect of relevant separation agreement law in relation to the matters dealt with by the corresponding provision in each agreement is consistent.

(2) See (among other things)—
- (a) Article 4 of the withdrawal agreement (methods and principles relating to the effect, the implementation and the application of the agreement),
- (b) Articles 158 and 160 of the withdrawal agreement (jurisdiction of the European Court in relation to Part 2 and certain provisions of Part 5 of the agreement),

(c) Articles 12 and 13 of the Protocol on Ireland/Northern Ireland in the withdrawal agreement (implementation, application, supervision and enforcement of the Protocol and common provisions),
(d) Article 4 of the EEA EFTA separation agreement (methods and principles relating to the effect, the implementation and the application of the agreement), and
(e) Article 4 of the Swiss citizens' rights agreement (methods and principles relating to the effect, the implementation and the application of the agreement).

(3) In this Act 'relevant separation agreement law' means—
(a) any of the following provisions or anything which is domestic law by virtue of any of them—
(i) section 7A, 7B, 8B or 8C or Part 1B or 1C of Schedule 2 or this section, or
(ii) Part 3, or section 20, of the European Union (Withdrawal Agreement) Act 2020 (citizens' rights and financial provision), or
(b) anything not falling within paragraph (a) so far as it is domestic law for the purposes of, or otherwise within the scope of—
(i) the withdrawal agreement (other than Part 4 of that agreement),
(ii) the EEA EFTA separation agreement, or
(iii) the Swiss citizens' rights agreement,

as that body of law is added to or otherwise modified by or under this Act or by other domestic law from time to time.

Main powers in connection with withdrawal

8 Dealing with deficiencies arising from withdrawal*

(1) A Minister of the Crown may by regulations make such provision as the Minister considers appropriate to prevent, remedy or mitigate—
(a) any failure of retained EU law to operate effectively, or
(b) any other deficiency in retained EU law,

arising from the withdrawal of the United Kingdom from the EU.

(2) Deficiencies in retained EU law are where the Minister considers that retained EU law—
(a) contains anything which has no practical application in relation to the United Kingdom or any part of it or is otherwise redundant or substantially redundant,
(b) confers functions on, or in relation to, EU entities which no longer have functions in that respect under EU law in relation to the United Kingdom or any part of it,
(c) makes provision for, or in connection with, reciprocal arrangements between—
(i) the United Kingdom or any part of it or a public authority in the United Kingdom, and
(ii) the EU, an EU entity, a member State or a public authority in a member State, which no longer exist or are no longer appropriate,
(d) makes provision for, or in connection with, other arrangements which—
(i) involve the EU, an EU entity, a member State or a public authority in a member State, or
(ii) are otherwise dependent upon the United Kingdom's membership of the EU or Part 4 of the withdrawal agreement, and which no longer exist or are no longer appropriate,
(e) makes provision for, or in connection with, any reciprocal or other arrangements not falling within paragraph (c) or (d) which no longer exist, or are no longer appropriate, as a result of the United Kingdom ceasing to be a party to any of the EU Treaties or as a result of either the end of the implementation period or any other effect of the withdrawal agreement,
(ea) is not clear in its effect as a result of the operation of any provision of sections 2 to 6 or Schedule 1,
(f) does not contain any functions or restrictions which—
(i) were in an EU directive and in force immediately before IP completion day (including any power to make EU tertiary legislation), and

* **Editor's Note:** Subject to amendment at end of 2023 by the Retained EU Law (Revocation and Reform) (REUL) Bill when enacted.

(ii) it is appropriate to retain, or

(g) contains EU references which are no longer appropriate.

(3) There is also a deficiency in retained EU law where the Minister considers that there is—

(a) anything in retained EU law which is of a similar kind to any deficiency which falls within subsection (2), or

(b) a deficiency in retained EU law of a kind described, or provided for, in regulations made by a Minister of the Crown.

(4) But retained EU law is not deficient merely because it does not contain any modification of EU law which is adopted or notified, comes into force or only applies on or after IP completion day.

(5) Regulations under subsection (1) may make any provision that could be made by an Act of Parliament.

(6) Regulations under subsection (1) may (among other things) provide for functions of EU entities or public authorities in member States (including making an instrument of a legislative character or providing funding) to be—

(a) exercisable instead by a public authority (whether or not established for the purpose) in the United Kingdom, or

(b) replaced, abolished or otherwise modified.

(7) But regulations under subsection (1) may not—

(a) impose or increase taxation or fees,

(b) make retrospective provision,

(c) create a relevant criminal offence,

(d) establish a public authority,

(e)

(f) amend, repeal or revoke the Human Rights Act 1998 or any subordinate legislation made under it, or

(g) amend or repeal the Scotland Act 1998, the Government of Wales Act 2006 or the Northern Ireland Act 1998 (unless the regulations are made by virtue of paragraph 21(b) of Schedule 7 to this Act or are amending or repealing any provision of those Acts which modifies another enactment).

(8) No regulations may be made under this section after the end of the period of two years beginning with IP completion day.

(9) The reference in subsection (1) to a failure or other deficiency arising from the withdrawal of the United Kingdom from the EU includes a reference to any failure or other deficiency arising from—

(a) any aspect of that withdrawal, including (among other things)—

(i) the end of the implementation period, or

(ii) any other effect of the withdrawal agreement, or

(b) that withdrawal, or any such aspect of it, taken together with the operation of any provision, or the interaction between any provisions, made by or under this Act or the European Union (Withdrawal Agreement) Act 2020.

8A Supplementary power in connection with implementation period

(1) A Minister of the Crown may by regulations—

(a) provide for other modifications for the purposes of section 1B(3)(f)(i) (whether applying in all cases or particular cases or descriptions of case),

(b) provide for subsection (3) or (4) of section 1B not to apply to any extent in particular cases or descriptions of case,

(c) make different provision in particular cases or descriptions of case to that made by subsection (3) or (4) of that section,

(d) modify any enactment contained in this Act in consequence of any repeal made by section 1A(5) or 1B(6), or

(e) make such provision not falling within paragraph (a), (b), (c) or (d) as the Minister considers appropriate for any purpose of, or otherwise in connection with, Part 4 of the withdrawal agreement.

(2) The power to make regulations under subsection (1) may (among other things) be exercised by modifying any provision made by or under an enactment.

(3) In subsection (2) 'enactment' does not include primary legislation passed or made after IP completion day.

(4) No regulations may be made under subsection (1) after the end of the period of two years beginning with IP completion day.

8B Power in connection with certain other separation issues

(1) A Minister of the Crown may by regulations make such provision as the Minister considers appropriate—

(a) to implement Part 3 of the withdrawal agreement (separation provisions),

(b) to supplement the effect of section 7A in relation to that Part, or

(c) otherwise for the purposes of dealing with matters arising out of, or related to, that Part (including matters arising by virtue of section 7A and that Part).

(2) A Minister of the Crown may by regulations make such provision as the Minister considers appropriate—

(a) to implement Part 3 of the EEA EFTA separation agreement (separation provisions),

(b) to supplement the effect of section 7B in relation to that Part, or

(c) otherwise for the purposes of dealing with matters arising out of, or related to, that Part (including matters arising by virtue of section 7B and that Part).

(3) Regulations under this section may make any provision that could be made by an Act of Parliament.

(4) Regulations under this section may (among other things) restate, for the purposes of making the law clearer or more accessible, anything that forms part of domestic law by virtue of—

(a) section 7A above and Part 3 of the withdrawal agreement, or

(b) section 7B above and Part 3 of the EEA EFTA separation agreement.

(5) But regulations under this section may not—

(a) impose or increase taxation or fees,

(b) make retrospective provision,

(c) create a relevant criminal offence,

(d) establish a public authority,

(e) amend, repeal or revoke the Human Rights Act 1998 or any subordinate legislation made under it, or

(f) amend or repeal the Scotland Act 1998, the Government of Wales Act 2006 or the Northern Ireland Act 1998 (unless the regulations are made by virtue of paragraph 21(b) of Schedule 7 to this Act or are amending or repealing any provision of those Acts which modifies another enactment).

(6) In this section references to Part 3 of the withdrawal agreement or of the EEA EFTA separation agreement include references to any provision of EU law which is applied by, or referred to in, that Part (to the extent of the application or reference).

8C Power in connection with Ireland/Northern Ireland Protocol in withdrawal agreement

(1) A Minister of the Crown may by regulations make such provision as the Minister considers appropriate—

(a) to implement the Protocol on Ireland/Northern Ireland in the withdrawal agreement,

(b) to supplement the effect of section 7A in relation to the Protocol, or

(c) otherwise for the purposes of dealing with matters arising out of, or related to, the Protocol (including matters arising by virtue of section 7A and the Protocol).

(2) Regulations under subsection (1) may make any provision that could be made by an Act of Parliament (including modifying this Act).

(3) Regulations under subsection (1) may (among other things) make provision facilitating the access to the market within Great Britain of qualifying Northern Ireland goods.

(4) Such provision may (among other things) include provision about the recognition within Great Britain of technical regulations, assessments, registrations, certificates, approvals and authorisations issued by—

(a) the authorities of a member State, or

(b) bodies established in a member State,

in respect of qualifying Northern Ireland goods.

(5) Regulations under subsection (1) may (among other things) restate, for the purposes of making the law clearer or more accessible, anything that forms part of domestic law by virtue of section 7A and the Protocol.

(6) A Minister of the Crown may by regulations define 'qualifying Northern Ireland goods' for the purposes of this Act.

(7) In this section any reference to the Protocol on Ireland/Northern Ireland includes a reference to—

(a) any other provision of the withdrawal agreement so far as applying to the Protocol, and

(b) any provision of EU law which is applied by, or referred to in, the Protocol (to the extent of the application or reference),

but does not include the second sentence of Article 11(1) of the Protocol (which provides that the United Kingdom and the Republic of Ireland may continue to make new arrangements that build on the provisions of the Belfast Agreement in other areas of North-South cooperation on the island of Ireland).

9 Implementing the withdrawal agreement [repealed by s. 36(a) EUWAA 2020]

Devolution

10 Protection for North-South co-operation and prevention of new border arrangements

(1) In exercising any of the powers under this Act, a Minister of the Crown or devolved authority must—

(a) act in a way that is compatible with the terms of the Northern Ireland Act 1998, and

(b) have due regard to the joint report from the negotiators of the EU and the United Kingdom Government on progress during phase 1 of negotiations under Article 50 of the Treaty on European Union.

(2) Nothing in section 8, or 23(1) or (6) of this Act authorises regulations which—

(a) diminish any form of North-South cooperation provided for by the Belfast Agreement, or

(b) create or facilitate border arrangements between Northern Ireland and the Republic of Ireland after exit day which feature physical infrastructure, including border posts, or checks and controls, that did not exist before exit day and are not in accordance with an agreement between the United Kingdom and the EU.

(3) A Minister of the Crown may not agree to the making of a recommendation by the Joint Committee under Article 11(2) of the Protocol on Ireland/Northern Ireland in the withdrawal agreement (recommendations as to North-South cooperation) to—

(a) alter the arrangements for North-South co-operation as provided for by the Belfast Agreement,

(b) establish a new implementation body, or

(c) alter the functions of an existing implementation body.

(4) In this section—

'the Belfast Agreement' has the meaning given by section 98 of the Northern Ireland Act 1998;

'implementation body' has the meaning given by section 55(3) of that Act.

11 Powers involving devolved authorities corresponding to sections 8 to 8C

Schedule 2 (which confers powers to make regulations involving devolved authorities which correspond to the powers conferred by sections 8 to 8C) has effect.

12 Retaining EU restrictions in devolution legislation etc.

(1) In section 29(2)(d) of the Scotland Act 1998 (no competence for the Scottish Parliament to legislate incompatibly with EU law) for 'with EU law' substitute 'in breach of the restriction in section 30A(1)'.

(2) After section 30 of that Act (legislative competence: supplementary) insert—

'30A Legislative competence: restriction relating to retained EU law

(1) An Act of the Scottish Parliament cannot modify, or confer power by subordinate legislation to modify, retained EU law so far as the modification is of a description specified in regulations made by a Minister of the Crown.

(2) But subsection (1) does not apply to any modification so far as it would, immediately before exit day, have been within the legislative competence of the Parliament.

(3) A Minister of the Crown must not lay for approval before each House of the Parliament of the United Kingdom a draft of a statutory instrument containing regulations under this section unless—

(a) the Scottish Parliament has made a consent decision in relation to the laying of the draft, or

(b) the 40 day period has ended without the Parliament having made such a decision.

(4) For the purposes of subsection (3) a consent decision is—

(a) a decision to agree a motion consenting to the laying of the draft,

(b) a decision not to agree a motion consenting to the laying of the draft, or

(c) a decision to agree a motion refusing to consent to the laying of the draft;

and a consent decision is made when the Parliament first makes a decision falling within any of paragraphs (a) to (c) (whether or not it subsequently makes another such decision).

(5) A Minister of the Crown who is proposing to lay a draft as mentioned in subsection (3) must—

(a) provide a copy of the draft to the Scottish Ministers, and

(b) inform the Presiding Officer that a copy has been so provided.

(6) See also paragraph 6 of Schedule 7 (duty to make explanatory statement about regulations under this section including a duty to explain any decision to lay a draft without the consent of the Parliament).

(7) No regulations may be made under this section after the end of the period of two years beginning with exit day.

(8) Subsection (7) does not affect the continuation in force of regulations made under this section at or before the end of the period mentioned in that subsection.

(9) Any regulations under this section which are in force at the end of the period of five years beginning with the time at which they came into force are revoked in their application to any Act of the Scottish Parliament which receives Royal Assent after the end of that period.

(10) Subsections (3) to (8) do not apply in relation to regulations which only relate to a revocation of a specification.

(11) In this section—

"the 40 day period" means the period of 40 days beginning with the day on which a copy of the draft instrument is provided to the Scottish Ministers,

and, in calculating that period, no account is to be taken of any time during which the Parliament is dissolved or during which it is in recess for more than four days.'

(3) In section 108A(2)(e) of the Government of Wales Act 2006 (no competence for the National Assembly for Wales to legislate incompatibly with EU law) for 'with EU law' substitute 'in breach of the restriction in section 109A(1)'.

(4) After section 109 of that Act (legislative competence: supplementary) insert—

'109A Legislative competence: restriction relating to retained EU law

(1) An Act of the Assembly cannot modify, or confer power by subordinate legislation to modify, retained EU law so far as the modification is of a description specified in regulations made by a Minister of the Crown.

(2) But subsection (1) does not apply to any modification so far as it would, immediately before exit day, have been within the Assembly's legislative competence.

(3) No regulations are to be made under this section unless a draft of the statutory instrument containing them has been laid before, and approved by a resolution of, each House of Parliament.

(4) A Minister of the Crown must not lay a draft as mentioned in subsection (3) unless—

(a) the Assembly has made a consent decision in relation to the laying of the draft, or

(b) the 40 day period has ended without the Assembly having made such a decision.

(5) For the purposes of subsection (4) a consent decision is—

(a) a decision to agree a motion consenting to the laying of the draft,

(b) a decision not to agree a motion consenting to the laying of the draft, or

(c) a decision to agree a motion refusing to consent to the laying of the draft;

and a consent decision is made when the Assembly first makes a decision falling within any of paragraphs (a) to (c) (whether or not it subsequently makes another such decision).

(6) A Minister of the Crown who is proposing to lay a draft as mentioned in subsection (3) must—

(a) provide a copy of the draft to the Welsh Ministers, and

(b) inform the Presiding Officer that a copy has been so provided.

(7) See also section 157ZA (duty to make explanatory statement about regulations under this section including a duty to explain any decision to lay a draft without the consent of the Assembly).

(8) No regulations may be made under this section after the end of the period of two years beginning with exit day.

(9) Subsection (8) does not affect the continuation in force of regulations made under this section at or before the end of the period mentioned in that subsection.

(10) Any regulations under this section which are in force at the end of the period of five years beginning with the time at which they came into force are revoked in their application to any Act of the Assembly which receives Royal Assent after the end of that period.

(11) Subsections (4) to (9) do not apply in relation to regulations which only relate to a revocation of a specification.

(12) In this section—

"the 40 day period" means the period of 40 days beginning with the day on which a copy of the draft instrument is provided to the Welsh Ministers,

and, in calculating that period, no account is to be taken of any time during which the Assembly is dissolved or during which it is in recess for more than four days.'

(5) In section 6(2)(d) of the Northern Ireland Act 1998 (no competence for the Northern Ireland Assembly to legislate incompatibly with EU law) for 'incompatible with EU law' substitute 'in breach of the restriction in section 6A(1)'.

(6) After section 6 of that Act (legislative competence) insert—

'6A Restriction relating to retained EU law

(1) An Act of the Assembly cannot modify, or confer power by subordinate legislation to modify, retained EU law so far as the modification is of a description specified in regulations made by a Minister of the Crown.

(2) But subsection (1) does not apply to any modification so far as it would, immediately before exit day, have been within the legislative competence of the Assembly.

(3) A Minister of the Crown must not lay for approval before each House of Parliament a draft of a statutory instrument containing regulations under this section unless—

(a) the Assembly has made a consent decision in relation to the laying of the draft, or

(b) the 40 day period has ended without the Assembly having made such a decision.

(4) For the purposes of subsection (3) a consent decision is—

(a) a decision to agree a motion consenting to the laying of the draft,

(b) a decision not to agree a motion consenting to the laying of the draft, or

(c) a decision to agree a motion refusing to consent to the laying of the draft;

and a consent decision is made when the Assembly first makes a decision falling within any of paragraphs (a) to (c) (whether or not it subsequently makes another such decision).

(5) A Minister of the Crown who is proposing to lay a draft as mentioned in subsection (3) must—

(a) provide a copy of the draft to the relevant Northern Ireland department, and

(b) inform the Presiding Officer that a copy has been so provided.

(6) See also section 96A (duty to make explanatory statement about regulations under this section including a duty to explain any decision to lay a draft without the consent of the Assembly).

(7) No regulations may be made under this section after the end of the period of two years beginning with exit day.

(8) Subsection (7) does not affect the continuation in force of regulations made under this section at or before the end of the period mentioned in that subsection.

(9) Any regulations under this section which are in force at the end of the period of five years beginning with the time at which they came into force are revoked in their application to any Act of the Assembly which receives Royal Assent after the end of that period.

(10) Subsections (3) to (8) do not apply in relation to regulations which only relate to a revocation of a specification.

(11) Regulations under this section may include such supplementary, incidental, consequential, transitional, transitory or saving provision as the Minister of the Crown making them considers appropriate.

(12) In this section—

"the relevant Northern Ireland department" means such Northern Ireland department as the Minister of the Crown concerned considers appropriate;

"the 40 day period" means the period of 40 days beginning with the day on which a copy of the draft instrument is provided to the relevant Northern Ireland department,

and, in calculating that period, no account is to be taken of any time during which the Assembly is dissolved or during which it is in recess for more than four days.'

(7) Part 1 of Schedule 3 (which makes corresponding provision in relation to executive competence to that made by subsections (1) to (6) in relation to legislative competence) has effect.

(8) Part 2 of Schedule 3 (which imposes reporting obligations on a Minister of the Crown in recognition of the fact that the powers to make regulations conferred by subsections (1) to (6) and Part 1 of Schedule 3, and any restrictions arising by virtue of them, are intended to be temporary) has effect.

(9) A Minister of the Crown may by regulations—

(a) repeal any of the following provisions—

(i) section 30A or 57(4) to (15) of the Scotland Act 1998,

(ii) section 80(8) to (8L) or 109A of the Government of Wales Act 2006, or

(iii) section 6A or 24(3) to (15) of the Northern Ireland Act 1998, or

(b) modify any enactment in consequence of any such repeal.

(10) Until all of the provisions mentioned in subsection (9)(a) have been repealed, a Minister of the Crown must, after the end of each review period, consider whether it is appropriate—

(a) to repeal each of those provisions so far as it has not been repealed, or

(b) to revoke any regulations made under any of those provisions so far as they have not been revoked.

(11) In considering whether to exercise the power to make regulations under subsection (9), a Minister of the Crown must have regard (among other things) to—

(a) the fact that the powers to make regulations conferred by the provisions mentioned in subsection (9)(a), and any restrictions arising by virtue of them, are intended to be temporary and, where appropriate, replaced with other arrangements, and

(b) any progress which has been made in implementing those other arrangements.

(12) Part 3 of Schedule 3 (which contains amendments of devolution legislation not dealt with elsewhere) has effect.

(13) In this section—

'arrangement' means any enactment or other arrangement (whether or not legally enforceable);

'review period' means—

(a) the period of three months beginning with the day on which subsection (10) comes into force, and

(b) after that, each successive period of three months.

Parliamentary oversight of withdrawal

13 Parliamentary approval of the outcome of negotiations with the EU [repealed by s. 31 EUWAA 2020]

13A Review of EU legislation during implementation period

(1) Subsection (2) applies where the European Scrutiny Select Committee of the House of Commons ('the ESC') publishes a report in respect of any EU legislation made, or which may be made, during the implementation period and the report—

(a) states that, in the opinion of the ESC, the EU legislation raises a matter of vital national interest to the United Kingdom,

(b) confirms that the ESC has taken such evidence as it considers appropriate as to the effect of the EU legislation and has consulted any Departmental Select Committee of the House of Commons which the ESC considers also has an interest in the EU legislation, and

(c) sets out the wording of a motion to be moved in the House of Commons in accordance with subsection (2).

(2) A Minister of the Crown must, within the period of 14 Commons sitting days beginning with the day on which the report is published, make arrangements for the motion mentioned in subsection (1)(c) to be debated and voted on by the House of Commons.

(3) Subsection (4) applies where the EU Select Committee of the House of Lords ('the EUC') publishes a report in respect of any EU legislation made, or which may be made, during the implementation period and the report—

(a) states that, in the opinion of the EUC, the EU legislation raises a matter of vital national interest to the United Kingdom,

(b) confirms that the EUC has taken such evidence as it considers appropriate as to the effect of the EU legislation, and

(c) sets out the wording of a motion to be moved in the House of Lords in accordance with subsection (4).

(4) A Minister of the Crown must, within the period of 14 Lords sitting days beginning with the day on which the report is published, make arrangements for the motion mentioned in subsection (3)(c) to be debated and voted on by the House of Lords.

(5) In this section—

'EU legislation' means—

(a) any amendment to the Treaty on European Union, the Treaty on the Functioning of the European Union, the Euratom Treaty or the EEA agreement,

(b) any EU directive, or

(c) any EU regulation or EU decision which is not EU tertiary legislation;

'the European Scrutiny Select Committee of the House of Commons' means the Select Committee of the House of Commons known as the European Scrutiny Select Committee or any successor of that committee;

'the EU Select Committee of the House of Lords' means the Select Committee of the House of Lords known as the EU Select Committee or any successor of that committee.

13B Certain dispute procedures under withdrawal agreement

(1) Subsection (2) applies if a request has been made under Article 170 of the withdrawal agreement to the other party in a dispute (request to establish an arbitration panel in relation to a dispute between the EU and the United Kingdom).

(2) A Minister of the Crown must, within the 14 day period beginning with the day on which the request is made, make a statement in writing to each House of Parliament that the request has been made and setting out the details of it.

(3) Subsection (4) applies if the European Court has given a ruling in response to a request by an arbitration panel under Article 174(1) of the withdrawal agreement (request for ruling by European Court on certain questions arising in a dispute submitted to arbitration).

(4) A Minister of the Crown must, within the 14 day period beginning with the publication in the Official Journal of the European Union of the ruling of the European Court, make a statement in writing to each House of Parliament that the ruling has been made and setting out the details of it contained in the Official Journal.

(5) After the end of each reporting period, a Minister of the Crown must lay before each House of Parliament a report setting out the number of times within the reporting period that the Joint Committee has been provided with notice under Article 169(1) of the withdrawal agreement (notice concerning the commencement of consultations in the Joint Committee to resolve a dispute between the EU and the United Kingdom about the interpretation and application of the withdrawal agreement).

(6) In this section—

'reporting period' means—

(a) the period of one year beginning with the day on which IP completion day falls, and

(b) each subsequent year;

'the 14 day period' means—

(a) in relation to the House of Commons, the period of 14 Commons sitting days, and

(b) in relation to the House of Lords, the period of 14 Lords sitting days.

*Financial and other matters**

15A Prohibition on extending implementation period

A Minister of the Crown may not agree in the Joint Committee to an extension of the implementation period.

15B Ministerial co-chairs of the Joint Committee

The functions of the United Kingdom's co-chair of the Joint Committee, under Annex VIII of the withdrawal agreement (rules of procedure of the Joint Committee and specialised committees), are to be exercised personally by a Minister of the Crown (and, accordingly, only a Minister of the Crown may be designated as a replacement under Rule 1(3)).

15C No use of written procedure in the Joint Committee

(1) The United Kingdom's co-chair of the Joint Committee may not consent to the Joint Committee using the written procedure provided for in Rule 9(1) of Annex VIII of the withdrawal agreement.

(2) In subsection (1) the reference to the United Kingdom's co-chair of the Joint Committee includes a reference to any designee of the co-chair designated under Rule 1(3) of Annex VIII of the withdrawal agreement.

16 Maintenance of environmental principles etc. [repealed by s. 36(b) EUWAA 2020]

17 Family unity for those seeking asylum or other protection in Europe

(1) A Minister of the Crown must, within the period of two months beginning with the day on which the European Union (Withdrawal Agreement) Act 2020 is passed, lay before Parliament a statement of policy in relation to any future arrangements between the United Kingdom and the EU about—

(a) unaccompanied children, who make an application for international protection to a member State, coming to the United Kingdom where it is in their best interests to join a relative who—

(i) is a lawful resident of the United Kingdom, or

(ii) has made a protection claim which has not been decided, and

* **Editor's Note:** Sections 14 and 15 omitted.

(b) unaccompanied children in the United Kingdom, who make a protection claim, going to a member State to join a relative there in equivalent circumstances.

(2) For the purposes of subsection (1)(a)(i) a person is not a lawful resident of the United Kingdom if the person requires leave to enter or remain in the United Kingdom but does not have it.

(3) For the purposes of subsection (1)(a)(ii), a protection claim is decided—

(a) when the Secretary of State notifies the claimant of the Secretary of State's decision on the claim, unless the claimant appeals against the decision, or

(b) if the claimant appeals against the Secretary of State's decision on the claim, when the appeal is disposed of.

(4) In this section—

'application for international protection' has the meaning given by Article 2(h) of Directive 2011/95/EU of the European Parliament and of the Council on standards for the qualification of third-country nationals or stateless persons as beneficiaries of international protection, for a uniform status for refugees or for persons eligible for subsidiary protection, and for the content of the protection granted;

'protection claim' has the same meaning as in Part 5 of the Nationality, Immigration and Asylum Act 2002 (see section 82(2) of that Act);

'relative', in relation to an unaccompanied child, means—

(a) a spouse or civil partner of the child or any person with whom the child has a durable relationship that is similar to marriage or civil partnership, or

(b) a parent, grandparent, uncle, aunt, brother or sister of the child;

'unaccompanied child' means a person under the age of 18 ('the child') who is not in the care of a person who—

(a) is aged 18 or over, and

(b) by law or custom of the country or territory in which the child is present, has responsibility for caring for the child.

18 Customs arrangement as part of the framework for the future relationship [repealed by s. 36(b) EUWAA 2020]

19 Future interaction with the law and agencies of the EU [repealed by s. 36(c) EUWAA 2020]

General and final provision

20 Interpretation [omitted]

21 Index of defined expressions [omitted]

22 Regulations

Schedule 7 (which makes provision about the scrutiny by Parliament and the devolved legislatures of regulations under this Act and contains other general provision about such regulations) has effect.

23 Consequential and transitional provision

(1) A Minister of the Crown may by regulations make such provision as the Minister considers appropriate in consequence of this Act.

(2) The power to make regulations under subsection (1) may (among other things) be exercised by modifying any provision made by or under an enactment.

(3) In subsection (2) 'enactment' does not include primary legislation passed or made after IP completion day.

(4) No regulations may be made under subsection (1) after the end of the period of 10 years beginning with IP completion day.

(5) Parts 1 and 2 of Schedule 8 (which contain consequential provision) have effect.

(6) A Minister of the Crown may by regulations make such transitional, transitory or saving provision as the Minister considers appropriate in connection with the coming into force of any provision of this Act (including its operation in connection with IP completion day).

(7) Parts 3 and 4 of Schedule 8 (which contain transitional, transitory and saving provision) have effect.

(8) The enactments mentioned in Schedule 9 (which contains repeals not made elsewhere in this Act) are repealed to the extent specified.

24 Extent

(1) Subject to subsections (2) and (3), this Act extends to England and Wales, Scotland and Northern Ireland.

(2) Any provision of this Act which amends or repeals an enactment has the same extent as the enactment amended or repealed.

(3) Regulations under section 8(1) or 23 may make provision which extends to Gibraltar—

(a) modifying any enactment which—

(i) extends to Gibraltar and relates to European Parliamentary elections, or

(ii) extends to Gibraltar for any purpose which is connected with Gibraltar forming part of an electoral region, under the European Parliamentary Elections Act 2002, for the purposes of such elections, or

(b) which is supplementary, incidental, consequential, transitional, transitory or saving provision in connection with a modification within paragraph (a).

25 Commencement and short title*

(5) This Act may be cited as the European Union (Withdrawal) Act 2018.

Section 5(6)

SCHEDULE 1**

FURTHER PROVISION ABOUT EXCEPTIONS TO SAVINGS AND INCORPORATION

Challenges to validity of retained EU law

1.—(1) There is no right in domestic law on or after IP completion day to challenge any retained EU law on the basis that, immediately before IP completion day an EU instrument was invalid.

(2) Sub-paragraph (1) does not apply so far as—

(a) the European Court has decided before IP completion day that the instrument is invalid, or

(b) the challenge is of a kind described, or provided for, in regulations made by a Minister of the Crown.

(3) Regulations under sub-paragraph (2)(b) may (among other things) provide for a challenge which would otherwise have been against an EU institution to be against a public authority in the United Kingdom.

General principles of EU law

2. No general principle of EU law is part of domestic law on or after IP completion day if it was not recognised as a general principle of EU law by the European Court in a case decided before IP completion day (whether or not as an essential part of the decision in the case).

3.—(1) There is no right of action in domestic law on or after IP completion day based on a failure to comply with any of the general principles of EU law.

(2) No court or tribunal or other public authority may, on or after IP completion day—

(a) disapply or quash any enactment or other rule of law, or

(b) quash any conduct or otherwise decide that it is unlawful,

because it is incompatible with any of the general principles of EU law.

* **Editor's Note:** Omitted as the 2020 Act has amended this.

** **Editor's Note:** Other Schedules omitted.

Rule in Francovich

4. There is no right in domestic law on or after IP completion day to damages in accordance with the rule in *Francovich*.

Interpretation

5.—(1) References in section 5 and this Schedule to the principle of the supremacy of EU law, the Charter of Fundamental Rights, any general principle of EU law or the rule in *Francovich* are to be read as references to that principle, Charter or rule so far as it would otherwise continue to be, or form part of, domestic law on or after IP completion day in accordance with this Act.

(2) Accordingly (among other things) the references to the principle of the supremacy of EU law in section 5(2) and (3) do not include anything which would bring into domestic law any modification of EU law which is adopted or notified, comes into force or only applies on or after IP completion day.

Agreement on the Withdrawal of the United Kingdom of Great Britain and Northern Ireland from the European Union and the European Atomic Energy Community 2020*

THE EUROPEAN UNION AND THE EUROPEAN ATOMIC ENERGY COMMUNITY

AND

THE UNITED KINGDOM OF GREAT BRITAIN AND NORTHERN IRELAND, HAVE AGREED AS FOLLOWS:

PART ONE COMMON PROVISIONS

Article 1 Objective

This Agreement sets out the arrangements for the withdrawal of the United Kingdom of Great Britain and Northern Ireland ('United Kingdom') from the European Union ('Union') and from the European Atomic Energy Community ('Euratom').

Article 2 Definitions [omitted]

Article 3 Territorial scope

1. Unless otherwise provided in this Agreement or in Union law made applicable by this Agreement, any reference in this Agreement to the United Kingdom or its territory shall be understood as referring to:

(a) the United Kingdom;
(b) Gibraltar, to the extent that Union law was applicable to it before the date of entry into force of this Agreement;
(c) the Channel Islands and the Isle of Man, to the extent that Union law was applicable to them before the date of entry into force of this Agreement;
(d) the Sovereign Base Areas of Akrotiri and Dhekelia in Cyprus, to the extent necessary to ensure the implementation of the arrangements set out in the Protocol on the Sovereign Base Areas of the United Kingdom of Great Britain and Northern Ireland in Cyprus annexed to the Act concerning the conditions of accession of the Czech Republic, the Republic of Estonia, the Republic of Cyprus, the Republic of Latvia, the Republic of Lithuania, the Republic of Hungary, the Republic of Malta, the Republic of Poland, the Republic of Slovenia and the Slovak Republic to the European Union;

* **Editor's Note**: Selected Extracts (Arts 1–29; and 86–91). As taken from OJ 2020 L29/7. https://ec.europa.eu/info/relations-united-kingdom/eu-uk-withdrawal-agreement_en.

(e) the overseas countries and territories listed in Annex II to the TFEU having special relations with the United Kingdom, where the provisions of this Agreement relate to the special arrangements for the association of the overseas countries and territories with the Union.

2. Unless otherwise provided in this Agreement or in Union law made applicable by this Agreement, any reference in this Agreement to Member States, or their territory, shall be understood as covering the territories of the Member States to which the Treaties apply as provided in Article 355 TFEU.

Article 4 Methods and principles relating to the effect, the implementation and the application of this Agreement

1. The provisions of this Agreement and the provisions of Union law made applicable by this Agreement shall produce in respect of and in the United Kingdom the same legal effects as those which they produce within the Union and its Member States.

Accordingly, legal or natural persons shall in particular be able to rely directly on the provisions contained or referred to in this Agreement which meet the conditions for direct effect under Union law.

2. The United Kingdom shall ensure compliance with paragraph 1, including as regards the required powers of its judicial and administrative authorities to disapply inconsistent or incompatible domestic provisions, through domestic primary legislation.

3. The provisions of this Agreement referring to Union law or to concepts or provisions thereof shall be interpreted and applied in accordance with the methods and general principles of Union law.

4. The provisions of this Agreement referring to Union law or to concepts or provisions thereof shall in their implementation and application be interpreted in conformity with the relevant case law of the Court of Justice of the European Union handed down before the end of the transition period.

5. In the interpretation and application of this Agreement, the United Kingdom's judicial and administrative authorities shall have due regard to relevant case law of the Court of Justice of the European Union handed down after the end of the transition period.

Article 5 Good faith

The Union and the United Kingdom shall, in full mutual respect and good faith, assist each other in carrying out tasks which flow from this Agreement.

They shall take all appropriate measures, whether general or particular, to ensure fulfilment of the obligations arising from this Agreement and shall refrain from any measures which could jeopardise the attainment of the objectives of this Agreement.

This Article is without prejudice to the application of Union law pursuant to this Agreement, in particular the principle of sincere cooperation.

Article 6 References to Union law

1. With the exception of Parts Four and Five, unless otherwise provided in this Agreement all references in this Agreement to Union law shall be understood as references to Union law, including as amended or replaced, as applicable on the last day of the transition period.

2. Where in this Agreement reference is made to Union acts or provisions thereof, such reference shall, where relevant, be understood to include a reference to Union law or provisions thereof that, although replaced or superseded by the act referred to, continue to apply in accordance with that act.

3. For the purposes of this Agreement, references to provisions of Union law made applicable by this Agreement shall be understood to include references to the relevant Union acts supplementing or implementing those provisions.

Article 7 References to the Union and to Member States

1. For the purposes of this Agreement, all references to Member States and competent authorities of Member States in provisions of Union law made applicable by this Agreement shall be understood as including the United Kingdom and its competent authorities, except as regards:

(a) the nomination, appointment or election of members of the institutions, bodies, offices and agencies of the Union, as well as the participation in the decision-making and the attendance in the meetings of the institutions;
(b) the participation in the decision-making and governance of the bodies, offices and agencies of the Union;
(c) the attendance in the meetings of the committees referred to in Article 3(2) of Regulation (EU) No 182/2011 of the European Parliament and of the Council, of Commission expert groups or of other similar entities, or in the meetings of expert groups or similar entities of bodies, offices and agencies of the Union, unless otherwise provided in this Agreement.

2. Unless otherwise provided in this Agreement, any reference to the Union shall be understood as including Euratom.

Article 8 Access to networks, information systems and databases

Unless otherwise provided in this Agreement, at the end of the transition period the United Kingdom shall cease to be entitled to access any network, any information system and any database established on the basis of Union law. The United Kingdom shall take appropriate measures to ensure that it does not access a network, information system or database which it is no longer entitled to access.

PART TWO CITIZENS' RIGHTS

Title I General provisions

Article 9 Definitions

For the purposes of this Part, and without prejudice to Title III, the following definitions shall apply:

(a) 'family members' means the following persons, irrespective of their nationality, who fall within the personal scope provided for in Article 10 of this Agreement:
  (i) family members of Union citizens or family members of United Kingdom nationals as defined in point (2) of Article 2 of Directive 2004/38/EC of the European Parliament and of the Council;
  (ii) persons other than those defined in Article 3(2) of Directive 2004/38/EC whose presence is required by Union citizens or United Kingdom nationals in order not to deprive those Union citizens or United Kingdom nationals of a right of residence granted by this Part;
(b) 'frontier workers' means Union citizens or United Kingdom nationals who pursue an economic activity in accordance with Article 45 or 49 TFEU in one or more States in which they do not reside;
(c) 'host State' means:
  (i) in respect of Union citizens and their family members, the United Kingdom, if they exercised their right of residence there in accordance with Union law before the end of the transition period and continue to reside there thereafter;
  (ii) in respect of United Kingdom nationals and their family members, the Member State in which they exercised their right of residence in accordance with Union law before the end of the transition period and in which they continue to reside thereafter;
(d) 'State of work' means:
  (i) in respect of Union citizens, the United Kingdom, if they pursued an economic activity as frontier workers there before the end of the transition period and continue to do so thereafter;
  (ii) in respect of United Kingdom nationals, a Member State in which they pursued an economic activity as frontier workers before the end of the transition period and in which they continue to do so thereafter;

(e) 'rights of custody' means rights of custody within the meaning of point (9) of Article 2 of Council Regulation (EC) No 2201/2003, including rights of custody acquired by judgment, by operation of law or by an agreement having legal effect.

Article 10 Personal scope

1. Without prejudice to Title III, this Part shall apply to the following persons:

(a) Union citizens who exercised their right to reside in the United Kingdom in accordance with Union law before the end of the transition period and continue to reside there thereafter;

(b) United Kingdom nationals who exercised their right to reside in a Member State in accordance with Union law before the end of the transition period and continue to reside there thereafter;

(c) Union citizens who exercised their right as frontier workers in the United Kingdom in accordance with Union law before the end of the transition period and continue to do so thereafter;

(d) United Kingdom nationals who exercised their right as frontier workers in one or more Member States in accordance with Union law before the end of the transition period and continue to do so thereafter;

(e) family members of the persons referred to in points (a) to (d), provided that they fulfil one of the following conditions:

(i) they resided in the host State in accordance with Union law before the end of the transition period and continue to reside there thereafter;

(ii) they were directly related to a person referred to in points (a) to (d) and resided outside the host State before the end of the transition period, provided that they fulfil the conditions set out in point (2) of Article 2 of Directive 2004/38/EC at the time they seek residence under this Part in order to join the person referred to in points (a) to (d) of this paragraph;

(iii) they were born to, or legally adopted by, persons referred to in points (a) to (d) after the end of the transition period, whether inside or outside the host State, and fulfil the conditions set out in point (2)(c) of Article 2 of Directive 2004/38/EC at the time they seek residence under this Part in order to join the person referred to in points (a) to (d) of this paragraph and fulfil one of the following conditions:

- both parents are persons referred to in points (a) to (d);
- one parent is a person referred to in points (a) to (d) and the other is a national of the host State; or
- one parent is a person referred to in points (a) to (d) and has sole or joint rights of custody of the child, in accordance with the applicable rules of family law of a Member State or of the United Kingdom, including applicable rules of private international law under which rights of custody established under the law of a third State are recognised in the Member State or in the United Kingdom, in particular as regards the best interests of the child, and without prejudice to the normal operation of such applicable rules of private international law;

(f) family members who resided in the host State in accordance with Articles 12 and 13, Article 16(2) and Articles 17 and 18 of Directive 2004/38/EC before the end of the transition period and continue to reside there thereafter.

2. Persons falling under points (a) and (b) of Article 3(2) of Directive 2004/38/EC whose residence was facilitated by the host State in accordance with its national legislation before the end of the transition period in accordance with Article 3(2) of that Directive shall retain their right of residence in the host State in accordance with this Part, provided that they continue to reside in the host State thereafter.

3. Paragraph 2 shall also apply to persons falling under points (a) and (b) of Article 3(2) of Directive 2004/38/EC who have applied for facilitation of entry and residence before the end of the

transition period, and whose residence is being facilitated by the host State in accordance with its national legislation thereafter.

4. Without prejudice to any right to residence which the persons concerned may have in their own right, the host State shall, in accordance with its national legislation and in accordance with point (b) of Article 3(2) of Directive 2004/38/EC, facilitate entry and residence for the partner with whom the person referred to in points (a) to (d) of paragraph 1 of this Article has a durable relationship, duly attested, where that partner resided outside the host State before the end of the transition period, provided that the relationship was durable before the end of the transition period and continues at the time the partner seeks residence under this Part.

5. In the cases referred to in paragraphs 3 and 4, the host State shall undertake an extensive examination of the personal circumstances of the persons concerned and shall justify any denial of entry or residence to such persons.

Article 11 Continuity of residence

Continuity of residence for the purposes of Articles 9 and 10 shall not be affected by absences as referred to in Article 15(2).

The right of permanent residence acquired under Directive 2004/38/EC before the end of the transition period shall not be treated as lost through absence from the host State for a period specified in Article 15(3).

Article 12 Non-discrimination

Within the scope of this Part, and without prejudice to any special provisions contained therein, any discrimination on grounds of nationality within the meaning of the first subparagraph of Article 18 TFEU shall be prohibited in the host State and the State of work in respect of the persons referred to in Article 10 of this Agreement.

Title II Rights and obligations

Chapter 1 Rights related to residence, residence documents

Article 13 Residence rights

1. Union citizens and United Kingdom nationals shall have the right to reside in the host State under the limitations and conditions as set out in Articles 21, 45 or 49 TFEU and in Article 6(1), points (a), (b) or (c) of Article 7(1), Article 7(3), Article 14, Article 16(1) or Article 17(1) of Directive 2004/38/EC.

2. Family members who are either Union citizens or United Kingdom nationals shall have the right to reside in the host State as set out in Article 21 TFEU and in Article 6(1), point (d) of Article 7(1), Article 12(1) or (3), Article 13(1), Article 14, Article 16(1) or Article 17(3) and (4) of Directive 2004/38/EC, subject to the limitations and conditions set out in those provisions.

3. Family members who are neither Union citizens nor United Kingdom nationals shall have the right to reside in the host State under Article 21 TFEU and as set out in Article 6(2), Article 7(2), Article 12(2) or (3), Article 13(2), Article 14, Article 16(2), Article 17(3) or (4) or Article 18 of Directive 2004/38/EC, subject to the limitations and conditions set out in those provisions.

4. The host State may not impose any limitations or conditions for obtaining, retaining or losing residence rights on the persons referred to in paragraphs 1, 2 and 3, other than those provided for in this Title. There shall be no discretion in applying the limitations and conditions provided for in this Title, other than in favour of the person concerned.

Article 14 Right of exit and of entry

1. Union citizens and United Kingdom nationals, their respective family members, and other persons, who reside in the territory of the host State in accordance with the conditions set out in this Title shall have the right to leave the host State and the right to enter it, as set out in Article 4(1) and the first subparagraph of Article 5(1) of Directive 2004/38/EC, with a valid passport or national

identity card in the case of Union citizens and United Kingdom nationals, and with a valid passport in the case of their respective family members and other persons who are not Union citizens or United Kingdom nationals.

Five years after the end of the transition period, the host State may decide no longer to accept national identity cards for the purposes of entry to or exit from its territory if such cards do not include a chip that complies with the applicable International Civil Aviation Organisation standards related to biometric identification.

2. No exit visa, entry visa or equivalent formality shall be required of holders of a valid document issued in accordance with Article 18 or 26.

3. Where the host State requires family members who join the Union citizen or United Kingdom national after the end of the transition period to have an entry visa, the host State shall grant such persons every facility to obtain the necessary visas. Such visas shall be issued free of charge as soon as possible, and on the basis of an accelerated procedure.

Article 15 Right of permanent residence

1. Union citizens and United Kingdom nationals, and their respective family members, who have resided legally in the host State in accordance with Union law for a continuous period of 5 years or for the period specified in Article 17 of Directive 2004/38/EC, shall have the right to reside permanently in the host State under the conditions set out in Articles 16, 17 and 18 of Directive 2004/38/EC. Periods of legal residence or work in accordance with Union law before and after the end of the transition period shall be included in the calculation of the qualifying period necessary for acquisition of the right of permanent residence.

2. Continuity of residence for the purposes of acquisition of the right of permanent residence shall be determined in accordance with Article 16(3) and Article 21 of Directive 2004/38/EC.

3. Once acquired, the right of permanent residence shall be lost only through absence from the host State for a period exceeding 5 consecutive years.

Article 16 Accumulation of periods

Union citizens and United Kingdom nationals, and their respective family members, who before the end of the transition period resided legally in the host State in accordance with the conditions of Article 7 of Directive 2004/38/EC for a period of less than 5 years, shall have the right to acquire the right to reside permanently under the conditions set out in Article 15 of this Agreement once they have completed the necessary periods of residence. Periods of legal residence or work in accordance with Union law before and after the end of the transition period shall be included in the calculation of the qualifying period necessary for acquisition of the right of permanent residence.

Article 17 Status and changes

1. The right of Union citizens and United Kingdom nationals, and their respective family members, to rely directly on this Part shall not be affected when they change status, for example between student, worker, self-employed person and economically inactive person. Persons who, at the end of the transition period, enjoy a right of residence in their capacity as family members of Union citizens or United Kingdom nationals, cannot become persons referred to in points (a) to (d) of Article 10(1).

2. The rights provided for in this Title for the family members who are dependants of Union citizens or United Kingdom nationals before the end of the transition period, shall be maintained even after they cease to be dependants.

Article 18 Issuance of residence documents

1. The host State may require Union citizens or United Kingdom nationals, their respective family members and other persons, who reside in its territory in accordance with the conditions set out in this Title, to apply for a new residence status which confers the rights under this Title and a document evidencing such status which may be in a digital form.

Applying for such a residence status shall be subject to the following conditions:

(a) the purpose of the application procedure shall be to verify whether the applicant is entitled to the residence rights set out in this Title. Where that is the case, the applicant shall have a right to be granted the residence status and the document evidencing that status;

(b) the deadline for submitting the application shall not be less than 6 months from the end of the transition period, for persons residing in the host State before the end of the transition period.

For persons who have the right to commence residence after the end of the transition period in the host State in accordance with this Title, the deadline for submitting the application shall be 3 months after their arrival or the expiry of the deadline referred to in the first subparagraph, whichever is later.

A certificate of application for the residence status shall be issued immediately;

(c) the deadline for submitting the application referred to in point (b) shall be extended automatically by 1 year where the Union has notified the United Kingdom, or the United Kingdom has notified the Union, that technical problems prevent the host State either from registering the application or from issuing the certificate of application referred to in point (b). The host State shall publish that notification and shall provide appropriate public information for the persons concerned in good time;

(d) where the deadline for submitting the application referred to in point (b) is not respected by the persons concerned, the competent authorities shall assess all the circumstances and reasons for not respecting the deadline and shall allow those persons to submit an application within a reasonable further period of time if there are reasonable grounds for the failure to respect the deadline;

(e) the host State shall ensure that any administrative procedures for applications are smooth, transparent and simple, and that any unnecessary administrative burdens are avoided;

(f) application forms shall be short, simple, user friendly and adapted to the context of this Agreement; applications made by families at the same time shall be considered together;

(g) the document evidencing the status shall be issued free of charge or for a charge not exceeding that imposed on citizens or nationals of the host State for the issuing of similar documents;

(h) persons who, before the end of the transition period, hold a valid permanent residence document issued under Article 19 or 20 of Directive 2004/38/EC or hold a valid domestic immigration document conferring a permanent right to reside in the host State, shall have the right to exchange that document within the period referred to in point (b) of this paragraph for a new residence document upon application after a verification of their identity, a criminality and security check in accordance with point (p) of this paragraph and confirmation of their ongoing residence; such new residence documents shall be issued free of charge;

(i) the identity of the applicants shall be verified through the presentation of a valid passport or national identity card for Union citizens and United Kingdom nationals, and through the presentation of a valid passport for their respective family members and other persons who are not Union citizens or United Kingdom nationals; the acceptance of such identity documents shall not be made conditional upon any criteria other than that of the validity of the document. Where the identity document is retained by the competent authorities of the host State while the application is pending, the host State shall return that document upon application without delay, before the decision on the application has been taken;

(j) supporting documents other than identity documents, such as civil status documents, may be submitted in copy. Originals of supporting documents may be required only in specific cases where there is a reasonable doubt as to the authenticity of the supporting documents submitted;

(k) the host State may only require Union citizens and United Kingdom nationals to present, in addition to the identity documents referred to in point (i) of this paragraph, the following supporting documents as referred to in Article 8(3) of Directive 2004/38/EC:

(i) where they reside in the host State in accordance with point (a) of Article 7(1) of Directive 2004/38/EC as workers or self-employed, a confirmation of engagement from the employer or a certificate of employment, or proof that they are self-employed;

(ii) where they reside in the host State in accordance with point (b) of Article 7(1) of Directive 2004/38/EC as economically inactive persons, evidence that they have sufficient resources for themselves and their family members not to become a burden on the social assistance system of the host State during their period of residence and that they have comprehensive sickness insurance cover in the host State; or

(iii) where they reside in the host State in accordance with point (c) of Article 7(1) of Directive 2004/38/EC as students, proof of enrolment at an establishment accredited or financed by the host State on the basis of its legislation or administrative practice, proof of comprehensive sickness insurance cover, and a declaration or equivalent means of proof, that they have sufficient resources for themselves and their family members not to become a burden on the social assistance system of the host State during their period of residence. The host State may not require such declarations to refer to any specific amount of resources.

With regard to the condition of sufficient resources, Article 8(4) of Directive 2004/38/EC shall apply;

(l) the host State may only require family members who fall under point (e)(i) of Article 10(1) or Article 10(2) or (3) of this Agreement and who reside in the host State in accordance with point (d) of Article 7(1) or Article 7(2) of Directive 2004/38/EC to present, in addition to the identity documents referred to in point (i) of this paragraph, the following supporting documents as referred to in Article 8(5) or 10(2) of Directive 2004/38/EC:

(i) a document attesting to the existence of a family relationship or registered partnership;

(ii) the registration certificate or, in the absence of a registration system, any other proof that the Union citizen or the United Kingdom national with whom they reside actually resides in the host State;

(iii) for direct descendants who are under the age of 21 or who are dependants and dependent direct relatives in the ascending line, and for those of the spouse or registered partner, documentary evidence that the conditions set out in point (c) or (d) of Article 2(2) of Directive 2004/38/EC are fulfilled;

(iv) for the persons referred to in Article 10(2) or (3) of this Agreement, a document issued by the relevant authority in the host State in accordance with Article 3(2) of Directive 2004/38/EC.

With regard to the condition of sufficient resources as concerns family members who are themselves Union citizens or United Kingdom nationals, Article 8(4) of Directive 2004/38/EC shall apply;

(m) the host State may only require family members who fall under point (e)(ii) of Article 10(1) or Article 10(4) of this Agreement to present, in addition to the identity documents referred to in point (i) of this paragraph, the following supporting documents as referred to in Articles 8(5) and 10(2) of Directive 2004/38/EC:

(i) a document attesting to the existence of a family relationship or of a registered partnership;

(ii) the registration certificate or, in the absence of a registration system, any other proof of residence in the host State of the Union citizen or of the United Kingdom nationals whom they are joining in the host State;

(iii) for spouses or registered partners, a document attesting to the existence of a family relationship or a registered partnership before the end of the transition period;

(iv) for direct descendants who are under the age of 21 or who are dependants and dependent direct relatives in the ascending line and those of the spouse or registered partner, documentary evidence that they were related to Union citizens or United Kingdom nationals before the end of the transition period and fulfil the conditions set out in point (c) or (d) of Article 2(2) of Directive 2004/38/EC relating to age or dependence;

(v) for the persons referred to in Article 10(4) of this Agreement, proof that a durable relationship with Union citizens or United Kingdom nationals existed before the end of the transition period and continues to exist thereafter;

(n) for cases other than those set out in points (k), (l) and (m), the host State shall not require applicants to present supporting documents that go beyond what is strictly necessary and proportionate to provide evidence that the conditions relating to the right of residence under this Title have been fulfilled;

(o) the competent authorities of the host State shall help the applicants to prove their eligibility and to avoid any errors or omissions in their applications; they shall give the applicants the opportunity to furnish supplementary evidence and to correct any deficiencies, errors or omissions;

(p) criminality and security checks may be carried out systematically on applicants, with the exclusive aim of verifying whether the restrictions set out in Article 20 of this Agreement may be applicable. For that purpose, applicants may be required to declare past criminal convictions which appear in their criminal record in accordance with the law of the State of conviction at the time of the application. The host State may, if it considers this essential, apply the procedure set out in Article 27(3) of Directive 2004/38/EC with respect to enquiries to other States regarding previous criminal records;

(q) the new residence document shall include a statement that it has been issued in accordance with this Agreement;

(r) the applicant shall have access to judicial and, where appropriate, administrative redress procedures in the host State against any decision refusing to grant the residence status. The redress procedures shall allow for an examination of the legality of the decision, as well as of the facts and circumstances on which the proposed decision is based. Such redress procedures shall ensure that the decision is not disproportionate.

2. During the period referred to in point (b) of paragraph 1 of this Article and its possible one-year extension under point (c) of that paragraph, all rights provided for in this Part shall be deemed to apply to Union citizens or United Kingdom nationals, their respective family members, and other persons residing in the host State, in accordance with the conditions and subject to the restrictions set out in Article 20.

3. Pending a final decision by the competent authorities on any application referred to in paragraph 1, and pending a final judgment handed down in case of judicial redress sought against any rejection of such application by the competent administrative authorities, all rights provided for in this Part shall be deemed to apply to the applicant, including Article 21 on safeguards and right of appeal, subject to the conditions set out in Article 20(4).

4. Where a host State has chosen not to require Union citizens or United Kingdom nationals, their family members, and other persons, residing in its territory in accordance with the conditions set out in this Title, to apply for the new residence status referred to in paragraph 1 as a condition for legal residence, those eligible for residence rights under this Title shall have the right to receive, in accordance with the conditions set out in Directive 2004/38/EC, a residence document, which may be in a digital form, that includes a statement that it has been issued in accordance with this Agreement.

Article 19 Issuance of residence documents during the transition period

1. During the transition period, a host State may allow applications for a residence status or residence document as referred to in Article 18(1) and (4) to be made voluntarily from the date of entry into force of this Agreement.

2. Decisions to accept or refuse such applications shall be taken in accordance with Article 18(1) and (4). Decisions under Article 18(1) shall have no effect until after the end of the transition period.

3. If an application under Article 18(1) is accepted before the end of the transition period, the host State may not withdraw the decision granting the residence status before the end of the transition period on any grounds other than those set out in Chapter VI and Article 35 of Directive 2004/38/EC.

4. If an application is refused before the end of the transition period, the applicant may apply again at any time before the expiry of the period set out in point (b) of Article 18(1).

5. Without prejudice to paragraph 4, the redress procedures under point (r) of Article 18(1) shall be available from the date of any decision to refuse an application referred to in paragraph 2 of this Article.

Article 20 Restrictions of the rights of residence and entry

1. The conduct of Union citizens or United Kingdom nationals, their family members, and other persons, who exercise rights under this Title, where that conduct occurred before the end of the transition period, shall be considered in accordance with Chapter VI of Directive 2004/38/EC.

2. The conduct of Union citizens or United Kingdom nationals, their family members, and other persons, who exercise rights under this Title, where that conduct occurred after the end of the transition period, may constitute grounds for restricting the right of residence by the host State or the right of entry in the State of work in accordance with national legislation.

3. The host State or the State of work may adopt the necessary measures to refuse, terminate or withdraw any right conferred by this Title in the case of the abuse of those rights or fraud, as set out in Article 35 of Directive 2004/38/EC. Such measures shall be subject to the procedural safeguards provided for in Article 21 of this Agreement.

4. The host State or the State of work may remove applicants who submitted fraudulent or abusive applications from its territory under the conditions set out in Directive 2004/38/EC, in particular Articles 31 and 35 thereof, even before a final judgment has been handed down in the case of judicial redress sought against any rejection of such an application.

Article 21 Safeguards and right of appeal

The safeguards set out in Article 15 and Chapter VI of Directive 2004/38/EC shall apply in respect of any decision by the host State that restricts residence rights of the persons referred to in Article 10 of this Agreement.

Article 22 Related rights

In accordance with Article 23 of Directive 2004/38/EC, irrespective of nationality, the family members of a Union citizen or United Kingdom national who have the right of residence or the right of permanent residence in the host State or the State of work shall be entitled to take up employment or self-employment there.

Article 23 Equal treatment

1. In accordance with Article 24 of Directive 2004/38/EC, subject to the specific provisions provided for in this Title and Titles I and IV of this Part, all Union citizens or United Kingdom nationals residing on the basis of this Agreement in the territory of the host State shall enjoy equal treatment with the nationals of that State within the scope of this Part. The benefit of this right shall be extended to those family members of Union citizens or United Kingdom nationals who have the right of residence or permanent residence.

2. By way of derogation from paragraph 1, the host State shall not be obliged to confer entitlement to social assistance during periods of residence on the basis of Article 6 or point (b) of Article 14(4) of Directive 2004/38/EC, nor shall it be obliged, prior to a person's acquisition of the right of permanent residence in accordance with Article 15 of this Agreement, to grant maintenance aid for studies, including vocational training, consisting in student grants or student loans to persons other than workers, self-employed persons, persons who retain such status or to members of their families.

Chapter 2 Rights of workers and self-employed persons

Article 24 Rights of workers

1. Subject to the limitations set out in Article 45(3) and (4) TFEU, workers in the host State and frontier workers in the State or States of work shall enjoy the rights guaranteed by Article 45 TFEU and the rights granted by Regulation (EU) No 492/2011 of the European Parliament and of the Council. These rights include:

(a) the right not to be discriminated against on grounds of nationality as regards employment, remuneration and other conditions of work and employment;
(b) the right to take up and pursue an activity in accordance with the rules applicable to the nationals of the host State or the State of work;
(c) the right to assistance afforded by the employment offices of the host State or the State of work as offered to own nationals;
(d) the right to equal treatment in respect of conditions of employment and work, in particular as regards remuneration, dismissal and in case of unemployment, reinstatement or re-employment;
(e) the right to social and tax advantages;
(f) collective rights;
(g) the rights and benefits accorded to national workers in matters of housing;
(h) the right for their children to be admitted to the general educational, apprenticeship and vocational training courses under the same conditions as the nationals of the host State or the State of work, if such children are residing in the territory where the worker works.

2. Where a direct descendant of a worker who has ceased to reside in the host State is in education in that State, the primary carer for that descendant shall have the right to reside in that State until the descendant reaches the age of majority, and after the age of majority if that descendant continues to need the presence and care of the primary carer in order to pursue and complete his or her education.

3. Employed frontier workers shall enjoy the right to enter and exit the State of work in accordance with Article 14 of this Agreement and shall retain the rights they enjoyed as workers there, provided they are in one of the circumstances set out in points (a), (b), (c) and (d) of Article 7(3) of Directive 2004/38/EC, even where they do not move their residence to the State of work.

Article 25 Rights of self-employed persons

1. Subject to the limitations set out in Articles 51 and 52 TFEU, self-employed persons in the host State and self-employed frontier workers in the State or States of work shall enjoy the rights guaranteed by Articles 49 and 55 TFEU. These rights include:

(a) the right to take up and pursue activities as self-employed persons and to set up and manage undertakings under the conditions laid down by the host State for its own nationals, as set out in Article 49 TFEU;
(b) the rights as set out in points (c) to (h) of Article 24(1) of this Agreement.

2. Article 24(2) shall apply to direct descendants of self-employed workers.

3. Article 24(3) shall apply to self-employed frontier workers.

Article 26 Issuance of a document identifying frontier workers' rights

The State of work may require Union citizens and United Kingdom nationals who have rights as frontier workers under this Title to apply for a document certifying that they have such rights under this Title. Such Union citizens and United Kingdom nationals shall have the right to be issued with such a document.

Chapter 3 Professional qualifications

Article 27 Recognised professional qualifications

1. The recognition, before the end of the transition period, of professional qualifications, as defined in point (b) of Article 3(1) of Directive 2005/36/EC of the European Parliament and of the Council, of Union citizens or United Kingdom nationals, and their family members, by their host

State or their State of work shall maintain its effects in the respective State, including the right to pursue their profession under the same conditions as its nationals, where such recognition was made in accordance with any of the following provisions:

(a) Title III of Directive 2005/36/EC in respect of the recognition of professional qualifications in the context of the exercise of the freedom of establishment, whether such recognition fell under the general system for the recognition of evidence of training, the system for the recognition of professional experience or the system for the recognition on the basis of coordination of minimum training conditions;

(b) Article 10(1) and (3) of Directive 98/5/EC of the European Parliament and of the Council in respect of gaining admission to the profession of lawyer in the host State or State of work;

(c) Article 14 of Directive 2006/43/EC of the European Parliament and of the Council in respect of the approval of statutory auditors from another Member State;

(d) Council Directive 74/556/EEC in respect of the acceptance of evidence of the knowledge and ability necessary to take up or pursue the activities of self-employed persons and of intermediaries engaging in the trade and distribution of toxic products or activities involving the professional use of toxic products.

2. Recognitions of professional qualifications for the purposes of point (a) of paragraph 1 of this Article shall include:

(a) recognitions of professional qualifications which have benefited from Article 3(3) of Directive 2005/36/EC;

(b) decisions granting partial access to a professional activity in accordance with Article 4f of Directive 2005/36/EC;

(c) recognitions of professional qualifications for establishment purposes made under Article 4d of Directive 2005/36/EC.

Article 28 Ongoing procedures on the recognition of professional qualifications

Article 4, Article 4d in respect of recognitions of professional qualifications for establishment purposes, Article 4f and Title III of Directive 2005/36/EC, Article 10(1), (3) and (4) of Directive 98/5/EC, Article 14 of Directive 2006/43/EC and Directive 74/556/EEC shall apply in respect of the examination by a competent authority of the host State or State of work of any application for the recognition of professional qualifications introduced before the end of the transition period by Union citizens or United Kingdom nationals and in respect of the decision on any such application.

Articles 4a, 4b and 4e of Directive 2005/36/EC shall also apply to the extent relevant for the completion of the procedures for the recognitions of professional qualifications for establishment purposes under Article 4d of that Directive.

Article 29 Administrative cooperation on recognition of professional qualifications

1. With regard to the pending applications referred to in Article 28, the United Kingdom and the Member States shall cooperate in order to facilitate the application of Article 28. Cooperation may include the exchange of information, including information on disciplinary action or criminal sanctions taken or any other serious and specific circumstances which are likely to have consequences for the pursuit of the activities falling under the Directives referred to in Article 28.

2. By way of derogation from Article 8, for a period not exceeding 9 months from the end of the transition period, the United Kingdom shall be entitled to use the internal market information system in respect of applications referred to in Article 28 insofar as they concern procedures for the recognition of professional qualifications for establishment purposes under Article 4d of Directive 2005/36/EC.

PART THREE SEPARATION PROVISIONS

Title I Goods placed on the market

Article 40 Definitions

For the purposes of this Title, the following definitions shall apply:

(a) 'making available on the market' means any supply of a good for distribution, consumption or use on the market in the course of a commercial activity, whether in return for payment or free of charge;

(b) 'placing on the market' means the first making available of a good on the market in the Union or the United Kingdom;

(c) 'supply of a good for distribution, consumption or use' means that an existing and individually identifiable good, after the stage of manufacturing has taken place, is the subject matter of a written or verbal agreement between two or more legal or natural persons for the transfer of ownership, any other property right, or possession concerning the good in question, or is the subject matter of an offer to a legal or natural person or persons to conclude such an agreement;

(d) 'putting into service' means the first use of a good within the Union or the United Kingdom by the end user for the purposes for which it was intended or, in the case of marine equipment, placing on board;

(e) 'market surveillance' means the activities carried out and measures taken by market surveillance authorities to ensure that goods comply with the applicable requirements and do not endanger health, safety or any other aspect of public interest protection;

(f) 'market surveillance authority' means an authority of a Member State or of the United Kingdom responsible for carrying out market surveillance on its territory;

(g) 'conditions for the marketing of goods' means requirements concerning the characteristics of goods such as levels of quality, performance, safety or dimensions, including on the composition of such goods or on the terminology, symbols, testing and testing methods, packaging, marking, labelling, and conformity assessment procedures used in relation to such goods; the term also covers requirements concerning production methods and processes, where these have an effect on product characteristics;

(h) 'conformity assessment body' means a body that performs conformity assessment activities including calibration, testing, certification and inspection;

(i) 'notified body' means a conformity assessment body authorised to carry out third-party conformity assessment tasks under Union law harmonising the conditions for the marketing of goods;

(j) 'animal products' means products of animal origin, animal by-products and derived products, as referred to in points (29), (30) and (31) of Article 4 of Regulation (EU) 2016/429 of the European Parliament and of the Council, respectively, feed of animal origin, and food and feed containing products of animal origin.

Article 41 Continued circulation of goods placed on the market

1. Any good that was lawfully placed on the market in the Union or the United Kingdom before the end of the transition period may:

(a) be further made available on the market of the Union or of the United Kingdom and circulate between these two markets until it reaches its end-user;

(b) where provided in the applicable provisions of Union law, be put into service in the Union or in the United Kingdom.

2. The requirements set out in Articles 34 and 35 TFEU and the relevant Union law governing the marketing of goods, including the conditions for the marketing of goods, applicable to the goods concerned shall apply in respect of the goods referred to in paragraph 1.

3. Paragraph 1 shall apply to all existing and individually identifiable goods within the meaning of Title II of Part Three of the TFEU, with the exception of the circulation between the Union market and the United Kingdom's market or vice-versa of:

(a) live animals and germinal products;

(b) animal products.

4. In respect of a movement of live animals or of germinal products between a Member State and the United Kingdom, or vice-versa, the provisions of Union law listed in Annex II shall apply, provided that the date of departure was before the end of the transition period.

5. This Article shall be without prejudice to the possibility for the United Kingdom, a Member State or the Union to take measures to prohibit or restrict the making available on its market of a good referred to in paragraph 1, or a category of such goods, where and to the extent permitted by Union law.

6. The provisions of this Title shall be without prejudice to any applicable rules on modalities of sale, intellectual property, customs procedures, tariffs and taxes.

Article 42 Proof of placing on the market

Where an economic operator relies on Article 41(1) with respect to a specific good, that operator shall bear the burden of proof of demonstrating, on the basis of any relevant document, that the good was placed on the market in the Union or the United Kingdom before the end of the transition period.

Article 43 Market surveillance

1. The market surveillance authorities of the Member States and the market surveillance authorities of the United Kingdom shall exchange without delay any relevant information collected with regard to the goods referred to in Article 41(1) in the context of their respective market surveillance activities. They shall, in particular, communicate to each other and to the European Commission any information relating to those goods presenting a serious risk, as well as any measures taken in relation to non-compliant goods, including relevant information drawn from networks, information systems and databases established under Union or United Kingdom law in relation to those goods.

2. The Member States and the United Kingdom shall transmit without delay any request from the market surveillance authorities of the United Kingdom or of a Member State, respectively, to a conformity assessment body established in their territory, where that request concerns a conformity assessment carried out by that body in its capacity as notified body before the end of the transition period. Member States and the United Kingdom shall ensure that any such request is promptly addressed by the conformity assessment body.

Article 44 Transfer of files and documents relating to ongoing procedures

The United Kingdom shall transfer without delay to the competent authority of a Member State designated in accordance with the procedures provided for in the applicable Union law all relevant files or documents in relation to assessments, approvals and authorisations ongoing on the day before the date of entry into force of this Agreement and led by a United Kingdom competent authority in accordance with Regulation (EU) No 528/2012, Regulation (EC) No 1107/2009, Directive 2001/83/EC and Directive 2001/82/EC of the European Parliament and of the Council.

Article 45 Making available of information in relation to past authorisation procedures for medicinal products

1. The United Kingdom shall, upon a reasoned request from a Member State or the European Medicines Agency, make available without delay the marketing authorisation dossier of a medicinal product authorised by a competent authority of the United Kingdom before the end of the transition period, where that dossier is necessary for the assessment of a marketing authorisation application in accordance with Articles 10 and 10a of Directive 2001/83/EC or Articles 13 and 13a of Directive 2001/82/EC.

2. A Member State shall, upon a reasoned request from the United Kingdom, make available without delay the marketing authorisation dossier of a medicinal product authorised by a competent authority of that Member State before the end of the transition period, where that dossier is necessary for the assessment of a marketing authorisation application in the United Kingdom in accordance with the United Kingdom's legislative requirements, to the extent that those legislative requirements replicate the circumstances of Articles 10 and 10a of Directive 2001/83/EC or Articles 13 and 13a of Directive 2001/82/EC.

Article 46 Making available of information held by notified bodies established in the United Kingdom or in a Member State

1. The United Kingdom shall ensure that information held by a conformity assessment body established in the United Kingdom in relation to its activities as a notified body under Union law before the end of the transition period is made available at the request of the certificate holder, without delay, to a notified body established in a Member State as indicated by the certificate holder.

2. Member States shall ensure that information held by a notified body established in the Member State concerned in relation to its activities before the end of the transition period is made available at the request of the certificate holder, without delay, to a conformity assessment body established in the United Kingdom as indicated by the certificate holder.

Title II Ongoing customs procedures

Article 47 Union status of goods

1. Regulation (EU) No 952/2013 of the European Parliament and of the Council shall apply in respect of Union goods referred to in point (23) of Article 5 of that Regulation, where such goods move from the customs territory of the United Kingdom to the customs territory of the Union, or vice versa, provided that the movement started before the end of the transition period and ended thereafter. A movement of goods which has started before the end of the transition period and ends thereafter shall be treated as an intra-Union movement regarding importation and exportation licencing requirements in Union law.

2. For the purposes of paragraph 1, the presumption of the customs status of Union goods as referred to in Article 153(1) of Regulation (EU) No 952/2013 shall not apply. The customs status of those goods as Union goods, as well as the fact that the movement referred to in paragraph 1 started before the end of the transition period, shall need to be proven for every movement by the person concerned by any of the means referred to in Article 199 of Commission Implementing Regulation (EU) 2015/2447. The proof of the start of the movement shall be provided by means of a transport document relating to the goods.

3. Paragraph 2 shall not apply in respect of Union goods that are carried by air and have been loaded or transhipped at an airport in the customs territory of the United Kingdom for consignment to the customs territory of the Union or have been loaded or transhipped at an airport in the customs territory of the Union for consignment to the customs territory of the United Kingdom, where such goods are carried under cover of a single transport document issued in either of the customs territories concerned, provided that the movement by air started before the end of the transition period and the movement ended thereafter.

4. Paragraph 2 shall not apply in respect of Union goods that are carried by sea and have been shipped between ports in the customs territory of the United Kingdom and ports in the customs territory of the Union by a regular shipping service, as referred to in Article 120 of Commission Delegated Regulation (EU) 2015/2446, provided that:

(a) the voyage comprising the ports in the customs territory of the United Kingdom and ports in the customs territory of the Union started before the end of the transition period and ended thereafter; and

(b) the regular shipping service vessel called at one or several ports in the customs territory of the United Kingdom or in the customs territory of the Union before the end of the transition period.

5. When during the voyage referred to in point (a) of paragraph 4 the regular shipping service vessel calls at one or several ports in the customs territory of the United Kingdom after the end of the transition period:

(a) for goods loaded before the end of the transition period and unloaded in those ports, the customs status of Union goods shall not be altered;

(b) for goods loaded in ports called after the end of the transition period, the customs status of Union goods shall not be altered provided that it is proven in accordance with paragraph 2.

Article 48 Entry summary declaration and pre-departure declaration

1. Regulation (EU) No 952/2013 shall apply in respect of entry summary declarations that were lodged at a customs office of first entry in accordance with Chapter I of Title IV of that Regulation before the end of the transition period, and those declarations shall produce the same legal effects in the customs territory of the Union and the customs territory of the United Kingdom after the end of the transition period.

2. Regulation (EU) No 952/2013 shall apply in respect of pre-departure declarations that were lodged in accordance with Chapter I of Title VIII of that Regulation before the end of the transition period and, where applicable, where the goods were released in accordance with Article 194 of that Regulation before the end of the transition period. Those declarations shall produce the same legal effects in the customs territory of the Union and the customs territory of the United Kingdom after the end of the transition period.

Article 49 Ending of temporary storage or customs procedures

1. Regulation (EU) No 952/2013 shall apply in respect of non-Union goods that were in temporary storage referred to in point (17) of Article 5 of that Regulation at the end of the transition period and in respect of goods that were under any of the customs procedures referred to in point (16) of Article 5 of that Regulation in the customs territory of the United Kingdom at the end of the transition period, until such temporary storage is ended, until one of the special customs procedures is discharged, until the goods are released for free circulation, or until the goods are taken out of the territory, provided that such event occurs after the end of the transition period but not later than within the corresponding time limit referred to in Annex III.

However, points (b) and (c) of Article 148(5) and Article 219 of Regulation (EU) No 952/2013 shall not apply in respect of movements of goods between the customs territory of the United Kingdom and the customs territory of the Union which end after the end of the transition period.

2. Regulation (EU) No 952/2013, Council Decision 2014/335/EU, Euratom, Council Regulation (EU, Euratom) No 608/2014 and Council Regulation (EU, Euratom) No 609/2014 shall apply in respect of any customs debt arising after the end of the transition period from the end of temporary storage or discharge referred to in paragraph 1.

3. Section 1 of Chapter 1 of Title II of Implementing Regulation (EU) 2015/2447 shall apply in respect of requests to benefit from tariff quotas which have been accepted by the customs authorities in the customs territory of the United Kingdom and where the required supporting documents have been provided in accordance with Article 50 of that Regulation by the customs authorities in the customs territory of the United Kingdom before the end of the transition period, and shall apply in respect of the cancellation of requests and returns of unused allocated quantities of such requests.

Article 50 Access to relevant networks, information systems and databases

By way of derogation from Article 8, the United Kingdom shall have access, to the extent strictly necessary to comply with its obligations under this Title, to the networks, information systems and databases listed in Annex IV. The United Kingdom shall reimburse the Union for the actual costs incurred by the Union as a consequence of facilitating that access. The Union shall communicate to the United Kingdom the amount of those costs by 31 March of each year until the end of the period referred to in Annex IV. In the event that the communicated amount of the actual costs incurred considerably diverges from the best estimates amount that was communicated by the Union to the United Kingdom before the signature of this Agreement, the United Kingdom shall pay without delay to the Union the best estimates amount and the Joint Committee shall determine the manner in which the difference between the actual costs incurred and the best estimates amount is to be addressed.

Title X Union judicial and administrative procedures

Chapter 1 Judicial procedures

Article 86 Pending cases before the Court of Justice of the European Union

1. The Court of Justice of the European Union shall continue to have jurisdiction in any proceedings brought by or against the United Kingdom before the end of the transition period. Such jurisdiction shall apply to all stages of proceedings, including appeal proceedings before the Court of Justice and proceedings before the General Court where the case is referred back to the General Court.

2. The Court of Justice of the European Union shall continue to have jurisdiction to give preliminary rulings on requests from courts and tribunals of the United Kingdom made before the end of the transition period.

3. For the purposes of this Chapter, proceedings shall be considered as having been brought before the Court of Justice of the European Union, and requests for preliminary rulings shall be considered as having been made, at the moment at which the document initiating the proceedings has been registered by the registry of the Court of Justice or the General Court, as the case may be.

Article 87 New cases before the Court of Justice

1. If the European Commission considers that the United Kingdom has failed to fulfil an obligation under the Treaties or under Part Four of this Agreement before the end of the transition period, the European Commission may, within 4 years after the end of the transition period, bring the matter before the Court of Justice of the European Union in accordance with the requirements laid down in Article 258 TFEU or the second subparagraph of Article 108(2) TFEU, as the case may be. The Court of Justice of the European Union shall have jurisdiction over such cases.

2. If the United Kingdom does not comply with a decision referred to in Article 95(1) of this Agreement, or fails to give legal effect in the United Kingdom's legal order to a decision, as referred to in that provision, that was addressed to a natural or legal person residing or established in the United Kingdom, the European Commission may, within 4 years from the date of the decision concerned, bring the matter to the Court of Justice of the European Union in accordance with the requirements laid down in Article 258 TFEU or the second subparagraph of Article 108(2) TFEU, as the case may be. The Court of Justice of the European Union shall have jurisdiction over such cases.

3. In deciding to bring matters under this Article, the European Commission shall apply the same principles in respect of the United Kingdom as in respect of any Member State.

Article 88 Procedural rules

The provisions of Union law governing the procedure before the Court of Justice of the European Union shall apply in respect of the proceedings and requests for preliminary rulings referred to in this Title.

Article 89 Binding force and enforceability of judgments and orders

1. Judgments and orders of the Court of Justice of the European Union handed down before the end of the transition period, as well as such judgments and orders handed down after the end of the

transition period in proceedings referred to in Articles 86 and 87, shall have binding force in their entirety on and in the United Kingdom.

2. If, in a judgment referred to in paragraph 1, the Court of Justice of the European Union finds that the United Kingdom has failed to fulfil an obligation under the Treaties or this Agreement, the United Kingdom shall take the necessary measures to comply with that judgment.

3. Articles 280 and 299 TFEU shall apply in the United Kingdom in respect of the enforcement of the judgments and orders of the Court of Justice of the European Union referred to in paragraph 1 of this Article.

Article 90 Right to intervene and participate in the procedure

Until the judgments and orders of the Court of Justice of the European Union in all proceedings and requests for preliminary rulings referred to in Article 86 have become final, the United Kingdom may intervene in the same way as a Member State or, in the cases brought before the Court of Justice of the European Union in accordance with Article 267 TFEU, participate in the procedure before the Court of Justice of the European Union in the same way as a Member State. During that period, the Registrar of the Court of Justice of the European Union shall notify the United Kingdom, at the same time and in the same manner as the Member States, of any case referred to the Court of Justice of the European Union for a preliminary ruling by a court or tribunal of a Member State.

The United Kingdom may also intervene or participate in the procedure before the Court of Justice of the European Union in the same way as a Member State:

(a) in relation to cases which concern a failure to fulfil obligations under the Treaties, where the United Kingdom was subject to the same obligations before the end of the transition period, and where such cases are brought before the Court of Justice of the European Union in accordance with Articles 258 TFEU before the end of the period referred to in Article 87(1) or, as the case may be, until the moment, after the end of that period, at which the last judgment or order rendered by the Court of Justice of the European Union on the basis of Article 87(1) has become final;

(b) in relation to cases which concern acts or provisions of Union law which were applicable before the end of the transition period to and in the United Kingdom and which are brought before Court of Justice of the European Union in accordance with Article 267 TFEU before the end of the period referred to in Article 87(1) or, as the case may be, until the moment, after the end of that period, at which the last judgment or order rendered by the Court of Justice on the basis of Article 87(1) has become final; and

(c) in relation to the cases referred to in Article 95(3).

Article 91 Representation before the Court

1. Without prejudice to Article 88, where, before the end of the transition period, a lawyer authorised to practise before the courts or tribunals of the United Kingdom represented or assisted a party in proceedings before the Court of Justice of the European Union or in relation to requests for preliminary rulings made before the end of the transition period, that lawyer may continue to represent or assist that party in those proceedings or in relation to those requests. This right shall apply to all stages of proceedings, including appeal proceedings before the Court of Justice and proceedings before the General Court after a case has been referred back to it.

2. Without prejudice to Article 88, lawyers authorised to practise before the courts or tribunals of the United Kingdom may represent or assist a party before the Court of Justice of the European Union in the cases referred to in Article 87 and Article 95(3). Lawyers authorised to practise before the courts or tribunals of the United Kingdom may also represent or assist the United Kingdom in the proceedings covered by Article 90 in which the United Kingdom has decided to intervene or participate.

3. When representing or assisting a party before the Court of Justice of the European Union in the cases referred to in paragraphs 1 and 2, lawyers authorised to practise before the courts or tribunals of the United Kingdom shall in every respect be treated as lawyers authorised to practise before courts or tribunals of Member States representing or assisting a party before the Court of Justice of the European Union.

PART SIX INSTITUTIONAL AND FINAL PROVISIONS

TITLE II INSTITUTIONAL PROVISIONS

Article 164 Joint Committee

1. A Joint Committee, comprising representatives of the Union and of the United Kingdom, is hereby established. The Joint Committee shall be co-chaired by the Union and the United Kingdom.

2. The Joint Committee shall meet at the request of the Union or the United Kingdom, and in any event shall meet at least once a year. The Joint Committee shall set its meeting schedule and its agenda by mutual consent. The work of the Joint Committee shall be governed by the rules of procedure set out in Annex VIII to this Agreement.

3. The Joint Committee shall be responsible for the implementation and application of this Agreement. The Union and the United Kingdom may each refer to the Joint Committee any issue relating to the implementation, application and interpretation of this Agreement.

4. The Joint Committee shall:
   (a) supervise and facilitate the implementation and application of this Agreement;
   (b) decide on the tasks of the specialised committees and supervise their work;
   (c) seek appropriate ways and methods of preventing problems that might arise in areas covered by this Agreement or of resolving disputes that may arise regarding the interpretation and application of this Agreement;
   (d) consider any matter of interest relating to an area covered by this Agreement;
   (e) adopt decisions and make recommendations as set out in Article 166; and
   (f) adopt amendments to this Agreement in the cases provided for in this Agreement.

5. The Joint Committee may:
   (a) delegate responsibilities to specialised committees, except those responsibilities referred to in points (b), (e) and (f) of paragraph 4;
   (b) establish specialised committees other than those established by Article 165, in order to assist the Joint Committee in the performance of its tasks;
   (c) change the tasks assigned to specialised committees and dissolve any of those committees;
   (d) except in relation to Parts One, Four and Six, until the end of the fourth year following the end of the transition period, adopt decisions amending this Agreement, provided that such amendments are necessary to correct errors, to address omissions or other deficiencies, or to address situations unforeseen when this Agreement was signed, and provided that such decisions may not amend the essential elements of this Agreement;
   (e) adopt amendments to the rules of procedure set out in Annex VIII; and
   (f) take such other actions in the exercise of its functions as decided by the Union and the United Kingdom.

6. The Joint Committee shall issue an annual report on the functioning of this Agreement.

(All other Articles omitted as these are covered in the Trade and Cooperation Agreement extracts of which are reproduced later.)

Protocol on Ireland/Northern Ireland/(The Windsor Framework)*

(RECITALS OMITTED)

The Union and the United Kingdom,

HAVE AGREED UPON the following provisions, which shall be annexed to the Withdrawal Agreement:

Article 1 Objectives

1. This Protocol is without prejudice to the provisions of the 1998 Agreement in respect of the constitutional status of Northern Ireland and the principle of consent, which provides that any change in that status can only be made with the consent of a majority of its people.

2. This Protocol respects the essential State functions and territorial integrity of the United Kingdom.

3. This Protocol sets out arrangements necessary to address the unique circumstances on the island of Ireland, to maintain the necessary conditions for continued North-South cooperation, to avoid a hard border and to protect the 1998 Agreement in all its dimensions.

Article 2 Rights of individuals

1. The United Kingdom shall ensure that no diminution of rights, safeguards or equality of opportunity, as set out in that part of the 1998 Agreement entitled Rights, Safeguards and Equality of Opportunity results from its withdrawal from the Union, including in the area of protection against discrimination, as enshrined in the provisions of Union law listed in Annex 1 to this Protocol, and shall implement this paragraph through dedicated mechanisms.

2. The United Kingdom shall continue to facilitate the related work of the institutions and bodies set up pursuant to the 1998 Agreement, including the Northern Ireland Human Rights Commission, the Equality Commission for Northern Ireland and the Joint Committee of representatives of the Human Rights Commissions of Northern Ireland and Ireland, in upholding human rights and equality standards.

Article 3 Common Travel Area

1. The United Kingdom and Ireland may continue to make arrangements between themselves relating to the movement of persons between their territories (the 'Common Travel Area'), while fully respecting the rights of natural persons conferred by Union law.

2. The United Kingdom shall ensure that the Common Travel Area and the rights and privileges associated therewith can continue to apply without affecting the obligations of Ireland under Union law, in particular with respect to free movement to, from and within Ireland for Union citizens and their family members, irrespective of their nationality.

Article 4 Customs territory of the United Kingdom

Northern Ireland is part of the customs territory of the United Kingdom.

Accordingly, nothing in this Protocol shall prevent the United Kingdom from including Northern Ireland in the territorial scope of any agreements it may conclude with third countries, provided that those agreements do not prejudice the application of this Protocol.

In particular, nothing in this Protocol shall prevent the United Kingdom from concluding agreements with a third country that grant goods produced in Northern Ireland preferential access to that country's market on the same terms as goods produced in other parts of the United Kingdom.

* **Editor's Notes**: Taken from OJ 2020 L29/102. Some provisions omitted as noted. Annexes omitted. The Protocol is proposed to be entitled "The Windsor Framework" and, once implemented, will amend the original protocol but mainly through Annexes. Although not finalised at the time of review (May 2023) the changes are predictable enough for me to have made the amendments to this text in advance of this and noted in footnotes following. A Statutory Instrument has now been drafted to put the Framework into law: https://www.legislation.gov.uk/ukdsi/2023/9780348246322.

Nothing in this Protocol shall prevent the United Kingdom from including Northern Ireland in the territorial scope of its Schedules of Concessions annexed to the General Agreement on Tariffs and Trade 1994.

Article 5 Customs, movement of goods

1. No customs duties shall be payable for a good brought into Northern Ireland from another part of the United Kingdom by direct transport, notwithstanding paragraph 3, unless that good is at risk of subsequently being moved into the Union, whether by itself or forming part of another good following processing.

The customs duties in respect of a good being moved by direct transport to Northern Ireland other than from the Union or from another part of the United Kingdom shall be the duties applicable in the United Kingdom, notwithstanding paragraph 3, unless that good is at risk of subsequently being moved into the Union, whether by itself or forming part of another good following processing.

No duties shall be payable by, as relief shall be granted to, residents of the United Kingdom for personal property, as defined in point (c) of Article 2(1) of Council Regulation (EC) No 1186/2009, brought into Northern Ireland from another part of the United Kingdom.

2. For the purposes of the first and second subparagraphs of paragraph 1, a good brought into Northern Ireland from outside the Union shall be considered to be at risk of subsequently being moved into the Union unless it is established that that good:

(a) will not be subject to commercial processing in Northern Ireland; and

(b) fulfils the criteria established by the Joint Committee in accordance with the fourth subparagraph of this paragraph.

For the purposes of this paragraph, 'processing' means any alteration of goods, any transformation of goods in any way, or any subjecting of goods to operations other than for the purpose of preserving them in good condition or for adding or affixing marks, labels, seals or any other documentation to ensure compliance with any specific requirements.

Before the end of the transition period, the Joint Committee shall by decision establish the conditions under which processing is to be considered not to fall within point (a) of the first subparagraph, taking into account in particular the nature, scale and result of the processing.

Before the end of the transition period, the Joint Committee shall by decision establish the criteria for considering that a good brought into Northern Ireland from outside the Union is not at risk of subsequently being moved into the Union. The Joint Committee shall take into consideration, *inter alia*:

(a) the final destination and use of the good;

(b) the nature and value of the good;

(c) the nature of the movement; and

(d) the incentive for undeclared onward-movement into the Union, in particular incentives resulting from the duties payable pursuant to paragraph 1.

The Joint Committee may amend at any time its decisions adopted pursuant to this paragraph.

In taking any decision pursuant to this paragraph, the Joint Committee shall have regard to the specific circumstances in Northern Ireland.

3. Legislation as defined in point (2) of Article 5 of Regulation (EU) No 952/2013 shall apply to and in the United Kingdom in respect of Northern Ireland (not including the territorial waters of the United Kingdom). However, the Joint Committee shall establish the conditions, including in quantitative terms, under which certain fishery and aquaculture products, as set out in Annex I to Regulation (EU) No 1379/2013 of the European Parliament and of the Council, brought into the customs territory of the Union defined in Article 4 of Regulation (EU) No 952/2013 by vessels flying the flag of the United Kingdom and having their port of registration in Northern Ireland are exempted from duties.

4. The provisions of Union law listed in Annex 2 to this Protocol shall also apply, under the conditions set out in that Annex, to and in the United Kingdom in respect of Northern Ireland.

5. Articles 30 and 110 TFEU shall apply to and in the United Kingdom in respect of Northern Ireland. Quantitative restrictions on exports and imports shall be prohibited between the Union and Northern Ireland.

6. Customs duties levied by the United Kingdom in accordance with paragraph 3 are not remitted to the Union.

Subject to Article 10, the United Kingdom may in particular:

(a) reimburse duties levied pursuant to the provisions of Union law made applicable by paragraph 3 in respect of goods brought into Northern Ireland;
(b) provide for circumstances in which a customs debt which has arisen is to be waived in respect of goods brought into Northern Ireland;
(c) provide for circumstances in which customs duties are to be reimbursed in respect of goods that can be shown not to have entered the Union; and
(d) compensate undertakings to offset the impact of the application of paragraph 3.

In taking decisions under Article 10, the European Commission shall take the circumstances in Northern Ireland into account as appropriate.

7. No duties shall be payable on consignments of negligible value, on consignments sent by one individual to another or on goods contained in travellers' personal baggage, under the conditions set out in the legislation referred to in paragraph 3.

Article 6 Protection of the UK internal market

1. Nothing in this Protocol shall prevent the United Kingdom from ensuring unfettered market access for goods moving from Northern Ireland to other parts of the United Kingdom's internal market. Provisions of Union law made applicable by this Protocol which prohibit or restrict the exportation of goods shall only be applied to trade between Northern Ireland and other parts of the United Kingdom to the extent strictly required by any international obligations of the Union. The United Kingdom shall ensure full protection under international requirements and commitments that are relevant to the prohibitions and restrictions on the exportation of goods from the Union to third countries as set out in Union law.

2. Having regard to Northern Ireland's integral place in the United Kingdom's internal market, the Union and the United Kingdom shall use their best endeavours to facilitate the trade between Northern Ireland and other parts of the United Kingdom, in accordance with applicable legislation and taking into account their respective regulatory regimes as well as the implementation thereof.

This includes specific arrangements for the movement of goods within the United Kingdom's internal market, consistent with Northern Ireland's position as part of the customs territory of the United Kingdom in accordance with this Protocol, where the goods are destined for final consumption or final use in Northern Ireland and where the necessary safeguards are in place to protect the integrity of the Union's internal market and customs union.*

The Joint Committee shall keep the application of this paragraph under constant review and shall adopt appropriate recommendations with a view to avoiding controls at the ports and airports of Northern Ireland to the extent possible.

3. Nothing in this Protocol shall prevent a product originating from Northern Ireland from being presented as originating from the United Kingdom when placed on the market in Great Britain.

4. Nothing in this Protocol shall affect the law of the United Kingdom regulating the placing on the market in other parts of the United Kingdom of goods from Northern Ireland that comply with or benefit from technical regulations, assessments, registrations, certificates, approvals or authorisations governed by provisions of Union law referred to in Annex 2 to this Protocol.

Article 7 Technical regulations, assessments, registrations, certificates, approvals and authorisations [7.1 and 7.2 omitted]

1. Without prejudice to the provisions of Union law referred to in Annex 2 to this Protocol, the lawfulness of placing goods on the market in Northern Ireland shall be governed by the law of the United Kingdom as well as, as regards goods imported from the Union, by Articles 34 and 36 TFEU.

* **Editor's Note:** As amended by the Joint EU-UK Withdrawal Agreement Committee (see Art 164 of the 2020 Withdrawal Agreement, extract reproduced above) Decision 1/2023, Art 1. https://commission.europa.eu/system/files/2023-03/Joint%20Committee%20Decision%20No%201-2023.pdf.

The first subparagraph does not prevent the test and release by a qualified person in Northern Ireland of a batch of a medicinal product imported into or manufactured in Northern Ireland.

Articles 8 to 10 [Omitted]

Article 11 Other areas of North-South cooperation

1. Consistent with the arrangements set out in Articles 5 to 10, and in full respect of Union law, this Protocol shall be implemented and applied so as to maintain the necessary conditions for continued North-South cooperation, including in the areas of environment, health, agriculture, transport, education and tourism, as well as in the areas of energy, telecommunications, broadcasting, inland fisheries, justice and security, higher education and sport.

In full respect of Union law, the United Kingdom and Ireland may continue to make new arrangements that build on the provisions of the 1998 Agreement in other areas of North-South cooperation on the island of Ireland.

2. The Joint Committee shall keep under constant review the extent to which the implementation and application of this Protocol maintains the necessary conditions for North-South cooperation. The Joint Committee may make appropriate recommendations to the Union and the United Kingdom in this respect, including on a recommendation from the Specialised Committee.

Article 12 Implementation, application, supervision and enforcement

1. Without prejudice to paragraph 4, the authorities of the United Kingdom shall be responsible for implementing and applying the provisions of Union law made applicable by this Protocol to and in the United Kingdom in respect of Northern Ireland.

2. Without prejudice to paragraph 4 of this Article, Union representatives shall have the right to be present during any activities of the authorities of the United Kingdom related to the implementation and application of provisions of Union law made applicable by this Protocol, as well as activities related to the implementation and application of Article 5, and the United Kingdom shall provide, upon request, all relevant information relating to such activities. The United Kingdom shall facilitate such presence of Union representatives and shall provide them with the information requested. Where the Union representative requests the authorities of the United Kingdom to carry out control measures in individual cases for duly stated reasons, the authorities of the United Kingdom shall carry out those control measures.

The Union and the United Kingdom shall exchange information on the application of Article 5 (1) and (2) on a monthly basis.

3. The practical working arrangements relating to the exercise of the rights of Union representatives referred to in paragraph 2 shall be determined by the Joint Committee, upon proposal from the Specialised Committee.

4. As regards the second subparagraph of paragraph 2 of this Article, Article 5 and Articles 7 to 10, the institutions, bodies, offices, and agencies of the Union shall in relation to the United Kingdom and natural and legal persons residing or established in the territory of the United Kingdom have the powers conferred upon them by Union law. In particular, the Court of Justice of the European Union shall have the jurisdiction provided for in the Treaties in this respect. The second and third paragraphs of Article 267 TFEU shall apply to and in the United Kingdom in this respect.

5. Acts of the institutions, bodies, offices, and agencies of the Union adopted in accordance with paragraph 4 shall produce in respect of and in the United Kingdom the same legal effects as those which they produce within the Union and its Member States.

6. When representing or assisting a party in relation to administrative procedures arising from the exercise of the powers of the institutions, bodies, offices, and agencies of the Union referred to in paragraph 4, lawyers authorised to practise before the courts or tribunals of the United Kingdom shall in every respect be treated as lawyers authorised to practise before courts or tribunals of Member States who represent or assist a party in relation to such administrative procedures.

7. In cases brought before the Court of Justice of the European Union pursuant to paragraph 4:

(a) the United Kingdom may participate in the proceedings before the Court of Justice of the European Union in the same way as a Member State;

(b) lawyers authorised to practise before the courts or tribunals of the United Kingdom may represent or assist a party before the Court of Justice of the European Union in such proceedings and shall in every respect be treated as lawyers authorised to practise before courts or tribunals of Member States representing or assisting a party before the Court of Justice of the European Union.

Article 13 Common provisions

1. For the purposes of this Protocol, any reference to the United Kingdom in the applicable provisions of the Withdrawal Agreement shall be read as referring to the United Kingdom or to the United Kingdom in respect of Northern Ireland, as the case may be.

Notwithstanding any other provisions of this Protocol, any reference to the territory defined in Article 4 of Regulation (EU) No 952/2013 in the applicable provisions of the Withdrawal Agreement and of this Protocol, as well as in the provisions of Union law made applicable to and in the United Kingdom in respect of Northern Ireland by this Protocol, shall be read as including the part of the territory of the United Kingdom to which Regulation (EU) No 952/2013 applies by virtue of Article 5(3) of this Protocol.

Titles I and III of Part Three and Part Six of the Withdrawal Agreement shall apply without prejudice to the provisions of this Protocol.

2. Notwithstanding Article 4(4) and (5) of the Withdrawal Agreement, the provisions of this Protocol referring to Union law or to concepts or provisions thereof shall in their implementation and application be interpreted in conformity with the relevant case law of the Court of Justice of the European Union.

3. Notwithstanding Article 6(1) of the Withdrawal Agreement, and unless otherwise provided, where this Protocol makes reference to a Union act, that reference shall be read as referring to that Union act as amended or replaced.

3a.* By derogation from paragraph 3, and subject to the fourth subparagraph of this paragraph, a Union act covered by this paragraph that has been amended or replaced by a specific Union act (hereinafter: "specific Union act") shall not apply as amended or replaced by the specific Union act as from two weeks after the day on which the United Kingdom has notified the Union in writing through the Joint Committee that the procedure set out in the unilateral declaration on involvement of the institutions of the 1998 Agreement made by the United Kingdom, as annexed as Annex I to Joint Committee Decision 1/2023, has been followed.

Such notification shall be made within two months of the publication of the specific Union act and shall include a detailed explanation of the United Kingdom's assessment as regards the conditions referred to in the third subparagraph of this paragraph, as well as of the procedural steps taken within the United Kingdom prior to the notification. If the Union considers that the United Kingdom's explanation is insufficient as regards the circumstances referred to in the third subparagraph of this paragraph, it may request further explanation within two weeks as of the date of notification and the United Kingdom shall provide that further explanation within two weeks as of the date of the request. In that case the Union act covered by this paragraph shall not apply as amended or replaced by the specific Union act as from the third day after the day on which the United Kingdom has provided that further explanation.

The United Kingdom shall make the notification referred to in the first subparagraph of this paragraph only where:

(a) the content or scope of the Union act as amended or replaced by the specific Union act significantly differs, in whole or in part, from the content or scope of the Union act as applicable before being amended or replaced; and

(b) the application in Northern Ireland of the Union act as amended or replaced by the specific Union act, or of the relevant part thereof as the case may be, would have a significant impact specific to everyday life of communities in Northern Ireland in a way that is liable to persist.

* **Editor's Note:** As amended by the Joint EU-UK Withdrawal Agreement Committee (see Art 164 of the 2020 Withdrawal Agreement, extract reproduced above) Decision 1/2023, Art 2. https://commission.europa.eu/system/files/2023-03/Joint%20Committee%20Decision%20No%201-2023.pdf

Where the conditions set out in points (a) and (b) are met in relation only to a part of the Union act as amended or replaced by the specific Union act, the notification shall be made only in respect of that part, provided that the latter is severable from the other parts of the Union act as amended or replaced by the specific Union act. If the latter is not severable, the notification shall be made in respect of the smallest severable element of the Union act as amended or replaced by the specific Union act containing the part in question.

Where the notification is made in respect of a part of the Union act as amended or replaced by the specific Union act, in accordance with the second sentence of the previous subparagraph, the Union act shall not apply as amended or replaced by the specific Union act only in respect of that part.

Where the notification referred to in the first subparagraph of this paragraph has been made, paragraph 4 shall apply with regard to the Union act as amended or replaced by the specific Union act; in case the Union act as amended or replaced by the specific Union act is added to this Protocol, this shall be in lieu of the Union act before being amended or replaced.

This paragraph covers Union acts referred to in the first indent of heading 1 and headings 7 to 47 of Annex 2 to this Protocol, and the third subparagraph of Article 5(1) thereof.

4. Where the Union adopts a new act that falls within the scope of this Protocol, but which neither amends nor replaces a Union act listed in the Annexes to this Protocol, the Union shall inform the United Kingdom of the adoption of that act in the Joint Committee. Upon the request of the Union or the United Kingdom, the Joint Committee shall hold an exchange of views on the implications of the newly adopted act for the proper functioning of this Protocol, within 6 weeks after the request.

As soon as reasonably practical after the Union has informed the United Kingdom in the Joint Committee, the Joint Committee shall either:

(a) adopt a decision adding the newly adopted act to the relevant Annex to this Protocol; or

(b) where an agreement on adding the newly adopted act to the relevant Annex to this Protocol cannot be reached, examine all further possibilities to maintain the good functioning of this Protocol and take any decision necessary to this effect.

If the Joint Committee has not taken a decision referred to in the second subparagraph within a reasonable time, the Union shall be entitled, after giving notice to the United Kingdom, to take appropriate remedial measures. Such measures shall take effect at the earliest 6 months after the Union informed the United Kingdom in accordance with the first subparagraph, but in no event shall such measures take effect before the date on which the newly adopted act is implemented in the Union.

5. By way of derogation from paragraph 1 of this Article and from Article 7 of the Withdrawal Agreement, unless the Union considers that full or partial access by the United Kingdom or the United Kingdom in respect of Northern Ireland, as the case may be, is strictly necessary to enable the United Kingdom to comply with its obligations under this Protocol, including where such access is necessary because access to the relevant information cannot be facilitated by the working group referred to in Article 15 of this Protocol or by any other practical means, in respect of access to any network, information system or database established on the basis of Union law, references to Member States and competent authorities of Member States in provisions of Union law made applicable by this Protocol shall not be read as including the United Kingdom or the United Kingdom in respect of Northern Ireland, as the case may be.

6. Authorities of the United Kingdom shall not act as leading authority for risk assessments, examinations, approvals and authorisation procedures provided for in Union law made applicable by this Protocol.

7. Articles 346 and 347 TFEU shall apply to this Protocol as regards measures taken by a Member State or by the United Kingdom in respect of Northern Ireland.

8. Any subsequent agreement between the Union and the United Kingdom shall indicate the parts of this Protocol which it supersedes. Once a subsequent agreement between the Union and the United Kingdom becomes applicable after the entry into force of the Withdrawal Agreement, this Protocol shall then, from the date of application of such subsequent agreement and in accordance with the provisions of that agreement setting out the effect of that agreement on this Protocol, not apply or shall cease to apply, as the case may be, in whole or in part.

Article 14 Specialised Committee

The Committee on issues related to the implementation of the Protocol on Ireland/Northern Ireland established by Article 165 of the Withdrawal Agreement ('Specialised Committee') shall:

(a) facilitate the implementation and application of this Protocol;
(b) examine proposals concerning the implementation and application of this Protocol from the North-South Ministerial Council and North-South Implementation bodies set up under the 1998 Agreement;
(c) consider any matter of relevance to Article 2 of this Protocol brought to its attention by the Northern Ireland Human Rights Commission, the Equality Commission for Northern Ireland, and the Joint Committee of representatives of the Human Rights Commissions of Northern Ireland and Ireland;
(d) discuss any point raised by the Union or the United Kingdom that is of relevance to this Protocol and gives rise to a difficulty; and
(e) make recommendations to the Joint Committee as regards the functioning of this Protocol.

Article 15 Joint consultative working group

1. A joint consultative working group on the implementation of this Protocol ('working group') is hereby established. It shall serve as a forum for the exchange of information and mutual consultation.

2. The working group shall be composed of representatives of the Union and the United Kingdom and shall carry out its functions under the supervision of the Specialised Committee, to which it shall report. The working group shall have no power to take binding decisions other than the power to adopt its own rules of procedure referred to in paragraph 6.

3. Within the working group:

(a) the Union and the United Kingdom shall, in a timely manner, exchange information about planned, ongoing and final relevant implementation measures in relation to the Union acts listed in the Annexes to this Protocol;
(b) the Union shall inform the United Kingdom about planned Union acts within the scope of this Protocol, including Union acts that amend or replace the Union acts listed in the Annexes to this Protocol;
(c) the Union shall provide to the United Kingdom all information the Union considers relevant to allow the United Kingdom to fully comply with its obligations under the Protocol; and
(d) the United Kingdom shall provide to the Union all information that Member States are required to provide to one another or to the institutions, bodies, offices or agencies of the Union pursuant to the Union acts listed in the Annexes to this Protocol.

4. The working group shall be co-chaired by the Union and the United Kingdom.

5. The working group shall meet at least once a month, unless otherwise decided by the Union and the United Kingdom by mutual consent. Where necessary, the Union and the United Kingdom may exchange information referred to in points (c) and (d) of paragraph 3 between meetings.

6. The working group shall adopt its own rules of procedure by mutual consent.

7. The Union shall ensure that all views expressed by the United Kingdom in the working group and all information provided by the United Kingdom in the working group, including technical and scientific data, are communicated to the relevant institutions, bodies, offices and agencies of the Union without undue delay.

Article 16 Safeguards

1. If the application of this Protocol leads to serious economic, societal or environmental difficulties that are liable to persist, or to diversion of trade, the Union or the United Kingdom may unilaterally take appropriate safeguard measures. Such safeguard measures shall be restricted with

regard to their scope and duration to what is strictly necessary in order to remedy the situation. Priority shall be given to such measures as will least disturb the functioning of this Protocol.

2. If a safeguard measure taken by the Union or the United Kingdom, as the case may be, in accordance with paragraph 1 creates an imbalance between the rights and obligations under this Protocol, the Union or the United Kingdom, as the case may be, may take such proportionate rebalancing measures as are strictly necessary to remedy the imbalance. Priority shall be given to such measures as will least disturb the functioning of this Protocol.

3. Safeguard and rebalancing measures taken in accordance with paragraphs 1 and 2 shall be governed by the procedures set out in Annex 7 to this Protocol.

Article 17 Protection of financial interests

The Union and the United Kingdom shall counter fraud and any other illegal activities affecting the financial interests of the Union or the financial interests of the United Kingdom.

Article 18 Democratic consent in Northern Ireland

1. Within 2 months before the end of both the initial period and any subsequent period, the United Kingdom shall provide the opportunity for democratic consent in Northern Ireland to the continued application of Articles 5 to 10.

2. For the purposes of paragraph 1, the United Kingdom shall seek democratic consent in Northern Ireland in a manner consistent with the 1998 Agreement. A decision expressing democratic consent shall be reached strictly in accordance with the unilateral declaration concerning the operation of the 'Democratic consent in Northern Ireland' provision of the Protocol on Ireland/Northern Ireland made by the United Kingdom on 17 October 2019, including with respect to the roles of the Northern Ireland Executive and Assembly.

3. The United Kingdom shall notify the Union before the end of the relevant period referred to in paragraph 5 of the outcome of the process referred to in paragraph 1.

4. Where the process referred to in paragraph 1 has been undertaken and a decision has been reached in accordance with paragraph 2, and the United Kingdom notifies the Union that the outcome of the process referred to in paragraph 1 is not a decision that the Articles of this Protocol referred to in that paragraph should continue to apply in Northern Ireland, then those Articles and other provisions of this Protocol, to the extent that those provisions depend on those Articles for their application, shall cease to apply 2 years after the end of the relevant period referred to in paragraph 5. In such a case the Joint Committee shall address recommendations to the Union and to the United Kingdom on the necessary measures, taking into account the obligations of the parties to the 1998 Agreement. Before doing so, the Joint Committee may seek an opinion from institutions created by the 1998 Agreement.

5. For the purposes of this Article, the initial period is the period ending 4 years after the end of the transition period. Where the decision reached in a given period was on the basis of a majority of Members of the Northern Ireland Assembly, present and voting, the subsequent period is the 4 year period following that period, for as long as Articles 5 to 10 continue to apply. Where the decision reached in a given period had cross-community support, the subsequent period is the 8-year period following that period, for as long as Articles 5 to 10 continue to apply.

6. For the purposes of paragraph 5, cross-community support means:

(a) a majority of those Members of the Legislative Assembly present and voting, including a majority of the unionist and nationalist designations present and voting; or

(b) a weighted majority (60 %) of Members of the Legislative Assembly present and voting, including at least 40 % of each of the nationalist and unionist designations present and voting.

Article 19 Annexes

Annexes 1 to 7 shall form an integral part of this Protocol.

(Annexes omitted.)

European Union (Withdrawal Agreement) Act 2020*

(2020 c. 1)

An Act to implement, and make other provision in connection with, the agreement between the United Kingdom and the EU under Article 50(2) of the Treaty on European Union which sets out the arrangements for the United Kingdom's withdrawal from the EU. [23rd January 2020]

PART 3 CITIZENS' RIGHTS

Rights in relation to entry and residence

7 Rights related to residence: application deadline and temporary protection

(1) A Minister of the Crown may by regulations make such provision as the Minister considers appropriate for any of the following purposes—

(a) specifying the deadline that applies for the purposes of—

(i) the first sub-paragraph of Article 18(1)(b) of the withdrawal agreement (deadline for the submission of applications for the new residence status described in Article 18(1));

(ii) the first sub-paragraph of Article 17(1)(b) of the EEA EFTA separation agreement (deadline for the submission of applications for the new residence status described in Article 17(1));

(iii) the first sentence of Article 16(1)(b) of the Swiss citizens' rights agreement (deadline for the submission of applications for the new residence status described in Article 16(1));

(b) implementing Article 18(2) of the withdrawal agreement (protection for Union citizens etc. in the period prior to the deadline for the submission of applications for the new residence status described in Article 18(1));

(c) implementing Article 17(2) of the EEA EFTA separation agreement (protection for EEA EFTA nationals etc. in the period prior to the deadline for the submission of applications for the new residence status described in Article 17(1));

(d) implementing Article 16(2) of the Swiss citizens' rights agreement (protection for Swiss nationals etc. in the period prior to the deadline for the submission of applications for the new residence status described in Article 16(1));

(e) implementing Article 18(3) of the withdrawal agreement (protection for Union citizens etc. pending a final decision on an application for the new residence status described in Article 18(1));

(f) implementing Article 17(3) of the EEA EFTA separation agreement (protection for EEA EFTA nationals etc. pending a final decision on an application for the new residence status described in Article 17(1));

(g) implementing Article 16(3) of the Swiss citizens' rights agreement (protection for Swiss nationals etc. pending a final decision on an application for the new residence status described in Article 16(1)).

(2) If the Minister considers it appropriate, regulations under subsection (1) relating to the implementation of a provision mentioned in subsection (1)(b), (c) or (d) may be made so as to apply both to—

(a) persons to whom the provision in question applies, and

* **Editor's Note:** The following sections which amended the EUWA 2018 (and can be found in situ within the 2018 Act) have been removed from here: ss. 1–6, 15–24, 28–31, and 33–36. The Schedules have been omitted.

(b) persons to whom that provision does not apply but who may be granted leave to enter or remain in the United Kingdom by virtue of residence scheme immigration rules (see section 17) and who do not have such leave.

(3) If the Minister considers it appropriate, regulations under subsection (1) relating to the implementation of a provision mentioned in subsection (1)(e), (f) or (g) may be made so as to apply both to—

(a) persons to whom the provision in question applies, and
(b) persons to whom that provision does not apply but who make an application for leave to enter or remain in the United Kingdom by virtue of residence scheme immigration rules.

(4) The power to make regulations under subsection (1) may (among other things) be exercised by modifying any provision made by or under an enactment.

8 Frontier workers

(1) A Minister of the Crown may by regulations make such provision as the Minister considers appropriate for the purpose of implementing any of the following—

(a) Articles 24(3) and 25(3) of the withdrawal agreement (rights of employed and self-employed frontier workers) other than as regards rights enjoyed as workers (see section 14(1));
(b) Articles 23(3) and 24(3) of the EEA EFTA separation agreement (rights of employed and self-employed frontier workers) other than as regards rights enjoyed as workers (see section 14(2));
(c) Article 20(2) of the Swiss citizens' rights agreement (rights of frontier workers to enter and exit).

(2) A Minister of the Crown may by regulations make such provision as the Minister considers appropriate for the purpose of implementing any of the following—

(a) Article 26 of the withdrawal agreement (issue of documents);
(b) Article 25 of the EEA EFTA separation agreement (issue of documents);
(c) Article 21(1)(a) and (2) of the Swiss citizens' rights agreement (issue of documents).

(3) The power to make regulations under subsection (1) or (2) may (among other things) be exercised by modifying any provision made by or under the Immigration Acts.

9 Restrictions of rights of entry and residence

(1) A Minister of the Crown may by regulations make such provision as the Minister considers appropriate for the purpose of implementing any of the following—

(a) Article 20(1), (3) and (4) of the withdrawal agreement (restrictions of the rights of entry and residence);
(b) Article 19(1), (3) and (4) of the EEA EFTA separation agreement (restrictions of the rights of entry and residence);
(c) Articles 17(1) and (3) and 20(3) of the Swiss citizens' rights agreement (restrictions of the rights of entry and residence).

(2) If the Minister considers it appropriate, regulations under subsection (1) relating to the implementation of a provision mentioned in subsection (1)(a), (b) or (c) may be made so as to apply both to—

(a) persons to whom the provision in question applies, and
(b) persons to whom that provision does not apply but who—
  (i) have entry clearance granted by virtue of relevant entry clearance immigration rules (see section 17),
  (ii) have leave to enter or remain in the United Kingdom granted by virtue of residence scheme immigration rules (see section 17), or
  (iii) otherwise have leave to enter granted after arriving with entry clearance granted by virtue of relevant entry clearance immigration rules.

(3) In subsection (2)(b), references to a person who has entry clearance or leave to enter or remain include references to a person who would have had entry clearance or leave to enter or remain but for—

(a) the making of a deportation order under section 5(1) of the Immigration Act 1971, or
(b) the making of any other decision made in connection with restricting the right of the person to enter the United Kingdom.

(4) The power to make regulations under subsection (1) may (among other things) be exercised by modifying any provision made—

(a) by or under the Immigration Acts, or
(b) under other primary legislation.

10 Retention of existing grounds for deportation

(1) Section 3 of the Immigration Act 1971 (general provisions for regulation and control) is amended in accordance with subsections (2) to (4).

(2) After subsection (5) insert—

'(5A) The Secretary of State may not deem a relevant person's deportation to be conducive to the public good under subsection (5) if the person's deportation—

(a) would be in breach of the obligations of the United Kingdom under Article 20 of the EU withdrawal agreement, Article 19 of the EEA EFTA separation agreement, or Article 17 or 20(3) of the Swiss citizens' rights agreement, or
(b) would be in breach of those obligations if the provision in question mentioned in paragraph (a) applied in relation to the person.'

(3) After subsection (6) insert—

'(6A) A court may not recommend under subsection (6) that a relevant person be deported if the offence for which the person was convicted consisted of or included conduct that took place before IP completion day.'

(4) After subsection (9) insert—

'(10) For the purposes of this section, a person is a "relevant person"—

(a) if the person is in the United Kingdom (whether or not they have entered within the meaning of section 11(1)) having arrived with entry clearance granted by virtue of relevant entry clearance immigration rules,
(b) if the person has leave to enter or remain in the United Kingdom granted by virtue of residence scheme immigration rules,
(c) if the person may be granted leave to enter or remain in the United Kingdom as a person who has a right to enter the United Kingdom by virtue of—
   (i) Article 32(1)(b) of the EU withdrawal agreement,
   (ii) Article 31(1)(b) of the EEA EFTA separation agreement, or
   (iii) Article 26a(1)(b) of the Swiss citizens' rights agreement,
   whether or not the person has been granted such leave, or
(d) if the person may enter the United Kingdom by virtue of regulations made under section 8 of the European Union (Withdrawal Agreement) Act 2020 (frontier workers), whether or not the person has entered by virtue of those regulations.

(11) In this section—

"EEA EFTA separation agreement" and "Swiss citizens' rights agreement" have the same meanings as in the European Union (Withdrawal Agreement) Act 2020 (see section 39(1) of that Act);

"relevant entry clearance immigration rules" and "residence scheme immigration rules" have the meanings given by section 17 of the European Union (Withdrawal Agreement) Act 2020.'

(5) In section 33 of the UK Borders Act 2007 (exceptions to automatic deportation), after subsection (6A), insert—

'(6B) Exception 7 is where—

(a) the foreign criminal is a relevant person, and
(b) the offence for which the foreign criminal was convicted as mentioned in section 32(1)(b) consisted of or included conduct that took place before IP completion day.

(6C) For the purposes of subsection (6B), a foreign criminal is a "relevant person"—

(a) if the foreign criminal is in the United Kingdom (whether or not they have entered within the meaning of section 11(1) of the Immigration Act 1971) having arrived with entry clearance granted by virtue of relevant entry clearance immigration rules,

(b) if the foreign criminal has leave to enter or remain in the United Kingdom granted by virtue of residence scheme immigration rules,

(c) if the foreign criminal may be granted leave to enter or remain in the United Kingdom as a person who has a right to enter the United Kingdom by virtue of—

(i) Article 32(1)(b) of the EU withdrawal agreement,

(ii) Article 31(1)(b) of the EEA EFTA separation agreement, or

(iii) Article 26a(1)(b) of the Swiss citizens' rights agreement,

whether or not the foreign criminal has been granted such leave, or

(d) if the foreign criminal may enter the United Kingdom by virtue of regulations made under section 8 of the European Union (Withdrawal Agreement) Act 2020 (frontier workers), whether or not the foreign criminal has entered by virtue of those regulations.

(6D) In this section—

"EEA EFTA separation agreement" and "Swiss citizens' rights agreement" have the same meanings as in the European Union (Withdrawal Agreement) Act 2020 (see section 39(1) of that Act);

"relevant entry clearance immigration rules" and "residence scheme immigration rules" have the meanings given by section 17 of the European Union (Withdrawal Agreement) Act 2020.'

(6) In section 3(10) of the Immigration Act 1971 and section 33(6C) of the UK Borders Act 2007 (for which see subsections (4) and (5) above), references to having leave to enter or remain in the United Kingdom granted by virtue of residence scheme immigration rules include references to having such leave granted by virtue of those rules before section 17 comes into force.

11 Appeals etc. against citizens' rights immigration decisions

(1) A Minister of the Crown may by regulations make provision for, or in connection with, appeals against citizens' rights immigration decisions of a kind described in the regulations.

(2) For the purposes of this section, each of the following is a 'citizens' rights immigration decision'—

(a) a decision made in connection with entry clearance by virtue of relevant entry clearance immigration rules (see section 17);

(b) a decision made in connection with leave to enter or remain in the United Kingdom by virtue of residence scheme immigration rules (see section 17);

(c) a decision made in connection with entry clearance for the purposes of acquiring leave to enter or remain in relation to a healthcare right of entry;

(d) a decision made in connection with leave to enter or remain in the United Kingdom in relation to a healthcare right of entry;

(e) a decision made in connection with a right to enter or remain in the United Kingdom by virtue of regulations made under section 8 (frontier workers);

(f) a decision to make, or a refusal to revoke, a deportation order under section 5(1) of the Immigration Act 1971 in relation to a relevant person;

(g) any other decision made in connection with restricting the right of a relevant person to enter the United Kingdom.

(3) A Minister of the Crown may also by regulations make provision for, or in connection with, reviews (including judicial reviews) of decisions within subsection (2)(g).

(4) The power to make regulations under subsection (1) or (3) may (among other things) be exercised by modifying any provision made by or under an enactment.

(5) Such regulations may, for example, apply with or without modifications any enactment which applies in relation to appeals under section 82 of the Nationality, Immigration and Asylum Act 2002 or section 2 of the Special Immigration Appeals Commission Act 1997.

(6) For the purposes of subsection (2), a 'healthcare right of entry' is a right to enter the United Kingdom that a person has by virtue of—

(a) Article 32(1)(b) of the withdrawal agreement,

(b) Article 31(1)(b) of the EEA EFTA separation agreement, or

(c) Article 26a(1)(b) of the Swiss citizens' rights agreement.

(7) For the purposes of subsection (2)(f) and (g), a person is a 'relevant person' if—

(a) Article 20 of the withdrawal agreement, Article 19 of the EEA EFTA separation agreement or (as the case may be) Articles 17 or 20(3) of the Swiss citizens' rights agreement (restrictions of the rights of entry and residence) applies to the person, or
(b) the person is not within paragraph (a) but—
(i) has entry clearance granted by virtue of relevant entry clearance immigration rules,
(ii) has leave to enter or remain in the United Kingdom granted by virtue of residence scheme immigration rules, or
(iii) otherwise has leave to enter granted after arriving with entry clearance granted by virtue of relevant entry clearance immigration rules.

(8) In subsection (7)(b), references to a person who has entry clearance or leave to enter or remain include references to a person who would have had entry clearance or leave to enter or remain but for—
(a) the making of a deportation order under section 5(1) of the Immigration Act 1971, or
(b) the making of any other decision made in connection with restricting the right of the person to enter the United Kingdom.

Professional qualifications

12 Recognition of professional qualifications

(1) An appropriate authority may by regulations make such provision as the authority considers appropriate—
(a) to implement Chapter 3 of Title II of Part 2 of the withdrawal agreement (professional qualifications),
(b) to supplement the effect of section 7A of the European Union (Withdrawal) Act 2018 in relation to that Chapter, or
(c) otherwise for the purposes of dealing with matters arising out of, or related to, that Chapter (including matters arising by virtue of section 7A of that Act and that Chapter).

(2) An appropriate authority may by regulations make such provision as the authority considers appropriate—
(a) to implement Chapter 3 of Title II of Part 2 of the EEA EFTA separation agreement (professional qualifications),
(b) to supplement the effect of section 7B of the European Union (Withdrawal) Act 2018 in relation to that Chapter, or
(c) otherwise for the purposes of dealing with matters arising out of, or related to, that Chapter (including matters arising by virtue of section 7B of that Act and that Chapter).

(3) An appropriate authority may by regulations make such provision as the authority considers appropriate—
(a) to implement professional qualification provisions of the Swiss citizens' rights agreement,
(b) to supplement the effect of section 7B of the European Union (Withdrawal) Act 2018 in relation to those provisions, or
(c) otherwise for the purposes of dealing with matters arising out of, or related to, those provisions (including matters arising by virtue of section 7B of that Act and those provisions).

(4) For the purposes of subsection (3) the following are 'professional qualification provisions' of the Swiss citizens' rights agreement—
(a) Part 4 of that agreement (mutual recognition of professional qualifications);
(b) Article 23(4) of that agreement as regards the recognition of professional qualifications.

(5) If an appropriate authority considers it appropriate, regulations under subsection (1) or (2) relating to the implementation of a provision of Chapter 3 of Title II of Part 2 of the withdrawal agreement or of the EEA EFTA separation agreement may be made so as to apply both to—
(a) persons to whom the provision in question applies, and

(b) persons to whom that provision does not apply but who may be granted leave to enter or remain in the United Kingdom by virtue of residence scheme immigration rules, whether or not they have been granted such leave (see section 17).

(6) The power to make regulations under subsection (1), (2) or (3) may (among other things) be exercised by modifying any provision made by or under an enactment.

(7) In subsection (6) 'enactment' does not include primary legislation passed or made after IP completion day.

(8) In this section, 'appropriate authority' means—

(a) a Minister of the Crown,

(b) a devolved authority, or

(c) a Minister of the Crown acting jointly with a devolved authority.

(9) Schedule 1 contains further provision about the power of devolved authorities to make regulations under this section.

Co-ordination of social security systems

13 Co-ordination of social security systems

(1) An appropriate authority may by regulations make such provision as the authority considers appropriate—

(a) to implement Title III of Part 2 of the withdrawal agreement (co-ordination of social security systems),

(b) to supplement the effect of section 7A of the European Union (Withdrawal) Act 2018 in relation to that Title, or

(c) otherwise for the purposes of dealing with matters arising out of, or related to, that Title (including matters arising by virtue of section 7A of that Act and that Title).

(2) An appropriate authority may by regulations make such provision as the authority considers appropriate—

(a) to implement Title III of Part 2 of the EEA EFTA separation agreement (co-ordination of social security systems),

(b) to supplement the effect of section 7B of the European Union (Withdrawal) Act 2018 in relation to that Title, or

(c) otherwise for the purposes of dealing with matters arising out of, or related to, that Title (including matters arising by virtue of section 7B of that Act and that Title).

(3) An appropriate authority may by regulations make such provision as the authority considers appropriate—

(a) to implement social security co-ordination provisions of the Swiss citizens' rights agreement,

(b) to supplement the effect of section 7B of the European Union (Withdrawal) Act 2018 in relation to those provisions, or

(c) otherwise for the purposes of dealing with matters arising out of, or related to, those provisions (including matters arising by virtue of section 7B of that Act and those provisions).

(4) For the purposes of subsection (3) the following are 'social security co-ordination provisions' of the Swiss citizens' rights agreement—

(a) Part 3 of that agreement (co-ordination of social security systems);

(b) Article 23(4) of that agreement as regards social security co-ordination.

(5) The power to make regulations under subsection (1), (2) or (3) may (among other things) be exercised by modifying any provision made by or under an enactment.

(6) In this section, 'appropriate authority' means—

(a) a Minister of the Crown,

(b) a devolved authority, or

(c) a Minister of the Crown acting jointly with a devolved authority.

(7) Schedule 1 contains further provision about the power of devolved authorities to make regulations under this section.

Equal treatment etc.

14 Non-discrimination, equal treatment and rights of workers etc.

(1) An appropriate authority may by regulations make such provision as the authority considers appropriate for the purpose of implementing any of the following provisions of the withdrawal agreement—

- (a) Article 12 (prohibition of discrimination on grounds of nationality);
- (b) Article 23 (right to equal treatment);
- (c) Articles 24(1) and 25(1) (rights of workers and the self-employed);
- (d) Articles 24(3) and 25(3) (rights of employed or self-employed frontier workers) as regards rights enjoyed as workers.

(2) An appropriate authority may by regulations make such provision as the authority considers appropriate for the purpose of implementing any of the following provisions of the EEA EFTA separation agreement—

- (a) Article 11 (prohibition of discrimination on grounds of nationality);
- (b) Article 22 (right to equal treatment);
- (c) Articles 23(1) and 24(1) (rights of workers and the self-employed);
- (d) Articles 23(3) and 24(3) (rights of employed or self-employed frontier workers) as regards rights enjoyed as workers.

(3) An appropriate authority may by regulations make such provision as the authority considers appropriate for the purpose of implementing any of the following provisions of the Swiss citizens' rights agreement—

- (a) Article 7 (prohibition of discrimination on grounds of nationality);
- (b) Article 18 (right to take up employment etc.);
- (c) Article 19 (rights of employed or self-employed persons etc.);
- (d) Article 20(1) (rights of frontier workers);
- (e) Article 23(1) (rights of persons providing services).

(4) If the appropriate authority considers it appropriate, regulations under subsection (1), (2) or (3) relating to the implementation of a provision mentioned in that subsection, may be made so as to apply both to—

- (a) persons to whom the provision in question applies, and
- (b) persons to whom that provision does not apply but who may be granted leave to enter or remain in the United Kingdom by virtue of residence scheme immigration rules, whether or not they have been granted such leave (see section 17).

(5) The power to make regulations under subsection (1), (2) or (3) may (among other things) be exercised by modifying any provision made by or under an enactment.

(6) In this section, 'appropriate authority' means—

- (a) a Minister of the Crown,
- (b) a devolved authority, or
- (c) a Minister of the Crown acting jointly with a devolved authority.

(7) Schedule 1 contains further provision about the power of devolved authorities to make regulations under this section.

Relationship to EUWA 2018

25 Retention of saved EU law at end of implementation period [Amendments made]

26 Interpretation of retained EU law and relevant separation agreement law [Amendments made]

27 Dealing with deficiencies in retained EU law [Amendments made]

32 Requirements in Part 2 of CRAGA

Section 20 of the Constitutional Reform and Governance Act 2010 (treaties to be laid before Parliament before ratification) does not apply in relation to the withdrawal agreement (but this does not affect whether that section applies in relation to any modification of the agreement).

Other matters

37 Arrangements with EU about unaccompanied children seeking asylum [Amendments made]

PART 5 GENERAL AND FINAL PROVISION

Parliamentary sovereignty

38 Parliamentary sovereignty

(1) It is recognised that the Parliament of the United Kingdom is sovereign.

(2) In particular, its sovereignty subsists notwithstanding—

(a) directly applicable or directly effective EU law continuing to be recognised and available in domestic law by virtue of section 1A or 1B of the European Union (Withdrawal) Act 2018 (savings of existing law for the implementation period),

(b) section 7A of that Act (other directly applicable or directly effective aspects of the withdrawal agreement),

(c) section 7B of that Act (deemed direct applicability or direct effect in relation to the EEA EFTA separation agreement and the Swiss citizens' rights agreement), and

(d) section 7C of that Act (interpretation of law relating to the withdrawal agreement (other than the implementation period), the EEA EFTA separation agreement and the Swiss citizens' rights agreement).

(3) Accordingly, nothing in this Act derogates from the sovereignty of the Parliament of the United Kingdom.

Interpretation

39 Interpretation

(1) In this Act—

'devolved authority' means—

(a) the Scottish Ministers,

(b) the Welsh Ministers, or

(c) a Northern Ireland department;

'EEA EFTA separation agreement' means (as modified from time to time in accordance with any provision of it) the Agreement on arrangements between Iceland, the Principality of Liechtenstein, the Kingdom of Norway and the United Kingdom of Great Britain and Northern Ireland following the withdrawal of the United Kingdom from the European Union, the EEA Agreement and other agreements applicable between the United Kingdom and the EEA EFTA States by virtue of the United Kingdom's membership of the European Union;

'enactment' means an enactment whenever passed or made and includes—

(a) an enactment contained in any Order in Council, order, rules, regulations, scheme, warrant, byelaw or other instrument made under an Act of Parliament,

(b) an enactment contained in any Order in Council made in exercise of Her Majesty's Prerogative,

(c) an enactment contained in, or in an instrument made under, an Act of the Scottish Parliament,

(d) an enactment contained in, or in an instrument made under, a Measure or Act of the National Assembly for Wales,
(e) an enactment contained in, or in an instrument made under, Northern Ireland legislation,
(f) an enactment contained in any instrument made by a member of the Scottish Government, the Welsh Ministers, the First Minister for Wales, the Counsel General to the Welsh Government, a Northern Ireland Minister, the First Minister in Northern Ireland, the deputy First Minister in Northern Ireland or a Northern Ireland department in exercise of prerogative or other executive functions of Her Majesty which are exercisable by such a person on behalf of Her Majesty,
(g) an enactment contained in, or in an instrument made under, a Measure of the Church Assembly or of the General Synod of the Church of England, and
(h) any retained direct EU legislation;

'IP completion day' means 31 December 2020 at 11.00 p.m. (and see subsections (2) to (5));

'Minister of the Crown' has the same meaning as in the Ministers of the Crown Act 1975 and also includes the Commissioners for Her Majesty's Revenue and Customs;

'modify' includes amend, repeal or revoke (and related expressions are to be read accordingly);

'primary legislation' means—
(a) an Act of Parliament,
(b) an Act of the Scottish Parliament,
(c) a Measure or Act of the National Assembly for Wales, or
(d) Northern Ireland legislation;

'subordinate legislation' means any Order in Council, order, rules, regulations, scheme, warrant, byelaw or other instrument made under any primary legislation;

'Swiss citizens' rights agreement' means (as modified from time to time in accordance with any provision of it) the Agreement signed at Bern on 25 February 2019 between the United Kingdom of Great Britain and Northern Ireland and the Swiss Confederation on citizens' rights following the withdrawal of the United Kingdom from—
(a) the European Union, and
(b) the free movement of persons agreement,

so far as the Agreement operates for the purposes of the case where 'specified date' for the purposes of that Agreement has the meaning given in Article 2(b)(ii) of that Agreement;

'withdrawal agreement' means the agreement between the United Kingdom and the EU under Article 50(2) of the Treaty on European Union which sets out the arrangements for the United Kingdom's withdrawal from the EU (as that agreement is modified from time to time in accordance with any provision of it).

(2) In this Act references to before, after or on IP completion day, or to beginning with IP completion day, are to be read as references to before, after or at 11.00 p.m. on 31 December 2020 or (as the case may be) to beginning with 11.00 p.m. on that day.

(3) Subsection (4) applies if, by virtue of any change to EU summer-time arrangements, the transition or implementation period provided for by Part 4 of the withdrawal agreement is to end on a day or time which is different from that specified in the definition of 'IP completion day' in subsection (1).

(4) A Minister of the Crown may by regulations—
(a) amend the definition of 'IP completion day' in subsection (1) to ensure that the day and time specified in the definition are the day and time that the transition or implementation period provided for by Part 4 of the withdrawal agreement is to end, and
(b) amend subsection (2) in consequence of any such amendment.

(5) In subsection (3) 'EU summer-time arrangements' means the arrangements provided for by Directive 2000/84/EC of the European Parliament and of the Council of 19 January 2001 on summer-time arrangements.

(6) In this Act any reference to an Article of the Treaty on European Union includes a reference to that Article as applied by Article 106a of the Euratom Treaty.

Supplementary and final

40 Regulations

Schedule 4 contains provision about regulations under this Act (including provision about procedure).

41 Consequential and transitional provision etc.

(1) A Minister of the Crown may by regulations make such provision as the Minister considers appropriate in consequence of this Act.

(2) The power to make regulations under subsection (1) may (among other things) be exercised by modifying any provision made by or under an enactment.

(3) In subsection (2) 'enactment' does not include primary legislation passed or made after IP completion day.

(4) Parts 1 and 2 of Schedule 5 contain minor and consequential provision.

(5) A Minister of the Crown may by regulations make such transitional, transitory or saving provision as the Minister considers appropriate in connection with the coming into force of any provision of this Act (including its operation in connection with exit day or IP completion day).

(6) Part 3 of Schedule 5 contains transitional, transitory and saving provision.

42 Extent, commencement and short title

(1) Subject to subsections (2) to (5), this Act extends to England and Wales, Scotland and Northern Ireland.

(2) Any provision of this Act which amends or repeals an enactment has the same extent as the enactment amended or repealed.

(3) Accordingly, section 1 (but not section 2) also extends to the Isle of Man, the Channel Islands and Gibraltar.

(4) The power in section 36 of the Immigration Act 1971 or (as the case may be) section 60(4) of the UK Borders Act 2007 may be exercised so as to extend (with or without modifications) to the Isle of Man or any of the Channel Islands the modifications made to that Act by section 10 above.

(5) Paragraphs 1 and 2 of Schedule 5, so far as they relate to the modification of any provision in subordinate legislation which extends outside England and Wales, Scotland and Northern Ireland, also extend there.

(6) The following provisions—

- (a) sections 3 and 4,
- (b) sections 11, 16 and 17,
- (c) sections 20, 29 and 31 to 40 (including Schedule 4),
- (d) section 41(1) to (3) and (5),
- (e) the following provisions of Schedule 5—
  - (i) paragraphs 1(3) to (6) and 2,
  - (ii) paragraph 3(2) to (8),
  - (iii) paragraph 4,
  - (iv) paragraphs 5 and 7(a) and (b),
  - (v) paragraphs 8 and 12(a) and (b),
  - (vi) paragraphs 17, 20, 22, 24, 27 and 31,
  - (vii) paragraphs 32, 36(a) and (b) and 37(b) and (c),
  - (viii) paragraphs 38, 41(1) and (3)(a), 42, 44(1), (2)(a), (d) and (e) and (3), 47(1), (2), (4) and (6) and 50,
  - (ix) paragraphs 51 and 56(1) and (7)(b) for the purposes of making regulations under section 8A of, or Part 1A of Schedule 2 to, the European Union (Withdrawal) Act 2018,
  - (x) paragraphs 52(1) and (3) to (7) and 53(1) to (4), (6), (7)(a), (8)(a) and (9) to (13),
  - (xi) paragraph 56(1) and (6)(b) to (d), and
  - (xii) paragraphs 65 to 68,

(and section 41(4) and (6) so far as relating to any provision so far as it falls within any of sub-paragraphs (i) to (xii)), and

(f) this section,

come into force on the day on which this Act is passed.

(7) The provisions of this Act, so far as they are not brought into force by subsection (6), come into force on such day as a Minister of the Crown may by regulations appoint; and different days may be appointed for different purposes.

(8) This Act may be cited as the European Union (Withdrawal Agreement) Act 2020.

The EU–UK Trade and Cooperation Agreement 2020* (Selected extracts)**

TRADE AND COOPERATION AGREEMENT

between the European Union and the European Atomic Energy Community, of the one part, and the United Kingdom of Great Britain and Northern Ireland, of the other part

Preamble

THE EUROPEAN UNION AND THE EUROPEAN ATOMIC ENERGY COMMUNITY

AND

THE UNITED KINGDOM OF GREAT BRITAIN AND NORTHERN IRELAND,

(RECITALS OMITTED)

HAVE AGREED AS FOLLOWS:

PART ONE COMMON AND INSTITUTIONAL PROVISIONS

Title I General provisions

Article 1 Purpose

This Agreement establishes the basis for a broad relationship between the Parties, within an area of prosperity and good neighbourliness characterised by close and peaceful relations based on cooperation, respectful of the Parties' autonomy and sovereignty.

Article 2 Supplementing agreements

1. Where the Union and the United Kingdom conclude other bilateral agreements between them, such agreements shall constitute supplementing agreements to this Agreement, unless otherwise provided for in those agreements. Such supplementing agreements shall be an integral part of the overall bilateral relations as governed by this Agreement and shall form part of the overall framework.

2. Paragraph 1 also applies to:

(a) agreements between the Union and its Member States, of the one part, and the United Kingdom, of the other part; and

(b) agreements between the European Atomic Energy Community, of the one part, and the United Kingdom, of the other part.

* **Editor's Note:** As published in OJ 2021 L149/10.

** **Editor's Note:** As indicated throughout the text. The decisions to omit or retain Articles are based on the Editor's view on their relevance to subjects covered in EU law modules.

Article 3 Good faith

1. The Parties shall, in full mutual respect and good faith, assist each other in carrying out tasks that flow from this Agreement and any supplementing agreement.

2. They shall take all appropriate measures, whether general or particular, to ensure the fulfilment of the obligations arising from this Agreement and from any supplementing agreement, and shall refrain from any measures which could jeopardise the attainment of the objectives of this Agreement or any supplementing agreement.

Title II Principles of interpretation and definitions

Article 4 Public international law

1. The provisions of this Agreement and any supplementing agreement shall be interpreted in good faith in accordance with their ordinary meaning in their context and in light of the object and purpose of the agreement in accordance with customary rules of interpretation of public international law, including those codified in the Vienna Convention on the Law of Treaties, done at Vienna on 23 May 1969.

2. For greater certainty, neither this Agreement nor any supplementing agreement establishes an obligation to interpret their provisions in accordance with the domestic law of either Party.

3. For greater certainty, an interpretation of this Agreement or any supplementing agreement given by the courts of either Party shall not be binding on the courts of the other Party.

Article 5 Private rights

1. Without prejudice to Article SSC.67 of the Protocol on Social Security Coordination and with the exception, with regard to the Union, of Part Three of this Agreement, nothing in this Agreement or any supplementing agreement shall be construed as conferring rights or imposing obligations on persons other than those created between the Parties under public international law, nor as permitting this Agreement or any supplementing agreement to be directly invoked in the domestic legal systems of the Parties.

2. A Party shall not provide for a right of action under its law against the other Party on the ground that the other Party has acted in breach of this Agreement or any supplementing agreement.

Article 6 Definitions

1. For the purposes of this Agreement and any supplementing agreement, and unless otherwise specified, the following definitions apply:

(a) 'data subject' means an identified or identifiable natural person; an identifiable person being a person who can be identified, directly or indirectly, in particular by reference to an identifier such as a name, an identification number, location data or an online identifier, or to one or more factors specific to the physical, physiological, genetic, mental, economic, cultural or social identity of that natural person;

(b) 'day' means a calendar day;

(c) 'Member State' means a Member State of the European Union;

(d) 'personal data' means any information relating to a data subject;

(e) 'State' means a Member State or the United Kingdom, as the context requires;

(f) 'territory' of a Party means in respect of each Party the territories to which this Agreement applies in accordance with Article 774;

(g) 'the transition period' means the transition period provided for in Article 126 of the Withdrawal Agreement; and

(h) 'Withdrawal Agreement' means the Agreement on the withdrawal of the United Kingdom of Great Britain and Northern Ireland from the European Union and the European Atomic Energy Community, including its Protocols.

2. Any reference to the 'Union', 'Party' or 'Parties' in this Agreement or any supplementing agreement shall be understood as not including the European Atomic Energy Community, unless otherwise specified or where the context otherwise requires.

Title III Institutional framework

Article 7 Partnership Council

1. A Partnership Council is hereby established. It shall comprise representatives of the Union and of the United Kingdom. The Partnership Council may meet in different configurations depending on the matters under discussion.

2. The Partnership Council shall be co-chaired by a Member of the European Commission and a representative of the Government of the United Kingdom at ministerial level. It shall meet at the request of the Union or the United Kingdom, and, in any event, at least once a year, and shall set its meeting schedule and its agenda by mutual consent.

3. The Partnership Council shall oversee the attainment of the objectives of this Agreement and any supplementing agreement. It shall supervise and facilitate the implementation and application of this Agreement and of any supplementing agreement. Each Party may refer to the Partnership Council any issue relating to the implementation, application and interpretation of this Agreement or of any supplementing agreement.

4. The Partnership Council shall have the power to:

(a) adopt decisions in respect of all matters where this Agreement or any supplementing agreement so provides;

(b) make recommendations to the Parties regarding the implementation and application of this Agreement or of any supplementing agreement;

(c) adopt, by decision, amendments to this Agreement or to any supplementing agreement in the cases provided for in this Agreement or in any supplementing agreement;

(d) except in relation to Title III of Part One, until the end of the fourth year following the entry into force of this Agreement, adopt decisions amending this Agreement or any supplementing agreement, provided that such amendments are necessary to correct errors, or to address omissions or other deficiencies;

(e) discuss any matter related to the areas covered by this Agreement or by any supplementing agreement;

(f) delegate certain of its powers to the Trade Partnership Committee or to a Specialised Committee, except those powers and responsibilities referred to in point (g) of this paragraph;

(g) by decision, establish Trade Specialised Committees and Specialised Committees, other than those referred to in Article 8 (1), dissolve any Trade Specialised Committee or Specialised Committee, or change the tasks assigned to them; and

(h) make recommendations to the Parties regarding the transfer of personal data in specific areas covered by this Agreement or any supplementing agreement.

5. The work of the Partnership Council shall be governed by the rules of procedure set out in Annex 1. The Partnership Council may amend that Annex.

Article 8 Committees [8.3 and 8.4 omitted]

1. The following Committees are hereby established:

(a) the Trade Partnership Committee, which addresses matters covered by Titles I to VII, Chapter 4 of Title VIII, Titles IX to XII of Heading One of Part Two, Heading Six of Part Two, and Annex 27;

(b) the Trade Specialised Committee on Goods which addresses matters covered by Chapter 1 of Title I of Heading One of Part Two and Chapter 4 of Title VIII of Heading One of Part Two;

(c) the Trade Specialised Committee on Customs Cooperation and Rules of Origin, which addresses matters covered by Chapters 2 and 5 of Title I of Heading One of Part Two, the Protocol on mutual administrative assistance in customs matters and the provisions on customs enforcement of intellectual property rights, fees and charges, customs valuation and repaired goods;

(d) the Trade Specialised Committee on Sanitary and Phytosanitary Measures, which addresses matters covered by Chapter 3 of Title I of Heading One of Part Two;

(e) the Trade Specialised Committee on Technical Barriers to Trade, which addresses matters covered by Chapter 4 of Title I of Heading One of Part Two and Article 323;
(f) the Trade Specialised Committee on Services, Investment and Digital Trade, which addresses matters covered by Titles II to IV of Heading One of Part Two and Chapter 4 of Title VIII of Heading One of Part Two;
(g) the Trade Specialised Committee on Intellectual Property, which addresses matters covered by Title V of Heading One of Part Two;
(h) the Trade Specialised Committee on Public Procurement, which addresses matters covered by Title VI of Heading One of Part Two;
(i) the Trade Specialised Committee on Regulatory Cooperation, which addresses matters covered by Title X of Heading One of Part Two;
(j) the Trade Specialised Committee on Level Playing Field for Open and Fair Competition and Sustainable Development, which addresses matters covered by Title XI of Heading One of Part Two and Annex 27;
(k) the Trade Specialised Committee on Administrative Cooperation in VAT and Recovery of Taxes and Duties, which addresses matters covered by the Protocol on administrative cooperation and combating fraud in the field of Value Added Tax and on mutual assistance for the recovery of claims relating to taxes and duties;
(l) the Specialised Committee on Energy,
  (i) which addresses matters covered by Title VIII of Heading One of Part Two, with the exception of Chapter 4, Article 323 and Annex 27, and
  (ii) which can discuss and provide expertise to the relevant Trade Specialised Committee on matters pertaining to Chapter 4 and Article 323;
(m) the Specialised Committee on Air Transport, which addresses matters covered by Title I of Heading Two of Part Two;
(n) the Specialised Committee on Aviation Safety, which addresses matters covered by Title II of Heading Two of Part Two;
(o) the Specialised Committee on Road Transport, which addresses matters covered by Heading Three of Part Two;
(p) the Specialised Committee on Social Security Coordination, which addresses matters covered by Heading Four of Part Two and the Protocol on Social Security Coordination;
(q) the Specialised Committee on Fisheries, which addresses matters covered by Heading Five of Part Two;
(r) the Specialised Committee on Law Enforcement and Judicial Cooperation, which addresses matters covered by Part Three; and
(s) the Specialised Committee on Participation in Union Programmes, which addresses matters covered by Part Five.

2. With respect to issues related to Titles I to VII, Chapter 4 of Title VIII, Titles IX to XII of Heading One of Part Two, Heading Six of Part Two and Annex 27, the Trade Partnership Committee referred to in paragraph 1 of this Article shall have the power to:

(a) assist the Partnership Council in the performance of its tasks and, in particular, report to the Partnership Council and carry out any task assigned to it by the latter;
(b) supervise the implementation of this Agreement or any supplementing agreement;
(c) adopt decisions or make recommendations as provided for in this Agreement or any supplementing agreement or where such power has been delegated to it by the Partnership Council;
(d) supervise the work of the Trade Specialised Committees referred to in paragraph 1 of this Article;
(e) explore the most appropriate way to prevent or solve any difficulty that may arise in relation to the interpretation and application of this Agreement or any supplementing agreement, without prejudice to Title I of Part Six;
(f) exercise the powers delegated to it by the Partnership Council pursuant to point (f) of Article 7(4);

(g) establish, by decision, Trade Specialised Committees other than those referred to in paragraph 1 of this Article, dissolve any such Trade Specialised Committee, or change the tasks assigned to them; and

(h) establish, supervise, coordinate and dissolve Working Groups, or delegate their supervision to a Trade Specialised Committee.

5. Committees shall comprise representatives of each Party. Each Party shall ensure that its representatives on the Committees have the appropriate expertise with respect to the issues under discussion.

6. The Trade Partnership Committee shall be co-chaired by a senior representative of the Union and a representative of the United Kingdom with responsibility for trade-related matters, or their designees. It shall meet at the request of the Union or the United Kingdom, and, in any event, at least once a year, and shall set its meeting schedule and its agenda by mutual consent.

7. The Trade Specialised Committees and the Specialised Committees shall be co-chaired by a representative of the Union and a representative of the United Kingdom. Unless otherwise provided for in this Agreement, or unless the co-chairs decide otherwise, they shall meet at least once a year.

8. Committees shall set their meeting schedule and agenda by mutual consent.

9. The work of the Committees shall be governed by the rules of procedure set out in Annex 1.

10. By way of derogation from paragraph 9, a Committee may adopt and subsequently amend its own rules that shall govern its work.

Article 9 Working Groups

1. The following Working Groups are hereby established:

(a) the Working Group on Organic Products, under the supervision of the Trade Specialised Committee on Technical Barriers to Trade;

(b) the Working Group on Motor Vehicles and Parts, under the supervision of the Trade Specialised Committee on Technical Barriers to Trade;

(c) the Working Group on Medicinal Products, under the supervision of the Trade Specialised Committee on Technical Barriers to Trade;

(d) the Working Group on Social Security Coordination, under the supervision of the Specialised Committee on Social Security Coordination.

2. Working Groups shall, under the supervision of Committees, assist Committees in the performance of their tasks and, in particular, prepare the work of Committees and carry out any task assigned to them by the latter.

3. Working Groups shall comprise representatives of the Union and of the United Kingdom and shall be co-chaired by a representative of the Union and a representative of the United Kingdom.

4. Working Groups shall set their own rules of procedure, meeting schedule and agenda by mutual consent.

Article 10 Decisions and recommendations

1. The decisions adopted by the Partnership Council, or, as the case may be, by a Committee, shall be binding on the Parties and on all the bodies set up under this Agreement and under any supplementing agreement, including the arbitration tribunal referred to in Title I of Part Six. Recommendations shall have no binding force.

2. The Partnership Council or, as the case may be, a Committee, shall adopt decisions and make recommendations by mutual consent.

Article 11 Parliamentary cooperation

1. The European Parliament and the Parliament of the United Kingdom may establish a Parliamentary Partnership Assembly consisting of Members of the European Parliament and of Members of the Parliament of the United Kingdom, as a forum to exchange views on the partnership.

2. Upon its establishment, the Parliamentary Partnership Assembly:

(a) may request relevant information regarding the implementation of this Agreement and any supplementing agreement from the Partnership Council, which shall then supply that Assembly with the requested information;

(b) shall be informed of the decisions and recommendations of the Partnership Council; and

(c) may make recommendations to the Partnership Council.

Article 12 Participation of civil society

The Parties shall consult civil society on the implementation of this Agreement and any supplementing agreement, in particular through interaction with the domestic advisory groups and the Civil Society Forum referred to in Articles 13 and 14.

Article 13 Domestic advisory groups

1. Each Party shall consult on issues covered by this Agreement and any supplementing agreement its newly created or existing domestic advisory group or groups comprising a representation of independent civil society organisations including non-governmental organisations, business and employers' organisations, as well as trade unions, active in economic, sustainable development, social, human rights, environmental and other matters. Each Party may convene its domestic advisory group or groups in different configurations to discuss the implementation of different provisions of this Agreement or of any supplementing agreement.

2. Each Party shall consider views or recommendations submitted by its domestic advisory group or groups. Representatives of each Party shall aim to consult with their respective domestic advisory group or groups at least once a year. Meetings may be held by virtual means.

3. In order to promote public awareness of the domestic advisory groups, each Party shall endeavour to publish the list of organisations participating in its domestic advisory group or groups as well as the contact point for that or those groups.

4. The Parties shall promote interaction between their respective domestic advisory groups, including by exchanging where possible the contact details of members of their domestic advisory groups.

Article 14 Civil Society Forum

1. The Parties shall facilitate the organisation of a Civil Society Forum to conduct a dialogue on the implementation of Part Two. The Partnership Council shall adopt operational guidelines for the conduct of the Forum.

2. The Civil Society Forum shall meet at least once a year, unless otherwise agreed by the Parties. The Civil Society Forum may meet by virtual means.

3. The Civil Society Forum shall be open for the participation of independent civil society organisations established in the territories of the Parties, including members of the domestic advisory groups referred to in Article 13. Each Party shall promote a balanced representation, including non-governmental organisations, business and employers' organisations and trade unions, active in economic, sustainable development, social, human rights, environmental and other matters.

PART TWO TRADE, TRANSPORT, FISHERIES AND OTHER ARRANGEMENTS

HEADING ONE TRADE

Title I Trade in goods

Chapter 1 National treatment and market access for goods (including trade remedies)

Article 15 Objective

The objective of this Chapter is to facilitate trade in goods between the Parties and to maintain liberalised trade in goods in accordance with the provisions of this Agreement.

Article 16 Scope

Except as otherwise provided, this Chapter applies to trade in goods of a Party.

Article 17 Definitions [Omitted]

Article 18 Classification of goods

The classification of goods in trade between the Parties under this Agreement is set out in each Party's respective tariff nomenclature in conformity with the Harmonised System.

Article 19 National treatment on internal taxation and regulation

Each Party shall accord national treatment to the goods of the other Party in accordance with Article III of GATT 1994 including its Notes and Supplementary Provisions. To that end, Article III of GATT 1994 and its Notes and Supplementary Provisions are incorporated into and made part of this Agreement, *mutatis mutandis*.

Article 20 Freedom of transit

Each Party shall accord freedom of transit through its territory, via the routes most convenient for international transit, for traffic in transit to or from the territory of the other Party or of any other third country. To that end, Article V of GATT 1994 and its Notes and Supplementary Provisions are incorporated into and made part of this Agreement, *mutatis mutandis*. The Parties understand that Article V of GATT 1994 includes the movement of energy goods via *inter alia* pipelines or electricity grids.

Article 21 Prohibition of customs duties

Except as otherwise provided for in this Agreement, customs duties on all goods originating in the other Party shall be prohibited.

Article 22 Export duties, taxes or other charges

1. A Party may not adopt or maintain any duty, tax or other charge of any kind imposed on, or in connection with, the exportation of a good to the other Party; or any internal tax or other charge on a good exported to the other Party that is in excess of the tax or charge that would be imposed on like goods when destined for domestic consumption.

2. For the purpose of this Article, the term 'other charge of any kind' does not include fees or other charges that are permitted under Article 23.

Article 23 Fees and formalities

1. Fees and other charges imposed by a Party on or in connection with importation or exportation of a good of the other Party shall be limited in amount to the approximate cost of the services rendered, and shall not represent an indirect protection to domestic goods or taxation of imports or exports for fiscal purposes. A Party shall not levy fees or other charges on or in connection with importation or exportation on an *ad valorem* basis.

2. Each Party may impose charges or recover costs only where specific services are rendered, in particular, but not limited to, the following:

- (a) attendance, where requested, by customs staff outside official office hours or at premises other than customs premises;
- (b) analyses or expert reports on goods and postal fees for the return of goods to an applicant, particularly in respect of decisions relating to binding information or the provision of information concerning the application of the customs laws and regulations;
- (c) the examination or sampling of goods for verification purposes, or the destruction of goods, where costs other than the cost of using customs staff are involved; and
- (d) exceptional control measures, if these are necessary due to the nature of the goods or to a potential risk.

3. Each Party shall promptly publish all fees and charges it imposes in connection with importation or exportation via an official website in such a manner as to enable governments, traders and other interested parties, to become acquainted with them. That information shall include the reason for the fee or charge for the service provided, the responsible authority, the fees and charges that will be applied, and when and how payment is to be made. New or amended fees and charges shall not be imposed until information in accordance with this paragraph has been published and made readily available.

4. A Party shall not require consular transactions, including related fees and charges, in connection with the importation of any good of the other Party.

Article 24 Repaired goods

1. A Party shall not apply a customs duty to a good, regardless of its origin, that re-enters the Party's territory after that good has been temporarily exported from its territory to the territory of the other Party for repair.

2. Paragraph 1 does not apply to a good imported in bond, into free trade zones, or in similar status, that is then exported for repair and is not re-imported in bond, into free trade zones, or in similar status.

3. A Party shall not apply a customs duty to a good, regardless of its origin, imported temporarily from the territory of the other Party for repair.

Article 25 Remanufactured goods

1. A Party shall not accord to remanufactured goods of the other Party treatment that is less favourable than that which it accords to equivalent goods in new condition.

2. Article 26 applies to import and export prohibitions or restrictions on remanufactured goods. If a Party adopts or maintains import and export prohibitions or restrictions on used goods, it shall not apply those measures to remanufactured goods.

3. A Party may require that remanufactured goods be identified as such for distribution or sale in its territory and that they meet all applicable technical requirements that apply to equivalent goods in new condition.

Article 26 Import and export restrictions

1. A Party shall not adopt or maintain any prohibition or restriction on the importation of any good of the other Party or on the exportation or sale for export of any good destined for the territory of the other Party, except in accordance with Article XI of GATT 1994, including its Notes and Supplementary Provisions. To that end, Article XI of GATT 1994 and its Notes and Supplementary Provisions are incorporated into and made part of this Agreement, *mutatis mutandis*.

2. A Party shall not adopt or maintain:

(a) export and import price requirements, except as permitted in enforcement of countervailing and anti-dumping duty orders and undertakings; or

(b) import licensing conditioned on the fulfilment of a performance requirement.

Article 27 Import and export monopolies

A Party shall not designate or maintain an import or export monopoly. For the purposes of this Article, import or export monopoly means the exclusive right or grant of authority by a Party to an entity to import a good from, or export a good to, the other Party.

Article 28 Import licensing procedures

1. Each Party shall ensure that all import licensing procedures applicable to trade in goods between the Parties are neutral in application, and are administered in a fair, equitable, non-discriminatory and transparent manner.

2. A Party shall only adopt or maintain licensing procedures as a condition for importation into its territory from the territory of the other Party, if other appropriate procedures to achieve an administrative purpose are not reasonably available.

3. A Party shall not adopt or maintain any non-automatic import licensing procedure, unless it is necessary to implement a measure that is consistent with this Agreement. A Party adopting such non-automatic import licensing procedure shall indicate clearly the measure being implemented through that procedure.

4. Each Party shall introduce and administer any import licensing procedure in accordance with Articles 1 to 3 of the WTO Agreement on Import Licensing Procedures ('the Import Licensing Agreement'). To that end, Articles 1 to 3 of the Import Licensing Agreement are incorporated into and made part of this Agreement *mutatis mutandis*.

5. Any Party introducing or modifying any import licensing procedure shall make all relevant information available online on an official website. That information shall be made available, whenever practicable, at least 21 days prior to the date of the application of the new or modified licensing procedure and in any event no later than the date of application. That information shall contain the data required under Article 5 of the Import Licensing Agreement.

6. At the request of the other Party, a Party shall promptly provide any relevant information regarding any import licensing procedures that it intends to adopt or that it maintains, including the information referred to in Articles 1 to 3 of the Import Licensing Agreement.

7. For greater certainty, nothing in this Article requires a Party to grant an import licence, or prevents a Party from implementing its obligations or commitments under United Nations Security Council Resolutions or under multilateral non-proliferation regimes and import control arrangements.

Article 29 Export licensing procedures [29.2–29.4 omitted]

1. Each Party shall publish any new export licensing procedure, or any modification to an existing export licensing procedure, in such a manner as to enable governments, traders and other interested parties to become acquainted with them. Such publication shall take place, whenever practicable, 45 days before the procedure or modification takes effect, and in any case no later than the date such procedure or modification takes effect and, where appropriate, publication shall take place on any relevant government websites.

Article 30 Customs valuation [omitted]

Article 31 Preference utilization [omitted]

Article 32 Trade remedies

1. The Parties affirm their rights and obligations under Article VI of GATT 1994, the Anti-Dumping Agreement, the SCM Agreement, Article XIX of GATT 1994, the Safeguards Agreement, and Article 5 of the Agreement on Agriculture.

2. Chapter 2 of this Title does not apply to anti-dumping, countervailing and safeguard investigations and measures.

3. Each Party shall apply anti-dumping and countervailing measures in accordance with the requirements of the Anti-Dumping Agreement and the SCM Agreement, and pursuant to a fair and transparent process.

4. Provided it does not unnecessarily delay the conduct of the investigation, each interested party in an anti-dumping or countervailing investigation[1] shall be granted a full opportunity to defend its interests.

5. Each Party's investigating authority may, in accordance with the Party's law, consider whether the amount of the anti-dumping duty to be imposed shall be the full margin of dumping or a lesser amount.

6. Each Party's investigating authority shall, in accordance with the Party's law, consider information provided as to whether imposing an anti-dumping or a countervailing duty would not be in the public interest.

7. A Party shall not apply or maintain, with respect to the same good, at the same time:

(a) a measure pursuant to Article 5 of the Agreement on Agriculture; and

(b) a measure pursuant to Article XIX of GATT 1994 and the Safeguards Agreement.

8. Title I of Part Six does not apply to paragraphs 1 to 6 of this Article.

Article 33 Use of existing WTO tariff rate quotas

1. Products originating in one Party shall not be eligible to be imported into the other Party under existing WTO Tariff Rate Quotas ('TRQs') as defined in paragraph 2. This shall include those

[1] For the purpose of this Article, interested parties shall be defined as per Article 6.11 of the Anti-dumping Agreement and Article 12.9 of the SCM Agreement.

TRQs as being apportioned between the Parties pursuant to Article XXVIII GATT negotiations initiated by the European Union in WTO document G/SECRET/42/Add.2 and by the United Kingdom in WTO document G/SECRET/44 and as set out in each Party's respective internal legislation. For the purposes of this Article, the originating status of the products shall be determined on the basis of non-preferential rules of origin applicable in the importing Party.

2. For the purposes of paragraph 1, 'existing WTO TRQs' means those tariff rate quotas which are WTO concessions of the European Union included in the draft EU28 schedule of concessions and commitments under GATT 1994 submitted to the WTO in document G/MA/TAR/RS/506 as amended by documents G/MA/TAR/RS/506/Add.1 and G/MA/TAR/RS/506/Add.2.

Article 34 Measures in case of breaches or circumventions of customs legislation

1. The Parties shall cooperate in preventing, detecting and combating breaches or circumventions of customs legislation, in accordance with their obligations under Chapter 2 of this Title and the Protocol on mutual administrative assistance in customs matters. Each Party shall take appropriate and comparable measures to protect its own and the other Party's financial interests regarding the levying of duties on goods entering the customs territories of the United Kingdom or the Union.

2. Subject to the possibility of exemption for compliant traders under paragraph 7, a Party may temporarily suspend the relevant preferential treatment of the product or products concerned in accordance with the procedure laid down in paragraphs 3 and 4 if:

(a) that Party has made a finding, based on objective, compelling and verifiable information, that systematic and large-scale breaches or circumventions of customs legislation have been committed, and;

(b) the other Party repeatedly and unjustifiably refuses or otherwise fails to comply with the obligations referred to in paragraph 1.

3. The Party which has made a finding as referred to in paragraph 2 shall notify the Trade Partnership Committee and shall enter into consultations with the other Party within the Trade Partnership Committee with a view to reaching a mutually acceptable solution.

4. If the Parties fail to agree on a mutually acceptable solution within three months after the date of notification, the Party which has made the finding may decide to suspend temporarily the relevant preferential treatment of the product or products concerned. In this case, the Party which made the finding shall notify the temporary suspension, including the period during which it intends the temporary suspension to apply, to the Trade Partnership Committee without delay.

5. The temporary suspension shall apply only for the period necessary to counteract the breaches or circumventions and to protect the financial interests of the Party concerned, and in any case not for longer than six months. The Party concerned shall keep the situation under review and, where it decides that the temporary suspension is no longer necessary, it shall bring it to an end before the end of the period notified to the Trade Partnership Committee. Where the conditions that gave rise to the suspension persist at the expiry of the period notified to the Trade Partnership Committee, the Party concerned may decide to renew the suspension. Any suspension shall be subject to periodic consultations within the Trade Partnership Committee.

6. Each Party shall publish, in accordance with its internal procedures, notices to importers about any decision concerning temporary suspensions referred to in paragraphs 4 and 5.

7. Notwithstanding paragraph 4, if an importer is able to satisfy the importing customs authority that such products are fully compliant with the importing Party's customs legislation, the requirements of this Agreement, and any other appropriate conditions related to the temporary suspension established by the importing Party in accordance with its laws and regulations, the importing Party shall allow the importer to apply for preferential treatment and recover any duties paid in excess of the applicable preferential tariff rates when the products were imported.

Article 35 Management of administrative errors [omitted]

Article 36 Cultural property [omitted]

Chapter 2 Rules of origin

Section 1 Rules of origin

Article 37 Objective

The objective of this Chapter is to lay down the provisions determining the origin of goods for the purpose of application of preferential tariff treatment under this Agreement, and setting out related origin procedures.

Article 38 Definitions [omitted]

Article 39 General requirements

1. For the purposes of applying the preferential tariff treatment by a Party to the originating good of the other Party in accordance with this Agreement, provided that the products satisfy all other applicable requirements of this Chapter, the following products shall be considered as originating in the other Party:

(a) products wholly obtained in that Party within the meaning of Article 41;
(b) products produced in that Party exclusively from originating materials in that Party; and
(c) products produced in that Party incorporating non-originating materials provided they satisfy the requirements set out in Annex 3.

2. If a product has acquired originating status, the non-originating materials used in the production of that product shall not be considered as non-originating when that product is incorporated as a material in another product.

3. The acquisition of originating status shall be fulfilled without interruption in the United Kingdom or the Union.

Article 40 Cumulation of origin

1. A product originating in a Party shall be considered as originating in the other Party if that product is used as a material in the production of another product in that other Party.

2. Production carried out in a Party on a non-originating material may be taken into account for the purpose of determining whether a product is originating in the other Party.

3. Paragraphs 1 and 2 do not apply if the production carried out in the other Party does not go beyond the operations referred to in Article 43.

4. In order for an exporter to complete the statement on origin referred to in point (a) of Article 54(2) for a product referred to in paragraph 2 of this Article, the exporter shall obtain from its supplier a supplier's declaration as provided for in Annex 6 or an equivalent document that contains the same information describing the non-originating materials concerned in sufficient detail to enable them to be identified.

Article 41 Wholly obtained products

1. The following products shall be considered as wholly obtained in a Party:

(a) mineral products extracted or taken from its soil or from its seabed;
(b) plants and vegetable products grown or harvested there;
(c) live animals born and raised there;
(d) products obtained from live animals raised there;
(e) products obtained from slaughtered animals born and raised there;
(f) products obtained by hunting or fishing conducted there;
(g) products obtained from aquaculture there if aquatic organisms, including fish, molluscs, crustaceans, other aquatic invertebrates and aquatic plants are born or raised from seed stock such as eggs, roes, fry, fingerlings, larvae, parr, smolts or other immature fish at a

post-larval stage by intervention in the rearing or growth processes to enhance production such as regular stocking, feeding or protection from predators;

(h) products of sea fishing and other products taken from the sea outside any territorial sea by a vessel of a Party;

(i) products made aboard of a factory ship of a Party exclusively from products referred to in point (h);

(j) products extracted from the seabed or subsoil outside any territorial sea provided that they have rights to exploit or work such seabed or subsoil;

(k) waste and scrap resulting from production operations conducted there;

(l) waste and scrap derived from used products collected there, provided that those products are fit only for the recovery of raw materials;

(m) products produced there exclusively from the products specified in points (a) to (l).

2. The terms 'vessel of a Party' and 'factory ship of a Party' in points (h) and (i) of paragraph 1 mean a vessel and factory ship which:

(a) is registered in a Member State or in the United Kingdom;

(b) sails under the flag of a Member State or of the United Kingdom; and

(c) meets one of the following conditions:

  (i) it is at least 50% owned by nationals of a Member State or of the United Kingdom; or

  (ii) it is owned by legal persons which each:

    (A) have their head office and main place of business in the Union or the United Kingdom; and

    (B) are at least 50% owned by public entities, nationals or legal persons of a Member State or the United Kingdom.

Articles 42–52 [Omitted]

Article 53 Review of drawback of, or exemption from, customs duties

Not earlier than two years from the entry into force of this Agreement, at the request of either Party, the Trade Specialised Committee on Customs Cooperation and Rules of Origin shall review the Parties' respective duty drawback and inward-processing schemes. For that purpose, at the request of a Party, no later than 60 days from that request, the other Party shall provide the requesting Party with available information and detailed statistics covering the period from the entry into force of this Agreement, or the previous five year period if that period is shorter, on the operation of its duty-drawback and inward-processing scheme. In the light of this review, the Trade Specialised Committee on Customs Cooperation and Rules of Origin may make recommendations to the Partnership Council for the amendment of the provisions of this Chapter and its Annexes, with a view to introducing limitations or restrictions with respect to drawback of or exemption from customs duties.

Section 2 Origin procedures

Articles 54–65 [Omitted]

Section 3 Other Provisions

Articles 66–68 [Omitted]

Chapter 3 Sanitary and phytosanitary measures [omitted]

Chapter 4 Technical barriers to trade

Article 88 Objective

The objective of this Chapter is to facilitate trade in goods between the Parties by preventing, identifying and eliminating unnecessary technical barriers to trade.

Article 89 Scope

1. This Chapter applies to the preparation, adoption and application of all standards, technical regulations and conformity assessment procedures, which may affect trade in goods between the Parties.

2. This Chapter does not apply to:

(a) purchasing specifications prepared by governmental bodies for production or consumption requirements of such bodies; or

(b) SPS measures that fall within the scope of Chapter 3 of this Title.

3. The Annexes to this Chapter apply in addition to this Chapter in respect of products within the scope of those Annexes. Any provision in an Annex to this Chapter that an international standard or body or organisation is to be considered or recognised as relevant shall not prevent a standard developed by any other body or organisation from being considered to be a relevant international standard pursuant to Article 91(4) and (5).

Article 90 Relationship with the TBT Agreement

1. Articles 2 to 9 of and Annexes 1 and 3 to the TBT Agreement are incorporated into and made part of this Agreement *mutatis mutandis*.

2. Terms referred to in this Chapter and in the Annexes to this Chapter shall have the same meaning as they have in the TBT Agreement.

Article 91 Technical regulations

1. Each Party shall carry out impact assessments of planned technical regulations in accordance with its respective rules and procedures. The rules and procedures referred to in this paragraph and in paragraph 8 may provide for exceptions.

2. Each Party shall assess the available regulatory and non-regulatory alternatives to the proposed technical regulation that may fulfil the Party's legitimate objectives, in accordance with Article 2.2 of the TBT Agreement.

3. Each Party shall use relevant international standards as a basis for its technical regulations except when it can demonstrate that such international standards would be an ineffective or inappropriate means for the fulfilment of the legitimate objectives pursued.

4. International standards developed by the International Organization for Standardization (ISO), the International Electrotechnical Commission (IEC), the International Telecommunication Union (ITU) and the Codex Alimentarius Commission (Codex) shall be the relevant international standards within the meaning of Article 2, Article 5 and Annex 3 of the TBT Agreement.

5. A standard developed by other international organisations may also be considered a relevant international standard within the meaning of Article 2, Article 5 and Annex 3 of the TBT Agreement, provided that:

(a) it has been developed by a standardising body which seeks to establish consensus either:

(i) among national delegations of the participating WTO Members representing all the national standardising bodies in their territory that have adopted, or expect to adopt, standards on the subject matter to which the international standardisation activity relates, or,

(ii) among governmental bodies of participating WTO Members; and

(b) it has been developed in accordance with the Decision of the WTO Committee on Technical Barriers to Trade on Principles for the Development of International Standards, Guides and Recommendations with relation to Articles 2, 5, and Annex 3 of the TBT Agreement.[2]

6. Where a Party does not use international standards as a basis for a technical regulation, on request of the other Party, it shall identify any substantial deviation from the relevant international standard, explain the reasons why such standards were judged inappropriate or ineffective for the objective pursued, and provide the scientific or technical evidence on which that assessment was based.

7. Each Party shall review its technical regulations to increase the convergence of those technical regulations with relevant international standards, taking into account, *inter alia*, any new

[2] G/TBT/9, 13 November 2000, Annex 4.

developments in the relevant international standards or any changes in the circumstances that have given rise to divergence from any relevant international standards.

8. In accordance with its respective rules and procedures and without prejudice to Title X of this Heading, when developing a major technical regulation which may have a significant effect on trade, each Party shall ensure that procedures exist that allow persons to express their opinion in a public consultation, except where urgent problems of safety, health, environment or national security arise or threaten to arise. Each Party shall allow persons of the other Party to participate in such consultations on terms that are no less favourable than those accorded to its own nationals, and shall make the results of those consultations public.

Article 92 Standards

1. Each Party shall encourage the standardising bodies established within its territory, as well as the regional standardising bodies of which a Party or the standardising bodies established in its territory are members:

(a) to participate, within the limits of their resources, in the preparation of international standards by relevant international standardising bodies;

(b) to use relevant international standards as a basis for the standards they develop, except where such international standards would be ineffective or inappropriate, for example because of an insufficient level of protection, fundamental climatic or geographical factors or fundamental technological problems;

(c) to avoid duplications of, or overlaps with, the work of international standardising bodies;

(d) to review national and regional standards that are not based on relevant international standards at regular intervals, with a view to increasing the convergence of those standards with relevant international standards;

(e) to cooperate with the relevant standardising bodies of the other Party in international standardisation activities, including through cooperation in the international standardising bodies or at regional level;

(f) to foster bilateral cooperation with the standardising bodies of the other Party; and

(g) to exchange information between standardising bodies.

2. The Parties shall exchange information on:

(a) their respective use of standards in support of technical regulations; and

(b) their respective standardisation processes, and the extent to which they use international, regional or sub-regional standards as a basis for their national standards.

3. Where standards are rendered mandatory in a draft technical regulation or conformity assessment procedure, through incorporation or reference, the transparency obligations set out in Article 94 and in Article 2 or 5 of the TBT Agreement shall apply.

Articles 93–100 [Omitted]

Chapter 5 Customs and trade facilitation

Article 101 Objective

The objectives of this Chapter are:

(a) to reinforce cooperation between the Parties in the area of customs and trade facilitation and to support or maintain, where relevant, appropriate levels of compatibility of their customs legislation and practices with a view to ensuring that relevant legislation and procedures, as well as the administrative capacity of the relevant administrations, fulfil the objectives of promoting trade facilitation while ensuring effective customs controls and effective enforcement of customs legislation and trade related laws and regulations, the proper protection of security and safety of citizens and the respect of prohibitions and restrictions and financial interests of the Parties;

(b) to reinforce administrative cooperation between the Parties in the field of VAT and mutual assistance in claims related to taxes and duties;

(c) to ensure that the legislation of each Party is non-discriminatory and that customs procedures are based upon the use of modern methods and effective controls to combat fraud and to promote legitimate trade; and
(d) to ensure that legitimate public policy objectives, including in relation to security, safety and the fight against fraud are not compromised in any way.

Article 102 Definitions

For the purposes of this Chapter and Annex 18 and the Protocol on mutual administrative assistance in customs matters and the Protocol on administrative cooperation and combating fraud in the field of Value Added Tax and on mutual assistance for the recovery of claims relating to taxes and duties, the following definitions apply:

(a) 'Agreement on Pre-shipment Inspection' means the Agreement on Pre-shipment Inspection, contained in Annex 1A to the WTO Agreement;
(b) 'ATA and Istanbul Conventions' means the Customs Convention on the ATA Carnet for the Temporary Admission of Goods done in Brussels on 6 December 1961 and the Istanbul Convention on Temporary Admission done on 26 June 1990;
(c) 'Common Transit Convention' means the Convention of 20 May 1987 on a common transit procedure;
(d) 'Customs Data Model of the WCO' means the library of data components and electronic templates for the exchange of business data and compilation of international standards on data and information used in applying regulatory facilitation and controls in global trade, as published by the WCO Data Model Project Team from time to time;
(e) 'customs legislation' means any legal or regulatory provision applicable in the territory of either Party, governing the entry or import of goods, exit or export of goods, the transit of goods and the placing of goods under any other customs regime or procedure, including measures of prohibition, restriction and control;
(f) 'information' means any data, document, image, report, communication or authenticated copy, in any format, including in electronic format, whether or not processed or analysed;
(g) 'person' means any person as defined in point (l) of Article 512[3];
(h) 'SAFE Framework' means the SAFE Framework of Standards to Secure and Facilitate Global Trade adopted at the June 2005 World Customs Organisation Session in Brussels and as updated from time to time; and
(i) 'WTO Trade Facilitation Agreement' means the Agreement on Trade Facilitation annexed to the Protocol Amending the WTO Agreement (decision of 27 November 2014).

Article 103 Customs cooperation

1. The relevant authorities of the Parties shall cooperate on customs matters to support the objectives set out in Article 101, taking into account the resources of their respective authorities. For the purpose of this Title, the Convention of 20 May 1987 on the Simplification of Formalities in Trade in Goods applies.

2. The Parties shall develop cooperation, including in the following areas:

(a) exchanging information concerning customs legislation, the implementation of customs legislation and customs procedures; particularly in the following areas:
  (i) the simplification and modernisation of customs procedures;
  (ii) the facilitation of transit movements and transhipment;
  (iii) relations with the business community; and
  (iv) supply chain security and risk management;
(b) working together on the customs-related aspects of securing and facilitating the international trade supply chain in accordance with the SAFE Framework;

[3] For greater certainty, it is understood that, in particular for the purposes of this Chapter, the notion of 'person' includes any association of persons lacking the legal status of a legal person but recognized under applicable law as having the capacity to perform legal acts.

(c) considering developing joint initiatives relating to import, export and other customs procedures including technical assistance, as well as towards ensuring an effective service to the business community;
(d) strengthening their cooperation in the field of customs in international organisations such as the WTO and the WCO, and exchanging information or holding discussions with a view to establishing where possible common positions in those international organisations and in UNCTAD, UNECE;
(e) endeavouring to harmonise their data requirements for import, export and other customs procedures by implementing common standards and data elements in accordance with the Customs Data Model of the WCO;
(f) strengthening their cooperation on risk management techniques, including sharing best practices, and, where appropriate, risk information and control results. Where relevant and appropriate, the Parties may also consider mutual recognition of risk management techniques, risk standards and controls and customs security measures; the Parties may also consider, where relevant and appropriate, the development of compatible risk criteria and standards, control measures and priority control areas;
(g) establishing mutual recognition of Authorised Economic Operator programmes to secure and facilitate trade;
(h) fostering cooperation between customs and other government authorities or agencies in relation to Authorised Economic Operator programmes, which may be achieved, *inter alia*, by agreeing on the highest standards, facilitating access to benefits and minimising unnecessary duplication;
(i) enforcing intellectual property rights by customs authorities, including exchanging information and best practices in customs operations focusing in particular on intellectual property rights enforcement;
(j) maintaining compatible customs procedures, where appropriate and practicable to do so, including the application of a single administrative document for customs declaration; and
(k) exchanging, where relevant and appropriate and under arrangements to be agreed, certain categories of customs-related information between the customs authorities of the Parties through structured and recurrent communication, for the purposes of improving risk management and the effectiveness of customs controls, targeting goods at risk in terms of revenue collection or safety and security, and facilitating legitimate trade; such exchanges may include export and import declaration data on trade between the Parties, with the possibility of exploring, through pilot initiatives, the development of interoperable mechanisms to avoid duplication in the submission of such information. Exchanges under this point shall be without prejudice to exchanges of information that may take place between the Parties pursuant to the Protocol on mutual administrative assistance in customs matters.

3. Without prejudice to other forms of cooperation envisaged in this Agreement, the customs authorities of the Parties shall provide each other with mutual administrative assistance in the matters covered by this Chapter in accordance with the Protocol on mutual administrative assistance in customs matters.

4. Any exchange of information between the Parties under this Chapter shall be subject to the confidentiality and protection of information set out in Article 12 of the Protocol on mutual administrative assistance in customs matters, *mutatis mutandis*, as well as to any confidentiality requirements set out in the legislation of the Parties.

Article 104 Customs and other trade related legislation and procedures

1. Each Party shall ensure that its customs provisions and procedures:
(a) are consistent with international instruments and standards applicable in the area of customs and trade, including the WTO Trade Facilitation Agreement, the substantive elements of the Revised Kyoto Convention on the Simplification and Harmonisation

of Customs Procedures, the International Convention on the Harmonised Commodity Description and Coding System, as well as the SAFE Framework and the Customs Data Model of the WCO;
(b) provide the protection and facilitation of legitimate trade taking into account the evolution of trade practices through effective enforcement including in case of breaches of its laws and regulations, duty evasion and smuggling and through ensuring compliance with legislative requirements;
(c) are based on legislation that is proportionate and non-discriminatory, avoids unnecessary burdens on economic operators, provides for further facilitation for operators with high levels of compliance including favourable treatment with respect to customs controls prior to the release of goods, and ensures safeguards against fraud and illicit or damageable activities while ensuring a high level of protection of security and safety of citizens and the respect of prohibitions and restrictions and financial interests of the Parties; and
(d) contain rules that ensure that any penalty imposed for breaches of customs regulations or procedural requirements is proportionate and non-discriminatory and that the imposition of such penalties does not result in unjustified delays.

Each Party should periodically review its legislation and customs procedures. Customs procedures should also be applied in a manner that is predictable, consistent and transparent.

2. In order to improve working methods and to ensure non-discrimination, transparency, efficiency, integrity and the accountability of operations, each Party shall:
(a) simplify and review requirements and formalities wherever possible with a view to ensuring the rapid release and clearance of goods;
(b) work towards the further simplification and standardisation of the data and documentation required by customs and other agencies; and
(c) promote coordination between all border agencies, both internally and across borders, to facilitate border-crossing processes and enhance control, taking into account joint border controls where feasible and appropriate.

Article 105 Release of goods

1. Each Party shall adopt or maintain customs procedures that:
(a) provide for the prompt release of goods within a period that is no longer than necessary to ensure compliance with its laws and regulations;
(b) provide for advance electronic submission and processing of documentation and any other required information prior to the arrival of the goods, to enable the release of goods promptly upon arrival if no risk has been identified through risk analysis or if no random checks or other checks are to be performed;
(c) provide for the possibility, where appropriate and if the necessary conditions are satisfied, of releasing goods for free circulation at the first point of arrival; and
(d) allow for the release of goods prior to the final determination of customs duties, taxes, fees and charges, if such a determination is not done prior to, or upon arrival, or as rapidly as possible after arrival and provided that all other regulatory requirements have been met.

2. As a condition for such release, each Party may require a guarantee for any amount not yet determined in the form of a surety, a deposit or another appropriate instrument provided for in its laws and regulations. Such guarantee shall not be greater than the amount the Party requires to ensure payment of customs duties, taxes, fees and charges ultimately due for the goods covered by the guarantee. The guarantee shall be discharged when it is no longer required.

3. The Parties shall ensure that the customs and other authorities responsible for border controls and procedures dealing with importation, exportation and transit of goods cooperate with one another and coordinate their activities in order to facilitate trade and expedite the release of goods.

Article 106 Simplified customs procedures

1. Each Party shall work towards simplification of its requirements and formalities for customs procedures in order to reduce the time and costs thereof for traders or operators, including small and medium-sized enterprises.

2. Each Party shall adopt or maintain measures allowing traders or operators fulfilling criteria specified in its laws and regulations to benefit from further simplification of customs procedures. Such measures may include *inter alia*:

(a) customs declarations containing a reduced set of data or supporting documents;
(b) periodical customs declarations for the determination and payment of customs duties and taxes covering multiple imports within a given period after the release of those imported goods;
(c) self-assessment of and the deferred payment of customs duties and taxes until after the release of those imported goods; and
(d) the use of a guarantee with a reduced amount or a waiver from the obligation to provide a guarantee.

3. Where a Party chooses to adopt one of these measures, it will offer, where considered appropriate and practicable by that Party and in accordance with its laws and regulations, these simplifications to all traders who meet the relevant criteria.

Articles 107–109 [Omitted]

Article 110 Authorised Economic Operators

1. Each Party shall maintain a partnership programme for operators who meet the specified criteria in Annex 18.

2. The Parties shall recognise their respective programmes for Authorised Economic Operators in accordance with Annex 18.

Article 111–122 [Omitted]

Title II Services and investment

Chapter 1 General provisions

Article 123 Objective and scope

1. The Parties affirm their commitment to establish a favourable climate for the development of trade and investment between them.

2. The Parties reaffirm the right to regulate within their territories to achieve legitimate policy objectives, such as: the protection of public health; social services; public education; safety; the environment, including climate change; public morals; social or consumer protection; privacy and data protection or the promotion and protection of cultural diversity.

3. This Title does not apply to measures affecting natural persons of a Party seeking access to the employment market of the other Party or to measures regarding nationality, citizenship, residence or employment on a permanent basis.

4. This Title shall not prevent a Party from applying measures to regulate the entry of natural persons into, or their temporary stay in, its territory, including those measures necessary to protect the integrity of its borders and to ensure the orderly movement of natural persons across them, provided that such measures are not applied in such a manner as to nullify or impair the benefits accruing to the other Party under the terms of this Title. The sole fact of requiring a visa for natural persons of certain countries and not for those of others shall not be regarded as nullifying or impairing benefits under this Title.

5. This Title does not apply to:

(a) air services or related services in support of air services[4], other than:
  (i) aircraft repair and maintenance services;
  (ii) computer reservation system services;
  (iii) ground handling services;

4 Air services or related services in support of air services include, but are not limited to, the following services: air transportation; services provided by using an aircraft whose primary purpose is not the transportation of goods or passengers, such as aerial fire-fighting, flight training, sightseeing, spraying, surveying, mapping, photography, parachute jumping, glider towing, helicopter-lift for logging and construction, and other airborne agricultural, industrial and inspection services; the rental of aircraft with crew; and airport operation services.

(iv) the following services provided using a manned aircraft, subject to compliance with the Parties' respective laws and regulations governing the admission of aircrafts to, departure from and operation within, their territory: aerial fire-fighting; flight training; spraying; surveying; mapping; photography; and other airborne agricultural, industrial and inspection services; and
(v) the selling and marketing of air transport services;

(b) audio-visual services;
(c) national maritime cabotage[5]; and
(d) inland waterways transport.

6. This Title does not apply to any measure of a Party with respect to public procurement of a good or service purchased for governmental purposes, and not with a view to commercial resale or with a view to use in the supply of a good or service for commercial sale, whether or not that procurement is 'covered procurement' within the meaning of Article 277.

7. Except for Article 132, this Title does not apply to subsidies or grants provided by the Parties, including government-supported loans, guarantees and insurance.

Article 124 Definitions [omitted]

Article 125 Denial of benefits

1. A Party may deny the benefits of this Title and Title IV of this Heading to an investor or service supplier of the other Party, or to a covered enterprise, if the denying Party adopts or maintains measures related to the maintenance of international peace and security, including the protection of human rights, which:

(a) prohibit transactions with that investor, service supplier or covered enterprise; or
(b) would be violated or circumvented if the benefits of this Title and Title IV of this Heading were accorded to that investor, service supplier or covered enterprise, including where the measures prohibit transactions with a natural or legal person which owns or controls any of them.

2. For greater certainty, paragraph 1 is applicable to Title IV of this Heading to the extent that it relates to services or investment with respect to which a Party has denied the benefits of this Title.

Article 126 Review

1. With a view to introducing possible improvements to the provisions of this Title, and consistent with their commitments under international agreements, the Parties shall review their legal framework relating to trade in services and investment, including this Agreement, in accordance with Article 776.

2. The Parties shall endeavour, where appropriate, to review the non-conforming measures and reservations set out in Annexes 19, 20, 21 and 22 and the activities for short term business visitors set out in Annex 21, with a view to agreeing to possible improvements in their mutual interest.

3. This Article shall not apply with respect to financial services.

Chapter 2 Investment liberalisation

Article 127 Scope

This Chapter applies to measures of a Party affecting the establishment of an enterprise to perform economic activities and the operation of such an enterprise by:

(a) investors of the other Party;
(b) covered enterprises; and

5 National maritime cabotage covers: for the Union, without prejudice to the scope of activities that may be considered cabotage under the relevant national legislation, transportation of passengers or goods between a port or point located in a Member State and another port or point located in that same Member State, including on its continental shelf, as provided for in the United Nations Convention on the Law of the Sea and traffic originating and terminating in the same port or point located in a Member State; for the United Kingdom, transportation of passengers or goods between a port or point located in the United Kingdom and another port or point located in the United Kingdom, including on its continental shelf, as provided for in the United Nations Convention on the Law of the Sea and traffic originating and terminating in the same port or point located in the United Kingdom.

(c) for the purposes of Article 132, any enterprise in the territory of the Party which adopts or maintains the measure.

Article 128 Market access

A Party shall not adopt or maintain, with regard to establishment of an enterprise by an investor of the other Party or by a covered enterprise, or operation of a covered enterprise, either on the basis of its entire territory or on the basis of a territorial sub-division, measures that:

(a) impose limitations on:

(i) the number of enterprises that may carry out a specific economic activity, whether in the form of numerical quotas, monopolies, exclusive rights or the requirement of an economic needs test;

(ii) the total value of transactions or assets in the form of numerical quotas or the requirement of an economic needs test;

(iii) the total number of operations or on the total quantity of output expressed in terms of designated numerical units in the form of quotas or the requirement of an economic needs test;[6, 7]

(iv) the participation of foreign capital in terms of maximum percentage limit on foreign shareholding or the total value of individual or aggregate foreign investment; or

(v) the total number of natural persons that may be employed in a particular sector or that an enterprise may employ and who are necessary for, and directly related to, the performance of an economic activity, in the form of numerical quotas or the requirement of an economic needs test; or

(b) restrict or require specific types of legal entity or joint venture through which an investor of the other Party may perform an economic activity.

Article 129 National treatment

1. Each Party shall accord to investors of the other Party and to covered enterprises treatment no less favourable than that it accords, in like situations, to its own investors and to their enterprises, with respect to their establishment and operation in its territory.

2. The treatment accorded by a Party under paragraph 1 means:

(a) with respect to a regional or local level of government of the United Kingdom, treatment no less favourable than the most favourable treatment accorded, in like situations, by that level of government to investors of the United Kingdom and to their enterprises in its territory; and

(b) with respect to a government of, or in, a Member State, treatment no less favourable than the most favourable treatment accorded, in like situations, by that government to investors of that Member State and to their enterprises in its territory.

Article 130 Most-favoured-nation-treatment

1. Each Party shall accord to investors of the other Party and to covered enterprises treatment no less favourable than that it accords, in like situations, to investors of a third country and to their enterprises, with respect to establishment in its territory.

2. Each Party shall accord to investors of the other Party and to covered enterprises treatment no less favourable than that it accords, in like situations, to investors of a third country and to their enterprises, with respect to operation in its territory.

3. Paragraphs 1 and 2 shall not be construed as obliging a Party to extend to investors of the other Party or to covered enterprises the benefit of any treatment resulting from:

(a) an international agreement for the avoidance of double taxation or other international agreement or arrangement relating wholly or mainly to taxation; or

[6] Points (a)(i) to (iii) of Article 128 do not cover measures taken in order to limit the production of an agricultural or fishery product. Point (a)(iii) of Article 128 does not cover measures by a Party which limit inputs for the supply of services.

[7] Point (a)(iii) of Article 128 does not cover measures by a Party which limit inputs for the supply of services.

(b) measures providing for recognition, including the recognition of the standards or criteria for the authorisation, licencing, or certification of a natural person or enterprise to carry out an economic activity, or the recognition of prudential measures as referred to in paragraph 3 of the GATS Annex on Financial Services.

4. For greater certainty, the 'treatment' referred to in paragraphs 1 and 2 does not include investor-to-state dispute settlement procedures provided for in other international agreements.

5. For greater certainty, the existence of substantive provisions in other international agreements concluded by a Party with a third country, or the mere formal transposition of those provisions into domestic law to the extent that it is necessary in order to incorporate them into the domestic legal order, do not in themselves constitute the 'treatment' referred to in paragraphs 1 and 2. Measures of a Party pursuant to those provisions may constitute such treatment and thus give rise to a breach of this Article.

Article 131 Senior management and boards of directors

A Party shall not require a covered enterprise to appoint individuals of any particular nationality as executives, managers or members of boards of directors.

Article 132 Performance requirements

1. A Party shall not impose or enforce any requirement, or enforce any commitment or undertaking, in connection with the establishment or operation of any enterprise in its territory:

(a) to export a given level or percentage of goods or services;

(b) to achieve a given level or percentage of domestic content;

(c) to purchase, use or accord a preference to goods produced or services provided in its territory or to purchase goods or services from natural or legal persons or any other entities in its territory;

(d) to relate in any way the volume or value of imports to the volume or value of exports or to the amount of foreign exchange inflows associated with such enterprise;

(e) to restrict sales of goods or services in its territory that such enterprise produces or supplies, by relating those sales in any way to the volume or value of its exports or foreign exchange inflows;

(f) to transfer technology, a production process or other proprietary knowledge to a natural or legal person or any other entity in its territory;[8]

(g) to supply exclusively from the territory of that Party a good produced or a service supplied by the enterprise to a specific regional or world market;

(h) to locate the headquarters for a specific region of the world which is broader than the territory of the Party or the world market in its territory;

(i) to employ a given number or percentage of natural persons of that Party;

(j) to achieve a given level or value of research and development in its territory;

(k) to restrict the exportation or sale for export; or

(l) with regard to any licence contract in existence at the time the requirement is imposed or enforced, or any commitment or undertaking is enforced, or with regard to any future licence contract freely entered into between the enterprise and a natural or legal person or any other entity in its territory, if the requirement is imposed or enforced or the commitment or undertaking is enforced, in a manner that constitutes direct interference with that licence contract by an exercise of non-judicial governmental authority of a Party, to adopt:

(i) a rate or amount of royalty below a certain level; or

(ii) a given duration of the term of a licence contract.

This point does not apply where the licence contract is concluded between the enterprise and the Party. For the purposes of this point, a 'licence contract' means any contract concerning the licensing of technology, a production process, or other proprietary knowledge.

[8] For greater certainty, point (f) of Article 132(1) is without prejudice to the provisions of Article 207.

2. A Party shall not condition the receipt or continued receipt of an advantage, in connection with the establishment or operation of an enterprise in its territory, on compliance with any of the following requirements:

(a) achieving a given level or percentage of domestic content;
(b) purchasing, using or according a preference to goods produced or services supplied in its territory, or to purchase goods or services from natural or legal persons or any other entity in its territory;
(c) relating in any way the volume or value of imports to the volume or value of exports or to the amount of foreign exchange inflows associated with that enterprise;
(d) restricting the sales of goods or services in its territory that that enterprise produces or supplies by relating those sales in any way to the volume or value of its exports or foreign exchange inflows; or
(e) restricting the exportation or sale for export.

3. Paragraph 2 shall not be construed as preventing a Party from conditioning the receipt or continued receipt of an advantage, in connection with the establishment or operation of any enterprise in its territory, on compliance with a requirement to locate production, supply a service, train or employ workers, construct or expand particular facilities, or carry out research and development, in its territory.

4. Points (f) and (l) of paragraph 1 of this Article do not apply where:

(a) the requirement is imposed or enforced, or the commitment or undertaking is enforced, by a court or administrative tribunal, or by a competition authority pursuant to a Party's competition law to prevent or remedy a restriction or a distortion of competition; or
(b) a Party authorises the use of an intellectual property right in accordance with Article 31 or Article 31bis of the TRIPS Agreement, or adopts or maintains measures requiring the disclosure of data or proprietary information that fall within the scope of, and are consistent with, paragraph 3 of Article 39 of the TRIPS Agreement.

5. Points (a) to (c) of paragraph 1 and points (a) and (b) of paragraph 2 do not apply to qualification requirements for goods or services with respect to participation in export promotion and foreign aid programmes.

6. For greater certainty, this Article does not preclude the enforcement by the competent authorities of a Party of any commitment or undertaking given between persons other than a Party which was not directly or indirectly imposed or required by that Party.

7. For greater certainty, points (a) and (b) of paragraph 2 do not apply to requirements imposed by an importing Party in relation to the content of goods necessary to qualify for preferential tariffs or preferential quotas.

8. Point (l) of paragraph 1 does not apply if the requirement is imposed or enforced, or the commitment or undertaking is enforced, by a tribunal as equitable remuneration under the Party's copyright laws.

9. A Party shall neither impose nor enforce any measure inconsistent with its obligations under the Agreement on Trade-Related Investment Measures (TRIMs), even where such measure has been listed by that Party in Annex 19 or 20.

10. For greater certainty, this Article shall not be construed as requiring a Party to permit a particular service to be supplied on a cross-border basis where that Party adopts or maintains restrictions or prohibitions on such provision of services which are consistent with the reservations, conditions or qualifications specified with respect to a sector, subsector or activity listed in Annex 19 or 20.

11. A condition for the receipt or continued receipt of an advantage referred to in paragraph 2 does not constitute a requirement or a commitment or undertaking for the purposes of paragraph 1.

Article 133 Non-conforming measures and exceptions

1. Articles 128, 129, 130, 131 and 132 do not apply to:

(a) any existing non-conforming measure of a Party at the level of:
  (i) for the Union:

(A) the Union, as set out in the Schedule of the Union in Annex 19;
(B) The central government of a Member State, as set out in the Schedule of the Union in Annex 19;
(C) a regional government of a Member State, as set out in the Schedule of the Union in Annex 19; or
(D) a local government, other than that referred to in point (C); and

(ii) for the United Kingdom:
(A) the central government, as set out in the Schedule of the United Kingdom in Annex 19;
(B) a regional government, as set out in the Schedule of the United Kingdom in Annex 19; or
(C) a local government;

(b) the continuation or prompt renewal of any non-conforming measure referred to in point (a) of this paragraph; or
(c) a modification to any non-conforming measure referred to in points (a) and (b) of this paragraph, to the extent that it does not decrease the conformity of the measure, as it existed immediately before the modification, with Article 128, 129, 130, 131 or 132.

2. Articles 128, 129, 130, 131 and 132 do not apply to a measure of a Party which is consistent with the reservations, conditions or qualifications specified with respect to a sector, subsector or activity listed in Annex 20.

3. Articles 129 and 130 of this Agreement do not apply to any measure that constitutes an exception to, or a derogation from, Article 3 or 4 of the TRIPS Agreement, as specifically provided for in Articles 3 to 5 of that Agreement.

4. For greater certainty, Articles 129 and 130 shall not be construed as preventing a Party from prescribing information requirements, including for statistical purposes, in connection with the establishment or operation of investors of the other Party or of covered enterprises, provided that it does not constitute a means to circumvent that Party's obligations under those Articles.

Chapter 3 Cross-border trade in services

Article 134 Scope

This Chapter applies to measures of a Party affecting the cross-border trade in services by service suppliers of the other Party.

Article 135 Market access

A Party shall not adopt or maintain, either on the basis of its entire territory or on the basis of a territorial sub-division, measures that:

(a) impose limitations on:
(i) the number of service suppliers that may supply a specific service, whether in the form of numerical quotas, monopolies, exclusive service suppliers or the requirement of an economic needs test;
(ii) the total value of service transactions or assets in the form of numerical quotas or the requirement of an economic needs test; or
(iii) the total number of service operations or on the total quantity of service output expressed in the terms of designated numerical units in the form of quotas or the requirement of an economic needs test[9]; or

(b) restrict or require specific types of legal entity or joint venture through which a service supplier may supply a service.

Article 136 Local presence

A Party shall not require a service supplier of the other Party to establish or maintain an enterprise or to be resident in its territory as a condition for the cross-border supply of a service.

[9] Point (a)(iii) of Article 135 does not cover measures by a Party which limit inputs for the supply of services.

Article 137 National treatment

1. Each Party shall accord to services and service suppliers of the other Party treatment no less favourable than that it accords, in like situations, to its own services and service suppliers.

2. A Party may meet the requirement of paragraph 1 by according to services and service suppliers of the other Party either formally identical treatment or formally different treatment to that it accords to its own services and service suppliers.

3. Formally identical or formally different treatment shall be considered to be less favourable if it modifies the conditions of competition in favour of services or service suppliers of the Party compared to services or service suppliers of the other Party.

4. Nothing in this Article shall be construed as requiring either Party to compensate for inherent competitive disadvantages which result from the foreign character of the relevant services or service suppliers.

Article 138 Most-favoured-nation treatment

1. Each Party shall accord to services and service suppliers of the other Party treatment no less favourable than that it accords, in like situations, to services and service suppliers of a third country.

2. Paragraph 1 shall not be construed as obliging a Party to extend to services and service suppliers of the other Party the benefit of any treatment resulting from:

(a) an international agreement for the avoidance of double taxation or other international agreement or arrangement relating wholly or mainly to taxation; or

(b) measures providing for recognition, including of the standards or criteria for the authorisation, licencing, or certification of a natural person or enterprise to carry out an economic activity, or of prudential measures as referred to in paragraph 3 of the GATS Annex on Financial Services.

3. For greater certainty, the existence of substantive provisions in other international agreements concluded by a Party with a third country, or mere formal transposition of those provisions into domestic law to the extent that it is necessary in order to incorporate them into the domestic legal order, do not in themselves constitute the 'treatment' referred to in paragraph 1. Measures of a Party pursuant to those provisions may constitute such treatment and thus give rise to a breach of this Article.

Article 139 Non-conforming measures

1. Articles 135, 136, 137 and 138 do not apply to:

(a) any existing non-conforming measure of a Party at the level of:

(i) for the Union:

(A) the Union, as set out in the Schedule of the Union in Annex 19;

(B) the central government of a Member State, as set out in the Schedule of the Union in Annex 19;

(C) a regional government of a Member State, as set out in the Schedule of the Union in Annex 19; or

(D) a local government, other than that referred to in point (C); and

(ii) for the United Kingdom:

(A) the central government, as set out in the Schedule of the United Kingdom in Annex 19;

(B) a regional government, as set out in the Schedule of the United Kingdom in Annex 19; or

(C) a local government;

(b) the continuation or prompt renewal of any non-conforming measure referred to in point (a) of this paragraph; or

(c) a modification to any non-conforming measure referred to in points (a) and (b) of this paragraph to the extent that it does not decrease the conformity of the measure, as it existed immediately before the modification, with Articles 135, 136, 137 and 138.

2. Articles 135, 136, 137 and 138 do not apply to any measure of a Party which is consistent with the reservations, conditions or qualifications specified with respect to a sector, subsector or activity listed in Annex 20.

Chapter 4 Entry and temporary stay of natural persons for business purposes

Article 140 Scope and definitions

1. This Chapter applies to measures of a Party affecting the performance of economic activities through the entry and temporary stay in its territory of natural persons of the other Party, who are business visitors for establishment purposes, contractual service suppliers, independent professionals, intra-corporate transferees and short-term business visitors.

2. To the extent that commitments are not undertaken in this Chapter, all requirements provided for in the law of a Party regarding the entry and temporary stay of natural persons shall continue to apply, including laws and regulations concerning the period of stay.

3. Notwithstanding the provisions of this Chapter, all requirements provided for in the law of a Party regarding work and social security measures shall continue to apply, including laws and regulations concerning minimum wages and collective wage agreements.

4. Commitments on the entry and temporary stay of natural persons for business purposes do not apply in cases where the intent or effect of the entry and temporary stay is to interfere with or otherwise affect the outcome of any labour or management dispute or negotiation, or the employment of any natural person who is involved in that dispute.

5. For the purposes of this Chapter:

(a) 'business visitors for establishment purposes' means natural persons working in a senior position within a legal person of a Party, who:

(i) are responsible for setting up an enterprise of such legal person in the territory of the other Party;

(ii) do not offer or provide services or engage in any economic activity other than that which is required for the purposes of the establishment of that enterprise; and

(iii) do not receive remuneration from a source located within the other Party;

(b) 'contractual service suppliers' means natural persons employed by a legal person of a Party (other than through an agency for placement and supply services of personnel), which is not established in the territory of the other Party and has concluded a bona fide contract, not exceeding 12 months, to supply services to a final consumer in the other Party requiring the temporary presence of its employees who:

(i) have offered the same type of services as employees of the legal person for a period of not less than one year immediately preceding the date of their application for entry and temporary stay;

(ii) possess, on that date, at least three years professional experience, obtained after having reached the age of majority, in the sector of activity that is the object of the contract, a university degree or a qualification demonstrating knowledge of an equivalent level and the professional qualifications legally required to exercise that activity in the other Party[10]; and

(iii) do not receive remuneration from a source located within the other Party;

(c) 'independent professionals' means natural persons engaged in the supply of a service and established as self-employed in the territory of a Party who:

(i) have not established in the territory of the other Party;

(ii) have concluded a bona fide contract (other than through an agency for placement and supply services of personnel) for a period not exceeding 12 months to supply services to a final consumer in the other Party[11], requiring their presence on a temporary basis; and

[10] Where the degree or qualification has not been obtained in the Party where the service is supplied, that Party may evaluate whether this is equivalent to a university degree required in its territory.

[11] Where the degree or qualification has not been obtained in the Party where the service is supplied, that Party may evaluate whether this is equivalent to a university degree required in its territory.

(iii) possess, on the date of their application for entry and temporary stay, at least six years professional experience in the relevant activity, a university degree or a qualification demonstrating knowledge of an equivalent level and the professional qualifications legally required to exercise that activity in the other Party[12];

(d) 'intra-corporate transferees' means natural persons, who:

(i) have been employed by a legal person of a Party, or have been partners in it, for a period, immediately preceding the date of the intra-corporate transfer, of not less than one year in the case of managers and specialists and of not less than six months in the case of trainee employees;

(ii) at the time of application reside outside the territory of the other Party;

(iii) are temporarily transferred to an enterprise of the legal person in the territory of the other Party which is a member of the same group as the originating legal person, including its representative office, subsidiary, branch or head company[13]; and

(iv) belong to one of the following categories:

(A) managers[14];

(B) specialists; or

(C) trainee employees;

(e) 'manager' means a natural person working in a senior position, who primarily directs the management of the enterprise in the other Party, receiving general supervision or direction principally from the board of directors or from shareholders of the business or their equivalent and whose responsibilities include:

(i) directing the enterprise or a department or subdivision thereof;

(ii) supervising and controlling the work of other supervisory, professional or managerial employees; and

(iii) having the authority to recommend hiring, dismissing or other personnel-related actions;

(f) 'specialist' means a natural person possessing specialised knowledge, essential to the enterprise's areas of activity, techniques or management, which is to be assessed taking into account not only knowledge specific to the enterprise, but also whether the person has a high level of qualification, including adequate professional experience of a type of work or activity requiring specific technical knowledge, including possible membership of an accredited profession; and

(g) 'trainee employee' means a natural person possessing a university degree who is temporarily transferred for career development purposes or to obtain training in business techniques or methods and is paid during the period of the transfer.[15]

6. The service contract referred to in points (b) and (c) of paragraph 5 shall comply with the requirements of the law of the Party where the contract is executed.

Article 141 Intra-corporate transferees and business visitors for establishment purposes

1. Subject to the relevant conditions and qualifications specified in Annex 21:

(a) each Party shall allow:

(i) the entry and temporary stay of intra-corporate transferees;

[12] Where the degree or qualification has not been obtained in the Party where the service is supplied, that Party may evaluate whether this is equivalent to a university degree required in its territory.

[13] Managers and specialists may be required to demonstrate they possess the professional qualifications and experience needed in the legal person to which they are transferred.

[14] While managers do not directly perform tasks concerning the actual supply of the services, this does not prevent them, in the course of executing their duties as described above, from performing such tasks as may be necessary for the provision of the services.

[15] The recipient enterprise may be required to submit a training programme covering the duration of the stay for prior approval, demonstrating that the purpose of the stay is for training. For AT, CZ, DE, FR, ES, HU and LT, training must be linked to the university degree which has been obtained.

(ii) the entry and temporary stay of business visitors for establishment purposes without requiring a work permit or other prior approval procedure of similar intent; and

(iii) the employment in its territory of intra-corporate transferees of the other Party;

(b) a Party shall not maintain or adopt limitations in the form of numerical quotas or economic needs tests regarding the total number of natural persons that, in a specific sector, are allowed entry as business visitors for establishment purposes or that an investor of the other Party may employ as intra-corporate transferees, either on the basis of a territorial subdivision or on the basis of its entire territory; and

(c) each Party shall accord to intra-corporate transferees and business visitors for establishment purposes of the other Party, during their temporary stay in its territory, treatment no less favourable than that it accords, in like situations, to its own natural persons.

2. The permissible length of stay shall be for a period of up to three years for managers and specialists, up to one year for trainee employees and up to 90 days within any six-month period for business visitors for establishment purposes.

Article 142 Short-term business visitors

1. Subject to the relevant conditions and qualifications specified in Annex 21, each Party shall allow the entry and temporary stay of short-term business visitors of the other Party for the purposes of carrying out the activities listed in Annex 21, subject to the following conditions:

(a) the short-term business visitors are not engaged in selling their goods or supplying services to the general public;

(b) the short-term business visitors do not, on their own behalf, receive remuneration from within the Party where they are staying temporarily; and

(c) the short-term business visitors are not engaged in the supply of a service in the framework of a contract concluded between a legal person that has not established in the territory of the Party where they are staying temporarily, and a consumer there, except as provided for in Annex 21.

2. Unless otherwise specified in Annex 21, a Party shall allow entry of short-term business visitors without the requirement of a work permit, economic needs test or other prior approval procedures of similar intent.

3. If short-term business visitors of a Party are engaged in the supply of a service to a consumer in the territory of the Party where they are staying temporarily in accordance with Annex 21, that Party shall accord to them, with regard to the supply of that service, treatment no less favourable than that it accords, in like situations, to its own service suppliers.

4. The permissible length of stay shall be for a period of up to 90 days in any six-month period.

Article 143 Contractual service suppliers and independent professionals

1. In the sectors, subsectors and activities specified in Annex 22 and subject to the relevant conditions and qualifications specified therein:

(a) a Party shall allow the entry and temporary stay of contractual service suppliers and independent professionals in its territory;

(b) a Party shall not adopt or maintain limitations on the total number of contractual service suppliers and independent professionals of the other Party allowed entry and temporary stay, in the form of numerical quotas or an economic needs test; and

(c) each Party shall accord to contractual service suppliers and independent professionals of the other Party, with regard to the supply of their services in its territory, treatment no less favourable than that it accords, in like situations, to its own service suppliers.

2. Access accorded under this Article relates only to the service which is the subject of the contract and does not confer entitlement to use the professional title of the Party where the service is provided.

3. The number of persons covered by the service contract shall not be greater than necessary to fulfil the contract, as it may be required by the law of the Party where the service is supplied.

4. The permissible length of stay shall be for a cumulative period of 12 months, or for the duration of the contract, whichever is less.

Article 144 Non-conforming measures

To the extent that the relevant measure affects the temporary stay of natural persons for business purposes, points (b) and (c) of Article 141(1), Article 142(3) and points (b) and (c) of Article 143(1) do not apply to:

(a) any existing non-conforming measure of a Party at the level of:
   (i) for the Union:
      (A) the Union, as set out in the Schedule of the Union in Annex 19;
      (B) the central government of a Member State, as set out in the Schedule of the Union in Annex 19;
      (C) a regional government of a Member State, as set out in the Schedule of the Union in Annex 19; or
      (D) a local government, other than that referred to in point (C); and
   (ii) for the United Kingdom:
      (A) the central government, as set out in the Schedule of the United Kingdom in Annex 19;
      (B) a regional subdivision, as set out in the Schedule of the United Kingdom in Annex 19; or
      (C) a local government;

(b) the continuation or prompt renewal of any non-conforming measure referred to in point (a) of this Article;

(c) a modification to any non-conforming measure referred to in points (a) and (b) of this Article to the extent that it does not decrease the conformity of the measure, as it existed immediately before the modification, with points (b) and (c) of Article 141(1), Article 142(3) and points (b) and (c) of Article 143(1); or

(d) any measure of a Party consistent with a condition or qualification specified in Annex 20.

Article 145 Transparency

1. Each Party shall make publicly available information on relevant measures that pertain to the entry and temporary stay of natural persons of the other Party, referred to in Article 140(1).

2. The information referred to in paragraph 1 shall, to the extent possible, include the following information relevant to the entry and temporary stay of natural persons:

(a) categories of visa, permits or any similar type of authorisation regarding the entry and temporary stay;
(b) documentation required and conditions to be met;
(c) method of filing an application and options on where to file, such as consular offices or online;
(d) application fees and an indicative timeframe of the processing of an application;
(e) the maximum length of stay under each type of authorisation described in point (a);
(f) conditions for any available extension or renewal;
(g) rules regarding accompanying dependants;
(h) available review or appeal procedures; and
(i) relevant laws of general application pertaining to the entry and temporary stay of natural persons for business purposes.

3. With respect to the information referred to in paragraphs 1 and 2, each Party shall endeavour to promptly inform the other Party of the introduction of any new requirements and procedures or of the changes in any requirements and procedures that affect the effective application for the grant of entry into, temporary stay in and, where applicable, permission to work in the former Party.

Chapter 5 Regulatory framework

Section 1 Domestic regulation

Article 146 Scope and definitions

1. This Section applies to measures by the Parties relating to licensing requirements and procedures, qualification requirements and procedures, formalities and technical standards that affect:
   - (a) cross-border trade in services;
   - (b) establishment or operation; or
   - (c) the supply of a service through the presence of a natural person of a Party in the territory of the other Party as set out in Article 140.

As far as measures relating to technical standards are concerned, this Section only applies to measures that affect trade in services. For the purposes of this Section, the term 'technical standards' does not include regulatory or implementing technical standards for financial services.

2. This Section does not apply to licensing requirements and procedures, qualification requirements and procedures, formalities and technical standards pursuant to a measure:
   - (a) that does not conform with Article 128 or 129 and is referred to in points (a) to (c) of Article 133(1) or with Article 135, 136 or 137 and is referred to in points (a) to (c) of Article 139(1) or with points (b) and (c) of Article 141(1), or Article 142(3) or with points (b) and (c) of Article 143(1) and is referred to in Article 144; or
   - (b) referred to in Article 133(2) or Article 139(2).

3. For the purposes of this Section, the following definitions apply:
   - (a) 'authorisation' means the permission to carry out any of the activities referred to in points (a) to (c) of paragraph 1 resulting from a procedure a natural or legal person must adhere to in order to demonstrate compliance with licensing requirements, qualification requirements, technical standards or formalities for the purposes of obtaining, maintaining or renewing that permission; and
   - (b) 'competent authority' means a central, regional or local government or authority or non-governmental body in the exercise of powers delegated by central, regional or local governments or authorities, which is entitled to take a decision concerning the authorisation referred to in point (a).

Article 147 Submission of applications

Each Party shall, to the extent practicable, avoid requiring an applicant to approach more than one competent authority for each application for authorisation. If an activity for which authorisation is requested is within the jurisdiction of multiple competent authorities, multiple applications for authorisation may be required.

Article 148 Application timeframes

If a Party requires authorisation, it shall ensure that its competent authorities, to the extent practicable, permit the submission of an application at any time throughout the year. If a specific time period for applying for authorisation exists, the Party shall ensure that the competent authorities allow a reasonable period of time for the submission of an application.

Article 149 Electronic applications and acceptance of copies

If a Party requires authorisation, it shall ensure that its competent authorities:
- (a) to the extent possible provide for applications to be completed by electronic means, including from within the territory of the other Party; and
- (b) accept copies of documents, that are authenticated in accordance with the Party's domestic law, in place of original documents, unless the competent authorities require original documents to protect the integrity of the authorisation process.

Article 150 Processing of applications

1. If a Party requires authorisation, it shall ensure that its competent authorities:
   - (a) process applications throughout the year. Where that is not possible, this information should be made public in advance, to the extent practicable;

(b) to the extent practicable, provide an indicative timeframe for the processing of an application. That timeframe shall be reasonable to the extent practicable;
(c) at the request of the applicant, provide without undue delay information concerning the status of the application;
(d) to the extent practicable, ascertain without undue delay the completeness of an application for processing under the Party's domestic laws and regulations;
(e) if they consider an application complete for the purposes of processing under the Party's domestic laws and regulations,[16] within a reasonable period of time after the submission of the application ensure that:
 (i) the processing of the application is completed; and
 (ii) the applicant is informed of the decision concerning the application, to the extent possible, in writing;[17]
(f) if they consider an application incomplete for the purposes of processing under the Party's domestic laws and regulations, within a reasonable period of time, to the extent practicable:
 (i) inform the applicant that the application is incomplete;
 (ii) at the request of the applicant identify the additional information required to complete the application or otherwise provide guidance on why the application is considered incomplete; and
 (iii) provide the applicant with the opportunity to provide the additional information that is required to complete the application;[18]

 however, if none of the actions referred to in points (i), (ii) and (iii) is practicable, and the application is rejected due to incompleteness, the competent authorities shall ensure that they inform the applicant within a reasonable period of time; and
(g) if an application is rejected, either upon their own initiative or upon request of the applicant, inform the applicant of the reasons for rejection and of the timeframe for an appeal against that decision and, if applicable, the procedures for resubmission of an application; an applicant shall not be prevented from submitting another application solely on the basis of a previously rejected application.

2. The Parties shall ensure that their competent authorities grant an authorisation as soon as it is established, on the basis of an appropriate examination, that the applicant meets the conditions for obtaining it.

3. The Parties shall ensure that, once granted, an authorisation enters into effect without undue delay, subject to the applicable terms and conditions.[19]

Article 151 Fees

1. For all economic activities other than financial services, each Party shall ensure that the authorisation fees charged by its competent authorities are reasonable and transparent and do not in themselves restrict the supply of the relevant service or the pursuit of any other economic activity. Having regard to the cost and administrative burden, each Party is encouraged to accept payment of authorisation fees by electronic means.

2. With regard to financial services, each Party shall ensure that its competent authorities, with respect to authorisation fees that they charge, provide applicants with a schedule of fees or information on how fee amounts are determined, and do not use the fees as a means of avoiding the Party's commitments or obligations.

3. Authorisation fees do not include fees for the use of natural resources, payments for auction, tendering or other non-discriminatory means of awarding concessions or mandated contributions to universal service provision.

[16] Balancing resource constraints against the potential burden on businesses, in cases where it is reasonable to do so, competent authorities may require that all information is submitted in a specified format to consider it 'complete for the purposes of processing'.

[17] Competent authorities may meet the requirement set out in point (ii) by informing an applicant in advance in writing, including through a published measure, that a lack of response after a specified period of time from the date of submission of the application indicates acceptance of the application. The reference to 'in writing' should be understood as including electronic format.

[18] Such 'opportunity' does not require a competent authority to provide extensions of deadlines.

[19] Competent authorities are not responsible for delays due to reasons outside their competence.

Article 152 Assessment of qualifications

If a Party requires an examination to assess the qualifications of an applicant for authorisation, it shall ensure that its competent authorities schedule such an examination at reasonably frequent intervals and provide a reasonable period of time to enable applicants to request to take the examination. To the extent practicable, each Party shall accept requests in electronic format to take such examinations and shall consider the use of electronic means in other aspects of examination processes.

Article 153 Publication and information available

1. If a Party requires authorisation, the Party shall promptly publish the information necessary for persons carrying out or seeking to carry out the activities referred to in Article 146(1) for which the authorisation is required to comply with the requirements, formalities, technical standards and procedures for obtaining, maintaining, amending and renewing such authorisation. Such information shall include, to the extent it exists:

(a) the licensing and qualification requirements and procedures and formalities;
(b) contact information of relevant competent authorities;
(c) authorisation fees;
(d) applicable technical standards;
(e) procedures for appeal or review of decisions concerning applications;
(f) procedures for monitoring or enforcing compliance with the terms and conditions of licences or qualifications;
(g) opportunities for public involvement, such as through hearings or comments; and
(h) indicative timeframes for the processing of an application.

For the purposes of this Section, 'publish' means to include in an official publication, such as an official journal, or on an official website. Parties shall consolidate electronic publications into a single online portal or otherwise ensure that competent authorities make them easily accessible through alternative electronic means.

2. Each Party shall require each of its competent authorities to respond to any request for information or assistance, to the extent practicable.

Article 154 Technical standards

Each Party shall encourage its competent authorities, when adopting technical standards, to adopt technical standards developed through open and transparent processes, and shall encourage any body, including relevant international organisations, designated to develop technical standards to do so through open and transparent processes.

Article 155 Conditions for authorisation

1. Each Party shall ensure that measures relating to authorisation are based on criteria which preclude the competent authorities from exercising their power of assessment in an arbitrary manner and may include, *inter alia*, competence and the ability to supply a service or any other economic activity, including to do so in compliance with a Party's regulatory requirements such as health and environmental requirements. For the avoidance of doubt, the Parties understand that in reaching decisions a competent authority may balance criteria.

2. The criteria referred to in paragraph 1 shall be:

(a) clear and unambiguous;
(b) objective and transparent;
(c) pre-established;
(d) made public in advance;
(e) impartial; and
(f) easily accessible.

3. If a Party adopts or maintains a measure relating to authorisation, it shall ensure that:

(a) the competent authority concerned processes applications, and reaches and administers its decisions objectively and impartially and in a manner independent of the undue influence of any person carrying out the economic activity for which authorisation is required; and

(b) the procedures themselves do not prevent fulfilment of the requirements.

Article 156 Limited numbers of licences

If the number of licences available for a given activity is limited because of the scarcity of available natural resources or technical capacity, a Party shall apply a selection procedure to potential candidates which provides full guarantees of impartiality, objectivity and transparency, including, in particular, adequate publicity about the launch, conduct and completion of the procedure. In establishing the rules for the selection procedure, a Party may take into account legitimate policy objectives, including considerations of health, safety, the protection of the environment and the preservation of cultural heritage.

Section 2 Provisions of general application

Article 157 Review procedures for administrative decisions

A Party shall maintain judicial, arbitral or administrative tribunals or procedures which provide, on request of an affected investor or service supplier of the other Party, for the prompt review of, and if justified appropriate remedies for, administrative decisions that affect establishment or operation, cross-border trade in services or the supply of a service through the presence of a natural person of a Party in the territory of the other Party. For the purposes of this Section, 'administrative decisions' means a decision or action with a legal effect that applies to a specific person, good or service in an individual case and covers the failure to take an administrative decision or take such action when that is so required by a Party's law. If such procedures are not independent of the competent authority entrusted with the administrative decision concerned, a Party shall ensure that the procedures in fact provide for an objective and impartial review.

Article 158 Professional qualifications

1. Nothing in this Article shall prevent a Party from requiring that natural persons possess the necessary professional qualifications specified in the territory where the activity is performed, for the sector of activity concerned[20].

2. The professional bodies or authorities, which are relevant for the sector of activity concerned in their respective territories, may develop and provide joint recommendations on the recognition of professional qualifications to the Partnership Council. Such joint recommendations shall be supported by an evidence-based assessment of:

(a) the economic value of an envisaged arrangement on the recognition of professional qualifications; and

(b) the compatibility of the respective regimes, that is, the extent to which the requirements applied by each Party for the authorisation, licensing, operation and certification are compatible.

3. On receipt of a joint recommendation, the Partnership Council shall review its consistency with this Title within a reasonable period of time. The Partnership Council may, following such review, develop and adopt an arrangement on the conditions for the recognition of professional qualifications by decision as an annex to this Agreement, which shall be considered to form an integral part of this Title.[21]

4. An arrangement referred to in paragraph 3 shall provide for the conditions for recognition of professional qualifications acquired in the Union and professional qualifications acquired in the United Kingdom relating to an activity covered by this Title and Title III of this Heading.

5. The Guidelines for arrangements on the recognition of professional qualifications set out in Annex 24 shall be taken into account in the development of the joint recommendations referred to in paragraph 2 of this Article and by the Partnership Council when assessing whether to adopt such an Arrangement, as referred to in paragraph 3 of this Article.

[20] For greater certainty, this Article shall not be construed to prevent the negotiation and conclusion of one or more agreements between the Parties on the recognition of professional qualifications on conditions and requirements different from those provided for in this Article.

[21] For greater certainty, such arrangements shall not lead to the automatic recognition of qualifications but shall set, in the mutual interest of both Parties, the conditions for the competent authorities granting recognition.

Section 3 Delivery services

Article 159 Scope and definitions

1. This Section applies to measures of a Party affecting the supply of delivery services in addition to Chapters 1, 2, 3 and 4 of this Title, and to Sections 1 and 2 of this Chapter.

2. For the purposes of this Section, the following definitions apply:

(a) 'delivery services' means postal services, courier services, express delivery services or express mail services, which include the following activities: the collection, sorting, transport, and delivery of postal items;

(b) 'express delivery services' means the collection, sorting, transport and delivery of postal items at accelerated speed and reliability and may include value added elements such as collection from point of origin, personal delivery to the addressee, tracing, possibility of changing the destination and addressee in transit or confirmation of receipt;

(c) 'express mail services' means international express delivery services supplied through the EMS Cooperative, which is the voluntary association of designated postal operators under Universal Postal Union (UPU);

(d) 'licence' means an authorisation that a regulatory authority of a Party may require of an individual supplier in order for that supplier to offer postal or courier services;

(e) 'postal item' means an item up to 31.5 kg addressed in the final form in which it is to be carried by any type of supplier of delivery services, whether public or private and may include items such as a letter, parcel, newspaper or catalogue;

(f) 'postal monopoly' means the exclusive right to supply specified delivery services within a Party's territory or a subdivision thereof pursuant to the law of that Party; and

(g) 'universal service' means the permanent supply of a delivery service of specified quality at all points in the territory of a Party or a subdivision thereof at affordable prices for all users.

Article 160 Universal service

1. Each Party has the right to define the kind of universal service obligation it wishes to maintain and to decide on its scope and implementation. Any universal service obligation shall be administered in a transparent, non-discriminatory and neutral manner with regard to all suppliers subject to the obligation.

2. If a Party requires inbound express mail services to be supplied on a universal service basis, it shall not accord preferential treatment to those services over other international express delivery services.

Article 161 Universal service funding

A party shall not impose fees or other charges on the supply of a delivery service that is not a universal service for the purposes of funding the supply of a universal service. This Article does not apply to generally applicable taxation measures or administrative fees.

Article 162 Prevention of market distortive practices

Each party shall ensure that suppliers of delivery services subject to a universal service obligation or postal monopolies do not engage in market distortive practices such as:

(a) using revenues derived from the supply of the service subject to a universal service obligation or from a postal monopoly to cross-subsidise the supply of an express delivery service or any delivery service which is not subject to a universal service obligation; or

(b) unjustifiably differentiating between consumers with respect to tariffs or other terms and conditions for the supply of a service subject to a universal service or a postal monopoly.

Article 163 Licences

1. If a Party requires a licence for the provision of delivery services, it shall make publicly available:

(a) all the licensing requirements and the period of time normally required to reach a decision concerning an application for a licence; and

(b) the terms and conditions of licences.

2. The procedures, obligations and requirements of a licence shall be transparent, non-discriminatory and based on objective criteria.

3. If a licence application is rejected by the competent authority, it shall inform the applicant of the reasons for the rejection in writing. Each Party shall establish an appeal procedure through an independent body available to applicants whose licence has been rejected. That body may be a court.

Article 164 Independence of the regulatory body

1. Each Party shall establish or maintain a regulatory body which shall be legally distinct from and functionally independent from any supplier of delivery services. If a Party owns or controls a supplier of delivery services, it shall ensure the effective structural separation of the regulatory function from activities associated with ownership or control.

2. The regulatory bodies shall perform their tasks in a transparent and timely manner and have adequate financial and human resources to carry out the task assigned to them. Their decisions shall be impartial with respect to all market participants.

Section 4 Telecommunications services

Article 165 Scope

This Section applies to measures of a Party affecting the supply of telecommunications services in addition to Chapters 1, 2, 3 and 4 of this Title, and to Sections 1 and 2 of this Chapter.

Article 166 Definitions

For the purposes of this Section, the following definitions apply:

(a) 'associated facilities' means associated services, physical infrastructure and other facilities or elements associated with a telecommunications network or telecommunications service which enable or support the supply of services via that network or service or have the potential to do so;

(b) 'end user' means a final consumer of, or subscriber to, a public telecommunications service, including a service supplier other than a supplier of public telecommunications services;

(c) 'essential facilities' means facilities of a public telecommunications network or a public telecommunications service that:

  (i) are exclusively or predominantly provided by a single or limited number of suppliers; and

  (ii) cannot feasibly be economically or technically substituted in order to provide a service;

(d) 'interconnection' means the linking of public telecommunications networks used by the same or different suppliers of telecommunications networks or telecommunications services in order to allow the users of one supplier to communicate with users of the same or another supplier or to access services provided by another supplier, irrespective of whether those services are provided by the suppliers involved or any other supplier who has access to the network;

(e) 'international mobile roaming service' means a commercial mobile service provided pursuant to a commercial agreement between suppliers of public telecommunications services that enables an end user to use its home mobile handset or other device for voice, data or messaging services while outside the territory in which the end user's home public telecommunications network is located;

(f) 'internet access service' means a public telecommunications service that provides access to the internet and thereby connectivity to virtually all end points of the internet, irrespective of the network technology and terminal equipment used;

(g) 'leased circuit' means telecommunications services or facilities, including those of a virtual nature, that set aside capacity for the dedicated use by, or availability to, a user between two or more designated points;

(h) 'major supplier' means a supplier of telecommunications networks or telecommunications services which has the ability to materially affect the terms of participation, having regard to price and supply, in a relevant market for telecommunications networks or telecommunications services as a result of control over essential facilities or the use of its position in that market;
(i) 'network element' means a facility or equipment used in supplying a telecommunications service, including features, functions and capabilities provided by means of that facility or equipment;
(j) 'number portability' means the ability of subscribers who so request to retain the same telephone numbers, at the same location in the case of a fixed line, without impairment of quality, reliability or convenience when switching between the same category of suppliers of public telecommunications services;
(k) 'public telecommunications network' means any telecommunications network used wholly or mainly for the provision of public telecommunications services which supports the transfer of information between network termination points;
(l) 'public telecommunications service' means any telecommunications service that is offered to the public generally;
(m) 'subscriber' means any natural or legal person which is party to a contract with a supplier of public telecommunications services for the supply of such services;
(n) 'telecommunications' means the transmission and reception of signals by any electromagnetic means;
(o) 'telecommunications network' means transmission systems and, where applicable, switching or routing equipment and other resources, including network elements which are not active, which permit the transmission and reception of signals by wire, radio, optical, or other electromagnetic means;
(p) 'telecommunications regulatory authority' means the body or bodies charged by a Party with the regulation of telecommunications networks and telecommunications services covered by this Section;
(q) 'telecommunications service' means a service which consists wholly or mainly in the transmission and reception of signals, including broadcasting signals, over telecommunications networks, including those used for broadcasting, but not a service providing, or exercising editorial control over, content transmitted using telecommunications networks and telecommunications services;
(r) 'universal service' means the minimum set of services of specified quality that must be made available to all users, or to a set of users, in the territory of a Party, or in a subdivision thereof, regardless of their geographical location and at an affordable price; and
(s) 'user' means any natural or legal person using a public telecommunications service.

Article 167 Telecommunications regulatory authority

1. Each Party shall establish or maintain a telecommunications regulatory authority that:
(a) is legally distinct and functionally independent from any supplier of telecommunications networks, telecommunications services or telecommunications equipment;
(b) uses procedures and issues decisions that are impartial with respect to all market participants;
(c) acts independently and does not seek or take instructions from any other body in relation to the exercise of the tasks assigned to it by law to enforce the obligations set out in Articles 169, 170, 171, 173 and 174;
(d) has the regulatory power, as well as adequate financial and human resources, to carry out the tasks mentioned in point (c) of this Article;
(e) has the power to ensure that suppliers of telecommunications networks or telecommunications services provide it, promptly upon request, with all the information[22], including financial information, which is necessary to enable it to carry out the tasks mentioned in point (c) of this Article; and

[22] Information requested shall be treated in accordance with the requirements of confidentiality.

(f) exercises its powers transparently and in a timely manner.

2. Each Party shall ensure that the tasks assigned to the telecommunications regulatory authority are made public in an easily accessible and clear form, in particular where those tasks are assigned to more than one body.

3. A Party that retains ownership or control of suppliers of telecommunications networks or telecommunications services shall ensure the effective structural separation of the regulatory function from activities associated with ownership or control.

4. Each Party shall ensure that a user or supplier of telecommunications networks or telecommunications services affected by a decision of the telecommunications regulatory authority has a right of appeal before an appeal body which is independent of the regulatory authority and other affected parties. Pending the outcome of the appeal, the decision shall stand, unless interim measures are granted in accordance with the Party's law.

Article 168 Authorisation to provide telecommunications networks or services

1. Each Party shall permit the provision of telecommunications networks or telecommunications services without a prior formal authorisation.

2. Each Party shall make publicly available all the criteria, applicable procedures and terms and conditions under which suppliers are permitted to provide telecommunications networks or telecommunications services.

3. Any authorisation criteria and applicable procedures shall be as simple as possible, objective, transparent, non-discriminatory and proportionate. Any obligations and conditions imposed on or associated with an authorisation shall be non-discriminatory, transparent and proportionate, and shall be related to the services or networks provided.

4. Each Party shall ensure that an applicant for an authorisation receives in writing the reasons for any denial or revocation of an authorisation or the imposition of supplier-specific conditions. In such cases, the applicant shall have a right of appeal before an appeal body.

5. Administrative fees imposed on suppliers shall be objective, transparent, non-discriminatory and commensurate with the administrative costs reasonably incurred in the management, control and enforcement of the obligations set out in this Section[23].

Article 169 Interconnection

Each Party shall ensure that a supplier of public telecommunications networks or public telecommunications services has the right and, when so requested by another supplier of public telecommunications networks or public telecommunications services, the obligation to negotiate interconnection for the purposes of providing public telecommunications networks or public telecommunications services.

Article 170 Access and use

1. Each Party shall ensure that any covered enterprise or service supplier of the other Party is accorded access to and use of public telecommunications networks or public telecommunications services on reasonable and non-discriminatory[24] terms and conditions. This obligation shall be applied, *inter alia*, to paragraphs 2 to 5.

2. Each Party shall ensure that covered enterprises or service suppliers of the other Party have access to and use of any public telecommunications network or public telecommunications service offered within or across its border, including private leased circuits, and to that end shall ensure, subject to paragraph 5, that such enterprises and suppliers are permitted:

(a) to purchase or lease and attach terminal or other equipment which interfaces with the network and which is necessary to conduct their operations;

[23] Administrative fees do not include payments for rights to use scarce resources and mandated contributions to universal service provision.

[24] For the purposes of this Article, 'non-discriminatory' means most-favoured-nation and national treatment as defined in Articles 129, 130, 136 and 137, as well as under terms and conditions no less favourable than those accorded to any other user of like public telecommunications networks or services in like situations.

(b) to interconnect private leased or owned circuits with public telecommunications networks or with circuits leased or owned by another covered enterprise or service supplier; and

(c) to use the operating protocols of their choice in their operations, other than as necessary to ensure the availability of telecommunications services to the public generally.

3. Each Party shall ensure that covered enterprises or service suppliers of the other Party may use public telecommunications networks and public telecommunications services for the movement of information within and across borders, including for their intra-corporate communications, and for access to information contained in databases or otherwise stored in machine-readable form in the territory of either Party.

4. Notwithstanding paragraph 3, a Party may take such measures as are necessary to ensure the security and confidentiality of communications, subject to the requirement that such measures are not applied in a manner which would constitute either a disguised restriction on trade in services or a means of arbitrary or unjustifiable discrimination or of nullification or impairment of benefits under this Title.

5. Each Party shall ensure that no condition is imposed on access to and use of public telecommunications networks or services other than as necessary:

(a) to safeguard the public service responsibilities of suppliers of public telecommunications networks or public telecommunications services, in particular their ability to make their services available to the public generally; or

(b) to protect the technical integrity of public telecommunications networks or services.

Article 171 Resolution of telecommunications disputes

1. Each Party shall ensure that, in the event of a dispute arising between suppliers of telecommunications networks or telecommunications services in connection with rights and obligations that arise from this Section, and upon request of either party involved in the dispute, the telecommunications regulatory authority issues a binding decision within a reasonable timeframe to resolve the dispute.

2. The decision by the telecommunications regulatory authority shall be made available to the public, having regard to the requirements of business confidentiality. The parties concerned shall be given a full statement of the reasons on which it is based and shall have the right of appeal referred to in Article 167(4).

3. The procedure referred to in paragraphs 1 and 2 shall not preclude either party concerned from bringing an action before a judicial authority.

Article 172 Competitive safeguards on major suppliers

Each Party shall introduce or maintain appropriate measures for the purpose of preventing suppliers of telecommunications networks or telecommunications services who, alone or together, are a major supplier from engaging in or continuing anti-competitive practices. These anti-competitive practices shall include in particular:

(a) engaging in anti-competitive cross-subsidisation;

(b) using information obtained from competitors with anti-competitive results; and

(c) not making available to other service suppliers on a timely basis technical information about essential facilities and commercially relevant information which are necessary for them to provide services.

Article 173 Interconnection with major suppliers

1. Each Party shall ensure that major suppliers of public telecommunications networks or public telecommunications services provide interconnection at any technically feasible point in the network. Such interconnection shall be provided:

(a) under non-discriminatory terms and conditions (including as regards rates, technical standards, specifications, quality and maintenance) and of a quality no less favourable than that provided for the own like services of such major supplier, or for like services of its subsidiaries or other affiliates;

(b) in a timely fashion, on terms and conditions (including as regards rates, technical standards, specifications, quality and maintenance) that are transparent, reasonable, having regard to economic feasibility, and sufficiently unbundled so that the supplier need not pay for network elements or facilities that it does not require for the service to be provided; and
(c) upon request, at points in addition to the network termination points offered to the majority of users, subject to charges that reflect the cost of construction of necessary additional facilities.

2. The procedures applicable for interconnection to a major supplier shall be made publicly available.

3. Major suppliers shall make publicly available either their interconnection agreements or their reference interconnection offers as appropriate.

Article 174 Access to major suppliers' essential facilities

Each Party shall ensure that major suppliers in its territory make their essential facilities available to suppliers of telecommunications networks or telecommunications services on reasonable, transparent and non-discriminatory terms and conditions for the purpose of providing public telecommunications services, except where this is not necessary to achieve effective competition on the basis of the facts collected and the assessment of the market conducted by the telecommunications regulatory authority. The major supplier's essential facilities may include network elements, leased circuits services and associated facilities.

Article 175 Scarce resources

1. Each Party shall ensure that the allocation and granting of rights of use of scarce resources, including radio spectrum, numbers and rights of way, is carried out in an open, objective, timely, transparent, non-discriminatory and proportionate manner and by taking into account general interest objectives. Procedures, and conditions and obligations attached to rights of use, shall be based on objective, transparent, non-discriminatory and proportionate criteria.

2. The current use of allocated frequency bands shall be made publicly available, but detailed identification of radio spectrum allocated for specific government uses is not required.

3. Parties may rely on market-based approaches, such as bidding procedures, to assign spectrum for commercial use.

4. The Parties understand that measures of a Party allocating and assigning spectrum and managing frequency are not in and of themselves inconsistent with Articles 128 and 135. Each Party retains the right to establish and apply spectrum and frequency management measures that may have the effect of limiting the number of suppliers of telecommunications services, provided that it does so in a manner consistent with this Agreement. This includes the ability to allocate frequency bands taking into account current and future needs and spectrum availability.

Article 176 Universal service

1. Each Party has the right to define the kind of universal service obligations it wishes to maintain and to decide on their scope and implementation.

2. Each Party shall administer the universal service obligations in a proportionate, transparent, objective and non-discriminatory way, which is neutral with respect to competition and not more burdensome than necessary for the kind of universal service defined by the Party.

3. Each Party shall ensure that procedures for the designation of universal service suppliers are open to all suppliers of public telecommunications networks or public telecommunications services. Such designation shall be made through an efficient, transparent and non-discriminatory mechanism.

4. If a Party decides to compensate the universal service suppliers, it shall ensure that such compensation does not exceed the net cost caused by the universal service obligation.

Article 177 Number portability

Each Party shall ensure that suppliers of public telecommunications services provide number portability on reasonable terms and conditions.

Article 178 Open internet access

1. Each Party shall ensure that, subject to its laws and regulations, suppliers of internet access services enable users of those services to:

(a) access and distribute information and content, use and provide applications and services of their choice, subject to non-discriminatory, reasonable, transparent and proportionate network management; and

(b) use devices of their choice, provided that such devices do not harm the security of other devices, the network or services provided over the network.

2. For greater certainty, nothing in this Article shall prevent the Parties from adopting measures with the aim of protecting public safety with regards to users online.

Article 179 Confidentiality of information

1. Each Party shall ensure that suppliers that acquire information from another supplier in the process of negotiating arrangements pursuant to Articles 169, 170, 173 and 174 use that information solely for the purpose for which it was supplied and respect at all times the confidentiality of information transmitted or stored.

2. Each Party shall ensure the confidentiality of communications and related traffic data transmitted in the use of public telecommunications networks or public telecommunications services subject to the requirement that measures applied to that end do not constitute a means of arbitrary or unjustifiable discrimination or a disguised restriction on trade in services.

Article 180 Foreign shareholding

With regard to the provision of telecommunications networks or telecommunications services through establishment and notwithstanding Article 133, a Party shall not impose joint venture requirements or limit the participation of foreign capital in terms of maximum percentage limits on foreign shareholding or the total value of individual or aggregate foreign investment.

Article 181 International mobile roaming[25]

1. The Parties shall endeavour to cooperate on promoting transparent and reasonable rates for international mobile roaming services in ways that can help promote the growth of trade among the Parties and enhance consumer welfare.

2. Parties may choose to take steps to enhance transparency and competition with respect to international mobile roaming rates and technological alternatives to roaming services, such as:

(a) ensuring that information regarding retail rates is easily accessible to end users; and

(b) minimising impediments to the use of technological alternatives to roaming, whereby end users visiting the territory of a Party from the territory of the other Party can access telecommunications services using the device of their choice.

3. Each Party shall encourage suppliers of public telecommunications services in its territory to make publicly available information on retail rates for international mobile roaming services for voice, data and text messages offered to their end users when visiting the territory of the other Party.

4. Nothing in this Article shall require a Party to regulate rates or conditions for international mobile roaming services.

Section 5 Financial services

Article 182 Scope

1. This Section applies to measures of a Party affecting the supply of financial services in addition to Chapters 1, 2, 3 and 4 of this Title, and to Sections 1 and 2 of this Chapter.

2. For the purposes of this Section, the term 'activities performed in the exercise of governmental authority' referred to in point (f) of Article 124 means the following[26]:

[25] This Article does not apply to intra-European Union roaming services, which are commercial mobile services provided pursuant to a commercial agreement between suppliers of public telecommunications services that enable an end user to use its home mobile handset or other device for voice, data or messaging services in a Member State other than that in which the end user's home public telecommunications network is located.

[26] For greater certainty, this modification applies to 'services supplied in the exercise of governmental authority' in point (o) of Article 124 as it applies to 'activities performed in the exercise of governmental authority' in point (f) of Article 124.

(a) activities conducted by a central bank or a monetary authority or by any other public entity in pursuit of monetary or exchange rate policies;
(b) activities forming part of a statutory system of social security or public retirement plans; and
(c) other activities conducted by a public entity for the account or with the guarantee or using the financial resources of the Party or its public entities.

3. For the purposes of the application of point (f) of Article 124 to this Section, if a Party allows any of the activities referred to in point (b) or (c) of paragraph 2 of this Article to be conducted by its financial service suppliers in competition with a public entity or a financial service supplier, 'activities performed in the exercise of governmental authority' does not include those activities.

4. Point (a) of Article 124 does not apply to services covered by this Section.

Article 183 Definitions [omitted]

Article 184 Prudential carve-out

1. Nothing in this Agreement shall prevent a Party from adopting or maintaining measures for prudential reasons[27], such as:
(a) the protection of investors, depositors, policy-holders or persons to whom a fiduciary duty is owed by a financial service supplier; or
(b) ensuring the integrity and stability of a Party's financial system.

2. Where such measures do not conform with the provisions of this Agreement, they shall not be used as a means of avoiding the Party's commitments or obligations under this Agreement.

Article 185 Confidential information

Without prejudice to Part Three, nothing in this Agreement shall be construed to require a Party to disclose information relating to the affairs and accounts of individual consumers or any confidential or proprietary information in the possession of public entities.

Article 186 International standards

The Parties shall make their best endeavours to ensure that internationally agreed standards in the financial services sector for regulation and supervision, for the fight against money laundering and terrorist financing and for the fight against tax evasion and avoidance, are implemented and applied in their territory. Such internationally agreed standards are, *inter alia*, those adopted by: the G20; the Financial Stability Board; the Basel Committee on Banking Supervision, in particular its 'Core Principle for Effective Banking Supervision'; the International Association of Insurance Supervisors, in particular its 'Insurance Core Principles'; the International Organisation of Securities Commissions, in particular its 'Objectives and Principles of Securities Regulation'; the Financial Action Task Force; and the Global Forum on Transparency and Exchange of Information for Tax Purposes of the Organisation for Economic Cooperation and Development.

Article 187 Financial services new to the territory of a Party

1. Each Party shall permit a financial service supplier of the other Party established in its territory to supply any new financial service that it would permit its own financial service suppliers to supply in accordance with its law in like situations, provided that the introduction of the new financial service does not require the adoption of a new law or the amendment of an existing law. This does not apply to branches of the other Party established in the territory of a Party.

2. A Party may determine the institutional and legal form through which the service may be supplied and require authorisation for the supply of the service. Where such authorisation is required, a decision shall be made within a reasonable time and the authorisation may only be refused for prudential reasons.

Article 188 Self-regulatory organisations

Where a Party requires membership of, participation in, or access to, any self-regulatory organisation in order for financial service suppliers of the other Party to supply financial services in its

[27] For greater certainty, this shall not prevent a Party from adopting or maintaining measures for prudential reasons in relation to branches established in its territory by legal persons in the other Party.

territory, the Party shall ensure observance by that self-regulatory organisation of the obligations under Articles 129, 130, 137 and 138.

Article 189 Clearing and payment systems

Under terms and conditions that accord national treatment, each Party shall grant to financial service suppliers of the other Party established in its territory access to payment and clearing systems operated by public entities, and to official funding and refinancing facilities available in the normal course of ordinary business. This Article does not confer access to the Party's lender of last resort facilities.

Section 6 International maritime transport services [omitted]

Section 7 Legal services

Article 192 Scope

1. This Section applies to measures of a Party affecting the supply of designated legal services in addition to Chapters 1, 2, 3 and 4 of this Title and to Sections 1 and 2 of this Chapter.

2. Nothing in this Section shall affect the right of a Party to regulate and supervise the supply of designated legal services in its territory in a non-discriminatory manner.

Article 193 Definitions

For the purposes of this Section, the following definitions apply:

(a) 'designated legal services' means legal services in relation to home jurisdiction law and public international law, excluding Union law;

(b) 'home jurisdiction' means the jurisdiction (or a part of the jurisdiction) of the Member State or of the United Kingdom in which a lawyer acquired their home jurisdiction professional title or, in the case of a lawyer who has acquired a home jurisdiction professional title in more than one jurisdiction, any of those jurisdictions;

(c) 'home jurisdiction law' means the law of the lawyer's home jurisdiction[28];

(d) 'home jurisdiction professional title' means:

  (i) for a lawyer of the Union, a professional title acquired in a Member State authorising the supply of legal services in that Member State; or

  (ii) for a lawyer of the United Kingdom, the title of advocate, barrister or solicitor, authorising the supply of legal services in any part of the jurisdiction of the United Kingdom;

(e) 'lawyer' means:

  (i) a natural person of the Union who is authorised in a Member State to supply legal services under a home jurisdiction professional title; or

  (ii) a natural person of the United Kingdom who is authorised in any part of the jurisdiction of the United Kingdom to supply legal services under a home jurisdiction professional title;

(f) 'lawyer of the other Party' means:

  (i) where 'the other Party' is the Union, a lawyer referred to in point (e)(i); or

  (ii) where 'the other Party' is the United Kingdom, a lawyer referred to in point (e)(ii); and

(g) 'legal services' means the following services:

  (i) legal advisory services; and

  (ii) legal arbitration, conciliation and mediation services (but excluding such services when supplied by natural persons as set out in Article 140).[29]

[28] For greater certainty, for the purposes of this Title, Union law is part of the home jurisdiction law of the lawyers referred to in point (e)(i) of this Article.

[29] 'Legal arbitration, conciliation and mediation services' means the preparation of documents to be submitted to, the preparation for and appearance before, an arbitrator, conciliator or mediator in any dispute involving the application and interpretation of law. It does not include arbitration, conciliation and mediation services in disputes not involving the application and interpretation of law, which fall under services incidental to management consulting. It also does not include acting as an arbitrator, conciliator or mediator. As a sub-category, international legal arbitration, conciliation or mediation services refers to the same services when the dispute involves parties from two or more countries.

'Legal services' do not include legal representation before administrative agencies, the courts, and other duly constituted official tribunals of a Party, legal advisory and legal authorisation, documentation and certification services supplied by legal professionals entrusted with public functions in the administration of justice such as notaries, 'huissiers de justice' or other 'officiers publics et ministériels', and services supplied by bailiffs who are appointed by an official act of government.

Article 194 Obligations

1. A Party shall allow a lawyer of the other Party to supply in its territory designated legal services under that lawyer's home jurisdiction professional title in accordance with Articles 128, 129, 135, 137 and 143.

2. Where a Party (the host jurisdiction) requires registration in its territory as a condition for a lawyer of the other Party to supply designated legal services pursuant to paragraph 1, the requirements and process for such registration shall not:

(a) be less favourable than those which apply to a natural person of a third country who is supplying legal services in relation to third country law or public international law under that person's third-country professional title in the territory of the host jurisdiction; and

(b) amount to or be equivalent to any requirement to requalify into or be admitted to the legal profession of the host jurisdiction.

3. Paragraph 4 applies to the supply of designated legal services pursuant to paragraph 1 through establishment.

4. A Party shall allow a legal person of the other Party to establish a branch in its territory through which designated legal services[30] are supplied pursuant to paragraph 1, in accordance with and subject to the conditions set out in Chapter 2 of this Title. This shall be without prejudice to requirements that a certain percentage of the shareholders, owners, partners, or directors of a legal person be qualified or practice a certain profession such as lawyers or accountants.

Article 195 Non-conforming measures

1. Article 194 does not apply to:

(a) any existing non-conforming measure of a Party at the level of:

(i) for the Union:

(A) the Union, as set out in the Schedule of the Union in Annex 19;

(B) the central government of a Member State, as set out in the Schedule of the Union in Annex 19;

(C) a regional government of a Member State, as set out in the Schedule of the Union in Annex 19; or

(D) a local government, other than that referred to in point (C); and

(ii) for the United Kingdom:

(A) the central government, as set out in the Schedule of the United Kingdom in Annex 19;

(B) a regional government, as set out in the Schedule of the United Kingdom in Annex 19; or

(C) a local government;

(b) the continuation or prompt renewal of any non-conforming measure referred to in point (a) of this paragraph; or

[30] For greater certainty, for the purposes of this paragraph 'designated legal services' means, for services supplied in the Union, legal services in relation to the law of the United Kingdom or any part of it and public international law (excluding Union law), and for services supplied in the United Kingdom, legal services in relation to the law of the Member States (including Union law) and public international law (excluding Union law).

(c) a modification to any non-conforming measure referred to in points (a) and (b) of this paragraph to the extent that it does not decrease the conformity of the measure, as it existed immediately before the modification, with Article 194.

2. Article 194 does not apply to any measure of a Party which is consistent with the reservations, conditions or qualifications specified with respect to a sector, subsector or activity listed in Annex 20.

3. This Section applies without prejudice to Annex 22.

Title III Digital trade

Chapter 1 General provisions

Article 196 Objective

The objective of this Title is to facilitate digital trade, to address unjustified barriers to trade enabled by electronic means and to ensure an open, secure and trustworthy online environment for businesses and consumers.

Article 197 Scope

1. This Title applies to measures of a Party affecting trade enabled by electronic means.
2. This Title does not apply to audio-visual services.

Article 198 Right to regulate

The Parties reaffirm the right to regulate within their territories to achieve legitimate policy objectives, such as the protection of public health, social services, public education, safety, the environment including climate change, public morals, social or consumer protection, privacy and data protection, or the promotion and protection of cultural diversity.

Article 199 Exceptions

For greater certainty, nothing in this Title prevents the Parties from adopting or maintaining measures in accordance with Articles 184, 412 and 415 for the public interest reasons set out therein.

Article 200 Definitions

1. The definitions in Article 124 apply to this Title.
2. For the purposes of this Title, the following definitions apply:

(a) 'consumer' means any natural person using a public telecommunications service for other than professional purposes;

(b) 'direct marketing communication' means any form of commercial advertising by which a natural or legal person communicates marketing messages directly to a user via a public telecommunications service and covers at least electronic mail and text and multimedia messages (SMS and MMS);

(c) 'electronic authentication' means an electronic process that enables the confirmation of:

(i) the electronic identification of a natural or legal person, or

(ii) the origin and integrity of data in electronic form;

(d) 'electronic registered delivery service' means a service that makes it possible to transmit data between third parties by electronic means and provides evidence relating to the handling of the transmitted data, including proof of sending and receiving the data, and that protects transmitted data against the risk of loss, theft, damage or any unauthorised alterations;

(e) 'electronic seal' means data in electronic form used by a legal person which is attached to or logically associated with other data in electronic form to ensure the latter's origin and integrity;

(f) 'electronic signature' means data in electronic form which is attached to or logically associated with other data in electronic form that:

(i) is used by a natural person to agree on the data in electronic form to which it relates; and

(ii) is linked to the data in electronic form to which it relates in such a way that any subsequent alteration in the data is detectable;

(g) 'electronic time stamp' means data in electronic form which binds other data in electronic form to a particular time establishing evidence that the latter data existed at that time;
(h) 'electronic trust service' means an electronic service consisting of:
  (i) the creation, verification and validation of electronic signatures, electronic seals, electronic time stamps, electronic registered delivery services and certificates related to those services;
  (ii) the creation, verification and validation of certificates for website authentication; or
  (iii) the preservation of electronic signatures, seals or certificates related to those services;
(i) 'government data' means data owned or held by any level of government and by non-governmental bodies in the exercise of powers conferred on them by any level of government;
(j) 'public telecommunications service' means any telecommunications service that is offered to the public generally;
(k) 'user' means any natural or legal person using a public telecommunications service.

Chapter 2 Data flows and personal data protection

Article 201 Cross-border data flows

1. The Parties are committed to ensuring cross-border data flows to facilitate trade in the digital economy. To that end, cross-border data flows shall not be restricted between the Parties by a Party:
(a) requiring the use of computing facilities or network elements in the Party's territory for processing, including by imposing the use of computing facilities or network elements that are certified or approved in the territory of a Party;
(b) requiring the localisation of data in the Party's territory for storage or processing;
(c) prohibiting the storage or processing in the territory of the other Party; or
(d) making the cross-border transfer of data contingent upon use of computing facilities or network elements in the Parties' territory or upon localisation requirements in the Parties' territory.

2. The Parties shall keep the implementation of this provision under review and assess its functioning within three years of the date of entry into force of this Agreement. A Party may at any time propose to the other Party to review the list of restrictions listed in paragraph 1. Such a request shall be accorded sympathetic consideration.

Article 202 Protection of personal data and privacy

1. Each Party recognises that individuals have a right to the protection of personal data and privacy and that high standards in this regard contribute to trust in the digital economy and to the development of trade.

2. Nothing in this Agreement shall prevent a Party from adopting or maintaining measures on the protection of personal data and privacy, including with respect to cross-border data transfers, provided that the law of the Party provides for instruments enabling transfers under conditions of general application[31] for the protection of the data transferred.

3. Each Party shall inform the other Party about any measure referred to in paragraph 2 that it adopts or maintains.

Chapter 3 Specific provisions

Article 203 Customs duties on electronic transmissions

1. Electronic transmissions shall be considered as the supply of a service within the meaning of Title II of this Heading.

2. The Parties shall not impose customs duties on electronic transmissions.

[31] For greater certainty, 'conditions of general application' refer to conditions formulated in objective terms that apply horizontally to an unidentified number of economic operators and thus cover a range of situations and cases.

Article 204 No prior authorisation

1. A Party shall not require prior authorisation of the provision of a service by electronic means solely on the ground that the service is provided online, and shall not adopt or maintain any other requirement having an equivalent effect.

A service is provided online when it is provided by electronic means and without the parties being simultaneously present.

2. Paragraph 1 does not apply to telecommunications services, broadcasting services, gambling services, legal representation services or to the services of notaries or equivalent professions to the extent that they involve a direct and specific connection with the exercise of public authority.

Article 205 Conclusion of contracts by electronic means

1. Each Party shall ensure that contracts may be concluded by electronic means and that its law neither creates obstacles for the use of electronic contracts nor results in contracts being deprived of legal effect and validity solely on the ground that the contract has been made by electronic means.

2. Paragraph 1 does not apply to the following:

(a) broadcasting services;
(b) gambling services;
(c) legal representation services;
(d) the services of notaries or equivalent professions involving a direct and specific connection with the exercise of public authority;
(e) contracts that require witnessing in person;
(f) contracts that establish or transfer rights in real estate;
(g) contracts requiring by law the involvement of courts, public authorities or professions exercising public authority;
(h) contracts of suretyship granted, collateral securities furnished by persons acting for purposes outside their trade, business or profession; or
(i) contracts governed by family law or by the law of succession.

Article 206 Electronic authentication and electronic trust services

1. A Party shall not deny the legal effect and admissibility as evidence in legal proceedings of an electronic document, an electronic signature, an electronic seal or an electronic time stamp, or of data sent and received using an electronic registered delivery service, solely on the ground that it is in electronic form.

2. A Party shall not adopt or maintain measures that would:

(a) prohibit parties to an electronic transaction from mutually determining the appropriate electronic authentication methods for their transaction; or
(b) prevent parties to an electronic transaction from being able to prove to judicial and administrative authorities that the use of electronic authentication or an electronic trust service in that transaction complies with the applicable legal requirements.

3. Notwithstanding paragraph 2, a Party may require that for a particular category of transactions, the method of electronic authentication or trust service is certified by an authority accredited in accordance with its law or meets certain performance standards which shall be objective, transparent and non-discriminatory and only relate to the specific characteristics of the category of transactions concerned.

Article 207 Transfer of or access to source code

1. A Party shall not require the transfer of, or access to, the source code of software owned by a natural or legal person of the other Party.

2. For greater certainty:

(a) the general exceptions, security exceptions and prudential carve-out referred to in Article 199 apply to measures of a Party adopted or maintained in the context of a certification procedure; and

(b) paragraph 1 of this Article does not apply to the voluntary transfer of, or granting of access to, source code on a commercial basis by a natural or legal person of the other Party, such as in the context of a public procurement transaction or a freely negotiated contract.

3. Nothing in this Article shall affect:

(a) a requirement by a court or administrative tribunal, or a requirement by a competition authority pursuant to a Party's competition law to prevent or remedy a restriction or a distortion of competition;

(b) a requirement by a regulatory body pursuant to a Party's laws or regulations related to the protection of public safety with regard to users online, subject to safeguards against unauthorised disclosure;

(c) the protection and enforcement of intellectual property rights; and

(d) the right of a Party to take measures in accordance with Article III of the GPA as incorporated by Article 277 of this Agreement.

Article 208 Online consumer trust

1. Recognising the importance of enhancing consumer trust in digital trade, each Party shall adopt or maintain measures to ensure the effective protection of consumers engaging in electronic commerce transactions, including but not limited to measures that:

(a) proscribe fraudulent and deceptive commercial practices;

(b) require suppliers of goods and services to act in good faith and abide by fair commercial practices, including through the prohibition of charging consumers for unsolicited goods and services;

(c) require suppliers of goods or services to provide consumers with clear and thorough information, including when they act through intermediary service suppliers, regarding their identity and contact details, the transaction concerned, including the main characteristics of the goods or services and the full price inclusive of all applicable charges, and the applicable consumer rights (in the case of intermediary service suppliers, this includes enabling the provision of such information by the supplier of goods or services); and

(d) grant consumers access to redress for breaches of their rights, including a right to remedies if goods or services are paid for and are not delivered or provided as agreed.

2. The Parties recognise the importance of entrusting their consumer protection agencies or other relevant bodies with adequate enforcement powers and the importance of cooperation between these agencies in order to protect consumers and enhance online consumer trust.

Article 209 Unsolicited direct marketing communications

1. Each Party shall ensure that users are effectively protected against unsolicited direct marketing communications.

2. Each Party shall ensure that direct marketing communications are not sent to users who are natural persons unless they have given their consent in accordance with each Party's laws to receiving such communications.

3. Notwithstanding paragraph 2, a Party shall allow natural or legal persons who have collected, in accordance with conditions laid down in the law of that Party, the contact details of a user in the context of the supply of goods or services, to send direct marketing communications to that user for their own similar goods or services.

4. Each Party shall ensure that direct marketing communications are clearly identifiable as such, clearly disclose on whose behalf they are made and contain the necessary information to enable users to request cessation free of charge and at any moment.

5. Each Party shall provide users with access to redress against suppliers of direct marketing communications that do not comply with the measures adopted or maintained pursuant to paragraphs 1 to 4.

Article 210 Open government data

1. The Parties recognise that facilitating public access to, and use of, government data contributes to stimulating economic and social development, competitiveness, productivity and innovation.

2. To the extent that a Party chooses to make government data accessible to the public, it shall endeavour to ensure, to the extent practicable, that the data:

(a) is in a format that allows it to be easily searched, retrieved, used, reused, and redistributed;
(b) is in a machine-readable and spatially-enabled format;
(c) contains descriptive metadata, which is as standard as possible;
(d) is made available via reliable, user-friendly and freely available Application Programming Interfaces;
(e) is regularly updated;
(f) is not subject to use conditions that are discriminatory or that unnecessarily restrict re-use; and
(g) is made available for re-use in full compliance with the Parties' respective personal data protection rules.

3. The Parties shall endeavour to cooperate to identify ways in which each Party can expand access to, and use of, government data that the Party has made public, with a view to enhancing and generating business opportunities, beyond its use by the public sector.

Article 211 Cooperation on regulatory issues with regard to digital trade

1. The Parties shall exchange information on regulatory matters in the context of digital trade, which shall address the following:

(a) the recognition and facilitation of interoperable authentication and electronic trust services;
(b) the treatment of direct marketing communications;
(c) the protection of consumers; and
(d) any other matter relevant for the development of digital trade, including emerging technologies.

2. Paragraph 1 shall not apply to a Party's rules and safeguards for the protection of personal data and privacy, including on cross-border transfers of personal data.

Article 212 Understanding on computer services

1. The Parties agree that, for the purpose of liberalising trade in services and investment in accordance with Title II of this Heading, the following services shall be considered as computer and related services, regardless of whether they are delivered via a network, including the internet:

(a) consulting, adaptation, strategy, analysis, planning, specification, design, development, installation, implementation, integration, testing, debugging, updating, support, technical assistance or management of or for computers or computer systems;
(b) computer programmes defined as the sets of instructions required to make computers work and communicate (in and of themselves), as well as consulting, strategy, analysis, planning, specification, design, development, installation, implementation, integration, testing, debugging, updating, adaptation, maintenance, support, technical assistance, management or use of or for computer programmes;
(c) data processing, data storage, data hosting or database services;
(d) maintenance and repair services for office machinery and equipment, including computers; and
(e) training services for staff of clients, related to computer programmes, computers or computer systems, and not elsewhere classified.

For greater certainty, services enabled by computer and related services, other than those listed in paragraph 1, shall not be regarded as computer and related services in themselves.

Title IV Capital movements, payments, transfers and temporary safeguard measures [omitted]

Title V Intellectual property

Chapter 1 General provisions

Article 219 Objectives

The objectives of this Title are to:

(a) facilitate the production, provision and commercialisation of innovative and creative products and services between the Parties by reducing distortions and impediments to such trade, thereby contributing to a more sustainable and inclusive economy; and

(b) ensure an adequate and effective level of protection and enforcement of intellectual property rights.

Article 220 Scope

1. This Title shall complement and further specify the rights and obligations of each Party under the TRIPS Agreement and other international treaties in the field of intellectual property to which they are parties.

2. This Title does not preclude either Party from introducing more extensive protection and enforcement of intellectual property rights than required under this Title, provided that such protection and enforcement does not contravene this Title.

Article 221 Definitions

For the purposes of this Title, the following definitions apply:

(a) 'Paris Convention' means the Paris Convention for the Protection of Industrial Property of 20 March 1883, as last revised at Stockholm on 14 July 1967;

(b) 'Berne Convention' means the Berne Convention for the Protection of Literary and Artistic Works of 9 September 1886 revised at Paris on 24 July 1971 and amended on 28 September 1979;

(c) 'Rome Convention' means the International Convention for the Protection of Performers, Producers of Phonograms and Broadcasting Organisations done at Rome on 26 October 1961;

(d) 'WIPO' means the World Intellectual Property Organisation;

(e) 'intellectual property rights' means all categories of intellectual property that are covered by Articles 225 to 255 of this Agreement or Sections 1 to 7 of Part II of the TRIPS Agreement. The protection of intellectual property includes protection against unfair competition as referred to in Article 10bis of the Paris Convention;

(f) 'national' means, in respect of the relevant intellectual property right, a person of a Party that would meet the criteria for eligibility for protection provided for in the TRIPS Agreement and multilateral agreements concluded and administered under the auspices of WIPO, to which a Party is a contracting party.

Article 222 International agreements

1. The Parties affirm their commitment to comply with the international agreements to which they are party:

(a) the TRIPS Agreement;

(b) the Rome Convention;

(c) the Berne Convention;

(d) the WIPO Copyright Treaty, adopted at Geneva on 20 December 1996;

(e) the WIPO Performances and Phonograms Treaty, adopted at Geneva on 20 December 1996;

(f) the Protocol Relating to the Madrid Agreement Concerning the International Registration of Marks, adopted at Madrid on 27 June 1989, as last amended on 12 November 2007;
(g) the Trademark Law Treaty, adopted at Geneva on 27 October 1994;
(h) the Marrakesh Treaty to Facilitate Access to Published Works for Persons Who Are Blind, Visually Impaired or Otherwise Print Disabled, adopted at Marrakesh on 27 June 2013;
(i) the Geneva Act of the Hague Agreement Concerning the International Registration of Industrial Designs, adopted at Geneva on 2 July 1999.

2. Each Party shall make all reasonable efforts to ratify or accede to the following international agreements:

(a) the Beijing Treaty on Audiovisual Performances, adopted at Beijing on 24 June 2012;
(b) the Singapore Treaty on the Law of Trademarks adopted at Singapore on 27 March 2006.

Article 223 Exhaustion

This Title does not affect the freedom of the parties to determine whether and under what conditions the exhaustion of intellectual property rights applies.

Article 224 National treatment

1. In respect of all categories of intellectual property covered by this Title, each Party shall accord to the nationals of the other Party treatment no less favourable than the treatment it accords to its own nationals with regard to the protection of intellectual property subject where applicable to the exceptions already provided for in, respectively, the Paris Convention, the Berne Convention, the Rome Convention and the Treaty on Intellectual Property in Respect of Integrated Circuits, done at Washington on 26 May 1989. In respect of performers, producers of phonograms and broadcasting organisations, this obligation only applies in respect of the rights provided for under this Agreement.

2. For the purposes of paragraph 1 of this Article, 'protection' shall include matters affecting the availability, acquisition, scope, maintenance, and enforcement of intellectual property rights as well as matters affecting the use of intellectual property rights specifically addressed in this Title, including measures to prevent the circumvention of effective technological measures as referred to in Article 234 and measures concerning rights management information as referred to in Article 235.

3. A Party may avail itself of the exceptions permitted pursuant to paragraph 1 in relation to its judicial and administrative procedures, including requiring a national of the other Party to designate an address for service in its territory, or to appoint an agent in its territory, if such exceptions are:

(a) necessary to secure compliance with the Party's laws or regulations which are not inconsistent with this Title; or
(b) not applied in a manner which would constitute a disguised restriction on trade.

4. Paragraph 1 does not apply to procedures provided in multilateral agreements concluded under the auspices of WIPO relating to the acquisition or maintenance of intellectual property rights.

Chapter 2 Standards concerning intellectual property rights

Section 1 Copyright and related rights

Article 225 Authors

Each Party shall provide authors with the exclusive right to authorise or prohibit:

(a) direct or indirect, temporary or permanent reproduction by any means and in any form, in whole or in part, of their works;
(b) any form of distribution to the public by sale or otherwise of the original of their works or of copies thereof;
(c) any communication to the public of their works by wire or wireless means, including the making available to the public of their works in such a way that members of the public may access them from a place and at a time individually chosen by them;

(d) the commercial rental to the public of originals or copies of their works; each Party may provide that this point does not apply to buildings or works of applied art.

Article 226 Performers

Each Party shall provide performers with the exclusive right to authorise or prohibit:

(a) the fixation of their performances;

(b) the direct or indirect, temporary or permanent reproduction by any means and in any form, in whole or in part, of fixations of their performances;

(c) the distribution to the public, by sale or otherwise, of the fixations of their performances;

(d) the making available to the public of fixations of their performances, by wire or wireless means, in such a way that members of the public may access them from a place and at a time individually chosen by them;

(e) the broadcasting by wireless means and the communication to the public of their performances, except where the performance is itself already a broadcast performance or is made from a fixation;

(f) the commercial rental to the public of the fixation of their performances.

Article 227 Producers of phonograms

Each Party shall provide phonogram producers with the exclusive right to authorise or prohibit:

(a) the direct or indirect, temporary or permanent, reproduction by any means and in any form, in whole or in part, of their phonograms;

(b) the distribution to the public, by sale or otherwise, of their phonograms, including copies thereof;

(c) the making available to the public of their phonograms, by wire or wireless means, in such a way that members of the public may access them from a place and at a time individually chosen by them;

(d) the commercial rental of their phonograms to the public.

Article 228 Broadcasting organisations

Each Party shall provide broadcasting organisations with the exclusive right to authorise or prohibit:

(a) the fixation of their broadcasts, whether these broadcasts are transmitted by wire or over the air, including by cable or satellite;

(b) the direct or indirect, temporary or permanent reproduction by any means and in any form, in whole or in part, of fixations of their broadcasts, whether those broadcasts are transmitted by wire or over the air, including by cable or satellite;

(c) the making available to the public, by wire or wireless means, of fixations of their broadcasts, whether those broadcasts are transmitted by wire or over the air, including by cable or satellite, in such a way that members of the public may access them from a place and at a time individually chosen by them;

(d) the distribution to the public, by sale or otherwise, of fixations, including copies thereof, of their broadcasts, whether these broadcasts are transmitted by wire or over the air, including by cable or satellite;

(e) the rebroadcasting of their broadcasts by wireless means, as well as the communication to the public of their broadcasts if such communication is made in places accessible to the public against payment of an entrance fee.

Article 229 Broadcasting and communication to the public of phonograms published for commercial purposes

1. Each Party shall provide a right in order to ensure that a single equitable remuneration is paid by the user to the performers and producers of phonograms, if a phonogram published for commercial purposes, or a reproduction of such phonogram, is used for broadcasting or any communication to the public.

2. Each Party shall ensure that the single equitable remuneration is shared between the relevant performers and phonogram producers. Each Party may enact legislation that, in the absence of an

agreement between performers and producers of phonograms, sets the terms according to which performers and producers of phonograms shall share the single equitable remuneration.

3. Each Party may grant more extensive rights, as regards the broadcasting and communication to the public of phonograms published for commercial purposes, to performers and producers of phonograms.

Article 230 Term of protection

1. The rights of an author of a work shall run for the life of the author and for 70 years after the author's death, irrespective of the date when the work is lawfully made available to the public.

2. For the purpose of implementing paragraph 1, each Party may provide for specific rules on the calculation of the term of protection of musical composition with words, works of joint authorship as well as cinematographic or audiovisual works. Each Party may provide for specific rules on the calculation of the term of protection of anonymous or pseudonymous works.

3. The rights of broadcasting organisations shall expire 50 years after the first transmission of a broadcast, whether this broadcast is transmitted by wire or over the air, including by cable or satellite.

4. The rights of performers for their performances otherwise than in phonograms shall expire 50 years after the date of the fixation of the performance or, if lawfully published or lawfully communicated to the public during this time, 50 years from the first such publication or communication to the public, whichever is the earlier.

5. The rights of performers for their performances fixed in phonograms shall expire 50 years after the date of fixation of the performance or, if lawfully published or lawfully communicated to the public during this time, 70 years from such act, whichever is the earlier.

6. The rights of producers of phonograms shall expire 50 years after the fixation is made or, if lawfully published to the public during this time, 70 years from such publication. In the absence of a lawful publication, if the phonogram has been lawfully communicated to the public during this time, the term of protection shall be 70 years from such act of communication. Each Party may provide for effective measures in order to ensure that the profit generated during the 20 years of protection beyond 50 years is shared fairly between the performers and the producers of phonograms.

7. The terms laid down in this Article shall be counted from the first of January of the year following the year of the event which gives rise to them.

8. Each Party may provide for longer terms of protection than those provided for in this Article.

Article 231 Resale right

1. Each Party shall provide, for the benefit of the author of an original work of graphic or plastic art, a resale right, to be defined as an inalienable right, which cannot be waived, even in advance, to receive a royalty based on the sale price obtained for any resale of the work, subsequent to the first transfer of the work by the author.

2. The right referred to in paragraph 1 shall apply to all acts of resale involving as sellers, buyers or intermediaries art market professionals, such as salesrooms, art galleries and, in general, any dealers in works of art.

3. Each Party may provide that the right referred to in paragraph 1 shall not apply to acts of resale, where the seller has acquired the work directly from the author less than three years before that resale and where the resale price does not exceed a certain minimum amount.

4. The procedure for collection of the remuneration and their amounts shall be determined by the law of each Party.

Article 232 Collective management of rights

1. The Parties shall promote cooperation between their respective collective management organisations for the purpose of fostering the availability of works and other protected subject matter in their respective territories and the transfer of rights revenue between the respective collective management organisations for the use of such works or other protected subject matter.

2. The Parties shall promote the transparency of collective management organisations, in particular regarding the rights revenue they collect, the deductions they apply to the rights revenue they collect, the use of the rights revenue collected, the distribution policy and their repertoire.

3. The Parties shall endeavour to facilitate arrangements between their respective collective management organisations on non-discriminatory treatment of right holders whose rights these organisations manage under representation agreements.

4. The Parties shall cooperate to support the collective management organisations established in their territory and representing another collective management organisation established in the territory of the other Party by way of a representation agreement with a view to ensuring that they accurately, regularly and diligently pay amounts owed to the represented collective management organisations and provide the represented collective management organisation with the information on the amount of rights revenue collected on its behalf and any deductions made to that rights revenue.

Article 233 Exceptions and limitations

Each Party shall confine limitations or exceptions to the rights set out in Articles 225 to 229 to certain special cases which do not conflict with a normal exploitation of the work or other subject-matter and do not unreasonably prejudice the legitimate interests of the right holders.

Article 234 Protection of technological measures

1. Each Party shall provide adequate legal protection against the circumvention of any effective technological measures, which the person concerned carries out in the knowledge, or with reasonable grounds to know, that he or she is pursuing that objective. Each Party may provide for a specific regime for legal protection of technological measures used to protect computer programs.

2. Each Party shall provide adequate legal protection against the manufacture, import, distribution, sale, rental, advertisement for sale or rental, or possession for commercial purposes of devices, products or components or the provision of services which:

(a) are promoted, advertised or marketed for the purpose of circumvention of;
(b) have only a limited commercially significant purpose or use other than to circumvent; or
(c) are primarily designed, produced, adapted or performed for the purpose of enabling or facilitating the circumvention of, any effective technological measures.

3. For the purposes of this Section, the expression 'technological measures' means any technology, device or component that, in the normal course of its operation, is designed to prevent or restrict acts, in respect of works or other subject-matter, which are not authorised by the right holder of any copyright or related right covered by this Section. Technological measures shall be deemed 'effective' where the use of a protected work or other subject matter is controlled by the right holders through application of an access control or protection process, such as encryption, scrambling or other transformation of the work or other subject-matter or a copy control mechanism, which achieves the protection objective.

4. Notwithstanding the legal protection provided for in paragraph 1 of this Article, each Party may take appropriate measures, as necessary, to ensure that the adequate legal protection against the circumvention of effective technological measures provided for in accordance with this Article does not prevent beneficiaries of exceptions or limitations provided for in accordance with Article 233 from enjoying such exceptions or limitations.

Article 235 Obligations concerning rights management information

1. Each Party shall provide adequate legal protection against any person knowingly performing without authority any of the following acts:

(a) the removal or alteration of any electronic rights-management information;
(b) the distribution, importation for distribution, broadcasting, communication or making available to the public of works or other subject-matter protected pursuant to this Section from which electronic rights-management information has been removed or altered without authority;

if such person knows, or has reasonable grounds to know, that by so doing he or she is inducing, enabling, facilitating or concealing an infringement of any copyright or any related rights as provided by the law of a Party.

2. For the purposes of this Article, 'rights-management information' means any information provided by right holders which identifies the work or other subject-matter referred to in this

Article, the author or any other right holder, or information about the terms and conditions of use of the work or other subject-matter, and any numbers or codes that represent such information.

3. Paragraph 2 applies if any of these items of information is associated with a copy of, or appears in connection with the communication to the public of, a work or other subject-matter referred to in this Article.

Section 2 Trade marks

Article 236 Trade mark classification

Each Party shall maintain a trade mark classification system that is consistent with the Nice Agreement Concerning the International Classification of Goods and Services for the Purposes of the Registration of Marks of 15 June 1957, as amended and revised.

Article 237 Signs of which a trade mark may consist

A trade mark may consist of any signs, in particular words, including personal names, or designs, letters, numerals, colours, the shape of goods or of the packaging of goods, or sounds, provided that such signs are capable of:

(a) distinguishing the goods or services of one undertaking from those of other undertakings; and

(b) being represented on the respective trade mark register of each Party, in a manner which enables the competent authorities and the public to determine the clear and precise subject matter of the protection afforded to its proprietor.

Article 238 Rights conferred by a trade mark

1. Each Party shall provide that the registration of a trade mark confers on the proprietor exclusive rights therein. The proprietor shall be entitled to prevent all third parties not having the proprietor's consent from using in the course of trade:

(a) any sign which is identical with the registered trade mark in relation to goods or services which are identical with those for which the trade mark is registered;

(b) any sign where, because of its identity with, or similarity to, the registered trade mark and the identity or similarity of the goods or services covered by this trade mark and the sign, there exists a likelihood of confusion on the part of the public, including the likelihood of association between the sign and the registered trade mark.

2. The proprietor of a registered trade mark shall be entitled to prevent all third parties from bringing goods, in the course of trade, into the Party where the trade mark is registered without being released for free circulation there, where such goods, including packaging, come from other countries or the other Party and bear without authorisation a trade mark which is identical to the trade mark registered in respect of such goods, or which cannot be distinguished in its essential aspects from that trade mark.

3. The entitlement of the proprietor of a trade mark pursuant to paragraph 2 shall lapse if during the proceedings to determine whether the registered trade mark has been infringed, evidence is provided by the declarant or the holder of the goods that the proprietor of the registered trade mark is not entitled to prohibit the placing of the goods on the market in the country of final destination.

Article 239 Registration procedure

1. Each Party shall provide for a system for the registration of trade marks in which each final negative decision taken by the relevant trade mark administration, including partial refusals of registration, shall be communicated in writing to the relevant party, duly reasoned and subject to appeal.

2. Each Party shall provide for the possibility for third parties to oppose trade mark applications or, where appropriate, trade mark registrations. Such opposition proceedings shall be adversarial.

3. Each Party shall provide a publicly available electronic database of trade mark applications and trade mark registrations.

4. Each Party shall make best efforts to provide a system for the electronic application for and processing, registration and maintenance of trade marks.

Article 240 Well-known trade marks

For the purpose of giving effect to protection of well-known trade marks, as referred to in Article 6bis of the Paris Convention and Article 16(2) and (3) of the TRIPS Agreement, each Party shall apply the Joint Recommendation Concerning Provisions on the Protection of Well-Known Marks, adopted by the Assembly of the Paris Union for the Protection of Industrial Property and the General Assembly of the WIPO at the Thirty-Fourth Series of Meetings of the Assemblies of the Member States of WIPO on 20 to 29 September 1999.

Article 241 Exceptions to the rights conferred by a trade mark

1. Each Party shall provide for limited exceptions to the rights conferred by a trade mark such as the fair use of descriptive terms including geographical indications, and may provide other limited exceptions, provided such exceptions take account of the legitimate interests of the proprietor of the trade mark and of third parties.

2. The trade mark shall not entitle the proprietor to prohibit a third party from using, in the course of trade:

(a) the name or address of the third party, where the third party is a natural person;

(b) signs or indications concerning the kind, quality, quantity, intended purpose, value, geographical origin, the time of production of goods or of rendering of the service, or other characteristics of goods or services; or

(c) the trade mark for the purpose of identifying or referring to goods or services as those of the proprietor of that trade mark, in particular where the use of that trade mark is necessary to indicate the intended purpose of a product or service, in particular as accessories or spare parts, provided the third party uses them in accordance with honest practices in industrial or commercial matters.

3. The trade mark shall not entitle the proprietor to prohibit a third party from using, in the course of trade, an earlier right which only applies in a particular locality if that right is recognised by the laws of the Party in question and is used within the limits of the territory in which it is recognised.

Article 242 Grounds for revocation

1. Each Party shall provide that a trade mark shall be liable to revocation if, within a continuous period of five years it has not been put to genuine use in the relevant territory of a Party by the proprietor or with the proprietor's consent in relation to the goods or services for which it is registered, and there are no proper reasons for non-use.

2. Each Party shall also provide that a trade mark shall be liable to revocation if within the period of five years following the date of completion of the registration procedure it has not been put to genuine use in the relevant territory by the proprietor or with the proprietor's consent, in relation to the goods or services for which it is registered, and there are no proper reasons for non-use.

3. However, no person may claim that the proprietor's rights in a trade mark should be revoked where, during the interval between expiry of the five-year period and filing of the application for revocation, genuine use of the trade mark has been started or resumed. The commencement or resumption of use within a period of three months preceding the filing of the application for revocation which began at the earliest on expiry of the continuous period of five years of non-use, shall, however, be disregarded where preparations for the commencement or resumption occur only after the proprietor becomes aware that the application for revocation may be filed.

4. A trade mark shall also be liable to revocation if, after the date on which it was registered:

(a) as a consequence of acts or inactivity of the proprietor, it has become the common name in the trade for a good or service in respect of which it is registered;

(b) as a consequence of the use made of the trade mark by the proprietor of the trade mark or with the proprietor's consent in respect of the goods or services for which it is registered, it is liable to mislead the public, particularly as to the nature, quality or geographical origin of those goods or services.

Article 243 The right to prohibit preparatory acts in relation to the use of packaging or other means

Where the risk exists that the packaging, labels, tags, security or authenticity features or devices, or any other means to which the trade mark is affixed could be used in relation to goods or services and that use would constitute an infringement of the rights of the proprietor of the trade mark, the proprietor of that trade mark shall have the right to prohibit the following acts if carried out in the course of trade:

(a) affixing a sign identical with, or similar to, the trade mark on packaging, labels, tags, security or authenticity features or devices, or any other means to which the mark may be affixed; or

(b) offering or placing on the market, or stocking for those purposes, or importing or exporting, packaging, labels, tags, security or authenticity features or devices, or any other means to which the mark is affixed.

Article 244 Bad faith applications

A trade mark shall be liable to be declared invalid where the application for registration of the trade mark was made in bad faith by the applicant. Each Party may provide that such a trade mark shall not be registered.

Section 3 Design

Article 245 Protection of registered designs

1. Each Party shall provide for the protection of independently created designs that are new and original. This protection shall be provided by registration and shall confer exclusive rights upon their holders in accordance with this Section.

For the purposes of this Article, a Party may consider that a design having individual character is original.

2. The holder of a registered design shall have the right to prevent third parties not having the holder's consent at least from making, offering for sale, selling, importing, exporting, stocking the product bearing and embodying the protected design or using articles bearing or embodying the protected design where such acts are undertaken for commercial purposes.

3. A design applied to or incorporated in a product which constitutes a component part of a complex product shall only be considered to be new and original:

(a) if the component part, once it has been incorporated into the complex product, remains visible during normal use of the latter; and

(b) to the extent that those visible features of the component part fulfil in themselves the requirements as to novelty and originality.

4. For the purposes of point (a) of paragraph 3, 'normal use' means use by the end user, excluding maintenance, servicing or repair work.

Article 246 Duration of protection

The duration of protection available for registered designs, including renewals of registered designs, shall amount to a total term of 25 years from the date on which the application was filed[32].

Article 247 Protection of unregistered designs

1. Each Party shall confer on holders of an unregistered design the right to prevent the use of the unregistered design by any third party not having the holder's consent only if the contested use results from copying the unregistered design in their respective territory[33]. Such use shall at least cover the offering for sale, putting on the market, importing or exporting the product.

2. The duration of protection available for the unregistered design shall amount to at least three years as from the date on which the design was first made available to the public in the territory of the respective Party.

[32] Each Party may determine the relevant date of filing of the application in accordance with its own legislation.

[33] This section does not apply to the protection known in the United Kingdom as a design right.

Article 248 Exceptions and exclusions

1. Each Party may provide limited exceptions to the protection of designs, including unregistered designs, provided that such exceptions do not unreasonably conflict with the normal exploitation of designs, and do not unreasonably prejudice the legitimate interests of the holder of the design, taking account of the legitimate interests of third parties.

2. Protection shall not extend to designs solely dictated by technical or functional considerations. A design shall not subsist in features of appearance of a product which must necessarily be reproduced in their exact form and dimensions in order to permit the product in which the design is incorporated or to which it is applied to be mechanically connected to or placed in, around or against another product so that either product may perform its function.

3. By way of derogation from paragraph 2 of this Article, a design shall, in accordance with the conditions set out in Article 245(1), subsist in a design, which has the purpose of allowing the multiple assembly or connection of mutually interchangeable products within a modular system.

Article 249 Relationship to copyright

Each Party shall ensure that designs, including unregistered designs, shall also be eligible for protection under the copyright law of that Party as from the date on which the design was created or fixed in any form. The extent to which, and the conditions under which, such a protection is conferred, including the level of originality required, shall be determined by each Party.

Section 4 Patents

Article 250 Patents and public health

1. The Parties recognise the importance of the Declaration on the TRIPS Agreement and Public Health, adopted on 14 November 2001 by the Ministerial Conference of the WTO at Doha (the 'Doha Declaration'). In interpreting and implementing the rights and obligations under this Section, each Party shall ensure consistency with the Doha Declaration.

2. Each Party shall implement Article 31bis of the TRIPS Agreement, as well as the Annex to the TRIPS Agreement and the Appendix to the Annex to the TRIPS Agreement.

Article 251 Extension of the period of protection conferred by a patent on medicinal products and on plant protection products

1. The Parties recognise that medicinal products and plant protection products[34] protected by a patent in their respective territory may be subject to an administrative authorisation procedure before being put on their respective markets. The Parties recognise that the period that elapses between the filing of the application for a patent and the first authorisation to place the product on the market, as defined for that purpose by the relevant legislation, may shorten the period of effective protection under the patent.

2. Each Party shall provide for further protection, in accordance with its laws and regulations, for a product which is protected by a patent and which has been subject to an administrative authorisation procedure referred to in paragraph 1 to compensate the holder of a patent for the reduction of effective patent protection. The terms and conditions for the provision of such further protection, including its length, shall be determined in accordance with the laws and regulations of the Parties.

3. For the purposes of this Title, 'medicinal product' means:

(a) any substance or combination of substances presented as having properties for treating or preventing disease in human beings or animals; or

(b) any substance or combination of substances which may be used in or administered to human beings or animals either with a view to restoring, correcting or modifying physiological functions by exerting a pharmacological, immunological or metabolic action, or to making a medical diagnosis.

[34] For the purposes of this Title, the term 'plant protection product' shall be defined for each Party by the respective legislations of the Parties.

Section 5 Protection of undisclosed information

Article 252 Protection of trade secrets

1. Each Party shall provide for appropriate civil judicial procedures and remedies for any trade secret holder to prevent, and obtain redress for, the acquisition, use or disclosure of a trade secret whenever carried out in a manner contrary to honest commercial practices.

2. For the purposes of this Section, the following definitions apply:

(a) 'trade secret' means information which meets all of the following requirements:

(i) it is secret in the sense that it is not, as a body or in the precise configuration and assembly of its components, generally known among or readily accessible to persons within the circles that normally deal with the kind of information in question;

(ii) it has commercial value because it is secret; and

(iii) it has been subject to reasonable steps under the circumstances, by the person lawfully in control of the information, to keep it secret;

(b) 'trade secret holder' means any natural or legal person lawfully controlling a trade secret.

3. For the purposes of this Section, at least the following conduct shall be considered contrary to honest commercial practices:

(a) the acquisition of a trade secret without the consent of the trade secret holder, whenever obtained by unauthorised access to, or by appropriation or copying of, any documents, objects, materials, substances or electronic files that are lawfully under the control of the trade secret holder, and that contain the trade secret or from which the trade secret can be deduced;

(b) the use or disclosure of a trade secret whenever it is carried out, without the consent of the trade secret holder, by a person who is found to meet any of the following conditions:

(i) having acquired the trade secret in a manner referred to in point (a);

(ii) being in breach of a confidentiality agreement or any other duty not to disclose the trade secret; or

(iii) being in breach of a contractual or any other duty to limit the use of the trade secret;

(c) the acquisition, use or disclosure of a trade secret whenever carried out by a person who, at the time of the acquisition, use or disclosure, knew, or ought to have known, under the circumstances that the trade secret had been obtained directly or indirectly from another person who was using or disclosing the trade secret unlawfully within the meaning of point (b).

4. Nothing in this Section shall be understood as requiring either Party to consider any of the following conducts as contrary to honest commercial practices:

(a) independent discovery or creation;

(b) the reverse engineering of a product that has been made available to the public or that is lawfully in the possession of the acquirer of the information, where the acquirer of the information is free from any legally valid duty to limit the acquisition of the trade secret;

(c) the acquisition, use or disclosure of a trade secret required or allowed by the law of each Party;

(d) the exercise of the right of workers or workers' representatives to information and consultation in accordance with the laws and regulations of that Party.

5. Nothing in this Section shall be understood as affecting the exercise of freedom of expression and information, including the freedom and pluralism of the media, as protected in each Party, restricting the mobility of employees, or as affecting the autonomy of social partners and their right to enter into collective agreements, in accordance with the laws and regulations of the Parties.

Article 253 Protection of data submitted to obtain an authorisation to put a medicinal product on the market

1. Each Party shall protect commercially confidential information submitted to obtain an authorisation to place medicinal products on the market ('marketing authorisation') against disclosure to third parties, unless steps are taken to ensure that the data are protected against unfair commercial use or except where the disclosure is necessary for an overriding public interest.

2. Each Party shall ensure that for a limited period of time to be determined by its domestic law and in accordance with any conditions set out in its domestic law, the authority responsible for the granting of a marketing authorisation does not accept any subsequent application for a marketing authorisation that relies on the results of pre-clinical tests or clinical trials submitted in the application to that authority for the first marketing authorisation, without the explicit consent of the holder of the first marketing authorisation, unless international agreements to which the Parties are both party provide otherwise.

3. Each Party shall also ensure that, for a limited period of time to be determined by its domestic law and in accordance with any conditions set out in its domestic law, a medicinal product subsequently authorised by that authority on the basis of the results of the pre-clinical tests and clinical trials referred to in paragraph 2 is not placed on the market without the explicit consent of the holder of the first marketing authorisation, unless international agreements to which the Parties are both party provide otherwise.

4. This Article is without prejudice to additional periods of protection which each Party may provide in that Party's law.

Articles 254–255 [Omitted]

Chapter 3 Enforcement of intellectual property rights

Section 1 General provisions

Article 256 General obligations

1. Each Party shall provide under its respective law for the measures, procedures and remedies necessary to ensure the enforcement of intellectual property rights. For the purposes of Sections 1, 2 and 4 of this Chapter, the term 'intellectual property rights' does not include rights covered by Section 5 of Chapter 2.

2. The measures, procedures and remedies referred to in paragraph 1 shall:

(a) be fair and equitable;
(b) not be unnecessarily complicated or costly, or entail unreasonable time-limits or unwarranted delays;
(c) be effective, proportionate and dissuasive;
(d) be applied in such a manner as to avoid the creation of barriers to legitimate trade and to provide for safeguards against their abuse.

Article 257 Persons entitled to apply for the application of the measures, procedures and remedies

Each Party shall recognise as persons entitled to seek application of the measures, procedures and remedies referred to in Sections 2 and 4 of this Chapter:

(a) the holders of intellectual property rights in accordance with the law of a Party;
(b) all other persons authorised to use those rights, in particular licensees, in so far as permitted by and in accordance with the law of a Party; and
(c) federations and associations[35], in so far as permitted by and in accordance with the law of a Party.

[35] For greater certainty, and in so far as permitted by the law of a Party, the term 'federations and associations' includes at least collective rights management bodies and professional defence bodies which are regularly recognised as having the right to represent holders of intellectual property rights.

Section 2 Civil and administrative enforcement [omitted]

Title VI Public procurement [omitted]

Title VII Small and medium-sized enterprises [omitted]

Title VIII Energy [omitted]

Title IX Transparency

Article 332 Objective

1. Recognising the impact that their respective regulatory environments may have on trade and investment between them, the Parties aim to provide a predictable regulatory environment and efficient procedures for economic operators, especially for small and medium-sized enterprises.

2. The Parties affirm their commitments in relation to transparency under the WTO Agreement, and build on those commitments in the provisions laid down in this Title.

Article 333 Definition

For the purposes of this Title, 'administrative decision' means a decision or action with legal effect that applies to a specific person, good or service in an individual case, and covers the failure to take a decision or take such action when that is so required by the law of a Party.

Article 334 Scope

This Title applies with respect to Titles I to VIII and Titles X to XII of this Heading and Heading Six.

Article 335 Publication

1. Each Party shall ensure that its laws, regulations, procedures and administrative rulings of general application are promptly published via an officially designated medium, and, where feasible, by electronic means, or are otherwise made available in such a manner as to enable any person to become acquainted with them.

2. To the extent appropriate, each Party shall provide an explanation of the objective of and rationale for measures referred to in paragraph 1.

3. Each Party shall provide a reasonable period of time between publication and entry into force of its laws and regulations, except when this is not possible for reasons of urgency.

Article 336 Enquiries

1. Each Party shall establish or maintain appropriate and proportionate mechanisms for responding to questions from any person regarding any laws or regulations.

2. Each Party shall promptly provide information and respond to questions by the other Party pertaining to any law or regulation whether in force or planned, unless a specific mechanism is established under another provision of this Agreement.

Article 337 Administration of measures of general application

1. Each Party shall administer its laws, regulations, procedures and administrative rulings of general application in an objective, impartial, and reasonable manner.

2. When administrative proceedings relating to persons, goods or services of the other Party are initiated in respect of the application of laws or regulations, each Party shall:

(a) endeavour to provide persons who are directly affected by the administrative proceedings with reasonable notice in accordance with its laws and regulations, including a description of the nature of the proceedings, a statement of the legal authority under which the proceedings are initiated and a general description of any issues in controversy; and

(b) afford such persons a reasonable opportunity to present facts and arguments in support of their positions prior to any final administrative decision insofar as time, the nature of the proceedings and the public interest permit.

Article 338 Review and appeal

1. Each Party shall establish or maintain judicial, arbitral or administrative tribunals and procedures for the purpose of the prompt review and, if warranted, correction of administrative decisions. Each Party shall ensure that its tribunals carry out procedures for appeal or review in a non-discriminatory and impartial manner. Those tribunals shall be impartial and independent of the authority entrusted with administrative enforcement.

2. Each Party shall ensure that the parties to the proceedings as referred to in paragraph 1 are provided with a reasonable opportunity to support or defend their respective positions.

3. In accordance with its law, each Party shall ensure that any decisions adopted in proceedings as referred to in paragraph 1 are based on the evidence and submissions of record or, where applicable, on the record compiled by the competent administrative authority.

4. Each Party shall ensure that decisions as referred to in paragraph 3 shall be implemented by the authority entrusted with administrative enforcement, subject to appeal or further review as provided for in its law.

Article 339 Relation to other Titles

The provisions set out in this Title supplement the specific transparency rules set out in those Titles of this Heading with respect to which this Title applies.

Title X Good regulatory practices and regulatory cooperation

Article 340 General principles

1. Each Party shall be free to determine its approach to good regulatory practices under this Agreement in a manner consistent with its own legal framework, practice, procedures and fundamental principles[36] underlying its regulatory system.

2. Nothing in this Title shall be construed as requiring a Party to:

(a) deviate from its domestic procedures for preparing and adopting regulatory measures;
(b) take actions that would undermine or impede the timely adoption of regulatory measures to achieve its public policy objectives; or
(c) achieve any particular regulatory outcome.

3. Nothing in this Title shall affect the right of a Party to define or regulate its own levels of protection in pursuit or furtherance of its public policy objectives in areas such as:

(a) public health;
(b) human, animal or plant life and health, and animal welfare;
(c) occupational health and safety;
(d) labour conditions;
(e) environment including climate change;
(f) consumer protection;
(g) social protection and social security;
(h) data protection and cybersecurity;
(i) cultural diversity;
(j) integrity and stability of the financial system, and protection of investors;
(k) energy security; and
(l) anti-money laundering.

For greater certainty, for the purposes of in particular point (c) and (d) of the first subparagraph, the different models of industrial relations, including the role and autonomy of social partners, as provided for in the law or national practices of a Party, shall continue to apply, including laws and practices concerning collective bargaining and the enforcement of collective agreements.

4. Regulatory measures shall not constitute a disguised barrier to trade.

[36] For the Union, such principles include the precautionary principle.

Article 341 Definitions

For the purposes of this Title, the following definitions apply:

(a) 'regulatory authority' means:
   (i) for the Union, the European Commission; and
   (ii) for the United Kingdom, Her Majesty's Government of the United Kingdom of Great Britain and Northern Ireland, and the devolved administrations of the United Kingdom.

(b) 'regulatory measures' means:
   (i) for the Union:
      (A) regulations and directives, as provided for in Article 288 TFEU; and
      (B) implementing and delegated acts, as provided for in Articles 290 and 291 TFEU, respectively; and
   (ii) for the United Kingdom:
      (A) primary legislation; and
      (B) secondary legislation.

Article 342 Scope

1. This Title applies to regulatory measures proposed or issued, as relevant, by the regulatory authority of each Party in respect of any matter covered by Titles I to IX, Title XI and Title XII of this Heading and Heading Six.

2. Articles 351 and 352 also apply to other measures of general application issued or proposed by the regulatory authority of a Party in respect of any matter covered by the Titles referred to in paragraph 1 of this Article which are relevant to regulatory cooperation activities, such as guidelines, policy documents or recommendations.

3. This Title does not apply to regulatory authorities and regulatory measures, regulatory practices or approaches of the Member States.

4. Any specific provisions in the Titles referred to in paragraph 1 of this Article shall prevail over the provisions of this Title to the extent necessary for the application of the specific provisions.

Article 343 Internal coordination

Each Party shall have in place internal coordination or review processes or mechanisms with respect to regulatory measures that its regulatory authority is preparing. Such processes or mechanisms should seek, *inter alia*, to:

(a) foster good regulatory practices, including those set forth in this Title;
(b) identify and avoid unnecessary duplication and inconsistent requirements between the Party's own regulatory measures;
(c) ensure compliance with the Party's international trade and investment obligations; and
(d) promote the consideration of the impact of the regulatory measures under preparation, including the impact on small and medium-sized enterprises[39], in accordance with its respective rules and procedures.

Article 344 Description of processes and mechanisms

Each Party shall make publicly available descriptions of the processes or mechanisms used by its regulatory authority to prepare, evaluate or review regulatory measures. Those descriptions shall refer to relevant rules, guidelines or procedures, including those regarding opportunities for the public to provide comments.

Article 345 Early information on planned regulatory measures

1. Each Party shall make publicly available, in accordance with its respective rules and procedures on at least an annual basis, a list of planned major[37] regulatory measures that its regulatory authority reasonably expects to propose or adopt within a year. The regulatory authority of each

[37] For the United Kingdom, 'small and medium-sized enterprises' means small and micro-sized businesses.

[38] In the case of the United Kingdom, major regulatory measures shall be understood as significant regulatory measures in accordance with the definition of such measures in the United Kingdom's rules and procedures.

Party may determine what constitutes a major regulatory measure for the purposes of its obligations under this Title.

2. With respect to each major regulatory measure included in the list referred to in paragraph 1, each Party should also make publicly available, as early as possible:

(a) a brief description of its scope and objectives; and
(b) if available, the estimated time for its adoption, including any opportunities for public consultation.

Article 346 Public consultation

1. When preparing a major regulatory measure, each Party, in accordance with its respective rules and procedures, shall ensure that its regulatory authority:

(a) publishes either the draft regulatory measure or consultation documents providing sufficient details about the regulatory measure under preparation to allow any person to assess whether and how that person's interests might be significantly affected;
(b) offers, on a non-discriminatory basis, reasonable opportunities for any person to provide comments; and
(c) considers the comments received.

2. Each Party shall ensure that its regulatory authority makes use of electronic means of communication and shall seek to maintain online services that are available to the public free of charge for the purposes of publishing the relevant regulatory measures or documents of the kind referred to in point (a) of paragraph 1 and of receiving comments related to public consultations.

3. Each Party shall ensure that its regulatory authority makes publicly available, in accordance with its respective rules and procedures, a summary of the results of the public consultations referred to in this Article.

Article 347 Impact assessment

1. Each Party affirms its intention to ensure that its regulatory authority carries out, in accordance with its respective rules and procedures, impact assessments for any major regulatory measures it prepares. Such rules and procedures may provide for exceptions.

2. When carrying out an impact assessment, each Party shall ensure that its regulatory authority has processes and mechanisms in place that promote the consideration of the following factors:

(a) the need for the regulatory measure, including the nature and the significance of the problem that the regulatory measure intends to address;
(b) any feasible and appropriate regulatory or non-regulatory options that would achieve the Party's public policy objectives, including the option of not regulating;
(c) to the extent possible and relevant, the potential social, economic and environmental impact of those options, including the impact on international trade and investment and, in accordance with its respective rules and procedures, the impact on small and medium-sized enterprises; and
(d) where appropriate, how the options under consideration relate to relevant international standards, including the reasons for any divergence.

3. With respect to an impact assessment that a regulatory authority has conducted for a regulatory measure, each Party shall ensure that its regulatory authority prepares a final report detailing the factors it considered in its assessment and its relevant findings. To the extent possible, each Party shall make such reports publicly available no later than when the proposal for a regulatory measure as referred to in point (b)(i)(A) or (b)(ii(A) of Article 341 or a regulatory measure as referred to in point (b)(i)(B) or (b)(ii)(B) of that Article has been made publicly available.

Article 348 Retrospective evaluation

1. Each Party shall ensure that its regulatory authority has in place processes or mechanisms for the purpose of carrying out periodic retrospective evaluations of regulatory measures in force, where appropriate.

2. When conducting a periodic retrospective evaluation, each Party shall endeavour to consider whether there are opportunities to more effectively achieve its public policy objectives and to reduce unnecessary regulatory burdens, including on small and medium-sized enterprises.

3. Each Party shall ensure that its regulatory authority makes publicly available any existing plans for and the results of such retrospective evaluations.

Article 349 Regulatory register

Each Party shall ensure that regulatory measures that are in effect are published in a designated register that identifies regulatory measures and that is publicly available online free of charge. The register should allow searches for regulatory measures by citations or by word. Each Party shall periodically update its register.

Article 350 Exchange of information on good regulatory practices

The Parties shall endeavour to exchange information on their good regulatory practices as set out in this Title, including in the Trade Specialised Committee on Regulatory Cooperation.

Article 351 Regulatory cooperation activities

1. The Parties may engage in regulatory cooperation activities on a voluntary basis, without prejudice to the autonomy of their own decision-making and their respective legal orders. A Party may refuse to engage in or it may withdraw from regulatory cooperation activities. A Party that refuses to engage in or that withdraws from regulatory cooperation activities should explain the reasons for its decision to the other Party.

2. Each Party may propose a regulatory cooperation activity to the other Party. It shall present its proposal via the contact point designated in accordance with Article 353. The other Party shall review that proposal within a reasonable period and shall inform the proposing Party whether it considers the proposed activity to be suitable for regulatory cooperation.

3. In order to identify activities that are suitable for regulatory cooperation, each Party shall consider:

(a) the list referred to in Article 345(1); and

(b) proposals for regulatory cooperation activities submitted by persons of a Party that are substantiated and accompanied by relevant information.

4. If the Parties decide to engage in a regulatory cooperation activity, the regulatory authority of each Party shall endeavour, where appropriate:

(a) to inform the regulatory authority of the other Party about the preparation of new or the revision of existing regulatory measures and other measures of general application referred to in Article 342(2) that are relevant to the regulatory cooperation activity;

(b) on request, to provide information and discuss regulatory measures and other measures of general application referred to in Article 342(2) that are relevant to the regulatory cooperation activity; and

(c) when preparing new or revising existing regulatory measures or other measures of general application referred to in Article 342(2), consider, to the extent feasible, any regulatory approach by the other Party on the same or a related matter.

Article 352 Trade Specialised Committee on Regulatory Cooperation

1. The Trade Specialised Committee on Regulatory Cooperation shall have the following functions:

(a) enhancing and promoting good regulatory practices and regulatory cooperation between the Parties;

(b) exchanging views with respect to the cooperation activities proposed or carried out under Article 351;

(c) encouraging regulatory cooperation and coordination in international fora, including, when appropriate, periodic bilateral exchanges of information on relevant ongoing or planned activities.

2. The Trade Specialised Committee on Regulatory Cooperation may invite interested persons to participate in its meetings.

Article 353 Contact points

Within a month after the entry into force of this Agreement, each Party shall designate a contact point to facilitate the exchange of information between the Parties.

Article 354 Non-application of dispute settlement

Title I of Part Six does not apply in respect of disputes regarding the interpretation and application of this Title.

Title XI Level playing field for open and fair competition and sustainable development

Chapter 1 General provisions

Article 355 Principles and objectives

1. The Parties recognise that trade and investment between the Union and the United Kingdom under the terms set out in this Agreement require conditions that ensure a level playing field for open and fair competition between the Parties and that ensure that trade and investment take place in a manner conducive to sustainable development.

2. The Parties recognise that sustainable development encompasses economic development, social development and environmental protection, all three being interdependent and mutually reinforcing, and affirm their commitment to promoting the development of international trade and investment in a way that contributes to the objective of sustainable development.

3. Each Party reaffirms its ambition of achieving economy-wide climate neutrality by 2050.

4. The Parties affirm their common understanding that their economic relationship can only deliver benefits in a mutually satisfactory way if the commitments relating to a level playing field for open and fair competition stand the test of time, by preventing distortions of trade or investment, and by contributing to sustainable development. However the Parties recognise that the purpose of this Title is not to harmonise the standards of the Parties. The Parties are determined to maintain and improve their respective high standards in the areas covered by this Title.

Article 356 Right to regulate, precautionary approach[39] and scientific and technical information

1. The Parties affirm the right of each Party to set its policies and priorities in the areas covered by this Title, to determine the levels of protection it deems appropriate and to adopt or modify its law and policies in a manner consistent with each Party's international commitments, including its commitments under this Title.

2. The Parties acknowledge that, in accordance with the precautionary approach, where there are reasonable grounds for concern that there are potential threats of serious or irreversible damage to the environment or human health, the lack of full scientific certainty shall not be used as a reason for preventing a Party from adopting appropriate measures to prevent such damage.

3. When preparing or implementing measures aimed at protecting the environment or labour conditions that may affect trade or investment, each Party shall take into account relevant and available scientific and technical information, international standards, guidelines and recommendations.

Article 357 Dispute settlement

Title I of Part Six does not apply to this Chapter, except for Article 356(2). Articles 408 and 409 apply to Article 355(3).

[39] For greater certainty, in relation to the implementation of this Agreement in the territory of the Union, the precautionary approach refers to the precautionary principle.

Chapter 2 Competition policy

Article 358 Principles and definitions

1. The Parties recognise the importance of free and undistorted competition in their trade and investment relations. The Parties acknowledge that anticompetitive business practices may distort the proper functioning of markets and undermine the benefits of trade liberalisation.

2. For the purposes of this Chapter, an 'economic actor' means an entity or a group of entities constituting a single economic entity, regardless of its legal status, that is engaged in an economic activity by offering goods or services on a market.

Article 359 Competition law

1. In recognition of the principles set out in Article 358, each Party shall maintain a competition law which effectively addresses the following anticompetitive business practices:

(a) agreements between economic actors, decisions by associations of economic actors and concerted practices which have as their object or effect the prevention, restriction or distortion of competition;

(b) abuse by one or more economic actors of a dominant position; and

(c) for the United Kingdom, mergers or acquisitions and, for the Union, concentrations, between economic actors which may have significant anticompetitive effects.

2. The competition law referred to in paragraph 1 shall apply to all economic actors irrespective of their nationality or ownership status.

3. Each Party may provide for exemptions from its competition law in pursuit of legitimate public policy objectives, provided that those exemptions are transparent and are proportionate to those objectives.

Article 360 Enforcement

1. Each Party shall take appropriate measures to enforce its competition law in its territory.

2. Each Party shall maintain an operationally independent authority or authorities competent for the effective enforcement of its competition law.

3. Each Party shall apply its competition law in a transparent and non-discriminatory manner, respecting the principles of procedural fairness, including the rights of defence of the economic actors concerned, irrespective of their nationality or ownership status.

Article 361 Cooperation

1. To achieve the objectives of this Chapter and to enhance the effective enforcement of their respective competition law, the Parties recognise the importance of cooperation between their respective competition authorities with regard to developments in competition policy and enforcement activities.

2. For the purposes of paragraph 1, the European Commission or the competition authorities of the Member States, on the one side, and the United Kingdom's competition authority or authorities, on the other side, shall endeavour to cooperate and coordinate, with respect to their enforcement activities concerning the same or related conduct or transactions, where doing so is possible and appropriate.

3. To facilitate the cooperation and coordination referred to in paragraphs 1 and 2, the European Commission and the competition authorities of the Member States, on the one side, and the United Kingdom's competition authority or authorities, on the other side, may exchange information to the extent permitted by each Party's law.

4. To implement the objectives of this Article, the Parties may enter into a separate agreement on cooperation and coordination between the European Commission, the competition authorities of the Member States and the United Kingdom's competition authority or authorities, which may include conditions for the exchange and use of confidential information.

Article 362 Dispute settlement

This Chapter shall not be subject to dispute settlement under Title I of Part Six.

Chapters 3 to 5 [omitted]

Chapter 6 Labour and social standards

Article 386 Definition

1. For the purposes of this Chapter, 'labour and social levels of protection' means the levels of protection provided overall in a Party's law and standards[40], in each of the following areas:

(a) fundamental rights at work;
(b) occupational health and safety standards;
(c) fair working conditions and employment standards;
(d) information and consultation rights at company level; or
(e) restructuring of undertakings.

2. For the Union, 'labour and social levels of protection' means labour and social levels of protection that are applicable to and in, and are common to, all Member States.

Article 387 Non-regression from levels of protection

1. The Parties affirm the right of each Party to set its policies and priorities in the areas covered by this Chapter, to determine the labour and social levels of protection it deems appropriate and to adopt or modify its law and policies in a manner consistent with each Party's international commitments, including those under this Chapter.

2. A Party shall not weaken or reduce, in a manner affecting trade or investment between the Parties, its labour and social levels of protection below the levels in place at the end of the transition period, including by failing to effectively enforce its law and standards.

3. The Parties recognise that each Party retains the right to exercise reasonable discretion and to make bona fide decisions regarding the allocation of labour enforcement resources with respect to other labour law determined to have higher priority, provided that the exercise of that discretion, and those decisions, are not inconsistent with its obligations under this Chapter.

4. The Parties shall continue to strive to increase their respective labour and social levels of protection referred to in this Chapter.

Article 388 Enforcement

For the purposes of enforcement as referred to in Article 387 each Party shall have in place and maintain a system for effective domestic enforcement and, in particular, an effective system of labour inspections in accordance with its international commitments relating to working conditions and the protection of workers; ensure that administrative and judicial proceedings are available that allow public authorities and individuals with standing to bring timely actions against violations of the labour law and social standards; and provide for appropriate and effective remedies, including interim relief, as well as proportionate and dissuasive sanctions. In the domestic implementation and enforcement of Article 387, each Party shall respect the role and autonomy of the social partners at a national level, where relevant, in line with applicable law and practice.

Article 389 Dispute settlement

1. The Parties shall make all efforts through dialogue, consultation, exchange of information and cooperation to address any disagreement on the application of this Chapter.

2. By way of derogation from Title I of Part Six, in the event of a dispute between the Parties regarding the application of this Chapter, the Parties shall have recourse exclusively to the procedures established under Articles 408, 409 and 410.

[40] For greater certainty, this Chapter and Article 411 do not apply to the Parties' law and standards relating to social security and pensions.

Chapter 7 Environment and climate [omitted]

Chapter 8 [Omitted]

Chapter 9 Horizontal and institutional provisions

Article 408 Consultations

1. A Party may request consultations with the other Party regarding any matter arising under Article 355(3), and Chapters 6, 7, and 8 by delivering a written request to the other Party. The complaining Party shall specify in its written request the reasons and basis for the request, including identification of the measures at issue, specifying the provisions that it considers applicable. Consultations must commence promptly after a Party delivers a request for consultations and in any event not later than 30 days after the date of delivery of the request, unless the Parties agree to a longer period.

2. The Parties shall enter into consultations with the aim of reaching a mutually satisfactory resolution of the matter. During consultations, each Party shall provide the other Party with sufficient information in its possession to allow a full examination of the matters raised. Each Party shall endeavour to ensure the participation of personnel of their competent authorities who have expertise in the matter subject to the consultations.

3. In matters relating to Article 355(3) or to the multilateral agreements or instruments referred to in Chapters 6, 7 or 8 the Parties shall take into account available information from the ILO or relevant bodies or organisations established under multilateral environmental agreements. Where relevant, the Parties shall jointly seek advice from such organisations or their bodies, or any other expert or body they deem appropriate.

4. Each Party may seek, when appropriate, the views of the domestic advisory groups referred to in Article 13 or other expert advice.

5. Any resolution reached by the Parties shall be made available to the public.

Article 409 Panel of experts

1. For any matter that is not satisfactorily addressed through consultations under Article 408, a Party may, after 90 days from the receipt of a request for consultations under that Article, request that a panel of experts be convened to examine that matter, by delivering a written request to the other Party. The request shall identify the measure at issue, specify and explain how that measure does not conform with the provisions of the relevant Chapter or Chapters in a manner sufficient to present the complaint clearly.

2. The panel of experts shall be composed of three panellists.

3. The Trade Specialised Committee on Level Playing Field for Open and Fair Competition and Sustainable Development shall, at its first meeting after the entry into force of this Agreement, establish a list of at least 15 individuals who are willing and able to serve as panellists. Each Party shall name at least five individuals to the list to serve as panellists. The Parties shall also name at least five individuals who are not nationals of either Party and who are willing and able to serve as chairperson of a panel of experts. The Trade Specialised Committee on Level Playing Field for Open and Fair Competition and Sustainable Development shall ensure that the list is kept up to date and that the number of experts is maintained at a minimum of 15 individuals.

4. The experts proposed as panellists must have specialised knowledge or expertise in labour or environmental law, other issues addressed in the relevant Chapter or Chapters, or in the resolution of disputes arising under international agreements. They must serve in their individual capacities and not take instructions from any organisation or government with regard to matters related to the dispute. They must not be affiliated with or take instructions from either Party. They shall not be persons who are members, officials or other servants of the Union institutions, of the Government of a Member State, or of the Government of the United Kingdom.

5. Unless the Parties agree otherwise within five days from the date of establishment of the panel of experts, the terms of reference shall be:

'to examine, in the light of the relevant provisions, the matter referred to in the request for the establishment of the panel of experts, and to deliver a report, in accordance with this Article that makes findings on the conformity of the measure with the relevant provisions.'

6. In respect of matters related to multilateral standards or agreements covered in this Title, the panel of experts should seek information from the ILO or relevant bodies established under those agreements, including any pertinent available interpretative guidance, findings or decisions adopted by the ILO and those bodies.

7. The panel of experts may request and receive written submissions or any other information from persons with relevant information or specialised knowledge.

8. The panel of experts shall make available such information to each Party allowing them to submit their comments within 20 days of its receipt.

9. The panel of experts shall issue to the Parties an interim report and a final report setting out the findings of fact, its determinations on the matter including as to whether the respondent Party has conformed with its obligations under the relevant Chapter or Chapters and the rationale behind any findings and determinations that it makes. For greater certainty, the Parties share the understanding that if the Panel makes recommendations in its report, the respondent Party does not need to follow these recommendations in ensuring conformity with this Agreement.

10. The panel of experts shall deliver to the Parties the interim report within 100 days after the date of establishment of the panel of experts. When the panel of experts considers that this deadline cannot be met, the chairperson of the panel of experts shall notify the Parties in writing, stating the reasons for the delay and the date on which the panel of experts plans to deliver its interim report. The panel of experts shall, under no circumstances, deliver its interim report later than 125 days after the date of establishment of the panel of experts.

11. Each Party may deliver to the panel of experts a reasoned request to review particular aspects of the interim report within 25 days of its delivery. A Party may comment on the other's Party's request within 15 days of the delivery of the request.

12. After considering those comments, the panel of experts shall prepare the final report. If no request to review particular aspects of the interim report is delivered within the time period referred to in paragraph 11, the interim report shall become the final report of the panel of experts.

13. The panel of experts shall deliver its final report to the Parties within 175 days of the date of establishment of the panel of experts. When the panel of experts considers that this time limit cannot be met, its chairperson shall notify the Parties in writing, stating the reasons for the delay and the date on which the panel of experts plans to deliver its final report. The panel of experts shall, under no circumstances, deliver its final report later than 195 days after the date of establishment of the panel of experts.

14. The final report shall include a discussion of any written request by the Parties on the interim report and clearly address the comments of the Parties.

15. The Parties shall make the final report available to the public within 15 days of its delivery by the panel of experts.

16. If the final report of the panel of experts determines that a Party has not conformed with its obligations under the relevant Chapter or Chapters, the Parties shall, within 90 days of the delivery of the final report, discuss appropriate measures to be implemented taking into account the report of the panel of experts. No later than 105 days after the report has been delivered to the Parties, the respondent Party shall inform its domestic advisory groups established under Article 13 and the complaining Party of its decision on any measures to be implemented.

17. The Trade Specialised Committee on Level Playing Field for Open and Fair Competition and Sustainable Development shall monitor the follow-up to the report of the panel of experts. The domestic advisory groups of the Parties established under Article 13 may submit observations to the Trade Specialised Committee on Level Playing Field for Open and Fair Competition and Sustainable Development in that regard.

18. When the Parties disagree on the existence of, or the consistency with, the relevant provisions of any measure taken to address the non-conformity, the complaining Party may deliver a

request, which shall be in writing, to the original panel of experts to decide on the matter. The request shall identify any measure at issue and explain how that measure is not in conformity with the relevant provisions in a manner sufficient to present the complaint clearly. The panel of experts shall deliver its findings to the Parties within 45 days of the date of the delivery of the request.

19. Except as otherwise provided for in this Article, Article 739(1), Article 740 and Articles 753 to 758, as well as Annexes 48 and 49, shall apply *mutatis mutandis*.

Article 410 Panel of experts for non-regression areas

1. Article 409 shall apply to disputes between the Parties concerning the interpretation and application of Chapters 6 and 7.

2. For the purposes of such disputes, in addition to the Articles listed in Article 409(19), Articles 749 and 750 shall apply *mutatis mutandis*.

3. The Parties recognise that, where the respondent Party chooses not [to] take any action to conform with the report of the panel of experts and with this Agreement, any remedies authorised under Article 749 continue to be available to the complaining Party.

Article 411 Rebalancing

1. The Parties recognise the right of each Party to determine its future policies and priorities with respect to labour and social, environmental or climate protection, or with respect to subsidy control, in a manner consistent with each Party's international commitments, including those under this Agreement. At the same time, the Parties acknowledge that significant divergences in these areas can be capable of impacting trade or investment between the Parties in a manner that changes the circumstances that have formed the basis for the conclusion of this Agreement.

2. If material impacts on trade or investment between the Parties are arising as a result of significant divergences between the Parties in the areas referred to in paragraph 1, either Party may take appropriate rebalancing measures to address the situation. Such measures shall be restricted with respect to their scope and duration to what is strictly necessary and proportionate in order to remedy the situation. Priority shall be given to such measures as will least disturb the functioning of this Agreement. A Party's assessment of those impacts shall be based on reliable evidence and not merely on conjecture or remote possibility.

3. The following procedures shall apply to rebalancing measures taken under paragraph 2:

(a) the concerned Party shall, without delay, notify the other Party through the Partnership Council of the rebalancing measures it intends to take, providing all relevant information. The Parties shall immediately enter into consultations. Consultations shall be deemed concluded within 14 days from the date of delivery of the notification, unless they are jointly concluded before that time limit;

(b) if no mutually acceptable solution is found, the concerned Party may adopt rebalancing measures no sooner than five days from the conclusion of the consultations, unless the notified Party requests within the same five day period, in accordance with Article 739(2)[41], the establishment of an arbitration tribunal by means of a written request delivered to the other Party in order for the arbitration tribunal to decide whether the notified rebalancing measures are consistent with paragraph 2 of this Article;

(c) the arbitration tribunal shall conduct its proceeding in accordance with Article 760 and deliver its final ruling within 30 days from its establishment. If the arbitration tribunal does not deliver its final ruling within that time period, the concerned Party may adopt the rebalancing measures no sooner than three days after the expiry of that 30 day time period. In that case, the other Party may take countermeasures proportionate to the adopted rebalancing measures until the arbitration tribunal delivers its ruling. Priority shall be given to such countermeasures as will least disturb the functioning of this Agreement. Point (a) shall apply *mutatis mutandis* to such countermeasures, which may be adopted no sooner than three days after the conclusion of consultations;

[41] For greater certainty, in this case the Party shall not have prior recourse to consultations in accordance with Article 738.

(d) if the arbitration tribunal has found the rebalancing measures to be consistent with paragraph 2, the concerned Party may adopt the rebalancing measures as notified to the other Party;
(e) if the arbitration tribunal has found the rebalancing measures to be inconsistent with paragraph 2 of this Article, the concerned Party shall, within three days from the delivery of the ruling, notify the complaining Party of the measures[42] it intends to adopt to comply with the ruling of the arbitration tribunal. Article 748(2) and Articles 749[43] and 750 shall apply *mutatis mutandis*, if the complaining Party considers that the notified measures are not in compliance with the ruling of the arbitration tribunal. The procedures under Article 748(2) and Articles 749 and 750 shall have no suspensive effect on the application of the notified measures pursuant to this paragraph;
(f) if rebalancing measures were adopted prior to the arbitration ruling in accordance with point (c), any countermeasures adopted pursuant to that point shall be withdrawn immediately, and in no case later than five days, after delivery of the ruling of the arbitration tribunal;
(g) a Party shall not invoke the WTO Agreement or any other international agreement to preclude the other Party from taking measures pursuant to paragraphs 2 and 3, including when those measures consist of suspension of obligations under this Agreement;
(h) if the notified Party does not submit a request pursuant to point (b) of this paragraph within the time period laid down therein, that Party may without having prior recourse to consultations in accordance with Article 738 initiate the arbitration procedure referred to in Article 739. An arbitration tribunal shall treat the issue as a case of urgency for the purpose of Article 744.

4. In order to ensure an appropriate balance between the commitments made by the Parties in this Agreement on a more durable basis, either Party may request, no sooner than four years after the entry into force of this Agreement, a review of the operation of this Heading. The Parties may agree that other Headings of this Agreement may be added to the review.

5. Such a review shall commence at a Party's request, if that Party considers that measures under paragraph 2 or 3 have been taken frequently by either or both Parties, or if a measure that has a material impact on trade or investment between the Parties has been applied for a period of 12 months. For the purposes of this paragraph, the measures in question are those which were not challenged or not found by an arbitration tribunal to be strictly unnecessary pursuant to point (d) or (h) of paragraph 3. This review may commence earlier than four years after the entry into force of this Agreement.

6. The review requested pursuant to paragraph 4 or 5 shall begin within three months of the request and be completed within six months.

7. A review on the basis of paragraph 4 or 5 may be repeated at subsequent intervals of no less than four years after the conclusion of the previous review. If a Party has requested a review under paragraph 4 or 5, it may not request a further review under either paragraph 4 or 5 for at least four years from the conclusion of the previous review or, if applicable, from the entry into force of any amending agreement.

8. The review shall address whether this Agreement delivers an appropriate balance of rights and obligations between the Parties, in particular with regard to the operation of this Heading, and whether, as a result, there is a need for any modification of the terms of this Agreement.

9. The Partnership Council may decide that no action is required as a result of the review. If a Party considers that following the review there is a need for an amendment of this Agreement, the Parties shall use their best endeavours to negotiate and conclude an agreement making the necessary amendments. Such negotiations shall be limited to matters identified in the review.

[42] Such measures may include withdrawal or adjustment of the rebalancing measures, as appropriate.
[43] Suspension of obligations under Article 749 shall be available only if rebalancing measures have in fact been applied.

10. If an amending agreement referred to in paragraph 9 is not concluded within one year from the date the Parties started negotiations, either Party may give notice to terminate this Heading or any other Heading of this Agreement that was added to the review, or the Parties may decide to continue negotiations. If a Party terminates this Heading, Heading Three shall be terminated on the same date. The termination shall take effect three months after the date of such notice.

11. If this Heading is terminated pursuant to paragraph 10 of this Article, Heading Two shall be terminated on the same date, unless the Parties agree to integrate the relevant parts of Title XI of this Heading in Heading Two.

12. Title I of Part Six does not apply to paragraphs 4 to 9 of this Article.

Title XII Exceptions [omitted]

HEADING TWO AVIATION [OMITTED]

Title II Aviation safety [omitted]

HEADING THREE ROAD TRANSPORT [OMITTED]

HEADING FOUR SOCIAL SECURITY COORDINATION AND VISAS FOR SHORT-TERM VISITS

Title I Social security coordination

Article 488 Overview

Member States and the United Kingdom shall coordinate their social security systems in accordance with the Protocol on Social Security Coordination, in order to secure the social security entitlements of the persons covered therein.

Article 489 Legally residing

1. The Protocol on Social Security Coordination applies to persons legally residing in a Member State or the United Kingdom.

2. Paragraph 1 of this Article shall not affect entitlements to cash benefits which relate to previous periods of legal residence of persons covered by Article SSC.2 of the Protocol on Social Security Coordination.

Article 490 Cross-border situations

1. The Protocol on Social Security Coordination only applies to situations arising between one or more Member States and the United Kingdom.

2. The Protocol on Social Security Coordination shall not apply to persons whose situations are confined in all respects either to the United Kingdom, or to the Member States.

Article 491 Immigration applications

The Protocol on Social Security Coordination applies without prejudice to the right of a Member State or the United Kingdom to charge a health fee under national legislation in connection with an application for a permit to enter, to stay, to work, or to reside in that State.

Title II Visas for short-term visits

Article 492 Visas for short-term visits

1. The Parties note that on the date of entry into force of this Agreement both Parties provide for visa-free travel for short-term visits in respect of their nationals in accordance with their domestic law. Each Party shall notify the other of any intention to impose a visa requirement for short-term

visits by nationals of the other Party in good time and, if possible, at least three months before such a requirement takes effect.

2. Subject to paragraph 3 of this Article and to Article 781, in the event that the United Kingdom decides to impose a visa requirement for short-term visits on nationals of a Member State, that requirement shall apply to the nationals of all Member States.

3. This Article is without prejudice to any arrangements made between the United Kingdom and Ireland concerning the Common Travel Area.

HEADING FIVE FISHERIES [OMITTED]

HEADING SIX OTHER PROVISIONS [OMITTED]

PART THREE LAW ENFORCEMENT AND JUDICIAL COOPERATION IN CRIMINAL MATTERS [OMITTED]

PART FOUR THEMATIC COOPERATION [OMITTED]

PART FIVE PARTICIPATION IN UNION PROGRAMMES, SOUND FINANCIAL MANAGEMENT AND FINANCIAL PROVISIONS [OMITTED]

PART SIX DISPUTE SETTLEMENT AND HORIZONTAL PROVISIONS

Title I Dispute settlement

Chapter 1 General provisions

Article 734 Objective

The objective of this Title is to establish an effective and efficient mechanism for avoiding and settling disputes between the Parties concerning the interpretation and application of this Agreement and supplementing agreements, with a view to reaching, where possible, a mutually agreed solution.

Article 735 Scope

1. This Title applies, subject to paragraphs 2, 3, 4 and 5, to disputes between the Parties concerning the interpretation and application of the provisions of this Agreement or of any supplementing agreement ('covered provisions').

2. The covered provisions shall include all provisions of this Agreement and of any supplementing agreement with the exception of:

(a) Article 32 (1) to (6) and Article 36;
(b) Annex 12;
(c) Title VII of Heading one of Part Two;
(d) Title X of Heading One of Part Two;
(e) Article 355(1), (2) and (4), Article 356(1) and (3), Chapter 2 of Title XI of Heading One of Part Two, Articles 371 and 372, Chapter 5 of Title XI of Heading One of Part Two, and Article 411(4) to (9);
(f) Part Three, including when applying in relation to situations governed by other provisions of this Agreement;
(g) Part Four;
(h) Title II of Part Six;
(i) Article 782; and

(j) the Agreement on security procedures for exchanging and protecting classified information;

3. The Partnership Council may be seized by a Party with a view to resolving a dispute with respect to obligations arising from the provisions referred to in paragraph 2.

4. Article 736 applies to the provisions referred to in paragraph 2 of this Article.

5. Notwithstanding paragraphs 1 and 2, this Title shall not apply with respect to disputes concerning the interpretation and application of the provisions of the Protocol on Social Security Coordination or its annexes in individual cases.

Article 736 Exclusivity

The Parties undertake not to submit a dispute between them regarding the interpretation or application of provisions of this Agreement or of any supplementing agreement to a mechanism of settlement other than those provided for in this Agreement.

Article 737 Choice of forum in case of a substantially equivalent obligation under another international agreement

1. If a dispute arises regarding a measure allegedly in breach of an obligation under this Agreement or any supplementing agreement and of a substantially equivalent obligation under another international agreement to which both Parties are party, including the WTO Agreement, the Party seeking redress shall select the forum in which to settle the dispute.

2. Once a Party has selected the forum and initiated dispute settlement procedures either under this Title or under another international agreement, that Party shall not initiate such procedures under the other international agreement with respect to the particular measure referred to in paragraph 1, unless the forum selected first fails to make findings for procedural or jurisdictional reasons.

3. For the purposes of this Article:

(a) dispute settlement procedures under this Title are deemed to be initiated by a Party's request for the establishment of an arbitration tribunal under Article 739;

(b) dispute settlement procedures under the WTO Agreement are deemed to be initiated by a Party's request for the establishment of a panel under Article 6 of the Understanding on Rules and Procedure Governing the Settlement of Disputes of the WTO; and

(c) dispute settlement procedures under any other agreement are deemed to be initiated if they are initiated in accordance with the relevant provisions of that agreement.

4. Without prejudice to paragraph 2, nothing in this Agreement or any supplementing agreement shall preclude a Party from suspending obligations authorised by the Dispute Settlement Body of the WTO or authorised under the dispute settlement procedures of another international agreement to which the Parties are party. The WTO Agreement or any other international agreement between the Parties shall not be invoked to preclude a Party from suspending obligations under this Title.

Chapter 2 Procedure

Article 738 Consultations

1. If a Party ('the complaining Party') considers that the other Party ('the respondent Party') has breached an obligation under this Agreement or under any supplementing agreement, the Parties shall endeavour to resolve the matter by entering into consultations in good faith, with the aim of reaching a mutually agreed solution.

2. The complaining Party may seek consultations by means of a written request delivered to the respondent Party. The complaining Party shall specify in its written request the reasons for the request, including the identification of the measures at issue and the legal basis for the request, and the covered provisions it considers applicable.

3. The respondent Party shall reply to the request promptly, and in any case no later than 10 days after the date of its delivery. Consultations shall be held within 30 days of the date of delivery of the request in person or by any other means of communication agreed by the Parties. If held in person, consultations shall take place in the territory of the respondent Party, unless the Parties agree otherwise.

4. The consultations shall be deemed concluded within 30 days of the date of delivery of the request, unless the Parties agree to continue consultations.

5. Consultations on matters of urgency, including those regarding perishable goods or seasonal goods or services, shall be held within 20 days of the date of delivery of the request. The consultations shall be deemed concluded within those 20 days unless the Parties agree to continue consultations.

6. Each Party shall provide sufficient factual information to allow a complete examination of the measure at issue, including an examination of how that measure could affect the application of this Agreement or any supplementing agreement. Each Party shall endeavour to ensure the participation of personnel of their competent authorities who have expertise in the matter subject to the consultations.

7. For any dispute concerning an area other than Titles I to VII, Chapter 4 of Title VIII, Titles IX to XII of Heading One or Heading Six of Part Two, at the request of the complaining Party, the consultations referred to in paragraph 3 of this Article shall be held in the framework of a Specialised Committee or of the Partnership Council. The Specialised Committee may at any time decide to refer the matter to the Partnership Council. The Partnership Council may also seize itself of the matter. The Specialised Committee, or, as the case may be, the Partnership Council, may resolve the dispute by a decision. The time periods referred to in paragraph 3 of this Article shall apply. The venue of meetings shall be governed by the rules of procedure of the Specialised Committee or, as the case may be, the Partnership Council.

8. Consultations, and in particular all information designated as confidential and positions taken by the Parties during consultations, shall be confidential, and shall be without prejudice to the rights of either Party in any further proceedings.

Article 739 Arbitration procedure

1. The complaining Party may request the establishment of an arbitration tribunal if:

(a) the respondent Party does not respond to the request for consultations within 10 days of the date of its delivery;
(b) consultations are not held within the time periods referred to in Article 738(3), (4) or (5);
(c) the Parties agree not to have consultations; or
(d) consultations have been concluded without a mutually agreed solution having been reached.

2. The request for the establishment of the arbitration tribunal shall be made by means of a written request delivered to the respondent Party. In its request, the complaining Party shall explicitly identify the measure at issue and explain how that measure constitutes a breach of the covered provisions in a manner sufficient to present the legal basis for the complaint clearly.

Article 740 Establishment of an arbitration tribunal

1. An arbitration tribunal shall be composed of three arbitrators.

2. No later than 10 days after the date of delivery of the request for the establishment of an arbitration tribunal, the Parties shall consult with a view to agreeing on the composition of the arbitration tribunal.

3. If the Parties do not agree on the composition of the arbitration tribunal within the time period provided for in paragraph 2 of this Article, each Party shall appoint an arbitrator from the sub-list for that Party established pursuant to Article 752 no later than five days after the expiry of the time period provided for in paragraph 2 of this Article. If a Party fails to appoint an arbitrator from its sub-list within that time period, the co-chair of the Partnership Council from the complaining Party shall select, no later than five days after the expiry of that time period, an arbitrator by lot from the sub-list of the Party that has failed to appoint an arbitrator. The co-chair of the Partnership Council from the complaining Party may delegate such selection by lot of the arbitrator.

4. If the Parties do not agree on the chairperson of the arbitration tribunal within the time period provided for in paragraph 2 of this Article, the co-chair of the Partnership Council from the complaining Party shall select, no later than five days after the expiry of that time period, the

chairperson of the arbitration tribunal by lot from the sub-list of chairpersons established pursuant to Article 752. The co-chair of the Partnership Council from the complaining Party may delegate such selection by lot of the chairperson of the arbitration tribunal.

5. Should any of the lists provided for in Article 752 not be established or not contain sufficient names at the time a selection is made pursuant to paragraph 3 or 4 of this Article, the arbitrators shall be selected by lot from the individuals who have been formally proposed by one Party or both Parties in accordance with Annex 48.

6. The date of establishment of the arbitration tribunal shall be the date on which the last of the three arbitrators has notified to the Parties the acceptance of his or her appointment in accordance with Annex 48.

Article 741 Requirements for arbitrators

1. All arbitrators shall:

(a) have demonstrated expertise in law and international trade, including on specific matters covered by Titles I to VII, Chapter 4 of Title VIII, Titles IX to XII of Heading One of Part Two or Heading Six of Part Two, or in law and any other matter covered by this Agreement or by any supplementing agreement and, in the case of a chairperson, also have experience in dispute settlement procedures;

(b) not be affiliated with or take instructions from either Party;

(c) serve in their individual capacities and not take instructions from any organisation or government with regard to matters related to the dispute; and

(d) comply with Annex 49.

2. All arbitrators shall be persons whose independence is beyond doubt, who possess the qualifications required for appointment to high judicial office in their respective countries or who are jurisconsults of recognised competence.

3. In view of the subject-matter of a particular dispute, the Parties may agree to derogate from the requirements listed in point (a) of paragraph 1.

Article 742 Functions of the arbitration tribunal

The arbitration tribunal:

(a) shall make an objective assessment of the matter before it, including an objective assessment of the facts of the case and the applicability of, and conformity of the measures at issue with, the covered provisions;

(b) shall set out, in its decisions and rulings, the findings of facts and law and the rationale behind any findings that it makes; and

(c) should consult regularly with the Parties and provide adequate opportunities for the development of a mutually agreed solution.

Article 743 Terms of reference

1. Unless the Parties agree otherwise no later than five days after the date of the establishment of the arbitration tribunal, the terms of reference of the arbitration tribunal shall be:

> 'to examine, in the light of the relevant covered provisions of this Agreement or of a supplementing agreement, the matter referred to in the request for the establishment of the arbitration tribunal, to decide on the conformity of the measure at issue with the provisions referred to in Article 735 and to issue a ruling in accordance with Article 745'.

2. If the Parties agree on terms of reference other than those referred to in paragraph 1, they shall notify the agreed terms of reference to the arbitration tribunal within the time period referred to in paragraph 1.

Article 744 Urgent proceedings

1. If a Party so requests, the arbitration tribunal shall decide, no later than 10 days after the date of its establishment, whether the case concerns matters of urgency.

2. In cases of urgency, the applicable time periods set out in Article 745 shall be half the time prescribed therein.

Article 745 Ruling of the arbitration tribunal

1. The arbitration tribunal shall deliver an interim report to the Parties within 100 days after the date of establishment of the arbitration tribunal. If the arbitration tribunal considers that this deadline cannot be met, the chairperson of the arbitration tribunal shall notify the Parties in writing, stating the reasons for the delay and the date on which the arbitration tribunal plans to deliver its interim report. The arbitration tribunal shall not deliver its interim report later than 130 days after the date of establishment of the arbitration tribunal under any circumstances.

2. Each Party may deliver to the arbitration tribunal a written request to review precise aspects of the interim report within 14 days of its delivery. A Party may comment on the other Party's request within six days of the delivery of the request.

3. If no written request to review precise aspects of the interim report is delivered within the time period referred to in paragraph 2, the interim report shall become the ruling of the arbitration tribunal.

4. The arbitration tribunal shall deliver its ruling to the Parties within 130 days of the date of establishment of the arbitration tribunal. When the arbitration tribunal considers that that deadline cannot be met, its chairperson shall notify the Parties in writing, stating the reasons for the delay and the date on which the arbitration tribunal plans to deliver its ruling. The arbitration tribunal shall not deliver its ruling later than 160 days after the date of establishment of the arbitration tribunal under any circumstances.

5. The ruling shall include a discussion of any written request by the Parties on the interim report and clearly address the comments of the Parties.

6. For greater certainty, a 'ruling' or 'rulings' as referred to in Articles 742, 743 and 753 and Article 754(1), (3), (4) and (6) shall be understood to refer also to the interim report of the arbitration tribunal.

Chapter 3 Compliance

Article 746 Compliance measures

1. If, in its ruling referred to in Article 745(4), the arbitration tribunal finds that the respondent Party has breached an obligation under this Agreement or under any supplementing agreement, that Party shall take the necessary measures to comply immediately with the ruling of the arbitration tribunal in order to bring itself in compliance with the covered provisions.

2. The respondent Party, no later than 30 days after delivery of the ruling, shall deliver a notification to the complaining Party of the measures which it has taken or which it envisages to take in order to comply.

Article 747 Reasonable Period of Time

1. If immediate compliance is not possible, the respondent Party, no later than 30 days after delivery of the ruling referred to in Article 745(4), shall deliver a notification to the complaining Party of the length of the reasonable period of time it will require for compliance with the ruling referred to in Article 745(4). The Parties shall endeavour to agree on the length of the reasonable period of time to comply.

2. If the Parties have not agreed on the length of the reasonable period of time, the complaining Party may, at the earliest 20 days after the delivery of the notification referred to in paragraph 1, request in writing that the original arbitration tribunal determines the length of the reasonable period of time. The arbitration tribunal shall deliver its decision to the Parties within 20 days of the date of delivery of the request.

3. The respondent Party shall deliver a written notification of its progress in complying with the ruling referred to in Article 745(4) to the complaining Party at least one month before the expiry of the reasonable period of time.

4. The Parties may agree to extend the reasonable period of time.

Article 748 Compliance Review

1. The respondent Party shall, no later than the date of expiry of the reasonable period of time, deliver a notification to the complaining Party of any measure that it has taken to comply with the ruling referred to in Article 745(4).

2. When the Parties disagree on the existence of, or the consistency with the covered provisions of, any measure taken to comply, the complaining Party may deliver a request, which shall be in writing, to the original arbitration tribunal to decide on the matter. The request shall identify any measure at issue and explain how that measure constitutes a breach of the covered provisions in a manner sufficient to present the legal basis for the complaint clearly. The arbitration tribunal shall deliver its decision to the Parties within 45 days of the date of delivery of the request.

Article 749 Temporary Remedies

1. The respondent Party shall, at the request of and after consultations with the complaining Party, present an offer for temporary compensation if:

(a) the respondent Party delivers a notification to the complaining Party that it is not possible to comply with the ruling referred to in Article 745(4); or
(b) the respondent Party fails to deliver a notification of any measure taken to comply within the deadline referred to in Article 746 or before the date of expiry of the reasonable period of time; or
(c) the arbitration tribunal finds that no measure taken to comply exists or that the measure taken to comply is inconsistent with the covered provisions.

2. In any of the conditions referred to in points (a), (b) and (c) of paragraph 1, the complaining Party may deliver a written notification to the respondent Party that it intends to suspend the application of obligations under the covered provisions if:

(a) the complaining Party decides not to make a request under paragraph 1; or
(b) the Parties do not agree on the temporary compensation within 20 days after the expiry of the reasonable period of time or the delivery of the arbitration tribunal decision under Article 748 if a request under paragraph 1 of this Article is made.

The notification shall specify the level of intended suspension of obligations.

3. Suspension of obligations shall be subject to the following conditions:

(a) Obligations under Heading Four of Part Two, the Protocol on Social Security Coordination or its annexes or Part Five may not be suspended under this Article;
(b) By way of derogation from point (a), obligations under Part Five may be suspended only where the ruling referred to in Article 745(4) concerns the interpretation and implementation of Part Five;
(c) Obligations outside Part Five may not be suspended where the ruling referred to in Article 745(4) concerns the interpretation and implementation of Part Five; and
(d) Obligations under Title II of Heading One of Part Two in respect of financial services may not be suspended under this Article, unless the ruling referred to in Article 745(4) concerns the interpretation and application of obligations under Title II of Heading One of Part two in respect of financial services.

4. Where a Party persists in not complying with a ruling of an arbitration panel established under an earlier agreement concluded between the Parties, the other Party may suspend obligations under the covered provisions referred to in Article 735. With the exception of the rule in point (a) of paragraph 3 of this Article, all rules relating to temporary remedies in case of non-compliance and to review of any such measures shall be governed by the earlier agreement.

5. The suspension of obligations shall not exceed the level equivalent to the nullification or impairment caused by the violation.

6. If the arbitration tribunal has found the violation in Heading One or Heading Three of Part Two, the suspension may be applied in another Title of the same Heading as that in which the tribunal has found the violation, in particular if the complaining party is of the view that such suspension is effective in inducing compliance.

7. If the arbitration tribunal has found the violation in Heading Two of Part Two:

(a) the complaining party should first seek to suspend obligations in the same Title as that in which the arbitration tribunal has found the violation;
(b) if the complaining party considers that it is not practicable or effective to suspend obligations with respect to the same Title as that in which the tribunal has found the violation, it may seek to suspend obligations in the other Title under the same Heading.

8. If the arbitration tribunal has found the violation in Heading One, Heading Two, Heading Three or Heading Five of Part Two, and if the complaining party considers that it is not practicable or effective to suspend obligations within the same Heading as that in which the arbitration tribunal has found the violation, and that the circumstances are serious enough, it may seek to suspend obligations under other covered provisions.

9. In the case of point (b) of paragraph 7 and paragraph 8, the complaining Party shall state the reasons for its decision.

10. The complaining Party may suspend the obligations 10 days after the date of delivery of the notification referred to in paragraph 2 unless the respondent Party made a request under paragraph 11.

11. If the respondent Party considers that the notified level of suspension of obligations exceeds the level equivalent to the nullification or impairment caused by the violation or that the principles and procedures set forth in point (b) of paragraph 7, paragraph 8 or paragraph 9 have not been followed, it may deliver a written request to the original arbitration tribunal before the expiry of the 10 day period set out in paragraph 10 to decide on the matter. The arbitration tribunal shall deliver its decision on the level of the suspension of obligations to the Parties within 30 days of the date of the request. Obligations shall not be suspended until the arbitration tribunal has delivered its decision. The suspension of obligations shall be consistent with that decision.

12. The arbitration tribunal acting pursuant to paragraph 11 shall not examine the nature of the obligations to be suspended but shall determine whether the level of such suspension exceeds the level equivalent to the nullification or impairment caused by the violation. However, if the matter referred to arbitration includes a claim that the principles and procedures set forth in point (b) of paragraph 7, paragraph 8 or paragraph 9 have not been followed, the arbitration tribunal shall examine that claim. In the event the arbitration tribunal determines that those principles and procedures have not been followed, the complaining party shall apply them consistently with point (b) of paragraph 7, paragraph 8 and paragraph 9. The parties shall accept the arbitration tribunal's decision as final and shall not seek a second arbitration procedure. This paragraph shall under no circumstances delay the date as of which the complaining Party is entitled to suspend obligations under this Article.

13. The suspension of obligations or the compensation referred to in this Article shall be temporary and shall not be applied after:

(a) the Parties have reached a mutually agreed solution pursuant to Article 756;
(b) the Parties have agreed that the measure taken to comply brings the respondent Party into compliance with the covered provisions; or
(c) any measure taken to comply which the arbitration tribunal has found to be inconsistent with the covered provisions has been withdrawn or amended so as to bring the respondent Party into compliance with those covered provisions.

Article 750 Review of any measure taken to comply after the adoption of temporary remedies

1. The respondent Party shall deliver a notification to the complaining Party of any measure it has taken to comply following the suspension of obligations or following the application of temporary compensation, as the case may be. With the exception of cases under paragraph 2, the complaining Party shall terminate the suspension of obligations within 30 days from the delivery of the notification. In cases where compensation has been applied, with the exception of cases under paragraph 2, the respondent Party may terminate the application of such compensation within 30 days from the delivery of its notification that it has complied.

2. If the Parties do not reach an agreement on whether the notified measure brings the respondent Party into compliance with the covered provisions within 30 days of the date of delivery of the notification, the complaining Party shall deliver a written request to the original arbitration tribunal to decide on the matter. The arbitration tribunal shall deliver its decision to the Parties within 46 days of the date of the delivery of the request. If the arbitration tribunal finds that the measure taken to comply is in conformity with the covered provisions, the suspension of obligations or compensation, as the case may be, shall be terminated. When relevant, the level of suspension of obligations or of compensation shall be adjusted in light of the arbitration tribunal decision.

Chapter 4 Common procedural provisions

Articles 751–753 [Omitted]

Article 754 Arbitration tribunal decisions and rulings

1. The deliberations of the arbitration tribunal shall be kept confidential. The arbitration tribunal shall make every effort to draft rulings and take decisions by consensus. If this is not possible, the arbitration tribunal shall decide the matter by majority vote. In no case shall separate opinions of arbitrators be disclosed.

2. The decisions and rulings of the arbitration tribunal shall be binding on the Union and on the United Kingdom. They shall not create any rights or obligations with respect to natural or legal persons.

3. Decisions and rulings of the arbitration tribunal cannot add to or diminish the rights and obligations of the Parties under this Agreement or under any supplementing agreement.

4. For greater certainty, the arbitration tribunal shall have no jurisdiction to determine the legality of a measure alleged to constitute a breach of this Agreement or of any supplementing agreement, under the domestic law of a Party. No finding made by the arbitration tribunal when ruling on a dispute between the Parties shall bind the domestic courts or tribunals of either Party as to the meaning to be given to the domestic law of that Party.

5. For greater certainty, the courts of each Party shall have no jurisdiction in the resolution of disputes between the Parties under this Agreement.

6. Each Party shall make the rulings and decisions of the arbitration tribunal publicly available, subject to the protection of confidential information.

7. The information submitted by the Parties to the arbitration tribunal shall be treated in accordance with the confidentiality rules laid down in Annex 48.

Article 755 Suspension and termination of the arbitration proceedings

At the request of both Parties, the arbitration tribunal shall suspend its work at any time for a period agreed by the Parties and not exceeding 12 consecutive months. The arbitration tribunal shall resume its work before the end of the suspension period at the written request of both Parties, or at the end of the suspension period at the written request of either Party. The requesting Party shall deliver a notification to the other Party accordingly. If a Party does not request the resumption of the arbitration tribunal's work at the expiry of the suspension period, the authority of the arbitration tribunal shall lapse and the dispute settlement procedure shall be terminated. In the event of a suspension of the work of the arbitration tribunal, the relevant time periods shall be extended by the same time period for which the work of the arbitration tribunal was suspended.

Article 756 Mutually agreed solution

1. The Parties may at any time reach a mutually agreed solution with respect to any dispute referred to in Article 735.

2. If a mutually agreed solution is reached during panel proceedings, the Parties shall jointly notify the agreed solution to the chairperson of the arbitration tribunal. Upon such notification, the arbitration proceedings shall be terminated.

3. The solution may be adopted by means of a decision of the Partnership Council. Mutually agreed solutions shall be made publicly available. The version disclosed to the public shall not contain any information either Party has designated as confidential.

4. Each Party shall take the measures necessary to implement the mutually agreed solution within the agreed time period.

5. No later than the date of expiry of the agreed time period, the implementing Party shall inform the other Party in writing of any measures thus taken to implement the mutually agreed solution.

Article 757 Time Periods

1. All time periods laid down in this Title shall be counted in days from the day following the act to which they refer.

2. Any time period referred to in this Title may be modified by mutual agreement of the Parties.

3. The arbitration tribunal may at any time propose to the Parties to modify any time period referred to in this Title, stating the reasons for the proposal.

Articles 758–759 [Omitted]

Chapter 5 Specific arrangements for unilateral measures

Article 760 Special procedures for remedial measures and rebalancing

1. For the purposes of Article 374 and Article 411(2) and (3), this Title applies with the modifications set out in this Article.

2. By way of derogation from Article 740 and Annex 48, if the Parties do not agree on the composition of the arbitration tribunal within two days, the co-chair of the Partnership Council from the complaining Party shall select, no later than one day after the expiry of the two-day time period, an arbitrator by lot from the sub-list of each Party and the chairperson of the arbitration tribunal by lot from the sub-list of chairpersons established pursuant to Article 752. The co-chair of the Partnership Council from the complaining Party may delegate such selection by lot of the arbitrator or chairperson. Each individual shall confirm his or her availability to both Parties within two days from the date on which he or she was informed of his or her appointment. The organisational meeting referred to in Rule 10 of Annex 48 shall take place within two days from the establishment of the arbitration tribunal.

3. By way of derogation from Rule 11 of Annex 48 the complaining Party shall deliver its written submission no later than seven days after the date of establishment of the arbitration tribunal. The respondent Party shall deliver its written submission no later than seven days after the date of delivery of the written submission of the complaining Party. The arbitration tribunal shall adjust any other relevant time periods of the dispute settlement procedure as necessary to ensure the timely delivery of the report.

4. Article 745 does not apply and references to the ruling in this Title shall be read as references to the ruling referred to in Article 374(10) or point (c) of Article 411(3).

5. By way of derogation from Article 748(2), the arbitration tribunal shall deliver its decision to the Parties within 30 days from the date of delivery of the request.

Article 761 Suspension of obligations for the purposes of Article 374(12), Article 501(5) and Article 506(7)

1. The level of suspension of obligations shall not exceed the level equivalent to the nullification or impairment of benefits under this Agreement or under a supplementing agreement that is directly caused by the remedial or compensatory measures from the date the remedial or compensatory measures enter into effect until the date of the delivery of the arbitration ruling.

2. The level of suspension of obligations requested by the complaining Party and the determination of the level of suspension of obligations by the arbitration tribunal shall be based on facts demonstrating that the nullification or impairment arises directly from the application of the remedial or compensatory measure and affects specific goods, service suppliers, investors or other economic actors and not merely on allegation, conjecture or remote possibility.

3. The level of nullified or impaired benefits requested by the complaining Party or determined by the arbitration tribunal:

(a) shall not include punitive damages, interest or hypothetical losses of profits or business opportunities;

(b) shall be reduced by any prior refunds of duties, indemnification of damages or other forms of compensation already received by the concerned operators or the concerned Party; and

(c) shall not include the contribution to the nullification or impairment by wilful or negligent action or omission of the concerned Party or any person or entity in relation to whom remedies are sought pursuant to the intended suspension of obligations.

Article 762 Conditions for rebalancing, remedial, compensatory and safeguard measures

Where a Party takes a measure under Article 374, Article 411, Article 469, Article 501, Article 506 or Article 773, that measure shall only be applied in respect of covered provisions within the meaning of Article 735 and shall comply, mutatis mutandis, with the conditions set out in Article 749(3).

Title II Basis for cooperation

Article 763 Democracy, rule of law and human rights

1. The Parties shall continue to uphold the shared values and principles of democracy, the rule of law, and respect for human rights, which underpin their domestic and international policies. In that regard, the Parties reaffirm their respect for the Universal Declaration of Human Rights and the international human rights treaties to which they are parties.

2. The Parties shall promote such shared values and principles in international forums. The Parties shall cooperate in promoting those values and principles, including with or in third countries.

Article 764 Fight against climate change

1. The Parties consider that climate change represents an existential threat to humanity and reiterate their commitment to strengthening the global response to this threat. The fight against human-caused climate change as elaborated in the United Nations Framework Convention on Climate Change (UNFCCC) process, and in particular in the Paris Agreement adopted by the Conference of the Parties to the United Nations Framework Convention on Climate Change at its 21st session (the 'Paris Agreement'), inspires the domestic and external policies of the Union and the United Kingdom. Accordingly, each Party shall respect the Paris Agreement and the process set up by the UNFCCC and refrain from acts or omissions that would materially defeat the object and purpose of the Paris Agreement.

2. The Parties shall advocate the fight against climate change in international forums, including by engaging with other countries and regions to increase their level of ambition in the reduction of greenhouse emissions.

Articles 765–766 [Omitted]

Article 767 The most serious crimes of concern to the international community

1. The Parties reaffirm that the most serious crimes of concern to the international community as a whole must not go unpunished and that their effective prosecution must be ensured by taking measures at the national level and by enhancing international cooperation, including with the International Criminal Court. The Parties agree to fully support the universality and integrity of the Rome Statute of the International Criminal Court and related instruments.

2. The Parties agree to establish a regular dialogue on those matters.

Article 768 Counter-terrorism

1. The Parties shall cooperate at the bilateral, regional and international levels to prevent and combat acts of terrorism in all its forms and manifestations in accordance with international law, including, where applicable, international counterterrorism-related agreements, international humanitarian law and international human rights law, as well as in accordance with the principles of the Charter of the United Nations.

2. The Parties shall enhance cooperation on counter-terrorism, including preventing and countering violent extremism and the financing of terrorism, with the aim of advancing their common security interests, taking into account the United Nations Global Counter-Terrorism Strategy and relevant United Nations Security Council resolutions, without prejudice to law enforcement and judicial cooperation in criminal matters and intelligence exchanges.

3. The Parties agree to establish a regular dialogue on those matters. This dialogue will, *inter alia*, aim to promote and facilitate:

(a) the sharing of assessments on the terrorist threat;

(b) the exchange of best practices and expertise on counter terrorism;
(c) operational cooperation and exchange of information; and
(d) exchanges on cooperation in the framework of multilateral organisations.

Article 769 Personal data protection

1. The Parties affirm their commitment to ensuring a high level of personal data protection. They shall endeavour to work together to promote high international standards.

2. The Parties recognise that individuals have a right to the protection of personal data and privacy and that high standards in this regard contribute to trust in the digital economy and to the development of trade, and are a key enabler for effective law enforcement cooperation. To that end, the Parties shall undertake to respect, each in the framework of their respective laws and regulations, the commitments they have made in this Agreement in connection with that right.

3. The Parties shall cooperate at bilateral and multilateral levels, while respecting their respective laws and regulations. Such cooperation may include dialogue, exchanges of expertise, and cooperation on enforcement, as appropriate, with respect to personal data protection.

4. Where this Agreement or any supplementing agreement provide for the transfer of personal data, such transfer shall take place in accordance with the transferring Party's rules on international transfers of personal data. For greater certainty, this paragraph is without prejudice to the application of any specific provisions in this Agreement relating to the transfer of personal data, in particular Article 202 and Article 525, and to Title I of Part Six. Where needed, each Party will make best efforts, while respecting its rules on international transfers of personal data, to establish safeguards necessary for the transfer of personal data, taking into account any recommendations of the Partnership Council under point (h) of Article 7(4).

Article 770 Global cooperation on issues of shared economic, environmental and social interest

1. The Parties recognise the importance of global cooperation to address issues of shared economic, environmental and social interest. Where it is in their mutual interest, they shall promote multilateral solutions to common problems.

2. While preserving their decision-making autonomy, and without prejudice to other provisions of this Agreement or any supplementing agreement, the Parties shall endeavour to cooperate on current and emerging global issues of common interest such as peace and security, climate change, sustainable development, cross-border pollution, environmental protection, digitalisation, public health and consumer protection, taxation, financial stability, and free and fair trade and investment. To that end, they shall endeavour to maintain a constant and effective dialogue and to coordinate their positions in multilateral organisations and forums in which the Parties participate, such as the United Nations, the Group of Seven (G-7) and the Group of Twenty (G-20), the Organisation for Economic Co-operation and Development, the International Monetary Fund, the World Bank and the World Trade Organization.

Article 771 Essential elements

Article 763(1), Article 764(1) and Article 765(1) constitute essential elements of the partnership established by this Agreement and any supplementing agreement.

Title III Fulfillment of obligations and safeguard measures

Article 772 Fulfilment of obligations described as essential elements

1. If either Party considers that there has been a serious and substantial failure by the other Party to fulfil any of the obligations that are described as essential elements in Article 771, it may decide to terminate or suspend the operation of this Agreement or any supplementing agreement in whole or in part.

2. Before doing so, the Party invoking the application of this Article shall request that the Partnership Council meet immediately, with a view to seeking a timely and mutually agreeable

solution. If no mutually agreeable solution is found within 30 days from the date of the request to the Partnership Council, the Party may take the measures referred to in paragraph 1.

3. The measures referred to in paragraph 1 shall be in full respect of international law and shall be proportionate. Priority shall be given to the measures which least disturb the functioning of this Agreement and of any supplementing agreements.

4. The Parties consider that, for a situation to constitute a serious and substantial failure to fulfil any of the obligations described as essential elements in Article 771, its gravity and nature would have to be of an exceptional sort that threatens peace and security or that has international repercussions. For greater certainty, an act or omission which materially defeats the object and purpose of the Paris Agreement shall always be considered as a serious and substantial failure for the purposes of this Article.

Article 773 Safeguard measures

1. If serious economic, societal or environmental difficulties of a sectorial or regional nature, including in relation to fishing activities and their dependent communities, that are liable to persist arise, the Party concerned may unilaterally take appropriate safeguard measures. Such safeguard measures shall be restricted with regard to their scope and duration to what is strictly necessary in order to remedy the situation. Priority shall be given to those measures which will least disturb the functioning of this Agreement.

2. The Party concerned shall, without delay, notify the other Party through the Partnership Council and shall provide all relevant information. The Parties shall immediately enter into consultations in the Partnership Council with a view to finding a mutually agreeable solution.

3. The Party concerned may not take safeguard measures until one month has elapsed after the date of notification referred to in paragraph 2, unless the consultation procedure pursuant to paragraph 2 has been jointly concluded before the expiration of the stated time limit. When exceptional circumstances requiring immediate action exclude prior examination, the Party concerned may apply forthwith the safeguard measures strictly necessary to remedy the situation.

The Party concerned shall, without delay, notify the measures taken to the Partnership Council and shall provide all relevant information.

4. If a safeguard measure taken by the Party concerned creates an imbalance between the rights and obligations under this Agreement or under any supplementing agreement, the other Party may take such proportionate rebalancing measures as are strictly necessary to remedy the imbalance. Priority shall be given to those measures which will least disturb the functioning of this Agreement. Paragraphs 2 to 4 shall apply *mutatis mutandis* to such rebalancing measures.

5. Either Party may, without having prior recourse to consultations pursuant to Article 738, initiate the arbitration procedure referred to in Article 739 to challenge a measure taken by the other Party in application of paragraphs 1 to 5 of this Article.

6. The safeguard measures referred to in paragraph 1 and the rebalancing measures referred to in paragraph 5 may also be taken in relation to a supplementing agreement, unless otherwise provided therein.

PART SEVEN FINAL PROVISIONS

Article 774 Territorial scope

1. This Agreement applies to:

(a) the territories to which the TEU, the TFEU and the Treaty establishing the European Atomic Energy Community are applicable, and under the conditions laid down in those Treaties; and

(b) the territory of the United Kingdom.

2. This Agreement also applies to the Bailiwick of Guernsey, the Bailiwick of Jersey and the Isle of Man to the extent set out in Heading Five of Part Two and Article 520.

3. This Agreement shall neither apply to Gibraltar nor have any effects in that territory.

4. This Agreement does not apply to the overseas territories having special relations with the United Kingdom: Anguilla; Bermuda; British Antarctic Territory; British Indian Ocean Territory; British Virgin Islands; Cayman Islands; Falkland Islands; Montserrat; Pitcairn, Henderson, Ducie and Oeno Islands; Saint Helena, Ascension and Tristan da Cunha; South Georgia and the South Sandwich Islands; and Turks and Caicos Islands.

Article 775 [Omitted]

Article 776 Review

The Parties shall jointly review the implementation of this Agreement and supplementing agreements and any matters related thereto five years after the entry into force of this Agreement and every five years thereafter.

Article 777 Classified information and sensitive non-classified information

Nothing in this Agreement or in any supplementing agreement shall be construed as requiring a Party to make available classified information.

Classified information or material provided by or exchanged between the Parties under this Agreement or any supplementing agreement shall be handled and protected in compliance with the Agreement on security procedures for exchanging and protecting classified information and any implementing arrangement concluded under it.

The Parties shall agree upon handling instructions to ensure the protection of sensitive non-classified information exchanged between them.

Article 778 Integral parts of this Agreement

1. The Protocols, Annexes, Appendices and footnotes to this Agreement shall form an integral part of this Agreement.

2. Each of the Annexes to this Agreement, including its appendices, shall form an integral part of the Section, Chapter, Title, Heading or Protocol that refers to that Annex or to which reference is made in that Annex.

(List of annexes omitted.)

Article 779 Termination

Either Party may terminate this Agreement by written notification through diplomatic channels. This Agreement and any supplementing agreement shall cease to be in force on the first day of the twelfth month following the date of notification.

Article 780 [Omitted]

Article 781 Future accessions to the Union

1. The Union shall notify the United Kingdom of any new request for accession of a third country to the Union.

2. During the negotiations between the Union and a third country regarding the accession of that country to the Union[44], the Union shall endeavour to:

(a) on request of the United Kingdom and, to the extent possible, provide any information regarding any matter covered by this Agreement and any supplementing agreement; and

(b) take into account any concerns expressed by the United Kingdom.

3. The Partnership Council shall examine any effects of accession of a third country to the Union on this Agreement and any supplementing agreement sufficiently in advance of the date of such accession.

4. To the extent necessary, the United Kingdom and the Union shall, before the entry into force of the agreement on the accession of a third country to the Union:

(a) amend this Agreement or any supplementing agreement,

[44] For greater certainty, paragraphs 2 to 9 apply in respect of negotiations between the Union and a third country for accession to the Union taking place after the entry into force of this Agreement, notwithstanding the fact a request for accession took place before the entry into force of this Agreement.

(b) put in place by decision of the Partnership Council any other necessary adjustments or transitional arrangements regarding this Agreement or any supplementing agreement; or
(c) decide within the Partnership Council whether:
  (i) to apply Article 492 to the nationals of that third country; or
  (ii) to establish transitional arrangements as regards Article 492 in relation to that third country and its nationals once it accedes to the Union.

5. In the absence of a decision under point (c)(i) or (ii) of paragraph 4 of this Article by the entry into force of the agreement on the accession of the relevant third country to the Union, Article 492 shall not apply to nationals of that third country.

6. In the event that the Partnership Council establishes transitional arrangements as referred to in point (c)(ii) of paragraph 4, it shall specify their duration. The Partnership Council may extend the duration of those transitional arrangements.

7. Before the expiry of the transitional arrangements referred to in point (c)(ii) of paragraph 4 of this Article, the Partnership Council shall decide whether to apply Article 492 to the nationals of that third country from the end of the transitional arrangements. In the absence of such a decision Article 492 shall not apply in relation to the nationals of that third country from the end of the transitional arrangements.

8. Point (c) of paragraph 4, and paragraphs 5 to 7 are without prejudice to the Union's prerogatives under its domestic legislation.

9. For greater certainty, without prejudice to point (c) of paragraph 4 and paragraphs 5 to 7, this Agreement shall apply in relation to a new Member State of the Union from the date of accession of that new Member State to the Union.

Article 782 [Omitted]

Article 783 Entry into force and provisional application

1. This Agreement shall enter into force on the first day of the month following that in which both Parties have notified each other that they have completed their respective internal requirements and procedures for establishing their consent to be bound.

2. The Parties agree to provisionally apply this Agreement from 1 January 2021 provided that prior to that date they have notified each other that their respective internal requirements and procedures necessary for provisional application have been completed. Provisional application shall cease on one of the following dates, whichever is the earliest:

(a) 28 February 2021 or another date as decided by the Partnership Council; or
(b) the day referred to in paragraph 1.

3. As from the date from which this Agreement is provisionally applied, the Parties shall understand references in this Agreement to 'the date of entry into force of this Agreement' or to 'the entry into force of this Agreement' as references to the date from which this Agreement is provisionally applied.

Done at Brussels and London on the thirtieth day of December in the year two thousand and twenty.
(Signatures and all annexes omitted.)

Index

A

Abuse of dominance
- Commission Notice on agreements appreciably affecting trade **336–7**
- Regulation on the conduct of proceedings **325–9**
- Regulation on the control of concentrations **312–24**
- Regulation implementing Arts 81 and 82 (1962) **291**
- Regulation implementing Arts 81 and 82 (2002) **303–12**

Abuse of rights **119**
Administrative cooperation **73**
Advisory bodies
- Treaty on the Functioning of the European Union (Consolidated version) **98–100**

Age discrimination **115**
Agreement on the Withdrawal of the United Kingdom of Great Britain and Northern Ireland from the European Union and the European Atomic Energy Community 2020 **365–83**
Agriculture and fisheries
- Treaty on the Functioning of the European Union (Consolidated version) **29–30**

Aid
- Treaty on the Functioning of the European Union (Consolidated version) **46–7, 77–8**

Anti-competitive agreements
- Commission Notice on agreements appreciably affecting trade **336–7**
- Commission Notice on agreements of minor importance (De Minimis Notice) **291–4**
- Commission Notice on cartel fines **337–44**
- Regulation on the conduct of proceedings **325–9**
- Regulation implementing Arts 81 and 82 (1962) **291**
- Regulation implementing Arts 81 and 82 (2002) **303–12**
- Regulation on vertical agreements and concerted practices (2010) **330–5**

Approximation of laws
- Directive on services in internal market **255–7**
- Treaty on the Functioning of the European Union (Consolidated version) **48–9**

Asylum and immigration
- Charter of Fundamental Rights **114**
- Treaty on the Functioning of the European Union (Consolidated version) **37–8**

B

Banks
- European Central Bank **92–3**
- European Investment Bank **100**

Brexit
- *see* Withdrawal (UK) from European Union

Budgetary provisions
- Treaty on European Union (Consolidated version) **15–16**
- Treaty on the Functioning of the European Union (Consolidated version) **101–6**

C

Capital movements
- Treaty on the Functioning of the European Union (Consolidated version) **34–5**

Charter of Fundamental Rights
- citizenship **117**
- equality **115**
- general provisions **118–19**
- justice **118**
- prohibition of slavery and forced labour **113**
- prohibition of torture **113**
- respect for private and family life **113**
- right to asylum **114**
- right to education **114**
- right to liberty and security **113**
- right to marry **113**
- right to property **114**

Children and young people
- Charter of Fundamental Rights **115**

Citizenship
- Charter of Fundamental Rights **117**
- Directive on family reunification **196–202**
- Directive on residence of EU citizens **213–25**
- Treaty on European Union (Consolidated version) **2**
- Treaty on the Functioning of the European Union (Consolidated version) **25–7**

Civil protection **73**
Codecision procedure **137–41**
Cohesion **68–9**
Collective bargaining
- Charter of Fundamental Rights **115**

Collective redundancies **285–8**
Commercial policy
- Treaty on the Functioning of the European Union (Consolidated version) **75–6**

Commission
- control of implementing powers (EU) (182/2011) **141–5**
- Joint declaration on codecision procedure **137–41**
- Joint declaration on public access to documents **136–7**
- Notice on agreements appreciably affecting trade **336–7**
- Notice on agreements of minor importance (De Minimis Notice) **291–94**
- Notice on cartel fines **337–44**
- Regulation on the conduct of competition proceedings **325–9**
- Treaty on European Union (Consolidated version) **7–8**
- Treaty on the Functioning of the European Union (Consolidated version) **85–6**

Committee of the Regions **99–100**

Common provisions
Treaty on European Union (Consolidated version) **2–4**
Treaty on the Functioning of the European Union (Consolidated version) **105**
Competences
Declaration 18 **133**
Protocol (No 25) **131**
Treaty on European Union (Consolidated version) **3**
Treaty on the Functioning of the European Union (Consolidated version) **22–3**
Competition rules
Commission Notice defining relevant markets **294–5**
Commission Notice on agreements of minor importance (De Minimis Notice) **291–94**
Commission Notice on cartel fines **337–44**
Regulation implementing Arts 81 and 82 (1962) **291**
Regulation implementing Arts 81 and 82 (2002) **303–12**
Regulation on the conduct of proceedings **325–9**
Regulation on the control of concentrations (Merger Regulation) **312–24**
Regulation on vertical agreements and concerted practices (2010) **330–5**
Treaty on the Functioning of the European Union (Consolidated version) **44–6**
Concentrations (Merger control) **312–24**
Concerted practices
Commission Notice on agreements of minor importance (De Minimis Notice) **291–94**
Commission Notice on cartel fines **337–44**
Regulation implementing Arts 81 and 82 (1962) **291**
Regulation implementing Arts 81 and 82 (2002) **303–12**
Regulation on the conduct of proceedings **325–9**
Regulation on vertical agreements and concerted practices (2010) **330–5**
Conduct of proceedings **325–9**
Consumer protection
Charter of Fundamental Rights **116**
Directive on provision of technical information and Information Society services **174–80**
Treaty on the Functioning of the European Union (Consolidated version) **66**
Cooperation
Directive on posted workers **188–93**
Directive on recognition of professional qualifications **239–40**
Directive on services in internal market **255–7**
EU–UK Trade and Cooperation Agreement 2020 **402–86**
national parliaments **124**
Treaty on the Functioning of the European Union (Consolidated version) **28, 38–42, 73, 76–7**
Council
European Parliament **84–5**
Joint declaration on codecision procedure **137–41**
Joint declaration on public access to documents **136–7**
Treaty on European Union (Consolidated version) **5–9**
Court of Auditors **93–5**
Court of Justice
Protocol (No 3) **127–31**
recommendations regarding preliminary rulings **145–52**
Rules of Procedure **152–67**
Treaty on European Union (Consolidated version) **9**
Treaty on the Functioning of the European Union (Consolidated version) **86–92**
Culture
Treaty on European Union (Consolidated version) **2**
Treaty on the Functioning of the European Union (Consolidated version) **64–5**
Customs duties **27–8**

D

Data protection
Charter of Fundamental Rights of the European Union **113**
De Minimis Notice **291–94**
Declarations
competences **133**
conferred powers **133**
human rights and fundamental freedoms **132**
Joint declaration on codecision procedure **137–41**
primacy principle **132–3**
Democratic principles **2, 4–5**
Dignity **2, 113**
Diplomatic protection
Charter of Fundamental Rights **117**
Treaty on European Union (Consolidated version) **14**
Direct actions **161–4**
Directives
collective redundancies (98/59/EC) **285–8**
equal access to goods and services (2004/113/EC) **268–72**
equal treatment for social security (79/7/EEC) **259–61**
equal treatment in employment and occupation (2000/78/EEC) **265–8**
equal treatment in employment and occupation (recast) (2006/54/EC) **272–8**
equal treatment of self-employed (2010/41/EU) **278–80**
family reunification (2003/86/EC) **196–202**
free movement of citizens (2004/38/EC) **213–25**
free movement of goods (70/50/EEC) **169–70**
freedom to provide legal services (77/249/EEC) **185–7**
lawyers' qualifications (98/5/EC) **193–6**
mutual recognition of goods (2019/515) **180–5**
posted workers (96/71/EC) **188–93**
pregnant workers (92/85/EEC) **283–5**
provision of technical information and Information Society services (2015/1535/EU) **174–80**
race discrimination (2000/43/EC) **261–5**
recognition of professional qualifications (2005/36/EC) **225–40**
services (2006/123/EC) **240–57**
status of third-country nationals (2003/109/EC) **203–13**

transfer of undertakings (2001/23/EC) **281–3**
working time (2003/88/EC) **288–90**
Disability discrimination **115**
Discrimination
see also Equality; Non-discrimination
age discrimination **115**
disability discrimination **115**
race discrimination **115, 261–5**
sex discrimination **115, 259–61, 265–8, 268–72, 272–8, 278–80**
Documents
Regulation on public access to documents **134–6**

E

Economic and Financial Committee **54–5**
Economic and Social Committee **98–9**
Economic policy **49–53**
Education
Directive on lawyers' qualifications **193–6**
Directive on recognition of professional qualifications **225–40**
Treaty on the Functioning of the European Union (Consolidated version) **63–4**
Elderly persons **115**
Elections **117**
Employment
Directive on collective redundancies **285–8**
Directive on equal treatment in employment and occupation (recast) **272–8**
Directive on health and safety of pregnant and nursing mothers **283–5**
Directive on posted workers **188–93**
Directive on transfer of undertakings **281–3**
Directive on working time **288–90**
Regulation on free movement of workers within Union **257–9**
Treaty on the Functioning of the European Union (Consolidated version) **58–60**
Energy
Treaty on the Functioning of the European Union (Consolidated version) **72**
Enhanced cooperation
Treaty on European Union (Consolidated version) **9**
Treaty on the Functioning of the European Union (Consolidated version) **106–8**
Environment
Charter of Fundamental Rights **116**
Treaty on the Functioning of the European Union (Consolidated version) **71–2**
Equality
Charter of Fundamental Rights **115**
Directive on equal treatment for social security **259–61**
Directive on equal treatment in access to and supply of goods and services **268–72**
Directive on equal treatment in employment and occupation **265–8**
Directive on equal treatment in employment and occupation (recast) **272–8**
Directive on race discrimination **261–5**
Treaty on European Union (Consolidated version) **2**
Establishment
Directive on lawyers' qualifications **193–6**
Directive on recognition of professional qualifications **225–40**
Directive on services in internal market **244–8**
Treaty on the Functioning of the European Union (Consolidated version) **32–3**
EU–UK Trade and Cooperation Agreement **402–86**
euro provisions **55–6**
European Central Bank **92–3**
European Communities Act 1972 **345**
European Council
European Parliament **83**
Treaty on European Union (Consolidated version) **5–9**
European Investment Bank **100**
European Parliament
European Council **83**
Joint declaration on codecision procedure **137–41**
Treaty on European Union (Consolidated version) **5–9**
Treaty on the Functioning of the European Union (Consolidated version) **81–3**
European Social Fund **63**
European System of Central Banks **53–4**
European Union (Withdrawal) Act 2018 **346–65**
European Union (Withdrawal Agreement) Act 2020 **392–402**
External action
Declaration 41 **133**
Treaty on European Union (Consolidated version) **10–11**
Treaty on the Functioning of the European Union (Consolidated version) **75–81**

F

Fair trial **118**
Family rights
Charter of Fundamental Rights **113, 116**
Directive on family reunification **196–202**
Directive on health and safety of pregnant and nursing mothers **283–5**
Directive on status of third-country nationals **203–13**
Foreign and security policy
Treaty on European Union (Consolidated version) **11–18**
Fraud **105–6**
Free movement of goods
Commission Directive **169–70**
Commission Practice Note on imports **171–2**
Council Regulation on internal market **172–3**
Directive on provision of technical information and Information Society services **174–80**
Regulation 2019/515 on mutual recognition of goods **180–5**
Treaty on the Functioning of the European Union (Consolidated version) **27–9**
Free movement of persons
Charter of Fundamental Rights **117**
Directive on family reunification **196–202**
Directive on lawyers' qualifications **193–6**
Directive on legal services **185–7**
Directive on posted workers **188–93**
Directive on recognition of professional qualifications **225–40**
Directive on residence of EU citizens **213–25**

Directive on services in internal market **240–57**
Directive on status of third-country nationals **203–13**
Regulation on free movement of workers within Union **257–9**
Treaty on the Functioning of the European Union (Consolidated version) **31–5**
Freedom of assembly and association **114,122**
Freedom of expression **114, 121–2**
Freedom of information
Charter of Fundamental Rights **114, 115, 117**
European Convention on Human Rights **121**
Regulation on public access to documents **134–6**
Freedom of the arts and sciences **114**
Freedom of thought, conscience and religion **113, 121**
Freedom to choose work **114**
Freedom to conduct business **114**
Fundamental freedoms
see also Charter of Fundamental Rights
Declarations 1 and 2 **132**
Protocol (No 8) (accession of the Union) **131**
Treaty on European Union (Consolidated version) **2, 3–4**

G

General provisions
Charter of Fundamental Rights **118–19**
Directive on equal treatment in access to and supply of goods and services **268–70**
Directive on equal treatment in employment and occupation **268–72**
Directive on equal treatment in employment and occupation (recast) **272–8**
Directive on services in internal market **226–9**
Treaty on European Union (Consolidated version) **10–11**
Treaty on the Functioning of the European Union (Consolidated version) **35–7, 108–12**

H

Health and safety at work
Directive on health and safety of pregnant and nursing mothers **283–5**
Directive on working time **290**
Health care **116**
Human rights and fundamental freedoms Declarations 1 and 2 **132**
Obligation to respect human rights **119**
Protocol (No 8) (accession of the Union) **131**
Rights and freedoms **119–22**
Treaty on European Union (Consolidated version) **2, 3–4**
Humanitarian aid **77–8**

I

Institutions
Directive on equal treatment in access to and supply of goods and services **271**
Directive on race discrimination **264**
Treaty on European Union (Consolidated version) **5–9**
Treaty on the Functioning of the European Union (Consolidated version) **54–5, 81–95**
Internal market
Council Regulation on free movement of goods **172–3**
Directive on services in internal market **240–57**
Treaty on the Functioning of the European Union (Consolidated version) **27**
International agreements **78–80**
International organisations **80**

J

Judicial cooperation **38–41**

L

Languages
Court of Justice **154–5**
recognition of professional qualifications (2005/36/EC) **238**
Lawyers
Directive on lawyers' qualifications **193–6**
Directive on legal services **185–7**
Legal acts and procedures
Joint declaration on codecision procedure **137–41**
Treaty on the Functioning of the European Union (Consolidated version) **95–8**
Luxembourg Accords **134**

M

Merger control **312–24**
Mutual recognition of goods
Regulation (2019/515) **180–5**

N

National court references **145–52**
National parliaments
Treaty on European Union (Consolidated version) **5**
Treaty on the Functioning of the European Union (Consolidated version) **123–4**
National security
Treaty on European Union (Consolidated version) **11–18**
Non-discrimination
see also Discrimination
Charter of Fundamental Rights **115**
Directive on race discrimination **261–5**
Treaty on European Union (Consolidated version) **2**
Treaty on the Functioning of the European Union (Consolidated version) **25–7**
Northern Ireland
Protocol (withdrawal from the European Union) **384–91**
Notices
agreements of minor importance (De Minimis Notice) **291–94**
defining relevant markets (97/C 372/03) **294–303**

O

Ombudsmen **117**

P

Police cooperation **41–2**
Pregnant and nursing mothers **283–5**
Preliminary rulings
recommendations from CJEU **145–52**
Rules of Court **156–61**

Primacy principle **132–3**
Product liability
  Directive on provision of technical information and Information Society services **174–80**
Prohibition of slavery and forced labour **113, 120**
Prohibition of torture **113, 119**
Proportionality **124–6**
Protocols
  Art 157 **132**
  Court of Justice **127–31**
  human rights and fundamental freedoms (accession of the Union) **131**
  national parliaments **123–4**
  shared competences **131**
  subsidiarity and proportionality **124–6**
Public health **65–6**

R

Race discrimination **261–5**
Redundancies **285–8**
Regulations
  conduct of proceedings (773/2004) **325–9**
  control of implementing powers (182/2011) **141–5**
  free movement of goods (2679/98) **172–3**
  free movement of workers (492/2011) **257–9**
  implementing Arts 81 and 82 (1/2003) **303–12**
  implementing Arts 81 and 82 (204/62) **291**
  merger control (139/2004) **312–24**
  mutual recognition of goods (2019/515) **180–5**
  public access to documents (1049/2001) **134–6**
  vertical agreements and concerted practices (2022/720) **330–5**
Relevant markets **294–303**
Research and development
  Treaty on the Functioning of the European Union (Consolidated version) **69–71**
Respect for private and family life **113**
Restrictive measures
  Commission Practice Note on imports **171–2**
  Treaty on the Functioning of the European Union (Consolidated version) **78**
Right not to be tried or punished twice in criminal proceedings for the same criminal offence **118**
Right of access to documents **117**
Right of access to placement services **115**
Right of collective bargaining and action **115**
Right to asylum **114**
Right to a fair trial **118, 120**
Right to an effective remedy **118, 122**
Right to education **114**
Right to good administration **117**
Right to liberty and security **113,120**
Right to life
  Charter of Fundamental Rights **113**
  European Convention on Human Rights **119**
Right to marry **113,122**
Right to petition **117**
Right to property **114**
Right to respect for private and family life **121**
Right to the integrity of the person **113**
Right to vote and to stand as a candidate **117**
Rights of the child **115**
Rights of the elderly **115**

S

Security
  Treaty on European Union (Consolidated version) **11–18**
Self-employment
  Directive on equal treatment for social security **259–61**
  Directive on equal treatment of self-employed **278–80**
Services
  Charter of Fundamental Rights **115, 116**
  Directive on equal treatment in access to and supply of goods and services **268–72**
  Directive on lawyers' qualifications **193–6**
  Directive on legal services **185–7**
  Directive on posted workers **188–93**
  Directive on recognition of professional qualifications **226–9**
  Directive on services in internal market **240–57**
  Treaty on the Functioning of the European Union (Consolidated version) **33–4**
Sex discrimination
  Directive on equal treatment for social security **259–61**
  Directive on equal treatment in access to and supply of goods and services **268–72**
  Directive on equal treatment in employment and occupation **265–8**
  Directive on equal treatment in employment and occupation (recast) **272–8**
  Directive on equal treatment of self-employed **278–80**
Social policy
  Directive on collective redundancies **285–8**
  Directive on equal treatment for social security **259–61**
  Directive on equal treatment in access to and supply of goods and services **268–72**
  Directive on equal treatment in employment and occupation **265–8**
  Directive on equal treatment in employment and occupation (recast) **272–8**
  Directive on equal treatment of self-employed **278–80**
  Directive on health and safety of pregnant and nursing mothers **283–5**
  Directive on race discrimination **261–5**
  Directive on transfer of undertakings **281–3**
  Directive on working time **288–90**
Solidarity
  Charter of Fundamental Rights **115–16**
  Treaty on European Union (Consolidated version) **2**
  Treaty on the Functioning of the European Union (Consolidated version) **80–1**
Space policy **69–71**
Sport **63–4**
State aid
  Treaty on the Functioning of the European Union (Consolidated version) **46–7, 77–8**
Subsidiarity **124–6**

T

Taxation
  Treaty on the Functioning of the European Union (Consolidated version) **47–8**
Technology
  provision of technical information and Information

Society services **174–80**
Treaty on the Functioning of the European Union (Consolidated version) **69–71**
Third countries
Directive on status of third-country nationals **203–13**
Treaty on European Union (Consolidated version) **4, 10–11**
Treaty on the Functioning of the European Union (Consolidated version) **74–5**
Time off work
Directive on health and safety of pregnant and nursing mothers **284**
Tourism
Treaty on the Functioning of the European Union (Consolidated version) **73**
Trade and Cooperation Agreement (EU–UK) **402–86**
Training
Directive on lawyers' qualifications **193–6**
Directive on recognition of professional qualifications **229–40**
Treaty on the Functioning of the European Union (Consolidated version) **63–4**
Trans-European networks **66–7**
Transfers of undertakings **281–3**
Transport **42–4**
Treaty on European Union (Consolidated version)
see also Declarations; Protocols
common provisions **2–4**
democratic principles **4–5**
enhanced cooperation **9**
external action **10–11**
final provisions **18–21**
foreign and security policy **11–18**
institutions **5–9**
preamble **1–2**
Treaty on the Functioning of the European Union (Consolidated version)
see also Declarations; Protocols
administrative cooperation **73**
agriculture and fisheries **29–30**
approximation of laws **48–9**
association with third countries **74–5**
budgetary provisions **101–6**
civil protection **73**
cohesion **68–9**
commercial policy **75–6**
Commission **85–6**
Committee of the Regions **99–100**
common provisions **105**
competences **22–3**
competition rules **44–6**
consumer protection **66**
cooperation **76–7**
Council **84–5**
Court of Auditors **93–5**
Court of Justice **86–92**
culture **64–5**
Economic and Social Committee **98–9**
economic policy **49–53**
education and training **63–4**
employment **58–60**
energy **72**
enhanced cooperation **106–8**
environment **71–2**
euro provisions **55–6**
European Central Bank **92–3**
European Investment Bank **100**
European Parliament **81–3**
European Social Fund **63**
external action **75–81**
fraud **105–6**
free movement of goods **27–9**
free movement of persons **31–5**
freedom, security and justice **35–42**
general and final provisions **108–12**
general provisions **23–5**
humanitarian aid **77–8**
industry **67**
institutions **54–5, 81–95**
internal market **27**
international agreements **78–80**
international organisations **80**
legal acts and procedures **95–8**
monetary policy **53–4**
non-discrimination and citizenship **25–7**
preamble **21**
Protocol (No 33) **132**
public health **65–6**
research and development **69–71**
restrictive measures **78**
social policy **60–3**
solidarity **80–1**
sport **63–4**
state aid **46–7**
taxation **47–8**
tourism **73**
trans-European networks **66–7**
transitional provisions **56–8**
transport **42–4**

V

Vertical agreements
Regulation on vertical agreements and concerted practices (2022/720) **330–5**
Vocational training
Directive on lawyers' qualifications **193–6**
Directive on recognition of professional qualifications **229–40**
Treaty on the Functioning of the European Union (Consolidated version) **63–4**
Voting
Charter of Fundamental Rights **117**
Treaty on European Union (Consolidated version) **4**

W

Windsor Framework
see Protocol on Ireland/Northern Ireland/(The Windsor Framework)
Withdrawal (UK) from European Union
Agreement on the Withdrawal of the United Kingdom of Great Britain and Northern Ireland from the European Union and the European Atomic Energy Community 2020 **365–83**
European Communities Act 1972 **345**
European Union (Withdrawal) Act 2018 **346–65**
European Union (Withdrawal Agreement) Act 2020 **392–402**

EU–UK Trade and Cooperation Agreement 2020 (Selected extracts) **402–86**
Protocol on Ireland/Northern Ireland/(The Windsor Framework) **384–91**
Workers
Charter of Fundamental Rights **115, 116**
Directive on collective redundancies **285–8**
Directive on equal treatment for social security **259–61**
Directive on equal treatment in employment and occupation **265–8, 268–72**
Directive on equal treatment in employment and occupation (recast) **272–8**
Directive on health and safety of pregnant and nursing mothers **283–5**
Directive on posted workers **188–93**
Directive on transfer of undertakings **281–3**
Directive on working time **288–90**
Regulation on free movement of workers within Union **257–9**
Treaty on the Functioning of the European Union (Consolidated version) **31–2**
Working time
Directive on health and safety of pregnant and nursing mothers **284**
Directive on working time **288–90**

Y

Young people
Charter of Fundamental Rights **115**
Equality **115**